Corporate Risk Management

Founded in 1807, John Wiley & Sons is the oldest independent publishing company in the United States. With offices in North America, Europe, Australia and Asia, Wiley is globally committed to developing and marketing print and electronic products and services for our customers' professional and personal knowledge and understanding.

The Wiley Finance series contains books written specifically for finance and investment professionals as well as sophisticated individual investors and their financial advisors. Book topics range from portfolio management to e-commerce, risk management, financial engineering, valuation and financial instrument analysis, as well as much more.

For a list of available titles, visit our website at www.WileyFinance.com.

Corporate Risk Management

Theories and Applications

GEORGES DIONNE

WILEY

Published by John Wiley & Sons, Inc., Hoboken, New Jersey.
Published simultaneously in Canada.

Library of Congress Cataloging-in-Publication Data

Names: Dionne, Georges, author.
Title: Corporate risk management : theories and applications / Georges Dionne.
Description: Hoboken, New Jersey : Wiley, [2019] | Series: The Wiley finance series | Includes index. |
Identifiers: LCCN 2019001984 (print) | LCCN 2019006503 (ebook) | ISBN 9781119583158 (ePub) | ISBN 9781119583172 (ePDF) | ISBN 9781119583127 (Hardcover)
Subjects: LCSH: Risk management.
Classification: LCC HD61 (ebook) | LCC HD61 .D56 2019 (print) | DDC 658.15/5—dc23
LC record available at https://lccn.loc.gov/2019001984

Cover Design: Wiley
Cover Image: © Danielle Blanchard

Printed in the United States of America.

V10008920_040219

To Danielle

Contents

Foreword

Risk management, which is omnipresent nowadays, as Georges Dionne rightly highlights, is nevertheless a relatively young field. Twenty or 30 years ago, the term would have seemed pretentious, and the natural reaction of a company director would have been to associate it with the management of insurance coverage. Not that insurance is no longer the anchor point for risk management—it still is—but the term *risk management* means a lot more than just insurance coverage. In this respect, three events have changed the content of risk management: the collapse of the Long-Term Capital Management fund in 1998, followed by that of Enron in 2001, and finally that of Lehman Brothers in 2008. These three companies were all among the best in their category, and were considered to have the most sophisticated risk management of the time. Lehman Brothers was thus rated "excellent" in risk management, a real role model. This made these failures all the more resounding. Three main lessons have been drawn from these incidents. First of all, good management of identified risks presupposes good overall governance of all the processes of the organization concerned. Next, sophistication is not enough for good risk management, because it can mask major deficiencies in terms of internal control. Finally, operational risk should not be underestimated and should be subjected to careful and reasoned assessment.

Risk management therefore goes beyond simple knowledge of the risks to which the company is exposed, their possible aggregate cost, and the techniques used to cover them. It covers governance, internal control, and compliance with regulatory requirements. In concrete terms, it covers complex processes that play out in seven logical steps:

1. First of all, a general system of good governance must be in place, which ensures the transparency of management and the rationality of the decisions made by those in charge of the organization.
2. Then the governing bodies need to set objectives for the organization concerned, in sufficient detail (what are the missions, and under what conditions they should be completed?).
3. Also, from these objectives, the governing bodies need to ascertain the organization's preferences in terms of risk or risk appetite (which risks to take or not take, minimise, etc.), bearing in mind that the objective of risk management is not to exclude risk but to control it.
4. After this, the current and emerging risks to which the organization is exposed need to be identified, and their impact on it measured in terms of frequency and severity.
5. The next step consists of deciding which measures are necessary to control these risks, by ruling them out, transferring them to other agents, or containing them within predefined limits.

6. Next, processes, thresholds, and controls must be implemented to ensure that risk control is in place throughout the organization.
7. Finally, there should be internal and external communication on risk management, depending on the legal obligations involved, market practices, and the prudential rules and standards specific to the organization and its reputation.

In this new understanding of "risk management," which emerged at the end of the twentieth century and the beginning of this one, risk management permeates the entire organization. It is thus an integral part of the company's values and culture, in which all of the company's employees, without exception, are now involved, to the point where judges may refer to it in their rulings. It is a very significant shift. This shift is not fully complete and will not be complete as long as it remains possible to hide from investors the risks to which you are exposed, and against which you are not protected. Decisions on insurance cover have become key variables with which to assess the strength of a company. They can no longer remain hidden within the departments in charge of negotiating the associated contracts. Investors, directors, and officers must be kept informed about them and must be able to assess their relevance to the company's objectives and risk appetite.

Today, good risk management forms part of a company's competitive advantages, particularly in the financial sector, and even more so in the insurance industry where you find risks on both the asset and the liability side of the balance sheet—this situation is particularly conducive to risk accumulation, which is at the root of the most extreme risks. Good risk management forms part of a company's capacity for strategic anticipation.

Georges Dionne's work fits into this renewed approach. It's important to emphasise the fact that although the consideration of risk has shaken the economy, economic analyses and works devoted to risk management and its impact on the behavior of organizations are still few and far between. Some examples are the pioneering work of the Nobel Prize–winners in Economics Lars Peter Hansen and Thomas Sargent, who raise questions in their book *Robustness* about the impact on capital management of considering risk management, and the works of Jean-Charles Rochet and Gilles Bénéplanc, who propose economic fundamentals consistent with risk management in their book *Risk Management in Turbulent Times*. It's clear that, for the purposes of optimization, risk management and capital management cannot be separated. The company seeks to maximize its current and future profitability, and therefore its growth, under the constraint of remaining solvent. And in general, the optimal situation is not one in which risk is excluded, but one where taking controlled risk enables the company to maximize its value.

Within the vast field covered by risk management, Georges Dionne's work concentrates on the motivation behind financial risk management and the measurement of its efficiency. It focuses on the management of market, credit, liquidity, and operational risk. This leads it to a detailed analysis of portfolio management and the calculation of optimal and regulatory capital. I recommend reading the entire work carefully, but I particularly appreciated the chapters devoted to analyzing the failures of LTCM and Enron, and to the subprime crisis. I also strongly recommend reading the chapters on capital and value at risk (VaR) and the most sophisticated developments in this regard within the framework of conditional value at risk (CVaR), which lies at the heart of the debate on the measurement of systemic risk. Georges Dionne talks about a textbook for students. In fact, *Corporate Risk Management: Theories and Applications* is not just a manual, it is also a faithful companion for academics wishing to update their knowledge and for all company directors who want the most appropriate instruments to manage both the risks they have decided to take on and those that are imposed on them.

Teachers, researchers, students, and decision makers will find in Georges Dionne's work a presentation of these instruments, their economic consistency, and their intrinsic limits that is at once pedagogical and comprehensive. Anyone who is allergic to quantitative techniques need not worry about the mathematical developments contained in the text: the author has stylized and simplified them so well that they are accessible to any enthusiastic reader, while retaining the flavor of mathematic discipline. This is therefore a work to read, to engage with, and to keep at hand.

Denis Kessler
Chairman and chief executive officer of the SCOR Group
April 12, 2018

Introduction

GENERAL PRESENTATION

The study of financial risk management began after World War II. This rather young discipline aims to reduce the costs associated with risk. It covers all risk categories.

Risks cause various types of costs: physical, economic, financial, and even psychological. Some are insurable and others are not. This book concentrates on economic and financial risks that businesses and individuals face, especially those that are not anticipated, although some anticipated risks are also discussed. The costs of risk are generated not only by passive exposure to hazards, but also by risk taking in hazardous environments linked notably to the competition, technology, debt, economic conditions, climatic conditions, market imperfections, and regulations, although regulations may also mitigate the social costs of some risks.

Risk management does not imply risk aversion. It may concern risk-averse decision makers, but risk aversion is not a necessary condition for its use. It is well known that an increase in risk (mean preserving spread) decreases the welfare of risk-averse decision makers, but it also reduces the value of firms that have a concave objective function. This concavity may be obtained by a moderate risk appetite along with an exposure to nonlinear financial products, and by market imperfections such as the convexity of tax functions, or information asymmetry in financial markets.

Under the regulations governing banks and insurance companies, the risk appetite of a financial institution must be stipulated and adopted by its board of directors. This should apply as well to all businesses, for the benefit of shareholders and various stakeholders. This exercise is important because its result determines the optimal risk management actions to take. An important corollary is that firms should not cover all risks automatically; they must take only the risk management actions that maximize firms' value.

Risk is ubiquitous. Individuals, businesses, communities, and governments all face it. Risk affects welfare and includes several dimensions. In finance, it combines hazards and opportunities. It is commonly measured by modeling different possible states of nature according to their probability of occurrence and the associated consequence. This combination is linked to a probability distribution of occurrences of states of nature that have different moments. Depending on the needs and preferences of decision-making agents, these moments may yield different costs and benefits. For losses related to pure risks, mathematical expectation or mean plays a determining role. Weighting of mean and volatility prevails in the estimation of opportunities related to financial assets. Higher moments may become important when all information is not contained in the first two moments. In the study of catastrophe risks, modeling extreme losses with very low probabilities is crucial. It often involves using higher moments of the probability distribution. When statistical information is lacking, these risk measures may become inapplicable. Other approaches of risk management must be used. Precaution is a form of risk management when agents lack information on the probabilities and consequences of the states of nature.

Information asymmetry and its consequences on risk management receive particular attention in this book. Banks cannot perfectly evaluate the risks posed by the individuals and businesses to which they make loans. This lack of information affects the risk premiums imposed by the banks, along with the forms of bank contracts and the default probabilities. Further, financial contracts affect borrowers' behavior. Choosing optimal forms of contracts is part of the risk management of financial institutions. The rating of clients' risks by banks is another form of credit risk management. In the years preceding the last financial crisis, banks put loans on the market using nonoptimal forms of securitization (without retention) in the presence of moral hazard. These choices affected their credit risk management behavior and greatly increased the probabilities of default on mortgage loans.

Information asymmetry also pertains to the governance of risk management. Do managers always choose the forms of risk management that maximize firm value? The answer may be partly linked to the different types of managerial compensation. Managers paid by stock options may not always be motivated to reduce the volatility of their firm value, compared with managers paid by shares or salary.

Information asymmetry can even justify risk management. For example, it may explain the hedging of internal financing of investment projects to avoid paying overly high interest rate premiums on external loans, arising from the difficulty that banks face when evaluating the risks associated with projects.

Information asymmetry affects risk prevention and reduces risk management when financing contracts are not written so as to give borrowers appropriate incentives. In some situations, risk becomes endogenous, which makes it more difficult to manage. Chapters 10 and 11 address this form of moral hazard.

The book is intended for graduate students in finance, financial economics, and financial engineering. It aims to provide a detailed presentation of the advanced literature on risk management. It does not use complex mathematics, but readers should have basic knowledge of statistical analysis, probability theory, applied econometrics, and finance, including portfolio management and the use of derivatives. This book does not discuss the risk management processes of risk identification, evaluation, prioritization, and control in detail, nor the execution of action plans to reduce risks under optimal scenarios. It does not address financial-product pricing or other activities related to financial engineering. Rather, it examines the motivation for risk management and the measurement of its efficiency. As the title indicates, the book is mainly dedicated to the corporate finance dimension of risk management by presenting different theoretical models that justify risk management, and by performing empirical verification of different theoretical propositions. It also proposes statistical modeling to identify the importance of different risks and of their variations according to economic cycles. Default, liquidity, and operational risks during the financial crisis that began in 2007 are analyzed in detail.

Obviously, this book cannot cover all financial risks. It focuses on market, credit, liquidity, and operational risk. It does not cover insurable risks. More specifically, it addresses portfolio market risk management and portfolio credit risk management, the use of derivatives and structured financial products, the calculation of optimal regulatory capital, prevention, conditional value at risk, regulation, and governance of risk management. It presents extreme examples that have cast doubt on the efficiency of risk management, like the financial crisis of 2007–2009, the Enron bankruptcy in 2001, and the failure of the fund Long-Term Capital Management (LTCM) in 1998.

CONTENTS OF THE BOOK

The book contains 21 chapters. The first chapter reviews the history of risk management and of derivatives and structured financial products. A definition of risk management for nonfinancial firms is proposed. It highlights the maximization of firm value by integrating internal activities of self-protection and self-insurance with external activities like the use of market insurance, derivatives, and structured financial products.

A large part of the book contains a detailed investigation of the motivations for risk management of nonfinancial firms. By taking into account managers' risk attitude and behavior, risk management generally aims to reduce the costs associated with various risks such as those of financial distress, premiums to different partners, taxes, and investment financing. Risk management also covers dividend payments, liquidity requirements, mergers and acquisitions and firm governance. These determinants are analyzed from a theoretical standpoint (Chapters 2 and 3), and their effects are estimated using empirical studies (Chapter 4).

The concepts of value at risk (VaR) and conditional value at risk (CVaR) are explored in Chapters 5 and 8. We also present the calculation of the VaR of a financial portfolio containing equity and derivatives (Chapter 7), and the optimal choices of a portfolio under the constraint of VaR (Chapter 6). Value at risk (VaR) and conditional value at risk (CVaR) are estimated and tested using exercises. The use of VaR is also documented in Chapter 9, dedicated to the regulation of banks' market risk under the Basel Accord. We examine whether financial institutions' should use internal models rather than the standard models proposed by the Basel regulation, depending on the diversification opportunities.

Chapters 10 and 11 analyze the effects of different forms of financial contracts on managers' risk prevention activities. Empirical applications to risks of air accidents and default by venture capital corporations are presented. Chapter 10 links air accidents to the financing contracts of airlines' investment projects, and Chapter 11 analyzes how financing of venture capital affects the default probabilities of new innovative or technological businesses that need financing. A test for the presence of residual asymmetric information in the portfolio of a venture capital firm is presented, using methodologies developed during the recent years.

Next, we analyze various risks. Chapters 12 and 13 cover credit risk. Chapter 12 proposes a theoretical and empirical model of scoring of bank borrowers' default risk, and Chapter 13 presents the CreditMetrics model of risk management of default of a bond portfolio. This type of model lets banks calculate the capital required to satisfy the regulatory requirements linked to the credit risk of their financial asset portfolio or loan portfolio. This model is distinguished by its consideration of correlations between different assets in the portfolio.

Chapters 14 and 15 present empirical analyses of operational and liquidity risk. In these chapters we propose regime models that we test on data collected during the financial crisis of 2007–2009. Data on operational risk come from American banks that hold assets of $1 billion or more. We show that consideration of Markov regimes reduces regulatory capital. Data on liquidity risk are taken from a private bond portfolio. We use CDS premiums to measure the default risk of bonds, and we apply principal component analysis to create an illiquidity index, based on different illiquidity measures. We show that liquidity risk was a key element in bonds' credit spreads during the most recent financial crisis.

Chapter 16 proposes an analysis of the LTCM fund debacle, caused by the exaggerated use of leverage and poor risk management. The managers exposed the aggregate portfolio to credit and liquidity risks by considering only very short-term market risk. Chapter 17 describes the mismanagement of different structured products, including CDOs (collateral debt obligations), during the years leading up to the financial crisis of 2007–2009.

Chapter 18 analyzes the governance of risk management at financial institutions in relation to the Enron bankruptcy and the last financial crisis. Chapter 19 reviews recent contributions on the industrial organization of risk management and Chapter 20 covers the effect of risk management on firm value. Lastly, five detailed exercises are presented in Chapter 21. The Excel files containing the solutions to these exercises are available at: https://chairegestiondesrisques.hec.ca/en/seminars-and-publications/book-Wiley.

ACKNOWLEDGMENTS

I would like to thank the late professor Jean-Claude Cosset, who strongly encouraged me to write this book during his tenure as Research Director at HEC Montréal. His outstanding intellectual rigor and tremendous kindness will forever be remembered.

Several sections of this book were developed jointly with coauthors in the field of risk management, to whom I am very grateful: Manuel Artis, Anne-Sophie Bergerès, Oussama Chakroun, Héla Dahen, Philippe d'Astous, Pascal François, Robert Gagné, François Gagnon, Martin Garand, Geneviève Gauthier, Montserrat Guillen, Khemais Hammami, Sadok Laajimi, Olfa Maalaoui-Chun, Sara Malekan, Mohamed Mnasri, Abdelhakim Nouira, Karima Ouederni, Nadia Ouertani, Maria Pacurar, Samir Saissi Hassani, Marc Santugini, Jean-Guy Simonato, Nabil Tahani, Thouraya Triki, Charles Vanasse, and Xiaozhou Zhou.

The contents of this book are drawn from the topics of the graduate-level risk management courses I have taught since 1996. Several students have read and reread different chapters in the past few years. I would like to thank in particular Julie Beaudoin, Anne-Sophie Clarisse, Katherine D'Onofrio, Marie-Ève Drolet-Mailhot, Geneviève Dussault, Alain-Philippe Fortin, David Gutkovsky, Jeanne Mutshioko, and Hassane Saddiki for their contribution to the book. Sabrina Mc Carthy was a very diligent reader of the latest versions of all chapters. Five research assistants were heavily involved in preparing and presenting the exercises: Alain-Philippe Fortin, Tom Imbernon, Martin Lebeau, Samir Saissi Hassani, and Faouzi Tharkani.

I am deeply indebted to Claire Boisvert for her invaluable help in formatting all of the versions of the book. She has produced a remarkable manuscript. Her extreme skill and congeniality facilitated the preparation of different versions over several years. Karen Sherman translated the manuscript in a highly professional manner. Their contribution was exemplary in many respects. The production of this book was partly financed by HEC Montréal, the Canada Research Chair in Risk Management, and the Social Sciences and Humanities Research Council of Canada (SSHRC).

My family has always encouraged me with great love and understanding. Thanks to my spouse Danielle and our two sons Jean-François and André-Pierre, together with Anne-Pier, Noah, Mila, and Zoë.

GENERAL REFERENCES

Bolton, P., and Dewatripont, M., 2005. *Contract Theory*. Cambridge, MA: MIT Press.

Chiappori, A.P., and Salanié, B., 2013. "Asymmetric Information in Insurance Markets: Predictions and Tests." In G. Dionne (Ed.), *Handbook of Insurance*, 2nd ed. New York: Springer, 397–422.

Christoffersen, P.F., 2012. *Elements of Financial Risk Management*, 2nd ed. Oxford, UK: Academic Press.

Courbage, C., Rey, B., and Treich, N., 2013. "Prevention and Precaution." In G. Dionne (Ed.), *Handbook of Insurance*, 2nd ed. New York: Springer, 185–204.

Crouhy, M., Galai, D., and Mark, R., 2000. *Risk Management*. New York: McGraw-Hill.

Cruz, M.G., 2002. *Modeling, Measuring and Hedging Operational Risk*. New York: John Wiley & Sons.

Dionne, G., 2013. "The Empirical Measure of Information Problems with Emphasis on Insurance Fraud and Dynamic Data." In G. Dionne (Ed.), *Handbook of Insurance*, 2nd. ed. New York: Springer, 423–448.

Dionne, G., 2013. *Handbook of Insurance*, 2nd ed. New York: Springer.

Dionne, G., and Harrington, S.E., 2014. "Insurance and Insurance Markets." In W.K. Viscusi and M. Machina (Eds.), *Handbook of the Economics of Risk and Uncertainty*. Amsterdam: North Holland, 203–261.

Doherty, N.A., 2000. *Integrated Risk Management: Techniques and Strategies for Reducing Risk*. New York: McGraw Hill.

Dowd, K., 1998. *Beyond Value at Risk*. New York: John Wiley & Sons.

Duffie, D., and Singleton, K.J., 2003. *Credit Risk: Pricing, Measurement, and Management*. Princeton, NJ: Princeton University Press.

Eeckhoudt, L., Gollier, C., and Schlesinger, H., 2005. *Economic and Financial Decisions under Risk*. Princeton, NJ: Princeton University Press.

Gouriéroux, C., and Jasiak, J., 2001. *Financial Econometrics: Problems, Models and Methods*. Princeton, NJ: Princeton University Press.

Jorion, P., 2000. *Value at Risk: The New Benchmark for Managing Financial Risk*, 2nd ed. New York: McGraw-Hill.

Laffont, J.J., 1989. *The Economics of Uncertainty and Information*. Cambridge, MA: MIT Press, MA.

Lando, D., 2004. *Credit Risk Modeling: Theory and Applications*. Princeton, NJ: Princeton University Press.

McNeil, A.J., Frey, R., and Embrechts, P., 2015. *Quantitative Risk Management: Concepts, Techniques and Tools*. Princeton, NJ: Princeton University Press.

Ritchken, P., 1996. *Derivative Markets: Theory, Strategy, and Applications*. New York: Harper Collins College Publishers.

Salanié, B., 2005. *The Economics of Contracts*, 2nd ed. Cambridge, MA: MIT Press.

Saunders, A., and Allen, L., 2010. *Credit Risk Measurement In and Out the Financial Crisis: New Approaches to Value at Risk and Other Paradigms*, 2nd ed. Hoboken, NJ: John Wiley & Sons.

Stulz, R., 2003. *Risk Management and Derivatives*. Mason, OH: Thomson South-Western.

Tirole, J., 2006. *The Theory of Corporate Finance*. Princeton, NJ: Princeton University Press, Princeton.

CHAPTER 1

Risk Management: Definition and Historical Development

Risk management began to be studied after World War II. Several sources (Crockford, 1982; Harrington and Niehaus, 2003; Williams and Heins, 1995) date the origin of modern risk management to the 1955–1964 period. Snider (1956) observed that there were no books on risk management at the time, and no universities offered courses in the subject. The first two academic books were published by Mehr and Hedges (1963) and Williams and Hems (1964). Their content covered pure risk management, which excluded financial risk. In parallel, engineers developed technological risk management models. Operational risk partly covers technological losses; today, operational risk has to be managed by firms and is regulated for banks and insurance companies. Professionals and academics also consider the political risk of projects.

Risk management has long been associated with the use of market insurance to protect individuals and companies from various losses associated with accidents (Harrington and Niehaus, 2003). In 1982, Crockford wrote: "Operational convenience continues to dictate that pure and speculative risks should be handled by different functions within a company, even though theory may argue for them being managed as one. For practical purposes, therefore, the emphasis of risk management continues to be on pure risks" (p. 171). In this remark, speculative risks were more related to financial risks than to the current definition of speculative risks, and pure risks were related to insurable risks.

New forms of pure risk management emerged during the mid-1950s as alternatives to market insurance when different types of insurance coverage became very costly and incomplete. Several business risks were costly or impossible to insure. During the 1960s, contingent planning activities were developed, and various risk prevention/self-protection and self-insurance activities against certain losses were put into place. Protection activities and coverage for work-related illnesses and accidents also began within companies during this period.

The use of derivatives as instruments to manage insurable and uninsurable risk began in the 1970s, and developed very quickly during the 1980s.[1] It was also in the 1980s that companies began to consider financial risk management or portfolio risk management. Financial risk management became complementary to pure risk management for many companies. Financial institutions, including banks and insurance

[1]Before the 1970s, derivatives were rarely used to cover financial products. They were mainly limited to agricultural products.

companies, intensified their market risk and credit risk management activities during the 1980s. Operational risk and liquidity risk management emerged in the 1990s.

International regulation of risk also began in the 1980s. Financial institutions developed internal risk management models and capital calculation formulas to protect themselves from unanticipated risks and reduce regulatory capital. At the same time, governance of risk management became essential, integrated risk management was introduced, and the chief risk officer (CRO) position was created.

In the wake of various scandals and bankruptcies resulting from poor risk management, the Sarbanes-Oxley regulation was introduced in the United States in 2002, stipulating governance rules for companies. Stock exchanges, including the New York Stock Exchange (NYSE) in 2002, also added risk management governance rules for listed companies (Blanchard and Dionne, 2004). However, all these regulations, rules, and risk management methods did not suffice to prevent the financial crisis that began in 2007. It is not necessarily the models of risk management that were inefficient, but rather their application and enforcement. It is well known that managers in various markets regularly skirt the regulation and rules. However, it seems that deviant actions had become much more common in the years preceding the financial crisis, a trend the regulatory authorities did not anticipate, notice, or, evidently, reprimand.

In this chapter, we review the history of corporate financial and nonfinancial risk management. We present the major milestones and analyze the main stages and events that fueled its development. Finally we propose a general definition of risk management.

1.1 HISTORY OF RISK MANAGEMENT

Risk management is a relatively recent corporate function. Historical milestones are helpful to illustrate its evolution. Modern risk management started after 1955. Since the early 1970s, the concept of financial risk management has evolved considerably. Notably, risk management has become less limited to market insurance coverage, which is now considered a competing protection tool that complements several other risk management activities. After World War II, large companies with diversified portfolios of physical assets began to develop self-insurance against risks, which they covered as effectively as insurers for many small risks. Self-insurance covers the financial consequences of an adverse event or losses from an accident (Ehrlich and Becker, 1972; Dionne and Eeckhoudt, 1985). A simple self-insurance activity involves creating a fairly liquid reserve of funds to cover losses resulting from an accident or a negative market fluctuation. Ex ante risk mitigation, now frequently used to reduce financial consequences related to natural catastrophes, is a form of self-insurance.

Self-protection activities have also become very important. This type of activity affects the probabilities of losses or costs before they arise. It can also affect the conditional distribution of losses ex ante. Accident prevention is the most natural form of self-protection. Precaution is a form of self-protection applied to suspected but undefined events for which the probabilities and financial consequences are unknown. For example, a pandemic is one such event (Courbage et al., 2013). All protection and prevention activities are part of risk management.

Insurers' traditional role was seriously questioned in the United States in the 1980s, particularly during the liability insurance crisis characterized by exorbitant premiums and partial risk coverage. In that decade, alternative forms of protection from various risks emerged, such as captives (company subsidiaries that insure various risks and reinsure the largest ones), risk retention groups (groups of companies in an industry or region that pool together to protect themselves from common risks), and finite insurance (distribution of risks over time for one unit of exposure to the risk rather than between many units of exposure).

The concept of risk management in the financial sector was revolutionized in the 1970s, when financial risk management became a priority for many companies including banks, insurers, and non-financial enterprises exposed to various price fluctuations such as risk related to interest rates, stock market returns, exchange rates, and the prices of raw materials or commodities.

This revolution was sparked by major increases in price fluctuations for the risks mentioned above. In particular, fixed currency parities disappeared, and prices of commodities became much more volatile. The risks of natural catastrophe also increased considerably. Historically, to protect themselves from these financial risks, companies used balance sheets or real activities (liquidity reserves). To increase flexibility or to reduce the cost of traditional hedging activities, derivatives were then increasingly used.

Derivatives are contracts that protect the holder of an underlying asset from certain risks. Their value depends on the value and volatility of the underlying asset, or of the value indices on which the contracts are based. The best-known derivatives are forward contracts, options, futures, and swaps. Derivatives were first viewed as forms of insurance to protect individuals and companies from major fluctuations in risks. However, speculation quickly emerged in various markets, creating other risks that are increasingly difficult to control or manage. In addition, the proliferation of derivatives made it very difficult to assess companies' global risks (specifically aggregating and identifying functional forms of distribution of prices or returns).

At the same time, the definition of risk management became more general. Risk management decisions are now financial decisions that must be evaluated based on their effect on firm or portfolio value, rather than on how well they cover certain risks. This change in the definition applies particularly to large public corporations, which, ironically, may be the companies that least need risk protection, because they are able to naturally diversify much more easily than small companies. In particular, shareholders can diversify their portfolios on financial markets at a much lower cost than that of managing the risk of companies whose shares they hold.

1.2 MILESTONES IN FINANCIAL RISK MANAGEMENT

The following tables present the important dates in the evolution of risk management (Table 1.1) and of derivatives or structured financial products (Table 1.2). The birth of modern financial theory is generally associated with the seminal work of Louis Bachelier in 1900; he was the first to use the concept of Brownian motion to analyze fluctuations in a financial asset. However, it was only in the 1930s that research on prices of financial assets began. The American Finance Association (AFA) met for the first time in 1939, in Philadelphia. Its first journal, *American Finance*, appeared in 1942. It became *The Journal of Finance* in 1946. At that time, research in finance specifically dealt with price setting, financial market efficiency, and detection of profitable strategies (including anticipation of stock prices). The year 1932 marked the

TABLE 1.1 Milestones in the history of risk management.

1730	First futures contracts on the price of rice in Japan
1864	First futures contracts on agricultural products at the Chicago Board of Trade
1900	Louis Bachelier's thesis "Théorie de la Spéculation"; Brownian motion
1932	First issue of the *Journal of Risk and Insurance*
1942	First issue of the *Journal of Finance*
1952	Publication of Markowitz's (1952) article "Portfolio Selection"
1961–1966	Treynor, Sharpe (1964), Lintner, and Mossin develop the CAPM
1963	Arrow (1963) introduces optimal insurance, moral hazard, and adverse selection
1972	Futures contracts on currencies at the Chicago Mercantile Exchange
1973	Option valuation formulas by Black and Scholes (1973) and Merton (1973)
1974	Merton's default risk model (1974)
1977	Interest rate models by Vasicek (1977) and Cox, Ingersoll, and Ross (1985)
1980–1990	Exotic options, swaptions, and stock derivatives
1979–1982	First OTC contracts in the form of swaps: currency and interest rate swaps.
1985	Creation of the Swap Dealers Association, which established the OTC exchange standards
1987	First risk management department in a bank (Merrill Lynch)
1988	Basel I
Late 1980s	Value at risk (VaR) and calculation of optimal capital
1992	Article by Heath, Jarrow, and Morton (1992) on the forward rate curve
1992	Integrated Risk Management
1992	RiskMetrics
1994–1995	First bankruptcies associated with misuse (or speculation) of derivatives: Procter & Gamble (manufacturer, rates derivatives, 1994), Orange County (management funds, derivatives on financial securities, 1994), and Barings (bank, forward contracts, 1995)
1997	CreditMetrics
1997–1998	Asian and Russian crisis and LTCM collapse
2001	Enron bankruptcy
2002	New governance rules by Sarbanes-Oxley and NYSE
2004	Basel II
2007	Beginning of the financial crisis
2009	Starting of CDS central clearing operations
2010	Basel III
2010	Dodd-Frank Act for regulating the US financial markets (including the Volcker Rule)
2011–2013	New rules for the governance of risk management
2016	Solvency II came into effect
2016	CVaR replaces VaR in Basel III regulation for market risk

Note: This table presents the main dates related to the history of risk management.

birth of the American Risk and Insurance Association. The first academic studies of insurance were published in *Journal of Insurance*, which was renamed *The Journal of Risk and Insurance* in 1964 (Weiss and Qiu, 2008). Other specialized journals followed, including *Risk Management* (formerly *The National Insurance Buyer*), published by the Risk and Insurance Management Society (RIMS), a professional association of risk managers founded in 1950, along with *The Geneva Papers of Risk and Insurance*, published by the Geneva Association since 1976.

TABLE 1.2 Main dates of the launching of derivatives and structured financial products.

1970s	Currency swaps
1972	Foreign currency futures
1973	Equity options
1979	Over-the-counter currency options
1981	Cross-currency interest rate swaps
1983	Equity index options
1983	Interest rate caps/floors
1983	Swaptions
1985	Asset-back securities (ABS)
1987	Path-dependent options (Asian, lookback, etc.)
1987	Collateralized debt obligations (CDO)
1992	CAT and futures insurance options
1993	Captions/Floortions
1994	Credit default swaps (CDS)
1994	CAT bonds
1997	Weather derivatives
2002	Collateralized fund obligations (CFO)
2017	Crypto derivatives

Note: This table presents the main appearance dates of derivative and structured financial products.

It was only in the 1950s and 1960s that researchers (Markowitz, Lintner, Treynor, Sharpe, and Mossin) undertook fundamental studies of financial decisions. This resulted in the modern theory of portfolio choice based on the Capital Asset Pricing Model (CAPM). This period was marked by revolutionary articles in finance, whose lead authors earned Nobel Prizes. Yet, it was only in the early 1970s that the main financial risk management products appeared and that the initial theoretical models of modern risk coverage were published.

Black and Scholes's model is undoubtedly the most popular of these early models. These authors were the first to propose an explicit formula for the pricing of a derivative, namely an option. This model was so revolutionary that the major finance journals refused to publish its first version. It was finally published in the *Journal of Political Economy*, in 1973. Later that year, Merton published an extension in the *Bell Journal of Economics and Management Science*. After that, risk coverage derivatives expanded quickly, spawning currency and interest rate swaps, and over-the-counter options (OTCs). Mathematical finance and the popularity of computers accelerated the growth and use of derivatives.

This period is the starting point for the intensive development of research on derivatives pricing. Although coverage of agricultural products began in Chicago in 1864 (and in Japan in 1730 for rice prices), it was only in 1972 that derivatives on financial assets surfaced in that American city (Chicago Board of Trade, CBOT). The year 1973 marked a turning point in financial history for another reason: the creation of the CBOE (Chicago Board Options Exchange), together with a clearinghouse.

The growth of the options market accelerated after the CBOE standardized contracts and developed secondary markets needed to generate sufficient liquid assets for market effectiveness (Smith, Smithson, and Wakeman, 1990). During the 1980s and 1990s, the implementation of these hedge products sensitized market players to the risk they incur in their regular investment activities.

Concomitantly, new statistical tools were put in place in banks and rating agencies to select the clientele (e.g., credit scoring) and manage credit risk. These tools facilitated assessment of default/credit and pricing risks. The Basel Accord of 1988 imposed an international regulatory vision of credit risk.

In the late 1980s, high market volatility spurred the large US investment banks to put in place risk management departments (Field, 2003). JP Morgan developed the two best-known internal risk management models—RiskMetrics for market risk and CreditMetrics for credit risk—in 1992 and 1997. These two models highlighted the idea of measuring risks in portfolio form by considering their dependencies and using value at risk to quantify aggregate portfolio risk. The publication of the RiskMetrics model prompted broad dissemination of the value-at-risk (VaR) measure among professionals and academics alike. It was imported from insurers, which used a similar risk measure to calculate their maximum losses (MPY, or maximum probable yearly aggregate Loss; Cummins and Freifelder, 1978). VaR is the maximum value that a portfolio or company can lose during a given period of time, at a specified level of confidence. This measure also allows one to measure the optimal capital required to protect companies or portfolios from anticipated and unanticipated losses (Scaillet, 2003).

These new risk measurement tools are important instruments for calculating banks' regulatory capital under Basel regulation. They were also used to analyze the first major losses sustained in 1994 and 1995 following the misuse of derivatives (Procter & Gamble, Orange County, and Barings). Three credit risk crises followed: the Asian crisis, the Russian crisis, and the collapse of Long-Term Capital Management (LTCM). The LTCM hedge fund was overexposed to various risks. When the Asians and Russians steadily defaulted on their obligations, LTCM began to run short of liquid assets to meet its obligations; this liquidity risk quickly turned into a default risk (Jorion, 2000).

Risk management became a corporate affair in the late 1990s. The major orientation decisions in firms' management policy (and monitoring) are now made by the board of directors. Most often, the audit committee monitors these decisions, although some large financial institutions have put risk committees in place. The position of Chief Risk Officer, or CRO, became more important.

Financial hedging products were developed to cover different types of risk. The four main risks for banks are credit risk (80% of the risk of banks, including default risk), market risk (5%), operational risk (15%), and liquidity risk (not yet well quantified). Market risk represents the risk of volatile prices or asset returns, and credit risk has been associated with default risk (although recent studies estimate that the default risk corresponds to a maximum ranging from 25% to 85% of the bond credit spread; Elton et al., 2001; Dionne et al., 2010). The Basel agreement of 2004 addresses these risks. Only credit risk was covered in 1988; market risk was considered years later, in 1996. It quickly became apparent that regulatory treatment (arbitrary capital) of market risk was ill-adapted to banks' portfolio management of this risk.

Regulatory authorities consequently authorized banks to use internal models to measure market risk. In contrast, the portfolio treatment of credit risk began only in 2004 under Basel II.

Adequate capital reserves became a major concern in the early 2000s following major defaults in the late 1990s and the Enron bankruptcy in 2001. Basel II introduced more rigorous rules for banks in 2004. In addition to modifying the credit risk management rules, the Accord introduced new rules for operational risk. However, the legislators have said little about managing the risks of various management and hedge funds, especially pension funds. Canada was equally lax: The Caisse de dépôt et placement du Québec, a major pension fund, lost over $30 billion CAD in the last financial crisis, including a $10 billion write-off caused by disastrous commercial paper risk management, involving misuse of this structured product with an AAA credit rating! US Federal Reserve Chairman Alan Greenspan was particularly negligent: he often gave contradictory speeches on the advantages and risks associated with the use of derivatives and on the financial market's capacity to absorb risks effectively, without additional regulation. In particular, OTC products proliferated without real or regulated verification of counterparty risk.

After the financial crisis, new rules for the governance of risk management were adopted in many countries. The firm board is now more involved in defining the risk appetite of the company and in adopting the main strategic decisions on risk-taking. Risk control is also under the responsibility of the board. Contrary to the 2002 rules, the emphasis is not limited to the presence of independent directors on the different committees but to their competencies in understanding different risks and risk management tools.

Table 1.2 presents the main dates that derivatives and structured products appeared. Its content is taken from Jorion (2001); Crouhy, Galai, and Mark (2000); Roncalli (2001); Field (2003); and electronic documents. Few derivatives and structured products have been launched since the 2000s. A special issue of *The Journal of Risk and Insurance* published in September 2009 focused on insurers' risk management and their use of derivatives, structured products, and their involvement in securitization. It featured survey articles by Cummins and Weiss (2009) and Cummins and Trainar (2009). On risk management and insurance demand, see MacMinn and Garven (2013) and on regulation of insurers, see Klein (2013).

1.3 CURRENT DEFINITION OF CORPORATE RISK MANAGEMENT

The goal of corporate risk management is to create a reference framework that will allow companies to handle risk and uncertainty. Risks are present in nearly all firms' financial and economic activities. The risk identification, assessment, and management process is part of companies' strategic development; it must be designed and planned at the highest level, namely the board of directors. The risk appetite of the company must also be defined by the board. An integrated risk management approach must evaluate, control, and monitor all risks and their dependencies to which the company is exposed. In general, a pure risk is a combination of the probability or frequency of an event and its consequences, which are usually negative. Risk can be measured by the volatility of results, but higher moments of the distribution are often necessary. Uncertainty is less precise because the probability of an uncertain event is often unknown or subjective, as is its consequence. In this case, we would refer to precautionary rather than preventive activities to protect against uncertainty. Lastly, financial risk management consists in undertaking opportunistic activities related to future risks that may generate positive or negative results.

In this book, corporate risk management is defined as a set of financial and operational activities that maximize the value of a company or a portfolio by reducing the costs associated with risk (Stulz, 1996, 2003). The main risk management activities are diversification and risk hedging using various instruments, including derivatives and structured products, market insurance, self-insurance, and self-protection. The main costs firms seek to minimize are costs of financial distress, risk premium to partners (stakeholders), expected income taxes, and investment financing. Managers' behavior toward risk (risk appetite and risk aversion) and corporate governance also affect the choice of risk management activities.

There are five main risks:

1. Pure risk (often insurable, and not necessarily exogenous in the presence of moral hazard and known in the presence of adverse selection);
2. Market risk (variation in prices of commodities, exchange rates, asset returns);
3. Default risk (probability of default, recovery rate, exposure at default);
4. Operational risk (employee or management errors, fraud, IT system breakdown, derivative mispricing);
5. Liquidity risk: risk of not possessing sufficient funds to meet short-term financial obligations without affecting prices. May degenerate into default risk.

1.4 CONCLUSION

The purpose of this chapter was to present a historical review of risk management. In addition to outlining the important dates, we discuss the objectives of risk management and criticize its application in the years preceding the latest financial crisis. The first conclusion is that risk management must encompass more than simply minimizing the company's risk exposure.

The objective of risk management is to maximize firm or portfolio value via the reduction of costs associated with different risks. The main costs that companies incur are financial distress, income taxes, financing of future investment projects, and premiums payable to stakeholders.

Risk management can also improve the firm's capital structure, which suggests that companies in good financial health should use their information advantage to establish strategies to hedge future prices. Companies also need integrated risk management, which would let them profit from different forms of natural coverage within the company.

Companies can use internal activities and market activities to protect themselves from risks. The most widespread internal activities are prevention of financial risks and accidents (self-protection) and the reduction of financial consequences resulting from bad events (risk retention, self-insurance, liquidity reserves). Market insurance is a form of protection for losses related to pure risks that cannot be covered by the company. Derivatives are financial instruments that protect companies from unanticipated financial losses.

Risk management is part of corporate governance. Its main orientations must be defined by the board of directors and must be monitored by independent and competent directors in the audit committee or the risk committee for companies highly exposed to various risks, such as financial institutions.

Financial institutions face a particular problem. Their risk positions, which are intended to increase their returns, expose their customers (holders of deposits and insurance contracts) to major losses. This justifies the current regulation of bank and insurance company risks. Recent history shows that international regulation of large financial institutions has failed in several respects: unfortunately, it is the taxpayers who have had to shoulder the cost of the indiscipline of executives of large financial institutions. Regulation can also create perverse and unanticipated effects on financial institutions.

In conclusion, effective regulation of financial institutions apparently remains elusive despite the immense progress seen in the past 25 years.

REFERENCES

Arrow, K.J., 1963. "Uncertainty and the Welfare Economics of Medical Care." *The American Economic Review* 53, 941–973.

Bank for International Settlements (BIS), 2005. *International Convergence of Capital Measurement and Capital Standards – A Revised Framework*. Basel Committee on Banking Supervision, Basel, Switzerland.

Bank for International Settlements (BIS), 2012. *Progress Report on Basel III Implementation*. Basel Committee on Banking Supervision.

Black, F., and Scholes M.S., 1973. "The Pricing of Options and Corporate Liabilities." *Journal of Political Economy* 81, 637–654.

Blanchard, D., and Dionne, G., 2004. "The Case for Independent Risk Management Committees." *Risk* 17, S19–S21.

Courbage, C., Rey-Fournier, B., and Treich, N., 2013. "Prevention and Precaution." In: Dionne, G. (Ed.), *Handbook of Insurance*, 2nd ed. New York: Springer, 185–204.

Cox, J.C., Ingersoll, J.E., and Ross, S.A., 1985. "A Theory of the Term Structure of Interest Rates." *Econometrica* 53, 385–408.

Crockford, G.N., 1982. "The Bibliography and History of Risk Management: Some Preliminary Observations." *Geneva Papers on Risk and Insurance* 7, 169–179.

Crouhy, M., Mark, R., and Galai, D., 2000. *Risk Management*. New York: McGraw Hill.

Cummins, J.D., and Freifelder, L.R., 1978. "A Comparative Analysis of Alternative Maximum Probable Yearly Aggregate Loss Estimators." *Journal of Risk and Insurance* 45, 27–52.

Cummins, J.D., and Trainar, P., 2009. "Securitization, Insurance, and Reinsurance." *Journal of Risk and Insurance* 76, 463–492.

Cummins, J.D. and Weiss, M.A., 2009. "Convergence of Insurance and Financial Markets: Hybrid and Securitized Risk-Transfer Solutions." *Journal of Risk and Insurance* 76, 493–545.

Dionne, G., 2009. "Structured Finance, Risk Management, and the Recent Financial Crisis." http://papers.ssrn.com/sol3/papers.cfm?abstract_id=1488767.

Dionne, G., 2004. "The Foundations of Risk Regulation for Banks: A Review of the Literature." In: *The Evolving Financial System and Public Policy*, 177–215. Proceedings of a conference held by the Bank of Canada, Ottawa, Canada, December 4–5.

Dionne, G., and Eeckhoudt, L., 1985. "Self-Insurance, Self-Protection and Increased Risk Aversion." *Economics Letters* 17, 39–42.

Dionne, G., Gauthier, G., Hammami, K., Maurice, M., and Simonato, J.G., 2011. "A Reduced Form Model of Default Spreads with Markov-Switching Macroeconomic Factors." *Journal of Banking and Finance* 35, 1984–2000.

Dionne, G., Hammami, K., Gauthier, G., Maurice, M., and Simonato, J.G., 2010. "Default Risk in Corporate Yield Spreads." *Financial Management* 39, 707–731.

Dionne, G. and Harrington, S.E., 2014. "Insurance and Insurance Markets." In Viscusi, W.K., and Machina, M. (Eds.), *Handbook of the Economics of Risk and Uncertainty*. Amsterdam: North Holland, 203–261.

Ehrlich, I., and Becker, G., 1972. "Market Insurance, Self-Insurance and Self-Protection." *Journal of Political Economy* 80, 623–648.

Elton, E., Gruber, M., Agrawal, D., and Mann, C., 2001. "Explaining the Rate Spread on Corporate Bonds." *Journal of Finance* 56, 247–277.

Field, P., 2003. *Introduction to Modern Risk Management, a History*. Incisive RWG. London: Haymarket House.

Harrington, S. and Niehaus, G.R., 2003. *Risk Management and Insurance*. Irwin/McGraw-Hill.

Heath, D., Jarrow, R., and Morton, A., 1992. "Bond Pricing and the Term Structure of Interest Rates: A New Methodology for Contingent Claims Valuation." *Econometrica* 60, 77–105.

Jorion, P., 2000. "Risk Management Lessons from the Long-Term Capital Management." *European Financial Management* 6, 277–300.

Jorion, P., 2001. *Value at Risk: The New Benchmark for Managing Financial Risk*. New York: McGraw-Hill.

Klein, R.W., 2013. "Insurance Market Regulation: Catastrophe Risk, Competition, and Systemic Risk." In: Dionne, G. (Ed.), *Handbook of Insurance*, 2nd ed. New York: Springer, 909–939.

MacMinn, R., and Garven, R., 2013. "On the Demand for Corporate Insurance – Creating Value." In: Dionne, G. (Ed.), *Handbook of Insurance*, 2nd ed. New York: Springer, 487–516.

Markowitz, H., 1952. "Portfolio Selection." *Journal of Finance* 7, 77–91.

Mehr, R.I., and Hedges, B.A., 1963. *Risk Management in the Business Enterprise*. Homewood, IL: Irwin.

Merton, R.C., 1973. "Theory of Rational Option Pricing." *Bell Journal of Economics and Management Science* 4, 141–183.

Merton, R.C., 1974. "On the Pricing of Corporate Debt: The Risk Structure of Interest Rates." *Journal of Finance* 29, 449–470.

Miller K.D., 1992. "A Framework for Integrated Risk Management in International Business." *Journal of International Business Studies* 23, 311–331.

Roncalli, T., 2001. "Introduction à la Gestion des Risques." Cours ENSAI, France. http://www.univ-evry.fr/modules/resources/download/default/m2if/roncalli/gdr.pdf.

Scaillet, O., 2003. *The Origin and Development of Value at Risk: Modern Risk Management: A History*. 15th Anniversary of Risk Magazine. London: Risk Publications, 151–158.

Sharpe, W.F., 1964. "Capital Asset Prices: A Theory of Market Equilibrium under Conditions of Risk." *Journal of Finance* 19, 425–442.

Smith, C., Smithson, C., and Wakeman L., 1990. "The Evolving Market for Swaps." In: Schwartz, R.J., and Smith, C.W. (Eds.), *The Handbook of Currency and Interest Rate Risk Management*. New York: New York Institute of Finance, 191–211.

Snider, H.W., 1956. "Reaching Professional Status: A Program for Risk Management." In: *Corporate Risk Management: Current Problems and Perspectives*. Insurance Series 112. American Management Association, 30–35.

Stulz, R.M., 1996. "Rethinking Risk Management." *Journal of Applied Corporate Finance* 9, 8–24.

Stulz, R.M., 2003. *Risk Management and Derivatives*. Thomson/South-Western.

Vasicek, O., 1977. "An Equilibrium Characterization of the Term Structure." *Journal of Financial Economics* 5, 177–188.

Weiss, M. and Qiu, J., 2008. "The Journal of Risk and Insurance: A 75-Year Historical Perspective." *Journal of Risk and Insurance* 75, 253–274.

Williams, A., and Heins, M.H., 1964. *Risk Management and Insurance*. New York: McGraw-Hill.

Williams, A., and Heins, M.H., 1995. *Risk Management and Insurance*. New York: McGraw-Hill.

CHAPTER 2

Theoretical Determinants of Risk Management in Non-Financial Firms

This chapter presents and analyzes the factors that motivate non-financial firms to hedge their risks based on arguments brought forth by Stulz (1996) in an important article on risk management. Stulz has also published a book on risk management (Stulz, 2003). He is one of the main contributors to the literature that explains why some non-financial firms choose to invest in risk management while others do not. Stulz expands on his 1996 paper with an article published in 2013 in which he analyzes examples of firm behavior with respect to risk management during the recent financial crisis.

Stulz's 1996 article sheds light on the differences between what the first risk management theorists proposed and what is observed in practice. In general, certain financial theorists suggested that firms should almost always use derivatives to hedge their currency risk, interest rate risk, and risk related to commodity prices, whereas others recommended routine use of market insurance to hedge against other risks such as pure risks.

Stulz (1996) argues that when making decisions pertaining to risk management, firms need to take a value-maximizing approach as opposed to focusing solely on the hedging efficiency of different tools.

As we will see, large non-financial firms use less market insurance than the amount recommended by traditional models and, oddly enough, tend to favor the use of derivatives more than smaller firms that have more volatile cash flows and a higher cost of capital. Smaller firms are also generally characterized by concentrated equity ownership. The shareholders of smaller firms are often less diversified than those of larger firms, which warrants greater use of risk management.

When firms use derivatives as hedging instruments, it is implied that they possess the knowledge of how these financial instruments function. It is rather difficult for small firms, as opposed to large firms, to acquire such competencies due to their limited resources. The requirements related to qualified personnel, software, and sophisticated computer systems are often impossible for smaller firms to meet, so they often have no other choice but to hire pricey consultants.

While studying the bankruptcy cases of the 1990s that were discussed in the previous chapter, it may be tempting to criticize the use of these financial instruments and to qualify them as dangerous even though they are intended to protect firms from such events.

The analysis of the events that occurred throughout Asia and the United States in the 1990s has left certain financiers perplexed. This subject requires prudence, and we should avoid hasty generalizations. In many cases, the critiques pertaining to the use of risk management (Barings, Orange County, Metallgesellschaft, and, more recently, Enron, LTCM, investment banks during the financial crisis, including Lehman Brothers, etc.) require us to take into account potential underlying problems related to corporate governance or to speculative (even fraudulent) activities that are often founded on management's outlook regarding future asset prices.

There are apparently improvements to be made to both the theory and practice in order to better harmonize predictions and observations; the simple minimization of the volatility of risks is not necessarily the most appropriate goal. This goal is the very essence of value at risk, or VaR, models.

Throughout his paper, Stulz (1996) corroborates this analysis. He argues that the minimization of variance has long dominated the academic discussions pertaining to hedging financial risks and that risk management should go beyond that approach.

Instead, we should focus on the probability of lower-tail events (downside risks or Conditional VaR, for example), namely those that incur significant financial costs or those that prevent firms from going forth with their investment projects (especially for non-financial firms). Simply counting the number of occurrences for which losses are greater than VaR is insufficient in many circumstances. Conditional VaR is useful to calculate the conditional losses associated with the outcomes of these lower-tail events. This subject will be discussed in further detail throughout the chapter dedicated to Conditional VaR (CVaR).

It is important to note that when we decrease the variability of a firm's earnings with forward contracts, we are simultaneously decreasing the probability of high earnings as well as low earnings, at least when the distribution is symmetrical. It is not evident that this is the best strategy; in fact, it may be sounder to concentrate on downside risk and use options.

Decisions pertaining to risk management need to be made jointly with those related to a firm's capital structure. The effect of a firm's risk management strategy on managerial incentives and decision making (corporate governance) also needs to be taken into account.

Further, certain firms that are in good financial health and that have comparative advantages (for instance, if a firm has privileged information regarding its industry risk) could use these advantages to take financial risks. Some have critiqued this opinion because it casts doubt on market efficiency; that is to say, asset prices already contain all information or that privileged (or asymmetrical) information simply may not exist.

Sellers of derivatives and structured products argue that such instruments are inexpensive and can increase firm value by decreasing the default probability. However, the recent financial crisis demonstrated that some of these instruments could be toxic and potentially even more dangerous than not hedging at all. The choice of appropriate hedging instruments in a dynamic environment is, in fact, crucial (Stulz, 2013; Mnasri, Dionne, and Gueyie, 2017; Dionne, Gueyie, and Mnasri, 2018).

2.1 VALUE OF RISK MANAGEMENT

The two pillars of modern risk management are the concepts of market efficiency and diversification.

The former postulates that asset prices contain all information, making it impossible to generate a profit by claiming to possess informational advantages.

Although this concept is widespread, many managers continue to believe that they possess comparative advantages in certain markets. Consequently, firms use their resources to develop investment strategies that are very risky because a high return is generally accompanied by high risk. However, these practices have been abandoned by many firms that realize they did not actually possess comparative advantages within their sector or because they had bad experiences resulting from the inappropriate use of hedging instruments.

In fact, firms do not necessarily need to hedge against all the financial risks they may face, particularly when they are already well diversified internally.

In order to maximize firm value, hedging should focus on the risks that are most difficult to diversify and that incur real costs for firms. Researchers have identified four of these costs:

1. Expected default costs (Smith and Stulz, 1985)
2. Supplementary payments or risk premiums to stakeholders (Stulz, 1996)
3. Expected tax payments (Graham and Smith, 1999; Graham and Rogers, 2002)
4. Investment financing (This last cost will be studied in parallel with the paper by Froot, Sharfstein, and Stein, 1993, in Chapter 3.)

More recently, risk management has been associated with:

5. Greater firm efficiency (Cummins et al., 2009)
6. The payment of dividends (Dionne and Ouederni, 2011)
7. Corporate governance (Dionne and Triki, 2013);
8. Industrial organization (Dionne and Santugini, 2014; Léautier and Rochet, 2014)
9. Mergers and acquisitions (Savor, 2002)
10. Market regulation (Basel II and III and Solvency II)

An efficient risk management strategy reduces the costs associated with the outcomes of the risks to which a firm is exposed. Throughout this chapter, we will concentrate on the first three costs.

2.1.1 Expected Default Costs

Default costs refer to the costs associated with default, not bankruptcy. Default costs can be divided into two categories: direct costs such as lawyer fees, consultant fees, and court-related expenses; and indirect costs incurred when a firm is under bankruptcy protection laws, such as reorganizational costs. Both these categories of costs are directly reflected in a firm's valuation. The goal of an efficient risk management strategy is to maintain these costs at an optimal level, while taking into consideration the cost of hedging instruments.

For example, if we evaluate that a firm's default costs are \$25 million and that without hedging, the firm's default probability is 10%, then the expected cost of default is \$2.5 million. If an efficient hedging strategy reduces the default probability to 0, the gross profit of the hedging activity is \$2.5 million. Now, if the firm is valued at \$100 million, this profit represents 2.5% of the firm's value. This example highlights the fact that risk management reduces default probability. It can also affect conditional default costs, but to a lesser extent.

Figure 2.1 illustrates that risk management contributes to reducing the volatility of a firm's value. The firm will default when its gross value (without distress costs) is

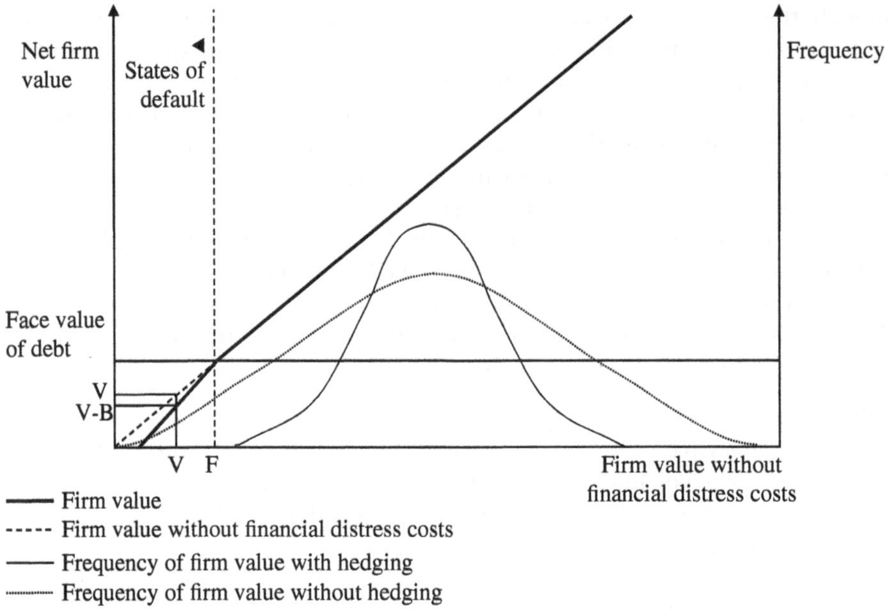

FIGURE 2.1 Hedging and firm value.
Source: Reproduced from Stulz (1996). © John Wiley & Sons, Inc. Reproduced with permission.

less than its face value F. In this example, hedging reduces the volatility of firm values and eliminates the default probability.

We observe two probability density functions of firm value in Figure 2.1. The density function represented by the dotted line corresponds to the density of firm value without hedging, whereas the full line represents the frequency with hedging. The first density function corresponds to a positive default probability (surface of the density function to the left of F), whereas the second function corresponds to a null default probability. We can see that the surface of the second density function seldom crosses F, implying that the firm value is always greater than F; this firm will thus never default.

Figure 2.1 compares the value of a firm with and without financial distress costs. It shows that the firm's net value (dark line) goes below the dotted line to the left of F. This signifies that the difference between the dotted line and the dark line to the left of F represents the financial distress costs. To the right of F, both values are identical; they overlap on the 45° line. To the left of F, the firm defaults and needs to disburse the required restructuring costs (for example, B for firm value V), which can be interpreted as conditional default costs.

Consequently, we observe that the least diversified firm has a positive default probability and therefore positive expected default costs. Its net firm value is consequently lower than that of a diversified firm.

2.1.2 Risk Premium to Stakeholders

Similar arguments can be made regarding stakeholders who may request higher salaries or risk premiums when a firm is less diversified because they face a higher risk of losing their job or their investment. Suppliers may also be less lenient with respect to credit terms and may also request a premium for this risk. These costs can be represented in the same manner as default costs, which is why we will not repeat the discussion here.

2.1.3 Expected Tax Payments

Risk management allows a firm to reduce the expected tax payments when the taxation function is convex with respect to profits or to firm value. This statement is demonstrated graphically in Figures 2.2 and 2.3.

Let us consider Figures 2.2 and 2.3. Figure 2.2 represents a strictly convex (progressive) tax function with a marginal taxation rate that increases continuously with firm value. In Figure 2.3, three taxation levels are illustrated with marginal rates of 0%, 20%, and 30%, for example.

Let us begin with Figure 2.2 and consider a firm whose value faces a binomial distribution with the following parameters: at the end of the period, if the retail price

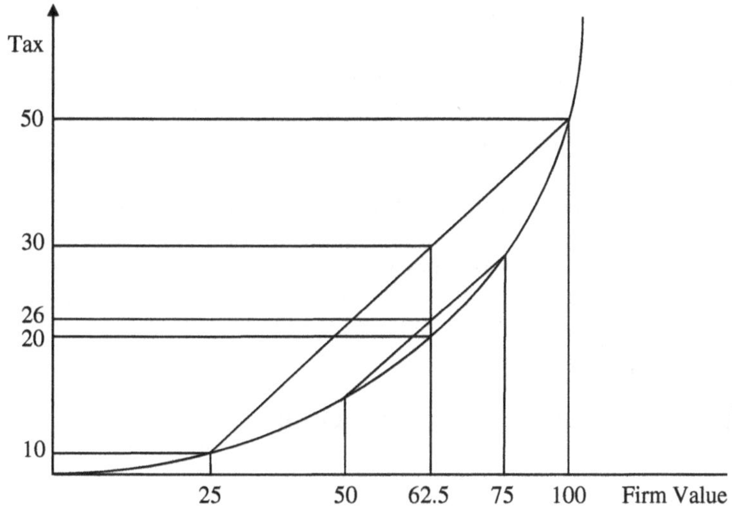

FIGURE 2.2 Benefit of hedging with a convex taxation function.

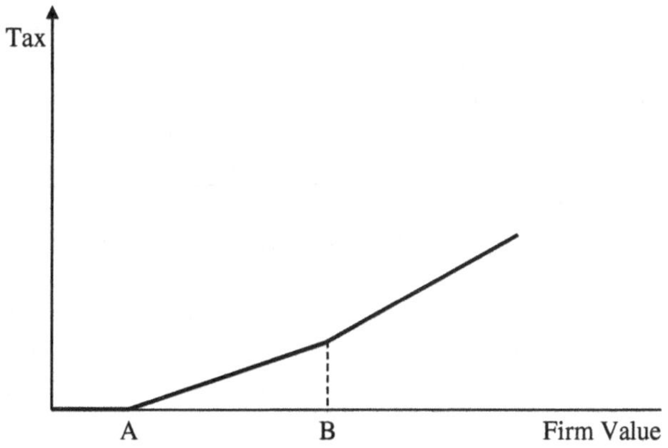

FIGURE 2.3 Piecewise linear taxation function.

of the product sold is high, the firm will be valued at $100 million with a probability of 0.5, and if the retail price is low, the firm's value will be reduced to $25 million with a probability of 0.5.

The average value of the firm is therefore $62.5 million. This value represents the halfway point between the values of $100 million and $25 million on the x-axis. The conditional amounts to be paid in taxes are $50 million and $10 million, with an average of $30 million represented on the y-axis.

Now, suppose that the firm decides to partially hedge its risk exposure, and the new distribution of the firm's value is $75 million with a probability of 0.5 and $50 million with a probability of 0.5. The average firm value remains equal to $62.5 million (no hedging cost). However, as the figure indicates, the average tax payment is reduced to $26 million. If the costs of hedging are null and if the firm is exposed to one risk factor, the optimal decision would be to hedge 100% of the firm's risk exposure, which gives an absolute (average) value of $62.5 million and taxes payable of $20 million. Here, it is the convexity of the tax function that explains the result, and not the level of taxes to be paid.

Let us consider Figure 2.3 to illustrate this last point. Figure 2.3 is a more realistic representation of the tax code observed in several countries. First, suppose that all the potential end-of-year values are to the right of point B. The local or effective tax function of the firm is therefore linear. Even though, on average, the firm pays a high amount in taxes, it does not have any incentive to hedge its risks in order to reduce its tax payment. However, a firm whose value can be to the right or left of point B (or A) would be motivated to hedge because its taxation function is convex when combining two or three linear sections. Again, it is the local convexity of the tax function that matters, not the average amount of taxes to be paid. We will return to this subject in Chapter 4 that discusses the empirical verifications of the determinants of corporate risk management.

2.2 COMPARATIVE ADVANTAGES IN RISK TAKING

The financial literature often maintains that firms cannot expect to generate profits based on prices that are perfectly anticipated by public information, because all information is revealed in these prices. What about private information held by specialists regarding the distribution of prices? For example, consider a firm that possesses private knowledge on the price fluctuations of a certain raw material. This firm is able to better anticipate the future movements in the price of the raw material (relative to other market participants) and can very well adjust its hedging strategy accordingly. For instance, the firm can protect 80% of its exposure to price increases of an input if it anticipates a price hike and only 20% of its exposure if it anticipates that the price of the raw material will decrease, rather than always hedging 50% of its exposure in the absence of privileged information or expertise.

However, before engaging in such activities, the firm must evaluate all its financial and operational risk factors and be in good financial health. In addition, the firm must be able to visualize the impact of its risk management strategy on its capital structure.

2.3 RISK MANAGEMENT AND CAPITAL STRUCTURE

As mentioned above, the goal of risk management is to maximize firm value, which implies that a firm can maintain the financial flexibility required to undertake new investment opportunities at competitive prices. Consequently, a good risk management strategy may increase a firm's debt capacity; risk management may be interpreted as a substitute for equity. An efficient risk management strategy can reduce the default probability and thus reduce lending costs because the default risk premium imposed by banks or investors can decrease.

Inversely, capital structure can also impact how a firm approaches risk management. To understand this argument, see Figure 2.4, proposed by Stulz (1996). It shows three density functions corresponding to three firms with very different valuation distributions. The AAA firm has a default probability of 0. BBB has a higher cost of capital, due to its higher default probability. Suppose that BBB's default probability is 5%. Finally, firm C is in financial difficulty with a high default probability, which we estimate at 95%.

Firm AAA does not need to diversify its activities to protect itself from financial distress because its default probability is 0. Thereby, the firm is able to borrow easily if need be and may even speculate if its managers hold private specialized information.

The situation of the firm BBB is very different. This firm should hedge in order to decrease its default probability and increase its affected value. Also, it should not engage in speculative activities.

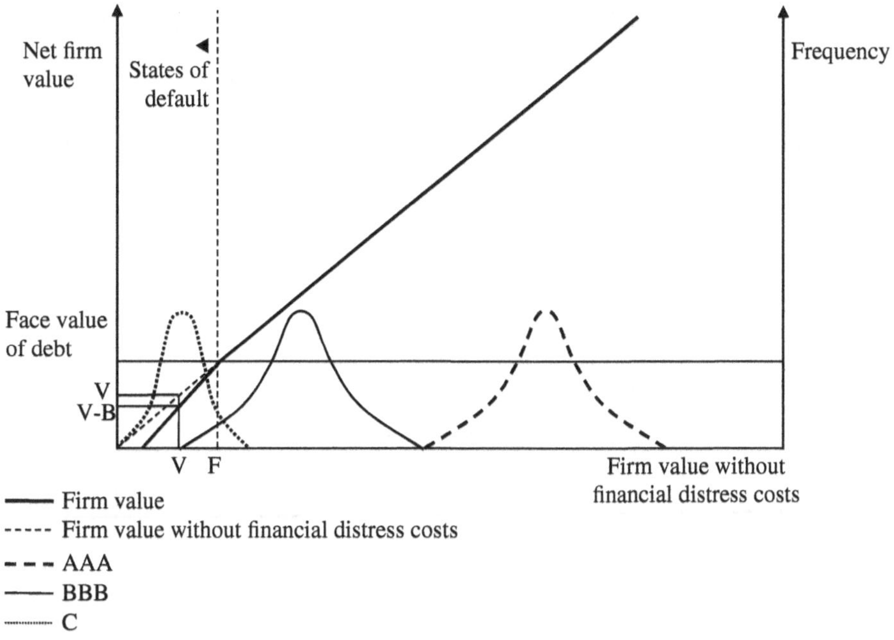

FIGURE 2.4 Hedging and firm capital structure.
Source: Reproduced from Stulz (1996). © John Wiley & Sons, Inc. Reproduced with permission.

What about firm C? It is seemingly impossible for this firm to use risk management as a tool to rectify its financial situation because hedging will actually increase its default probability. Some managers may even speculate in the hopes of being very lucky (last chance) in order to help the firm find a way out. Speculation would consequently have the opposite effect of hedging because it increases the probability of non-default (greater surface to the right of F) by increasing the volatility of the firm's value.

If we were to increase external debt (BBB), managers would be more disciplined, and risk management would be intensified within the firm. However, this option should be considered prudently because too much debt can cause extreme behavior (Jensen and Meckling, 1976).

2.4 RISK MANAGEMENT AND MANAGERIAL INCENTIVES

Firms whose managers are also shareholders (meaning that they also benefit from the firm's profits) are apparently the most diversified. Tufano (1996) tested this premise for firms in the gold mining industry. He found that managers who have a large portion of their human capital and compensation invested within their firm wish to protect themselves more. Attributing firm equity to managers is beneficial when it comes to risk management, yet this incentive is often more costly than stock options.

In addition, Figure 2.5 (Stulz, 1996) explains why firms that compensate managers with stock options may engage in more speculation or may be more lax with respect to risk management. Managers who hold stock options with a strike price equal to F′ are less inclined to hedge because hedging decreases the volatility of the

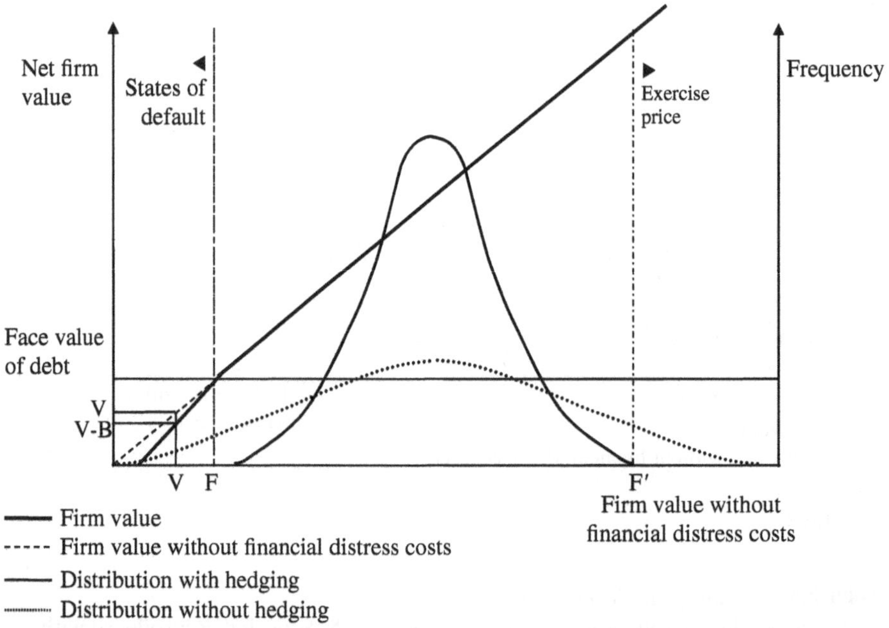

FIGURE 2.5 Impact of manager call options on risk management.
Source: Reproduced from Stulz (1996). © John Wiley & Sons, Inc. Reproduced with permission.

firm's shares (which consequently decreases the value of the stock options) as well as the probability of undertaking personal projects after having exercised the options.

The darker density corresponds to a null default probability (to the right of F), but also to a null probability of exercising the managers' stock options (to the left of F′), hence the conflict of interest between managers and shareholders. Given that managers hold stock options, they may prefer the dotted density function, whereas shareholders may prefer the darker density function. As we will see later, this potential conflict of interest will be more significant when options are out-of-the-money.

2.5 CONCLUSION

This chapter presents a corporate finance approach to risk management. The goal was to highlight that risk management should be broader than the simple minimization of variance, which is suggested by the VaR approach for non-financial firms.

The objective is to maximize firm value by reducing the risk of default and improving financial health. This, in turn, enables the firm to undertake its investment projects as planned, at a reasonable cost. Hedging may also allow firms to reduce the average amount of taxes payable when the tax function is convex.

Risk management may help firms better manage their capital structure. Moreover, certain firms in good financial health may use their informational advantage to speculate on future asset prices. But this activity is often dangerous.

In conclusion, non-financial firms can hedge their risk exposure using both internal activities and market activities. The most common internal activities are the prevention of financial risks and accidents (self-protection) and the reduction of financial consequences in the case of an accident (risk retention, self-insurance, and cash reserves).

Insurance is a form of market protection against the losses incurred by pure risks or accidents (Harrington and Niehaus, 2003). Derivatives can also be used to hedge against unanticipated financial risks.

REFERENCES

Cummins, D., Dionne, G., Gagné, R., and Nouira, A., 2009. "Efficiency of Insurance Firms with Endogenous Risk Management and Financial Intermediation Activities." *Journal of Productivity Analysis* 32, 145–159.

Dionne, G., Gueyie, J.P., and Mnasri, M., 2018. "Dynamic Corporate Risk Management: Motivations and Real Implications." *Journal of Banking and Finance* 95, 97–111.

Dionne, G., and Ouederni, K., 2011. "Corporate Risk Management and Dividend Signaling Theory." *Finance Research Letters* 8, 188–195.

Dionne, G., and Santugini, M., 2014. "Entry, Imperfect Competition, and Futures Market for the Input." *International Journal of Industrial Organization* 35, 70–83.

Dionne, G., and Triki, T., 2013. "On Risk Management Determinants: What Really Matters?" *European Journal of Finance* 19, 145–164.

Froot, K.A., Scharfstein, D., and Stein, J., 1993. "Risk Management: Coordinating Corporate Investment and Financing Policies." *Journal of Finance* 48, 1629–1658.

Graham, J.R., and Rogers, D.A., 2002. "Do Firms Hedge in Response to Tax Incentives?" *Journal of Finance* 57, 815–839.

Graham, J.R., and Smith, C., 1999. "Tax Incentives to Hedge." *Journal of Finance* 54, 2241–2263.

Harrington, S., and Niehaus, G.R., 2003. *Risk Management and Insurance*. Irwin/McGraw-Hill.

Jensen, M.C., and Meckling, W.H., 1976. "Theory of the Firm: Managerial Behavior, Agency Costs and Ownership Structure." *Journal of Financial Economics* 3, 305–360.

Léautier, T.O., and Rochet, J.C., 2014. "On the Strategic Value of Risk Management." *International Journal of Industrial Organization* 37, 153–169.

Mnasri, M., Dionne, G., and Gueyie, J.P., 2017. "The Use of Nonlinear Hedging Strategies by US Oil Producers: Motivations and Implications." *Energy Economics* 63, 348–364.

Savor, M., 2002."Risk Management and Its Effect on Mergers and Acquisitions." PhD Thesis, HEC Montréal.

Smith, C., and Stulz, R., 1985. "The Determinants of Firm Hedging Policies." *Journal of Financial and Quantitative Analysis* 20, 391–405.

Stulz, R.M., 1996. "Rethinking Risk Management." *Journal of Applied Corporate Finance* 9, 8–25.

Stulz, R.M., 2003. *Risk Management and Derivatives*. Thomson/South-Western.

Stulz, R.M., 2013. "How Companies Can Use Hedging to Create Shareholder Value." *Journal of Applied Corporate Finance* 25, 21–29.

Tufano, P., 1996. "Who Manages Risk? An Empirical Examination of Risk Management Practices in the Gold Mining Industry." *Journal of Finance* 51, 1097–1137.

CHAPTER 3

Risk Management and Investment Financing

This chapter explores the technical aspects of the relationship between investment and external financing, in order to help hedging design and optimize risk management policies.

Froot, Sharfstein, and Stein (1993) argue that it may be optimal to protect oneself (or hedge) from fluctuations of different risks if the external sources of investment financing are more costly than the internal sources. This conclusion is pertinent in the presence of high expected default costs, for example concave payoffs or concave profit functions, even if the entrepreneurs are risk-neutral.

Financial hedging with derivatives is not indispensable. In the presence of multiple risks, the correlations between the investment possibilities and the various sources of business risk play an important role in calculating the optimal hedging rate.

As part of integrated or enterprise risk management, it is important to consider all risks simultaneously. For example, the higher the (positive) correlations between cash flows and investment opportunities, the less businesses will need to hedge. Similarly, firms will hedge more if the cash flows and value of the collateral are strongly correlated (or if risk management increases their borrowing opportunities).

Nonlinear risk management instruments provide more precise results in risk hedging than do linear instruments. For example, options are more precise and especially more flexible than futures contracts. They also let the firm retain the advantages of favorable events. However, they are more expensive than other hedging instruments.[1]

3.1 BASIC MODEL

The model includes two periods. In period 1, the firm holds a random cash flow amount $\tilde{w}$ and plans to invest an amount I in a project at the beginning of period 2, which will be financed by internal financing w and external financing e. We therefore

[1]See the article by Rampini, Amir, and Viswanathan (2014) for a critique of Froot, Sharfstein, and Stein (1993). Dionne, Gueyie, and Mnasri (2018) and Mnasri, Dionne, Gueyie (2017) conducted empirical studies on the choice between linear vs. non-linear derivatives and on the dynamic management of derivatives.

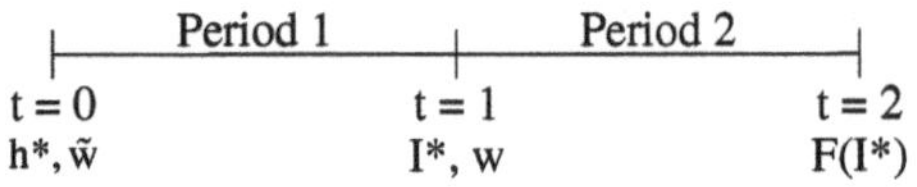

FIGURE 3.1 Temporal diagram of decisions and realizations.

have: I = w + e. Figure 3.1 reproduces the dates *t* of the decisions and the realizations of the random variables. The firm chooses an optimal hedging rate *h* of $\widetilde{w}$ at the start of period 1. The realized value of *w* is known at the end of period 1.

At the start of period 2, the size of the investment I* is selected, and it depends on the sources of financing. The output of the project (F(I*)) is realized, and the creditors are paid at the end of period 2.

The net value of the investment project is given by:

$$F(I) = f(I) - I,$$

where I represents the investment amount and f(I) the return on the investment in dollars, with $f_1 > 0$ and $f_{11} < 0$, where f_1 indicates the first derivative and f_{11} the second derivative of the function f(I). The realization of F(I) is not random here, but it will become random later in the presentation.

The concavity of the payoff may be interpreted either by convex taxes or by decreasing returns on investments. In this chapter, we favor the second interpretation. The discount rate is zero.

To make the problem more interesting, Froot, Sharfstein, and Stein (1993) add imperfections to the external sources of financing, by considering a supplementary cost: C(e), with $C_e > 0$ and $C_{ee} > 0$. The cost function is strictly convex. In other words, the risk premium requested by the bank increases at an increasing rate. These costs can be interpreted as the expected default costs (the default risk premium increases with the amount borrowed), or other costs related to information asymmetry between managers and creditors. For example, the effort of the manager may not be observed by the banks. In the presence of this information asymmetry the manager may have less incentive to be efficient because if the project fails, the losses will be shared with banks (residual claimants' argument).

We can also use the standard debt model that includes information asymmetries between entrepreneurs and creditors about the results of the project. In this second case, we emphasize the interpretation of ex post default costs rather than ex ante incentives (ex post rather than ex ante moral hazard), which implies the interpretation of the standard debt.

From now we write $\widetilde{w}$ as *w* to simplify the notation. The risk management problem is linked to the fact that *w* is a random variable at the start of period 1, namely when the internal financing is planned.

We will now examine three distinct situations concerning the hedging rate of *w*: case 1, in which there is no hedging; case 2, characterized by full hedging; and case 3, where we obtain an optimal hedging level.

CASE 1: NO HEDGING OF w

Without hedging of w, for simplicity we assume that two realizations are possible (w_1 and w_2), each of which has a probability of 0.5, which gives an expected value of w equal to E(w). In this case, the entrepreneur has an expected profit equal to E(P(w)) ex ante, as Figure 3.2 illustrates. We assume that P(w) is concave. We can see that the entrepreneur's welfare improves by going from E(P(w)) to P(E(w)), where P(E(w)) is the value of expected w under certainty. No hedging reduces the value of the firm having a concave payoff function.

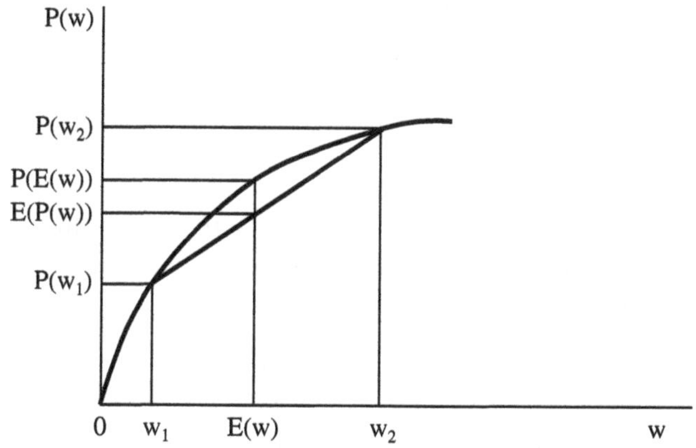

FIGURE 3.2 Concave profit function in relation to internal financing.

CASE 2: FULL HEDGING OF w

Now, let us assume that *w* can be protected from fluctuations and that the hedging activities do not affect its mean. This is a case of pure hedging. Assume that the entrepreneur chooses full risk hedging. Given that he is now in certainty, the entrepreneur obtains E(w) at the end of the period with a probability equal to 1 and the value of the profit function is now equal to P(E(w)). Hedging reduces the spread between the $P(w_i)$ and is beneficial only when the profit function is concave in *w* because $P(E(w)) > E(P(w))$, as indicated by Figure 3.2. We can also demonstrate that partial hedging increases the average payoff of the business. We now revisit the problem of investment financing.

CASE 3: OPTIMAL HEDGING DECISION

Because we face a problem covering two periods, we will use backward induction to first calculate the optimal investment amount for a given value of *w* and then calculate the optimal hedging of *w*.

At date t = 1, in certainty, the firm's problem is to maximize the net profit function linked to the project:

$$\max_{I} F(I) - C(e), \tag{3.1}$$

under the following constraint:

$$I = w + e.$$

For a given *w*, the optimal investment amount I* is the solution to the problem in equation (3.1) after substituting the above constraint in C(e). The first-order condition of the maximization problem is equal to:

$$F_I \equiv f_I - 1 - C_e de/dI = 0, \tag{3.2}$$

where de/dI = 1, which implies that additional costs linked to external financing give a lower investment level than that of full information, characterized by $f_I = 1$ because $C_e = 0$ for all *e* without information asymmetry. Let us write the solution for full information as I**.

Figure 3.3 clearly shows the negative effect of additional financing costs on the optimal investment level. We observe that the external financing costs reduce the investment possibilities from I** to I*.

Another way to represent the result is shown in Figure 3.4. When $C_e = 0$, the marginal benefit (f_I, marginal productivity) must equal the marginal cost equal to 1 at level I**. However, when $C_e > 0$, the marginal benefit must be higher, to cover the

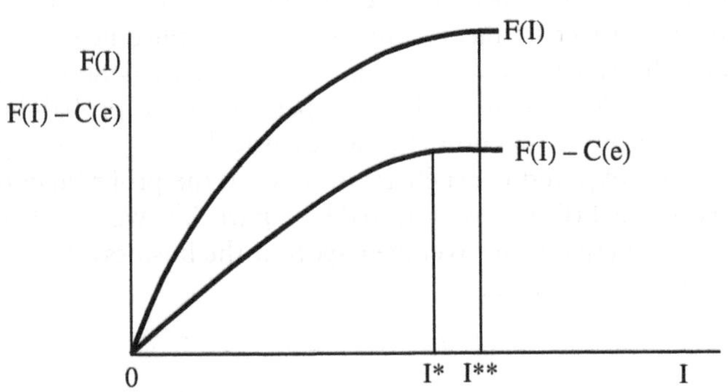

FIGURE 3.3 Effect of external financing cost on optimal investment.

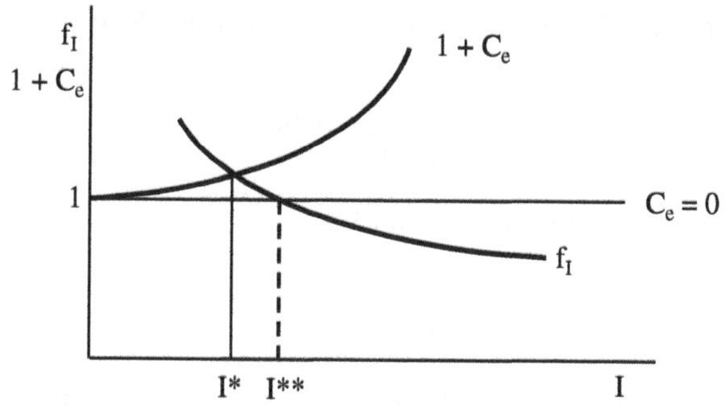

FIGURE 3.4 Marginal benefit and marginal cost of the investment.

additional marginal cost requested by the creditors, which can translate into a higher risk premium and a lower investment I^*.

Now let us return to date $t = 0$, when the firm must decide on the risk management policy for w. The objective is to reduce the spread between I^{**} and I^* by using internal financing as much as possible. Because the maximization problem of equation (3.1) is a function of w, we can write the optimal solution as:

$$P(w) = F(I^*(w)) - C(I^*(w) - w), \quad \text{for } I^*(w).$$

Similarly:

$$P(w) = F(I^{**}(w)), \quad \text{for } I^{**}(w).$$

We observe that, at equilibrium, the function P depends on w because $I^*(w)$ is a function of w at the optimum. If this function is concave in w, the entrepreneur should hedge against the fluctuations of w to reduce, on average, the use of external financing.

We will now verify whether P is concave in w in our problem of investment choice. The first derivative of P, evaluated at $I^*(w)$, relative to w gives:

$$P_w = (f_I - 1)\left(\frac{dI^*}{dw}\right) - C_e\left(\frac{dI^*}{dw} - 1\right) > 0. \tag{3.3}$$

It is positive because increasing the portion of internal financing increases profits (reduces the gap between I^* and I^{**}). To verify this result, we can rewrite this expression and obtain, by the envelope theorem:

$$P_w = (f_I - 1 - C_e)\left(\frac{dI^*}{dw}\right) + C_e > 0,$$

because $f_1 - 1 - C_e = 0$ (first-order condition in (3.2)). The second derivative is equal to:

$$P_{ww} = f_{II}\left(\frac{dI^*}{dw}\right)^2 - C_{ee}\left(\frac{dI^*}{dw} - 1\right)^2. \tag{3.4}$$

Using the fact that dI^*/dw is equal to (see Appendix A of the chapter):

$$\frac{-C_{ee}}{f_{II} - C_{ee}} > 0,$$

and by substitution of this expression in (3.4), we obtain:

$$P_{ww} = f_{II}\frac{dI^*}{dw}. \tag{3.5}$$

Two factors are important to obtain a negative value for P_{ww}: 1) the marginal return on the investment must be decreasing ($f_{11} < 0$), and 2) the level of internal financing must have a positive impact on the investment level, a sensitivity obtained when the external financing cost is increasing ($dI^*/dw > 0$). We therefore affirm that $P_{ww} < 0$ or that the optimal profit function is concave in w, which indicates that the entrepreneur should hedge. We now compute the optimal hedging solution.

We assume that the hedging cost is nil. Let us begin with a simple example of hedging. Let $w = w_0(h + (1 - h)\varepsilon)$ with $E(\varepsilon) = 1$ and $\sigma_\varepsilon^2 > 0$. The hedging rate is h. When $h = 0$, $w = w_0\varepsilon$ is completely random, and when $h = 1$, $w = w_0$ is a constant. The use of h as a hedge may be interpreted as a combination of forward contract. Let us assume that ε may take two values:

$$\varepsilon = 0,\ p = 0.5$$
$$\varepsilon = 2,\ p = 0.5$$

with $E(\varepsilon) = 1$.

When $h = 0$, w becomes:

$$\varepsilon = 0,\ w = 0,\ p = 0.5$$
$$\varepsilon = 2,\ w = w_0 2,\ p = 0.5.$$

When $h = 1/2$, we obtain:

$$\varepsilon = 0,\ w = w_0 0.5,\ p = 0.5$$
$$\varepsilon = 2,\ w = w_0 1.5,\ p = 0.5.$$

When $h = 1$, we obtain $w = w_0$ in both states of nature. Figure 3.5 describes the three cases of hedging and shows that $E_i P(w), i = a, b, c$, increases with h when $P(w)$ is concave: a) $h^* = 0$; b) $h^* = 1/2$; and c) $h^* = 1$.

The optimal choice of h corresponds to maximizing $E(P(w))$ for a given investment level:

$$\max_h EP(w_0(h + (1 - h)\varepsilon)).$$

The first-order condition gives:

$$E(P_w(1 - \varepsilon)) = 0 \tag{3.6}$$

where P_w is given by (3.3). Here P_w is random because it contains $I^*(w)$ and w is now random. The first-order condition corresponds to the expected value of the product of two random variables.

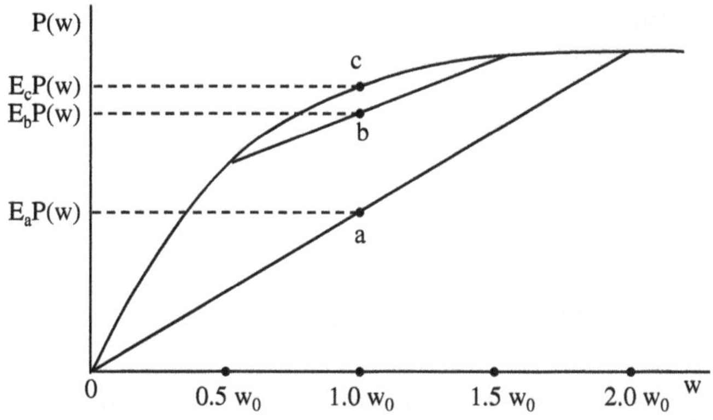

FIGURE 3.5 Example of forward contracts.

We know that:

$$E(xy) = E(x)E(y) + \text{cov}(x, y)$$

by definition of the covariance. If we apply this definition to the first-order condition (3.6), we verify that:

$$E(P_w(1 - \varepsilon)) = E(P_w)E(1 - \varepsilon) + \text{cov}(P_w, 1 - \varepsilon) = 0.$$

By assumption, $E(1 - \varepsilon) = 0$, which implies that $\text{cov}(P_w, 1 - \varepsilon)$ must be equal to zero at the optimum. Because P_w and $(1 - \varepsilon)$ are correlated when $h < 1$ and non-correlated when $h = 1$, we obtain:

$$h^* = 1 \text{ and } E(P(w^*)) = P(w_0),$$

as indicated at point *c* of Figure 3.5, because P_w must be a constant for the first-order condition to be verified.

In this case, it is therefore optimal for a business firm with a concave profit function to hedge fully because the hedging costs are zero.[2] Thus, at date $t = 1$, the business firm will know the precise amount of internal financing that will be available, namely $E(w)$.

3.2 ILLUSTRATION WITH THE STANDARD DEBT CONTRACT

We can show that the standard debt contract gives an increasing cost function $C(e)$ in *e* (see Appendix B of the chapter for more details).

In fact, if the loan contract is a debt contract or a standard bond:

$$C(e) = c\,G(D) \text{ with } D = D(e)$$

[2]Full hedging may also be optimal with low hedging costs.

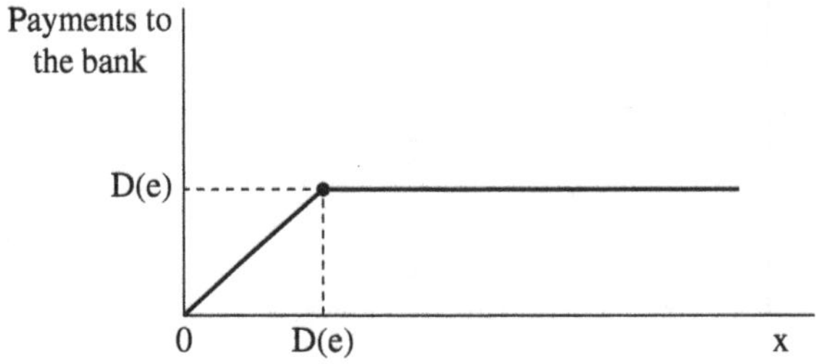

FIGURE 3.6 Standard debt contract.

where G(x) is the profit distribution function, D is the face value of the debt, *c* is the audit cost, and *e* still represents the level of external financing. G(D) is the default probability defined by:

$$G(D) = \int_{-\infty}^{D} g(x)dx.$$

Figure 3.6 illustrates a standard debt contract where *x* corresponds to the profits associated to the project.

We can verify that:

$$C'(e) = cG'(D)D'(e) > 0$$

if the external finance function is increasing in *e* or if its face value (D) increases with the amount borrowed, because a distribution function is always increasing ($G'(D) > 0$).

Froot, Scharfstein, and Stein (1993) impose a technical condition on the hazard rate so that dI^*/dw is positive, thus verifying that the profit function is concave in w (equation (3.5)) when $f_{II} < 0$.

3.3 MODEL WITH TWO RANDOM VARIABLES

Up to now, we have supposed that the investment opportunities F(I) were nonrandom and consequently independent of w. We will now examine the choice of optimal hedging when the investment opportunities are random as well.

Consider a petroleum company. Its current revenue (w, also associated with the internal financing amount available) and the profits from its investment opportunities (F(I)) depend positively on the price of oil. Therefore, when the oil price is high, the business experiences both higher internal revenue (which enables it to finance its investments) and higher returns on its investments. The opposite result occurs when the price of oil is low. When internal financing and investment opportunities are individually correlated with the price of oil, we can observe a positive correlation between the possibilities of internal financing and investment opportunities.

It therefore seems that the company in this example would need less external financial protection from fluctuations of internal financing than another company that has the same fluctuations of current revenue according to the price of oil, but with an investment project whose opportunities are independent of fluctuations in oil prices. Accordingly, when investment opportunities are high, financing is also high, and when these opportunities are low, the business has less need for internal and external financing. The firm therefore profits from natural diversification of its risks. We will now demonstrate this intuition and its consequence on optimal hedging.

To formalize this discussion, we use the following model. Namely:

$$w = w_0(h + (1 - h)\varepsilon) \tag{3.7}$$

where *h* is the hedging rate. F(I) also becomes a function of ε when the investment opportunities are correlated with the sale price of the good:

$$F(I) = \theta f(I) - I$$

with:

$$\theta = \alpha(\varepsilon - 1) + 1 \tag{3.8}$$

where θ measures the effect of price risk on investment opportunities and α is interpreted as the measure of the correlation between the investment opportunities and the risk to be hedged, namely fluctuations in internal financing. The two functions, equations (3.7) and (3.8), are dependent on ε, which may be interpreted as the oil price in our example. The value 1 is the mean of ε, as in the previous case. Therefore, $E(\theta) = 1$ as well. When $\alpha = 0$ and $\theta = 1$, we obtain the same result as in the previous case. When $\alpha > 0, \theta \neq 1$, and $h < 1$, we observe that θ and *w* are positively correlated when they are affected in the same direction by ε. If $h = 1$, the two variables become independent in the profit function of the business because w is a constant.

As before, we proceed in two steps to find the optimal values of I and *h*. We calculate the optimal investment amount for a given *w* and decide on the optimal hedge.

For the choice of investment, the problem does not change much, except that we must add the variable θ, which implies that P_w becomes:

$$P_w = \underbrace{(\alpha(\varepsilon - 1) + 1)}_{\theta} \; f_I \frac{dI^*}{dw} - C_e \left(\frac{dI^*}{dw} - 1 \right) - \frac{dI^*}{dw} \tag{3.9}$$

and

$$P_{ww} = \underbrace{(\alpha(\varepsilon - 1) + 1)}_{\theta} \; f_{II} \left(\frac{dI^*}{dw} \right)^2 - C_{ee} \left(\frac{dI^*}{dw} - 1 \right)^2 \tag{3.10}$$

Now, the choice of hedging is more complicated because we must not simply verify the concavity of the profit function. We must also take into account the correlation between *w* and the investment opportunities F(I) to calculate the optimal *h*.

To find the optimal hedging rate *h*, we maximize the function:

$$\underset{h}{\text{Max}} E(P(w))$$

and obtain:

$$E\left(P_w \frac{dw}{dh} \right) = 0.$$

This equation can be simplified by using the explicit value of *w* and its derivative:

$$E(P_w(1-\varepsilon)) = 0,$$

which can be rewritten as:

$$\mathrm{cov}(P_w, (1-\varepsilon)) = 0,$$

because we have seen that:

$$E(xy) = E(x)E(y) + \mathrm{cov}(x, y) \text{ and } E(1-\varepsilon) = 0.$$

The solution to the problem must consider the fact that the production decision is a function of another random variable, namely investment opportunities. In equation (3.9), P_w is now a function of ε via $I^*(w)$ and $\theta = \alpha(\varepsilon - 1) + 1$. To obtain an explicit value of h^*, we will use another property of the covariance.

Assume that a(x) and b(y) are two functions of random variables *x* and *y*. If the random variables are normal, we know, from Stein's lemma, that it is possible to write the covariance between the two functions as follows:

$$\mathrm{cov}(a(x), b(y)) = E(a_x)E(b_y)\mathrm{cov}(x, y),$$

where a_x and b_y are derivatives.

In our application, this covariance is equal to:

$$\mathrm{cov}(P_w(\varepsilon), 1-\varepsilon) = E(P_{w\varepsilon})E(-1)\sigma_\varepsilon^2 = 0, \tag{3.11}$$

because the covariance $\mathrm{cov}(\varepsilon, \varepsilon) = \sigma_\varepsilon^2$.

Since $I(w(\varepsilon))$ and $w = w_0(h + (1-h)\varepsilon)$ are both functions of ε, we can therefore explicitly rewrite the previous covariance by differentiating P_w in (3.9) with respect to ε and by omitting $E(-1)$ and σ_ε^2 in (3.11) because they are constants. We obtain:

$$E(P_{w\varepsilon}) = E\left[\alpha f_1 \frac{dI^*}{dw} + \theta f_{II}\left(\frac{dI}{dw}\right)^2 (1-h)w_0 - C_{ee}\left(\frac{dI}{dw} - 1\right)^2 (1-h)w_0\right] = 0. \tag{3.12}$$

We isolate an explicit value of h^* after substitution of the value P_{ww} given by (3.10) in (3.12):

$$E\left[\alpha f_1 \frac{dI^*}{dw} + P_{ww}(1-h^*)w_0\right] = 0 \tag{3.13}$$

We can rewrite the expression in (3.13) as $\alpha E\left[f_1 \frac{dI^*}{dw}\right] + (1-h^*)w_0E(P_{ww}) = 0$ and isolate h^*:

$$h^* = 1 + \frac{\alpha E\left[f_1 \frac{dI^*}{dw}\right]}{w_0 E(P_{ww})} = 1 + \frac{\alpha E\left[f_1 \frac{P_{ww}}{\theta f_{II}}\right]}{w_0 E(P_{ww})}. \tag{3.14}$$

We note from equation (3.14) that if α is equal to zero, we obtain the previous result, which gives full hedging without dependence ($h^* = 1$).

Further, if α is positive, the term added to 1 in equation (3.14) is negative when $P_{ww} < 0$ and $f_{II} < 0$ and we verify that h^* is generally lower than 1, but not necessarily greater than 0. If we have a positive correlation, hedging is natural, so financial hedging (h) is less necessary.

The higher the α, the weaker the h^* (it may even be zero or negative), implying that the entrepreneur either increases the firm's risk exposure or exposes it to additional risks. If α is negative, h^* may be higher than 1. The entrepreneur increases hedging because the introduction of the second random variable increases the firm's risk.

3.4 CONCLUSION

Before launching into the use of derivatives to reduce profit fluctuations, entrepreneurs should check whether this activity increases the value of their business and determine which risks should be diversified.

Here, the necessary condition for risk management is the concavity of the profit function due to decreasing returns on investments. With a concave function P(w), risk management increases the firm value. This concavity may also be induced by financial market imperfections such as taxes. Standard debt contracts introduce higher external financing costs than those of internal financing.

In conclusion, full risk hedging is not always the best choice. The optimal hedging rate notably depends on the correlations between the random internal funds and the investment opportunities. When both of these variables are strongly positively correlated, the hedging rate should be low.

Before proceeding directly with the analysis of management of market, credit, liquidity, and operational risk, a test of theoretical conclusions about determinants of risk management using data from a high-risk industry is presented in the next chapter.

REFERENCES

Dionne, G., Gueyie, J.P., and Mnasri, M., 2018. "Dynamic Corporate Risk Management: Motivations and Real Implications." *Journal of Banking and Finance* 95, 97–111.

Froot, K.A., Sharfstein, D.A., and Stein, J.C., 1993. "Risk Management: Coordinating Corporate Investment and Financing Policies." *The Journal of Finance* 48, 1629–1641 and conclusion.

Mnasri, M., Dionne, G., and Gueyie, J.P., 2017. "The Use of Nonlinear Hedging Strategies by US Oil Producers: Motivations and Implications." *Energy Economics* 63, 348–364.

Rampini, A.A., Amir, S., and Viswanathan, S., 2014. "Dynamic Risk Management." *Journal of Financial Economics* 111, 271–296.

APPENDIX A: VALUE OF dI^*/dw

Consider the problem:

$$\underset{I}{\text{Max}}\ f(I) - I - C(I - w).$$

The first-order condition H is equal to:

$$H \equiv f_I - 1 - C_e = 0.$$

Its total differentiation with respect to I* and *w* gives:

$$H_I dI^* + H_w dw = 0$$

or:

$$(f_{II} - C_{ee})dI^* + C_{ee}dw = 0,$$

because

$$dC/dI^* = 1 \text{ and } dC/dw = -1.$$

We obtain:

$$\frac{dI^*}{dw} = -\frac{H_w}{H_I} = -\frac{C_{ee}}{f_{II} - C_{ee}}.$$

This expression is positive because $f_{II} - C_{ee} < 0$ (second-order condition of the maximization problem) and $C_{ee} > 0$ according to the hypothesis of convexity of C(e).

APPENDIX B: STANDARD DEBT CONTRACT

C(e) = cG(D).	*c* is the cost of the audit and D is the face value of the debt. G(x) is the profit distribution of *x*.

We assume that D is a function of *e*:

D(e) with D′(e) > 0.	This implies that the face value increases with external financing because an increase in external financing from the bank increases the default probability.

Figure A3.1 represents the portion of profits R that the entrepreneur retains under a debt contract. When $x < D$, $R = 0$. When $x \geq D$, $R = x - D \geq 0$.

The problem of optimal choice of I and of D can be written as follows:

$$L = \underset{I,D}{\text{Max}} f(I) + \int_D^{\overline{x}} (x - D)g(x)dx,$$

under the constraint of zero profit for the bank offering a standard debt contract:

$$\int_{\underline{x}}^{D} (x - c)g(x)dx + \int_D^{\overline{x}} Dg(x)dx = I - w$$

or:

$$\int_{\underline{x}}^{D} (x - c)g(x)dx + D(1 - G(D)) = I - w,$$

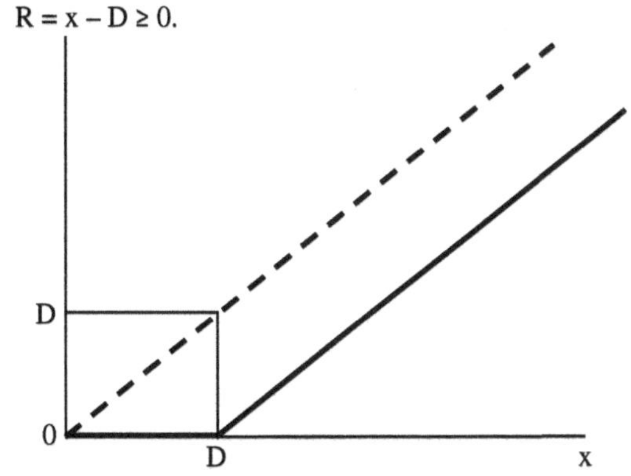

FIGURE A3.1 Payoff function of the entrepreneur who has a standard debt contract.

where $\underline{x}$ is the minimum value of x, $\overline{x}$ is the maximum value and x represents the entrepreneur's revenue.

The first-order conditions of the problem can be written as follows, by using λ as the Lagrange multiplier:

$$\frac{\partial L}{\partial I} = f_I - \lambda = 0$$

$$\frac{\partial L}{\partial D} = -\int_D^{\overline{x}} g(x)dx + \lambda(D - c)g(D) + (1 - G(D))\lambda - Dg(D)\lambda = 0$$

$$= -(1 - G(D)) - cg(D)\lambda + (1 - G(D))\lambda = 0,$$

or:

$$(1 - G(D))(\lambda - 1) - \lambda cg(D) = 0.$$

We can rewrite the two first-order conditions:

$$\lambda = f_I$$

$$\lambda = \frac{1 - G(D)}{1 - G(D) - cG(D)} \Rightarrow f_I = \frac{1 - G(D)}{1 - G(D) - cG(D)} > 1.$$

Froot, Sharfstein, and Stein (1993) show that:

$$L_{ww} = \frac{d\lambda}{dw} = f_{II}\frac{dI^*}{dw} < 0 \text{ if } f_{II} < 0 \text{ and } \frac{dI^*}{dw} > 0.$$

This result is obtained if the hazard rate $g(x)/(1 - G(x))$ is increasing in x, which is verified for the normal, exponential and uniform distributions.

CHAPTER 4

Significant Determinants of Risk Management of Non-Financial Firms

This chapter presents empirical studies of risk management within a specific industry. We show that the use of adequate data to measure the benefits generated by risk management may be crucial.[1]

The industry examined is that of gold producers in North America, and the risk variable is the final sale price of the product, namely one ounce of gold. We analyze only one risk because high-quality data on the other business risks and on their correlations were not available.

First, we limit our analysis to a single financial decision variable for the company: the optimal risk hedging. The empirical tests published in the literature provide contradictory results regarding the effect of risk hedging on firm value and shareholder welfare. Studies that did not address the simultaneous effects of risk hedging and other financial decisions at the company may have drawn incorrect conclusions about the effects of risk management.

The article by Dionne and Triki (2013) proposes a theoretical model of risk management that analyses the simultaneous choices of risk hedging and firm debt. The empirical results show that simultaneous analysis of decisions affects the analysis of determinants of risk management in the gold mining industry. They also shed light on the effects of corporate governance on risk management.

4.1 RATIONALE FOR THE RESEARCH

For more than 30 years, the finance literature has discussed the theoretical determinants of risk management of non-financial firms, but very few studies have measured the significance of the various determinants proposed.

One of the first empirical studies was done by Tufano (1996). It identifies two classes of arguments used to show why non-financial firms might undertake risk-management activities: (1) to maximize the firm's value and (2) to protect risk-averse managers.

These two classes of arguments are important when making decisions to hedge against operational risk, exchange rate risk, default risk, interest rate risk, insurable or pure risk, liquidity risk, and so on, and for the integration of these risks in a global risk management process.

[1]The research projects discussed in this chapter were conducted with Martin Garand and Thouraya Triki.

For now, we will try to quantify the net benefits of risk management for a single risk. The two main results of Tufano's study are that:

1. The determinants proposed to maximize the firm's value have practically no significance;
2. Determinants related to managers' risk aversion are significant.

Dionne and Garand (2003) revisit Tufano's study with a considerably expanded database compared to the one he used, and they conclude that his first result no longer holds. Their research concerning determinants that maximize firm value let them obtain a larger number of observations than Tufano, together with better variables to estimate the different determinants. The article by Dionne and Garand (2003) did not examine managers' risk aversion. However, Dionne and Triki (2013) took risk aversion into account. This study also considered variables of governance and the simultaneity of debt and risk management decisions.

Both studies use the method described in the article by Graham and Smith (1999) to build a measure of the convexity of the tax function and demonstrate that it provides better results than that suggested by Tufano (1996).[2]

The article by Campello et al. (2011) on risk management also analyzes the convexity of taxation and isolates its effect on risk management. The authors show that firms that choose to hedge pay lower interest rates and have fewer restrictions on their capital when they contract bank loans. Banks therefore seem to consider firms' risk management when they calculate the risk premiums to add to the base interest rate.

The article by Cliche (2000) proposes the first review of the main empirical studies of determinants of risk management. One conclusion of her article, demonstrating that very few determinants are significant and have signs in the right direction, proves that the data and statistical methods used to measure the pertinence of different determinants do not always measure up to the authors' ambitions.

We agree with this conclusion. It is very difficult to obtain pertinent data and to construct samples of sufficient size so as to isolate statistically significant effects. It is therefore quite probable that the absence of significant effects on firm value are explained more by the weakness of the empirical studies published and the lack of precise data than by the weakness of the theoretical arguments proposed to justify the measures of risk management at a firm.[3]

4.2 SIGNIFICANT DETERMINANTS

4.2.1 Target Variable or Dependent Variable

The variable to hedge is the price of an ounce of gold, an important source of risk for a mining company whose main production is gold. It is well known that this price has

[2]Also see the articles by Graham and Rogers (2002) and Adam (2009).

[3]Readers interested in the explicit effect of risk management on firm value may consult Hoyt and Liebenberg (2011), Pérez-Gonzalez and Yun (2013), Allayannis and Weston (2001), Mnasri, Dionne, and Gueyie (2017), and Dionne, Gueyie, and Mnasri (2018). See also Chapter 20 of this book.

varied significantly over time. The principal hedging method is the use of financial instruments that let a firm deliver part of its production at a price that maximizes its value:

- Futures contracts (forward contracts) that fix the sale price
- Repayment of bank loans in ounces of gold at a fixed price
- Put options on the price of gold
- Call options on the price of gold

The use of collars was not very advanced at that time, but was practiced implicitly by buying puts and by selling calls. In general, production firms consider the hedging of the sale price of anticipated gold production for the next three years. The question of determining which percentage of production to be hedged then arises.

The aggregate measure of firm hedging is the Delta%. There is a direct analogy between the Delta% and the Delta of an option. The Delta is the variation in the value of an option relative to the variation of one dollar of the price of one ounce of gold, which is the underlier in this case. The Delta% is an aggregate value over many hedging instruments.

We will now look at the main risk hedging activity in this industry. Table 4.1, taken from Tufano (1996), gives an example of the calculation of the Delta% of a firm on a given date. Panel A of the table describes the main instruments used by the firm on March 30, 1991. The firm uses forward contracts, gold loans with reimbursements in ounces of gold at a fixed price, and put and call options. The hedging horizon is three years. Panel A shows the quantity of ounces of gold that the business decided to hedge, and the price hedged. Note that the price of an ounce of gold on that date was US$367. Panel A shows the future selling prices negotiated.

Panel B of Table 4.1 presents the calculation of the Delta%. Specifically, we standardize the hedging obtained from the different instruments and add them together to obtain an aggregate hedging measure at a given date. This method considers the probability that the option is in-the-money at maturity (European option); in other words, that the hedge will be exercised. For futures contracts and repayments in ounces of gold, since they are already in-the-money, the probability is equal to 1, hence the value of the Delta = 1 in absolute value. For options, Tufano uses the formula of Black and Scholes to calculate the Delta. Given that the exercise value of puts is already in-the-money, the delta is very high, whereas calls are largely out-of-the-money. Lastly, we obtain the Delta% by adding the Delta-ounces covered and by dividing this quantity by the total planned production of ounces of gold for the next three years, which gives a fairly low Delta% for the firm, at 21%.

Table 4.2 provides the distribution of the Delta% observed in the industry. It indicates that firms hedge on average 24% of the price of anticipated production. The standard deviation is 27%. Because all these firms are in the same industry, namely the North American mining industry, they all face the same price risk. The differences observed can therefore be explained only by firm-specific factors, hence the interest in studying the determinants of risk management. The quarterly data in Table 4.2 come from 48 firms over seven years, from 1993 to 1999. This is a fairly large panel with much repetition of firm characteristics. Thus, time and firm-specific effects must be taken into account.

TABLE 4.1 Risk management position of a firm in the industry.

Panel A: Data from the Global Gold Hedging Survey for a firm at March 30, 1991

	1991			1992			1993		
Instrument	**Ounces**	**Price ($US/ounce)**	**% of production**	**Ounces**	**Price ($US/ounce)**	**% of production**	**Ounces**	**Price ($US/ounce)**	**% of production**
Futures contracts	96,000	443							
Loans repaid in ounces of gold	22,353	476		44,706	476		44,706	476	
Puts (buy)	20,000	425							
Total	138,353	446	61.2	44,706	476	10.3	44,706	476	11.0
Calls (sell)	20,000	455							

Panel B: Calculation of the Delta% of the firm at March 30, 1991

Position	**Ounces**	**Delta**	**Delta-ounces**
Futures contracts: 1991	96,000	−1.0	−96,000
Gold loan: payable 1991	22,353	−1.0	−22,353
Gold loan: payable 1992	44,706	−1.0	−44,706
Gold loan: payable 1993	44,706	−1.0	−44,706
Options put with a maturity in 1991	20,000	−0.957	−19,140
Options call with a maturity in 1991	20,000	−0.003	−60
Aggregate position of the hedged portfolio (ounces)			−226,965
Total production until December 1993 (ounces)			1,066,524
Delta%: percentage of production predicted (absolute value) of ounces of gold whose price is hedged			21%

Source: Tufano (1996), who used the document by Ted Reeve: Global Gold Hedging Survey, First Boston Equity Research, June 10, 1991, page 11.
Notes: The delta of the future sales positions and loan repayments in ounces of gold have a value of −1, because the probability of exercising these contracts is 100%. The delta of options is calculated using the formula of Black and Scholes. The two signs are identical because the firm has a long position on puts and a short one on calls. The delta takes into account the probability of exercising the option.

TABLE 4.2 Distribution of Delta% values.

Value	Number of observations		% of observations
Delta% = 0	152		16.9
0 < Delta% < 10%	193		21.5
10% ≤ Delta% < 20%	154		17.1
20% ≤ Delta% < 30%	127		14.1
30% ≤ Delta% < 60%	178		19.8
60% ≤ Delta% < 80%	53		5.9
80% ≤ Delta% < 100%	22		2.4
Delta% ≥ 100%	19		2.1
Total	898		100
Mean		24%	
Standard deviation		27%	

4.2.2 Main Determinants and Their Measurement

We will now identify the determinants and show how they can be measured to conduct our statistical analysis. Individual firms probably cannot replicate this study over the short term (because they have insufficient observations), but the measurement of the different coefficients estimated may be useful to help firms identify the main determinants that are relevant for them.

The analyses of the statistical correlations between historical hedging decisions and the main determinants discussed here may benefit firms in this industry. The results should convince firms to retain statistical information regarding their main variables on a quarterly basis, and perhaps weekly or daily, particularly for firms with major financial risks and that frequently carry out market transactions.

Risk Behavior

First, note that shareholders' risk aversion is not a relevant factor here, even as a theoretical argument. It is easier and less costly for shareholders to diversify their portfolios directly on financial markets than via the firm whose shares they hold.

Evidently, small and medium firm owners who have all of their assets in one firm may see things differently. The arguments developed for managers, presented below, may apply to them.

Further, even if shareholders do not need to use business risk management to diversify their portfolio, this does not mean that they should not be interested in it. On the contrary, because risk management increases both firm value and share value, shareholders should support this activity. Here, a first-order argument prevails, as opposed to a second-order or hedging argument, in the sense that shareholders value variation in the mean value of the firm associated with risk management.

Managers paid in equity and who hold a large number of shares have a portfolio that is only slightly diversified relative to the firm's risk. Their risk management decisions may thus be influenced by their own needs or behaviors toward risk, given that a portion of their assets is directly correlated with firm value.

PROPOSITION 1:

In firms whose risk-averse executives are paid in equity that they hold, we should observe more financial risk hedging (and insurance purchases) than in firms whose managers do not hold company equity.

Another dimension of the problem of managers' risk-related behavior is compensation by stock options. Two aspects of the problem should be considered here. First, as long as managers hold options, they are sheltered from the downside risks, which implies that the risk aversion effect described for shares does not really affect the firm's hedging decisions.

Further, these managers may want to see fluctuations in profits or firm value, which may raise the share price. The managers would then make a larger profit by exercising their options. We obtain an effect contrary to the preceding one for holders of options that are out-of-the-money.

PROPOSITION 2:

Firms whose managers are paid in stock options should hedge less against various risks to maintain high volatility of firm value and thus increase the value of their options.

Figure 4.1 illustrates the value of a stock option at the exercise time. If the value of the firm's share, at A_1, is below K (the exercise price of the option), the value of the option will be zero because the manager cannot exercise it. If the value of the firm's share is greater than K, at A_2, the manager who holds a stock option will buy the share at the price K and resell it at the price A_2. We can clearly see that managers who hold stock options that are out-of-the-money (at A_1, for example) would benefit from maintaining high volatility of the firm's stock to increase the probability of exercising the option and realizing private gains. In contrast, managers who hold options in-the-money (at A_2, for example) would behave differently: they would benefit from practicing more risk management at the firm to reduce stock volatility and improve their chances of exercising their options at year-end (Carpenter, 2000; Nguyen, 2015).

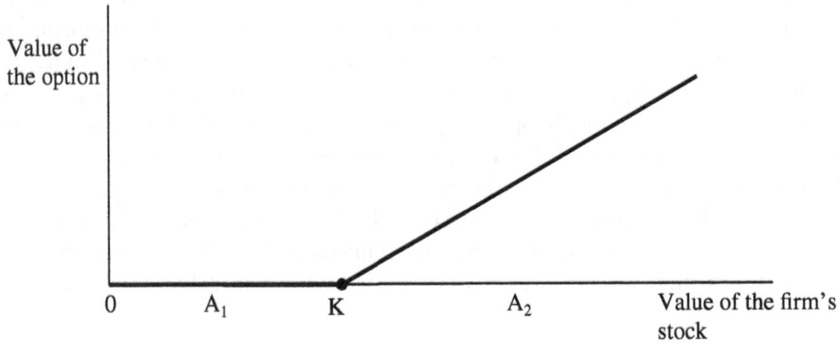

FIGURE 4.1 Stock option

Compensation by options may engender a countereffect on the anticipated value of this form of compensation for managers, which would also affect firm value. The main objective of this form of compensation is to introduce incentives to increase firm value. Most empirical studies show that this effect is weak or even ambiguous, which may be explained by managers' disincentive to undertake risk hedging activities when they are compensated with stock options.

Tufano (1996) tested propositions 1 and 2 and obtained significant effects for these two variables with signs of the coefficients in the direction predicted by the arguments presented above. We confirm these results below using the study by Dionne and Triki (2013).

Maximization of Firm Value

We will now look at arguments for maximization of firm value. Four principal determinants are often cited in the literature to justify risk-management activities:

1. Reducing the expected costs of financial distress;
2. Reducing the risk premiums payable to various partners;
3. Increasing investment possibilities;
4. Reducing expected tax payments.

After discussing the motivations behind these determinants, we will show how these theoretical effects can be measured in a statistical study. Other determinants have been developed in recent years:

- Reduction of dividends payable (Dionne and Ouederni, 2011);
- Financing of mergers and acquisitions (Savor, 2002);
- Entry into various markets (Dionne and Santugini, 2014);
- Reduction of project financing costs (Campello et al., 2011);
- Choices of forms of hedging (Adam, 2009; Mnasri, Dionne, and Gueyie, 2017); and
- Dynamic hedging behavior (Dionne, Gueyie, and Mnasri, 2018).

Now, we will look at the variables used to measure the main determinants.

Reduction of Anticipated Costs of Financial Distress and Premiums to Partners

In the studies consulted, the first two determinants are often grouped together because there are no variables that allow them to be easily distinguished.

We have shown in Chapter 2 that the probability of default is an important argument to justify risk management. We have also demonstrated that a firm with a dashed frequency like the one in Figure 4.2 would benefit from reducing its probability of having firm value to the left of the face value F of the debt by reducing the volatility of its value through the use of risk management. In the empirical analysis, we use two variables to measure this determinant.

Long-term debt weighted by the firm market value (L-T debt/MV) is the first variable used to measure the cost of financial distress. The debt level influences the face value, and greater face value introduces higher anticipated costs of financial distress. As Figure 4.2 indicates, the higher F is, the more important it is to use risk management to reduce the costs of financial distress.

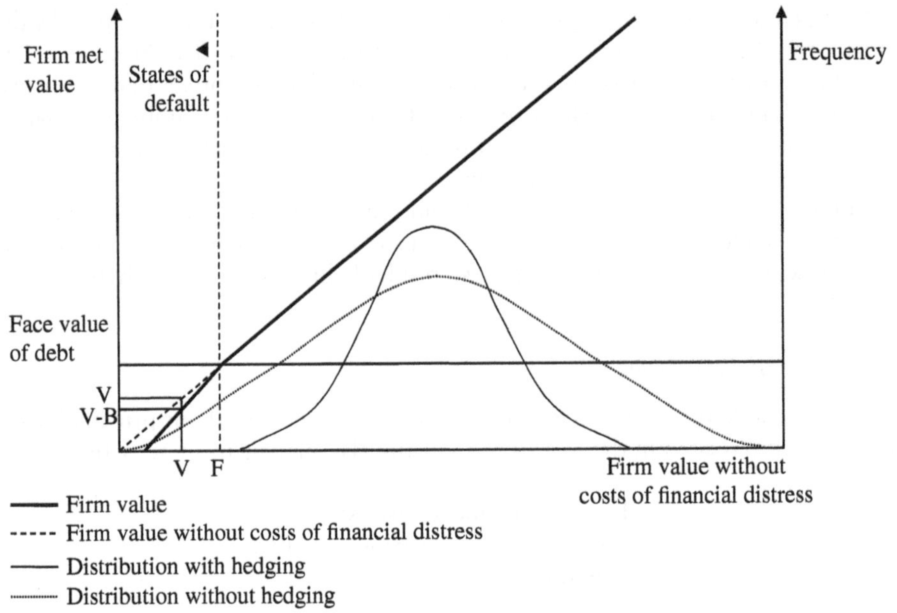

FIGURE 4.2 Risk management and costs of financial distress.
Source: Reproduced from Stulz (1996). © John Wiley & Sons, Inc. Reproduced with permission.

The second variable is associated mainly with the probability of short-term financial distress. The direct average monetary cost of production of one ounce of gold measures the efficiency of the firm: firms with higher costs are less efficient. They therefore have a higher probability of financial distress, and consequently pay partners higher risk premiums.

The average cost of production of one ounce of gold represents the mining company's technology. Interest and nonmonetary costs like amortization are not included in the construction of the variable. If the price of gold falls below the minimum monthly average cost of the business ($300 in Figure 4.3), the firm will find itself in financial difficulty when it repays its debt.

We can therefore predict, for these two variables, a positive sign on risk management for businesses with a capital structure that encourages hedging, namely indebted companies.

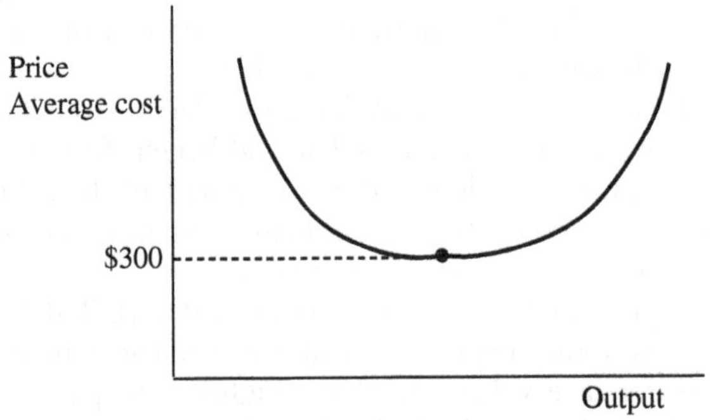

FIGURE 4.3 Average cost of production of one ounce of gold.

PROPOSITION 3:

Companies with high average production costs and that are more heavily indebted over the long term should practice more risk management to reduce their anticipated costs of financial failure.

The capital structure is not controlled in this study. We will see below how endogenous debt can influence the results. Two other variables are introduced in our model to consider the good financial health of the firm.

Ratio of Dividends Announced and the Use of Preferred Shares to Finance Investments

When companies announce dividend payments, this means they are able to make such payments regardless of the states of nature. They therefore need less diversification. This is an important measure of the financial health of the firm. Nonetheless, to handle pressure from competing firms that pay dividends, some firms may announce dividends even if they cannot afford to pay them. These firms should practise more risk management.

The use of preferred shares to finance investments is another measure of the financial health of the firm and a substitute for external debt without constraints on interest payments.

PROPOSITION 4:

Firms in good financial health (that announce dividends and finance their investments with preferred shares) have a lesser need for external debt and consequently need less hedging or risk management to protect themselves from the costs of financial distress.

Increase in Investment Possibilities

The major argument used here is the reduction in fluctuations of internal financing of investment projects (in other words their volatility) by risk hedging or the use of insurance to minimize the need for external financing, which is more costly in the presence of information asymmetry.

Therefore, consistent with the findings of Froot, Scharfstein, and Stein (1993), if we have only one random variable, like the price of the product sold, we should observe a positive relationship between investment opportunities and risk hedging. (See Chapter 3 of this book for more details.)

However, this relationship may be very weak or even negative if the returns on the investment opportunities are random. In particular, if the investment returns are also a function of the price of gold, as in our application, natural diversification occurs within the firm, thus lowering the needs for coverage by financial markets.

PROPOSITION 5:

Firms with more investment projects should hedge more, but this effect may be weak for firms having natural sources of diversification.

Two variables are used to measure investment opportunities: mining exploration activities and business acquisition activities in the industry; a positive sign is predicted for each variable.

Reduction of Tax Payments

The use of risk hedging may reduce the expected value of taxes payable by lowering the fluctuation of income in firms with convex tax functions. The simplest argument is linked to the asymmetric treatment of taxes between profits and losses, which creates the desired convexity.

Nonetheless, measuring the incentives linked to taxes is very complex, and it is not evident that the variables used by researchers, such as level of taxes paid, are always appropriate, which may explain the counterintuitive empirical results. Measuring the convexity of the tax function is difficult, as Figure 4.4 demonstrates. We can observe that the local tax function of a firm may be linear, convex and even concave.

In the upper portion of Figure 4.4, we have two tax functions: a base and an extended function. The extended function considers the different legal accounting rules that may be applied to reduce taxes payable. The use of these legal rules seems to make the tax function more convex, but this is not always the case. The enlargement

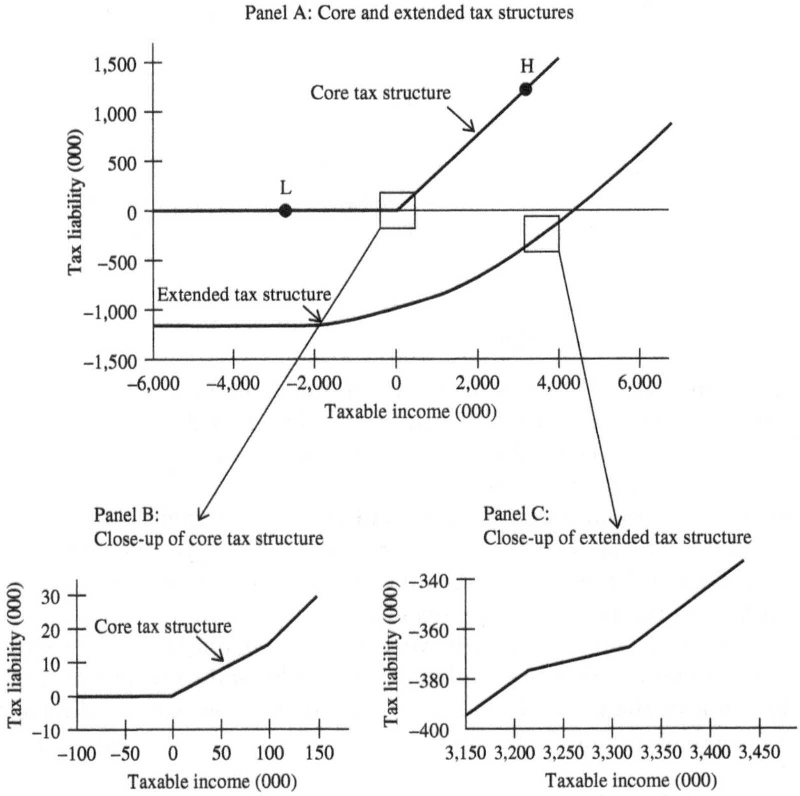

FIGURE 4.4 Tax Structure.
Source: Reproduced from Graham and Smith (1999). © John Wiley & Sons, Inc. Reproduced with permission.

of the figure in panel B clearly shows that a local curve may be linear in parts, but panel C indicates that the curve can also take a concave form locally.

PROPOSITION 6:

Firms with convex local taxation structures should undertake more risk management activities.

Tufano uses the variable tax loss carryforwards as a measure of the convexity of firms' tax function. A positive sign is predicted, but it is not evident that the variable clearly measures the convexity of a tax function.

We used two variables to consider the effect of taxes:

1. Deferred taxes, which replaces the tax loss carryforwards variable. It is the inverse of the tax loss variable. A negative sign is predicted.
2. Tax save, which measures, more directly, the convexity of the tax function for firms that pay taxes. This is the variable suggested by Graham and Smith (1999) to measure the convexity of the taxation function. A positive sign is predicted.

Tax save measures the real tax savings as a percentage following a 5% drop in the volatility of profits. It does not measure the degree of convexity directly, but, at best, may indicate that the function is convex if the tax savings is positive.

We can use equation 4A.1 in the appendix, taken from the article by Graham and Smith (1999), to create the tax save variable. The dependent variable of this equation measures the tax savings of 84,200 firms on COMPUSTAT following risk management that reduces the volatility of taxable income by 5%. The mean is 3.1% for all firms and 5.4% for firms with a convex local tax structure (55,059 firms). The results of the regression in the appendix indicate that the firms with more volatile income obtain greater tax savings. However, this is the marginal effect of one variable; the other variables may also affect the level of tax savings. Dionne and Garand (2003) have used this equation to predict the tax save variable with the data from their firms, corresponding to 898 observations.

The dependent variable of Equation 4A.1 was predicted with all the variables of the regression. We can therefore obtain positive, nil, or negative values depending on the convexity structure of the tax function of the firm. The results of Dionne and Garand (2003) calculations are presented in Table 4.3, where TS is the measure of tax save.

For each firm in their sample (at each quarter), they have documented the values of the independent variables in equation (4A.1) and used the regression coefficients to calculate the value of the dependent variable. The mean calculated is 4.9%, which is not very far from the values presented by Graham and Smith (1999). In Table 4.3, we observe that 27 observations have concave structures (negative TS) and that about 60% of observations present values of between 2% and 6%.

Firm Size

Firm size is a control variable that can be an indirect measure of the financing cost. This variable can also measure the firm's ability to access different risk diversification methods. Most empirical studies show that large firms are more diversified, although

TABLE 4.3 Distribution of the tax save (TS) variable.

Value	Number of observations	% of observations
TS < 0%	27	3.01
0 ≤ TS < 1%	0	0.00
1 ≤ TS < 2%	12	1.34
2 ≤ TS < 3%	165	18.37
3 ≤ TS < 4%	97	10.80
4 ≤ TS < 5%	153	17.04
5 ≤ TS < 6%	140	15.59
6 ≤ TS < 7%	74	8.24
7 ≤ TS < 8%	101	11.25
8 ≤ TS < 9%	78	8.69
9 ≤ TS < 10%	32	3.56
TS ≥ 10%	19	2.12
Total	898	100
Mean TS	4.9	
Standard deviation	3.3	
Volatility of income	6.164	
Standard deviation	24.58	
Temporal correlation of income	0.309	
Standard deviation	0.460	
Mean market value	1,207.08	
Standard deviation	1,953.86	
Mean debt/firm value ratio	0.105	
Standard deviation	0.113	
Percentage with ITC	0.0%	
Percentage with NOL	44.8%	

it is the smaller ones that would need diversification the most. The largest firms are financially able to recruit qualified staff, whereas the use of external consultants is very costly for small firms. We predict an ambiguous sign for this variable.

PROPOSITION 7:

Firm size has an ambiguous effect on the level of risk management.

Dionne and Garand (2003) used one variable to take firm size into account: gold reserves. They do not predict the sign of the coefficient.

Another variable discussed in the literature is the financial constraint

---

PROPOSITION 8:

Firms with tight financial constraints have a greater need to hedge from price declines to be able to pay their debt and satisfy their other financial needs. We predict a positive sign because, in general, a higher financial constraint implies a lower probability of repaying the debt and other commitments.

The financial constraint is a binary variable that takes the value of 1 when firms have an L-T debt/MV ratio that is higher than the industry median and a liquidity ratio below the median.

Finally, firms with more liquidity need less financial hedging because keeping liquidity in their financial statements is a form of hedging.

PROPOSITION 9:

We predict a negative sign for the variable liquidity ratio.

Table 4.4 presents the definitions of the variables used in the empirical analysis. The estimation results are presented in the next section.

TABLE 4.4 Definitions of variables.

Delta%

The Delta is the variation in the value of the portfolio of derivative products for every $1 variation in the price of gold; this value, calculated quarterly, is measured by the ratio of the sum of ounces of gold to produce during the next three years for which the price is hedged, divided by the total anticipated gold production for the next three years. The Delta % measures the level of derivatives used: that is, the degree to which risks are managed. Table 4.2 provides the distribution of the Delta% calculated.

Market value (MV)

The market value is defined by the number of common shares multiplied by their unit market value at quarter end plus the number of preferred shares issued multiplied by their value at par plus the book value of debt ($US). This variable is used to scale many variables. There are fixed components in both the costs of financial distress and in the costs of implementing a hedging program. For a large (small) firm, the relative costs of financial distress are smaller (larger), which means that the firm requires less (more) hedging. Conversely, the entry barrier to implement a hedging program is smaller (larger) for a large (small) firm because the relative costs are lower (higher).

Tax save

This variable measures the real tax savings as a percentage following a 5% drop in the volatility of profits. It does not measure the degree of convexity directly, but at best may indicate that the function is convex if it is positive or concave if it is negative. Values are given in Table 4.3.

Deferred income taxes/assets

The deferred income item of the statement divided by total assets. Given that tax credits for losses reduce deferred income, the ratio measures the inverse of the tax function's convexity. We consequently predict a negative relationship. In our computations, this variable was selected because it was available on a quarterly basis, unlike the tax-credits variable.

L-T debt/MV

The book value of the long-term debt divided by the firm's market value. Debt generates interest payments and principal repayments. If the firm is unable to make these payments, it may experience financial distress. This ratio therefore captures the financial distress factor. A positive sign is predicted.

TABLE 4.4 (*Continued*)

Cash-cost

Average cash-cost in $US to produce an ounce of gold. The variable is repeated in the four quarters of each year because it is available only on an annual basis. Production costs determine the firm's productivity; they thus capture the short-term financial distress factor. A positive sign is predicted.

Financial constraint

A binary variable that equals 1 when the "L-T debt/MV" variable and the liquidity ratio are respectively above and below the industry median. Otherwise it is equal to 0. A firm with high indebtedness and a thin liquidity cushion is a firm operating within the limits of financial constraint. The variable captures the financial-distress factor. A positive sign is predicted.

Dividend ratio

This ratio represents the annual per-share dividend announced divided by the share price at the end of the quarter. By announcing a dividend, the firm promises to pay said dividend in the future. To ensure that it can pay the dividend, it should practice hedging. A negative relationship is thus expected. This ratio can also be a good indicator of the firm's financial health, which reduces the need for hedging.

Preferred shares/MV

The number of preferred shares issued, multiplied by the value at par and then divided by the firm's market value. The preferred share is a substitute for external financing that is more flexible than debt because payment of dividends is optional. Given that an increase in the total value of preferred shares generally translates into a reduction in the ratio of indebtedness, a negative relationship is expected.

Reserves

The firm's proven and probable gold reserves (in ounces) at year-end, as a measure of firm size. The variable is repeated for the four quarters of each year because it is available only on an annual basis. Similar to the "market-value" variable, *reserves* refers to theories related to the costs of financial distress and to hedging costs. The sign is indeterminate.

Acquisition/MV

The value of acquisitions announced during the quarter and aimed at firms in the same sector, divided by market value. The variable captures the investment opportunities factor. A weak positive relationship or even a negative relationship is presumed because the correlation between investment opportunities and cash flow is generally positive in the gold mining industry: that is, gold producers benefit from natural hedging.

Exploration expenditures/MV

Exploration expenditures, divided by the firm's market value. The variable is repeated for the four quarters of each year, because it is available only on an annual basis. The variable captures the growth-opportunities factor to the extent that exploration efforts are profitable. A weak positive relationship or even a negative relationship is presumed because the correlation between investment opportunities and cash flow is generally positive in the gold mining industry: that is, gold producers benefit from natural hedging.

Liquidity ratio

The sum of cash on hand, short-term investments, and accounts receivable, divided by short-term liabilities. Liquidities can act as a cushion for financial losses. They are thus substitutes for risk management, and a negative relationship is expected.

4.2.3 Results of Estimations

Table 4.5 presents the results of the regressions.

TABLE 4.5 Regressions results, Tobit panel.

	All observations				Without Barrick Gold			
	A		B		C		D	
	Coef.	P(Z > z)	Coef.	P(Z > z)	Coef.	P(Z > z)	Coef.	P(Z > z)
Constant	−0.1771	0.003	−0.1624	0.0071	−0.2218	0.0000	−0.1986	0.0002
Taxes								
Deferred taxes /assets	−0.6314	0.0265	−0.6470	0.0382	−0.4040	0.1894	−0.4597	0.1212
Tax savings	0.0118	0.0000	0.0129	0.0004	0.0089	0.0081	0.0086	0.0000
Costs of financial distress								
LT debt /MV			0.3067	0.0000			0.3687	0.0000
Cash-cost	1.0658	0.0000	1.0851	0.0000	1.2498	0.0000	1.2703	0.0000
Financial constraint	0.0936	0.0000			0.1201	0.0000		
Dividend ratio	−4.8635	0.0000	−4.7762	0.0000	−1.8921	0.0616	−1.8597	0.0820
Preferred shares/MV	−1.2495	0.0001	−1.3903	0.0000	−0.5286	0.0701	−0.7521	0.0247
Size								
Reserves	0.1080	0.0000	0.1082	0.0000	0.0361	0.0413	0.0467	0.0306
Investment opportunity								
Acquisition/MV	−0.0640	0.8174	−0.0329	0.9119	−0.0312	0.9112	−0.0094	0.9713
Exploration expenses/MV	−0.3581	0.3481	−0.4936	0.2594	0.3779	0.4417	0.1447	0.7667
Substitute								
Liquidity ratio			−0.5043	0.0879			−0.6878	0.0072
Statistics								
Sigma (ν)	0.2023	0.0000	0.2047	0.0000	0.2012	0.0000	0.2026	0.0000
Sigma (μ)	0.1699	0.0000	0.1624	0.0000	0.1626	0.0000	0.1533	0.0000
Number of observations	898		898		868		868	
Chi-square	522.32		516.33		421.53		433.79	
p value of the regression	0.0000		0.0000		0.0000		0.0000	

Notes: The cash-cost and reserve variables were divided by 1,000 and 10 respectively for reasons related to the use of the software. Evidently, this operation does not affect the results. However, the coefficient must be transformed to obtain the real effect sizes.

We limit the detailed interpretation to the results in columns A and B. Regressions C and D were done to verify the effect of Barrick Gold on the industry. This firm is one of the largest in the industry, and was notorious for its very high hedging rate for the price of gold. It was even suspected of speculation during a particular period.

Let us interpret results in columns A and B. We can observe that the results are very significant with the predicted sign, apart from the two investment opportunity variables, which are not significant. There are two possible interpretations of these two variables: either they do not measure investment opportunities correctly, or firms in the industry profit from natural diversification explained by a potential correlation between the anticipated income from investment opportunities and internal financing. Both variables are positively correlated with the price of gold.

Columns A and B differ as follows: column A includes the financial constraint variable, whereas column B integrates the long-term debt and liquidity ratio variables. The three variables cannot be part of the same regression because the financial constraint variable is built from information on debt and liquidity. We can notice that the coefficients of the other variables remain stable between the two columns, which is a sign that the estimates are highly reliable. Lastly, the two sigma variables are significant, confirming that we had to control for temporal and individual effects in the panel data.

To summarize, firms that hedge more are those with higher indebtedness, a convex tax structure, and a tight financial constraint; they are also larger and less efficient at production. Firms that hedge less defer income taxes, announce dividends, use preferred shares to finance their projects, and have higher liquidity.

4.3 GOVERNANCE AND ENDOGENEITY OF DEBT

4.3.1 Model

Let us consider the model of Dionne and Triki (2013). As in the previous section, we assume that the mining firm produces gold. It also produces copper, for example, whose price, by assumption, cannot be hedged by derivative instruments. The total revenue w of the firm is equal to the sum of the income from the two goods x and y, two random variables that may be dependent:

$$w = w_0[h + (1 - h)x] + y \tag{4.1}$$

where:

w_0 corresponds to the firm's revenues from gold in certainty;
x to the random gold return;
h to the hedge ratio of the gold return;
y to the random revenue generated by the second good in place.

In line with Froot, Scharfstein, and Stein (1993), we assume that x is distributed normally with a mean of 1 and a standard deviation $\sigma > 0$. In addition, we assume that y is equal to $\alpha x w_0$, where α is a measure of the dependence between both revenues. When $\alpha > 0$, the two risks are positively correlated, and the inverse is true when $\alpha < 0$. In this characterization of the two risks, a negative correlation represents natural hedging between the risks.

To maximize its value, the firm chooses its hedging rate *h* and the face value of its debt F simultaneously, which is equivalent to solving the following program:

$$\underset{F,h}{\text{Max}} \int_{x_F}^{+\infty} [w_0[h + (1-h)x] + \alpha x w_0 - F]\ g(x)dx, \tag{4.2}$$

under the constraint that the economic profits of the bank are nil:

$$\int_{-\infty}^{x_F} [w_0[h + (1-h)x] + \alpha x w_0 - c]\ g(x)dx + F[1 - G(x_F)] = D(1+r), \tag{4.3}$$

where:

D	is the amount of debt contracted by the firm at the time the debt is issued;
c	are the audit costs paid by the bank when the firm declares default;
r	is the interest rate of T-bills during the period;
D(1 + r)	represents the bank's opportunity cost;
g(x) and G(x)	are respectively the density and cumulative distribution function of *x*;
F	is the face value of the debt;
x_F	is defined such that $w_0[h + (1-h)x_F] + \alpha x_F w_0 - F = 0$ and corresponds to the minimal value of gold return that allows the firm to avoid default. If $\alpha = 0$ and $h = 1$, then $x_F = F/w_0$, which is the minimum return to avoid default under certainty. However, it is not evident that $h = 1$ is an optimal solution, in this framework, even when $\alpha = 0$.

The maximization of (4.2) under the constraint (4.3) gives the following first-order conditions, where λ corresponds to the Lagrange multiplier for the constraint:

$$\begin{cases} \lambda = \dfrac{1 - G(x_F)}{1 - G(x_F) - cg(x_F)\dfrac{1}{w_0(1-h+\alpha)}} > 1 \\ \lambda = \dfrac{w_0\sigma^2}{w_0\sigma^2 - c\dfrac{F - w_0(1+\alpha)}{w_0(1-h+\alpha)^2}} > 1. \end{cases} \tag{4.4}$$

To simplify the discussion, we assume that:

$$F - w_0(1+\alpha) > 0 \text{ and } (1 - h + \alpha) > 0.$$

Solving the system of equations in (4.4) yields:[4]

$$\begin{cases} h^* = 1 + \alpha - \dfrac{1}{\sigma^2}\left[\dfrac{1 - G(x_f)}{g(x_f)}\right]\left[\dfrac{F^* - w_0(1+\alpha)}{w_0}\right] & (4.5a) \\ F^* = w_0\left[1 + \alpha + \sigma^2\dfrac{g(x_f)}{1 - G(x_f)}(1 - h^* + \alpha)\right] & (4.5b) \end{cases}$$

[4]See the appendix of the article by Dionne and Triki (2013) for more details.

According to equation (4.5a), the firm's optimal hedge ratio (h*) is increasing in σ^2, the volatility of x, and in the hazard rate (or conditional default probability), equal to $\frac{g(x_f)}{1-G(x_f)}$. This result is consistent with that of Leland (1998) in that hedging increases with the anticipated default costs.

Equation (4.5a) also shows that even if the firm faces only a single source of risk by selling only gold ($\alpha = 0$), its optimal hedging rate (h*) is different from 1 for a given F*. This result contrasts with the conclusion reached by Froot, Scharfstein, and Stein (1993) because in their model, optimal hedging is equal to 1 when the firm faces only one risk in the presence of low hedging costs. Here, when ($\alpha = 0$), the firm will hedge 100% of its income only if $F^* = w_0$: that is, F is equal to the mean expected income. A higher face value of the debt reduces the incentives to hedge. For a given debt level, firms with a higher F/w_0 hedge less because part of their hedging protects the bank. In contrast with the model of Froot, Scharfstein, and Stein (1993), here the firm hedges its total income and not only internal financing. As a result, a portion of the hedging benefits is reimbursed to the creditors, which explains why firms have a lesser incentive to finance such activities.

Equation (4.5a) shows that when $\alpha < 0$, the optimal hedge ratio will be lower than in the $\alpha = 0$ case, meaning that firms that have negatively correlated revenues will benefit from natural internal hedging. This decreases their need to turn to financial markets for hedging. When the two sources of revenues are positively correlated ($\alpha > 0$), the optimal hedge ratio will be greater than in the previous two cases and can even be greater than 1.

Similarly, equation (4.5b) shows that F*, the face value of a standard debt contract, is increasing in σ^2 and in the hazard rate. In addition, for a fixed value of the hazard rate, F* is a decreasing function of h*: an increase in h reduces the risk and the face value of the debt. However, variation of the hazard rate could modify this first conclusion. In fact, the derivative of F* relative to h* is equal to:

$$\frac{\partial F^*}{\partial h^*} = \underbrace{-\sigma^2 \frac{g(x_F)}{1 - G(x_F)}}_{\substack{<0 \\ \text{debt capacity}}} + \underbrace{(1 - h^* + \alpha)\frac{d\left(\frac{g(x_F)}{1-G(x_F)}\right)}{dx_F}\frac{dx_F}{dh^*}}_{\substack{? \\ \text{default intensity}}}. \tag{4.6}$$

From the previous discussion, we obtain two new empirical propositions.

PROPOSITION 10:

The firm's hedging ratio is an increasing function of the firm's default propensity, as shown in equation (4.5a). Because financially distressed firms support higher distress costs we should observe a positive relation between h (the hedge ratio) and the firm's financial default costs.

PROPOSITION 11:

More intensive hedging does not automatically decrease the face value of the debt, as shown in (4.6). This will occur only if the negative effect of the debt capacity on F outweighs the increase in the default intensity effect (if there is a positive effect).*

In other words, an increase in hedging reduces the cost of debt by reducing the risk premium (and by lowering the face value), but the reduction in the cost of debt may increase indebtedness (default intensity) because the firm can borrow more if the face value of the debt decreases sufficiently first.

4.3.2 Statistical Analysis

Measures of Hedging Rate and of Debt

As mentioned above, in Dionne and Triki (2013) we also test the propositions on a sample of data coming from North American gold producers. We estimate two equations: a hedging equation and a debt equation. The first equation uses the Delta% as a dependent variable. It measures, on a quarterly basis, the hedged fraction of gold production planned for the next three years. The dependent variable in the debt equation is long-term debt measured by the book value of debt divided by the firm's market value.

We will now describe the independent variables of the hedging equation.

Information Asymmetry

As did Graham and Rogers (2002), we measure information asymmetry by the percentage of shares held by institutional investors. Indeed, institutional investors typically have privileged access to management information and facilitate its diffusion in financial markets. Their presence should therefore reduce the need for financial hedging of the price of an ounce of gold associated with information asymmetry between the officers and the board. Moreover, institutional investors are usually well diversified and need less hedging. Therefore, we expect a negative coefficient for this variable.

Taxes

We calculate the tax savings resulting from a 5% reduction in the volatility of profits, as did Graham and Smith (1999). We scale the tax reduction calculated by the firms' sales in the regression analysis and expect a positive coefficient for this variable.

Costs of Financial Distress

Equation (4.5a) confirms the finding of Smith and Stulz (1985) that hedging increases firm value because it decreases the expected costs of financial distress. We measure these costs with two variables: the operating costs of producing one ounce of gold and long-term debt. We should observe a positive relationship between the hedging rate and both variables measuring the expected costs of financial distress. This prediction also supports Proposition 10.

Firm Size

We use the logarithm of revenues from sales to determine firm size. For the reasons stated in the article by Dionne and Garand (2003), we expect this variable to have an ambiguous effect on risk management.

Investment Opportunities

Froot, Scharfstein, and Stein (1993) argue that firms with investment opportunities are more likely to hedge to reduce external financing costs of projects that are more costly than internal financing. However, this positive effect may be attenuated by natural diversification within the firm.

Morellec and Smith (2002) demonstrate that hedging has two opposite effects on managers' risk-reduction incentive:

1. In the short run, hedging decreases the firm's free cash flow level and therefore constrains managers' investment policy;
2. In the long run, hedging decreases the firm's financial distress costs and improves its default risk, which leads to an increase in the investment level. This second effect prevails when investment opportunities are most attractive.

We therefore predict an ambiguous effect linking investment opportunities to financial hedging. We use two measures of investment opportunities of the firm, namely mining exploration expenses and business acquisition expenses, both scaled by the market value of the firm.

Managers' Risk Aversion

Smith and Stulz (1985) and Tufano (1996) argue that managers will hedge less if their expected utility is a convex function of the firm value. However, compensation packages that lead to a concave function between the manager's expected utility and the firm's value will encourage managers to hedge more. Consequently, managers who hold more of the firm's shares would engage in hedging more often, whereas those who hold options to purchase the firm's stock will hedge less when their options are out-of-the-money.[5]

We measure managerial risk aversion by two variables: the value of the common shares owned by directors and officers at the quarter end, and the number of options held by directors and officers.

Makeup of the Board of Directors

Several factors related to governance rules are associated with risk management. We use two variables to consider the makeup of the board of directors: the percentage of unrelated directors sitting on the board, and a dummy variable equal to 1 if the CEO is also the chairman of the board. A member of the board (including the president) is considered unrelated if he/she does not participate in firm management or does not belong to another firm that has ties to the firm on whose board that person sits. Former employees are considered related. If the rules are intended to increase shareholder wealth by reducing governance problems, these two variables should have a positive sign. They will be negative if the governance observed is mainly in officers' interest, particularly those who hold options that are out-of-the-money.

Liquidity

We use a liquidity index measured by the value of the cash on hand, short-term investments, and accounts receivable, divided by the short-term debt. We foresee a negative sign for the coefficient of this variable because liquidity is a substitute for risk management.

[5]See Dionne, Maalaoui Chun, and Triki (2018) for a more detailed discussion of governance problems associated with risk management.

Country

Lastly, we add a dummy variable equal to 1 to identify American firms and 0 for Canadian firms, to take into account the different markets between the countries. We do not make a prediction for this variable.

Determinants of Debt Level

We incorporate the percentage of hedging as an explanatory variable of debt. As stated in Proposition 11, the effect of greater hedging is ambiguous on the face value of debt. Whereas it first reduces the cost of debt or F* (and increases debt capacity), it may eventually affect the default intensity.

The other explanatory variables are the regular variables used in the literature (Titman and Wessels, 1988). We control for the collateral on firm debt, debt-related and other tax deductions, operational risk, firm's growth opportunities, and particularities of the firm such as size, profitability and country of origin.

Table 4.6 presents a description of the variables used in the multivariate analysis of debt and of risk management, along with the prediction of the effect of the variables selected. Some of the variables are weighted by the firm value, calculated as the number of common shares multiplied by their market price, plus the number of preferred shares multiplied by their value at par, plus the book value of the debt.

Data

For each firm-quarter observation, Dionne and Triki (2013) collected data from COMPUSTAT on the firm's market value, leverage, liquidity, expenses, operating income, selling and acquisition, depreciation, amortization, and general expenses, along with data on the book value of its property, equipment and sales.

The initial database describes, on a quarterly basis, hedging activities of 48 gold producers in North America during the 1993–1999 period. The aggregate variable of hedging, the Delta% for one quarter, measures the hedging of production of ounces of gold planned in the next three years using derivatives or bank loans reimbursed in ounces of gold whose value is set in the quarter studied. Table 4.7 presents the statistics of the Delta%. The sample is smaller than in the study by Dionne and Garand (2003) because we have many more variables here and potential missing values. We observe that the mean and standard deviation are not significantly affected when compared with values in Table 4.2. Table 4.8 describes the evolution of the Delta% over time. We can observe that hedging activities increased considerably after 1996. Table 4.9 details the descriptive statistics of different variables used in the econometric model.

Methodology

The methodology consists of estimating, simultaneously, the two equations of the reduced form obtained from the structural model derived by Dionne and Triki (2013). The reduced form of the model can be described as:

$$\begin{cases} y_{1it}^{*} = X_{it}'\eta_1 + l_{1i} + \gamma_{1it} & (4.7) \\ y_{2it}^{*} = X_{it}'\eta_2 + l_{2i} + \gamma_{2it} & (4.8) \end{cases}$$

where X_{it}' represents the vector including all the explanatory variables of the system, η_1 and η_2 are the vectors' parameters of the reduced system, l_{1i} and l_{2i} are the random

TABLE 4.6 Definition of the variables used by Dionne and Triki (2013).

Variable	Definition	Predicted sign	
		Risk management	Long-term Debt
Risk management activity			
Delta%	Gold production hedged divided by the total expected gold production for the next three years.		?
Costs of financial distress			
Long-term debt	The book value of the firm's long-term debt divided by its market value.	+	
Average cost of producing one ounce of gold	The average cost of producing one ounce of gold, excluding all non-cash items such as depreciation, amortization, and other financial costs.	+	
Information asymmetry			
Shares held by institutions	Percentage of firms' shares held by institutions.	–	
Tax effect			
Tax save	The tax savings resulting from a 5% reduction in the volatility of the taxable income. This variable is constructed using a modified version of the model by Graham and Smith (1999) to include Canadian tax law.	+	
Firm size			
Log (sales)	The natural logarithm of the firm's sales revenues.	?	
Investment opportunities			
Mining exploration expenses	The firm's exploration expenditures scaled by the firm's market value.	?	
Acquisitions of mining firms	The firm's acquisition expenditures scaled by the firm's market value.	?	
Managerial risk aversion			
Value of listed shares held by D&O	The number of common shares held by D&O multiplied by their market price.	+	
Value of options held by D&O	The value of options held by D&O on firm's common stock.	– (+)	

TABLE 4.6 (*Continued*)

Variable	Definition	Predicted sign	
		Risk management	Long-term Debt
Governance			
% unrelated	Percentage of unrelated directors on the board.	+ (–)	
CEO and COB	Dummy equal to 1 if the CEO is also the COB.	+ (–)	
Liquidity			
Liquidity ratio	The value of short-term investments and accounts receivable divided by the short-term liabilities.	–	
Firm's collateral value			
Collateral value	The book value of property divided by the book value of total assets.		+
Non-debt tax shield			
Depreciation and amortization	Depreciation and amortization divided by the book value of total assets.		–
Investments with debt			
Tax advantage	The firm's marginal tax rate measured by the additional taxes paid resulting from a variation in income.		+
Firm uniqueness			
Administration expenses	Selling and administrative expenses divided by net sales.		–
Profitability			
Operating income	Operating income scaled by the firm's sales.		–
Operational risk			
Volatility in OI	Volatility of the change in operating income.		–
Nationality			
US dummy variable	A dummy equal to 1 if the firm is US, 0 if it is Canadian.	?	?

TABLE 4.7 Descriptive statistics of the Delta%.

Delta%(1993–1999)	Number of observations
0	88
0–0.1	125
0.1–0.2	89
0.2–0.3	59
0.3–0.4	32
0.4–0.5	23
0.5–0.6	29
0.6–0.7	16
0.7–0.8	12
0.8–0.9	6
Higher than 0.9	29
Number of observations: 508	
Mean: 0.2451	
Median: 0.1381	
Standard deviation: 0.2808	

TABLE 4.8 Distribution of the Delta% over the sample period (1993–1999).

Year	Number of observations	Mean	Median	Standard deviation
1993	16	0.0233	0.0000	0.0448
1994	50	0.1992	0.0777	0.3003
1995	52	0.1632	0.0754	0.2618
1996	55	0.1886	0.1076	0.2446
1997	108	0.2374	0.1692	0.2342
1998	123	0.3068	0.2309	0.2864
1999	105	0.3058	0.1854	0.3209

TABLE 4.9 Descriptive statistics of the independent variables.

Variable	Number of observations	Mean	Median	Standard deviation
Cash cost	516	247	239	61.7266
Tax save	494	0.1381	0.0371	0.2822
Long-term debt	506	0.1186	0.0842	0.1271
Ln (Sales)	513	3.3220	3.1247	1.3674
Acquisition	517	0.0119	0.0000	0.0774
Exploration	517	0.0037	0.0022	0.0088
Quick ratio	517	3.1937	2.2022	3.0946
Institutional shareholding	517	0.1766	0.0000	0.2536
D&O shares value	517	16.9145	2.3021	46.8042
D&O options value	485	2.1	0.0390	6.98
% of unrelated directors	517	0.7018	0.7143	0.1580
Operating income	513	−0.0761	0.1797	1.1046
Administration expenses	513	0.1483	0.1105	0.1854
Volatility of % change in OI	485	12.9680	2.1128	125.3759
Depreciation	516	0.0181	0.0152	0.0176

firm effects of the reduced model, and γ_{1it} and γ_{2it} the error terms. The two variables explained are y^*_{1it}, the hedging rate selected, and y^*_{2it}, the long-term debt selected, divided by the firm value. More details on the derivation of this model are presented in the study by Dionne and Triki (2013). The empirical results are described in the next section.

4.3.3 Empirical Results

The results in Table 4.10 indicate that risk management (Delta %) and debt level (long-term debt) influence each other. A higher debt level increases risk management, and more risk management activities provide access to a higher debt capacity. However, these results assume that debt and risk management are exogenous as explanatory variables, and do not really take into account the feedback effect of the variation of each variable on the other. The results of Table 4.11 integrate this feedback effect, and show that a higher debt level still increases the need for risk management, whereas more risk management does not affect the debt level. It seems that the two theoretical effects of equation (4.6) cancel each other out: first, more risk management reduces the risk premium and increases the debt capacity (reduces F), but second, using more debt capacity increases the face value of debt and reduces the indebtedness possibilities (Proposition 11). The results also suggest that the variable

TABLE 4.10 Empirical results without the simultaneous equations model.

Variable	Risk management		Debt	
	Coefficient	*p value*	Coefficient	*p value*
Constant	−0.310	0.021**	0.010	0.842
Tax save	0.078	0.173		
Long-term debt	0.855	0.000***		
Delta%			0.119	0.000***
Average production cost	0.001	0.000***		
Ln (Sales)	0.055	0.015**	0.016	0.115
Acquisition expenses	0.099	0.341	0.003	0.927
Exploration expenses	−0.001	0.576	0.001	0.009***
Liquidity ratio	−0.010	0.024**		
Institutional shareholding	−0.348	0.000***		
D&O shares value	0.002	0.001***		
D&O options value	−0.010	0.000***		
% of unrelated directors	0.152	0.187		
CEO and COB dummy variable	0.083	0.012**		
Operating income			−0.007	0.020**
Administration expenses			0.086	0.035**
Depreciation and amortization			−0.380	0.082*
Value of collateral			0.006	0.860
Tax advantage			0.007	0.839
Volatility of % change in OI			0.0001	0.253
US dummy variable	−0.025	0.761	−0.042	0.191
Number of observations	485		485	
Uncensored variables	404		401	
p value	0.000		0.000	

Note: *, ** and *** denote that the variable is significant at 10%, 5%, and 1% respectively.

TABLE 4.11 Results with the simultaneous equations model.

Variable	Risk management		Debt	
	Coefficient	*p value*	Coefficient	*p value*
Constant	−0.255	0.000***	−0.042	0.332
Tax save	0.119	0.122		
Long-term debt	1.711	0.024**		
Delta%			−0.061	0.138
Average production cost	−0.0002	0.414		
Ln (Sales)	0.016	0.395	0.014	0.020**
Acquisition expenses	1.027	0.006***	−0.652	0.094*
Exploration expenses	−0.002	0.142	0.003	0.000***
Liquidity ratio	−0.013	0.000***		
Institutional shareholding	−0.370	0.000***		
D&O shares value	0.002	0.000***		
D&O options value	−0.007	0.000***		
% of unrelated directors	0.146	0.000***		
CEO and COB dummy variable	0.069	0.000***		
Operating income			−0.001	0.826
Administration expenses			−0.080	0.001***
Depreciation and amortization			−0.473	0.058*
Value of collateral			0.057	0.017**
Tax advantage			−0.126	0.000***
Volatility of % change in OI			−0.001	0.000***
US dummy variable	0.022	0.555	0.009	0.564
Number of observations	485		485	
Uncensored variables	404		401	

Note: *, ** and *** denote that the variable is significant at 10%, 5%, and 1% respectively.

D&O share value has a positive coefficient and the D&O options value variable has a negative coefficient, which may be explained by the fact that 63% of the options in the sample were out-of-the-money. The two governance variables in Table 4.11 (% of unrelated directors and CEO and COB dummy variable) have positive effects on hedging.

4.4 CONCLUSION

One valid criticism of the literature on risk management of non-financial firms is that it is still far from the portfolio approach, which could shed light on all of firms' diversification options. To implement integrated risk management, firms must first be able to quantify the different risks and their correlations.

For example, is exchange rate risk independent of interest rate risk in a country with an open economy like Canada? What is the correlation between fluctuations in exchange rates and the price of raw materials in a raw-material-producing country? These correlations between different risks should be central to future research if we want additional arguments to integrate the management of different risks.

The results of the estimates confirm the model developed by Tufano (1996), showing that managers' risk aversion affects risk management. They also show that the costs of financial distress, information asymmetry, and liquidity are important determinants of firms' risk management. In addition, governance variables like director independence and the fact that the CEO is also the chairman of the board of the firm also encourage risk management.

Our results demonstrate that even if financial distress costs favor risk management, greater risk hedging does not increase debt capacity in the simultaneous model. This conclusion runs counter to the results obtained from the non-simultaneous equations along with those predicted in the literature.

Even if our results are associated with a single industry, they highlight the importance of simultaneously modelling debt and risk management decisions in empirical studies identifying the determinants of risk management.

REFERENCES

Adam, T., 2009. "Capital Expenditures, Financial Constraints, and the Use of Options." *Journal of Financial Economics* 92, 238–251.

Allayannis, G., and Weston, J.P., 2001. "The Use of Foreign Currency Derivatives and Firm Market Value." *The Review of Financial Studies* 14, 243–276.

Campello, M., Lin, C., Yire, M., and Zou, H., 2011. "The Real and Financial Implications of Corporate Hedging." *Journal of Finance* 66, 1615–1647.

Carpenter, J.N., 2000. "Does Option Compensation Increase Managerial Risk Appetite?" *The Journal of Finance* LV, 2311–2331.

Cliche, J.A., 2000. "Les déterminants de la gestion des risques par les entreprises non financières: une revue de la littérature." *Insurance and Risk Management* 67, 595–636.

Dionne, G., and Garand, M., 2003. "Risk Management Determinants Affecting Firms' Values in the Gold Mining Industry: New Empirical Results." *Economics Letters* 79, 43–52.

Dionne, G., Gueyie, J.P., and Mnasri, M., 2018. "Dynamic Corporate Risk Management: Motivations and Real Implications." *Journal of Banking and Finance* 95, 97–111.

Dionne, G., Maalaoui Chun, O., and Triki, T., 2018. "The Governance of Risk Management: The Importance of Directors' Independence and Financial Knowledge." Mimeo, HEC Montreal.

Dionne, G., and Ouederni, K, 2011. "Corporate Risk Management and Dividend Signaling Theory." *Finance Research Letter* 8, 188–195.

Dionne, G., and Santugini, M., 2014. "Entry, Imperfect Competition, and Futures Market for the Input." *International Journal of Industrial Organization* 35, 70–83.

Dionne, G., and Triki, T., 2013. "On Risk Management Determinants: What Really Matters?" *European Journal of Finance* 19, 145–164.

Froot, K.A, Scharfstein, D.S., and Stein, J.C., 1993. "Risk Management: Coordinating Corporate Investment and Financing Policies." *Journal of Finance* 48, 1629–1658.

Graham, J.R., and Rogers, D.A., 2002. "Do Firms Hedge in Response to Tax Incentives?" *Journal of Finance* 57, 815–839.

Graham, J.R., and Smith, C.W., 1999. "Tax Incentives to Hedge." *Journal of Finance* 54, 2241–2262.

Hoyt, R.E., and Liebenberg, A.P., 2011. "The Value of Enterprise Risk Management." *Journal of Risk and Insurance* 78, 795–822.

Leland, H., 1998. "Agency Costs, Risk Management, and Capital Structure." *The Journal of Finance* 53, 1213–1244.

Mnasri, M., Dionne, G., and Gueyie, J.P., 2017. "The Use of Nonlinear Hedging Strategies by US Oil Producers: Motivations and Implications." *Energy Economics* 63, 348–364.

Morellec, E., and Smith, C., 2007. "Agency Conflicts and Risk Management." *Review of Finance* 11, 1–23.

Nguyen, N., 2015. "Effet de la rémunération des CEOs par options d'achat d'actions sur leur comportement de gestion du risque des entreprises d'énergie." Master supervised project report, HEC Montréal.

Pérez-Gonzalez, F., and Yun, H., 2013. "Risk Management and Firm Value: Evidence from Weather Derivatives." *Journal of Finance* 68, 2143–2176.

Savor, M., 2002. "Risk Management and Its Effect on Mergers and Acquisitions." Ph.D thesis, HEC Montréal.

Shue, K. and Townsend, R., 2017. "How Do Quasi-Random Option Grants Affect CEO Risk-Taking? *Journal of Finance* LXXII, 2551–2588.

Smith, C., and Stulz, R., 1985. "The Determinants of Firms' Hedging Policies." *Journal of Financial and Quantitative Analysis* 20, 391–405.

Stulz, R.M., 1996. "Rethinking Risk Management." *Journal of Applied Corporate Finance* 9, 8–25.

Titmans, S. and Wessels, R., 1988. "Determinants of Capital Structure Choice." *Journal of Finance* 43, 1–19.

Tufano, P., 1996. "Who Manages Risk? An Empirical Examination of Risk Management Practices in the Gold Mining Industry." *Journal of Finance* 51, 1097–1137.

APPENDIX: CONSTRUCTION OF THE TAX-SAVE VARIABLE

$$\text{Tax save }(5\%) = 4.88 + 7.15\ \text{TI(NEG)} + 1.60\ \text{TI(POS)} + 0.019\ \text{VOL} - 5.50\ \text{RHO}$$
$$- 1.28\ \text{ITC} + \text{NOL}(3.29 - 4.77\ \text{TI(NEG)} - 1.93\ \text{TI(POS)}) \quad (4\text{A}.1)$$

The regression taken from Graham and Smith (1999) is estimated on 84,200 firm-years. The adjusted R^2 is 8.2%. Researchers who have access to these independent variables and who cannot simulate the tax savings of the firms in their sample may use the coefficients of this regression to compute the dependent variable, and use this approximation as a measure of the convexity of the taxation function resulting from a 5% reduction in the volatility of firm revenue. The variable calculated may be positive (local convexity), nil, or negative (local concavity).

Regression (4A.1) links the tax save variable to different firm characteristics. Tax save is the variation in taxes for a firm following a 5% reduction in the volatility of its income. Explanatory variables are as follows, with their *t* value in parentheses:

TI (NEG)	dummy variable for firms with taxable income between −\$500,000 and \$0 (40.3);
TI (POS)	dummy variable for firms with taxable income between \$0 and +\$500,000 (11.3);
VOL	volatility of income (10.9);
RHO	first-order temporal correlation in revenue (−41.1);
ITC	dummy variable for the presence of an investment tax credit (−9.5); the authors find this sign counterintuitive;
NOL	dummy variable for the existence of carryforwards of operating losses (36.5); positive sign is counterintuitive but reversed with the interaction variables;
NOL(TI(NEG))	NOL variable in interaction with the dummy variable negative taxable income (−18.3);
NOL(TI(POS))	NOL variable in interaction with the dummy variable positive taxable income (−8.1).

CHAPTER 5

Value at Risk

The main role of value at risk (VaR) is to provide summary information on the risk of a firm, a portfolio, or a stock. This information is generally given to a firm's top management or to a portfolio manager or stockholder. It may also be used by regulatory agencies.

Some managers wish to be informed of their firm's VaR at 4:30 p.m. daily, while others would rather be given this information on Friday afternoons. Regulatory agencies require the banks that calculate their market risk using an internal method to transmit their market VaR every two weeks (or 10 business days). However, market risk VaR is now replaced by CVaR for Basel market risk regulation. This does not mean that the VaR is becoming useless. In fact, it is still very useful for backtesting the CVaR (Fortin, Simonato, and Dionne, 2018).

VaR is the maximum loss calculated for a given time period at a certain confidence level. It contains a time component (intraday, daily, weekly, monthly, or even annually for credit risk), and takes into account the opinion of a firm's management or of a portfolio holder to set the confidence level. The more conservative the opinion, the greater the required confidence level and the higher the VaR.

For many years, VaR was the most popular method used to measure market risk. However, this measurement focuses on the minimization of variance, which contradicts the model suggested in Stulz's (1996) article. Stulz suggests that we should instead focus on minimizing the risk of conditional losses (CVaR) or the downside risk. We will present an intuitive version of the CVaR at the end of the chapter. A more formal presentation of the CVaR will be discussed in Chapter 8. VaR is more appropriate for stock or bond portfolios than for non-financial firms with risk management horizons ranging from four months to few years (Christoffersen, 2012; Dionne, Pacurar, and Zhou, 2015; Jorion, 2001; Dowd, 1998, 2002).

5.1 EXAMPLE OF VaR

Let us consider the monthly returns of a portfolio over 10 years. The histogram of the data is presented in Figure 5.1. The average return $\mu = 1.23\%$, and the standard deviation $\sigma = 4.3\%$.

If we suppose that the distribution is normal, then two-thirds of the mass or of the surface is comprised within the two boundaries of one standard deviation: that is, a loss of 3.07% and a gain of 5.53%.

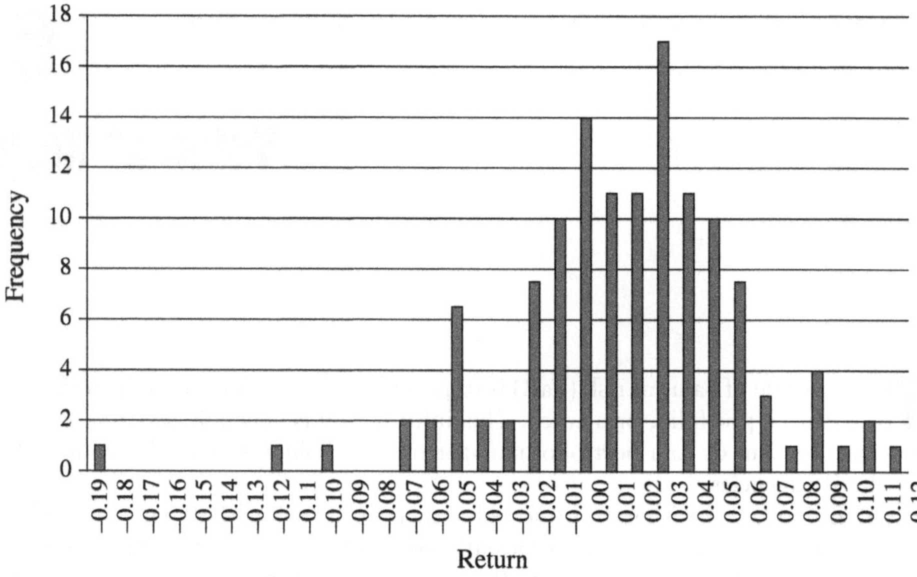

FIGURE 5.1 Monthly returns of a global portfolio September 1985–December 1995.

The VaR calculates, for instance, the maximum amount that a portfolio manager can lose during the next month with a confidence level of (1 – p). The relative parametric VaR can be written as follows:

$$VaR_r = \alpha\sigma\sqrt{\Delta t},$$

where σ is the standard deviation of the distribution and $\sqrt{\Delta t}$ measures the temporal variation, which we suppose is presently equal to 1. The value α is the weight that takes into account the chosen confidence level (α is equal to 1.65 for a confidence level of 95%). VaR_r is the VaR relative to the average. It covers the losses and the expected returns. VaR_r at 95% is equal to 7.1% $(1.65 \times 4.3\%)$ in the data of Figure 5.1. The absolute VaR only takes losses into account:

$$VaR_a = \alpha\sigma\sqrt{\Delta t} - \mu.$$

The absolute VaR corresponds to the VaR_r from which we subtract the average of the distribution. We can verify that $VaR_a = -1.23\% + 1.65(4.3\%) = 5.9\%$ of return loss in the above example.

Figure 5.2 illustrates the two values at risk when we do not reject that the returns in the histogram are normally distributed.

Given a $100 million initial portfolio, the maximum loss calculated with a confidence level of 95% is $7.1 million over the course of the next month, while the average expected return is $1.23 million. The VaR can be used to create a capital reserve in order to protect against the worst possible unanticipated outcome at a confidence level of 95%.

However, this concept is not very useful for general aspects of risk management of a non-financial firm. What is the probability of default over the next three years

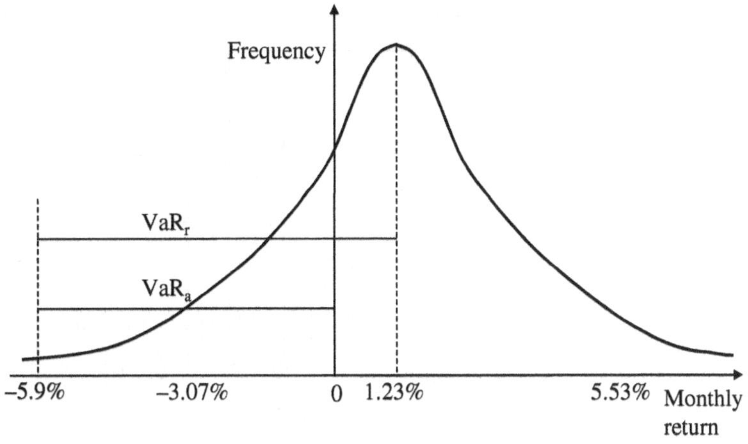

FIGURE 5.2 Value at risk.

for a BBB-rated firm? The market VaR calculated above does not allow us to answer this question.

VaR is very simple to use and is precise for intraday, daily, and monthly time periods, but it cannot be used for yearly time periods or for periods of three years for market risk. Technically, most non-financial firms do not possess a sufficient number of annual observations to establish good statistical approximations of their distribution of annual returns.

In addition, the performance of VaR presented here rests on the assumption of normally distributed returns, which is a strong assumption for many portfolios. Generally, the tails of return distributions are thicker than those of a normal distribution, particularly for default risk. This suggests a sensitivity approach using Monte Carlo simulations or more sophisticated parametric approaches. There are many ways to calculate the VaR; we will address two in the following sections, and others will be covered in the exercises.

5.2 NUMERICAL METHOD

This method consists of using the histogram of returns over a given time period. For example, Figure 5.3 represents the histogram of JP Morgan's daily revenue in 1995.

The average income is $7.6 million, but the observations are very dispersed. Most of the observations are between –$15M and $30M. There is even one daily loss greater than $26 million.

If we choose a confidence level of 95% to calculate the VaR, this implies that we are covering 95% of potential values. There is a 5% probability that the maximum loss calculated or VaR will be surpassed; the firm thus has five chances in a hundred of surpassing the maximum loss calculated over the next 100 transaction days (if the distribution remains stable).

The maximum value calculated is a daily loss of $11.4 million (5% of the 250 observations = 12.5 observations from the left). As discussed before, VaR can be defined in absolute terms and in relative terms with respect to the average. Absolute VaR was calculated above. It corresponds to the maximum loss with respect to zero.

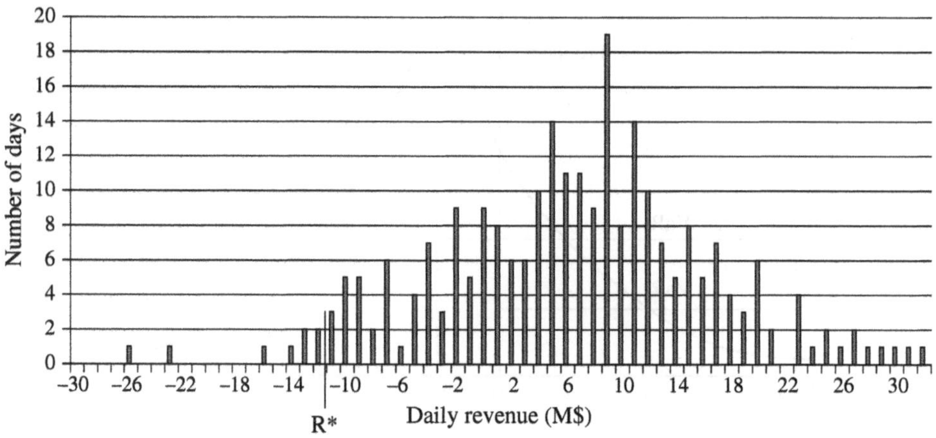

FIGURE 5.3 Histogram of JP Morgan's daily revenue in 1995.

Now, if we wish to calculate the maximum loss with respect to the mathematical expected revenue (E(R)), VaR will be equal to E(R) + VaR (absolute) = \$19 million for this example. To protect itself, the firm must create a \$19 million capital reserve. This numerical method is not frequently used in practice due to its lack of precision.

Let us now suppose that we are able to estimate the parameters of the distribution of revenues. This will allow us to address parametric VaR.

5.3 PARAMETRIC METHOD

Let us denote *R* as the returns and f(R) as the density function of the distribution. We may define the probability that *R* is inferior to a given R*, where R* is defined by the chosen confidence level 1 – p. R* corresponds to the maximum loss quantile. The probability *p* that *R* is inferior to R* is equal to:

$$F(R^*) = \text{Prob}[R < R^*] = \int_{-\infty}^{R*} f(R)dR = p,$$

where F(R) is the cumulative distribution function. If we choose a confidence level (1 – p) of 95%, we have a 5% probability of obtaining a loss greater than R* or a 95% probability that the end of period revenue will be greater than R*. In order to calculate parametric VaR, we now need to make an assumption about the distribution of *R*.

Let us suppose that R is normally distributed $N(\mu, \sigma^2)$ with a mean equal to μ and a variance equal to σ^2. The standard normal distribution table directly gives us the value of the limit variable (Z*) corresponding to R*, and associated with the given confidence level. For example, for a confidence level of 95%, the variable Z* is equal to –1.65, or Prob [Z < Z*] = 0.05. It is therefore beneficial to transform *R* in order to obtain *Z* where:

$$Z = \frac{R - \mu}{\sigma}.$$

Consequently, if we write F(Z) as the standard normal distribution function of Z:

$$
\begin{aligned}
F(Z^*) &= \text{Prob}\,[Z < Z^*] \\
&= \text{Prob}\,[Z < Z^*] \qquad = 0.05 \\
&= \text{Prob}\,[Z < -1.65] \qquad = 0.05 \\
&= \text{Prob}\left[Z < \left(\frac{R^* - \mu}{\sigma}\right)\right] = 0.05.
\end{aligned}
$$

Therefore, by definition of a monotonic increasing function:

$$\frac{R^* - \mu}{\sigma} = -1.65 \text{ or } F^{-1}(0.05) = -1.65$$

and

$$R^* = \mu - 1.65\sigma$$

or, by normalizing to obtain positive VaR:

$$-R^* = 1.65\sigma - \mu,$$

which implies that the VaR relative to the mean (or the relative VaR_r) is equal to:

$$VaR_r = 1.65\sigma = \mu - R^*,$$

and the absolute VaR_a is equal to:

$$VaR_a = 1.65\sigma - \mu = -R^*.$$

Using the values in the example presented at the beginning of this chapter, we obtain:

$$
\begin{aligned}
VaR_r &= -R^* + \mu = 1.65\sigma = 7.13\% \\
VaR_a &= -R^* = 1.65\sigma - \mu = 5.9\%
\end{aligned}
$$

where $\mu = 1.23\%$ and $\sigma = 4.32\%$.

5.4 TAKING TIME PERIODS INTO CONSIDERATION

In order to calculate VaRs of a time period using data from a different time unit, we need to adjust our model. We will suppose that our observations are not correlated from one period to another. This implies that if we have data over two six-month periods, for example, we can calculate the annual average as $E(x) = E(x_1) + E(x_2)$, where $x = x_1 + x_2$. Similarly, the variance can be calculated as $Var(x) = Var(x_1) + Var(x_2)$, because $cov(x_1, x_2) = 0$ under the assumption that our observations are independent between the two periods. In addition, if we suppose that the x_i have the same distribution (i.i.d.) from one period to another, we can write:

$$\sigma^2(x) = Var(x) = 2Var(x_i)$$
$$E(x) = 2E(x_i).$$

Consequently:

$$\sigma(x) = \sqrt{2}\ \sigma(x_i) = \sqrt{\Delta t}\ \sigma(x_i)$$

and inversely:

$$\sigma(x_i) = \sigma(x)\ 1/\sqrt{2} = \sigma(x)\ \left(\sqrt{2}\right)^{-1}.$$

Therefore, if we have monthly data and we wish to calculate the annual relative VaR_{ra}:

$$VaR_{ra} = \sigma_m\ \alpha\ \sqrt{12}$$

where σ_m is the monthly standard deviation. Inversely, if we have annual data, we can calculate the relative monthly VaR and obtain:

$$VaR_{rm} = \sigma_a \alpha \left(\sqrt{12}\right)^{-1}$$

where σ_a is the annual standard deviation.

5.5 CONFIDENCE INTERVAL OF THE VaR

If we build a data sample comprised of our observations of a normal population, the variable $(n-1)\,s^2/\sigma^2$ will be distributed according to a χ^2 with $(n-1)$ degrees of freedom, where *n* is the sample size and s^2 is the sample variance. There is a 95% chance that this variable takes a value within the following boundaries:

$$[\chi^2_{0.025},\ \chi^2_{0.975}]$$

$$\chi^2_{0.025} < (n-1)s^2/\sigma^2 < \chi^2_{0.975},$$

where σ^2 is the population variance (not necessarily known). We can invert the above equation and obtain the following ratios:

$$1/\chi^2_{0.975} < \sigma^2/(n-1)s^2 < 1/\chi^2_{0.025}$$

This allows us to calculate a confidence interval for the variance, and we obtain:

$$(n-1)\ s^2/\chi^2_{0.975} < \sigma^2 < (n-1)\ s^2/\chi^2_{0.025}$$

or, for the standard deviation:

$$s\sqrt{(n-1)/\chi^2_{0.975}} < \sigma < s\sqrt{(n-1)/\chi^2_{0.025}}.$$

Consequently, setting $\sqrt{\Delta t} = 1$, we can obtain a confidence interval for the relative VaR:

$$\alpha s\sqrt{(n-1)/\chi^2_{0.975}} < VaR_r = \alpha\sigma < \alpha s\sqrt{(n-1)/\chi^2_{0.025}}.$$

5.6 CVaR

Conditional VaR (CVaR) allows us to calculate the average loss beyond VaR. It measures the cost of surpassing VaR. CVaR indicates that VaR underestimates the average cost of surpassing VaR. VaR is an indicator that lets us measure a frequency rather than a cost. For continuous distributions, CVaR is equivalent to expected shortfall (ES).

Instead of limiting ourselves to counting the number of times where we would surpass the VaR for a given confidence level, we can calculate the average loss related to each surpassing of the VaR. The calculation of CVaR is more complex than that of VaR and will be the subject of a next chapter. For now, we will specify the nature of CVaR using an intuitive demonstration proposed by Dowd (2002). For instance, we wish to calculate CVaR of a standard normal distribution of losses N(0,1). We know that the VaR of this distribution is 1.645, as illustrated in Figure 5.4.

An intuitive and simple method to calculate CVaR is to calculate the different values of VaR beyond the chosen VaR and to then calculate their average. Table 5.1 demonstrates an example of the calculation of 10 VaR values (including the value of 1.645) of a N(0,1) distribution. CVaR or average VaR is equal to 1.9870.

Table 5.2 indicates that the precision can be improved by increasing the number of trials. The value of 2.061 shown in Figure 5.4 is obtained using 1,000 trials, which

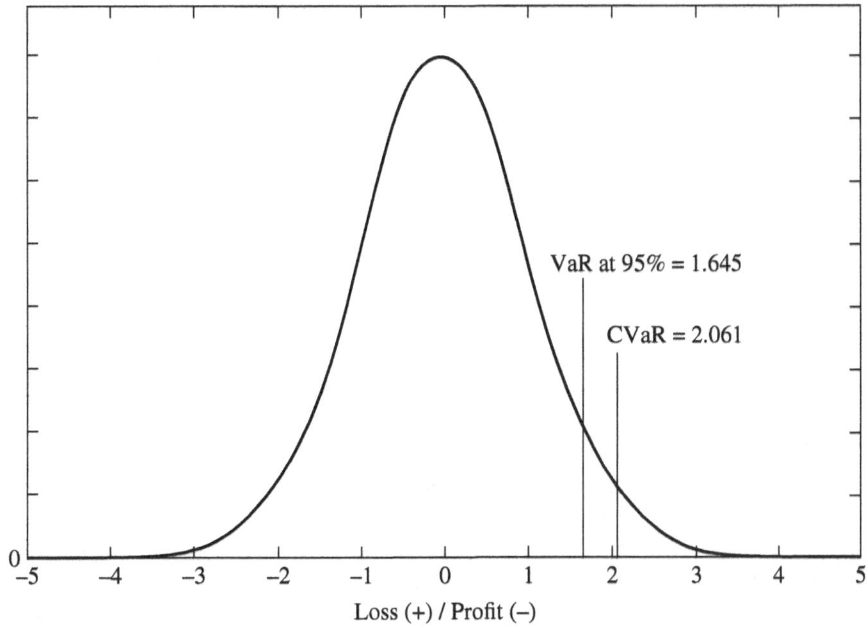

FIGURE 5.4 Conditional VaR or CVaR with 1,000 trials.

TABLE 5.1 Estimating CVaR as the average of VaR of the distribution tail.

VaRs	Value of VaR
VaR at 95.0%	1.6449
VaR at 95.5%	1.6954
VaR at 96.0%	1.7507
VaR at 96.5%	1.8119
VaR at 97.0%	1.8808
VaR at 97.5%	1.9600
VaR at 98.0%	2.0537
VaR at 98.5%	2.1701
VaR at 99.0%	2.3263
VaR at 99.5%	2.5758
Average VaR	1.9870

Note: VaRs are estimated under the assumption that the random variable follows a N(0,1) distribution.

TABLE 5.2 Estimating CVaR as a function of the number of trials of VaR.

Number of trials used	CVaR
n = 10	1.9820
n = 25	2.0273
n = 50	2.0432
n = 100	2.0521
n = 250	2.0580
n = 500	2.0602
n = 1,000	2.0614
n = 2,500	2.0621
n = 5,000	2.0624

Note: VaR is estimated under the assumption that the random variable follows a N(0,1) distribution. CVaR is an average of the calculated VaRs.

represents a good enough approximation of the actual CVaR, because the exact real value is $f(1.645)/1 - F(1.645) = 2.062$ using the density and cumulative distribution functions of a N(0,1).

5.7 CONCLUSION

We have presented an important concept of risk measurement, the value at risk (VaR). It is applied in many financial institutions to compute the necessary capital for optimal risk management. However, the concept has some methodological gaps, particularly for discontinuous functions. Moreover, VaR is not useful to compute the conditional loss and may underestimate the necessary capital for extreme events.

In a next chapter, we will address these failures by considering the conditional value at risk or CVaR. For recent analyses of VaR forecasting under portfolio management, see Kole et al. (2017), Santos, Nogales, and Ruiz (2013), Nieto and Ruiz (2016), and Fortin, Simonato, and Dionne (2018).

REFERENCES

Christoffersen, P., 2012. *Elements of Financial Risk Management*. Academic Press.

Dionne, G., Pacurar, M., and Zhou, X., 2015. "Liquidity-Adjusted Intraday Value at Risk Modeling and Risk Management: An Application to Data from Deutsche Börse." *Journal of Banking and Finance* 59, 202–219.

Dowd, K., 1998. *Beyond Value at Risk: The New Science of Risk Management*. John Wiley & Sons.

Dowd, K., 2002. *An Introduction to Market Risk Measurement*. Wiley Finance.

Fortin, A.P., Simonato, J.G., and Dionne, G., 2018. "Forecasting Expected Shortfall: Should We Use a Multivariate Model for Stock Market Factors?" Mimeo, Canada Research Chair in Risk Management, HEC Montréal.

Jorion, P., 2001. *Value at Risk*, 2nd ed. McGraw-Hill.

Kole, E., Markwat, T., Opschoor, A., and van Dijk, D., 2017. "Forecasting Value-at-Risk under Temporal and Portfolio Aggregation." *Journal of Financial Econometrics* 15, 649–677.

Nieto, M.R., and Ruiz, E., 2016. "Frontiers in VaR Forecasting and Backtesting." *International Journal of Forecasting* 32, 475–501.

Santos, A.A.P., Nogales, F.J., and Ruiz, E., 2013. "Comparing Univariate and Multivariate Models to Forecast Portfolio Value-at-Risk." *Journal of Financial Econometrics* 11, 400–441.

Stulz, R.M., 1996. "Rethinking Risk Management." *Journal of Applied Corporate Finance* 9, 8–25.

CHAPTER 6

Choice of Portfolio and VaR Constraint

In this chapter, we show how VaR can be used to make portfolio managers comply with the capital requirements of a brokerage firm, for example.[1]

6.1 OPTIMAL BENCHMARK PORTFOLIO OF THE FIRM

Consider the president of a brokerage firm with several portfolio managers. The president wants to constrain the firm's managers not to form overly risky portfolios.

To simplify, suppose they all have the same efficient frontier in a (E, σ) space but they have different risk aversion levels: $U(E, \sigma)$ differs between managers. E designates the mathematical expectation of the portfolio return, σ the standard deviation, and U the utility function of a risk-averse manager with the following partial derivatives: $U'_E > 0$, $U'_\sigma < 0$, indicating risk aversion.

The benchmark portfolio chosen by management is the solution maximizing the following program:

$$\underset{\beta_i}{\text{Max}}\ U(E, \sigma)$$

$$\text{subject to} \sum_{i=1}^{n} \beta_i = 1; \quad \beta_i \gtreqless 0$$

where:

$$E = \sum_{i=1}^{n} \beta_i E_i$$

$$\sigma^2 = \sum_{i=1}^{n} \beta_i^2 \sigma_i^2 + \sum_{i=1}^{n} \sum_{\substack{j=1 \\ j \neq i}}^{n} \beta_i \beta_j \sigma_{ij}$$

[1]For additional references, see Akume, Luderer, and Wunderlich (2009), Huisman, Koedijk, and Pownall (1999), Leibowitz and Henriksson (1989).

and where β_i is the portion of the asset *i* in the portfolio, *n* is the total number of assets, E_i the expected return on the asset *i*, σ_i its standard deviation, and σ_{ij} the covariance between the assets *i* and *j*.

Suppose that, for given values of the parameters $(U, \sigma_i, \sigma_{ij}, E_i)$, the president's optimal portfolio corresponds to the following values: $E^* = 8\%$ and $\sigma^* = 10\%$. The optimal solution is represented in Figure 6.1, where F is the efficient frontier.

This choice implies that statistically, ex post, we should have average realizations of the portfolio or of returns $\tilde{E}$ that will have a mathematical expectation of E^* (8%) and a standard deviation of σ^* (10%).

In other words, ex ante, $\tilde{E}$ is a random variable. Suppose that it follows a normal distribution of parameters $N(E^*, \sigma^*)$.

$$E(\tilde{E}) = \int_{-\infty}^{+\infty} \tilde{E} f(\tilde{E}) d\tilde{E} = E^*$$

$$Var(\tilde{E}) = \sigma^{2*}.$$

Under this hypothesis, we can verify that:

$$\int_{E^*-\sigma^*}^{E^*+\sigma^*} f(\tilde{E})\, d\tilde{E} = 68.28\%$$

$$\int_{E^*-2\sigma^*}^{E^*+2\sigma^*} f(\tilde{E})\, d\tilde{E} = 95.44\%.$$

We can therefore calculate the absolute VaR of the optimal portfolio with a degree of confidence of 90% and obtain:

$$p(\tilde{E} \geq E^* - 1.28\sigma^*) = \int_{E^*-1.28\sigma^*}^{+\infty} f(\tilde{E})\, d\tilde{E} = 90\%$$

or:

$$p(\tilde{E} < E^* - 1.28\sigma^*) = \int_{-\infty}^{E^*-1.28\sigma^*} f(\tilde{E})\, d\tilde{E} = 10\%$$

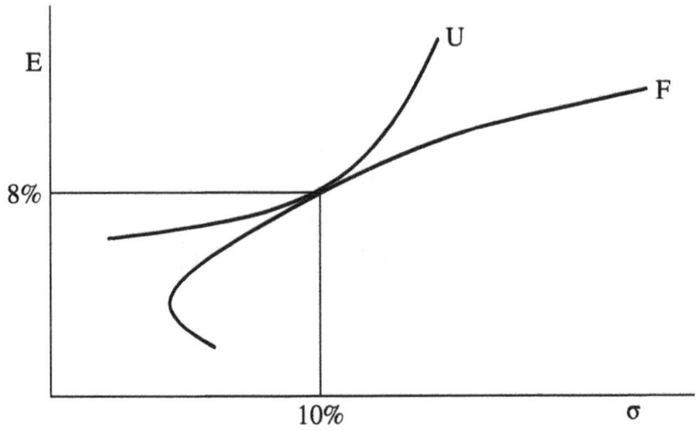

FIGURE 6.1 President's optimal portfolio.

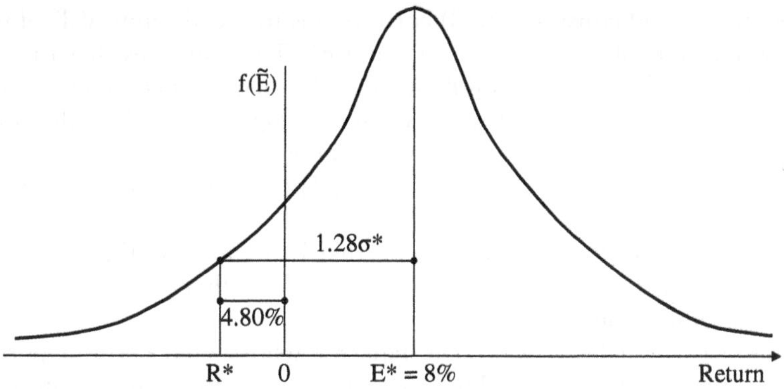

FIGURE 6.2 Representation of absolute and relative VaR.

with the percentile corresponding to 10%. We can write:

$$E^* - 1.28\ \sigma^* = R^*.$$

Note that −1.28 is the value of the 10th percentile of a standard normal distribution. By using the values of the optimal solution, we get:

$$R^* = E^* - 1.28\ \sigma^* = -4.80\%. \tag{6.1}$$

By the parametric approach, the absolute VaR, VaR_a, is equal to 4.80%, and the relative VaR, VaR_r, is equal to 12.80%, or 1.28 σ*. These solutions are depicted in Figure 6.2.

6.2 OPTIMAL PORTFOLIO OF A CONSTRAINED MANAGER

Now, we will look at the optimal portfolio choice of a portfolio manager belonging to this firm. For a manager *k*, if we introduce a VaR constraint, the portfolio manager's problem becomes:

$$\underset{\beta_{ik}}{\text{Max}}\ U_k(E_k, \sigma_k).$$

Under the constraints:

$$\sum_{i=1}^{n} \beta_{ik} = 1;\ \beta_{ik} \gtreqless 0 \tag{6.2}$$

$$E_k - 1.28\sigma_k \geq -4.80\% \tag{6.3}$$

where:

$$E_k = \sum_{i=1}^{n} \beta_{ik} E_i$$

$$\sigma_k^2 = \sum_{i=1}^{n} \beta_{ik}^2\ \sigma_i^2 + \sum_{i=1}^{n} \sum_{\substack{j=1 \\ j \neq i}}^{n} \beta_{ik} \beta_{jk} \sigma_{ij}$$

and where the second constraint (6.3) corresponds to the absolute VaR of the president's optimal portfolio by choosing E* and σ*. This indicates that the manager cannot have a return less than −4.80% with a 90% degree of confidence. The set of possible choices of the manager *k* is represented in Figure 6.3, where the dotted line represents the VaR constraint. This line is from equation (6.3), which has a slope equal to 1.28 and a constant equal to −4.80%. This line necessarily passes through the point (10%, 8%).

Managers who have utility functions U that let them be in the zone between B and D are not constrained and will choose a portfolio that gives a solution that is tangent to the continuous curve DB.

In contrast, for a less risk-averse manager who would chose a portfolio in section BC, the constraint is tighter (or active), and the manager must take it into account when solving his maximization problem. In general, the managers who are less risk-averse and who give σ less negative weight are the ones that the president wants to constrain. They demand a lower relative return and accept higher risk exposure. For example, a manager may choose an average return of 9% for a standard deviation of 12%, whereas this return is too low to meet the VaR constraint. The VaR_a constraint implicit in this choice (G) in Figure 6.4 solves:

$$9\% - 1.28\ (12\%) = -6.36\% < -4.80\%$$

A graphic representation of a solution (B) with a tight constraint for this manager is represented in Figure 6.4.

Evidently, portfolio G, which gives this manager more welfare than portfolio B, is not acceptable for the president. The manager must therefore choose a portfolio at the B level to meet the president's constraint. Portfolio B represents a loss of welfare for this manager.

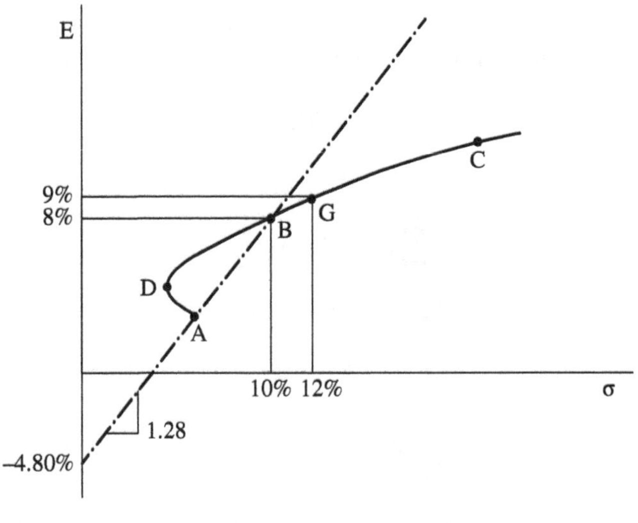

FIGURE 6.3 Possible choices for the manager *k*.

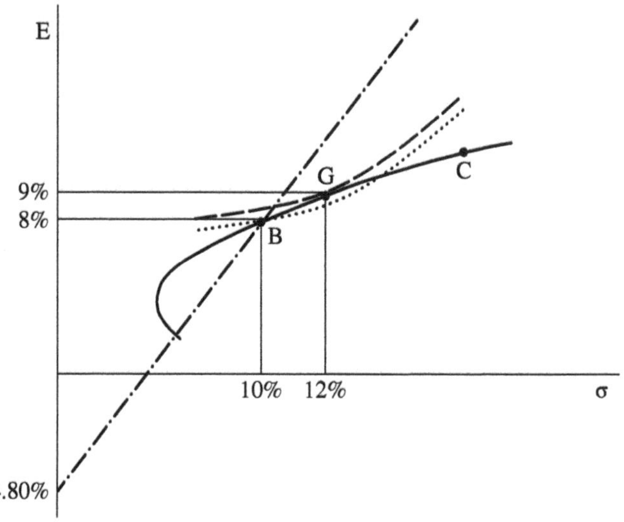

FIGURE 6.4 Choice of portfolio in the presence of a VaR constraint.

6.3 CONCLUSION

In this chapter, we have shown how to use the VaR as a constraint for optimal portfolio management. The constraint is more restrictive for less risk-averse portfolio managers who are willing to take greater risks to obtain higher returns. Akume, Luderer, and Wunderlich (2009) show how to generalize the above analysis to a shortfall constraint.

REFERENCES

Akume, D., Luderer, B., and Wunderlich, R., 2009. "Optimal Portfolio Strategies under a Shortfall Constraint." *ORiON* 25, 31–44.

Huisman, R., Koedijk, K.G., and Pownall, R.A.J., 1999. "Asset Allocation in a Value-at-Risk Framework." *Working paper*, Erasmus University, Rotterdam.

Leibowitz, M.L., and Henriksson, R.D., 1989. "Portfolio Optimization with Shortfall Constraints: A Confidence-Limit Approach to Managing Downside Risk." *Financial Analysts Journal* 45, 34–41.

CHAPTER 7

VaR in Portfolios of Assets and Options

To study market risk, we must calculate the capital required to protect a business or portfolio from adverse states of nature, or negative situations, associated with price variations.

In this chapter, we consider only the risks associated with variations in prices or returns. We do not consider default risk: that is, the default probability of the counterparties or liquidity risk.

First, we will explore the concept of risk measurement for an asset portfolio. We will then look at asset portfolios without derivatives. In the third part, we will discuss derivatives (particularly options) in an asset portfolio.

7.1 VaR AS A RISK MEASURE

To calculate the capital required by a portfolio, we need a measure that is easy to understand. VaR meets this criterion because it summarizes all the information in a single number expressed in monetary units or in returns. For example, according to the formula of J.P. Morgan's RiskMetrics model, relative VaR is the maximum amount that one can lose over the next unit of time at a given degree of confidence. This measure can be expressed as the following equation:

$$\mathrm{VaR} = \alpha\sigma_p\sqrt{\Delta t}$$

where:

σ_p is the standard deviation of the portfolio market risk, which we will revisit later;
α represents the weight assigned to the statistical risk measure of the portfolio to take the degree of confidence into account.

If we suppose that prices follow a normal distribution, weights α are given directly by the standard normal distribution table N(0, 1). We only consider one tail of the distribution because we calculate the probability of being to the left of a given number. In other words, we are interested only in the probability of losses and not of being statistically different from a number. For example, a degree of confidence of 99% implies that we have a 1% chance of being to the left of the number calculated and the absolute weight associated with this level is equal to 2.33. At 95%, we use 1.645; at 97.5%, we use 1.96; and 1.28 at 90%. On the other hand, if we have tests based on two distribution tails, we would take the values of 1.96 for 95%; 2.33 for 97.5%; 2.58 for 99%; and 1.645 for 90%.

$\sqrt{\Delta t}$ is a weight that converts the units of time used for the parametric or other calculation methods into units of time to measure VaR. If we suppose that the prices or returns are distributed identically over time (which implies that the prices follow a random walk with identical means and variances from one period to another) or if we do not have temporal correlations, then the expected value of the price and its deviations over two periods will be equal to $2E(R_p)$ and $2\sigma_p^2$, which means that the two measures increase linearly over time whereas the standard deviation is equal to $\sqrt{2}\sigma_p$.

7.2 MODELS WITHOUT DERIVATIVES

This section is based on Beckers' (1998) text. The objective of this study is to review the main models of financial markets equilibrium and link them to measures of market risk. In particular, Beckers studied the mean-variance model, the CAPM, and the multifactor model (APT), to measure market risk. He also shows how to use a market portfolio as a reference point (or benchmark) to evaluate portfolio managers' performance. In principle, people do not pay portfolio managers to replicate the market index but rather to earn superior returns. This portion of Beckers' analysis will not be covered here but may be consulted by readers who are interested in this problem.

7.2.1 Markowitz's Mean-Variance Model

We will not discuss this classic model of portfolio choice in detail since it is included in the exercises at the end of this book. It involves maximizing $E - rV$ by choosing the weights for different assets subject to the constraint that the sum of the weights is equal to 1, where E is the mathematical expectation of the portfolio return, V the variance and r a risk aversion parameter. This modeling implies that the decision-maker's utility function is quadratic for all distributions of returns or that the distribution of returns is elliptical, regardless of the decision-maker's utility function.

With two assets, the expected portfolio return is equal to:

$$E(R_p) = \delta_1 E(R_1) + \delta_2 E(R_2),$$

where:

$E(R_i), i = 1,2,$ is the expected return on asset *i*;
δ_i is the weight of asset *i*, with $\delta_1 + \delta_2 = 1$.

The variance is equal to:

$$\text{Var}(R_p) = \delta_1^2\sigma_1^2 + \delta_2^2\sigma_2^2 + 2\delta_1\delta_2\text{cov}(R_1, R_2).$$

It can also be expressed in matrix form as:

$$\mathrm{Var}(R_p) = (\delta_1, \delta_2) \begin{pmatrix} \sigma_1^2 & \sigma_{12} \\ \sigma_{21} & \sigma_2^2 \end{pmatrix} \begin{pmatrix} \delta_1 \\ \delta_2 \end{pmatrix}$$
$$= A' SA$$

where:

A is a vector of weights;
A′ is the transpose of A;
S is the variance-covariance matrix.

With *n* assets, this variance is equal to:

$$\mathrm{Var}(R_p) = (\delta_1, \ldots, \delta_n) \begin{pmatrix} \sigma_1^2 & \sigma_{12} & & \sigma_{1n} \\ \sigma_{j1} & & \sigma_j^2 & \sigma_{jn} \\ \sigma_{n1} & \sigma_{n2} & & \sigma_n^2 \end{pmatrix} \begin{pmatrix} \delta_1 \\ \\ \delta_n \end{pmatrix}.$$

In this model, risk is measured by calculating the variance-covariance matrix of the portfolio. The major difficulty in estimating the variance-covariance matrix is that it requires many observations. To be certain that the variance-covariance matrix has all the right properties (portfolio variance that is positive and stable over time), the number of observations must be much higher than the number of assets.

With 30 assets, we have 900 potential entries or 435 covariances (that is, (900 − 30)/2) to estimate. We therefore need much more than 30 observation periods on the 30 assets results to get results that present adequate properties.

If, for example, we use observations on the returns of 30 assets for 12 days, this gives us a 12 by 30 matrix of information on returns (R) observed. We cannot calculate all the covariances, and the usable matrix as a maximum rank of 12 if we want it to be defined as semi-positive and generate positive estimated variance ($\hat{V}$ar). The following R matrix of returns does not have good properties to estimate the total portfolio risk.

$$R = \begin{pmatrix} r_{11} \; r_{21} & \cdots & r_{301} \\ r_{1t} \cdots \cdots & \cdots & r_{30t} \\ r_{112} \cdots & \cdots & r_{3012} \end{pmatrix}_{12\times 30}.$$

To be sure that we have a positive value variance-covariance $\hat{S}$ matrix, the rank cannot exceed 12 in the previous example, namely the min (12, 30), implying a maximum number of entries of 144, which lets us calculate 66 covariances out of 435, or (144 − 12)/2.[1] The 99 ((360 − 30)/2 − 66) remaining estimates represent only white noise or 0 risk measures.

To get stable estimates, we suggest more than 3,000 lines of observations, which can give us a stable rank 30 matrix.[2] The corresponding VaR is equal to:

$$\alpha\sqrt{A'\hat{S}A} \times \sqrt{\Delta t} \times V_0$$

[1]The rank of a matrix is the number of linearly independent columns. To be certain that the $\hat{S}$ matrix is positive, the number of columns should not exceed the number of lines. Therefore, for 30 assets, we need more than 30 lines of information.

[2]See DeMiguel, Garlappi, and Uppal (2009) for an analysis with simulations.

where:

$\hat{S} \approx (1/m)R'R$ is the measure of the covariance matrix obtained from the sample;
V_0 is the amount invested in the portfolio;
m is the number of observations;
α is the weight for the degree of confidence.

7.2.2 CAPM

The CAPM supposes that all agents have the same anticipations, which represents both an advantage of, and a restriction on, this model. All agents should therefore choose the same market risk portfolio in the presence of a risk-free asset.

This normative model indicates how individuals should act if they were rational in efficient markets. Only the portion of the non-diversifiable risk (systematic risk) is compensated by a premium.

We thus obtain at equilibrium:

$$E(R_j) = R_f + \beta_j \; [E(R_m) - R_f]$$

where:

$E(R_j)$ is the expected return of asset *j*;
$E(R_m)$ is the expected return of the market portfolio that contains all of the assets with weightings;
R_f is the risk-free interest rate;
$[E(R_m) - R_f]$ is the risk premium;
$\beta_j = \frac{cov(R_j,R_m)}{Var(R_m)}$ is the Beta coefficient of the asset *j*.

Note that if β_j is equal to 1, then $E(R_j)$ is equal to $E(R_m)$. The required expected return will be equal to the expected return of the market portfolio.

This model is very difficult to validate empirically because it is impossible to construct the real market portfolio, which should include (in theory) not only all assets traded but also those that are not (Roll's critique).

However, this model can be useful to estimate (approximate) the risk of an asset by applying an econometric version of the equilibrium equation, namely:

$$R_{jt} - R_{ft} = \alpha_j + \beta_j(I_{mt} - R_{ft}) + \varepsilon_{jt}.$$

If I_{mt} is the observed return of the market portfolio, often measured by a market index, we can calculate the variance of this equation to get:

$$\sigma_j^2 = \beta_j^2 \sigma_I^2 + \sigma_{\varepsilon_j}^2.$$

As a measure of the risk of the asset *j*, we get $\sqrt{\sigma_j^2} = \sigma_j = \sqrt{\beta_j^2 \sigma_I^2 + \sigma_{\varepsilon_j}^2}$. Note that the two risks are orthogonal by construction. We can use σ_j directly to calculate the VaR of the asset. This procedure is explained in the following section, as this model can be reinterpreted as a one-factor model. Some authors recommend ignoring the specific risk ($\sigma^2_{\varepsilon_j}$). However, the Basel regulation requires that specific or idiosyncratic risk be considered in the calculation of regulatory capital with a higher weight than the systematic risk ($\beta_j^2\sigma_I^2$), to encourage banks to reduce the specific risk inherent in their portfolio.

This model has been criticized in many respects. The two main criticisms argue that the model contains only one factor and that the index used does not necessarily correspond to the market portfolio. In addition, the explanatory power of the model is often quite weak, characterized by a relatively low R^2.

7.2.3 Multifactor Model

Now suppose that the return on the asset *j* is explained by two factors:

$$E(R_j) = R_f + \beta_{1j}(E(F_1) - R_f) + \beta_{2j}(E(F_2) - R_f).$$

β_{ij} is the sensitivity of asset *j* to factor *i* and $E(F_i)$ is the return of factor *i*. Examples of factors are given in Table 6.1 in Beckers (1998). They include: historical volatility, recent performance, market capitalization, liquidity, and revenue growth. We can also add the Fama-French factors (relative capitalization, book value relative to market value) to the market index.

If we have two assets, we get, in statistical terms with two factors:

$$(R_{1t} - R_{ft}) = \gamma_1 + \beta_{11}(F_{1t} - R_{ft}) + \beta_{21}(F_{2t} - R_{ft}) + \varepsilon_{1t}$$
$$(R_{2t} - R_{ft}) = \gamma_2 + \beta_{12}(F_{1t} - R_{ft}) + \beta_{22}(F_{2t} - R_{ft}) + \varepsilon_{2t}.$$

In matrix form, if we suppose that the constants γ_j are not significant, we can write:

$$\begin{bmatrix} R_{1t} - R_{ft} \\ R_{2t} - R_{ft} \end{bmatrix} = \begin{bmatrix} \beta_{11} & \beta_{21} \\ \beta_{12} & \beta_{22} \end{bmatrix} \begin{bmatrix} F_{1t} - R_{ft} \\ F_{2t} - R_{ft} \end{bmatrix} + \begin{bmatrix} \varepsilon_{1t} \\ \varepsilon_{2t} \end{bmatrix}$$

$$R_t = Bf_t + E_t$$

where:

R_t is the vector of excess returns of the portfolio at period *t*;
B is the matrix of exposures to different factors;
f_t is the vector of the risk premium of the factors relative to a specific interest rate;
E_t is the vector of residual returns.

The variance-covariance matrix and the VaR_t of the portfolio are equal to:

$$V_t = \begin{bmatrix} \beta_{11} & \beta_{12} \\ \beta_{21} & \beta_{22} \end{bmatrix} \begin{bmatrix} \hat{\sigma}_{11} & \hat{\sigma}_{12} \\ \hat{\sigma}_{21} & \hat{\sigma}_{22} \end{bmatrix} \begin{bmatrix} \beta_{11} & \beta_{21} \\ \beta_{12} & \beta_{22} \end{bmatrix} + \begin{bmatrix} \sigma^2_{\varepsilon_1} & 0 \\ 0 & \sigma^2_{\varepsilon_2} \end{bmatrix}$$

$$V_t = B'F_tB + \Omega$$

$$VaR_t = \alpha V_0 \sqrt{B'F_tB + \Omega}\sqrt{\Delta t}.$$

where:

V_t is the variance-covariance matrix of the portfolio returns at period *t*;
F_t is the variance-covariance matrix of the factors' risks;
B' is the transpose of B;
Ω is the diagonal matrix of residual risks; the covariance between factors' residuals cannot be different from zero;
V_0 is the amount invested in the portfolio;
VaR_t is the relative value at risk of the portfolio.

There are at least three approaches to estimate V_t and R_t.

Fundamental Approach

This approach involves determining the factors to which firms are exposed and estimating the associated premiums. We get a linear regression of returns according to the factors retained, and we interpret the coefficients as risk premiums associated with the different factors. We thus estimate the equations by supposing the known β_{ij}. These are the observations in the regression.

We use data from several periods to calculate the significant factor premiums, along with the F_t matrix. One difficulty that arises is associated with the fact that we need an exhaustive list of factors. Otherwise, Ω may not be diagonal (non-zero covariance between the residuals), which potentially biases the total risk because the diversification of the total specific risk may be different from that corresponding to a diagonal Ω matrix. Nonetheless, this approach is used most often by practitioners.

Macroeconomic Approach

This approach calculates the factor premiums using temporal aggregated macroeconomic models. This first step identifies the significant factors to explain the variation in cash flows or in assets. We then use the premiums calculated to estimate the β_{ij}. The factors may include the index portfolio or other significant economic factors in the fundamental approach. Some of the most frequently used factors are inflation, industrial production, and investor confidence.

Statistical Analysis

This more general approach is linked to the estimation of the model used in APT (Arbitrage Pricing Theory). It serves to calculate the V matrix by factor analysis or principal component analysis. We thus identify the factors in B and can then calculate the premiums of the factors (f_t), as in the fundamental approach. Here, however, the factors are identified with a statistical model without any a priori hypothesis. In addition, because the factor premiums result from a principal component analysis, they are orthogonal, implying that the matrix of residual risk is diagonal.

The factors are identified endogenously rather than determined exogenously or randomly. We can then use aggregation to calculate the portfolio risk and the corresponding VaR.

7.3 VaR WITH OPTIONS

We are interested in an equity portfolio that contains put and call options. We will focus on call options, but adaptations can be easily made. Below, we limit the discussion to European call options, which can be exercised on the option's expiration date. However, the analysis may be easily transposed to American options. The role of dividends will not be discussed in detail. Lastly, transaction costs are zero.

Introducing options in a portfolio means including nonlinearities that greatly complicate the calculations of portfolio values and the VaR.

First, we will present a few definitions. In certainty, when a call option is exercised, its value at time *t* is equal to $C_t = \text{Max}(S_t - K, 0)$ where:

C_t is the value of the option at exercise time *t* or the intrinsic value of the option;
S_t is the value of the underlying asset at time *t*;
K is the exercise price of the option set at the start of the contract (of course, its value does not depend on the expiration date);
$t = T$ for a European option, where T is the expiration date.

By definition, the intrinsic value of an option C_t is always positive or zero. In the case of a European option, C_t corresponds to the value at expiration, which does not contain a time premium linked to uncertainty. It is therefore a minimal value. As indicated in Figure 7.1, if the value of the share is equal to S_1 at the end of the period, the option holder will not exercise the option. The value of the option is thus zero. If, in contrast, the value of the share is equal to S_2, the holder will buy the share at price K and resell it at price S_2. The value of the option is equal to $S_2 - K$.

In general, the value of call options increases when the share price, the time horizon $(T - t)$ (corresponding to a time premium), the volatility of the share price, or interest rates increase, or when the value of holding the share (substitute for an option) decreases. The value of these options also decreases when the exercise price increases (Ritchken, 1996).

Option prices can be calculated in different ways. We will limit the discussion to the Black-Scholes model (B-S), which presumes that transactions can be done continuously.

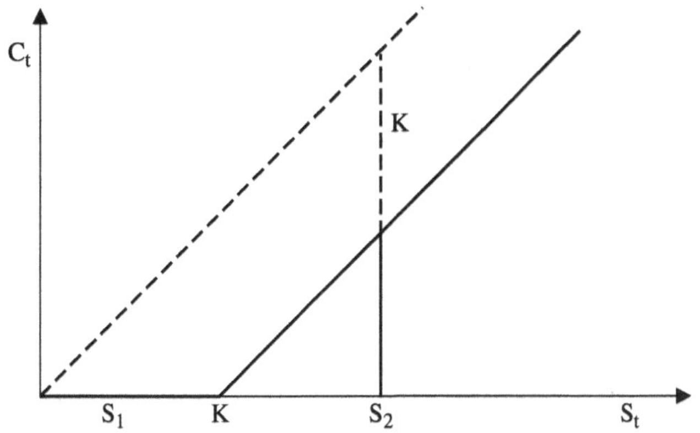

FIGURE 7.1 Intrinsic value of an option at time *t*.

The main variable that determines the option value is the price of the underlying share. This is also the primary cause of nonlinearity.

The main hypotheses of the B-S model are:

The return on the underlying share is continuous and follows a normal distribution at each date. In addition, this price is supposed to follow a random process over time, called a Brownian geometric motion. Accordingly, the instantaneous value of the return on the share is given by:

$$dS/S = \mu dt + \sigma \varepsilon \sqrt{dt}$$

with:

$$E(dS/S) = \mu dt \text{ et } Var(dS/S) = \sigma^2 dt\, Var(\varepsilon)$$

where:

dS/S is the instantaneous value of the return on the underlying share;
dS is the instantaneous variation in the underlying share price;
μ is the instantaneous mathematical expectation of the return on the share;
σ is its standard deviation;
$\varepsilon\sqrt{dt} \equiv dw$;
dw follows a Wiener process or a Brownian motion;

ε is a random variable $\sim N(0, 1)$; therefore, $Var(\varepsilon) = 1$.

Consequently, the return follows a normal distribution, and the equation tells us that dS/S is determined by a process with mean μdt and standard deviation $\sigma\sqrt{dt}$. It is important to note that this hypothesis eliminates shocks or large variations in returns.

Two other hypotheses are important in the B–S model:

1. The interest rate and volatility are known and constant.
2. Capital markets are perfect (no transaction costs or taxes, short selling is permitted, etc.).

Based on these hypotheses, we can derive the B–S formula and get the value C_t of a European call option at date *t*:

$$C_t = C(S_t, K, r, \sigma, T - t) \geq Max(S_T - K, 0)$$

where the difference corresponds to the time premium. Figure 7.2 shows a graphic representation of a call option. This representation includes the time premium. C_t may be explicitly written as:

$$C_t = S_t N(d_1) - Ke^{-r(T-t)} N(d_2)$$

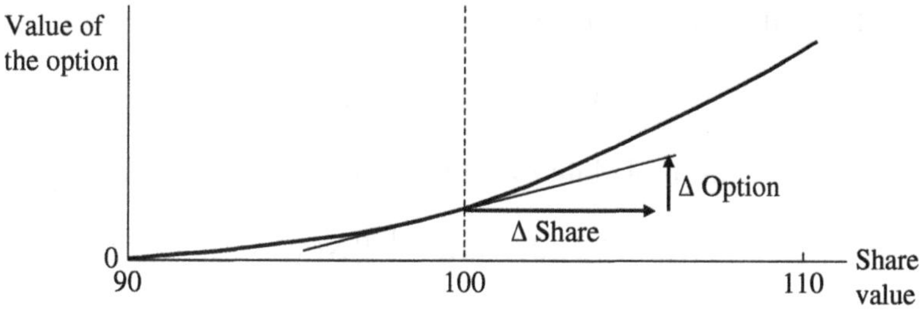

FIGURE 7.2 Current value of a call option according to the value of the underlier.

where T – t is the time to maturity, *r* is the risk-free interest rate, N(d) is the cumulative distribution function of the normal distribution where d_1 and d_2 take the following values:

$$d_1 = \frac{\ln\left(\frac{S_t}{K}\right) + \left(r + \frac{\sigma^2}{2}\right)(T - t)}{\sigma\sqrt{T - t}}$$

$$d_2 = d_1 - \sigma\sqrt{T - t}; N(d) = \int_{-\infty}^{d} f(x)dx.$$

In general, $d_1 > d_2$; this difference is explained by volatility and time to maturity. $N(d_1)$ is the probability that the option is in-the-money and $N(d_2)$ the probability that the option is exercised. $N(d_1)$ is higher than $N(d_2)$ because a European option may be in-the-money several times during its lifetime, without necessarily being in-the-money at maturity or when it is exercised. In addition, it must be in-the-money to be exercised.

Note that if the company pays dividends, the rate of return on the dividends must be incorporated in d_1. The B-S formula must also be adapted to include the return on the dividends.

It is possible to interpret the formula by saying that the price of the option at date *t* corresponds to the expected present value of the cash flow that the option generates. In other words, the value of the option corresponds to the net present sum of the probabilities that the option will be in-the-money and exercised (conditional on the fact that it is in-the-money), multiplied by the cash flow inherent to both cases.

Accordingly, the B–S formula calculates, at date *t*, the mathematical expectation of the exercise value at date T:

$$C_t = e^{-r(T-t)} E_t\{Max(S_T - K, 0)\}.$$

Another simple way to illustrate the development of the B–S value function is as follows. In certainty, we can write:

$$S_T = S_t e^{r(T-t)}$$

$$C_T = S_t e^{r(T-t)} - K.$$

By calculating the net present value, we get:

$$C_t = S_t - Ke^{-r(T-t)}.$$

Now, if we add the probabilities $N(d_1)$ and $N(d_2)$ to take uncertainty into account, we get:

$$C_t = S_t N(d_1) - Ke^{-r(T-t)} N(d_2).$$

7.4 BLACK AND SCHOLES MODEL AND RISK MANAGEMENT

The B–S formula links the value of an option to several factors:

$$C_t = f(S_t, \sigma, r, K, T - t).$$

In general, changes in the value of an option can be obtained using a Taylor expansion:

$$dC_t = \frac{\partial C_t}{\partial S_t} dS_t + \frac{1}{2} \frac{\partial^2 C_t}{\partial S_t^2} dS_t^2 + \frac{\partial C_t}{\partial \sigma} d\sigma + \frac{\partial C_t}{\partial r} dr + \frac{\partial C_t}{\partial t} dt.$$

1. The first important factor is the price of the underlying share S_t. The first derivative $\left(\frac{\partial C_t}{\partial S_t}\right)$ is called Delta; its value is equal to:

   $$\Delta = N(d_1) > 0.$$

   Figure 7.2 represents this derivative at the value 100 of the underlier.

   This first term does not pose a major difficulty because it corresponds to a first-order variation similar to those seen in the portfolio models. Delta can also be interpreted as the equivalent of a fraction of a share for small variations in price. For example, if $\Delta = 0.5$, a stock option is equivalent to half a share in terms of variations in the share price on the portfolio value. However, its value is not constant over time; it varies with the price of the underlier.

   The effect of the Delta has a curve similar to that of a normal distribution function, as in Figure 7.3, because $N(d_1)$ is the distribution function of a normal distribution.
2. The variation in the slope is the derivative of a distribution function and is therefore similar to a density function that has the form shown in Figure 7.3.

   Its value, called Gamma $\left(\frac{\partial^2 C_t}{\partial S_t^2}\right)$, is equal to:

   $$\Gamma = \frac{n(d_1)}{S_t \sigma \sqrt{T-t}} > 0.$$

Figure 7.4 shows how the sum of the two derivatives gives an approximation of the curve that links the share price to the current value of the option. It also shows how the Delta approach underestimates the variation when one moves away from

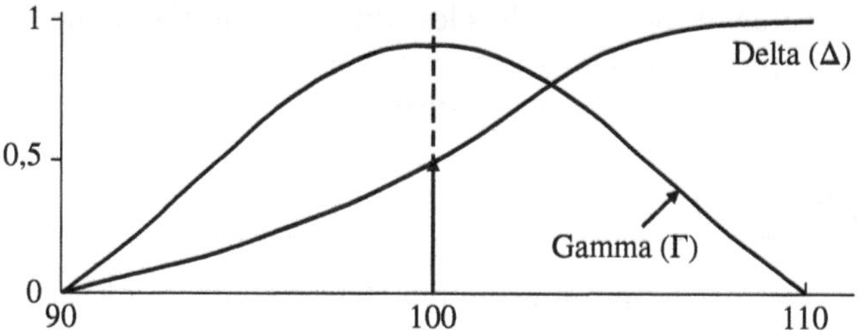

FIGURE 7.3 Delta and Gamma.

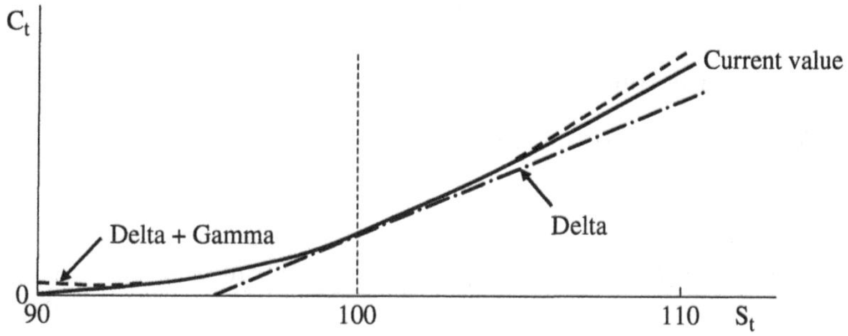

FIGURE 7.4 Delta-Gamma estimation.

the value 100. The disadvantage of the Delta-Gamma approach is that it exaggerates the extreme values, as the figure shows. We would therefore need a third derivative of the value relative to S_t to get a better approximation. Some authors have calculated this third derivative, which they call the Speed.

3. The third effect is that of volatility, called Lambda or Vega. It is a first-order effect whose positive value is given by:

$$\Lambda = n(d_1)\sqrt{T-t}\,S_t > 0.$$

   Λ is the derivative of C_t relative to σ $\left(\frac{\partial C_t}{\partial \sigma}\right)$. If the volatility increases, it increases both the probability that the option is in-the-money and that it is exercised.

4. Options are also sensitive to interest rates $\left(\frac{\partial C_t}{\partial r}\right)$, and the positive value of the variation, called Rho, is equal to:

$$\rho = Ke^{-r(T-t)}(T-t)\,N(d_2) > 0.$$

   This positive value mainly indicates that a higher *r* reduces the present value of the exercise cost K of an option and increases the net value of the option.

5. Lastly, negative variation relative to the time *t* $\left(\frac{\partial C_t}{\partial t}\right)$ is equal to Theta:

$$\theta = \frac{-S_t n(d_1)\,\sigma}{2\sqrt{T-t}} - r\,Ke^{-r(T-t)}N(d_2) = -\frac{\partial C_t}{\partial (T-t)} < 0$$

because the value of the option has less time to be in-the-money when the expiration date approaches. Theta can also be interpreted as the negative value of the derivative relative to time to maturity.

7.5 DELTA-GAMMA VaR

Calculating the VaR of an option using the Delta-Gamma approach involves using the variance of the variation of the value of the option, by supposing that factors other than S are constants. We are interested only in the variations of the price of the underlying S on the value of the option:

$$dC = \Delta dS + 1/2\,\Gamma dS^2,$$

which gives a variance equal to:

$$V(dC) = \Delta^2 V(dS) + (1/2\Gamma)^2 V(dS^2) + 2(\Delta \times 1/2\Gamma)\mathrm{cov}(dS, dS^2).$$

If we suppose that dS follows a standard normal distribution (zero odd moments), the third term is zero (namely, for two random variables x and x^2, the covariance is equal to $2\sigma^2(x)\mu(x) = 0$ if x has a mean $\mu(x)$ equal to 0) and the expression of the variance can be summarized (approximation) as follows if we define σ^2 as the variance of dS/S (Jorion, 2006):

$$V(dC) = \Delta^2\sigma^2 S^2 + 1/2[\Gamma\sigma^2 S^2]^2$$

and if we write $V(dS^2) = 2[V(dS)]^2$ because dS is normally distributed. Indeed, $\mathrm{Var}(x^2) = 2\sigma^2(x)(2\mu^2(x) + \sigma^2(x)) = 2(\sigma^2(x))^2$ if x has a mean ($\mu(x)$) equal to 0. We can therefore write the Delta-Gamma VaR as:

$$\mathrm{VaR}(dC) = \alpha\sqrt{\Delta^2 S^2\sigma^2 + 1/2\,[\Gamma S^2\sigma^2]^2}$$

where $\sqrt{\Delta t} = 1$.

The nonlinearity between the VaR of the option and the value of the underlying asset can be observed directly.

If $\Gamma = 0$, $V(dC) = \Delta^2\sigma^2 S^2$ and $\sigma(dC) = \Delta\sigma S$. When Gamma is zero, the formula is reduced to a linear relation between the VaR and S:

$$\mathrm{VaR}(dC) = \alpha\Delta S\sigma.$$

The VaR Gamma of an option is proportionate to that of the underlying share.

7.6 VaR OF A GENERAL PORTFOLIO

Now, if we want to generalize the analysis to a stocks and options portfolio, we can first write the value of a stock portfolio without options:

$$V = \sum_{i=1}^{m} x_i\ S_i$$

where x_i is the number of shares *i* and S_i is the value of the share *i*.

The variation in V, linked to market risk, can be written as equal to:

$$dV = \sum_{i=1}^{m} x_i \; dS_i$$

or, in the form of a return:

$$dV/V = 1/V \sum_{i=1}^{m} x_i dS_i$$
$$= \sum_{i=1}^{m} y_i r_i$$

with

$$r_i = dS_i/S_i \text{ et } y_i = \frac{x_i S_i}{V}.$$

The variance of dV/V can be written as:

$$\sigma_p^2 = [y_1 \cdots y_m] \sum \begin{bmatrix} y_1 \\ y_m \end{bmatrix} = Y' \sum Y$$

where $\sum$ is the variance-covariance matrix. This gives the following value of the VaR of the portfolio (in returns):

$$\text{VaR} = \alpha\sigma_p.$$

To translate this into monetary value, we need to multiply the VaR of the portfolio measured in returns by the initial value of the portfolio V_0. Now, if we introduce *n* call options in a portfolio of *m* shares, V and dV become respectively:

$$V = \sum_{i=1}^{m} \left[\sum_{j=1}^{n} w_{ij} C_{ij} + x_i S_i \right];$$
$$dV = \sum_{i=1}^{m} \left[\sum_{j=1}^{n} w_{ij} \, dC_{ij} + x_i \, dS_i \right]$$

where:

w_{ij} is the number of options *j* on share *i*;
C_{ij} is the value of option *j* on share *i*;
x_i is the number of shares *i*;
S_i is the value of the share *i*.

We have shown that dC_{ij} is equal to:

$$dC_{ij} = \Delta_{ij} \, dS_i + 1/2\,\Gamma_{ij}(dS_i)^2 + \Lambda_{ij} \, d\sigma_i + \rho_{ij} \, dr_{ij} + \theta_{ij} \, dt.$$

By substitution, we can write:

$$dV = \sum_{i=1}^{m}\left[\sum_{j=1}^{n} w_{ij}[\Delta_{ij}dS_i + 1/2\Gamma_{ij}(dS_i)^2 + \Lambda_{ij}d\sigma_i + \rho_{ij}dr_{ij} + \theta_{ij}dt] + x_i dS_i\right]$$

and by aggregation, we get:

$$dV = \sum_{i=1}^{m}\left[\Delta_i dS_i + 1/2\Gamma_i(dS_i)^2 + \Lambda_i d\sigma_i + \sum_{j=1}^{n} w_{ij}\,\rho_{ij}\,dr_{ij}\right] + \theta_p dt$$

where:

$$\Delta_i = \sum_{j=1}^{n} w_{ij}\,\Delta_{ij} + x_i$$

$$\Gamma_i = \sum_{j=1}^{n} w_{ij}\,\Gamma_{ij}$$

$$\Lambda_i = \sum_{j=1}^{n} w_{ij}\,\Lambda_{ij}$$

$$\theta_p = \sum_{i=1}^{m}\sum_{j=1}^{n} w_{ij}\,\theta_{ij}.$$

θ_p is a common value because time advances the same way for each asset. However, ρ cannot be aggregated because the different options may have different expiration dates or different interest rate exposures. The next step is to calculate the variance of this expression to get the VaR.

7.7 APPLICATION

Table 7.1 gives the data on five stocks and several related options. The portfolio contains quantities of shares of two stocks: American Air and Ford. The remaining positions are made up of call and put options with long and short positions. The value of the shares held is \$9,562,500, which represents 97% of the total portfolio value. The remaining 3% consists of hedging positions.

Investment in Ford stock is protected by a long put position with an exercise price of \$30, whereas the stock purchase price was \$28.38. The long call position of Time Warner, with an exercise price of \$40, is almost in-the-money, whereas that of Seagram is already in-the-money. We invite readers to look at the other options to get an idea of the market risk of this portfolio.

Table 7.2 provides the details of the Greek values to various risk factors of the different options. For American Air, made up of shares exclusively, the Delta value is \$100,000 because the Delta of one share is equal to one. For Ford, the put has a negative Delta of \$60,525, which gives a net position of \$39,475 for the Delta. Consider the example of a long call position on Time Warner, a stock not present

TABLE 7.1 Description of portfolio with stocks and options.

	Stock		Options						Portfolio		
Stock name	Market price ($)	Dividend yield	Option type	Option price ($)	Exercise price ($)	Expiration date	Settlement date	Risk-free rate	Units of assets	Position	Value ($)
American Air	67.25	0							100,000	Long	6,725,000
Option 1			None						0		
Option 2			None						0		
Ford	28.38	0.046							100,000	Long	2,837,500
Option 1			Put	2.50	30	1995-09-15	1995-05-19	0.0585	100,000	Long	250,000
Option 2			None						0		
IBM	93.25	0.011							0		—
Option 1			Put	0.0625	80	1995-07-14	1995-05-19	0.0561	100,000	Long	6,250
Option 2			Put	0.25	85	1995-07-14	1995-05-19	0.0561	100,000	Short	(25,000)
Time Warner	39.25	0.009							0		—
Option 1			Call	1.8125	40	1995-10-15	1995-05-19	0.0585	10,000	Short	(18,125)
Option 2			Call	1.00	40	1995-07-14	1995-05-19	0.0561	10,000	Long	10,000
Seagram	28.50	0.021							0		—
Option 1			Call	4.50	25	1995-11-17	1995-05-19	0.0590	20,000	Long	90,000
Option 2			None						0		
											9,875,625

Source: Table 8.13 in Jordan and Mackay (1997).

TABLE 7.2 Market risk exposures for the portfolio with stocks and options.

Company	Type	Quantity	Position	Market price ($)	Market value ($)	Delta	Gamma	Theta	Vega	Rho	Rho of dividend
American Air	Stock	100,000	Long	67.25	6,725,000	100,000	0	0	0	0	0
Option 1		0		0	0	0	0	0	0	0	0
Option 2		0		0	0	0	0	0	0	0	0
Position 1					6,725,000	100,000	0	0	0	0	0
Ford	Stock	100,000	Long	28.38	2,837,500	100,000	0	0	0	0	0
Option 1	*Put*	100,000	Long	2.50	250,000	(60,525)	9,234	(556)	610,376	(678,948)	619,851
Option 2		0		0	0	0	0	0	0	0	0
Position 2					3,087,500	39,475	9,234	(556)	610,376	(678,948)	619,851
IBM		0		93.25	0	0	0	0	0	0	0
Option 1	*Put*	100,000	Long	0.0625	6,250	(2,173)	689	(324)	189,650	(33,842)	26,963
Option 2	*Put*	100,000	Short	0.25	(25,000)	7,942	(2,189)	799	(539,821)	124,054	(104,721)
Position 3					(18,750)	5,769	(1,501)	474	(350,172)	(90,212)	(77,758)
Time Warner		0		39.25	0	0	0	0	0	0	0
Option 1	*Call*	10,000	Short	1.8125	(18,125)	(5,114)	(843)	102	(89,099)	(63,015)	67,295
Option 2	*Call*	10,000	Long	1.00	10,000	4,536	1,299	(128)	60,846	27,229	(28,091)
Position 4					(8,125)	(578)	455	(26)	(28,254)	(35,786)	39,204
Seagram		0		28.50	0	0	0	0	0	0	0
Option 1	*Call*	20,000	Long	4.50	90,000	16,093	995	(110)	106,980	194,672	(204,875)
Option 2		0		0	0	0	0	0	0	0	0
Position 5					90,000	16,093	995	(110)	106,980	194,672	(204,875)

Source: Table 8.14 in Jordan and Mackay (1997).

in the portfolio. As Table 7.1 indicates, the portfolio contains 10,000 options with a unit value of $1, which gives the total position a market value of $10,000. The total value of the Delta (Δ) is $4,536, which implies that the individual value of the Delta is $0.4536, whereas that of the Gamma is $0.1299. As seen above, the value of Theta (θ) is negative for a long call position, albeit fairly weakly, like all the values in this column compared with those of other columns. This is largely explained by the short expiration dates of options in this portfolio.

The Vega (or Lambda) is positive and very high ($6.00 individual), clearly indicating the importance of stock volatility to explain the value of an option. The more volatile the stock, the higher the probability of exercising the option. The Rho of the interest rate also has a positive effect because it reduces the discounted cost of exercising the option at expiration, but its effect here is practically canceled by the Rho of the dividend, which reduces the value of a call via its negative effect on the underlier.

Table 7.3 gives the values of the VaR for different time horizons and degrees of risk tolerance. We will concentrate our interpretation on the right-hand column, which represents risk tolerance of 10%, or a degree of confidence of 90%. Three values of absolute VaR are given by the time to expiration. Note that weekly and monthly values are obtained by using two different approaches.

Daily data correspond to two years of observations. Share prices and returns are obtained from the Center for Research in Security Prices (CRSP) for the period of

TABLE 7.3 VaR for alternative risk horizons and tolerance levels.

Risk tolerance	2.5% ($)	5.0% ($)	10.0% ($)
Daily			
Delta only	257,356	208,629	156,199
Delta-Gamma	256,225	210,397	158,473
All parameters	256,201	210,765	158,576
Weekly (non-overlapping data)			
Delta only	465,325	434,293	381,945
Delta-Gamma	487,834	428,188	383,227
All parameters	497,549	431,524	384,139
(Bootstrapped)			
Delta only	591,680	506,099	393,515
Delta-Gamma	607,856	504,508	397,471
All parameters	609,702	508,830	404,632
Monthly (non-overlapping data)			
Delta only	1,276,646	1,179,623	635,332
Delta-Gamma	1,265,527	1,175,090	711,765
All parameters	1,261,727	1,171,588	664,824
(Bootstrapped)			
Delta only	959,943	832,126	699,169
Delta-Gamma	1,038,865	875,136	706,497
All parameters	1,077,823	886,771	723,865

Source: Table 8.15 in Jordan and Mackay (1997).

January 2, 1992, to December 31, 1993. The daily data represent 507 observations, whereas the weekly and monthly data (non-overlapping) represent 104 and 24 observations respectively, which is very few.

The bootstrap method lets us increase the number of weekly and monthly observations using random draws in the corresponding data to form new observations. The results of the tables are thus obtained with 500 monthly and weekly observations via this method.

The Delta approach alone takes into account the first-order variations of options. It also integrates evolution over time (θ). The Delta-Gamma approach considers the nonlinearity of options, whereas the All approach adds Theta, Vega, and the two Rhos.

Note that the Delta approach alone is fairly precise with the daily data, explaining nearly 99% of the VaR of the All approach (10% tolerance). The Delta-Gamma approach is almost complete, which seems to suggest that using the other Greek parameters is not necessary with daily data, at least for this portfolio. We observe a similar trend with the weekly data.

The difference is greater between the Delta approach only and that of All with monthly data, in which the VaR with the Delta approach represents only about 96% of the total. Even if the variance in percentage seems low, it represents about $30,000 in capital with the non-overlapping data (10%) and over $100,000 with the bootstrap approach at 2.5%.

Table 7.4 calculates the VaR values according to the mean variance approach to portfolio management. This approach does not integrate the Gamma, Theta, Rho, and Vega values, but allows the Delta to be used to transform option values into share values. VaR values can therefore be compared to those of Delta only in Table 7.3. The differences are very large for the weekly and monthly VaR. It therefore seems that this portfolio approach is precise only for very short periods, such as for daily VaR, where the variance is less important, regardless of the risk tolerance.

Lastly, Table 7.5 presents the calculations of VaR using the single-factor financial equilibrium model. The results are far inferior to those obtained in the preceding tables because the authors deliberately used only the systematic risk portion of the model, whereas the previous approaches implicitly take idiosyncratic risk into account.

TABLE 7.4 VaR with mean-variance model for alternative risk horizons and tolerance levels.

Risk tolerance			2.5%		5.0%		10.0%	
Maturity/Parameters	Mean (μ_p)	Standard deviation (σ_p)	VaR(%)**	VaR($)*	VaR(%)**	VaR($)*	VaR(%)**	VaR($)*
Daily	0.000229	0.013317	−0.025871	255,712	−0.021675	214,274	−0.016837	166,496
Weekly								
(non−overlapping data)	0.001035	0.026595	−0.051092	506,081	−0.042711	423,322	−0.033049	327,904
(Bootstrapped)	−0.002366	0.027865	−0.056982	564,250	−0.048201	477,538	−0.038078	377,563
Monthly								
(non-overlapping data)	0.004080	0.049142	−0.092238	917,423	−0.076753	764,504	−0.058900	588,193
(Bootstrapped)	0.008612	0.058118	−0.105299	1,046,408	−0.086986	865,557	−0.065872	657,041

*For a $9,875,625 portfolio.

**VaR(%) = $\mu_p - k\sigma_p$ where k = 1.96, 1.6449, and 1.2816 for 2.5%, 5% and 10% respectively.

Source: Table 8.16 in Jordan and Mackay (1997).

TABLE 7.5 VaR with market equilibrium model for alternative risk horizons and tolerance levels.

Risk tolerance			2.5%		5.0%		10.0%	
Maturity/Parameters	Mean (μ_p)	Standard deviation (σ_p)	VaR(%)**	VaR($)*	VaR(%)**	VaR($)*	VaR(%)**	VaR($)*
Daily	0.000240	0.006276	−0.01206		−0.01008		−0.00780	
Delta only				99,834		83,500		64,667
Delta-Gamma				119,353		99,818		77,295
Weekly								
(non-overlapping data)	0.001256	0.013820	−0.02583		−0.02148		−0.01646	
Delta only				214,857		178,892		137,426
Delta-Gamma				256,659		213,647		164,056
(Bootstrapped)	0.001042	0.013634	−0.02568		−0.02138		−0.01643	
Delta only				213,619		178,138		137,228
Delta-Gamma				255,179		212,745		163,819
Monthly								
(non-overlapping data)	0.004848	0.019044	−0.03248		−0.02648		−0.01956	
Delta only				274,756		225,196		168,054
Delta-Gamma				327,316		268,045		199,706
(Bootstrapped)	0.008616	0.029166	−0.04855		−0.03936		−0.02876	
Delta only				407,503		331,599		244,084
Delta-Gamma				486,074		395,297		290,634

*For a $9,875,625 portfolio.
**VaR(%) = $\mu_p - k\sigma_p$ where k = 1.96, 1.6449, and 1.2816 for 2.5%, 5% and 10% respectively.
Source: Table 8.17 in Jordan and Mackay (1997).

Note that the Basel regulation of market risk requires that both idiosyncratic risk and systematic or general market risk be considered, and it demands more capital for the former than the latter, to encourage banks to hold shares with low idiosyncratic risk.

7.8 CONCLUSION

In this chapter, we have analyzed market risk management in greater depth by introducing models of market equilibrium and options. We have not considered futures contracts because their treatment is direct or linear, which refers to the same models as for stocks. For options, we have seen that nonlinearity (Gamma) may affect the calculation of capital, especially for expiration dates that are longer than daily. Moreover, the effects of the other Greeks were mainly observed for Vega and Rho.

Exercise 4, at the end of the book, shows how to calculate the Delta-Gamma VaR with Bloomberg data.

REFERENCES

Beckers, S., 1998. "A Survey of Risk Measurement Theory and Practice." In C. Alexander (Ed.), *Risk Management and Analysis,* volume 1: *Measuring and Modeling Financial Risk.* New York; John Wiley & Sons, 39–60.

Christoffersen, P., 2012. *Elements of Financial Risk Management.* Academic Press.

DeMiguel, V., Garlappi, L., and Uppal, R., 2009. "Optimal versus Naïve Diversification: How Inefficient Is the 1/N Portfolio Strategy?" *Review of Financial Studies* 22, 1915–1953.

Jordan, J.V., and Mackay, R.J., 1997. "Assessing Value at Risk for Equity Portfolios: Implementing Alternative Techniques." In *Derivatives Handbook*. Toronto: John Wiley & Sons, 265–309.

Jorion, P., 2006. *Value at Risk: The New Benchmark for Managing Financial Risk*, 3rd ed. New York: McGraw-Hill.

Ritchken, P., 1996. *Derivative Markets: Theory, Strategy, and Applications*. New York: Harper Collins College Publishers.

CHAPTER 8

Conditional VaR

This chapter discusses conditional VaR (CVaR), which is needed because VaR presents methodological gaps. The main gaps can be summarized by the following points.[1]

- When losses are not distributed continuously (for example, do not follow normal or elliptical distributions), VaR is difficult to use and is often unstable. Since it may underestimate or overestimate risk, it is less appropriate for credit risk, operational risk, and some forms of market risk.
- Analysts can verify the number of times that VaR is exceeded, but this statistic does not specify the loss amounts. It may thus be exceeded by $1 or $1 million.
- VaR is not coherent mathematically. VaR of two assets may exceed the sum of individual VaRs. It thus implies that VaR does not respect subadditivity or the principle of diversification, which is very useful in finance. It may give more diversified portfolios higher maximum capital!

8.1 MOTIVATION FOR CVaR AND COHERENCE IN RISK MEASURES

CVaR is more difficult to calculate and to test, but offers several advantages:

- CVaR is the expected conditional loss greater than VaR. It may also be interpreted as the mean of VaRs that exceed a given VaR.
- The same portfolio maximization results are obtained with relative CVaR as for relative VaR with a normal distribution and for elliptical distributions, because we minimize the portfolio variance in all cases.
- CVaR may be useful for very asymmetric distributions (market risk, credit risk, operational risk).
- CVaR respects the property of subadditivity and can yield convex solutions: if the loss function f(x, y) is convex relative to the decision variable x for a random variable y, then CVaR(x) is also convex, which represents an important property for optimization.

[1]The research discussed in this chapter was conducted with Samir Saissi Hassani and Alain-Philippe Fortin.

- For distributions with potential discontinuities, the analysis becomes more complicated; the CVaR falls within two limits, $CVaR^-$ and $CVaR^+$, where $CVaR^+$ is the *Expected Shortfall* (*upper* CVaR), a concept used in actuarial sciences, and the $CVaR^-$ (tailVaR) is the lower limit (*lower* CVaR). We can write: $CVaR^- \leq CVaR \leq CVaR^+$ with equal signs when there is no *jump* in the loss distribution.

For continuous distributions, CVaR is therefore identical to the *Expected Shortfall*. As mentioned above, CVaR is a coherent measure of risk, as defined by Artzner et al. (1999), whereas $CVaR^-$ and $CVaR^+$ are not (and nor is VaR). For more information on this topic, Rockafellar and Uryasev (2002) present a fine application of portfolio replication; see also Rockafellar and Uryasev (2000).

The four conditions of coherence for g(•), which represents any risk measure, are:

1. Positive homogeneity (respect for scales):

$$g(\lambda y) = \lambda g(y),$$

where *y* is a random variable. g(•) is a positive homogeneous function of degree 1 if $\lambda > 0$.
2. Subadditivity:

$$g(y_1 + y_2) \leq g(y_1) + g(y_2).$$

A positive homogeneous risk measure g(•) is convex only if it is subadditive. Subadditivity encourages diversification. We can also rewrite this condition using homogeneity:

$$g(\lambda y_1 + (1-\lambda)y_2) \leq \lambda g(y_1) + (1-\lambda)g(y_2) \text{ for all } 0 \leq \lambda \leq 1.$$

The VaR is subadditive for elliptical distributions.
3. Monotonic:

$$y_1 \leq y_2 \text{ implies that } g(y_1) \leq g(y_2).$$

4. Addition of a constant:

$$g(y_1 + k) = g(y_1) - k.$$

Before we go further, here is an example where the VaR is not coherent in the sense of subadditivity. Two random variables *x* and *y* are defined as in Table 8.1. They are independent from each other. Each variable may take the values of 10, 20, or 30. Consider a third random variable *z*, which is the sum of *x* and *y*. The variable *z* may have the modalities 20, 30, 40, 50, and 60, with the probabilities summarized in Table 8.1.

The variable *z* may take the value of 20 when $x_i = 10$ and $y_i = 10$. The resulting probability is 0.0299 (0.23×0.13). In contrast, $z_i = 40$ when $(x_i, y_i) = (10.30)$, (20.20) or (30.10). The corresponding probability is 0.6291 ($(0.23 \times 0.05) + (0.75 \times 0.82) + (0.02 \times 0.13)$).

We can calculate the VaR at 95% of *x*, *y*, and *z*. By definition, $VaR_{95\%}(x) = \min\{x_i : Pr(x \leq x_i) \geq 95\%\} = 20$. Similarly, $VaR_{95\%}(y) = 20$. The sum of the two VaRs at 95% is therefore 40. Further, $VaR_{95\%}(z) = 50$, because at $z_i = 40$ the cumulative probability does not yet reach 95%. Consequently, $VaR_{95\%}(x + y) > VaR(x) + VaR(y)$, which clearly constitutes a violation of the subadditivity axiom for the VaR in

TABLE 8.1 Example of non-subadditivity.

	10	20	30	40	50	60
x_i						
$Pr(x = x_i)$	0.23	0.75	0.02			
$Pr(x \leq x_i)$	0.23	0.98	1.00			
y_i						
$Pr(y = y_i)$	0.13	0.82	0.05			
$Pr(y \leq y_i)$	0.13	0.95	1.00			
$z_i = x_i + y_i$						
$Pr(z = z_i)$		0.0299	0.2861	0.6291	0.0539	0.0001
$Pr(z \leq z_i)$		0.0299	0.3160	0.9451	0.9990	1.0000

this precise case. Intuitively, this means that simply putting x and y together increases global risk, which is not usual in finance.

8.2 NOTATION AND VaR

Consider a random variable y (that may be a vector) and the decision variable x (that may be a vector). Let the loss function be equal to $f(x, y) = z$ (it is not necessarily linear in y). Below, we assume that $E(f(x, y)) < \infty$ for all x. When the function $f(x, y)$ is negative, it represents a gain. Because y is a random variable, z is also a random variable that depends on the decision variable x. Consider the distribution function $\Psi(x, \cdot)$ with a density function $\psi(x, \cdot)$. The probability that $f(x, y)$ does not exceed the VaR, denoted as ς, is equal to:

$$\Psi(x, \varsigma) = P\{y | f(x, y) \leq \varsigma\} \tag{8.1}$$

or

$$\Psi(x, \varsigma) = \int_{-\infty}^{\varsigma} \psi(x, \cdot)\ dy.$$

Also let

$\Psi(x, \varsigma^-)$, the left limit of $\Psi(x, \varsigma)$ at ς

or

$$\Psi(x, \varsigma^-) = P\{y | f(x, y) < \varsigma\}. \tag{8.2}$$

When the difference:

$$\Psi(x, \varsigma) - \Psi(x, \varsigma^-) = P\{y | f(x, y) = \varsigma\} \tag{8.3}$$

is positive, this means that there is a jump (mass point or probability atom) at ς. Without discontinuity and for a value of x, the value at risk $\varsigma_p(x)$, at a degree of confidence $p(x)$ for a loss distribution, solves:

$$\int_{\varsigma_p(x)}^{+\infty} \psi(x, y)\, dy = 1 - p(x),$$

where 1 – p(x) is the probability that the VaR is exceeded. This implies that:

$$\Psi(x, \varsigma_p(x)) = p(x) \tag{8.4}$$

is the probability of being to the left of $\varsigma_p(x)$ or the degree of confidence. Figure 8.1 gives a representation of the VaR for a continuous distribution of y. The corresponding CVaR is equal to:

$$\phi_p(x) = \int_{\varsigma_p(x)}^{+\infty} f(x, y)\ \psi(x, \cdot)dy \frac{1}{1 - p(x)}. \tag{8.5}$$

When Ψ is continuous, we have strict equality as in (8.4). Figure 8.2, corresponding to a continuous distribution, always has a single solution with equality as in equation (8.4). With a discontinuous distribution, we do not necessarily have this equality, which creates problems for VaR. We may not have a solution or we may have an infinite number of VaRs.

These two extreme cases are represented in Figures 8.3 and 8.4. In Figure 8.3, $p^- = \Psi(x, \varsigma_p^-(x))$ and $p^+ = \Psi(x, \varsigma_p(x))$.

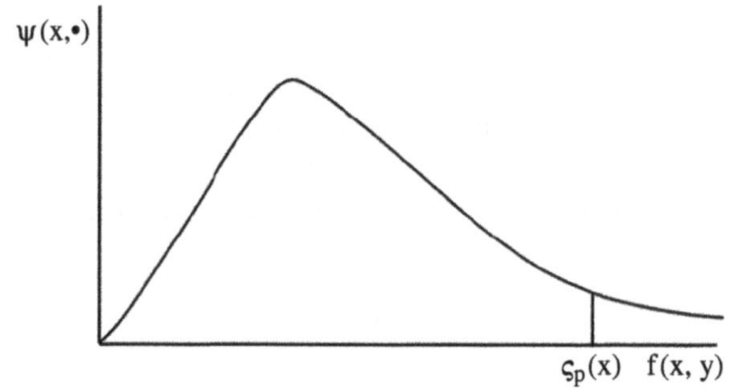

FIGURE 8.1 Value at risk.

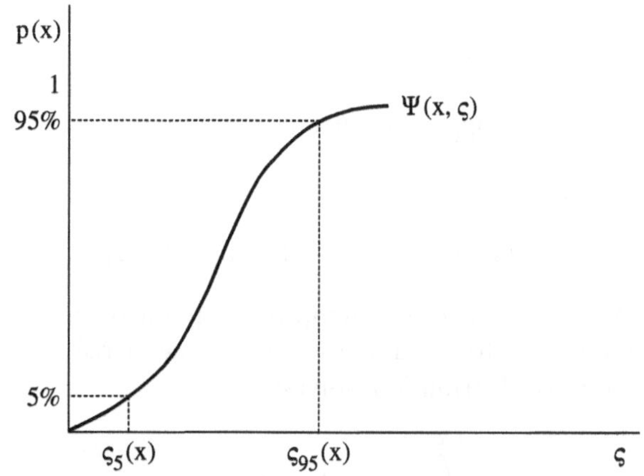

FIGURE 8.2 Equation $\Psi(x, \varsigma_p) = p(x)$ has a solution.

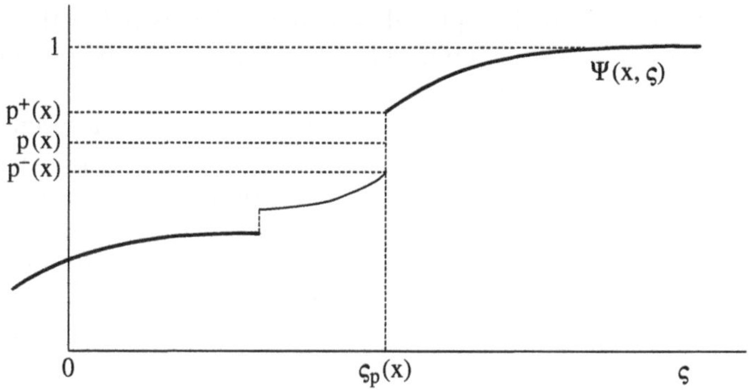

FIGURE 8.3 Equation $\Psi(x, \varsigma_p) = p(x)$ has no solution in ς, meaning that the VaR corresponds to different measures of confidence.
Source: Reproduced from Rockafellar and Uryasev (2002).
© Elsevier. Reproduced with permission.

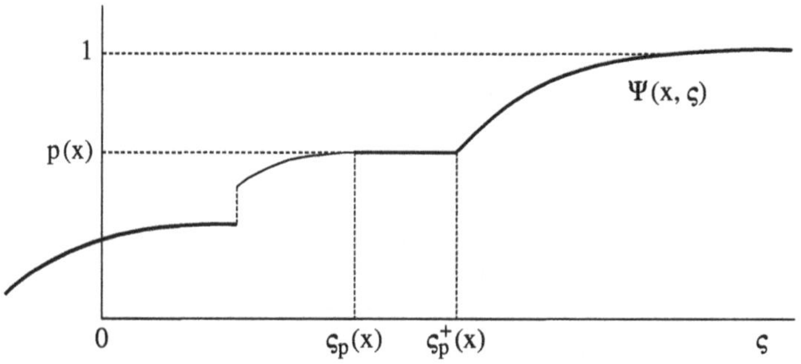

FIGURE 8.4 Equation $\Psi(x, \varsigma_p) = p(x)$ has several solutions in p, meaning that many VaR correspond to the same confidence level.
Source: Reproduced from Rockafellar and Uryasev (2002).
© Elsevier. Reproduced with permission.

In Figure 8.3, there is no solution because we have the same VaR for several degrees of confidence. Figure 8.4 represents a case with several VaRs for a single degree of confidence. These two cases are discussed in detail in the study by Rockafellar and Uryasev (2002).

Another concept used to define VaR is VaR^+:

$$\varsigma_p^+(x) = \inf\{\varsigma | \Psi(x, \varsigma) > p\},$$

which is defined as a function of the probability of being strictly to the right of $\varsigma_p(x)$.

This value is represented in Figure 8.4. Evidently, for a continuous distribution like the normal distribution, $\varsigma_p^+(x) = \varsigma_p(x)$. Otherwise, $\varsigma_p^+(x) \geq \varsigma_p(x)$. The last inequality is often observed for discrete distributions, because the function $\Psi(x, \cdot)$ may have jumps.

We can also define CVaR as being equal to:

$$\text{CVaR}(x) = \lambda_p(x)\text{VaR}_p(x) + (1 - \lambda_p(x))\text{CVaR}_p^+(x). \tag{8.6}$$

The difficulty is to find the optimal weight (λ) that is a function of x. It is interesting to note that CVaR, a coherent risk measure, may be obtained from a combination of two incoherent measures!

Investors use VaR to optimize their capital by choosing x, a weight vector of risky assets. They often minimize the portfolio risk for a given expected return. We can show that for a continuous and elliptical distribution of returns, minimizing variance, relative VaR or relative CVaR gives the same results in a parametric model. This is to be expected, because the two relative risk measures (VaR and CVaR) are proportional to the standard deviation of the portfolio.

8.3 DEFINITION OF CVaR

CVaR is the mean of losses (associated with decision x) that exceed the VaR.

$$\phi_p(x) = \text{CVaR}_p(x) = \text{mean of } p\text{-tail distribution of } z = f(x, y) \tag{8.7}$$

where the distribution is defined based on (8.1) as:

$$\Psi_p(x, \varsigma) = \begin{cases} 0 & \text{for } \varsigma < \varsigma_p(x) \\ [\Psi(x, \varsigma) - p]/(1 - p) & \text{for } \varsigma \geq \varsigma_p(x). \end{cases} \tag{8.8}$$

This redefinition of the distribution function lets us create a continuous distribution from a discontinuous distribution.

Figure 8.5 illustrates the distribution function $\Psi_p(x, \varsigma)$ obtained from the distribution tail in Figure 8.3, where we observed a mass point at $\varsigma_p(x)$.

The distribution function in (8.8) is that of Figure 8.3 rescaled. It is non-decreasing and right-continuous. We have two particular cases of the general definition $\phi_p(x)$.

$$\phi_p^+(x) = E\{f(x, y) | f(x, y) > \varsigma_p(x)\} \tag{8.9}$$

(often called "mean" or "expected shortfall" in the actuarial literature)

$$\phi_p^-(x) = E\{f(x, y) | f(x, y) \geq \varsigma_p(x)\} \tag{8.10}$$

(defined as the Tail VaR (TVaR) by Artzner et al., 1999).

These two particular definitions may pose the same problems of coherency as VaR. If there is no mass point at $\varsigma_p(x)$:

$$\phi_p^-(x) = \phi_p(x) = \phi_p^+(x). \tag{8.11}$$

If there is a mass point at $\varsigma_p(x)$:

$$\phi_p^-(x) < \phi_p(x) = \phi_p^+(x) \text{ when } p = \Psi(x, \varsigma_p(x)), \tag{8.12}$$

which signifies, in this situation, that the CVaR corresponds to the CVaR$^+$ and that the VaR is not really useful to measure risk. This is illustrated below.

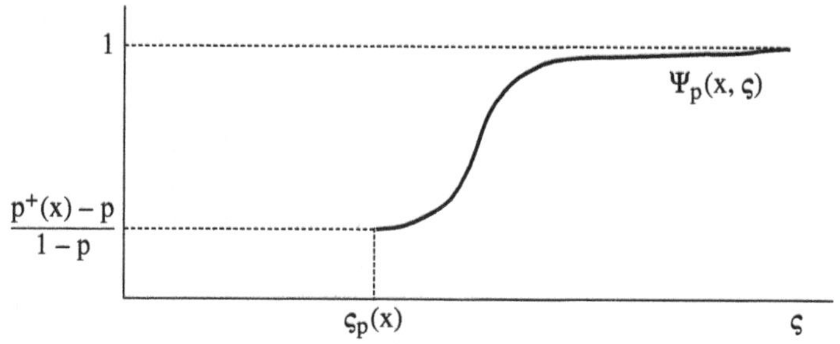

FIGURE 8.5 The distribution function of $\Psi_p(x, \varsigma)$ is obtained by redefining the function $\Psi(x, \varsigma)$ in the interval $[p, 1]$.
Source: Reproduced from Rockafellar and Uryasev (2002).
© Elsevier. Reproduced with permission.

As mentioned above, another way to define the CVaR is to use a weighted average of VaR and CVaR$^+$. Let $\lambda_p(x)$ be the probability that the loss $y = \varsigma_p(x)$, as defined in (8.14) and based on (8.8). Then:

$$\phi_p(x) = \lambda_p(x)\varsigma_p(x) + (1 - \lambda_p(x))\phi_p^+(x) \tag{8.13}$$

where:

$$\lambda_p(x) = [\Psi(x, \varsigma_p(x)) - p]/(1 - p) \quad \in [0,1]. \tag{8.14}$$

We observe that $\phi_p(x) = \phi_p^+(x)$ when $p = \Psi(x, \varsigma_p(x))$. The VaR has no weight. According to the definition (8.8), $\Psi(x, \varsigma_p(x)) \geq p$ in the presence of discrete distributions. Therefore, a gap between these two positive values indicates that $\Psi(\cdot, \cdot)$ evaluated at VaR is higher than p and therefore partly takes the discontinuity into account.

However, if $\Psi(x, \varsigma_p(x)) = 1$, that is, if there are no possible losses higher than $\varsigma_p(x)$, then $\lambda_p(x) = 1$ and $\phi_p(x) = \varsigma_p(x)$. In general $\phi_p(x) > \varsigma_p(x)$.

The article by Rockafellar and Uryasev (2002) formally shows that CVaR is convex, stable, and a coherent risk measure. Figure 8.6 summarizes the previous discussion. We observe that VaR_p may considerably underestimate risk and therefore has a low weight, whereas CVaR_p^+ overestimates it. CVaR_p represents a better risk measure because it is a weighted sum of the two other risk measures.

We now present an example to illustrate the continuity of the CVaR measure in the case of a discrete or discontinuous distribution.

Consider a sample of 100 observations of a loss distribution L. We categorize losses in increasing order: L_1 and L_{100} designate the smallest and the largest loss respectively. We want to estimate the risk based on the degree of confidence of 97%. The four largest losses are $L_{97} = 0.5$, $L_{98} = 0.66$, $L_{99} = 0.8$ and $L_{100} = 1.5$. The $\text{VaR}_{97\%}$ is estimated at 0.5. To estimate the $\text{CVaR}_{97\%}$, we have $\lambda_{97\%} = 0$, because the point 0.97 exists in the sample:

$$\lambda_{97\%} = (0.97 - 0.97)/(1 - 0.97) = 0,$$

therefore:

$$\text{CVaR}_{97\%} = (0.66 + 0.80 + 1.50)/3 = 0.9867.$$

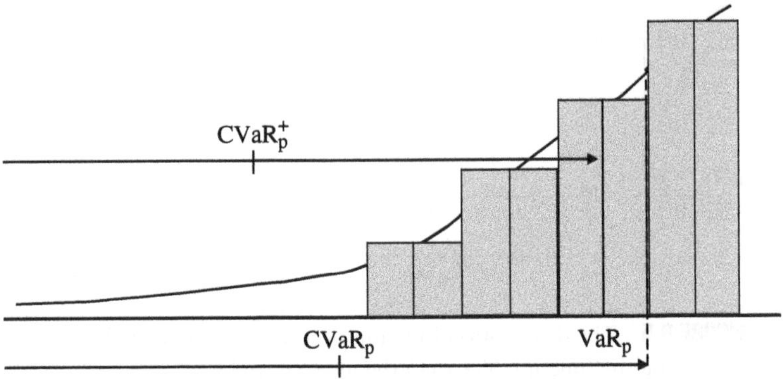

FIGURE 8.6 $CVaR_p$ as a weighted measure of VaR_p and of $CVaR_p^+$.

Now we want to do the calculations at a degree of confidence of 97.1%, for example. The $VaR_{97,1\%}$ is estimated at 0.66. There is a leap of $0.66 - 0.50 = 0.16$.

To estimate the $CVaR_{97,1\%}$, we use equation (8.6) and start by calculating $\lambda_{97.1\%} = (98\% - 97.1\%)/(1 - 97.1\%) = 0.3103$, from which we get $CVaR_{97.1\%} = 0.9979$, because $CVaR^+_{97.1\%} = (0.8 + 1.5)/2 = 1.15$. Note that this value is close to the $CVaR_{97\%}$ and that there are no jumps. Intuitively, the continuity of CVaR results from equation (8.6) because the weight λ_p is continuous relative to p and we can evaluate it at all degrees of intermediate confidence.

Table 8.2 summarizes the calculations at different degrees of confidence.

TABLE 8.2 VaR and CVaR for different p.

L_i		0.40	0.50	0.66	0.80	1.50
$P(L \le L_i)$		96%	97%	98%	99%	100%
p	L_i	VaR_p	λ	$1 - \lambda$	$CVaR_p^+$	$CVaR_p$
0.970	0.50	0.50	0	1	0.9867	0.9867
0.971		0.66	0.3103	0.6897	1.1500	0.9979
0.972		0.66	0.2857	0.7143	1.1500	1.0100
0.973		0.66	0.2593	0.7407	1.1500	1.0230
0.974		0.66	0.2308	0.7692	1.1500	1.0369
0.975		0.66	0.2000	0.8000	1.1500	1.0520
0.976		0.66	0.1667	0.8333	1.1500	1.0683
0.977		0.66	0.1304	0.8696	1.1500	1.0861
0.978		0.66	0.0909	0.9091	1.1500	1.1055
0.979		0.66	0.0476	0.9524	1.1500	1.1267
0.980	0.66	0.66	0	1	1.1500	1.1500
0.981		0.80	0.4737	0.5263	1.5000	1.1684
0.982		0.80	0.4444	0.5556	1.5000	1.1889
0.983		0.80	0.4118	0.5882	1.5000	1.2118
0.984		0.80	0.3750	0.6250	1.5000	1.2375
0.985		0.80	0.3333	0.6667	1.5000	1.2667
0.986		0.80	0.2857	0.7143	1.5000	1.3000
0.987		0.80	0.2308	0.7692	1.5000	1.3385
0.988		0.80	0.1667	0.8333	1.5000	1.3833
0.989		0.80	0.0909	0.9091	1.5000	1.4364
0.990	0.80	0.80	0	1	1.5000	1.5000

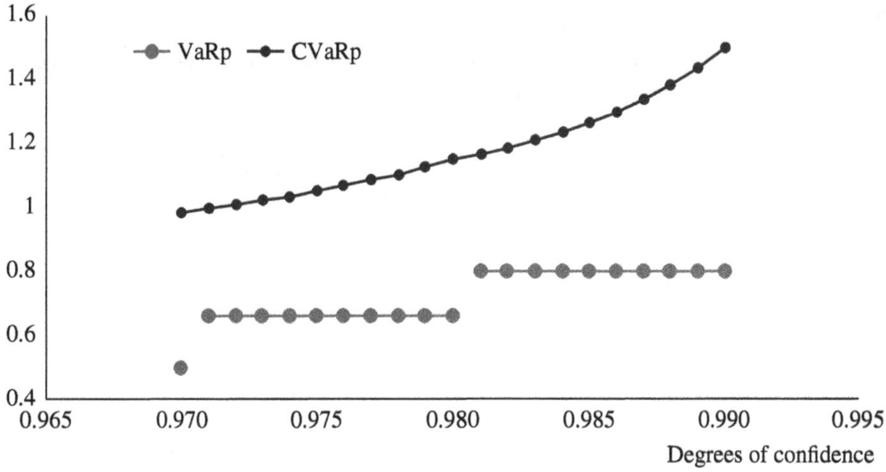

FIGURE 8.7 Continuity of CVaR for different degrees of confidence.

Figure 8.7 shows the continuity of CVaR whereas VaR is discontinuous.

8.4 ANOTHER WAY TO DERIVE CVaR WITH A RETURN DISTRIBUTION

We now consider the gains and returns rather than a loss function. Let (1 − p) be the probability that r_h is less than $-VaR_h$:

$$\Pr(r_h < -VaR_h) = (1 - p)$$

where:

$VaR_h > 0$;
p is the level of confidence;
h is the time horizon;

$r_h = \ln(V_{0+h}/V_0)$;
V_0 is the value of the portfolio at date 0;
V_{0+h} is its value at date *h*.

We can define the VaR relative to 0 or in absolute value:

$$VaR_h = -\sigma_h \phi^{-1}(1 - p) - \mu_h$$

where:

$\phi^{-1}(1-p)$ is the inverse quantile function of the normal standard distribution;
σ_h is the standard deviation of the return;
μ_h is the mean.

For example, $\phi^{-1}(1-p) = -2.33$ if $p = 99\%$. Subsequently, VaR_h is replaced by VaR for the sake of simplicity. We can define CVaR as:

$$CVaR = -E(r_h | r_h \leq -VaR) = \int_{-\infty}^{-VaR} -\frac{rf(r)dr}{Pr(r_h < -VaR)}$$
$$= -\frac{1}{Pr(r_h < -VaR)} \int_{-\infty}^{-VaR} rf(r)dr$$

where $E(r_h | r_h \leq -VaR)$ is the conditional expected value of the returns to the left of $-VaR$.

We now use a standardized definition of the return:

$$z_h = \frac{r_h - \mu_h}{\sigma_h}.$$

We can define *q*:

$$q = \frac{-VaR - \mu_h}{\sigma_h}$$

and get the CVaR:

$$CVaR = -\mu_h - \sigma_h \frac{\int_{-\infty}^{q} z_h f(z_h) dz_h}{1-p}.$$

8.5 EXAMPLE WITH STUDENT'S *t*-DISTRIBUTION AND OTHER EXAMPLES

Student's *t*-distribution can take into account kurtosis (or *excess kurtosis*) different from zero. For a normal distribution, when the mean is zero and the variance is unitary, we have, at the quantile $q < 0$:

$$CVaR_N = -\frac{f(q)}{F(q)} < 0$$

where F(q) is the distribution function of the standard normal distribution evaluated at *q* and f(q) its density function:

$$F(q) = \int_{-\infty}^{q} f(x)\,dx.$$

What interests us here is considering moments higher than two.[2]

For the Student's *t*-distribution, the conditional loss equals:

$$\int_{-\infty}^{q} yf(y)\,dy = \int_{-\infty}^{q} y\frac{\Gamma((\nu+1)/2)}{\Gamma(n/2)\sqrt{\pi\beta\nu}}(1+y^2/\beta\nu)^{-\left(\frac{1+\nu}{2}\right)}dy$$

where:

β is a dispersion parameter;

ν indicates the degrees of freedom.

For $\nu > 1$, we get the following value for CVaR:

$$\frac{\int_{-\infty}^{q} yf(y)\,dy}{F(q)} = \frac{-\beta\nu}{\nu-1}(1+q^2/\beta\nu)\frac{f(q)}{F(q)}. \tag{8.15}$$

For $\nu > 2$:

$$m_2 = \beta\nu/\nu - 2,$$

and CVaR becomes:

$$\text{CVaR} = -((1-\omega)m_2 + \omega q^2)\frac{f(q)}{F(q)}\text{ , where } \omega = \frac{1}{\nu-1}.$$

For $\nu > 4$, ω is a function of kurtosis (kur):

$$\omega = \text{kur}/(6+3\,\text{kur}) \text{ and } \nu = 4 + 6/\text{kur} \text{ or } \text{kur} = 6/(\nu-4).$$

For this distribution, *skewness* is zero for $\nu > 3$ and not defined otherwise. Given the estimators:

$$\hat{s}^2,\ \ \text{k}\hat{\text{u}}\text{r},\ \ \hat{\omega} = \text{k}\hat{\text{u}}\text{r}/(6+3\text{k}\hat{\text{u}}\text{r}),$$

we get:

$$\text{CV}\hat{\text{a}}\text{R} = -((1-\hat{\omega})\hat{s}^2 + \hat{\omega}q^2)\frac{f(q)}{F(q)},$$

or, by using the definition of kûr:

$$\text{CV}\hat{\text{a}}\text{R} = -\left(\frac{2\text{k}\hat{\text{u}}\text{r}+6}{6+3\text{k}\hat{\text{u}}\text{r}}\ \hat{s}^2 + \frac{\text{k}\hat{\text{u}}\text{r}}{6+3\text{k}\hat{\text{u}}\text{r}}\ q^2\right)\frac{f(q)}{F(q)}.$$

When kûr $= 0$, we get the formula of CVaR for the standard normal distribution because $\hat{s}^2 \approx 1$.

Table 8.3 gives the explicit values of CVaR for different known standard distributions in an application proposed by Andreev, Kanto, and Malo (2005).

[2]An application for CVaR for a term structure model of short-term interest rates with reversion to the mean and a diffusion process is presented in Andreev and Kanto (2004) and Andreev, Kanto, and Malo (2005).

TABLE 8.3 CVaR for the most common distributions.[1]

Name and support	Density function f(x)	Mean μ	Squared diffusion[2] $\sigma^2(x)$	CVaR (q < 0)	CVaR (q > 0)
Normal $(-\infty, \infty)$	$\frac{1}{\sqrt{2\pi}} e^{-1/2z^2}$	0	2θ	$-\frac{f(q)}{F(q)}$	$\frac{f(q)}{1-F(q)}$
Student $(-\infty, \infty)$	$\frac{\Gamma\left(\frac{v+1}{2}\right)}{\sqrt{v\pi}\Gamma(v/2v/2)}(1+1/_y x^2)^{-\frac{(v+1)}{2}}$ $v > 1$	0	$\frac{2\theta}{v-1}(v+x^2)$	$-\frac{v+q^2}{v-1}\frac{f(q)}{F(q)}$	$\frac{v+q^2}{v-1}\frac{f(q)}{1-F(q)}$
Pareto $(0, \infty)$	$\alpha(1+x)^{-\alpha-1}$ $\alpha > 1$	$\frac{1}{\alpha-1}$	$2\theta\mu x(1+x)$		$\frac{1}{\alpha-1}\left[1+q(1+q)\frac{f(q)}{1-F(q)}\right]$
Exponential $(0, \infty)$	$\lambda e^{-\lambda x}$ $\lambda > 0$	$\frac{1}{\lambda}$	$\frac{2\theta}{\lambda}x$		$\frac{1}{\lambda}+q$
Gamma $(0, \infty)$	$\frac{\lambda^\alpha}{\Gamma(\alpha)}x^{\alpha-1}e^{-\lambda x}$ $\alpha \geq 1,\ \lambda > 0$	$\frac{\alpha}{\lambda}$	$\frac{2\theta}{\lambda}x$		$\frac{1}{\lambda}\left[\alpha+q\frac{f(q)}{1-F(q)}\right]$
Log-normal $(0, \infty)$	$\frac{1}{\sqrt{2\pi\sigma^2}x}e^{-\frac{1}{2\sigma^2}(\log x-\delta)^2}$	$e^{\delta+2\sigma^2}$	$\frac{2\theta\mu}{f(x)}\left(\Phi\left(\frac{\log x-\delta}{\sigma}\right)-\Phi\left(\frac{\log x-\delta}{\sigma}-\sigma\right)\right)$		$e^{\delta+2\sigma^2}+\mu\left[\Phi\left(\frac{\log q-\delta}{\sigma}\right)-\Phi\left(\frac{\log q-\delta}{\sigma}-\sigma\right)\right]\frac{1}{1-F(q)}$
Weibull $(0, \infty)$	$cx^{c-1}e^{x^c}$ $c > 0$	$\Gamma\left(\frac{1}{c}+1\right)$	$\frac{2\theta}{f(x)}\left(\Gamma\left(\frac{1}{c}+1\right)(1-e^{-x^c})-\Gamma\left(x^c;\frac{1}{c}+1\right)\right)$		$\Gamma\left(\frac{1}{c}+1\right)+\frac{1}{1-F(q)}\left[\Gamma\left(\frac{1}{c}+1\right)(1-e^{-q^c})-\Gamma\left(q^c;\frac{1}{c}+1\right)\right]$

Notes:
[1] Φ represents the distribution function of the standardized normal distribution, Γ is the gamma function, and q is the quantile of VaR.
[2] The differential stochastic equation is equal to $dx_t = -\theta(x_t - \mu)dt + \sigma(x_t)dW_t$ with $\theta > 0$ and where W_t is the Brownian movement. Diffusion is defined in equation 3.3 of the article.
Source: Andreev, Kanto, and Malo (2005).

8.6 CONCLUSION: CVaR IN BASEL REGULATION

The 2008 financial crisis highlighted major gaps in the prevailing models for market risk of financial institutions (*trading books*). Most of these gaps are linked to estimation of risk by VaR combined with the thickness of distribution tails (*tail risks*) that are not adequately considered.

In 2012, Basel published a consultation document for a transition from VaR to CVaR concerning market risk. In January 2016, a new regulation took effect (BCBS352, STANDARDS Minimum capital requirements for market risk, January 2016). For internal market models, risk estimations by VaR and the *Stress* VaR are no longer used. The new approach is based on CVaR (called *Expected Shortfall* in the Basel documents).

The calculations are done relative to a degree of confidence of 97.5% for CVaR, which corresponds roughly to the degree of confidence of 99% for VaR of a normal distribution. The calculations for a standard normal distribution give $\text{VaR}_{0.99} = -\Phi^{-1}(1\%) = 2.326$. The $\text{CVaR}_{0.975} = 2.338$, which amounts to a slight increase in capital. But the normal distribution is very restrictive.

An important change is occurring in conjunction with this shift to CVaR. Basel is tightening up its model validation process, including models based on the standard normal distribution. In other words, in case of a proven thick tail, the increase in hedging capital may be large. To get a value, consider the shift from a VaR model based on a normal distribution to a CVaR built on a Student's t-distribution, with a degree of freedom of 20. Expression (8.15) of CVaR relative to the Student's t-distribution gives $\text{CVaR}_{0.975}\,\text{Student}(\nu = 20) = 2.556$. This represents an increase in capital of $(2.556 - 2.326)/2.326 = 9.89\% \approx 10\%$. Other aspects are added to calibrate the new internal CVaR models relative to a period of significant stress, which implies that the increase in hedging capital following the new regulation may be even greater. Overall, Basel estimates an increase in capital ranging from 7.3% to 19% depending on the case (BCBS352_note, Explanatory note on the revised minimum capital requirements for market risk, January 2016).

In closing, note that for now Basel does not plan to use CVaR to estimate capital for risks other than market risk. However, this first shift to CVaR may herald a new era of generalized CVaR. Lastly, Basel expects that the preparations for the shift to the new regulation will be finalized around January 2019 for an official application in late 2019.[3]

REFERENCES

Acerbi, C., and Tasche, D., 2002a. "On the Coherence of Expected Shortfall." *Journal of Banking and Finance* 26, 1487–1503.

Acerbi, C., and Tasche, D., 2002b. "Expected Shortfall: A Natural Coherent Alternative to Value at Risk." *Economic Notes Banca Monte dei Paschi di Siena SpA* 31, 379–388.

Andersson, F., Mausser, H., Rosen, D., and Uryasev, S., 2001. "Credit Risk Optimization with Conditional Value-at-Risk Criterion." *Mathematical Programming Springer B* 89, 273–291.

[3]For backtest theory and applications related to the CVaR, see Fortin, Simonato, and Dionne (2018), Acerbi and Tasche (2002a, 2002b), and Simonato (2011).

Andreev, A., and Kanto, A., 2004. "A Note on Calculation of CVaR for Student's Distribution." Working paper W-369, Helsinki School of Economics, http://hsepubl.lib.hse.fi/pdf/wp/w369.pdf. .

Andreev, A., Kanto, A., and Malo, P., 2005. "On Closed-Form Calculation of CVaR." Working paper W-389, Helsinki School of Economics, http://hsepubl.lib.hse.fi/pdf/wp/w389.pdf.

Artzner, P., Delbaen, F., Eber, J.M., and Heath, D., 1999. "Coherent Measures of Risk." *Mathematical Finance* 9, 203–228.

Basel Committee on Banking Supervision, 2016. "STANDARDS: Minimum Capital Requirements for Market Risk." http://www.bis.org/bcbs/publ/d352.pdf.

Fortin, A.P., Simonato, J.G., and Dionne, G., 2018. "Forecasting Expected Shortfall: Should We Use a Multivariate Model for Stock Expected Shortfall?" Mimeo, Canada Research Chair in Risk Management, HEC Montréal.

Rockafellar, R.T., and Uryasev, S., 2000. "Optimization of Conditional Value-at-Risk." *Journal of Risk*, http://www.risk.net/journal-of-risk/technical-paper/2161159/optimization-conditional-value-risk.

Rockafellar, R.T., and Uryasev, S., 2002. "Conditional Value-at-Risk for General Loss Distributions." *Journal of Banking and Finance* 26, 1443–1471.

Simonato, J.G., 2011. "The Performance of Johnson Distributions for Computing Value at Risk and Expected Shortfall." *Journal of Derivatives* 19, 7–24.

Uryasev, S., 2001. "Conditional Value-at-Risk (CVaR): Algorithms and Applications." Presentation for the Risk Management and Financial Engineering Lab, University of Florida.

CHAPTER 9

Regulation of Bank Risk and Use of VaR

Banks have been regulated for many years. This chapter discusses the regulation of bank risk rather than that of competition between banks. Even if some risks affect shareholders and banks' creditors, this does not justify regulation because these agents are compensated for the risks they take and have access to monitoring instruments that give them sufficient information to protect themselves. In addition, these actors can diversify their portfolios at costs lower than those incurred by other banks partners.

In contrast, deposit holders do not necessarily have access to the same private monitoring instruments and to the same diversification possibilities. Notably, private information on banks' default costs are lower for shareholders and creditors, who have direct access to some information. An inexpensive way to monitor a bank is to buy its stock. Investors thus receive quarterly and annual reports, and can attend shareholder meetings. However, this information may not be sufficient. It is better to be a board member!

It is crucial to keep in mind that small savers have fewer diversification options than shareholders, creditors, and bank managers. In addition, deposits are traditionally recognized or described as risk-free assets. Deposit insurance was introduced in several countries to protect depositors. However, this insurance may have generated ex ante moral hazard and induced risk-taking behavior in bank managers that does not necessarily serve the interests of deposit holders and the overall financial system. In other words, deposit insurance may encourage banks to take more risks because they have already paid deposit insurance premiums (at a fixed rate). Deposit insurance was eliminated in New Zealand to discipline banks, but savers were no longer protected. A new provisional deposit insurance system was reintroduced in 2008 in response to the financial crisis. In Canada, the Canada Deposit Insurance Corporation (CDIC), a federal Crown corporation founded in 1967, is responsible for this insurance.[1] In the United States, the deposit insurance has been provided by the Federal Deposit Insurance Corporation since 1933.

In general, regarding insurance problems, there is always a trade-off between prevention and risk level for the insured in the presence of moral hazard. For example, holders of auto theft or accident insurance policies often have fewer incentives to

[1]For more information about deposit insurance systems, see the International Association of Deposit Insurers website (http://www.iadi.org/di.aspx).

reduce the risk of accidents than do car owners without such insurance. However, it is still possible to demonstrate that, in the presence of moral hazard, insurance with well controlled incentive mechanisms grants insured better welfare than non-insurance. This happens because several risks are not truly diversifiable on financial markets. In the presence of risk aversion, a certain loss of efficiency in prevention is accepted in exchange for more risk protection.

Contrary to other types of insurance contracts, in deposit insurance contracts, the insured and the agents who make risk-related decisions are not the same. Deposit holders (who may be harmed by the risks taken by the bank) or the insured who are protected by deposit insurance do not have the problem of an incentive to protect themselves from bank default because, technically, they cannot affect the default probabilities of banks by their actions (except in the extreme case where most deposit holders withdraw their deposits). The only prevention they may exercise is diversification of deposits between banks (which is not encouraged since this activity has become costly due to increasing transaction costs). Moreover, deposit insurance does not encourage customers to diversify their deposits because they are covered for up to $250,000 per depositor in the United States ($100,000 in Canada), representing full insurance coverage for most customers.

Bank executives have very few incentives to limit risk when deposit insurance is present. They can consequently take high risks and conserve minimal capital to increase the bank's profitability. These actions generate higher bank default probabilities and potential negative externalities in the financial system, which justifies regulation of bank risks. Since 1967, more than 45 banks have declared bankruptcy in Canada, and during the last financial crisis (June 2007 to March 2009), more than 150 banks have failed, mainly in the United States.

Banks play an important role in the functioning of the financial system. In the presence of systemic risk, the bankruptcy of one or more large banks may incur sizable losses for the whole financial system by generating other bankruptcies via the simple domino effect. This more macro-economic dimension has become increasingly important since the financial crisis of 2007–2009 and has reinforced the need to regulate bank risks.

Systemic risk is the risk that a large portfolio or financial institution imposes on the financial system and even the whole economy. It generally affects default risk and even bankruptcy risk. If a major bank fails, nonpayment of its financial obligations to other financial institutions may result in huge losses, hence the commonly used expression "Too Big to Fail!" This phrase clearly illustrates the various precautions that the American government had to take when it forced Lehman Brothers to file for bankruptcy in September 2008. It also explains why other banks and AIG were bailed out using public funds or personal income taxes. Systemic risk is also defined as the risk of collapse of the financial system. It is very different from the systematic risk or general market risk. It is more related to the interlinkage of financial institutions and to their idiosyncratic risk. Network models have been proposed to measure systemic risk. The next section describes the evolution of bank regulation.

9.1 BASEL ACCORDS

The evolution of international regulation (Basel Accords) of banks is shown in Figure 9.1.

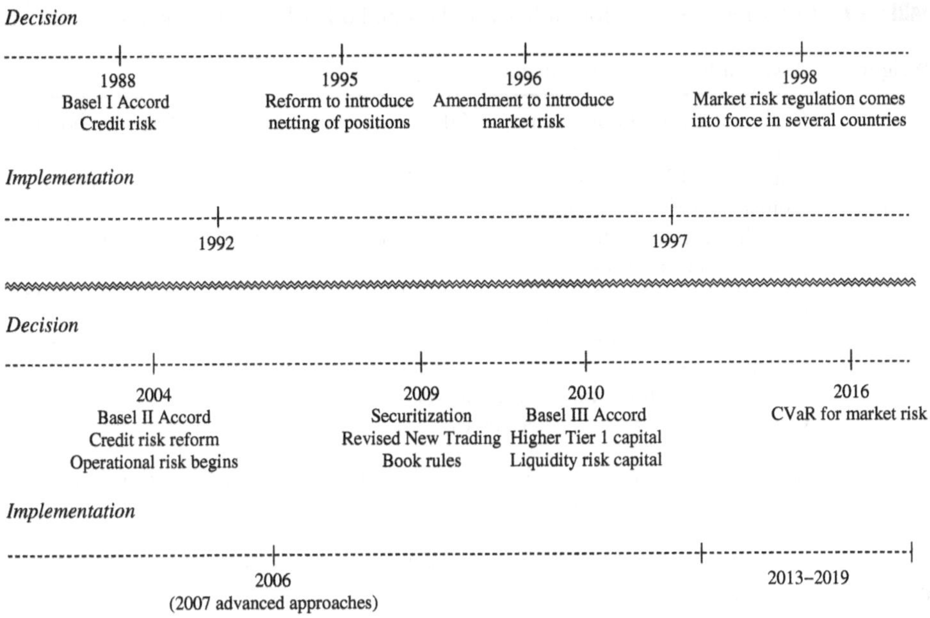

FIGURE 9.1 Important dates in Basel regulation

Basel I in 1988. In 1988, the group of the 10 most industrialized countries signed an accord to regulate banks (which took effect in 1992). Although the member countries of the accord may introduce more stringent regulation in their respective banking markets, they must abide by the minimum criteria of the international accord. The accord stipulates that banks in member nations must hold a minimum amount of required capital.

The definition of capital that is used to create reserves extends beyond bank equity. In 1988, two forms of capital were considered:

1. Tier 1 or core capital

Top-quality capital, which includes bank stocks, interest in subsidiaries and some reserves reported to the regulators.

2. Tier 2 or supplementary capital

Hybrid capital instruments (debentures with long maturities), subordinated debt with an original average maturity of at least five years, other instruments, and other reserves.

The Basel I Accord requires that 50% of the capital be covered by Tier 1 capital and that the sum of the sources of capital represent at least 8% (Cooke ratio) of weighted risky assets. In addition to the reserves required, the accord imposes restrictions on excessive risk-taking behavior:

- No holding may exceed 25% of a company's capital.
- The total high-risk positions may not exceed eight times the required capital, whereas the Cooke ratio allows banks to exceed the set of all weighted risks by up to 12.5 times.

TABLE 9.1 Risk capital weights for on-balance-sheet and off-balance-sheet assets.

Weight	Asset on-balance-sheet category
0%	Cash and gold bullion, claims on OECD governments such as Treasury bonds, insured residential mortgages
20%	Claims on OECD banks and OECD public sector entities like municipalities
50%	Uninsured residential mortgages.
100%	All other claims such as corporate bonds and less developed country debt, claims on non-OECD banks
	Off-balance-sheet category
0%	OECD governments.
20%	OECD banks and public sector entities
50%	Corporate and other counterparties.

Note: Surprisingly, private off-balance-sheet assets have lesser weights than on-balance-sheet securities. The argument put forth is that the institutions that issue these securities are more diversified.
Source: Reproduced from Crouhy, Galai, and Mark (1998). © John Wiley & Sons, Inc. Reproduced with permission.

The Basel I Accord was strongly criticized because it did not take market risk into account and had a very conservative approach to credit risk. In addition, it neglected the possibilities of risk diversification and of netting positions (that is, the presence of natural hedges between long and short positions).

From Basel I to Basel II, regulations and reforms were put in place to fill gaps in the first accord

This first accord was limited to credit risk. Each bank was required to keep a capital reserve of 8% (Cooke ratio)[2] of the exposures to different credit risks weighted by securities held. The weight depends on the risk of the assets. Some weights are given in Table 9.1, which comes from Crouhy, Galai, and Mark (1998).[3]

In 1995, netting was authorized on risky positions, including those associated with derivatives. In 1996, a first reform was proposed to consider market risk, and the use of an internal model for market risk was permitted.

The internal model supposes that the bank calculates four VaRs associated with the following four market risks: return risk of financial instruments, interest rate risk, foreign exchange risk, and commodities risk. Total VaR is the sum of the four VaRs. This approach is also very conservative because it does not allow diversification between blocks of risks.

In Canada, the new form of market risk regulation took effect in January 1998. It is overseen by the Office of the Superintendent of Financial Institutions (OSFI) in Ottawa. In the United States, bank regulation has undergone major changes during these years. Contrary to many other countries, US banking regulation is highly fragmented between different regulatory entities.

[2]The Cooke ratio is a measure that protects the bank from insolvency. It defines the minimum amount of capital that the bank must set aside depending on its risk level.

[3]These weights were modified in 2006 for banks still using this standard approach to calculate capital linked to credit risk. They are now based on external risk ratings obtained from independent rating agencies.

A reform for operational and credit risk was introduced in 2004 (Basel II) and implemented in 2006, but several countries had not enacted the new reform before the financial crisis of 2007–2009. It is important to note that Basel II authorized the use of internal models for credit risk (of the CreditMetrics type) and for operational risk, which we will revisit in subsequent chapters.

In this chapter, we will focus on the reform of 1996 and particularly on the market risk portion, although the regulation also covers standard credit risk. We will compare the internal model approach and the standardized approach for market risk. The standardized approach is linked to capital ratios calculated by the Basel committee, whereas the internal model approach is based on VaR. The main characteristics of this reform for market risk are still operational in many countries. Before analyzing Basel II, we will summarize the main characteristics of regulatory VaR.

In 1996, the reform allowed banks to use internal formulas to calculate the global VaR of bank market risk, providing that it included certain rules:

- The VAR horizon covers 10 market days or two weeks.
- The degree of confidence is 99%.
- Historical data must cover one year, and the model parameters must be updated every three months.
- Correlations between all forms of market risk can be used.
- The capital required for market risk is determined by $\mathrm{Max}(\mathrm{VaR}_{t-1};\ k * \overline{\mathrm{VaR}})$, that is, by the highest value between the VaR of the previous period or $k * \overline{\mathrm{VaR}}$, where $\overline{\mathrm{VaR}}$ represents the mean VaR of the last 60 market periods. If the risk rises rapidly, so does the VaR, and the bank must therefore set aside more capital. If the risk drops quickly, the VaR decreases, but the capital will not decrease as quickly because the bank will use the weighted 60-period average. Note that the factor $k = 3$ in many countries. However, this factor may increase if the losses observed exceed those predicted by the VaR too often, or if the internal model of the bank is inadequate.
- The introduction of market risk requires more capital. Banks can use Tier 3 capital to form the reserves, which mainly correspond to short-term subordinated debt. The capital used in Tier 2 and Tier 3 must not exceed 250% of the Tier 1 capital for market risk.

Basel II in 2004. The main goal of the reform is to make the capital calculation more risk sensitive. The calculation of capital for credit risk using the internal method (CreditMetrics type model) has also been added to consider the diversification of bond and loan portfolios. The calculation of capital (standard and advanced) for operational risk is also part of Basel II.

Total bank risk is estimated to consist of 80% credit risk, 15% operational risk, and 5% market risk. Since the financial crisis of 2008, banks must also consider liquidity risk. Note that the capital ratio remained at 8% for risky assets (weighted) under Basel II.

The three pillars of Basel II are:

- Calculation of capital: based more on financial models than on accounting rules.
- Supervision (implementation): heightened validation of statistical methods and data, translated by more tests of the validity of equity, particularly in a crisis situation.
- Market discipline: improvement of communication of financial or market information. In other words, more transparency regarding bank risk.

For credit risk, banks can use internal ratings, which are much more flexible than those of rating agencies because they may vary according to economic cycles.

Two methods are used to calculate capital:

1. Standardized approach.
2. Internal model approach, which may use Internal Ratings Based (IRB).
   Calculation of capital with the IRB model involves a detailed calculation of:
   - PD: probability of default;
   - EAD: exposure to credit risk at default;
   - LGD: loss given default rate or % of exposure to credit risk at default.

The internal model approach distinguishes unanticipated and anticipated losses; capital is calculated based on unanticipated losses. This is a very detailed approach with separate treatments for different types of debt: government, corporate, bank, and personal.

There are two sub-approaches in Internal Ratings-Based (IRB):

1. Advanced: the bank calculates PD, LGD, and EAD.
2. Less advanced: the bank calculates PD and takes the other values from the Basel II documents.

There are two forms of securitization:

1. Traditional: creates tranches of assets with different credit risks.
2. Synthetic: credit risk is transferred using derivatives like CDSs (credit default swaps).

A bank that uses securitization can reduce its required capital under certain conditions, including transfer of credit risk to third parties. It may not keep direct or indirect control over the positions transferred, nor use them to calculate its capital.

Basel III in 2010. Following the financial crisis, the Basel III Accord was ratified. It is being implemented over several years. Here are its main characteristics:

- New rules on capital adequacy and better control of liquidity risk.
- Closer management of risks and bank oversight. The CRO (Chief Risk Officer) becomes more independent.
- More transparency in risk management.
- Increased capital in reserves (long term):
  - Minimum total Tier 1 capital: equity portion increases from 2% to 3.5% in 2013, and the total Tier 1 should increase from 4% to 6% in 2019;
  - Total minimum capital: 8% in 2013, but its composition changes;
  - A buffer has been added: total of 10.5% in 2019 for periods of recession or financial crisis.
- Tier 3 capital is eliminated.
- Liquidity coverage ratio (LCR, 30 days):
  - As of 2011 (observation of banks' experience);
  - As of 2015 (minimum capital).
- Net stable funding ratio (NSFR, liquidity over one year):
  - As of 2012 (observation of banks' experience);
  - As of 2017 (minimum capital).

- Introduction of a new control standard for banks' debt ratio.
- Regulation more procyclical.
- Consideration of systemic risk.
- Banking book: more capital for securitization.
- More centralized transactions (clearing houses or central counterparties) and more control over OTC (over the counter) transactions, including those of CDS.
- More capital for market risk in the trading book.
- Main anticipated effects of Basel III on banks' capital and behavior.
- Substitution for assets with lower returns but more liquidity.
- Increased capital by issuing shares, fewer dividends, and decreased compensation of top managers is expected.
- Lower debt ratios, which should reduce the default risk level of banks and the associated costs, including deposit insurance.
- New liquidity standards that should foster development of new management and liquidity risk control policies.
- New stress test requirements based on economic cycles, which should allow better capital management to absorb potential losses during recessions or crises.
- Focus on a more macroeconomic approach to bank regulation.

Table 9.2 summarizes the proposed evolution of different capital ratios.

TABLE 9.2 Incremental implementation of Basel III.

	2011	2012	2013	2014	2015	2016	2017	2018	2019
Capital	Supervisory monitoring		Parallel run: 1 January 2013 to 1 January 2017					Migration to Pillar 1	
Common equity capital			3.5%	4.0%	4.5%	4.5%	4.5%	4.5%	4.5%
Capital conservation buffer						0.625%	1.25%	1.875%	2.5%
Common equity plus conservation buffer			3.5%	4.0%	4.5%	5.125%	5.750%	6.375%	7.0%
Phase-in deduction from Tier 1				20.0%	40.0%	60.0%	80.0%	100.0%	100.0%
Minimum Tier 1 capital			4.5%	5.5%	6.0%	6.0%	6.0%	6.0%	6.0%
Minimum total capital			8.0%	8.0%	8.0%	8.0%	8.0%	8.0%	8.0%
Total capital plus conservation buffer			8.0%	8.0%	8.0%	8.625%	9.250%	9.875%	10.50%
Liquidity coverage ratio	A				B				
Net stable funding ratio		A					B		

Notes: This table presents the implementation dates of Basel III and the changes to the calculation of capital. A: Observation period begins; B: Minimum standard introduced.
Source: Based on data from Basel Committee on Banking Supervision (2010) and Went (2010).

9.2 MARKET RISK REGULATION OF 1996

Two approaches can be used to comply with the regulation: the internal model approach and the standardized approach. The internal model approach is defined by the bank but monitored by the regulator. The second approach is both defined and monitored by the regulator.

The standardized approach is much more conservative than the internal model approach because it does not allow risk diversification. The capital amounts required for the different risks are calculated individually and added linearly without considering correlation between risks, which reduces the possibilities of diversification. However, some forms of "netting" (balancing between positions) are now permitted.

Regulators are fairly flexible about the types of transactions to include in the transaction book for calculations, but ask institutions to multiply their VaR by a factor of three for assessment purposes. This multiplier is a form of insurance for the use of internal models against nonperformance.

The model must be designed and managed by a risk management department (back office) that is independent of the traders. It must also be updated constantly.

Market risks are divided into four types:

1. Interest rate risk
2. Equity price or return risk based on a model of financial asset equilibrium
3. Exchange rate risk
4. Commodity price risk, mainly concerning raw materials

The VaR must be calculated at a confidence level of 99% with a 10-day horizon. During the initial phase, daily VaR can be used and multiplied by the square root of 10 to estimate the VaR over 10 days.

The principle is as follows: If the observations are independent and identically distributed over time, and if the parameters of the distributions are stable between periods, then the expected return on an asset can be calculated over 10 days based on daily expected returns. It is equal to 10 times the daily expected return. The same is true for the variance, which implies that a standard deviation over 10 days is 3.16 times the daily standard deviation $\left(\sqrt{10}\right)$. In other words, the expected return and variance increase linearly with time.

9.3 SPECIFIC RISKS

According to the regulation, specific (idiosyncratic) risks of stocks and bonds must be considered, and a capital amount must be used to support them.

Specific risks are due to variations in prices of stocks or bonds not foreseen by general market movements but explained by events specific to individual asset issuers.

Because not all these risks are considered by the traditional market models used to calculate them, the regulators require higher capital for the specific risk calculated by the banks' internal model. It is also easier for a bank to influence the specific risks of its portfolio through its choices of assets. In this case, regulation thus provides an incentive to reduce this risk.

For banks that use the internal model, the general formula for market risk can be the following, for example:

$$\text{capital for market risk} = 3\ (\overline{\text{VaR}}\ \text{general market risk}) + 4\ (\overline{\text{VaR}}\ \text{specific risk}),$$

hence the need to separate general market risk (or systematic risk) from the specific risk of financial assets (or idiosyncratic risk).

For bonds, readers are invited to consult the J.P. Morgan approach. Regarding stocks, their prices and returns incorporate general market risk and specific risk. To be able to separate these risks (in order to adequately weight them according to their respective effect), we can use the CAPM-type market equilibrium model or a more general financial markets equilibrium model. Alternatively, we can use a simple market index model like the one presented by Crouhy, Galai, and Mark (1998).

Consider asset *i*, whose return is linked to that of the market index I by a linear equation of the form:

$$R_i = \alpha_i + \beta_i I + \mu_i \tag{9.1}$$

where:

R_i is the rate of return of the asset *i*;
α_i is the component of the rate of return that is not explained by the index I;
I is the return of the index;
β_i is the marginal change in the rate of return of *i* following a unit variation of I;
μ_i is an error term that is assumed to be $N(0, \sigma_{\mu_i})$.

Two important hypotheses (underlying the ordinary least squares method) are used in this model: the error terms of the assets have zero covariances, and the covariance between I and μ_i is zero.

If we use historical data and the ordinary least squares method, we obtain:

$$\beta_i = \frac{\text{cov}(R_i, I)}{\text{Var}(I)}.$$

In addition, by taking the variance of both sides of equation (9.1), we obtain:

$$\sigma_i^2 = \beta_i^2\sigma_I^2 + \sigma_{\mu_i}^2.$$

The total risk can be divided into two components: $\beta_i^2\sigma_I^2$, which represents the systematic or non-diversifiable market risk, and $\sigma_{\mu_i}^2$, which characterizes the specific (idiosyncratic) risk that can be eliminated through diversification. However, $\sigma_{\mu_i}^2$ is generally not observable.

If we want to express these risks in value and if we use S_i as the value of a share *i*, we obtain:

$$GMR_i = S_i \times \beta_i \times \sigma_I$$

for the value of the General Market Risk, and:

$$SR_i = S_i\sqrt{\sigma_i^2 - \beta_i^2\sigma_I^2}$$

for the value of Specific Risk, where $\sigma_i^2 - \beta_i^2\sigma_I^2$ is used to obtain an approximation of $\sigma_{\mu_i}^2$.

Note that for a portfolio of *n* assets, the aggregated value of the general market risk is equal to:

$$GMR_p = \sum_{i=1}^{n} S_i\beta_i\sigma_I = \sum_{i=1}^{n} \frac{S_i}{P} \beta_i\sigma_I P = P\beta_p\sigma_I$$

where:

$$\beta_p = \sum_{i=1}^{n} \frac{S_i}{P} \beta_i$$

and P is the total value of the portfolio. The specific risk aggregate value is equal to:

$$SR_p = P\sum_{i=1}^{n} \sqrt{x_i^2\sigma_{\mu_i}^2} = P\sum_{i=1}^{n} \sqrt{x_i^2(\sigma_i^2 - \beta_i^2\sigma_I^2)}$$

where:

$$x_i = \frac{S_i}{P}.$$

9.4 TOTAL REQUIRED CAPITAL

Three capital tiers are permitted to create the capital reserve required under the regulation of 1996:

1. Tier 1: Core capital comprised of equity, holdings in subsidiaries, etc.
2. Tier 2: Perpetual debentures and subordinated debt of at least five years.
3. Tier 3: Short-term subordinated debt with a maturity of at least two years.

Tier 3 was added to the rules that took effect in 1996, when market risk was included in the calculation of the required capital. The use of Tier 3 capital is limited to market risk. Note that this tier was eliminated by Basel III.

To summarize, banks must take the following steps to form their capital reserve:

1. They must use Tier 1 and can use Tier 2 capital for credit risk and satisfy the ratio of 8% of risk-weighted assets. At least 50% of this capital must come from Tier 1.
2. They must then consider market risk included or not in the balance sheet by weighting it. However, sources of capital differ. The bank can now use capital from Tiers 1, 2, and 3.

Therefore, banks use Tier 1 capital only when necessary, then a maximum of Tier 2 capital while meeting the constraint that Tier 2 capital not exceed 50% of Tier 1 capital required for credit risk. For market risk, banks must set aside all of the

TABLE 9.3 Calculation of capital under the 1996 amendment.

Risk-weighted assets ($ billion)	Minimum capital charge (8%) ($ million)	Available capital ($ million)	Minimum capital for meeting requirement ($ million)	Eligible capital (excluding unused Tier 3) ($ million)	Unused but eligible Tier 3 ($ million)	Unused but not eligible Tier 3 ($ million)
Credit risk 7.500	600	Tier 1 700	Tier 1 500	Tier 1 700		
		Tier 2 100	Tier 2 100	Tier 2 100		
Market risk 4.375	350	Tier 3 600	Tier 1 100	Tier 3 250	Tier 3 250	Tier 3 100
(i.e. 350 × 12.5)			Tier 3 250			
				Capital ratio:	Excess Tier 3 capital ratio	
				1050/11,875 = 8.8%	250/11,875 = 2.1%	
Total 11.875	950	1,400	950	1,050	250	100

Source: Reproduced from Crouhy, Galai, and Mark (1998). © John Wiley & Sons, Inc. Reproduced with permission.

Tier 3 capital available. The sum of Tier 2 and 3 capital allotted to market risk must not exceed 250% of the amount of Tier 1 capital used for market risk.

An illustration shown in Table 9.3 supposes that the bank holds $7.5 billion in risky assets exposed to credit risk along with $4.375 billion in risky assets exposed to market risk. This implies required capital of $350 million for market risk and $600 million for credit risk.

The bank has set aside $700 million in Tier 1 capital, $100 million in Tier 2 capital, and $600 million in Tier 3 capital. Will it meet the required regulatory capital?

The detailed calculations are found in column 4 of Table 9.3. To comply with the global ratio of 8%, the bank needs $950 million (column 2), given that it holds invested assets equal to $11.875 billion.

To satisfy the need for capital of $600 million for credit risk, the bank can use $100 million of Tier 2 capital and $500 million of Tier 1 capital because it may not use Tier 3 capital (column 4) for this type of risk.

For the $350 million of market risk, it cannot use Tier 3 capital exclusively, because the sum of Tiers 2 and 3 for market risk must not exceed 250% of the sum of Tier 1 for market risk (column 4).

If we have $200 million of Tier 1 capital that can cover market risk, the maximum for Tier 3 is therefore $500 million. The bank should nonetheless conserve as much Tier 1 capital as possible. It will therefore use $100 million of Tier 1 and $250 million of Tier 3 to obtain the $350 million required. $100 million in eligible Tier 1 capital will remain, along with $250 million in eligible capital of the $350 million remaining in Tier 3. In fact, the additional \$100 million in Tier 3 capital is ineligible because, once again, Tiers 3 and 2 may not exceed 250% of the value of Tier 1 (column 5). Total eligible capital is 8.8%, which slightly exceeds the 8% required because the bank used \$100 million of the remaining Tier 1 capital, which represents a form of additional security. Some banks like to show that they have a moderate risk appetite and that they are more prudent than what the regulation requires.

9.5 TESTS

The use of VaR requires continuous tests because this statistical measure is very local and volatile (these tests became mandatory only after 1999).

The first kind of test is backtesting, which can validate the use of VaR. It compares, using historical data, the number of times that daily losses exceeded the maximum loss amount predicted by the VaR, and the number of times the VaR would have been exceeded in theory, according to the degree of confidence chosen $(1 - p)$. If the model is adequate and the market is stable, the absolute size of the amount observed should not exceed that of the VaR_p adjusted to the time horizon. For example, for a degree of confidence of 99%, the $VaR_{1\%}$ should be exceeded on average 2.5 times over a period of 250 days (1% of 250 days). Some regulations allow up to five overtakings to avoid overly penalizing the bank because a large k is costly (we will see this later on). If the VaR is exceeded too many times, the k multiplier of the VaR may reach 4.

The second kind of test is stress testing, which consists of verifying the robustness of the parameters used to calculate the VaR and of verifying the extent that the calculations vary following different extreme scenarios like those of the market crises of 1987, 1989, 1997, and 2007–2009, or political crises like that of the US budget in 2013.

9.6 COMPARISON BETWEEN STANDARD AND INTERNAL METHODS WITH INTEREST RATE RISK

9.6.1 Standard and Internal Methods

For this comparison, we will not discuss the detailed calculation of the internal method; they are obtained from VaR computation.

In this exercise, an AAA company has the same weight as a BB company because our application does not consider credit risk, apart from that of private counterparties of derivatives (not taken into account by Basel I). We thus assign a weight to different sources of market risk as Table 9.4 indicates for the standard approach and compare it with the VaR method.

The internal method can reduce the amount of required capital by the standard method in banks where portfolios are quite diversified. The two methods consider all forms of market risk associated with interest rates: fixed interest rate, variable interest rate, zero coupon, derivatives, swaps, options, and so on. They consider specific risk and general market risk simultaneously: specific risk integrates the net position of each instrument, and general market risk allows the use of netting of positions.

For capital allotted to specific risk, the rates in Table 9.4 are applied to the market value of securities. We do not insist on this calculation because it is not used to

TABLE 9.4 Specific risk for net debt positions.

Debt category	Remaining maturity	Capital charge %
OECD Government	—	0
OECD public services	6 months or less	0.25
G-10 Regulated firms	6 to 24 months	1.00
Qualifying instruments	over 2 years	1.60
Non-qualifying instruments	---	8.00

Source: Reproduced from Crouhy, Galai, and Mark (1998).

compare the two methods. This calculation of capital uses market value rather than notional value and is applied to net positions.

The portion of capital allotted to (systematic) general market risk takes into account interest rate fluctuations according to classic finance models. The capital required for interest rate risk is the amount needed to be protected against future rate fluctuations. The method retained in this example is the one concerning the maturity of securities, but Crouhy, Galai, and Mark (1998) mentioned that the approach by durations gives similar results.

The first step of the standard method of maturities is to identify maturity zones like those presented in Table 9.5. These zones take into account volatilities between different maturities to fix the core (or basic) capital needed. This first step in the evaluation is to allot market values to each maturity and make them comparable.

Derivatives are transformed into equivalent bonds on the balance sheet using two entries. For example, swaps derivatives should be converted into long positions

TABLE 9.5 Maturities and weights for market risk (core capital).

Zone	Coupon 3% or more	Coupon less than 3%	Capital charged (%)
1	1 month or less	1 month or less	0.00
	1 to 3 months	1 to 3 months	0.20
	3 to 6 months	3 to 6 months	0.40
	6 to 12 months	6 to 12 months	0.70
2	1 to 2 years	1 to 1.9 years	1.25
	2 to 3 years	1.9 to 2.8 years	1.75
	3 to 4 years	2.8 to 3.6 years	2.25
3	4 to 5 years	3.6 to 4.3 years	2.75
	5 to 7 years	4.3 to 5.7 years	3.25
	7 to 10 years	5.7 to 7.3 years	3.75
	10 to 15 years	7.3 to 9.3 years	4.50
	15 to 20 years	9.3 to 10.6 years	5.25
	over 20 years	10.6 to 12 years	6.00
		12 to 20 years	8.00
		over 20 years	12.50

Source: Reproduced from Crouhy, Galai, and Mark (1998).

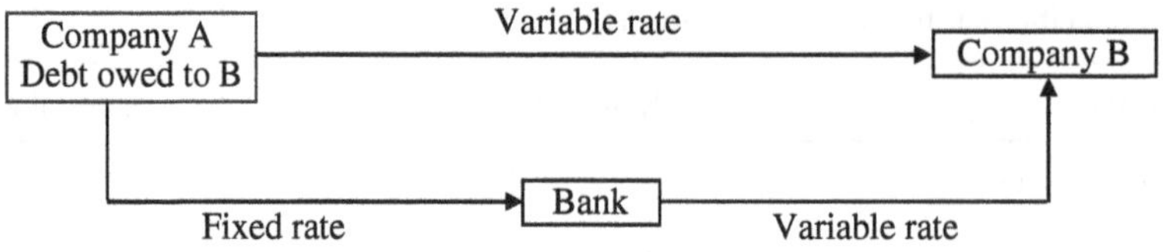

FIGURE 9.2 Standard interest rate swap contract
Company A transforms its variable-rate debt toward B into a fixed-rate debt toward the bank by using a swap with the bank. The bank receives the fixed rate from A and pays the variable rate to B. To calculate the regulated capital for the swap, the bank has a long position on the first asset and a short position on the second one.

or short positions in the underlying positions. In an interest rate swap,[4] a bank that receives the fixed portion will have a long position, in a manner similar to holding a bond with the maturity of a swap, and will have a short position over the short term for the variable portion. It will thus benefit from interest rate reductions. Figure 9.2 illustrates the standard interest rate swap contract where the bank receives the fix rate and pays the variable rate.

The second step consists of calculating the possibilities of diversification between zones. Table 9.6 shows the capital disallowances between zones. Suppose the bank has a long position of 100 million and a short position of 50 million, both in Zone 1 with a maturity of four months, where the capital charged without diversification is 0.40% for each position (Table 9.5). The capital charged for the diversification of the two positions will be 40% of 0.40% of 50 million. It will remain 0.40% of 50 million for the non-diversified position. For vertical diversification, only 10% of the capital of the diversified portion is charged. In step 3, the required capital is calculated.

Let us consider an example with four assets. The description of the four assets is in Table 9.7. The calculations of the capital amounts are presented in Table 9.8.

The positions taken on standard bonds A and B represent long positions for the bank. Holding these two bonds carries an interest rate risk resulting in a positive sign in Table 9.8. The maturity of the asset is used from Table 9.5 to measure the basic required capital.

Contract C is a swap whose maturity is fixed at eight years, in which the bank pays a fixed rate and receives a variable rate at each payment date. The next payment date is nine months later. Because it pays a fixed rate, it is considered a long-term (short) issuer and because it receives random interest, it is considered a short-term bond holder for this (long) portion. The intuitive idea for a swap is to use the fixed

[4]An interest rate swap is an arrangement among three parties who would benefit from trading. For example, the market maker, or intermediary, receives a fixed interest payment (predetermined fixed rate) of the first portion and pays an amount based on the market interest rate (variable rate) to a third party. In practice, an interest rate swap is negotiated between a market maker and two counterparties. One party may be a company that borrows at a variable rate and that anticipates that rates will increase. It may therefore be willing to pay the market maker a risk premium to swap its variable-rate contract for a fixed-rate contract. This arrangement may help companies manage market risk that may cause large liquidity risks if interest rates rise rapidly. The variable rate may be based on the LIBOR, which stands for the London Interbank Offered Rate.

TABLE 9.6 Capital calculation rates for disallowances between zones.

Zone	Time band	Within the Zone	Between adjacent zones	Between Zones 1 and 3
1	1 month or less			
	1 to 3 months	40%		
	3 to 6 months			
	6 to 12 months		40%	
2	1 to 2 years			
	2 to 3 years	30%		100%
	3 to 4 years			
3	4 to 5 years		40%	
	5 to 7 years			
	7 to 10 years			
	10 to 15 years	30%		
	15 to 20 years			
	over 20 years			

Source: Reproduced from Crouhy, Galai, and Mark (1998).

portion to determine whether a position is long or short. Receiving the fixed portion corresponds to holding a bond and vice versa. This contract is the mirror image of the example presented in Figure 9.2.

Security D is a futures contract on interest rates with delivery in six months (short position). The bond matures in 3.5 years. This is a long position with a long-term interest rate risk. The bank's short position is similar to that of issuing a bond.

Only A and C are vertically diversified (matched). For the vertical portion, the bank is charged 10% for diversified risk netting if applicable. It can therefore use the vertical risk weight of 10%, giving a total capital of $0.05 million for the diversified portion. This vertical basis risk is due to a natural hedging of $0.5 million between two instruments with the same maturity.

TABLE 9.7 Portfolios analyzed.

Portfolio	
A	Qualifying bond with a $13.3 million market value, a residual maturity of eight years, and a coupon of 8%. According to Table 9.5, the core capital required for general market risk is 3.75% of the market value.
B	Government bond with a market value of $75 million, a residual maturity of two months, and a coupon of 7%. Its core capital is 0.20% of $75 million.
C	Interest rate swap with a notional value of $150 million, where the bank receives the floating rate and pays the fixed rate, and where the next fixing is in nine months with a residual life of eight years.
D	A long position in an interest rate futures contract with a six-month delivery date, for which the underlying instrument is a government bond with a 3.5-year maturity and a market value of $50 million.

Source: Reproduced from Crouhy, Galai, and Mark (1998).

TABLE 9.8 Illustration of the calculation of general market interest rate risk capital for different assets.

Portfolio		Zone 1 (months)				Zone 2 (years)				Zone 3 (years)					
Coupon > 3%	0–1	1–3	3–6	6–12	1–2	2–3	3–4	4–5	5–7	7–10	10–15	15–20	> 20		
Coupon < 3%	0–1	1–3	3–6	6–12	1–1.9	1.9–2.8	2.8–3.6	3.6–4.3	4.3–5.7	5.7–7.3	7.3–9.3	9.3–10.6	10.6–12	12–20	> 20
A										+13,33 Bond					
B		+75 Gov.													
C				+150 Swap						−150 Swap					
D			−50 Fut.				+50 Fut.								
Weight (%)	0.00	0.20	0.40	0.70	1.25	1.75	2.25	2.75	3.25	3.75	4.50	5.25	6.00	8.00	12.5
Position × Weight		+0.15	−0.20	+1.05			+1.125			+0.5 −5.625					
Vertical diversification										0.5 × 10% = 0.05; −5.125 remaining in Zone 3					
Horizontal diversification 1	0.20 × 40% = 0.08; 1.0 remaining in Zone 1														
Horizontal diversification 2										1.125 × 40% = 0.45; −4.0 remaining in Zone 3					
Horizontal diversification 3					1.0 × 100% = 10; −3.0 remaining										

Source: Reproduced from Crouhy, Galai, and Mark (1998). © John Wiley & Sons, Inc. Reproduced with permission.

Now, we will examine the details of Table 9.8 for the horizontal portion of netting or additional diversification possibilities to reduce the required capital. In Zone 1, there are three positions. An absolute total of 0.20 is diversified, resulting in an amount of $0.08 million of capital. Diversification at a rate of 40% is possible for $1.125 million of capital between Zones 2 and 3, which equals to $0.45 million.

Diversification between Zones 1 and 3 gives $1 million and an unbalanced total gives $3 million (balance of the non-diversified capital of Zone 3), for a grand total of $4.580 million of capital required by the standard method for market risk (see recap in Table 9.9 for the calculation of the $4.580 million and the different interpretations of interest rate risks), whereas the total amount without diversification would be $8.5 million, namely the sum of the base amounts calculated before the possibility of diversification.

9.6.2 Comparison of the Two Methods

The comparison of the two methods shows that the internal method can help banks save considerable capital when portfolios are well diversified. We will look at the four portfolios in Table 9.10. Note that these examples do not include specific risk. The analysis is limited to general market risk; exchange rate risk is not addressed.

The calculation of capital according to the internal method is based on the VaR, and the calculation of the standard method for portfolio 1 is presented in Table 9.11. Table 9.13 compares the two methods. There is no credit risk on core products, but there is a counterparty risk on private derivatives not foreseen in Basel I. The computation details are not provided here; they are available in the study by Crouhy, Galai, and Mark (1998).

1. Calculation of capital required for portfolio 1

   The first portfolio contains a single asset: a 10-year US$100 million swap, for which the bank receives a fixed payment (long position) and is exposed to a Libor on which it pays a variable rate (short position).

TABLE 9.9 Total capital (in $ million).

Vertical diversification (basis risk)	0.050
Horizontal diversification in Zone 1 (curve risk)	0.080
Horizontal diversification between adjacent zones (curve risk)	0.450
Horizontal diversification between Zones 1 and 3 (steepening of the curve risk)	1.000
Capital for the overall net open position (parallel shift risk)	3.000
Total	4.580

Notes:

The total cost of capital, without considering diversification possibilities, is $8.65 million. Netting positions reduce this capital by about 47%.

Basis risk: Imperfect correspondence in the adjustment of rates received and paid on different products, including derivatives, may cause variance in cash flows.

Curve risk or butterfly: Change of zero coupon rate curves (1.5% of the market risk).

Steepening of the curve risk: Nonparallel movement of zero coupon rate curves (also known as twist of the curve) (8.5% of the market risk).

Parallel shift risk: Change in rate of returns associated with parallel shifts of zero coupon rate curve (90% of the market risk).

TABLE 9.10 Four portfolios of fixed-income instruments.

Portfolios	
1	An interest rate swap where the bank receives the fixed rate and pays the variable rate based on a three-month Libor. The core security has a market value of $100 million US and a maturity of 10 years. The counterparty is private and represents a credit risk.
2	Portfolio 1 plus an interest-rate swap with a five-year maturity on an asset of US$100 million, where the bank pays the fixed rate based on a three-month Libor. The counterparty is risky.
3	The bank has a long position on a US$100 million government bond with a semi-annual 6.5% coupon and a swap on another US$100 million bond, where the bank pays the fixed rate based on a three-month Libor. The bond and the swap have a 10-year maturity. The counterparty is risky.
4	The bank pays the fixed rate portion of a 10-year interest rate swap on a US$100 million bond on a three-month Libor. The counterparty is risky. It holds another 10-year swap for CAD$140 million and receives the fixed rate on a three-month Libor. The counterparty is risky.

Payments to the counterparty, here a private risky firm, are made on a quarterly basis. Similarly, we can calculate the differences for the four portfolios.

Table 9.11 indicates that there is no compensation between the assets (no netting or diversification because there is only one asset), only simple diversification between zones. The swap corresponds to high required capital: $3.75 million for a $100 million swap, whereas in the example in Table 9.8, the bank had to keep $4.5 million in capital for almost $300 million in assets, corresponding to approximately 1.5%.

The VaR of $927,000 represents the capital amount required by the internal method for portfolio 1 (Table 9.13). As we have seen, this amount must be multiplied by $\sqrt{10}$ for the 10-day VaR and by $k = 3$ to satisfy the requirements of the regulation.

Total capital is $8,854,294, whereas that obtained by the standard method is $3,810,000. The internal model approach requires 132% more than the standard method.

2. Calculation of capital required for portfolio 2

   The second portfolio consists of the first portfolio plus a five-year US$100 million swap for which the bank pays a fixed interest rate for a three-month Libor on which it receives variable rate payments. In both cases, the counterparty is a private risky firm. This portfolio is more diversified than the first one, and the capital required by the standard method declines accordingly from $3.75 million to $1.845 million (see Table 9.12 for the details).

   Table 9.13 indicates that the difference in required capital between the two methods decreases with portfolio 2, which is more diversified than portfolio 1.

3. Calculation of capital required for portfolio 3

   The third portfolio consists of US$100 million in a government bond with semi-annual coupons of 6.5% and a 10-year US$100 million swap for which the bank pays a fixed interest rate for a three-month Libor on which it receives variable-rate payments. The counterparty is a private risky firm.

TABLE 9.11 Standardized approach of portfolio 1 of Table 9.10.

Portfolio 1	Zone 1 (months)				Zone 2 (years)			Zone 3 (years)							
Coupon > 3%	0–1	1–3	3–6	6–12	1–2	2–3	3–4	4–5	5–7	7–10	10–15	15–20	> 20		
Coupon < 3%	0–1	1–3	3–6	6–12	1–1.9	1.9–2.8	2.8–3.6	3.6–4.3	4.3–5.7	5.7–7.3	7.3–9.3	9,3–10,6	10,6–-12	12–20	> 20
10-year swap, fixed receiver		(100)								100					
$US															
Weight (%)	0.00	0.20	0.40	0.70	1.25	1.75	2.25	2.75	3.25	3.75	4.50	5.25	6.00	8.00	12.5
Position × Weight															
Long position										3.75					
Short position		(0.20)													
Vertical disallowance = 0															
Horizontal disallowance 1		0 × 40% = 0				0 × 30% = 0					0 × 30% = 0				
Horizontal disallowance 2						0 × 40% = 0					0 × 40% = 0				
Horizontal disallowance 3									0.2 × 100% = 0.20						
Total net position									3.55 × 100% = 3.55						
				Total capital charge for general market risk = 3,75											

Source: Reproduced from Crouhy, Galai, and Mark (1998). © John Wiley & Sons, Inc. Reproduced with permission.

TABLE 9.12 Standardized approach of portfolio 2 of Table 9.10.

Portfolio 2	Zone 1 (months)				Zone 2 (years)			Zone 3 (years)							
Coupon > 3%	0–1	1–3	3–6	6–12	1–2	2–3	3–4	4–5	5–7	7–10	10–15	15–20	> 20		
Coupon < 3%	0–1	1–3	3–6	6–12	1–1.9	1.9–2.8	2.8–3.6	3.6–4.3	4.3–5.7	5.7–7.3	7.3–9.3	9.3–10.6	10.6–12	12–20	> 20
Positions															
A		(100)								100					
B		100						(100)							
Weight (%)	0.00	0.20	0.40	0.70	1.25	1.75	2.25	2.75	3.25	3.75	4.50	5.25	6.00	8.00	12.5
Position × Weight															
Long position		0.20								3.75					
Short position		(0.20)						(2.75)							
Vertical disallowance		0.20 × 10% = 0.02													
Horizontal disallowance		0 × 40% = 0				0 × 30% = 0					2.75 × 30% = 0.825				
Horizontal disallowance						0 × 40% = 0					0 × 40% = 0				
Horizontal disallowance									0 × 100% = 0						
Total net position									1 × 100% = 1						
Total capital charge for general market risk = 1.845															

Source: Reproduced from Crouhy, Galai, and Mark (1998). © John Wiley & Sons, Inc. Reproduced with permission.

TABLE 9.13 Comparison of the internal model and the standardized approach: capital required from portfolios 1, 2, 3, 4.

		Portfolio 1 ($US)	Portfolio 2 ($US)	Portfolio 3 ($US)	Portfolio 4 ($US)
Internal model					
(1) VaR	=	927,000	407,532	19,068	970,333
(2) General market risk: $3 \times \text{Var} \times \sqrt{10}$	=	8,794,294	3,866,188	180,898	9,205,390
(3) Counterparty risk[1] (1988 Basel Accord)	=	60,000	120,000	60,000	166,800
Required capital: (2) + (3)	=	8,854,294	3,986,188	240,898	9,372,190
Standard approach					
(4) General market risk	=	3,750,000	1,845,000	575,000	10,425,000
(5) Counterparty risk[1] (1988 Basel Accord)	=	60,000	120,000	60,000	166,800
Required capital: (4) + (5)	=	3,810,000	1,965,000	635,000	10,591,800
Capital variation[2]	=	132%	103%	(62%)	(11.5%)

[1]Calculation of capital required for counterparty risk: This capital was necessary before 2004 because it could not be calculated in the model used to calculate capital for credit risk under Basel I. The details can be found in the article by Crouhy, Galai, and Mark (1998).
[2]Variation in capital if banks adopt the internal model approach instead of the standardized approach. The more diversified the portfolio, the more profitable the internal model approach.
Source: Reproduced from Crouhy, Galai, and Mark (1998). © John Wiley & Sons, Inc. Reproduced with permission.

Build your own table. In the 7–10 years column you will have two entries for two maturities: a positive entry of \$100 million for the bond and a negative entry for the swap. There is a vertical counterparty here for the bond, which implies that the required capital may be calculated at 10% for the rate risk, which equals \$100 million × 3.75% × 10% = \$375,000.

Regarding the zone disallowances (Table 9.6), in Zone 3 the amounts cancel each other out. There is 0.20 of \$100 million remaining × 1 = \$200,000. The standard method gives \$575,000 for market risk, plus \$60,000 for counterparty risk, equal to \$635,000, whereas the internal method gives \$240,898, equal to 62% of the preceding amount. In Table 9.13, we notice that the internal method effectively gives lower required capital because the portfolio is better diversified.

4. Calculation of required capital for portfolio 4

   Table 9.13 also compares the calculations for portfolio 4, where the internal method reduces the required capital, but by a smaller amount than for portfolio 3.

9.7 CONCLUSION

The internal method lets banks limit their required capital by holding well diversified portfolios and having good teams of risk management analysts. However, the internal method must be approved and monitored by regulators and must provide continuous updates.

The calculations of capital in the four cases analyzed demonstrate that good portfolio diversification is crucial to reduce regulatory capital. The calculations also show that the internal method considers portfolio diversification more effectively. The more diversified the portfolios, the less capital the internal method requires, and the more advantageous the method is relative to the standard method, which rewards diversification to a lesser extent. We thus observed that for portfolio 3, which is the most diversified, the internal method allows banks to reduce the required capital by 62% compared with the standard method. An interesting extension of the discussion would be to apply the different cases by using CVaR instead of VaR.

REFERENCES

Angelini, P., Clerc, L., Curdia, V., Gambacorta, L., Gerali, A., Locarno, A., Motto, R., Roeger, W., van den Heuvel S., and Vlček, J., 2011. "Basel III: Long-Term Impact on Economic Performance and Fluctuations." BIS Working Papers No. 338.

Bank for International Settlements, 2006. "International Convergence of Capital Measurement and Capital Standards." https://www.bis.org/publ/bcbs128.pdf.

Bank for International Settlements, 2016. "Minimum Capital Requirement for Market Risk." https://www.bis.org/bcbs/publ/d352.pdf.

Basel Committee on Banking Supervision, 2010. "Basel III: A Global Regulatory Framework for More Resilient Banks and Banking Systems." https://www.bis.org/publ/bcbs/189.pdf.

Crouhy, M., Galai, D., and Mark, R., 1998. "The New 1998 Regulatory Framework for Capital Adequacy: 'Standardized Approach' versus 'Internal Model.'" In: C. Alexander (Ed.), *Risk Management and Analysis*, Vol. 1, *Measuring and Modelling Financial Risk*. New York: John Wiley.

Jorion, P., 2001. *Value at Risk*. New York: McGraw-Hill, chap. 3.

Went, P., 2010. "Basel III Accord: Where Do We Go from Here?" Jersey City, NJ: GARP Research Center.

CHAPTER 10

Optimal Financial Contracts and Incentives under Moral Hazard

Up to now, we have focused on the analysis of managers' actions that can reduce the dispersion of distributions of random variables.[1] These actions, which affect the volatility of results, are called second-order actions because they affect only the moments of distributions greater than one, which are mainly limited to variance.

The means of distributions are notably affected by risk management actions that introduce first-order variations of distributions (Courbage, Rey, and Treich, 2013; Winter, 2013). They are generally associated with loss prevention, self-protection, precaution, or efforts to obtain higher profits or lower losses. Many of these actions do not involve the use of financial instruments.

Obviously, entrepreneurs who finance 100% of a project have very strong incentives to maximize the expected profits and to reduce the default probability. In contrast, when a project is financed by third parties with partial guarantees, incentives may be weaker, particularly when the managers' actions are not perfectly observable by creditors. This incentive problem is called ex ante moral hazard. Moral hazard is present when the prevention actions of one party (business, individual, worker, or agent) are not observable by another party associated with the risks of a contract (bank, insurance company, employer, or principal), but may suffer the financial consequences associated with these risks. Moral hazard is often present in debt contracts, insurance contracts, and in the relationship between the board of a company and the officers. Moral hazard was present in securitization activities of banks before and during the financial crisis because banks had no incentives to monitor the credit risk of loans, particularly that of mortgage subprime loans (Dionne and Malekan, 2017; Dionne and Harchaoui, 2008; Malekan and Dionne, 2014; Keys et al, 2009, 2010; Keys, Seru, and Vig, 2012; Bubb and Kaufman, 2014).

In investment projects, the entrepreneur's action or effort may move the revenue frequency g(R) to the right, or the revenue distribution function G(R) downward. As Figures 10.1 and 10.2 illustrate, the agent increases the expected value of revenues by exerting more effort, which can be represented by e_2 instead of e_1.

The lender's problem is to write a loan contract that maximizes the entrepreneur's incentive to make the greatest effort. This is because if the project or the business fails, both parties will lose.

[1]The research in this chapter has been done with Robert Gagné, François Gagnon, and Charles Vanasse.

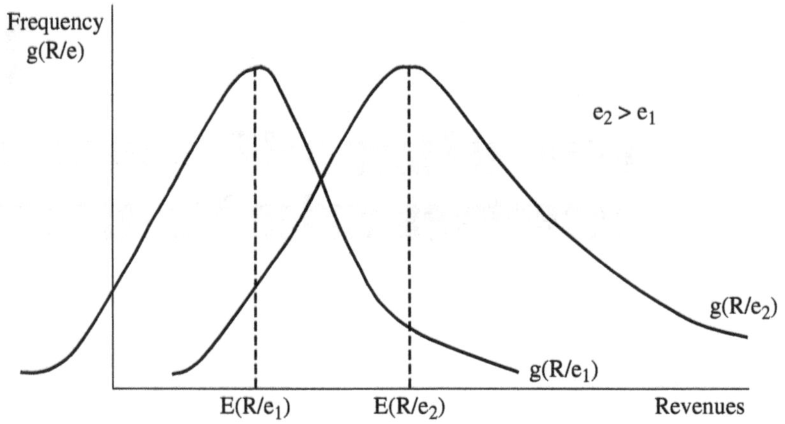

FIGURE 10.1 Movement of revenue frequency to the right by making more effort (e) to obtain higher expected revenues E(R/e) conditional on higher effort.

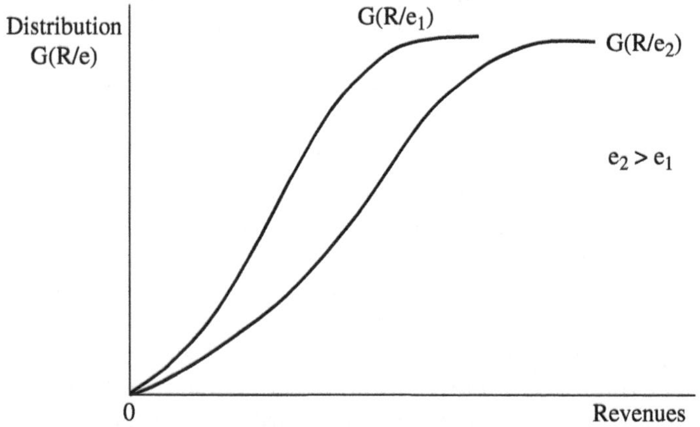

FIGURE 10.2 Downward movement of the revenue distribution function by making more effort (e).

We are not addressing the question of collateral although it is very important. In general, for commercial loans, the collateral requested may reach a large percentage of the loan amount. It is clear that when the collateral is 100%, the problem of incentives no longer arises. But incentives are generally less than those under full information with a lower collateral under moral hazard.

10.1 OPTIMAL FINANCIAL CONTRACTS AND MORAL HAZARD

Suppose that the stakeholders are risk neutral. We are interested in financial contracts in the presence of information asymmetry. The agent (borrower) may influence the result of the project by actions that cannot be observed by the principal (lender). A more detailed description of the contracts studied is presented in Appendix A.

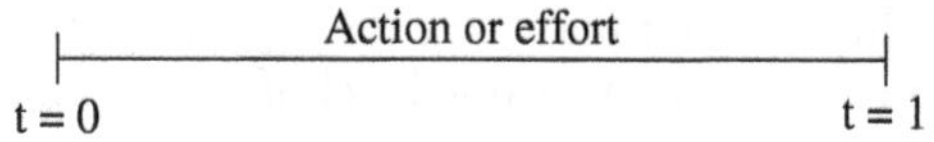

FIGURE 10.3 Sequence of a loan contract.

Here, we are interested in the action of the better informed party (agent). This action is not observable by the other contracting party (principal), but affects its revenues nonetheless.

Let us first define the two forms of moral hazard currently observed in the literature:

1. Ex ante: The action (prevention) is done before the realization of the random variable (here the project revenues) but after the signing of the contract.
2. Ex post: The action (reporting of realized revenues) is done after the realization of the random variable.

We can illustrate the sequence of a loan contract as in Figure 10.3:

The contract between the principal (bank) and the agent (entrepreneur) is signed at t = 0, and the realization of the random variable (profits of the project, for example) takes place on date t = 1. During the interim period, the agent may exert an effort that the principal cannot observe. This is a situation of ex ante moral hazard. Ex post moral hazard occurs after t = 1 and is explained by the fact that the principal does not observe the realization of the random variable. We now describe three types of contracts explained by moral hazard.

Case 1: The results of the investment or profits are perfectly observable by the creditor, but the action is not observable.

This first case implies that audit costs are zero: the entrepreneur must be transparent about the profits realized, and the only persistent information problem is that of ex ante incentives (that is, before the realization of the profits from the project) related to actions affecting the distribution of profits.

In this case, the optimal contract is a Live or Die contract (Innes, 1990) as illustrated in Figure 10.4. The entrepreneur keeps all the profits above a certain threshold (R^*), otherwise he keeps none of the profits. In general, the R^* threshold is higher than F, the face value of a standard debt contract.

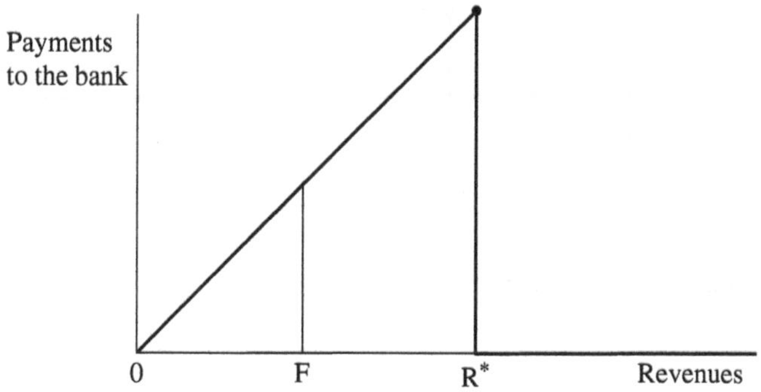

FIGURE 10.4 Live or Die contract.

We can show that this contract may have the same incentive properties as equity: that is, the entrepreneur will exert the same level of effort under certain conditions:

$$e^0 < e^* \leq e^i$$

where:

e^0 is the nonoptimal effort of a contract with moral hazard;
e^* is the optimal effort of a Live or Die financial contract with moral hazard;
e^i is the optimal effort in the presence of perfect information. Here, the principal observes the effort and offers the agent the following contract: the parties sign an optimal financial contract in which the observable level of effort e^i is specified. If this level is met by the agent, the contract will be executed until its maturity; otherwise it will be canceled. This contract is often labeled as Take It or Leave It!

Intuitively, the agent has a strong incentive to exert great effort under the Live or Die contract, because it will retain all the profits or revenues if the revenue realized is to the right of R^*. In other words, the entrepreneur is motivated to move the revenue density g(R/e) as far to the right as possible to increase the probability of retaining all revenues.

However, this type of contract is rare in practice because it would be very costly to audit if R is not observable. The bank would have to audit all reported *R* except R^*. Otherwise, the agent would say that revenues are low on the 45° line, or at 0, or to the right of R^*.

Case 2: Effort is perfectly observable, but the results are not.

The optimal contract is that of standard debt or financing by standard bonds. The objective is to minimize the audit costs, as shown by Gale and Hellwig (1985) (Figure 10.5).

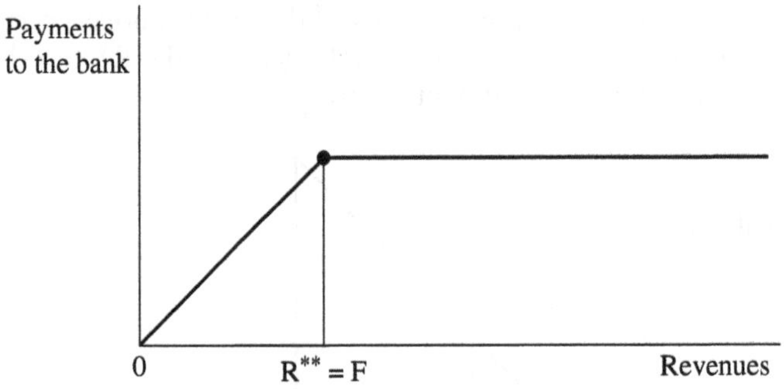

FIGURE 10.5 Standard debt contract.

The standard debt contract motivates agents to tell the truth about the realization of project revenues R, even if such revenues are not observable by the bank. When the revenue realized is to the right of F, the face value of the debt, the agent has no reason to hide anything because the payment to the bank is not a function of the agent's reporting. The debtholder pays F, whatever the value of R ≥ F. The bank therefore does not need to audit R in this revenue zone because it receives F for all R ≥ F. If the agent tells the bank that (because it is not able to pay F) R < F, the bank will put the debtholder in default and audit it. In this case, the audit will be necessary because the payment to the bank increases with R; in the absence of an audit, the agent would say that it defaulted and that its R is equal to zero or very low on the 45° line. The principle of limited liability is represented by the 45° line to the left of F. This is because the bank cannot take more than what the debtholder owns at the time of default. Each point on the 45° line may be interpreted as a recovery by the bank at the time of default.

This contract generates less effort than the Live or Die contract when effort is not observable. Notably, the agent begins to receive revenues at $R^{**} < R^{*}$, which provides a lesser incentive to move the revenue frequency to the right. In addition, the agent never can keep all the revenue from the project. The moral hazard generated by this contract thus makes it less efficient than the Live or Die contract ex ante, $e^{**} < e^{*}$, but more efficient ex post, by allowing a minimization of the audit costs because only the points to the left of F will be audited.

Case 3: Neither the action nor the results are perfectly observable.

There is an intermediate contract between the standard debt and Live or Die, called the Plateau (Figure 10.6; Dionne and Viala, 1992, 1994). This contract generates fewer incentives than the Live or Die or equity financing, but more effort than the standard debt contract, because a very efficient agent (to the right of R^{****} in Figure 10.6) can still retain all the revenues from the project. It is less costly to audit than the Live or Die contract because the bank does not have to audit the revenues between R^{***} and R^{****}. This contract is similar to the standard debt contract when the audit costs are very high (Figure 10.5). The optimal effort of this contract is e^{***} with:

$$e^{**} \leq e^{***} < e^{*}$$

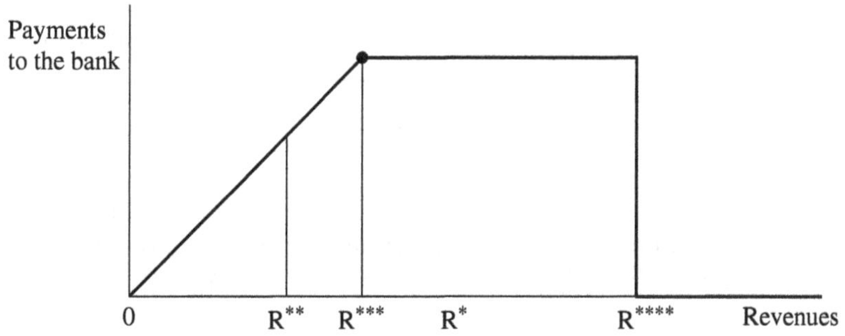

FIGURE 10.6 Plateau contract.

where:

e^* is the effort corresponding to the Live or Die contract (Figure 10.4);
e^{**} is the effort corresponding to the standard debt contract (Figure 10.5);
e^{***} is the effort corresponding to the Plateau contract (Figure 10.6).

We can thus understand why the standard debt contract is used so often, along with financing by standard bonds, whose structure is similar to that of standard debt. The high costs of auditing revenues seem to be the main cause. However, this contract may not provide very strong incentives to make an effort.

Froot, Scharfstein, and Stein (1993) mentioned that two forms of imperfections may create concave profit functions and justify financial risk management: (1) cost of external financing by debt; (2) and the convex tax structure. Here, the nature of financial contracts affects incentives to be prudent or to undertake risk management and a first-order effect is observed.

An empirical question is whether the negative effects of standard debt on incentives are important. Dionne et al (1997) propose an empirical test of air accidents to determine how significant ex ante moral hazard is: Do airlines that carry more debt perform less efficiently in prevention and have more accidents? In the case of airlines, purchases and rentals of new aircraft are financed either by bonds or by standard debt, as are investments in prevention.

10.2 THEORETICAL MODEL

We will now examine whether debt can have significant negative effects on prevention. In other words, does the debt/equity ratio explain the firms' results (specifically the number of air accidents)? We will analyze whether a higher debt-equity ratio reduces incentives to make an effort. Before performing the empirical application, we will present a theoretical model of optimal investment behavior in the presence of standard debt and moral hazard (Brander and Spencer, 1989). In this contribution, the form of the standard debt contract is set exogenously.

We have a business that must finance an investment project with a value of I by debt (bank loan or bonds) D and equity E. We can therefore write:

$$I = D + E.$$

The letter F designates the face value of the debt. In a competitive market, F solves the constraint of zero profits of the bank according to the following formula:

$$D(1+i) = \int_0^{z*} R(I, z)\ g(z/e)\,dz + F(1 - G(z^*/e)) - CG(z^*/e),$$

where i is the risk-free interest rate and z a random variable affecting revenues. The left side of the constraint is the bank's opportunity cost, where the bank places the amount D in Treasury bills that yield a return i. The right side of the constraint represents the bank's net expected revenues linked to the loan. The bank thus extends a loan to the entrepreneur who wants to carry out the project I only if the anticipated net revenues from the project (right side of the equation) are as high as $D(1+i)$.

R(I, z) represents the revenue from the project net of current costs; it is a random variable because *z* is a random variable. Here, *z* positively affects R and can be interpreted as the level of demand for the firm's good. The business cannot perfectly control *z* but can influence its mean by the effort *e*, which is the quality of the good or service that the company wants to produce. C represents the audit costs of the bank at the time of default.

G(z/e) is the distribution function of *z*; this distribution is a function of the effort or the action *e* with $G'_e < 0$ for all *z* (as in Figure 10.2); g(z/e) is the corresponding density function. Here, producing more effort increases the mathematical expectation for the level of sales of the product and moves *z*'s density function to the right (along with that of revenues, as in Figure 10.1).

At the lender's equilibrium, its economic profits are zero. In addition, there is a z^* such that for all $z > z^*$, the entrepreneur can repay the creditors. Otherwise, the company defaults. In other words, the face value of the debt $F = R(I, z^*)$. If R(I, z) is greater than F, the company can repay its debt or F and if R(I, z) is less than F, the company will default. This contract is illustrated in Figure 10.7.

If the default probability is zero, $z^* = 0$ and $G(0/e) = 0$. This enables us to verify that $D(1 + i) = F$ because the first term to the right of the bank's profit equation is equal to zero. The same applies to the last term because $G(0/e) = 0$ and $(1 - G(0/e)) = 1$.

In other words, $D(1 + i) < F$ when the default probability is positive because F takes the risk of default and the corresponding audit costs into account. Therefore, under uncertainty, the firm repays F. This amount is higher than the amount of capitalized debt (namely D(1 + i)) at the end of the period when the firm is not in default. The firm repays R(I, z) in the situations corresponding to a default. $R(I, z) < F$ can be interpreted as the debt recovery by the bank at the time of default. The more the company uses debt to finance its project, the higher the face value. The inverse is true for financing a project with equity.

We can demonstrate that:

$$dF/dD > 0 \text{ et } dF/dE < 0.$$

By taking the total derivative of the bank's zero-profit equation, we obtain:

$$dF/dD = (1 + i)/(1 - G(z^*/e)) > 0.$$

Because dD = –dE, this also completes the demonstration for dF/dE.

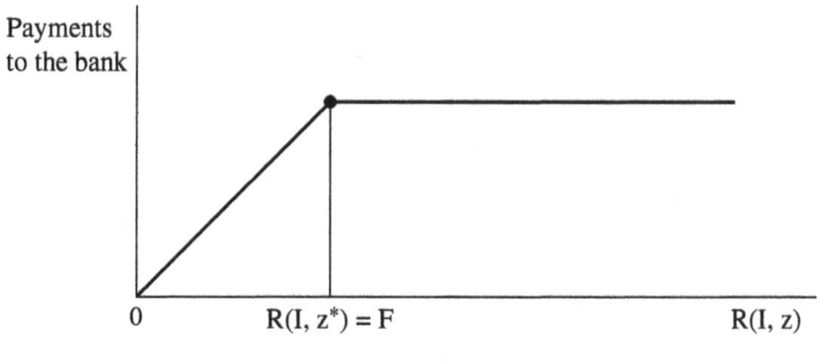

FIGURE 10.7 Optimal debt contract.

We will now look at the entrepreneur's optimal effort, namely the variable e*. As mentioned above, more effort or prevention actions move the density function of revenue, net of current costs, to the right, or increases the mathematical expectation of net income.

We can write the net revenue function of the entrepreneur's project as:

$$\int_{z*}^{\infty} (R(I,z) - F)\, g(z/e)\, dz - V(E) - c(e) \qquad (10.1)$$

where the first term is what the entrepreneur retains or the portion of the revenues net of F that goes to the bank; c(e)is the cost of the effort and V(E) the opportunity cost of equity. This opportunity cost is not limited to E(1 + i). It takes into account the default probability and the effect of E on the reduction of the default probability as well as the default costs. Therefore, the marginal cost V′(E) is equal to:[2]

$$V'(E) = (1 + i)\, G(z/e)/H > 0$$

where:

$$0 < H = G(z^*/e) + \overset{<0}{\frac{de}{dD}} \int_{0}^{z*} \underset{>0}{R(I,z)\, g_e(z/e)\, dz} < G(z^*/e) < 1.$$

H is positive and, in general, V′(E) ≠ (1 + i). When the default probability is less than 1, z* < ∞. In the presence of moral hazard, de/dD < 0, V′(E) > (1 + i), and the shareholders prefer to use more debt to finance the project. The entrepreneur's *payoff* function is shown in Figure 10.8. When R(I, z) > F, the firm retains R(I, z) − F, and when R(I, z) ≤ F, it is in default and receives nothing.

The optimal choice for the level of action is the solution to:

$$\underset{e}{\text{Max}}(10.1)$$

with, as a first-order condition:

$$\int_{z*}^{\infty} (R(I,z) - F)\, g_e(z/e) dz - c'(e) = 0, \qquad (10.2)$$

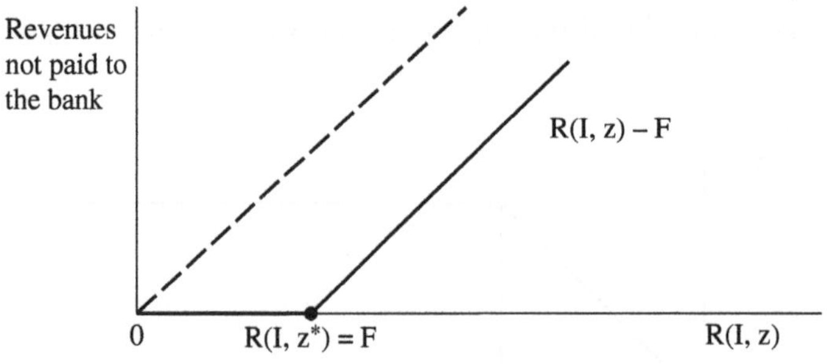

FIGURE 10.8 Entrepreneur's payoff function.

[2]See Brander and Spencer (1989) for more details.

where the marginal revenue from the effort equals its marginal cost. Marginal revenue is associated with the profits from moving the density function g(z/e) to the right.

Let e^* be the solution to this problem. It is important to determine how an increase in indebtedness or a decrease in equity will affect this choice. By differentiation of (10.2), we can show that de^*/dF is negative, an intuitive result considering that an increase in F decreases the share of earnings that goes to the entrepreneur. This is the effect of ex ante moral hazard. Similarly, we can show that de^*/dI is positive under certain conditions: increasing the investment enhances the productivity of the effort, and consequently the effort itself. We call this the investment effect.

We can therefore write e^* as a function of I and of F:

$$e^* = h(I, F) \text{ with } dh/dI > 0 \text{ and } dh/dF < 0.$$

We also know that:

$$I = D + E \text{ and } F(D, E).$$

By substitution, we obtain:

$$e^* = h(D + E, F(D, E)).$$

We can verify that the increased use of equity to finance the project increases the entrepreneur's optimal effort for a given D:

$$de^*/dE = \underset{>0}{dh/dI} + \underset{<0}{dh/dF} \times \underset{<0}{dF/dE} > 0.$$

Increasing equity increases I and the efficiency of the effort at first. This is the effect of I on the productivity of effort. In addition, increasing E decreases F for a given size of project I and increases *e* because F has a negative effect on *e*.

Now, if we increase the debt financing for a given E:

$$de^*/dD = \underset{>0}{dh/dI} + \underset{<0}{dh/dF} \times \underset{>0}{dF/dD}?$$

Initially, increasing the debt increases I and the effort. However, increasing D raises F and reduces the effort. The total effect is therefore ambiguous. As a result, de/d(D/E) (debt/equity ratio) is also ambiguous for businesses in good financial health: that is, those that use external financing for investment projects.

Further, for businesses in financial difficulty that must substitute debt for equity to survive (using debt to pay current expenses), we observe that an increase in debt undeniably reduces effort because, in this case, there is no possible investment effect.

Therefore, from the zero-profit constraint of the bank, we obtain, if $dI = 0$:

$$dF/dD - dF/dE = (1 + i)/H$$

and

$$de/dD - de/dE = dh/dF(dF/dD - dF/dE)$$

or

$$de/dD - de/dE = dh/dF \times (1 + i)/H < 0,$$

because we have already seen that $H > 0$.

The use of debt to finance current expenses provides a lesser incentive to produce effort than for businesses that use debt to finance their investments and even a lesser incentive than for enterprise that use equity.

10.3 EMPIRICAL APPLICATION TO AIR ACCIDENT RISK

In the application to air accidents, the number of accidents during the project is represented by z; z now has a negative effect on R, and there is one z^* such that for all $z > z^*$, $R(I, z^*) < F$, and the enterprise defaults.

In addition, more effort or prevention reduces the mathematical expectation of the number of accidents; more effort can move the accident distribution function upward, or the density function to the left.

Figure 10.9 summarizes the theoretical predictions regarding accident distribution made by the model from the previous section (where more accidents represent less effort).

The right-hand portion of Figure 10.9 corresponds to businesses in good financial health: that is, those with a ratio of $D/E > 0$, where E is book equity since many airlines in the empirical study were not public firms. Note that we suppose that book equity can be negative, which generally corresponds to cumulative losses, as in the left-hand section. The right-hand section of the figure indicates that a higher D/E is associated with higher prevention efficiency (fewer accidents) via the investment effect and less prevention via the moral hazard effect. The dominant effect will be empirically tested with the data. The left-hand portion illustrates similar relations: a more negative D/E introduces more accidents (moral hazard) and much less investment effect.

Here are the characteristics of a Canadian airline that had a terrible accident in the Middle East:

- Chartered medium airline operating with seven rented airplanes.
- Accident with 261 fatalities, including all crew members.

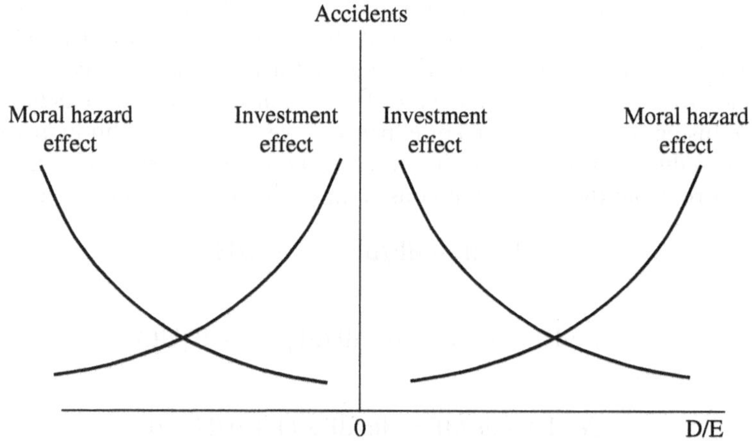

FIGURE 10.9 Predictions of the theoretical model.

- Negligence in the hours preceding the accident, determined by the regulatory authorities. Necessary maintenance was not done on the airplane tires, despite several requests by the maintenance manager. The accident was caused by a punctured tire during takeoff, which ignited all tires of the landing gear.
- The business failed about two years after the accident because it could no longer afford to procure insurance.

The study by Dionne et al (1997) found that the debt/equity ratio is a significant variable to explain the distribution of air accidents, particularly for businesses in financial difficulty. We will now examine this study in closer detail.

The database was developed in cooperation with Transport Canada, Statistics Canada, and the Transportation Safety Board of Canada. The authors had data on all Canadian carriers in levels 1, 2, and 3, from 1976 to 1987, corresponding to about 120 companies. Data are quarterly, for a total of over 5,000 observations. Table 10.1 presents the variables used and gives their predicted effect on the accident distribution. Model 2 in Table 10.2 gives the complete estimation results. We will interpret this model. Appendix B provides the detailed description of the variables.

TABLE 10.1 Means and standard deviations.

		3,116 observations		2,157 observations	
Variables	Effect predicted	Mean	Standard deviation	Mean	Standard deviation
NACC (number of accidents)		0.1091	0.3524	0.1043	0.3470
HOURS (flight hours)	+	3,747.89	10,828.32	4,367.71	12,341.67
NORTH (northern region of Canada)	+	0.3110	0.4630	0.3227	0.4676
SPEED (airplane speed)	–	293.65	140.43	301.85	145.85
SMALL (small business)	?	0.8569	0.3503	0.8359	0.3705
TIME (evolution over time)	–	7.819	3.475	8.166	3.300
ME (maintenance expenses)	–	505.46	1,263.28	503.63	1,168.58
OMARG (profit margin)	–	–0.0190	0.4326	–0.0113	0.4094
LOMARG (lag profit margin)	–	–	–	–0.0098	0.4070
DERATIOP[a] (positive D/E)	?	2.832	5.642	2.784	5.652
DERATION[b] (negative D/E)	?	–6.235	7.685	–6.733	7.813
LMDEP (lag mean positive D/E)	?	–	–	3.014	8.053
LMDEN (lag mean negative D/E)	?	–	–	–8.660	15.760
DUM (dummy variable)	+	0.1402	0.3473	0.1349	0.3417
DUMLMDE (DUM lag mean D/E)	+	–	–	0.1280	0.3341
WC (working capital)	–	–0.0328	0.2201	–0.0298	0.2086
LMWC (lag mean working capital)	–	–	–	–0.0383	0.1916

Note:

[a] Calculations based on the fact that book equity is negative or positive.

[b] Calculations based on observations for which the average book equity of the preceding four quarters is negative (LMDEN) or positive (LMDEP).

TABLE 10.2 Maximum likelihood estimates of Poisson regression coefficients (asymptotic *t*-ratios in parentheses).

Variables	Model 1		Model 2	
INTERCEPT	−0.9226	(−2.35)	−1.2017	(−2.25)
HOURS (flight hours)	0.25E-4	(4.86)	0.28E-4	(4.59)
SPEED (airplane speed)	−0.37E-2	(−5.46)	−0.35E-2	(−4.00)
TIME (evolution over time)	−0.0919	(−6.04)	−0.0860	(−4.30)
NORTH (northern region of Canada)	0.7965	(6.91)	0.7556	(5.24)
SMALL (small business)	0.0528	(0.18)	0.3356	(0.82)
ME-S[a] (maintenance expenses)	−0.54E-3	(−2.46)	−0.48E-3	(−2.01)
ME-B (maintenance expenses)	0.17E-3	(1.55)	0.15E-3	(0.96)
OMARG-S (profit margin)	0.6373	(3.31)	0.5943	(2.51)
OMARG-B (profit margin)	−0.1858	(−0.15)	0.4813	(0.28)
LOMARG-S (lag profit margin)			−0.1675	(−1.28)
LOMARG-B (lag profit margin)			−0.3547	(−0.20)
DERATION (negative D/E)	−0.0155	(−0.74)	0.0136	(0.40)
DERATIOP-S positive D/E for S)	−0.0333	(−1.71)	−0.0561	(−1.96)
DERATIOP-B (positive D/E for B)	−0.0154	(−0.57)	−0.0094	(−0.12)
LMDEN (lag mean negative D/E)			−0.0279	(−3.90)
LMDEP-S (lag mean positive D/E)			0.0018	(0.13)
LMDEP-B (lag mean positive D/E)			−0.0257	(−0.38)
DUM (dummy variable)	−0.1311	(−0.62)	−0.0197	(−0.40)
DUMLMDE (DUM lag mean D/E)			−0.7196	(−1.58)
WC-S (working capital)	−0.0767	(−0.27)	0.1756	(0.27)
WC-B (working capital)	0.7369	(0.54)	2.5574	(1.14)
LMWC-S (lag mean working capital)			−0.4530	(−0.65)
LMWC-B (lag mean working capital)			−3.2145	(−1.29)
Log likelihood	−1,017.98		−682.61	
No. observations	3,116		2,157	
χ^2 of fit	2.04		3.16	
Test statistic of dispersion	1.11		1.26	

Note:
[a]S represents SMALL and B represents 1 – SMALL.

The first three independent variables of Table 10.1, Hours, North, and Speed, are control variables for risk exposure. The more flight hours a company accumulates and the more these hours are flown in northern Canada, the higher its risks of accidents. In contrast, average speed of airplanes in the fleet, measured by the proportion of jet planes, should reduce the number of accidents because jet planes pose fewer risks than do propeller-driven aircraft. The authors did not make a prediction about the sign for firm size (SMALL). Further, they suppose that the passage of time (TIME) has a negative effect on accidents because new planes are becoming safer than ever. The maintenance expenses (ME) variable should certainly reduce the number of accidents, along with the profit margin and its logarithm, since businesses in good financial health can do more prevention.

Positive D/E and negative D/E are the two important variables in the theoretical model. Their signs are ambiguous because they depend on the relative effect of investment in prevention in relation to the moral hazard effect. However, positive D/E should have a negative effect on accidents if the investment effect dominates the effect of moral hazard for businesses in good financial health. Dionne et al (1997) make the inverse prediction for negative D/E, which is generally seen among companies that are in financial difficulty. The same predictions should be confirmed for lag mean positive D/E and lag mean negative D/E, which are the lagged mean variables of the D/E variables over four quarters. The two dummy variables (DUM and DUMLMDE) that follow should have a positive sign on accidents because they separate businesses in good financial health (positive D/E) from those that are not (negative D/E). The value 1 is attributed to companies in poor financial health (negative D/E). Lastly, the two working capital variables (WC) should have a negative sign for accidents because they should indicate good financial health for companies with positive working capital. However, we observe that they both have negative means, although it is the variation that counts.

The first column of Model 2 in Table 10.2 indicates the estimated coefficient, and the second column gives the Student's t values. We can see that the three risk exposure variables (Hours, Speed, and North) are all significant, which indicates that companies with fewer flight hours, more jet aircraft, and that mostly do not fly in the northern Canada region have fewer accidents. The Time variable, measuring the evolution of technology over time, also has a negative effect on the number of accidents. The other interesting variable is ME, which measures the average maintenance expenses per flight. It has a negative and significant coefficient for small airlines and nonsignificant for other companies, which are probably monitored more closely by the regulatory agencies in large airports. We observe that the coefficient of debt ratio to positive equity (DERATIOP-S) for small businesses is negative, indicating that the investment effect dominates the moral hazard effect for small businesses in good financial health. Further, the variable LMDNE, lagged debt ratio to negative equity, has a very significant negative coefficient, which implies that moral hazard dominates for companies in financial difficulty.

We can therefore graphically represent the empirical results as in Figure 10.10. The two lines in each chart meet because the dummy variables that separate the two zones are not significant.

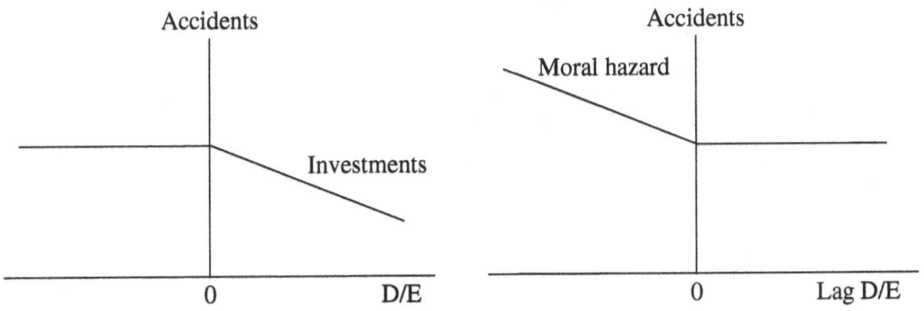

FIGURE 10.10 Representation of econometric results.

We can conclude that financing by standard debt introduces ex ante moral hazard in firm behavior, which justifies severe regulation of air transport.

10.4 CONCLUSION

In this chapter, we analyze the effect of debt contracts on debtholder risk management incentives. We show that the existence of the standard debt contract is mainly explained by large auditing costs of results. The debt contract reduces these costs at a minimal level. However, it is not the best contract to implement strong incentives for prevention or strong risk management by airlines. In fact, we empirically observe that airlines with more debt have more accidents. This may explain why safety activities of airlines are regulated.

REFERENCES

Brander, J., and Spencer, B., 1989. "Moral Hazard and Limited Liability: Implications for the Theory of the Firm." *International Economic Review* 30, 833–849.

Bubb, R., and Kaufman, A., 2014. "Securitization and Moral Hazard: Evidence from Credit Score Cutoff Rules." *Journal of Monetary Economics* 63, 1–18.

Caillaud, B., Dionne, G., and Jullien, B., 2000. "Corporate Insurance with Optimal Financial Contracting." *Economic Theory* 16, 77–105.

Courbage, C., Rey, C., and Treich, N., 2013. "Prevention and Precaution." In G. Dionne (Ed.), *Handbook of Insurance*, 2nd ed. New York: Springer, 185–204.

Dionne, G., Gagné, R., Gagnon, F., and Vanasse, C., 1997. "Debt, Moral Hazard and Airline Safety: An Empirical Evidence." *Journal of Econometrics* 79, 379–402.

Dionne, G., and Malekan, S., 2017. "Optimal Form of Retention for Securitized Loans under Moral Hazard." *Risks*, http://www.mdpi.com/2227-9091/5/4/55/pdf.

Dionne, G., and Harchaoui, T.M., 2008. "Banks' Capital, Securitization and Credit Risk: An Empirical Evidence for Canada." *Insurance and Risk Management* 75, 459–485.

Dionne, G., and Viala, P., 1992. "Optimal Design of Financial Contracts and Moral Hazard." Mimeo, Université de Montréal.

Dionne, G., and Viala, P., 1994. "Moral Hazard, Renegotiation and Debt." *Economics Letters* 46, 113–119.

Freixas X., and Rochet, J.C., 1997. *Microeconomics of Banking*. Cambridge: MIT Press.

Froot, K.A, Scharfstein, D.S., and Stein, J.C., 1993. "Risk Management: Coordinating Corporate Investment and Financing Policies." *Journal of Finance* 48, 1629–1658.

Gale, D., and Hellwig, M., 1985. "Incentive-Compatible Debt Contracts: The One-Period Problem." *Review of Economic Studies* 52, 647–663.

Innes, R.D., 1990. "Limited Liability and Incentive Contracting with Ex-Ante Action Choices." *Journal of Economic Theory* 52, 45–67.

Keys, B.J., Mukherjee, T., Seru, A., and Vig, V., 2009. "Financial Regulation and Securitization: Evidence from Subprime Loans." *Journal of Monetary Economics* 56, 700–720.

Keys, B.J., Mukherjee, T., Seru, A., and Vig, V., 2010. "Did Securitization Lead to Lax Screening? Evidence from Subprime Loans." *Quarterly Journal of Economics* 125, 307–362.

Keys, B.J., Seru, A., and Vig, V., 2012. "Lender Screening and the Role Of Securitization: Evidence from Prime and Subprime Mortgage Markets." *Review of Financial Studies* 25, 2071–2108.

Malekan, S., and Dionne, G., 2014. "Securitization and Optimal Retention under Moral Hazard." *Journal of Mathematical Economics* 55, 74–85.
Winter, R.A., 2013. "Optimal Insurance Contracts under Moral Hazard." In G. Dionne (Ed.), *Handbook of Insurance*, 2nd ed. New York: Springer, 205–230.

APPENDIX A: SYNTHESIS OF FORMS OF FINANCIAL CONTRACTS

Let:

z: be a random variable;

R: profits or net revenues of companies; this variable is random at date t_0; it is a function of *z*;

e: level of effort (or prevention) of the entrepreneur that is not observable by the bank;

C: audit cost of observing R at date t_1;

E(C): expected audit costs at date t_0.

In competition, the expected profit of the investor (the bank) is the same, regardless of the contract. The entrepreneur's welfare is maximized under the constraint that the investor has zero profits on each contract.

1. Situation where R is perfectly observable (C = 0) and *e* is not observable by the investor.

   The optimal contract is the Live or Die contract that maximizes the level of effort chosen by the entrepreneur. The entrepreneur would benefit from moving the density function as far right as possible to avoid paying the bank.

   We can show that the optimal level of effort e^* may be equal to that of a project financed by the entrepreneur's working capital or equity (e^i), which implies that the effect of ex ante moral hazard is low or practically zero.

   In practice, this contract is not observed often because the hypothesis that R is perfectly observable is too strong. If this contract is applied with C > 0, it would be very onerous to audit because the entrepreneur never benefits from telling the truth about the realization of R. Only the R^* statement will not be audited by the bank. Therefore, ex ante, at date t_0, the expected audit cost, E(C), is very high and almost equal to C, because the probability of audit is almost 1.
2. Situation where R is not perfectly observable (C > 0) and *e* is observable

   The optimal financial contract is the standard debt contract. For one, this contract does not effectively encourage effort in the presence of moral hazard. In addition, it minimizes E(C); these costs are equal to CG(F) where G(F) is the firm's probability of default. It is evident that CG(F) < C, because $0 \leq G(F) < 1$.

   In practice, the standard debt contract is very frequent, even when *e* is not observable, because it is the most efficient contract to minimize E(C). However, we can demonstrate that the optimal level of effort with a debt contract (e^{**}), when *e* is not observable, is equal to $e^{**} < e^* \leq e^i$. Therefore, if we have projects financed partly by debt, we should observe less effort or prevention than when they are financed uniquely by equity. We thus observe residual ex ante moral hazard.

3. Situation where neither *e* and R are observable

A hybrid contract, called the Plateau contract, has been proposed in the literature. This contract generates an optimal level of effort e*** that is greater than e** and less than e*, but that may incur high expected audit costs. In addition, it implies the use of very complex financing packages. As a result, this contract is used infrequently.

In practice, we mainly observe the standard debt contract (or financing of projects by bonds) combined with equity, although this contract is known to be not very effective at encouraging entrepreneurs to exert maximum effort.

APPENDIX B: DEFINITIONS OF VARIABLES

NACC	The total number of accidents in which the carrier is involved during a quarter. The definition of the Canadian Safety Board is used: an accident is an event in which there is material damages and/or casualties (deaths or injuries). Observations for this variable range from 0 to 4 which justifies the use of count data econometric models.
HOURS	The total number of hours flown. This variable accounts for risk exposure. HOURS is used instead of the total number of departures because the former was more accurate and reliable (particularly for charter activities). HOURS and departures are highly correlated (0.95) in the sample. Finally, the number of departures was introduced in the definition of FE (see below). A positive sign is predicted for the coefficient or HOURS.
NORTH	A dummy variable with NORTH = 1, if the carrier regularly served (50% or more of the activities) the designated northern area (National Transportation Act, 1987). NORTH = 0, otherwise. This variable captures the effect of particular weather conditions of this region on airline safety. A positive sign is predicted.
SPEED	The ratio of total number of kilometers over total number of hours flown. This variable is a proxy for the average type of aircraft used by a carrier. A negative sign is predicted since, in general, jets are safer.
SMALL	A dummy variable with SMALL = 1 if total operating revenues (quarterly) are less than \$5,000,000 (in 1986 dollars).[3] SMALL = 0, otherwise. This variable acts as a complement to SPEED and NORTH since, in general, smaller carriers fly with smaller planes and more often in the designated northern area. Since SPEED is not a perfect measure of the fleet of a carrier and NORTH cannot take into account all the effects of bad weather conditions, we expect a positive sign for SMALL.

[3]Variables expressed in dollars have been deflated with the GDP price index, 1986 = 100. Source: Statistics Canada, CANSIM D 20556.

TIME	A time trend with t = 1 in 1976, t = 2 in 1977, etc. This variable controls mainly the evolution of technology over time. A negative sign is predicted since technological change helps to improve safety.
FE	The total maintenance expenditures per departure (in 1986 dollars). Total maintenance expenditures include expenditures on flight equipment maintenance and ground and property maintenance. It is a proxy for flight equipment maintenance since both types of maintenance are not reported separately in all cases. However, when data were available, we verified that more than 80% of maintenance expenditures were for flight equipment. More maintenance expenditures per departure means more safety and therefore fewer accidents.
OMARG:	Operating margin defined as 1 – (operating expenses/operating revenues). Operating margin is a profitability measure. More profits may indicate that airlines reduced their expenditures on safety during the period under study. Therefore, OMARG may have a positive sign.
LOMARG	Operating margin of the preceding quarter. More profits in the past may indicate that airlines have more funds today for safety; therefore LOMARG should have a negative sign.
DERATIOP	Debt over equity when equity is positive. Since both debt and equity come from the balance sheet of the carriers, it is reported on an annual basis. Thus, for a given year, the same value of DERATIOP appears at each quarter for a carrier. Equity can be positive or negative because it corresponds to accounting equity (or book equity), which is financial equity plus accumulated profits. Accounting equity can be negative when a carrier has experienced recurrent financial losses. From the theoretical model, the effect of DERATIOP on accidents is ambiguous. On the one hand, a higher debt-equity ratio may indicate more investments, which in turn may increase the efficiency of safety activities (negative effect on accidents; investment effect). On the other hand, a higher ratio may signal fewer incentives for safety under moral hazard (positive effect on accidents).
DERATION	Debt over equity when equity is strictly negative (annual values repeated quarterly). Like DERATIOP, the effect of this variable on the number of accidents is ambiguous. But it is more likely to be negative because the investment effect should be low.
LMDEP	The ratio of the average debt and the average equity of the four preceding quarters when the average equity is strictly positive. This variable serves two purposes: it permits the introduction of lags in the analysis, and it offers a method for converting annual values to quarterly ones. LMDEP helps to capture the effect of persistent financial conditions on safety. It has the same interpretation as the current debt-equity ratio.

LMDEN	The ratio of the average debt and the average equity of the four preceding quarters when the average equity is strictly negative. Like LMDEP, it captures the effect of persistent financial conditions. In particular, when LMDEN is low, it may indicate that the carrier is in a near-bankruptcy situation. In this case, the coefficient of LMDEN can be interpreted as the effect of near bankruptcy on accidents.
DUM	A dummy variable with DUM = 1 if current equity is strictly negative. DUM = 0, otherwise; this variable was introduced to take into account the intercept differences between positive and negative debt-equity ratios.
DUMLMDE	A dummy variable with DUMLMDE = 1 if the average equity of the four preceding quarters is strictly negative. DUMLMDE = 0, otherwise; same role as DUM.
WC	Working capital defined as (total current assets – total current liabilities)/total assets (annual value repeated quarterly). This is a liquidity measure. Working capital is a complement variable to operating margin. More liquidities may mean less (or more) expenditures on safety and therefore more (fewer) accidents; we do not have an a priori hypothesis for the sign of the coefficient.
LMWC	Average working capital of the four preceding quarters. More liquidity in the past may allow carriers to put more funds into safety today. LMWC should therefore reduce the number of accidents.

CHAPTER 11
Venture Capital Risk with Optimal Financing Structure

External financing of venture capital projects that include considerable research and development is difficult because entrepreneurs have no loan guarantees or collateral to offer.[1] In addition, it is hard for them to convince potential shareholders to buy shares at a price that represents the value of the project. When projects are characterized by high uncertainty, traditional sources of external financing are generally unavailable. As a result, entrepreneurs are consequently obliged to turn to venture capital firms.

Investors require a high anticipated rate of return because investing in this type of project is very risky. Unlike banks, venture capital firms want to manage the business financed in order to increase the profitability of their projects. These firms generally have more business experience and financial knowledge than do the entrepreneurs/researchers who developed new ideas or inventions.

Venture capital financing contracts often differ in form from simple debt and equity. One form discussed in the literature is nonguaranteed debt (debentures) convertible into shares where the investor, often via the venture capital firm, becomes a shareholder when the profits reach a certain level. This form of financing lets investors protect themselves when the profits are low (or at least provides more protection than if they held shares) and obtain a higher return (than they would get from standard debt) in favorable situations.

Warrants are another source of financing whereby a venture capital firm buys the shares issued by the business. The investee thus obtains seed capital without the need to pay interest; it may not even need to repay the capital. However, the value of the firm may be diluted if the warrant holder exercises the option and receives capital stock. Equity financing is also possible from the start, even for the most risky projects.

More recently, venture debt has become more popular. This is a form of debt financing for venture equity-backed companies that do not have the necessary cash flow for traditional debt and that want flexibility. It usually includes warrants for company stocks. Venture debt is not convertible.

Finally, venture debt is usually used for incremental capital in the purchase of equipment, acquisitions, or when the new capital needed is not large enough for an equity round.

---

[1]The research discussed in this chapter was done with Jeanne Mutshioko, Anne-Sophie Clarisse, and Yann Furic.

The recent literature on venture capital specifies the optimal forms of project financing contracts, along with problems of information asymmetry between entrepreneurs and investors in this market. Venture capital financing is still a very risky activity. Bamford and Douthett (2013) show how risk management can reduce the costs of various sources of risk.

11.1 SOME STATISTICS ABOUT VENTURE CAPITAL

United States

- Venture capital investment is highly concentrated in California and the northeastern United States (which host 43% and 21% of the funds respectively), specifically in the San Francisco and Boston areas.
- Investors are very selective: only 12 projects out of 1,000 are accepted.
- In 1988, venture capital investments totaled $3 billion, 33% of which came from IBM's research and development budget.
- Since then, the amount of venture capital funds grew steadily until 2000, when it peaked at $105 billion before plunging by 65% in 2001, and then by 49% in 2002. The sharp drop in these amounts is attributable to the 2001 recession, which severely affected technology firms.
- A slight upward trend in amounts invested was observed after 2003, which is not as pronounced as before the crisis linked to the tech bubble.
- A plunge of 33% between 2008 and 2009, following the financial crisis, was the only obstacle to the growth of venture capital investments after 2001.
- More recently, interest in venture capital has rebounded. Investments practically doubled between 2013 and 2015 from $30 billion to $59.1 billion. However, in 2014 the US venture capital industry was about half as active as it was in 2000.
- Note that in 2009, 70% of investments were made in high tech businesses, and only 15% of the financing was granted to firms in the startup phase: venture capital plays a weak role in new business development.
- Venture capital funds seek to accelerate the development of businesses with high growth potential and to take them public as quickly as possible, thus realizing a high return (successful exit). The market plunges in 2001 and 2008 made it more difficult for venture capital firms to make successful exits.
- The US initial public offering (IPO) market has rebounded since 2010, thus enabling venture capital investors to recover the funds invested a few years earlier, despite a slight drop in amounts raised and the number of IPOs between 2014 and 2015.

Canada ($CAD)

- In 1995, $669 million in venture capital investments were made in Canada.
- In 1996, $1.1 billion was invested in Canada, including 56% in the high tech sector (this rate rose to 65% just before the tech bubble burst in 2000).
- In 1996, venture capital corporations held, on average, 35% of the equity of the companies concerned.
- In 2000, at the start of the tech bubble, venture capital investments stood at $5.8 billion. This equates to about 5% of the US total, down from 10% in 1996.
- Since the crisis of 2008, amounts invested have grown steadily, reaching $2.26 billion in 2015.

- In 2014, Ontario invested $906 million in 154 transactions, Quebec invested $604 million in 87 transactions, and British Columbia invested $506 million in 72 transactions. The average investment in Canada was $5.7 million per transaction.
- In 2014, funds were mainly invested in the information and communications technologies (ICT) (66%), life sciences (22%), and clean tech (7%) sectors.
- Venture-backed companies have an average debt/equity ratio of 0.81.

Quebec ($CAD)

- Venture capital was almost nonexistent in Quebec in 1985.
- The amounts invested in Quebec exhibit the same trends as those invested in Canada, after eliminating the most extreme variance.
- Amounts invested in Quebec represent on average about 30% of the Canadian total since 1995 (these amounts vary between 25% and 39%).
- In 1996, 38% of Canadian investment projects were carried out in Quebec (still 30% of total value for Canada, equal to $323 million), 69% of which were in the high tech sector (including 20% in biotechnology and 11% in computer software and hardware).
- Owing to large tax benefits, the supply of venture capital is large in Quebec. For example, $486 million was injected in 1996 with a reserve of $1 billion.
- Most of the funds raised in 2009 come from workers' funds, which have the largest tax benefits. Historically, the most active venture capital investors in Quebec were T2C2 (a subsidiary of the Caisse de dépôt et placement du Québec), Hydro-Québec CapiTech (a subsidiary of Hydro-Québec), BDC Capital Inc., Innovatech Québec, FTQ Solidarity Fund, FIER (Regional Economic Intervention Fund), and private venture capital firms. The technological orientation was less prevalent than in North America overall.
- Of the $604 million invested in Quebec in 2014, 62% was injected in the ICT sector (versus only 47% in 2009), 14% in life sciences, and 13% in clean tech.
- In 2014, the most active venture capital investors in Quebec were: Real Ventures, FTQ Solidarity Fund, BDC Capital Inc., Fondaction CSN, and iNovia Capital Inc.

11.2 ROLE OF VENTURE CAPITAL FIRMS

Venture capital firms are financial intermediaries between investors (pension funds, insurers, individuals, banks, etc.) seeking high returns (which therefore entail high risk) and innovating businesses with high growth potential that do not have much financial capital or collateral.

Entrepreneurs are often researchers who lack project management experience. They are very heterogeneous and difficult to evaluate, and cannot offer guarantees because their capital is between their ears.

Venture capital firms must try to identify good risks (through screening, which can reduce adverse selection), monitor investments to reduce ex ante and ex post moral hazard, and make a successful exit by making firms public or selling them to realize high returns (Bernstein, Giroux, and Townsend, 2016). Further, some venture capital firms get directly involved in business management, in addition to being represented on the board of directors. They are particularly involved in formulating marketing strategies and distributing new products. For example, they may represent their clients at exhibitions or trade fairs to sell the innovations.

Given the high risks, venture capital investors aim to achieve an average rate of return of 20%, which implies a required rate of 40% ex ante. At the same time, the default rate observed is high, at 30% of projects (Barry, 1994). An investment project lasts 5 to 10 years on average.

To protect themselves, many venture capital firms create financial syndicates to finance the most risky projects. They use the basic principles of portfolio management and partner with banks that agree to join the financial syndicates.

11.3 VENTURE CAPITAL FIRMS AND ADDED VALUE

Does the presence of venture capital firms add value to firms?

As financial intermediaries, yes, venture capital firms reduce information asymmetry in markets. We will try to measure this effect in the last section of this chapter. Van Pottelsberghe de la Potterie and Romain (2004) assess the impact of venture capital on the economy from a macroeconomic standpoint. They test their model using data from 16 OECD countries for the period of 1990 to 2001. They show that venture capital contributes significantly to boosting productivity in the studied countries. Gornall and Stebulaev (2015) conclude that the companies funded by venture capital represent an important part of the US economy with respect to research and development, employment, and revenue.

11.4 ROLE OF CONVERTIBLE DEBT

Private venture capital firms are invited to participate in a percentage of the capital invested and are repaid with a share of the profits. For example, they are asked to invest less than 10% of the capital required and receive an average share of the profits of over 20%. Financial contracts often take the form of convertible debentures whose exercise price is higher than the face value of the debt. To encourage entrepreneurs, investors offer them stock options in addition to their salary.

In addition to providing incentives for venture capital managers, convertible debt combines the advantages of debt and equity for entrepreneurs. In fact, there are two schools of thought in the literature; their interpretations of the convertible debt contract complement rather than substitute each other.

The first interpretation of the convertible debt contract says that this contract is debt-like and that it protects investors from the risks of the project by introducing limited liability. In general, adding a conversion option whose value increases with the return on the investment reduces the investors' expected costs of default by lowering the face value of the debt. This value decreases simply because investors perceive the project as less risky and demand a lower risk premium on the interest rate, or because they anticipate a sufficiently high probability of being able to exercise the option. Graphically, the convertible contract can be represented as in Figure 11.1, where F is the face value of the debt. A standard debt contract (Figure 11.2), has a face value of $B > F$ for the same loan or investment value.

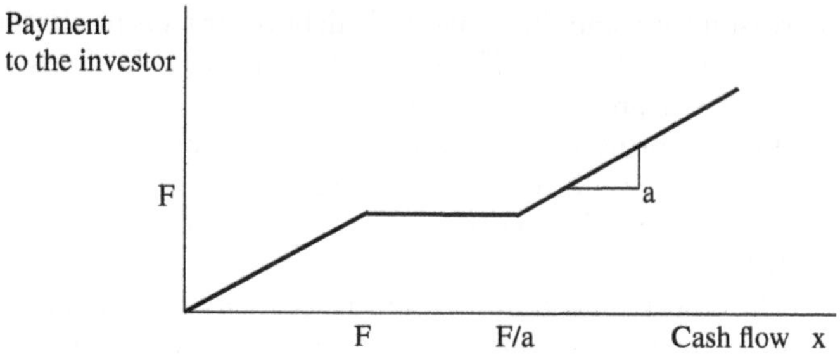

FIGURE 11.1 Payment function of convertible debt.
Note: a is the percentage of revenues transferred to the investor at the time of conversion;
F is the face value of a contract with convertible debt;
F/a is the critical value of revenues that makes it advantageous for the venture capital firm to exercise the option;
x is the cash flow of the project.

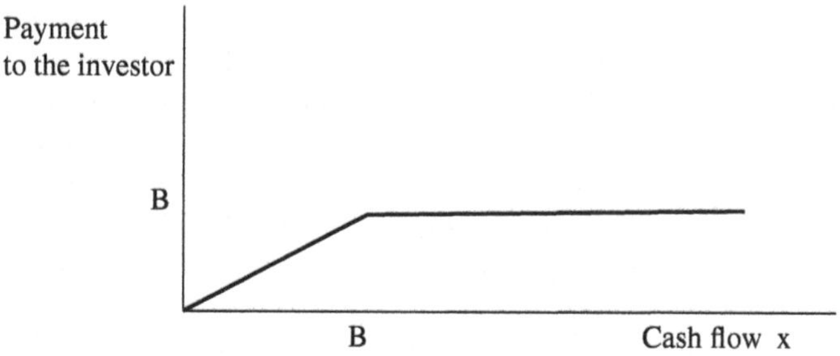

FIGURE 11.2 Payment function of standard debt.

Mathematically, the financial contract of Figure 11.1 becomes:

$$D(1+i) = \int_0^F (x-c)g(x)dx + F(G(F') - G(F)) + \int_{F'}^{\infty} axg(x)dx$$

where:

$F' = F/a$ and $dF/da < 0$.

x represents the cash flow of the project;
D is the amount borrowed;
i is the risk-free interest rate;
c is the audit cost;
g(x) is the density function of the cash flows;
G(x) is the distribution function.

This contract may be compared directly to a standard debt contract, as shown in Figure 11.2:

$$D(1+i) = \int_0^B (x-c)g(x)dx + B(1 - G(B)).$$

The second reason for using the convertible debt contract is to attract shareholders indirectly, or by the back door. The idea is that if a new business issues shares immediately to finance a project, the issue price will be too low because the real potential of the firm or project is not well known or is not easily quantifiable by the market and will not be reflected in the share price. This financing would be too expensive in terms of profit sharing (excessive dilution). Convertible debt lets the entrepreneur distribute preferred shares when the business is in a better position or when the market has more information about its capacity to generate profits. Once the project reaches maturity, the company can make a public offering.

In addition, the convertible debt contract gives venture capital (VC) managers more incentives than the standard debt contract. Convertible debt thus lets VC managers convert debt into a fraction of the shares depending on the capital invested, if the results are high enough.

It is important to note that we are talking about the incentives of the financial intermediary, and not the entrepreneur, as we did before. As mentioned above, venture capital firms may make important management decisions in the entrepreneurs' place.

Lastly, Bagella and Beccheti (1998) propose that the convertible debt approach be improved by suggesting the use of warrants when the steps of a project can be easily broken down ex ante. The advantage is that the entrepreneur does not have to pay interest on the portion of the debt in the early periods, unlike convertible debt. Over the long term, this should not change anything because this gain should be anticipated in the prices, but in the short term it will help small businesses that have no liquid assets to avoid paying interest during the startup phase of the project or business.

A warrant lets an investor buy the shares of a company at a fixed exercise price until the expiration date. It is like a stock option. Warrants differ from equity options on some points. The option is exercised on private shares, whereas convertible debt allows units of debt to be converted into a predetermined fixed number of shares. Warrants are issued by private companies and not by a public option exchange. Warrants are over-the-counter financial instruments. They are dilutive and owners do not have voting rights. They benefit the owners only when the company has growth opportunities.

11.5 INFORMATION ASYMMETRY AND VENTURE CAPITAL

In this section, we propose a model that can verify the presence of residual information asymmetry in the portfolio of a large investment firm that provides venture capital financing. We define the private investor as an investment bank or venture capital firm.

In the presence of information asymmetry, investors' main objective is to determine under which circumstances it is preferable to use a particular financial vehicle. The investor selects the financial vehicles based on the degree of risk and perceived adverse selection. Investors can also face moral hazard. Here, moral hazard is defined as the entrepreneur's propensity not to make sufficient effort to obtain an optimal return on the project. We assume that the venture capital firm is passive in the management of the project. Below, we use the term "information asymmetry" to refer to either adverse selection or moral hazard because the test used does not allow us to separate these two forms of information asymmetry (Dionne, 2013; Chiappori and Salanié, 2013; Dionne, Michaud, and Dahchour, 2013).

Once the investor has found a viable project, it must choose the type of financial vehicle to use. Five main types of financing are available: standard debt, convertible debt, standard debt with a warrant, short-term standard debt followed by a capital stock issue, and the use of common shares. A sixth vehicle is convertible preferred shares; it is similar to convertible debt.

We therefore want to verify that the investor, given the diverse information that it has ex ante, is able to accurately manage risks and thus avoid the adverse effects of the inefficiencies of residual information asymmetry. This happens because it expects that the business will negotiate the type of financial vehicle that represents its risk level.[2] Table 11.1 summarizes the main conclusions found in the literature.

TABLE 11.1 Summary of researchers' conclusions.

Author	Year	Type of risk	Conclusion
Stein	1992	Adverse selection	The inclusion of convertible debt instruments lets investors find a balance among firms that differ in terms of results. The main premise is the existence of positive and significant financial distress costs.
Bagella and Becchetti	1998	Adverse selection and moral hazard	High tech firms prefer to issue debentures with warrants. The market perceives the issuance of convertible securities less negatively than the issuance of common shares.
Brennan and Kraus	1987	Adverse selection	The negative effect of the issuance of convertible debt is inversely correlated with the conversion ratio and positively correlated with the face value of this debt.
Trester	1998	Moral hazard	The use of convertible preferred shares can eliminate Hold Up problems. If entrepreneurs cannot meet their obligations, all of the funds will be diverted away from them, thus causing the bankruptcy of the firm and the exclusion of bondholders. Convertible instruments do not let entrepreneurs get rid of lenders when the lenders convert their debt into shares.
Thakor	1998	Moral hazard	Replicates the article by Trester (1998). Trester's work is pertinent, but the Hold Up problem does not suffice to explain the use of convertible preferred shares.
Kaplan and Stromberg	2000, 2002	Adverse selection and moral hazard	The use of performance contracts for business managers can limit adverse selection and moral hazard.

[2]See the paper by Bourgeon and Dionne (2013) on the negotiation of financial contracts.

11.5.1 Methodology

The general objective of the empirical test is to verify the presence of residual information asymmetry (moral hazard or adverse selection) in the portfolio of a venture capital firm.

We use the models of Dionne, Gouriéroux, and Vanasse (1999, 2001) and of Dionne and Gagné (2001). The goal is to test whether a correlation exists between the financial vehicles selected and the realization of default. If there is no residual correlation, this implies that the selection of projects by the venture capital firm effectively eliminates information asymmetry between the entrepreneur and the investor. We use a latent variable model of the Probit type to estimate the probability of default. In this type of model, the dependent variable Y takes only two values: 0 in case of non-default and 1 otherwise. Using this estimate, we can calculate the expected value of Y, or the conditional predicted probability of default, E(Y/X). In the second step, we can use a linear regression model to explain the choice of the financial vehicle Z as a function of X and Y. The conditional distribution of Z can be as follows:

$$l(Z/X, Y) = l(Z/X) \tag{11.1}$$

$$l(Z/X, Y) = l(Z; Xa + Yb + E(Y/X)c) \tag{11.2}$$

where:

Z is the type of financial vehicle chosen by the investor;
X are the observable characteristics of the entrepreneur and the investor;
Y is the state of default: (1) for default and (0) for non-default;
E(Y/X) is the predicted default probability obtained from the estimation of the Probit model.

Equation (11.1) is verified when there is no residual information asymmetry in the data. In fact, Z's distribution is the same regardless of the presence of the default risk variable Y. This means that observing Y does not provide any information and that X contains all the necessary information to choose the appropriate financial vehicle. This result is obtained when the estimated coefficient *b*, in the second equation (11.2), is zero. The variable E(Y/X) must be used to take into account the fact that we impose a linear specification on the regression. It can also consider the fact that X does not contain all the variables needed to correctly estimate Z (poor econometric specification). Its coefficient *c* can be significant or not. The absence of E(Y/X) can generate false conclusions. Notably, *b* can be significantly different from zero in the absence of E(Y/X) and equal to zero when it is present. The conclusion obtained without E(Y/X) would probably be false (Dionne, Gouriéroux, and Vanasse, 2001).

11.5.2 Financial Vehicle Variables

In the empirical analysis we consider three financial vehicles.

1. CS: Contains only the common shares of listed or private companies. This type of financial vehicle should be used for businesses with a high default probability (highest earnings variance).

2. CD: Contains convertible debentures exclusively. The theory states that this type of instrument is best suited to businesses whose earnings variance is lower than that financed by common shares, but higher than that of firms that use standard debt. Therefore, the theory assumes that a business that procures financing by standard debt attains its objectives more often and that its earnings variance is lower.
3. LSB: Loans to sponsored businesses. This type of loan is identical to standard debt, but has a higher interest rate and a shorter maturity than a bank loan. It targets small businesses whose operations are too risky for bank financing.

11.5.3 Control Variables

Asset Size

T05: Companies whose assets are between \$0 and \$5 million (reference group).

T525: Companies whose assets are between \$5 million and \$25 million.

T2510: Companies whose assets are between \$25 million and \$100 million.

T1020: Companies whose assets are between \$100 million and \$200 million.

T2050: Companies whose assets are between \$200 million and \$500 million.

T500: Companies whose assets are over \$500 million.

Industrial Sectors

Industrial sectors (identified by S1 ... S12), identical to those of the TSE 300.

Financing Goal

DEM: Concerns businesses in the startup phase: that is companies that are new, or in a precarious position, and require funds to start up properly.

DEVL: Refers to companies that seek financing for their development, at a more advanced stage than startup companies. These companies use funds for various objectives ranging from a marketing campaign to improvement of their equipment in place, but may also serve to reinforce the human potential of the company by hiring specialists, for example.

REOR: Refers to companies in the reorganization phase, usually financial (rebalancing of liabilities and capital), along with firms that face problems of succession or change of leader (reference group).

Ownership

PRI: A binary variable that takes the value of 1 if the business is private and 0 otherwise.

Information Variables

Each of the variables below represents a different team of managers in the venture capital firm. The files studied are distributed based on the size of the firm's assets and its sector, such that each firm is reviewed by a specialized team.

G1: This team of managers invests in businesses with large capitalization, listed or not. It specializes in debt financing (reference group).

G2: These managers can finance businesses in all industrial sectors. Minimum placements are usually above $5 million. Assets are the stocks of large companies.

G3: This team studies businesses working in the public services sector, communications, and media. These firms usually have significant assets. The team also invests in midsize companies.

G4: These managers invest in biotechnology, industrial technology, and software firms. The firms are either in the startup phase or looking for additional funds to undertake subsequent development phases.

G5: This team finances businesses within any industrial sector, as long as they are small. Loans to sponsored businesses are found almost exclusively in this category. Investments peak at about $1 million. These firms are mainly startups and family-run businesses.

G6: As a complement to G5, these managers mainly invest in businesses working far from large centers.

Risk Variables

DEF: A binary variable that takes the value of 1 when the business defaults and 0 otherwise.

PROB: The predicted default probability E(Y/X). It is calculated based on the auxiliary equation that estimates default probabilities.

11.5.4 Results

Table 11.2 presents the default frequencies of the three financial vehicles retained.[3] The categorization is consistent with the theory that attributes higher default risk to businesses financed by stock and lower risk to those that use debt. In the analysis that follows, we group debentures and debt because the number of LSB contracts is low.

Table 11.3 presents the first regression regarding the choice of financial vehicle with a minimal specification where the dependent variable is equal to 1 for private common shares and 0 otherwise. Note that the default variable (DEF) explaining the probability that financing by common shares is significant. It confirms that businesses with the highest risk are financed by equity in the presence of residual information

TABLE 11.2 Frequency of default by financial vehicle.

Vehicle	Default frequency	Standard deviation
Private common shares	15.49%	36.27%
Convertible debentures	10.53%	31.53%
LSB	4.00%	20.00%

[3]See Mutshioko (2016) for more details about the data.

TABLE 11.3 Results of the first model.

	Model 1	
Variable	Coefficient	T-ratio
DEF	**0.4966**	**3.1221**
PRI	**−0.7717**	**−5.1272**
DEM	0.0775	0.4855
DEVL	0.1081	0.7034
Constant	**0.7230**	**9.1015**
Log likelihood	−574.02	
Observations	867	

Notes: Dependent variable: 1 if common shares; 0 if other vehicles. Variables in bold are significant at 5%.

asymmetry. But this result can be explained by the fact that the regression does not contain all the independent variables available or that the predicted default variable is not present. In other words, the result can be attributed to a weak specification or a linear regression component.

Model 2 of Table 11.4 improves the econometric specification, but the default variable remains significant. Model 3 considerably improves the econometric specification by adding information related to the project management teams and the prediction for the default probability. We can observe that the default variable is no longer significant (at 5%), indicating that there is no residual information asymmetry in the venture capital firm's portfolio. The venture capital firm knows the default risks of the businesses that it finances, and so does the entrepreneur. If the default variable is not significant, this means that the venture capital firm obtains sufficient information from the other observable variables (including its managers' judgment) to select the optimal financial vehicle. In fact, all Gi variables are highly significant when compared to G1.

11.6 CONCLUSION

In conclusion, because the number of observations was too small, we could not study all the financial vehicles. We therefore cannot conclude about the presence or absence of information asymmetry when choosing a convertible debenture, for example.

We have estimated the choice of whether or not to use common shares when financing a business, versus convertible debentures *and* standard debt. The size of the assets, the goal of financing, and the industrial sector are pertinent, but these variables do not eliminate the presence of information asymmetry. Only the inclusion of variables that consider managers' judgment (in addition to the predicted default probability) can eliminate residual information asymmetry.

The results of Model 3 indicate that the coefficient of the default variable (DEF) is not significant at 5%, which implies that there is no residual information asymmetry between the venture capital firm and the entrepreneurs when the model is well specified. In other words, the venture capital firm can effectively manage risks and create value in this industry.

TABLE 11.4 Regression results of models 2 and 3.

	Model 2		Model 3	
Variable	Coefficient	T-ratio	Coefficient	T-ratio
DEF	**0.3649**	**2.2139**	0.3144	1.8566
PROB			0.5017	0.1378
PRI	**−0.9704**	**−5.8520**	**−1.2123**	**−3.3039**
T525	0.1800	1.4223	0.0572	0.2433
T2550	−0.0655	−0.3166	−0.2402	−1.0899
T5010	0.1332	0.6129	0.2337	0.9791
T1020	**−0.4008**	**−1.9809**	**−0.4809**	**−2.1581**
T2050	0.2870	1.0743	0.4548	1.5731
T500	−0.0452	−0.2146	0.0587	0.2626
S1	5.9581	0.0195	5.3473	0.0162
S2	0.7012	1.5269	0.5095	0.7572
S3	**1.0450**	**2.3520**	**1.2190**	**2.6186**
S4	0.5703	1.9224	0.4594	1.5009
S5	**0.8404**	**5.1736**	**0.7093**	**3.7940**
S6	**1.1021**	**8.0825**	**0.9383**	**6.0060**
S7	−1.0441	−1.7102	−1.0488	−1.6772
S10	0.0142	0.0618	−0.3044	−1.2724
S11	**0.5954**	**3.2954**	0.3046	1.4570
S12	**1.0873**	**5.0773**	**0.9958**	**4.3360**
G2			**1.2612**	**6.7505**
G3			**1.0807**	**2.0865**
G4			**0.5642**	**3.0975**
G5			**0.6868**	**3.4211**
G6			**0.9999**	**3.3721**
DEM	−0.0434	−0.2519	−0.3094	−1.6180
DEVL	0.0034	0.0205	−0.2307	−1.2535
Constant	0.2180	1.7693	0.0641	0.4432
Log likelihood	−488.64		−457.06	
Observations	867		867	

Note: Variables in bold are significant at 5%.

REFERENCES

Asquith, P., and Mullins, D.W., 1986. "Equity Issues and Offering Dilution." *Journal of Financial Economics* 15, 61–89.

Bagella, M., and Becchetti, L., 1998. "The Optimal Financing Strategy of a High-Tech Firm: The Role of Warrants." *Journal of Economic Behavior and Organization* 35, 1–23.

Bamford, C.E., and Douthett, E.B. Jr., 2013. "Venture Capital and Risk Management: Evidence from Initial Public Offerings." *Journal of Managerial Issues* 25, 220–240.

Barry, C.B., 1994. "New Directions in Research on Venture Capital Finance." *Financial Management* 23, 3–15.

Bernstein, S., Giroud, X., and Townsend, R., 2016. "The Impact of Venture Capital Monitoring." *Journal of Finance* 71, 1591–1622.

Bourgeon, J.M., and Dionne, G., 2013. "On Debt Service and Renegotiation When Debt-Holders Are More Strategic." *Journal of Financial Intermediation* 22, 353–372.

Brennan, M. and Kraus, A., 1987. "Efficient Financing under Asymmetric Information." *Journal of Finance* 42, 1225–1243.
Chiappori, P.A., and Salanié, B., 2013. "Asymmetric Information in Insurance Markets: Predictions and Tests." In: G. Dionne (Ed.), *Handbook of Insurance*, 2nd ed. New York: Springer, 397–422.
Dionne, G., 2013. "The Empirical Measure of Information Problems with Emphasis on Insurance Fraud and Dynamic Data." In: G. Dionne (Ed.), *Handbook of Insurance*, 2nd ed. New York: Springer, 423–448.
Dionne, G., and Gagné, R., 2001. "Deductible Contracts against Fraudulent Claims: Evidence from Automobile Insurance." *Review of Economics and Statistics* 83, 290–301.
Dionne, G., Gouriéroux, C., and Vanasse, C. 1999. "Evidence of Adverse Selection in Automobile Insurance Markets." In: G. Dionne and C. Laberge-Nadeau (Eds.), *Automobile Insurance: Road Safety, New Drivers, Risks, Insurance Fraud and Regulation*, 13–46.
Dionne, G., Gouriéroux, C., and Vanasse, C., 2001. "Testing for Evidence of Adverse Selection in the Automobile Insurance Market: A Comment." *Journal of Political Economy* 109, 444–453.
Dionne, G., Michaud, P.C., and Dahchour, M., 2013. "Separating Moral Hazard from Adverse Selection and Learning in Automobile Insurance: Longitudinal Evidence from France." *Journal of the European Economic Association* 11, 897–917.
Gornall, W. and Strebulaev, I.A., 2015. "The Economic Impact of Venture Capital: Evidence from Public Companies." Working paper, Stanford University.
Kaplan, S.N., and Stromberg, P., 2000. "How Do Venture Capitalists Choose Investments?" Working paper, University of Chicago.
Kaplan, S.N. and Stromberg, P., 2002. "Financial Contracting Theory Meets the Real World: An Empirical Analysis of Venture Capital Contracts." *Review of Economics Studies* 15, 1–35.
Mutshioko, A.J., 2016. "Impact du niveau de risque sur le choix de financement des firmes privées." Supervised project, HEC Montréal.
Statista, 2017. "Venture capital in North America – Statistics & Facts." https://www.statista.com/topics/2565/venture-capital-in-north-america/.
Stein, J.C., 1992. "Convertible Bond as Backdoor Equity Financing." *Journal of Financial Economics* 32, 3–21.
Thakor, A.V., 1998. "Comment on Trester." *Journal of Banking and Finance* 22, 700–701.
Thomson Reuters, 2016. *National Venture Capital Association, Yearbook 2016.*
Trester, J.J., 1998. "Venture Capital Contracting under Asymmetric Information." *Journal of Banking and Finance* 22, 675–699.
Van Pottelsberghe de la Potterie, B. and Romain, A., 2004. "The Economic Impact of Venture Capital." Discussion paper Series 1/Volkswirtschaftliches Forschungszentrum der Deutschen Bundesbank, no. 2004, 18.

CHAPTER 12

Bank Credit Risk: Scoring of Individual Risks

Default risk generally refers to the default probability of the counterparty in a contractual relationship.[1] In bank credit, it refers to the borrower's probability of default or loan nonpayment. The recovery rate and the loan value at the time of default are also important to consider for computing the recovery value.

Bankers or lenders must evaluate individual default probabilities, a difficult risk management task. Most often, the borrower is more informed about its own default probability than the lender is. This situation of information asymmetry may generate adverse selection.

Several mechanisms are available to let banks protect themselves from this information problem:

1. Self-selection of risks[2]
2. Collateral or loan guarantees
3. Bank scoring

In this chapter, we will emphasize bank scoring, also known as risk classification by banks, which is a form of risk management.

This method consists of classifying risks using information that is inexpensive and that is correlated with the real unobservable risk that potential customers represent. The same method is used by insurers that, for example, price automobile insurance via different classification variables such as age, territory, type of car, and so on. This process has been shown to reduce asymmetric information within risk classes (Dionne, Gouriéroux, and Vanasse, 2001; Chiappori and Salanié, 2000; Dionne and Rothschild, 2014). It can even eliminate asymmetric information if the number of variables used and their different combinations allow the construction of homogeneous risk classes: that is, ones that do not contain any residual information problem. This statistical method for testing the presence of residual asymmetric information in different risk classes is presented in Chapter 11 for classification of risks associated with different financing contracts for investment projects in venture capital.

---

[1]The research discussed in this chapter was done with Manuel Artis, Anne-Sophie Bergerès, Philippe d'Astous, and Montserrat Guillen.

[2]Self-selection of risks: In automobile insurance, the insured can choose from among several contracts that offer different deductible amounts. The higher the deductible, the lower the premium that the insured will have to pay. High-risk individuals (or poor risks) will deliberately select the contract with the lowest deductible because they know that they have a greater probability of accidents. High-risk individuals will also chose a low collateral for their loan.

Rating agencies also use scoring when they give credit grades or ratings to businesses and governments.

Default risk includes three important components:

1. Default probability (1 – p);
2. Exposure at Default (EAD);
3. Proportion of risk exposure lost at default (LGD, Loss Given Default); (1 – LGD) is the recovery rate.

The expected loss of a loan contract is therefore:

$$(1-p)\ \text{EAD} \times \text{LGD}.$$

Default risk is a type of credit risk. Credit risk explains the yield spread between government bonds and private bonds. It also explains the risk premiums on interest rates of bank loans.

Figure 12.1 illustrates the yield spread required to cover credit risk and its different components. Take, for example, a BBB bond (or Baa, its equivalent) having a default spread representing about 25% of total credit spread. The yield spread shown in Figure 12.1 (credit risk) can also be explained by factors other than the default premium required by investors, such as the premium for default risk aversion, liquidity risk, taxes, or general market risk. Indeed, it would be unrealistic to think that yield spreads are associated with default risk only (Elton et al, 2001; Collin-Dufresne, Goldstein, and Martin, 2001; Huang and Huang, 2012; Dionne et al, 2010, 2011).

In a recent study, Maalaoui-Chun, Dionne, and François (2014) show that default, liquidity, and market risk are three important factors that can explain bond credit risk. In the rest of the chapter, however, we only analyze default risk as an explanation for the lending rate premium.

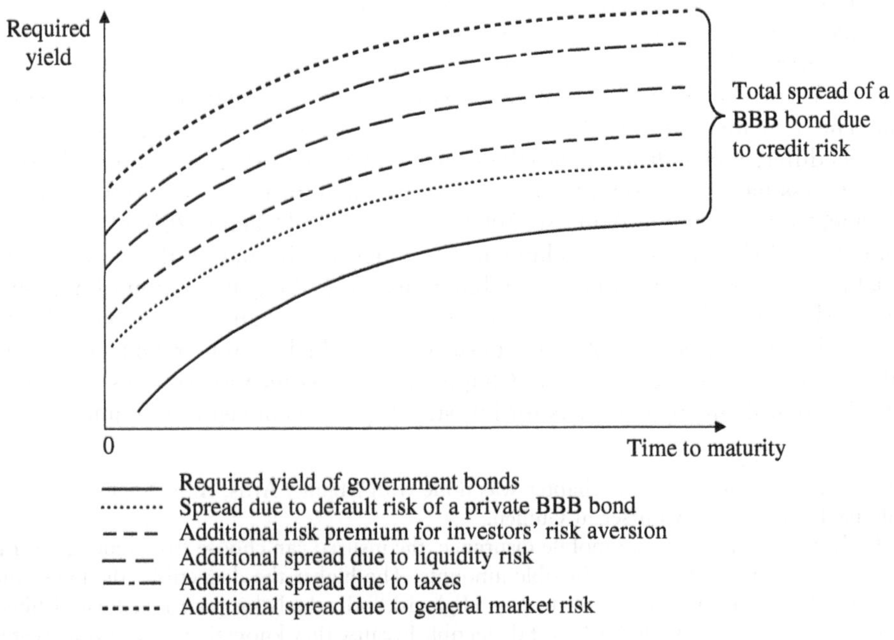

FIGURE 12.1 Required yield of a BBB bond.

The opportunity cost demanded by the investor is also important. In the literature, government bonds are often used as reference securities. However, this approach has been criticized by Hull, Petrescu, and White (2004), who point out that the government bond market is regulated. The prices observed, and consequently the yields required, may thus be biased. For example, the Central Bank may require banks to buy its bonds as an element of its monetary policy. This would effectively increase the government bond prices, reduce yields, and increase yield spreads relative to private bonds.

The swap interest rate and the LIBOR rate are often used by market participants to replace Treasury bills. However, recent observations on LIBOR rate manipulation by some banks has reduced its use as a substitute for the risk-free asset. Moreover, LIBOR can be associated with counterparty risk, as observed during the 2007–2009 financial crisis. The Overnight Indexed Swap (OIS) is now considered less risky than the LIBOR rate because it contains a lower counterparty risk.

12.1 THEORETICAL MODEL

The article by Dionne, Artis, and Guillen (1996) examines a problem inherent to consumer loans.[3]

Consider the following hypotheses:

- Only consumer loans are considered, thus no mortgage financing.
- Borrowers may have collateral or not, just as they may or may not be new borrowers.
- A priori, the bank does not observe the default probability directly when it signs the loan contract.
- What complicates the analysis for the bank (as for most banks) is the fact that it permits the customer to miss three monthly payments before considering it as defaulting or in default. For our purposes, we consider any borrower who has four or more nonpayments to be in default.

The article also studies the distribution of nonpayments conditional on whether there is default or not, to model the costs of bank loan management.

The type of loan contract considered is a variant of a standard debt model. The bank lends D dollars to a customer at an interest rate r, which is a function of its default probability $(1 - p)$. This value is not known initially, but will be determined by the risk classification. The opportunity cost of the bank is $D(1 + \mu)$, where μ is the Treasury bill rate, for example. We assume that the bank is in competition and gains zero economic profits from this bank loan. It therefore evens out its opportunity cost with the potential net earnings from granting a loan:

$$D(1 + \mu) = D(1 + r) - p\ E_0(C_0) - (1 - p)\ E_1(C_1) - (1 - p)\,D\ (1 + r)\ \pi. \quad (12.1)$$

The right-hand side of equation (12.1) contains the gross earnings from the loan $D(1 + r)$, less different costs:

- $(1 - p)\ D(1 + r)\pi$ is the expected cost of the loan default, where π is the fraction of the loan that will not be repaid (LGD). We assume here that exposure at default (EAD) is equal to the capitalized loan amount $(D(1 + r))$.

[3]For an extension of this model, see Roszbach (2004).

- $pE_0(C_0)$ is the expected value of the administrative costs linked to the first three nonpayments. The realization of (C_0) is random. In the empirical portion, we suppose that it follows a Poisson process.
- $(1 - p)\ E_1(C_1)$ is the expected value of the administrative costs linked to nonpayments higher than or equal to four (in the state of default). The realization of (C_1) is also random.

We can rewrite equation (12.1) to obtain relation (12.2):

$$D(r - \mu) - pE_0(C_0) - (1 - p)E_1(C_1) - (1 - p)D(1 + r)\pi = 0, \qquad (12.2)$$

which lets us isolate r*, the equilibrium interest rate corresponding to a given default risk:

$$r^* = \frac{D\mu + D\pi(1 - p) + pE_0(C_0) + (1 - p)E_1(C_1)}{D(1 - \pi(1 - p))}. \qquad (12.3)$$

We can verify that r* is an increasing function of the default probability $(1 - p)$, of π, and of the expected administrative costs $E_0(C_0)$ and $E_1(C_1)$. We also note that if $(1 - p) = 0$ and if $E_0(C_0) = 0$, $r^* = \mu$.

As mentioned above, the equilibrium interest rate includes a premium linked to the default risk and to the corresponding administrative costs. In other words, r* is strictly higher than μ at equilibrium when $(1 - p)$, administrative costs, and π are positive. It is difficult for the bank to estimate $(1 - p)$, $E(C_0)$, and $E(C_1)$. We assume here that $\pi > 0$ is known.

Before proceeding with the estimation of $(1 - p)$, $E_0(C_0)$ and $E_1(C_1)$, let us see how this bank loan model is linked to the standard debt model discussed in the previous chapters.

We can rewrite the equation of the standard debt contract as follows:

$$D(1 + \mu) = \int_0^F (x - c)g(x)dx + (1 - G(F))F, \qquad (12.4)$$

where F is the face value of the debt, x represents the revenue from a loan, $c = E_1(C_1)$, and $E_0(C_0)$ is zero. Here, only one nonpayment is sufficient to put the borrower in default, and the borrower is entitled to a single nonpayment in the state of default.

$(1 - G(F))$ corresponds to the non-default probability (namely p in our consumer loan model), and $G(F)$ to the probability of default. We can rewrite equation (12.4) and obtain:

$$D(1 + \mu) = \int_0^F xg(x)dx - c\int_0^F g(x)dx + (1 - G(F))\ F \qquad (12.5)$$

or, if we write that $\int_0^F xg(x)dx = F(1 - \pi)G(F)$:

$$D(1 + \mu) = F(1 - \pi)G(F) - cG(F) + (1 - G(F))\ F$$

$$D(1 + \mu) = F - \pi G(F)\ F - cG(F)$$

$$F \approx D\ (1 + \mu) + \pi G(F)\ F + cG(F)$$

$$F \approx \frac{D(1 + \mu) + cG(F)}{1 - \pi G(F)} > D(1 + \mu). \qquad (12.6)$$

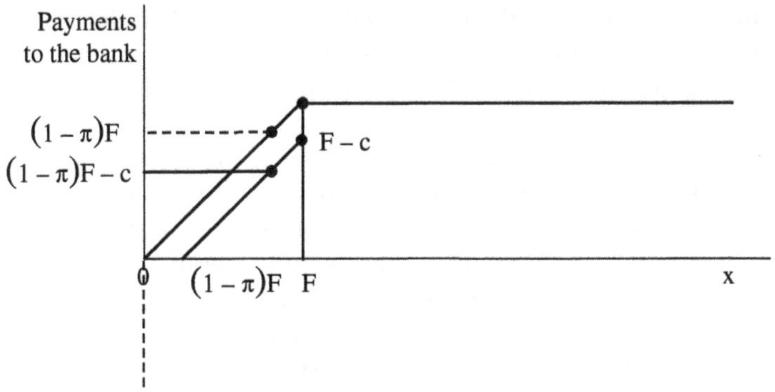

FIGURE 12.2 Standard debt contract adjusted to the consumer loan model.

This is an approximation because F is included in G(F). We represent this solution in Figure 12.2. Here there is only one recovery that gives the bank a recovery value of $(1 - \pi)F$.

Note that from the development of equation (12.6), the face value of the debt is a function of the loan amount D, of the opportunity cost $D(1 + \mu)$, of the default probability G(F), of the LGD, and of the audit cost *c*. It must be higher than $D(1 + \mu)$ when there is a default risk and management fees or audit costs associated with the default.

We can rewrite relation (12.6) in the following form if we replace F with $D(1 + r^*)$ and G(F) with $(1 - p)$:

$$D(1 + \mu) = D(1 + r^*) - \pi(1 - p)D(1 + r) - c\ (1 - p). \tag{12.7}$$

Here, the face value of the debt is equivalent to $D(1 + r^*)$, because the default risk is reflected in the equilibrium loan rate. Therefore, we can rewrite the previous relation to obtain:

$$r^* = \frac{D\mu + c(1 - p) + \pi(1 - p)\ D}{D\ (1 - \pi(1 - p))}. \tag{12.8}$$

Again, if $(1 - p) = 0, r^* = \mu$. If $(1 - p)$, *c*, and π are positive, the optimal pricing of the loan implies a risk premium explained by the default risk, audit costs, and loss given default.

12.2 EMPIRICAL ANALYSIS

The data come from a Spanish bank. We have the status of the loan files for 2,446 customers at a given date, in May 1989. The durations of individual loans at that date vary between 1 and 60 months.

The starting dates of the contracts vary, and some customers have nonpayments in their files. We must therefore consider the different contract durations to make the data comparable. In other words, we must carefully control the different risk exposures of the contracts to eliminate potential bias in the estimation of default probability. In addition, we know some of the customers' characteristics on the contract signing dates. We can therefore predict the individual default probabilities at the signing date by estimating the parameters of a Logit model, for example, which allows two possible events: default or non-default. Here, note that default does not correspond to a bankruptcy.

Table 12.1 shows nonpayment frequencies. It is interesting to note that there is a jump at the value 4, which clearly shows that the distribution of nonpayments is not a simple Poisson process. Rather, it contains a barrier at this value, which is explained by the fact that the loan defaults at the fourth nonpayment. Let us separate non-defaults from defaults, signifying that the best way to estimate the distribution of nonpayments to predict default risk is to proceed in two steps: 1) estimate the probability of obtaining more than three nonpayments by a Logit model, and 2) estimate the conditional distributions of nonpayments by using truncated counting distributions: one distribution for the values 0, 1, 2, and 3 and another for values equal to or greater than 4.

The main variables used are described in Table 12.2. The signs of the predicted effects of these variables on the default probability are also shown. We discuss here only the main variables; the others are considered as control variables. Y represents our truncated counting variable, modeled by a truncated Poisson process. YDUM is a dichotomous dummy variable used as a dependent variable to estimate the default probability and its complement, the probability of non-default for fewer than four nonpayments.

As mentioned above, it is important to control risk exposure. We have two variables measuring risk exposure, DURA and TD4. The latter variable identifies borrowers present for more than four years, whereas the first measures the seniority of the loan in months. The two variables should positively influence the default probability. Note that here we limit the predictions of the variables to their effects on the default probability because they are more related to risk management. We do not discuss their effects on the conditional distributions of nonpayments, but we interpret some empirical results.

COLL is a dummy variable indicating whether the borrowers offered collateral on the loan, in which case they represent a better risk because in case of default they will lose their collateral.

TABLE 12.1 Frequency of the number of nonpayments.

Number	Frequency	Percentage
0	1,665	68.1
1	271	11.1
2	101	4.1
3	73	3.0
4	106	4.3
5	72	2.9
6	43	1.8
7	31	1.3
8	31	1.3
9	25	1.0
10	19	0.8
11	9	0.4

TABLE 12.2 List of variables used in the econometric analysis and the predicted sign to explain the default probability.

Variable	Description	Predicted sign
Y	Number of nonpayments	
YDUM	1 if the number of nonpayments is ≥ 4; 0 otherwise	
TD4	1 if the total duration of the loan contract is > 4 years; 0 otherwise (reference group)	+
DURA	Number of months to count from the start of the contract until the sampling date	+
AGE1	1 if in the 18-to-24 age group; 0 otherwise	+
AGE2	1 if in the 25-to-39 age group; 0 otherwise	+
AGE3	1 if in the 40+ age group (reference group); 0 otherwise	
COLL	1 if credit is used to buy a good with a loan guarantee (collateral); 0 otherwise	–
EDU1	1 if the customer has not completed elementary school; 0 otherwise	+
EDU2	1 if the customer has completed elementary school; 0 otherwise	+
EDU3	1 if the customer has completed high school or college; 0 otherwise	+
EDU4	1 if the customer has a university degree (reference group); 0 otherwise	
RECSAL	1 if the customer receives a salary by direct deposit in their bank account; 0 otherwise	–
M1	1 if married, non-homeowner, salary below $3,000 per month; 0 otherwise	+
M2	1 if married, non-homeowner, salary above $3,000 per month; 0 otherwise	+
M3	1 if married, homeowner, salary below $3,000 per month; 0 otherwise	+
M4	1 if married, homeowner, salary above $3,000 (reference group); 0 otherwise	
NM1	1 if not married, non-homeowner; 0 otherwise	+
NM2	1 if not married, homeowner (reference group); 0 otherwise	
CENTRE	1 if credit is not granted by a bank (by a store, for example); 0 otherwise	+
RESID	1 if the resident has been living in his home for at least four years; 0 otherwise	–
Z1	1 the person resides in the south (Andalusia, Canaries, Castilla-La Mancha, Extremadura, Murcia) (reference group); 0 otherwise	
Z2	1 the person resides in the north (Aragon, Asturias, Cantabria, Castilla-Leon, Galicia, Pais, Vasco); 0 otherwise	+/–
Z3	1 the person resides in the east (Baleares, Catalunya, Valencia); 0 otherwise	+/ –
Z4	1 if the person resides in the center (Madrid); 0 otherwise	+/ –

RECSAL indicates that the borrowers receive their salary at the lending bank. Again, this is proof that they represent a better risk because their reputation may suffer in case of default if they contract a loan from the bank that receives their salary.

CENTER indicates whether the loan was negotiated directly with the bank or by an intermediary. We suppose that good risks negotiate directly with banks.

RESID indicates whether the borrowers have been living in their present home for more than four years. We suppose that such borrowers represent better risks because in Spain, stability is an important characteristic.

Other variables represent age, education, area of residence, marital status, home ownership and monthly salary. We suppose that individuals who are owners, married and whose salaries are higher represent lower risks of default.

Table 12.3 gives the means and variances of the variables used. These numbers indicate that the average age of loans is 19 months, and that one-third of the loans last more than four years. More than 45% of the loans have collateral, and more than 40% of borrowers do business with the bank where their salary is deposited. Slightly fewer than 74% of borrowers have been in their home for at least four years, and 16% negotiated their loan with a non-bank lender.

Tables 12.4 and 12.6 give the main results of the estimation of the model. Table 12.4 presents the econometric results of the estimation of the default probability and the parameters of the distribution of nonpayments of borrowers who did not default. Table 12.6 shows the same information as that presented in Table 12.4, but for borrowers who defaulted.

TABLE 12.3 Descriptive statistics

Variable	Mean	Variance
TD4	0.335	0.223
DURA	18.812	117.690
AGE1	0.087	0.080
AGE2	0.483	0.250
AGE3	0.439	0.245
COLL	0.453	0.248
EDU1	0.043	0.041
EDU2	0.486	0.250
EDU3	0.320	0.218
EDU4	0.152	0.129
RECSAL	0.403	0.241
M1	0.206	0.164
M2	0.020	0.019
M3	0.079	0.073
M4	0.695	0.212
NM1	0.219	0.171
NM2	0.781	0.171
CENTRE	0.158	0.133
RESID	0.738	0.193
Z1	0.282	0.202
Z2	0.292	0.207
Z3	0.297	0.209
Z4	0.129	0.113

TABLE 12.4 Truncated negative binomial barrier for non-defaults.

Variable	Barrier 1		Barrier 2	
	(Logit)	(TrunNB)	(Logit)	(TrunNB)
Constant	−1.8373	−0.48086	−2.305	−0.794
	(−31.280)	(−2.425)	(−7.791)	(−1.550)
TD4	—	—	0.516	0.244
			(4.045)	(0.950)
DUREEA	—	—	0.028	0.009
			(4.879)	(0.740)
AGE1	—	—	0.223	0.200
			(0.893)	(0.452)
AGE2	—	—	0.061	0.561
			(0.443)	(2.100)
AGE3	—	—	—	—
COLL	—	—	−0.573	−1.156
			(−4.364)	(−4.055)
EDU1	—	—	0.761	−0.016
			(2.500)	(−0.030)
EDU2	—	—	0.374	0.823
			(1.866)	(2.347)
EDU3	—	—	0.231	0.179
			(1.075)	(0.563)
EDU4	—	—	—	—
RECSAL	—	—	−0.932	−0.611
			(−6.540)	(−2.419)
M1	—	—	0.619	0.404
			(3.948)	(1.325)
M2	—	—	0.486	−0.167
			(1.119)	(−0.214)
M3	—	—	0.509	1.133
			(2.205)	(2.282)
M4	—	—	—	—
NM1	—	—	0.348	0.504
			(2.004)	(1.658)
NM2	—	—	—	—
CENTRE	—	—	0.038	−0.845
			(0.207)	(−2.684)
RESID	—	—	−0.250	−0.198
			(−1.811)	(−0.672)
Z1	—	—	—	—
Z2	—	—	−0.086	0.187
			(−0.568)	(0.609)
Z3	—	—	−0.425	0.245
			(−2.584)	(0.800)
Z4	—	—	−0.646	−0.633
			(−2.569)	(−1.809)
Alpha	—	4.7566	—	4.089
		(7.796)		(8.017)
Number of parameters	1	2	19	20
Number of observations	2,446	2,110	2,446	2,110
Log-likelihood	−978.8	−1,505.1	−896.4	−1,446.7
Total log-likelihood	−2,483.9		−2,363.1	

For each barrier, the first column (Logit) of Table 12.4 gives the results of the estimation of the default probability, and the second column presents the results of the estimation of nonpayments (0, 1, 2, 3) when there is no default, where TrunNB means Truncated Negative Binomial.

The first regression of Table 12.4 (Barrier 1) presents the results of a basic model without explanatory variables. This model confirms that we can reject the Poisson distribution for nonpayments, because the Alpha parameter is statistically significant. This indicates overdispersion in the data; the variance is greater than the mean (λ). In general, we can write the variance of a negative binomial distribution (BN) as:

$$\text{Var} = \lambda(1 + \text{Alpha})$$

where λ is the mean of the distribution and Alpha the dispersion parameter. When the estimated Alpha is equal to zero, we do not reject the Poisson distribution (Boyer, Dionne, and Vanasse, 1992), and, in this case, λ measures the mean and the variance.

The second regression group (Barrier 2) confirms the rejection of the Poisson distribution. It also shows that several variables are significant to explain the two regressions (Student's *t*-test statistics are presented in parentheses), which is confirmed by a higher log-likelihood for Barrier 2 than for Barrier 1. The results indicate that it is not necessarily the same variables that explain the two distributions. For example, the two risk exposure variables (TD4 and DURA) are positive and significant to explain default probabilities but not nonpayments. The COLL (collateral) and RECSAL (salary at the bank) variables are significant in both regressions, with negative signs indicating that they lower borrowers' risks. The variable M3 (married, homeowner, and salary below \$3,000) has a positive sign, indicating that this group of borrowers is more risky than the M4 group (married, homeowner, salary over \$3,000). The same is true for the variable NM1 relative to NM2, although the degree of significance is lower.

Tables 12.4 and 12.6 present similar results, with the exception of the variables RECSAL, NM1, and Alpha. The Poisson distribution is not rejected in Table 12.6. It seems there is more homogeneity in the default group. We can also observe a few differences for the geographic location variables (Z_i). Tables 12.5 and 12.7 give

TABLE 12.5 Chi-square statistic for non-defaults.

Value	Observed frequency	Estimated frequency	
		Barrier 1	Barrier 2
0	1,665	1,665.80	1,665.08
1	271	261.34	264.52
2	101	118.01	115.93
3	73	64.88	64.47
4+	336	335.99	336.00
Chi- square		3.83	3.21
P-value (4d.l.)		0.430	0.523
Cumulative frequency			
0	1,665	1,665.80	1,665.08
1	1,936	1,927.13	1,929.60
2	2,037	2,045.14	2,045.53
3	2,110	2,110.02	2,110.00
4+	2,446	2,446.01	2,446.00

TABLE 12.6 Truncated negative binomial model for defaults.

Variable	Barrier 3		Barrier 4	
	(Logit)	(TrunNB)	(Logit)	(TrunNB)
Constant	−1.8373	−1.4208	−2.305	−1.487
	(−31.280)	(−11.418)	(−7.791)	(6.982)
TD4	—	—	0.516	−0.102
			(4.045)	(−1.165)
DURA	—	—	0.028	0.007
			(4.879)	(1.515)
AGE1	—	—	0.223	0.273
			(0.893)	(1.961)
AGE2	—	—	0.061	0.231
			(0.443)	(2.489)
AGE3	—	—	—	—
COLL	—	—	−0.573	−0.234
			(−4.364)	(−2.481)
EDU1	—	—	0.761	0.065
			(2.500)	(0.339)
EDU2	—	—	0.374	0.054
			(1.866)	(0.424)
EDU3	—	—	0.231	−0.170
			(1.075)	(−1.168)
EDU4	—	—	—	—
RECSAL	—	—	−0.932	−0.139
			(−6.540)	(−1.530)
M1	—	—	0.619	0.103
			(3.948)	(1.023)
M2	—	—	0.486	0.070
			(1.119)	(0.122)
M3	—	—	0.509	0.341
			(2.205)	(2.330)
M4	—	—	—	—
NM1	—	—	0.348	0.040
			(2.004)	(0.392)
NM2	—	—	—	—
CENTRE	—	—	0.038	0.017
			(0.207)	(0.147)
RESID	—	—	−0.250	−0.045
			(−1.811)	(−0.532)
Z1	—	—	—	—
Z2	—	—	−0.086	−0.180
			(−0.568)	(−1.980)
Z3	—	—	−0.425	−0.278
			(−2.584)	(−2.292)
Z4	—	—	−0.646	0.049
			(−2.569)	(0.313)
Alpha	—	0.16248	—	0.049
		(1.392)		(0.907)
Number of parameters	1	2	19	20
Number of observations	2,446	336	2,446	336
Log-likelihood	−978.8	−638.9	−896.4	−617.8
Total log-likelihood	−1,617.7		−1,514.2	

TABLE 12.7 Chi-square statistic for defaults.

Value	Observed frequency	Estimated frequency	
		Barrier 1	Barrier 2
0-1-2-3	2,110	2,110.03	2,110.00
4	106	94.14	92.20
5	72	76.89	76.99
6	43	57.49	58.08
7	31	40.14	40.62
8	31	26.55	26.81
9	25	16.79	16.92
10+	28	24.00	24.38
Chi- square		12.97	13.64
P-value (7d.l.)		0.073	0.058
Cumulative frequency			
0-1-2-3	2,110	2,110.03	2,110.00
4	2,216	2,204.17	2,202.20
5	2,288	2,281.06	2,279.19
6	2,331	2,338.54	2,337.27
7	2,362	2,378.69	2,377.89
8	2,393	2,405.24	2,404.70
9	2,418	2,422.03	2,421.62
10+	2,446	2,446.03	2,446.00

the detailed tests for the results of the regressions obtained in tables 12.4 and 12.6. Tables 12.5 and 12.7 present the adequacy test of the truncated negative binomial (TrunNB) or Poisson regressions for non-defaults and defaults respectively. In both cases, the estimated distributions are not rejected, which indicates that they closely represent the raw data.

Table 12.8 analyzes Type 1 and Type 2 errors of the model that estimates default probabilities, using three thresholds: average frequency of defaults observed, default probability of the average individual, and a threshold of 12.5% suggested by bank managers. We will focus on the average frequency threshold, which seems to provide the best results. Note that other thresholds may also be used; the choice is up to

TABLE 12.8 Classification of results.

		Prediction	
		Good No default	Bad Default
Threshold equal to average default frequency			
Observation	Good	1,376	734
	Bad	107	229
Threshold equal to default probability of average individual			
Observation	Good	1,152	958
	Bad	72	264
Threshold equal to 0.125, as suggested by bank managers			
Observation	Good	1,258	852
	Bad	88	248

banks' credit risk managers. The 336 bad risks (107 + 229) represent customers who already defaulted, and the 2,110 good risks (1,376 + 734) are those who did not default.

The model predicts 1,376 good risks, which are indeed good risks. It also predicts 229 bad risks, which are indeed bad risks. However, it considers 107 individuals to be good risks whereas they were actually bad risks (Type 2 error). This error may be costly because it implies that the bank will charge lower interest rates to bad risks. In addition, the model classifies 734 individuals as bad risks although they are good risks (Type 1 error). This result implies that the bank should demand a higher risk premium for good risks, which may be costly because these customers may leave the bank. The trade-off relationship between Type 1 and Type 2 errors can be managed in greater detail by considering the associated costs and benefits. Different levels of risk tolerance can be used (Touré, 2013).

Tables 12.9–12.11 indicate how to use these results to calculate the parameters required for risk management. The parameters of the econometric model allow us to calculate the expected management costs associated with the different risks, along with the risk premiums on interest rates. Table 12.9 confirms that young people, ages 25–39, have expected costs of management fees that are $7 higher in the case of nonpayment before default than do customers with ages of 40 and over. These extra

TABLE 12.9 Conditional estimated cost of nonpayment ($E_0(C_0)$) for different individuals (before default).

Age 2 (25–39)	$29
Age 3 (40+)	$22
RECSAL = 0	$38
RECSAL = 1	$21

TABLE 12.10 Conditional estimated cost of nonpayment ($E_1(C_1)$) for different individuals (after default)

Age 2 (25–39)	$489
Age 3 (40+)	$396
RECSAL = 0	$585
RECSAL = 1	$427

TABLE 12.11 Equilibrium interest rates (r^*) for different average borrowers D = $10,000, π = 40%.

	μ = 9%	μ = 5%
Age 1 (18–24)	16.03%	11.81%
Age 3 (40+)	14.61%	10.42%
RECSAL = 0	17.44%	13.17%
RECSAL = 1	12.55%	8.44%

costs rise to \$93 after default, according to Table 12.10. Individuals who receive their salary at the bank have expected costs that are \$17 (before default) and \$158 (after default) lower than individuals who do not receive their salary at the bank, according to both scenarios.

Table 12.11 gives the interest rate premiums according to two levels of Treasury bill rates (μ); we discuss the case of 5%. The interest rate charged to the 40+ group should be 10.42%, whereas that charged to the age group of 18 to 24 should be 11.81%. Different rates are also charged depending on whether the borrowers receive their salary at the bank. Note that these results are explained by the fact that the age groups are statistically significant (relative to Age3) to explain nonpayment in case of default ($E_1(C_1)$) and that the variable RECSAL is significant to explain nonpayment and default probabilities.

12.3 CREDIT LINE AND LOAN DEFAULT

Table 12.13 presents additional econometric results obtained from another database that comes from a Canadian bank (Bergerès, d'Astous, and Dionne, 2011). The variables are defined in Table 12.12. Bergerès, d'Astous, and Dionne (2011)

TABLE 12.12 Definition of variables.

Variable	Definition	Usage rate (Expected Sign)	Default probability (Expected Sign)
Usage rate	Usage rate of the line of credit $\text{Usage rate} = \dfrac{\text{line of credit used}}{\text{total authorized amount}}$		+
Default probability	Probability that the loan is in default	+	
Seniority	Seniority as a customer at the bank (measured in months)	+	–
Employee	Employment status: 1 if employee; 0 otherwise	+	–
Dependents	Number of dependents	+	+
Age	Six age groups; 66+ age group is the reference category	+	+
Sex	1 if the person is male 0 otherwise	+	+
Payment capacity ratio	$\dfrac{\text{monthly loan payment}}{\text{payment capacity}}$ payment capacity = revenue + tangible assets – expenses. A ratio < 0.127, indicating high payment capacity, is the reference category	–	–
Loan maturity	$\dfrac{\text{maturity date} - \text{observation date}}{30}$		–
Loan guarantee	1 if the loan is guaranteed (collateral); 0 otherwise		–
Number of lines of credit	Counting variable		+
Line of credit balance	Amount available to use	+	
Line of credit guarantee	1 if the line is guaranteed; 0 otherwise	–	

estimate the default probability of loan holders at a financial institution according to their observable characteristics. We can see that a lower risk rating, worse payment capacity, and the number of lines of credit held by the borrower increase the default probability. The authors propose an index of payment capacity that takes into account the borrowers' monthly income and financial commitment: the higher the monthly payments are relative to income, the worse their payment capacity. A better payment capacity is used as a reference group. A weaker payment capacity increases the default probability and the line of credit's usage rate.

A key contribution of this study is that it analyzes individual default probability and the use of the customer's main line of credit at the same bank. The two equations are estimated simultaneously. We observe that customers who use their line of credit the most have a higher default probability on their loan. Inversely, those with a higher default probability use their line of credit more. It is possible that individuals who have difficulties making payments use their line of credit to repay their loan. In addition, customers who must use their line of credit to cover their current expenses do not have sufficient funds to repay the loan. Bad risks (high risk score) use their line of credit more. Conversely, those that provided a larger guarantee on their line of credit use it less.

TABLE 12.13 Coefficients of marginal effects.

	Use of line of credit (instrumented Tobit)	Default probability (instrumented Probit)
Usage rate		0.4585 (0.006)***
Default probability	0.5891 (0.000)***	
Risk rating	0.0104 (0.034)**	0.1818 (0.000)***
Seniority	0.0001 (0.000)***	−0.0001 (0.792)
Employee	0.0172 (0.131)	0.0282 (0.828)
Dependents	0.0088 (0.134)	−0.0862 (0.185)
Age 24 and under	−0.0090 (0.658)	0.2323 (0.257)
25 to 35	−0.0164 (0.330)	0.3823 (0.018)**
36 to 45	0.0053 (0.754)	0.3983 (0.012)**
46 to 55	−0.0160 (0.396)	0.6196 (0.001)***
56 to 65	−0.0351 (0.060)*	0.5700 (0.005)***
Sex	−0.0331 (0.000)***	0.2224 (0.003)***
Payment capacity	0.0592 (0.000)***	0.3882 (0.002)***
Payment capacity $0.498 \leq$ Ratio < 1	0.0537 (0.010)***	0.2983 (0.013)**
Payment capacity $0.249 \leq$ Ratio < 0.498	0.0554 (0.000)***	−0.0516 (0.698)
Payment capacity $0.127 \leq$ Ratio < 0.249	0.0240 (0.017)**	0.1679 (0.170)
Loan maturity		−0.0058 (0.004)***
Loan guarantee		−0.0374 (0.645)
Number of lines of credit		0.2623 (0.000)***
Line of credit balance	0.0331 (0.000)***	
Line of credit guarantee	−0.0343 (0.010)***	
Number of observations	14,827	14,827
Adjusted pseudo-R^2	0.0136	0.4371
Prob > chi2		0.000
Prob > F	0.000	

12.4 CONCLUSION

In this chapter, we analyze risk selection in consumer credit, which is a form of credit risk management done by banks. We show that several easily observable characteristics may affect a consumer's default probability and the conditional distributions of monthly nonpayments of loans. We also show how to calculate the expected costs of nonpayments and the risk premiums to charge on interest rates. Lastly, we confirm that line of credit availability has an adverse effect on individuals' default risk.

We show how difficult it is for a lender to estimate a borrower's default probability. The same problem exists for corporate credit risk. However, it is accentuated by higher loan amounts and fewer clients, which reduces the statistical reliability.

REFERENCES

Agarwal, S., Ambrose, B.W. Chomsisengphet, S. and Liu, C., 2006. "An Empirical Analysis of Home Equity Loan and Line Performance." *Journal of Financial Intermediation* 15, 444–469.

Agarwal, S., Ambrose, B.W., and Liu, C., 2006. "Credit Lines and Credit Utilization." *Journal of Money, Credit and Banking*, 1–22.

Bergerès, A.S., d'Astous, P., and Dionne, G., 2011. "Is There Any Dependence between Consumer Credit Line Utilization and Default Probability on a Term Loan? Evidence from Bank-Level Data." Working paper 11-03, Canada Research Chair in Risk Management, HEC Montréal, Montreal, Canada. A different version has been published in the *Journal of Empirical Finance* 33 (September 2015), 276–286.

Boyer, M., Dionne, G., and Vanasse, C., 1992. "Econometric Models of Accident Distributions." In: G. Dionne (Ed.), *Contributions to Insurance Economics*. Boston: Kluwer Academic Press.

Chiappori, P.A., and Salanié, B., 2000. "Testing for Asymmetric Information in Insurance Markets." *Journal of Political Economy* 108, 56–78.

Collin-Dufresne, P., Goldstein, R.S., and Martin, J.S., 2001. "The Determinants of Credit Spread Changes." *Journal of Finance* 56, 2177–2207.

D'Astous, P., and Shore, S.H., 2017. "Liquidity Constraints and Credit Card Delinquency: Evidence from Raising Minimum Payments." *Journal of Financial and Quantitative Analysis* 52, 1705–1730.

Dionne, G., Artis, M., and Guillen, M., 1996. "Count Data Models for a Credit Scoring System." *Journal of Empirical Finance* 3, 303–325.

Dionne, G., Gauthier, G., Hammami, K., Maurice, M. and Simonato, J.G., 2010. "Default Risk in Corporate Yield Spreads." *Financial Management* 39, 707–731.

Dionne, G., Gauthier, G., Hammami, K., Maurice, M., and Simonato, J.G., 2011. "A Reduced Form Model of Default Spreads with Markov-Switching Macroeconomic Factors." *Journal of Banking and Finance* 35, 1984–2000.

Dionne, G., Gouriéroux, C., and Vanasse, C., 2001. "Testing for Evidence of Adverse Selection in the Automobile Insurance Market: A Comment." *Journal of Political Economy* 109, 444–453.

Dionne, G., and Rothschild, C., 2014. "Economic Effects of Risk Classification Bans." *The Geneva Risk and Insurance Review* 39, 184–221.

Elton, E., Gruber, M., Agrawal, D., and Mann, C., 2001. "Explaining the Rate Spread on Corporate Bonds." *Journal of Finance* 56, 247–277.

Huang, J.Z., and Huang, M., 2012. "How Much of Corporate-Treasury Yield Spread Is Due to Credit Risk?" *The Review of Asset Pricing Studies* 2, 153–202.

Hull, H., Petrescu, M., and White, A., 2005. "The Relationship between Credit Default Swap Spreads, Bond Yields, and Credit Risk Announcements." *Journal of Banking and Finance* 28, 2789–2811.

Jagtiani, J., and Lang, W.W., 2011. "Strategic Defaults on First and Second Lien Mortgages during the Financial Crisis." *The Journal of Fixed Income* 20, 7–23.

Jiménez, G., Lopez, J.A., and Saurina, J., 2009. "Empirical Analysis of Corporate Credit Lines." *The Review of Financial Studies* 22, 5069–5098.

Jiménez, G., Lopez, J.A., and Saurina, J., 2009. "Calibrating Exposure at Default for Corporate Credit Lines." *Journal of Risk Management in Financial Institutions* 2, 121–129.

Maalaoui Chun, O., Dionne, G., and François, P., 2014. "Credit Spread Changes within Switching Regimes." *Journal of Banking and Finance* 49, 41–55.

Measter, L.J., Nakamura, L.I., and Renault, M., 2006. "Transactions Accounts and Loan Monitoring." *The Review of Financial Studies* 20, 529–556.

Norden, L., and Weber, M., 2010. "Credit Line Usage, Checking Account Activity, and Default Risk of Bank Borrowers." *The Review of Financial Studies* 23, 3665–3699.

Roszbach, K., 2004. "Bank Lending Policy, Credit Scoring, and the Survival of Loans." *Review of Economics and Statistics* 4, 946–958.

Strahan, P.E., 1999. "Borrower Risk And Price and Nonprice Terms of Bank Loans." Mimeo, Federal Reserve Bank of New York.

Touré, F., 2013. "Modèle de probabilité de default des prêts d'une banque canadienne." Supervised project report, HEC Montréal.

CHAPTER 13

Portfolio Management of Credit Risk

This chapter presents the first model for portfolio management of credit risk, developed by J.P. Morgan in the 1990s to meet capital requirements of the Basel regulation. This model arose because investment banks found that the capital requirements for credit risk stipulated in Basel I were too severe in evaluating default risk asset by asset, without considering dependencies between asset risks. The CreditMetrics (CM) model consequently proposes a portfolio management approach to bond management for a given bank. It shows how considering the correlations between default probabilities and bond credit migration can reduce optimal capital. Several banks currently use extensions of this model to manage credit risk under the Basel II Accord, which was put in place in 2004. No major changes were put in place for credit risk under Basel III.

13.1 CREDITMETRICS

CreditMetrics (CM) is an analytical model for the credit risk of a bond portfolio based on Value at Risk. It can calculate the required regulatory capital for banks and can also be used for optimal portfolio management, either for investment decisions or to protect portfolios from overly high default risks. It can also calculate credit limits.

Developed by the business bank J.P. Morgan for education and promotion purposes, this model does not necessarily correspond to the real model that the bank uses to manage its credit risk. The complete CM document can be found on the bank's website. An abridged version is presented here.

CM is based on mark-to-market values rather than historical book values. It can thus consider market variations associated with credit risk continuously, unlike the historical approach. The model considers default probabilities of financial instruments, along with their credit migrations.

In general, the density function of credit risk has a thicker left tail than that of market risk, which implies that only considering the standard deviation may be an insufficient method to measure this risk. Analysts therefore need more statistical information to evaluate the real density of credit risk than they do to evaluate market risk.

To illustrate the differences associated with credit risk, the global risk of a portfolio is presented in two ways: the standard deviation of the portfolio and the value of the first percentile of the distribution. The time horizon is annual.

The procedure is composed of three main steps:

1. Evaluation of the risk exposure of each instrument;
2. Evaluation of the volatility of each instrument by considering changes in default probabilities and credit migration probabilities;
3. Consideration of the correlations of default and credit migration risks between different bonds to calculate the portfolio risk.

The first step consists of assigning a default probability, a recovery rate at default, and the probabilities of credit migration (for example, those from Moody's tables) to each bond.

We must then calculate the value of the bond for each credit migration scenario, including default. For example, a BBB bond that becomes an A bond acquires a new value by discounting the projected cash flows from the coupons and from the face value using the zero-coupon curve rates of an A asset. In general, when assets are upgraded, their values increase, and the opposite happens when they are downgraded.

In the third step, we calculate the mathematical expectation and standard deviation for the value of the bond using migration probabilities and the corresponding values. We can also calculate the risk of a bond or portfolio using the first percentile of the values obtained if we assume a degree of confidence of 99%.

Now, suppose that the portfolio contains several assets or bonds. Each asset includes eight values corresponding to eight possible ratings, including that of default. For two assets, it is therefore possible to build an 8×8 matrix containing 64 entries to obtain the joint probabilities of migration and default. Inside the value matrix, each cell contains the sum of the values for the two assets corresponding to each of the joint scenarios.

Next, we calculate the joint probabilities of the 64 cells. If the two distributions are independent, the probability of one cell is the simple product of the migration probabilities of both assets. Otherwise, we must consider the correlations between the two assets.

If we have several bonds, the previous method would be difficult to generalize. For a portfolio of three assets, this would represent 512 joint probabilities (or 8^3) and for a portfolio of n assets, a total of 8^n joint probabilities. Fortunately, we can derive much information from the joint analyses of two by two assets as the CM document does. Simulations can also be used to calculate the risk of a portfolio containing many assets.

CM uses the firm assets value or its approximations to calculate the correlations of the default and credit migration probabilities by applying the KMV (Kealhofer, McQuown, Vasicek) approach and by supposing that asset variations (approximated by the variations of stock values) follow normal distributions.

In the following pages, we present chapters 2, 3, and 8 of CM.

13.2 REVIEW OF CHAPTERS 2 AND 3 OF CREDITMETRICS

13.2.1 Chapter 2 of CreditMetrics

Chapter 12 of this book discusses credit risk. It shows that three concepts are important when evaluating credit risk:

1. Default probabilities;
2. Loss given default (LGD which corresponds to the rate of losses at default);
3. Risk exposure at default (EAD).

Now, we will see how CM evaluates this risk with a portfolio containing one bond. In the next steps, we will use the main elements of this evaluation, which could also describe a more general portfolio.

Once again, our study is limited to the default risk of bonds; other components of credit risk are not considered. Credit risk and default risk are therefore considered synonymous in this chapter. We do not consider variations in bond prices associated with market and liquidity risk, only those linked to changes in default rating. We suppose that the interest rate spreads of private bonds relative to those of public risk-free bonds are due uniquely to the default risk of bonds. The best rated bonds require a smaller rate spread than do riskier bonds.

Figure 13.1, taken from the CM document, illustrates the main steps to follow in calculating the credit risk of a bond rated by a rating agency.

First, we must know the rating of the asset chosen and must follow its evolution via a credit migration table like that shown in Table 13.1. For example, the probability that the asset's rating remains AA is 90.65% or that the rating for the same asset drops to A is equal to 7.79%. Table 13.1 also shows the default probabilities of different ratings at the end of the period. We observe that for an AA or AAA asset, the default probability is zero, whereas that of a B asset is equal to 5.20%. It is important to note that what we call a probability is in fact a frequency, estimated using historical data from previous years.[1]

We must then evaluate the recovery rate (1 – LGD) for the bond at default. CM uses the seniority of the bond to evaluate the mean recovery rates and their

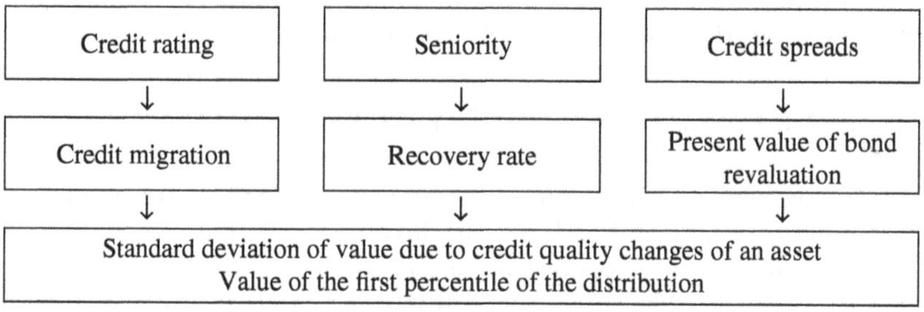

FIGURE 13.1 Elements used to calculate asset credit risk.
Source: Gupton, Finger, and Bhatia (1997). Reproduced with permission of Greg Gupton.

TABLE 13.1 One-year transition matrix (%).

	Rating at year-end							
Initial rating	AAA	AA	A	BBB	BB	B	CCC	Default
AAA	90.81	8.33	0.68	0.06	0.12	0	0	0
AA	0.70	90.65	7.79	0.64	0.06	0.14	0.02	0
A	0.09	2.27	91.05	5.52	0.74	0.26	0.01	0.06
BBB	0.02	0.33	5.95	86.93	5.30	1.17	0.12	0.18
BB	0.03	0.14	0.67	7.73	80.53	8.84	1.00	1.06
B	0	0.11	0.24	0.43	6.48	83.46	4.07	5.20
CCC	9.22	0	0.22	1.30	2.38	11.24	64.86	19.79

Source: Standard & Poor's CreditWeek (1996). Reproduced in CreditMetrics (1997).

[1]To calculate the probabilities using a generator, see Dionne et al. (2010).

TABLE 13.2 Recovery rates by seniority class.

Seniority class	Mean (%)	Standard deviation (%)
Senior Secured	53.80	26.86
Senior Unsecured	51.13	25.45
Senior Subordinated	38.52	23.81
Subordinated	32.74	20.18
Junior Subordinated	17.09	10.90

Source: Gupton, Finger, and Bhatia (1997). Reproduced with permission of Greg Gupton.

variabilities. Examples are given in Table 13.2. Because standard deviations are very high (owing to the scarcity of default events), this implies heterogeneity within the different classes, an important consideration when calculating capital. We can observe that the recovery rate increases with the seniority of the bond. In theory, the recovery value is equal to the face value of the bond multiplied by the recovery rate.

The third step is to calculate the present value of bonds corresponding to the different ratings using zero-coupon curves (examples of rates are found in Table 13.3).

Table 13.3 indicates the required rates for different ratings during the next four years. We use this table to calculate the present value of a bond corresponding to a rating, like the A rating given by equation ((13.1)). It is important to note that the coupons used in this equation are those of a BBB bond. The exercise consists of calculating the new present value of a BBB bond if it becomes an A bond. This value is \$108.66, whereas the real value of a BBB bond that does not migrate is \$107.55.

$$V = \$6 + \frac{\$6}{(1+3.72\%)} + \frac{\$6}{(1+4.32\%)} + \frac{\$6}{(1+4.93\%)} + \frac{\$106}{(1+5.32\%)} = \$108.66 \tag{13.1}$$

Now that we have these values for different ratings and the corresponding migration probabilities for a given bond, we can directly calculate its mean value, which considers its credit risk and its potential migrations.

Table 13.4 shows all the values that a BBB bond can have in the coming year if it changes ratings or if it stays at BBB. For example, \$51.13 represents its recovery value at default obtained using a recovery rate taken from Table 13.2. It is the mean

TABLE 13.3 Examples of zero-coupon rates by credit rating category (%).

Category	Year 1	Year 2	Year 3	Year 4
AAA	3.60	4.17	4.73	5.12
AA	3.65	4.22	4.78	5.17
A	3.72	4.32	4.93	5.32
BBB	4.10	4.67	5.25	5.63
BB	5.55	6.02	6.78	7.27
B	6.05	7.02	8.03	8.52
CCC	15.05	15.02	14.03	13.52

Source: Gupton, Finger, and Bhatia (1997). Reproduced with permission of Greg Gupton.

TABLE 13.4 Possible values of a BBB bond according to the risk class at the end of the year.

Year-end rating	Value ($)
AAA	109.37
AA	109.19
A	108.66
BBB	107.55
BB	102.02
B	98.10
CCC	83.64
Default	51.13

Source: Gupton, Finger, and Bhatia (1997). Reproduced with permission of Greg Gupton.

value of recovery of a senior unsecured bond. We can now calculate the mean of these values and the standard deviation for a BBB bond using the credit migration probabilities in Table 13.1. These values are given in Table 13.5.

Whereas the initial value of the BBB bond was $107.55, it has a mean value of $107.09 when we consider the probable changes in risk class. The standard deviation obtained is $2.99, which may represent a measure of credit risk equivalent to that of the parametric approach to market risk. The VaR_r corresponding to 99% is equal to $2.33 × $2.99 = $7.00, as illustrated in Table 13.6. We obtain a corresponding R* of $107.09 – $7.00 = $100.09. However, this R* does not necessarily correspond to the 1st percentile of the distribution because the distribution may be asymmetrical.

We can directly use the first percentile of the distribution if we work at a 99% degree of confidence. To obtain the value associated with the first percentile, we proceed as follows by using the data from Table 13.5. When the cumulative probability

TABLE 13.5 Calculating the mean and standard deviation of a BBB bond associated with changes in risk class.

Year-end rating	Probability of credit migration (%)	Value of BBB bond ($)
AAA	0.02	109.37
AA	0.33	109.19
A	5.95	108.66
BBB	86.93	107.55
BB	5.30	102.02
B	1.17	98.10
CCC	0.12	83.64
Default	0.18	51.13
Mean = $107.09		
Variance = 8.9477		
Standard deviation = $2.99		

Source: Gupton, Finger, and Bhatia (1997). Reproduced with permission of Greg Gupton.

TABLE 13.6 Capital according to the Credit Metrics model.

	VaR_r	R*
Chapter 2 BBB		
Parametric	\$7.00	\$100.09
SD \$2.99; μ = \$107.09		
Parametric (correction % recovery)	\$7.41	\$99.62
VaR_r 1st percentile; μ = \$107,09	\$8.99	\$98.10
Chapter 3 BBB and A		
Parametric (correlation 30%)	\$7.81	\$205.81
SD = \$3.35 (joint estimation)		
SD = \$4.48 (isolated estimations)		
SD BBB = \$2.99		
SD A = \$1.49; μ = \$213.63		
VaR_r 1st percentile	\$9.23	\$204.40
Marginal risk of A	Parametric	Percentile
\$0.36 < \$1.49	\$0.81 < \$3.47	\$0.24 < \$3.39
	\$1.49 × 2.33	\$106.54 – \$103.15

Note: SD signifies standard deviation and μ is the mean.

of credit migration, starting from that associated with default, exceeds 1%, we retain the bond value associated with the probability that lets us pass this threshold. For example, the default probability of a BBB bond is 0.18% and that of it becoming a CCC bond is 0.12%. This equates to a cumulative probability of 0.30%, which is still less than 1%. By adding the probability that the bond becomes a B, at 1.17%, we thus obtain a total probability of 1.47%. Because we have just exceeded the 1% threshold, we retain the value associated with the probability that the bond becomes B, namely \$98.10. This therefore implies a required capital of \$8.99 (\$107.09 – \$98.10) versus a value of \$7.00 with the parametric approach if we use 2.33 to consider the degree of confidence.

The comparison of the two VaR_rs in Table 13.6 clearly shows that the use of standard deviation (in assuming a normal distribution) underestimates the default risk of this bond. Table 13.6 also indicates how to adjust the parametric VaR if we consider the imprecision of the calculation associated with the recovery rate at default. The parametric VaR goes from \$7 to \$7.41 because the standard deviation increases to 3.18.[2]

13.2.2 Chapter 3 of CreditMetrics

When dealing with several assets, we must compute the correlations between credit risks of different bonds to correctly represent portfolio diversification in the calculation of required capital. The fourth column of Figure 13.2 indicates that we must consider the correlations between credit migrations when we calculate the portfolio value of the credit VaR. The probabilities of credit migration and default may be affected by common factors (credit cycle, recession), creating dependencies in their

[2]See CreditMetrics (2007) for more details.

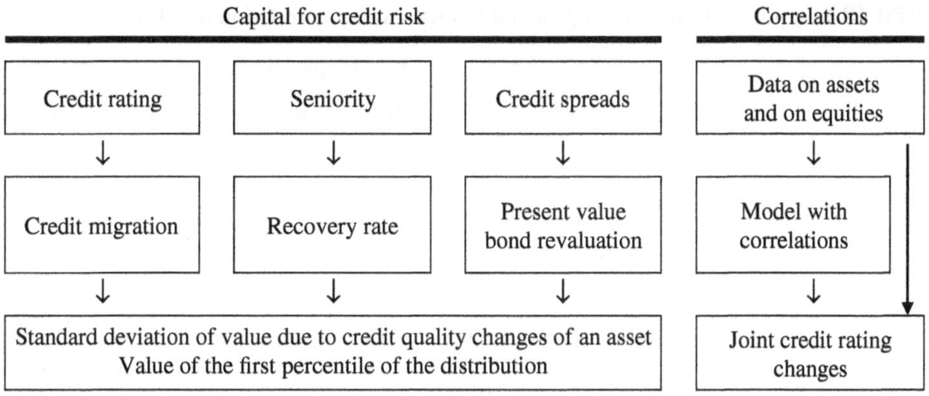

FIGURE 13.2 CreditMetrics model with correlations between risks.
Source: Gupton, Finger, and Bhatia (1997). Reproduced with permission of Greg Gupton.

variations. First, we consider these correlations as data to calculate capital; we then describe how the CM model is extended to calculate these correlations explicitly.

Consider a portfolio with two bonds. Each bond has a credit rating and a corresponding credit migration row in the retained matrix of migrations. We can then calculate the joint probabilities of being in one of the 64 cells of the joint migration matrix by supposing, for example, that the correlations are zero (Table 13.7), or by supposing a correlation equal to 0.30 between firms with two different ratings (Table 13.8).

The joint probabilities calculated in Table 13.7 are obtained from the product of the two bonds' probabilities under the assumption of independence. The probabilities in Table 13.8 are obtained from the calculation of a joint probability, by assuming a dependency of 30% for credit risk between the two bonds. Three characteristics of the two tables are important: 1) considering correlations mainly affects values situated on the diagonal (79.69, 0.39, and 0.64, instead of 79.15, 0.14, and 0.29 in Table 13.7); 2) the sum of the probabilities of each column and row is equal to the probability that the bond issuer is found in this row or column; 3) the sum of the joint 64 probabilities of the tables is equal to 1.

TABLE 13.7 Joint credit migration probabilities with zero correlation (%).

		Bond A rating							
Bond BBB rating		AAA 0.09	AA 2.27	A 91.05	BBB 5.52	BB 0.74	B 0.26	CCC 0.01	Default 0.06
AAA	0.02	0.00	0.00	0.02	0.00	0.00	0.00	0.00	0.00
AA	0.33	0.00	0.01	0.30	0.02	0.00	0.00	0.00	0.00
A	5.95	0.01	0.14	5.42	0.33	0.04	0.02	0.00	0.00
BBB	86.93	0.08	1.98	79.15	4.80	0.64	0.23	0.01	0.05
BB	5.30	0.00	0.12	4.83	0.29	0.04	0.01	0.00	0.00
B	1.17	0.00	0.03	1.06	0.06	0.01	0.00	0.00	0.00
CCC	0.12	0.00	0.00	0.11	0.01	0.00	0.00	0.00	0.00
Default	0.18	0.00	0.00	0.16	0.01	0.00	0.00	0.00	0.00

Source: Gupton, Finger, and Bhatia (1997). Reproduced with permission of Greg Gupton.

TABLE 13.8 Joint credit migration probabilities with assets correlation of 30% (%).

		Bond rating A							
		AAA	AA	A	BBB	BB	B	CCC	Default
Bond rating BBB		0.09	2.27	91.05	5.52	0.74	0.26	0.01	0.06
AAA	0.02	0.00	0.00	0.02	0.00	0.00	0.00	0.00	0.00
AA	0.33	0.00	0.04	0.29	0.00	0.00	0.00	0.00	0.00
A	5.95	0.02	0.39	5.44	0.08	0.01	0.00	0.00	0.00
BBB	86.93	0.07	1.81	79.69	4.55	0.57	0.19	0.01	0.04
BB	5.30	0.00	0.02	4.47	0.64	0.11	0.04	0.00	0.01
B	1.17	0.00	0.00	0.92	0.18	0.04	0.02	0.00	0.00
CCC	0.12	0.00	0.00	0.09	0.02	0.00	0.00	0.00	0.00
Default	0.18	0.00	0.00	0.13	0.04	0.01	0.00	0.00	0.00

Source: Gupton, Finger, and Bhatia (1997). Reproduced with permission of Greg Gupton.

TABLE 13.9 Joint values of a portfolio containing two bonds ($)according to year-end ratings.

		Bond rating A							
		AAA	AA	A	BBB	BB	B	CCC	Default
Bond rating BBB		106.59	106.49	106.30	105.64	103.15	101.39	88.71	51.13
AAA	109.37	215.96	215.86	215.67	215.01	212.52	210.76	198.08	160.50
AA	109.19	215.78	215.68	215.49	214.83	212.34	210.58	197.90	160.32
A	108.66	215.25	215.15	214.96	214.30	211.81	210.05	197.37	159.79
BBB	107.55	214.14	214.04	213.85	213.19	210.70	208.94	196.26	158.68
BB	102.02	208.61	208.51	208.33	207.66	205.17	203.41	190.73	153.15
B	98.10	204.69	204.59	204.40	203.74	201.25	199.49	186.81	149.23
CCC	83.64	190.23	190.13	189.94	189.28	186.79	185.03	172.35	134.77
Default	51.13	157.72	157.62	157.43	156.77	154.28	152.52	139.84	102.26

Source: Gupton, Finger, and Bhatia (1997). Reproduced with permission of Greg Gupton.

Calculating the mean value and standard deviation of the portfolio is simple: the process is the same as that of a bond, but using 64 values instead of 8. The joint values of bonds are the sum of the amounts of individual bonds, as Table 13.9 demonstrates.

The required capital values are presented in Table 13.6. We can observe that the mean values correspond to the sum of the two expectations calculated separately ($213.63). However, the joint standard deviation of $3.35 (with correlation) is less than the sum of the two independent values ($4.48), hence the advantage of diversification. The first percentile (0.92 in Table 13.8) has a value of $204.40 in Table 13.9, which represents about $9.23 of required capital, whereas by the parametric method the capital is $3.35 \times 2.33 = \$7.81$. This seems to indicate that imposing a joint normal distribution on credit risk underestimates the required capital.

Table 13.6 shows how to calculate the marginal risk on a portfolio when an A bond is added to a BBB bond. In the first column, we observe that the joint standard deviation (with correlation) is $3.35, whereas that of the BBB bond is $2.99 and that of an A bond is $1.49. The addition of an A bond therefore increases the marginal risk of the diversified portfolio by \$0.36. Column 2 restates the values under the parametric VaR_r, whereas column 3 shows the values in terms of the first percentile. Column 2 compares the variation of the parametric VaR_r by adding an A bond alone (\$3.47) to that of the variation in the portfolio (\$0.81), while column 3 compares the variation of the portfolio's 1st percentile VaR (\$9.23 – \$8.99) to the A bond's 1st percentile VaR (\$106.54 – \$103.15), where \$106.54 is the mean value and \$103.15 is the 1st percentile level value. Again, considering correlations reduces the required capital.

We will now look at the calculation of the correlations between the migration and default probabilities in transition matrices. These correlations are obtained by using the KMV approach.

13.3 KMV APPROACH

The basic idea behind the KMV approach is to use the value of listed stocks and option theory to assess business's default risk (Saunders and Allen, 2002) because firms' assets are not continuously observable (audited financial statements are annual or quarterly). Stock values are used to infer the values of firms' assets. However, this model applies uniquely to listed companies whose stock values are directly observable and liquid.

Consider a company that issued bonds (or made a bank loan) with a face value equal to F, as shown in Figure 13.3. As we have seen several times, this implies that the company must disburse F if it is not in default (A_2) or must default if the asset value (A_1) is below F. A_1 is the recovery (or residual) value of the bond at default. CM supposes that the mean of this value is a function of the seniority of that debt.

For Merton (1974), when a bank signs a debt contract or buys a bond, this amounts to writing a put option on the assets of the borrower or the bond issuer. The borrower has the option to default when the value of its assets is lower than F.

We can also represent the debt contract as a put option written by the bondholder or the bank on the value of the stock of the firm that issued the debt. If the equity value is higher than the exercise price X, the borrower keeps the premium of the option. However, if the value falls below X, the bondholder or the bank retains a value below X, as Figure 13.4 indicates.

We can take the analogy further and confirm that the same variables, used to evaluate a put option on shares, can also be used to evaluate the default option on

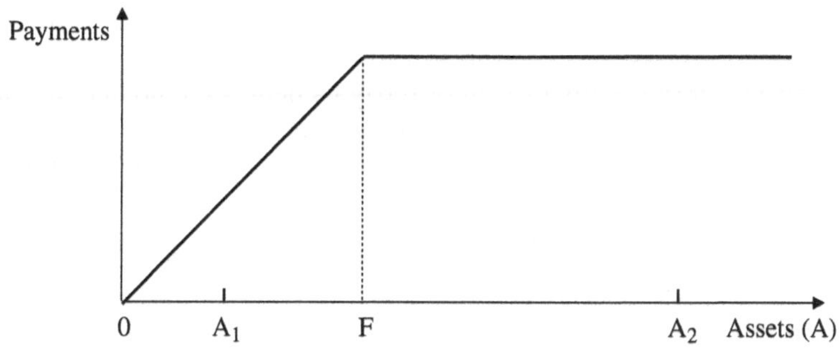

FIGURE 13.3 Standard debt contract.

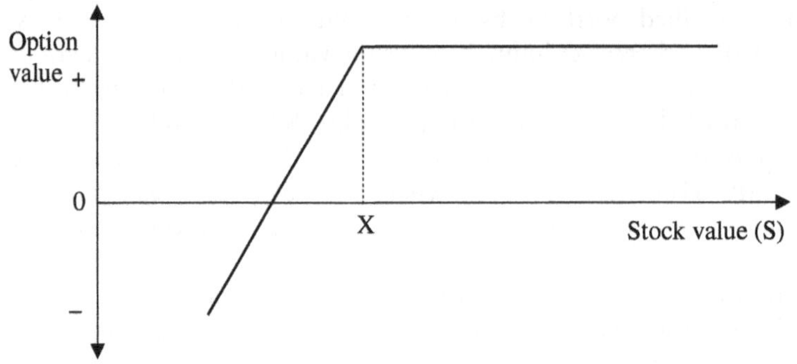

FIGURE 13.4 Put option on the value of the firm shares.

a bond issued or on a loan. We can write the value of a stock option on shares as $\overline{O}_1 = f(\overline{S}, \overline{X}, \overline{r}, \overline{\sigma}_S, \overline{\tau})$, whereas the value of an option on assets is $\overline{O}_2 = g(A, \overline{B}, \overline{r}, \sigma_A, \overline{\tau})$, where:

- S and A represent the values of the underliers, namely the shares and assets respectively;
- X and B are the exercise values of the options;
- r is the risk-free interest rate;
- σ_A and σ_S are the underlying volatilities;
- τ is the time to maturity;
- $\overline{\ }$ indicates that the variable is observable.

The five variables of a stock option ($\overline{O}_1$) are observable whereas the value of assets A and its volatility σ_A are not observable for an option on assets ($\overline{O}_2$). Some authors have tried to solve the problem of missing information by supposing that the market value of assets is equal to the book value. However, it is difficult to obtain the value of σ_A and to solve for $\overline{O}_2$.

KMV innovates by eliminating the interpretation of a put option on a debt issuer. Instead, they consider the value of equity as a call option for the indebted company. It thus solves the problem of two unknowns by using structural relations between: 1) the market value of the firm equity and that of its assets, and 2) the volatility of the firm's equity and that of its assets.

Consider Figure 13.5, which represents the repayment problem of the loan for the borrower (shareholders). If the value of the assets is at point A_2, for example, the company can repay its debt, and shareholders may conserve $A_2 - B$. The higher the value of the firm's assets, the larger the residual portion or the premium to shareholders. However, if the company cannot repay its debt, shareholders will lose their investment, namely a maximum of L, given the constraint of limited liability. This call option therefore has parameters like all options on the equity of the firm that issues the debt.

$$\overline{O}_3 = h(A, \overline{B}, \overline{r}, \sigma_A, \overline{\tau}). \tag{13.2}$$

The option's value is a function of the same five variables that were observed for the put option on the assets. A and σ_A are not yet observable. To solve the problem of identification (one equation, two unknowns), KMV supposes that the equity's

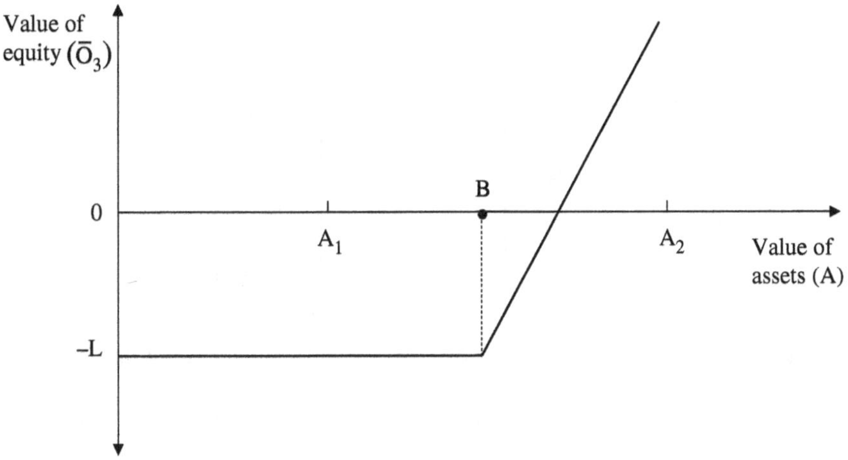

FIGURE 13.5 Call option on the value of firm assets.

observable volatility is a function of the same firm assets value $\bar{\sigma}_E = g(\sigma_A)$. By using these two equations (13.2 and the value $\bar{\sigma}_E$), we can therefore solve the system of equations and obtain values for A and σ_A by successive iterations. We substitute $\sigma_A = g^{-1}(\bar{\sigma}_E)$ in equation (13.2) to obtain one equation with one unknown. One difficulty in this case is to find explicit forms for the two equations.[3]

For CM, it is not necessary to know A because, in their framework, firm equity serves solely to calculate the volatility of assets and their correlations between firms with different risk classes.

By observing the value of listed stocks, we can infer the value of the firm's assets and calculate the default probability. This probability is illustrated in Figure 13.6; it corresponds to the area under the density function to the left of point F for a BB firm. Z_{def} in Figure 13.7 is the equivalent of F in Figure 13.6.

CM extends this analysis to calculate the credit migration probabilities. These probabilities are represented in Figure 13.7. Therefore, for a BB firm, the probability

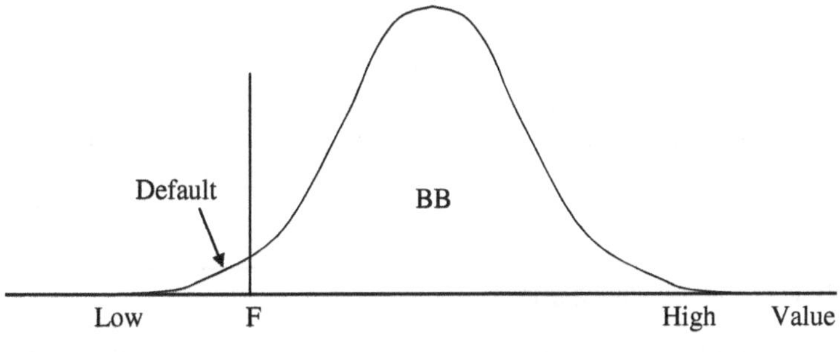

FIGURE 13.6 Distribution of the value of the firm assets and the face value of debt F.
Source: Gupton, Finger, and Bhatia (1997). Reproduced with permission of Greg Gupton.

[3]See Saunders and Allen (2002) for a more detailed discussion.

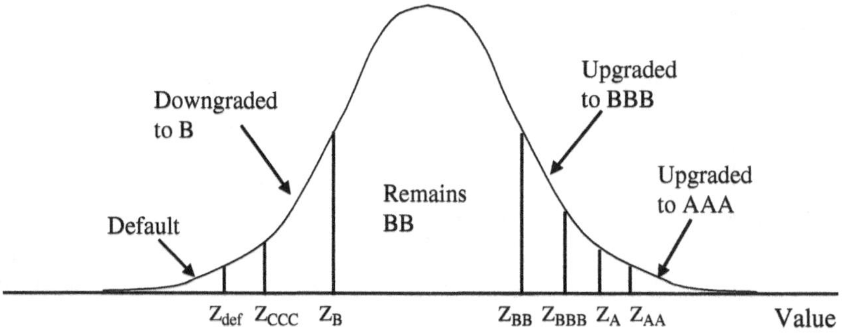

FIGURE 13.7 Distribution of firm assets value and the boundaries of the credit ratings.
Source: Gupton, Finger, and Bhatia (1997). Reproduced with permission of Greg Gupton.

of being a CCC corresponds to the area under the density function to the left of point Z_{ccc}. The transition probability is the area of the difference between the two values Z_{def} and Z_{ccc} under the density function. We also observe the area representing the probability that the bond remains a BB, and so on. The value of the sum of the areas under the density is equal to 1, like the sum of the credit and default migration probabilities in a transition matrix.

13.4 CALCULATION OF CORRELATIONS

In section 13.2, we have seen that the consideration of correlations may affect the capital calculations for credit risk. The correlations were introduced via the transition matrix, by supposing the same correlation between all bonds with two different ratings, namely an A and a BBB, for example. It is not evident that the same correlation exists between all A and BBB firms, especially if the portfolio is made up of bonds from different industries and different countries. This is the implied hypothesis of the model that we will now present. In the last section, we will discuss and distinguish the strategies proposed by CM to extend the model with more heterogeneity between firms.

This section presents the calculation of correlations between the values of firms' equity to obtain joint credit migration probabilities. Although the CM document dates back to 1997, it is still up to date because the study of this problem has practically not evolved due to a lack of adequate data. Chapter 8 of CM begins by discussing default correlations.

Approximation of Default Correlations

Table 13.10 presents the correlations of the annual default rates obtained from Moody's for the 1970–1995 period. The correlations implied within these ratings are weak, but significantly different from zero at a degree of confidence of 97.5%. They are all positive, which may suggest cyclical effects. However, this approach is not satisfactory to obtain default correlations for the following reasons:

- There are very few observations, and consequently the standard deviations and their confidence intervals are high.

TABLE 13.10 Default correlations with confidence intervals.

Category	Default rate μ	Standard deviation σ	Implied default correlation ρ	Lower confidence $\Pr\{\rho < X\} = 2.5\%$	Upper confidence $\Pr\{\rho > X\} = 2.5\%$
AA	0.03%	0.1%	0.33%	0.05%	1.45%
A	0.01%	0.1%	1.00%	0.15%	4.35%
BBB	0.13%	0.3%	0.69%	0.29%	1.83%
BB	1.42%	1.4%	1.40%	0.79%	2.91%
B	7.62%	4.8%	3.27%	1.95%	6.47%

Source: Moody's 1970–1995 1-year default rates and volatilities; Gupton, Finger, and Bhatia (1997). Reproduced with permission of Greg Gupton.

- A normal approximation of the standard deviations may be incorrect, especially for BBB and B bonds.
- The mean μ is supposed to be identical for all firms with the same rating.
- The approach is sensitive to economic cycles.
- This approach does not take credit migrations into account.

Direct Estimation of Joint Probabilities

Tables 13.11 (numbers) and 13.12 (percentages) show the joint movements of 1,234 firms with A and BBB ratings for 40 quarters. For a rating system with 8 possibilities, this implies a need for 28 tables of this type ((64 – 8)/2) to cover all the risk ratings. This process may be interesting but requires many observations from rating agencies, which are not available to holders of large bond portfolios. Nonetheless, several large banks are currently developing their own internal rating systems.

Another criticism comes, again, from the fact that this method still supposes that firms are identical within risk classes. Lastly, we can note that many cells have zero values, including those of defaults, due to the scarcity of observations.

Model Based on Firms Assets

We now re-examine the credit risk of a portfolio with two bonds. CM supposes that the changes in the value of firms assets follows a normal distribution. We have

TABLE 13.11 Credit quality co-movements.

	Firms starting with A rating							
Initial rating BBB	AAA	AA	A	BBB	BB	B	CCC	Default
AAA	0	0	0	0	0	0	0	0
AA	0	15	1,105	54	4	0	0	0
A	0	978	44,523	2,812	414	224	0	0
BBB	0	12,436	621,477	40,584	5,075	2,507	0	0
BB	0	839	41,760	2,921	321	193	0	0
B	0	175	7,081	532	76	48	0	0
CCC	0	55	2,230	127	18	15	0	0
Default	0	29	981	67	7	0	0	0

Source: Gupton, Finger, and Bhatia (1997). Reproduced with permission of Greg Gupton.

TABLE 13.12 Historical joint credit quality co-movements (%).

	Initial rating A							
Initial rating	AAA	AA	A	BBB	BB	B	CCC	Default
AAA	–	–	–	–	–	–	–	–
AA	–	0.00	0.14	0.01	0.00	–	–	–
A	–	0.12	5.64	0.36	0.05	0.03	–	–
BBB	–	1.57	78.70	5.14	0.64	0.32	–	–
BB	–	0.11	5.29	0.37	0.04	0.02	–	–
B	–	0.02	0.90	0.07	0.01	0.01	–	–
CCC	–	0.01	0.28	0.02	0.00	0.00	–	–
Default	–	0.00	0.12	0.01	0.00	–	–	–

Source: Gupton, Finger, and Bhatia (1997). Reproduced with permission of Greg Gupton.

seen in Table 13.7 that the joint probability of remaining A and BBB is 79.15% if the correlation is zero, and is 79.69% (Table 13.8) if the correlation between the two ratings is 0.30. CM underlines the empirical importance of correlations between different default and migration risks. We will now show how we obtain a correlation value as a result and how we can use this value to calculate the joint credit migration probabilities.

CM begins by calculating the distribution of asset values and then uses the correlations between the firm's assets (measured by correlations between stock returns) to obtain the values of the correlations on credit migrations, including default probabilities. The underlying idea is that the value of the assets of a firm (determined by its stock value) adequately reflects its capacity to repay its future debt (KMV approach).

Figure 13.8 establishes the links between the values of an asset and the credit ratings of a BB firm with a current value of $100 million. For example, if the (standardized) market value falls to a level of $18 million or less, the firm may not be able

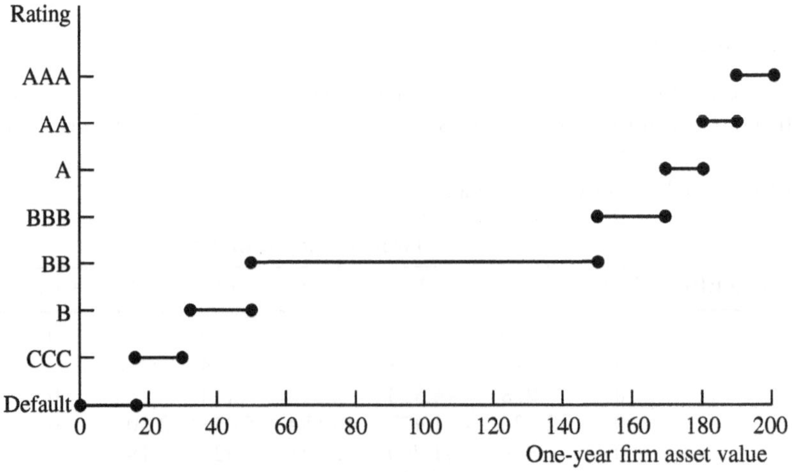

FIGURE 13.8 Credit migration of a BB firm.
Source: Gupton, Finger, and Bhatia (1997). Reproduced with permission of Greg Gupton.

to repay its debts. By extension, if the value is between \$50 million and \$150 million, its rating will remain BB. The authors use the term *thresholds* to refer to the values that can change a firm's credit class.

By assuming that the changes in the returns of asset values follow a normal distribution with a zero mean and positive standard deviation σ (this hypothesis on the mean is not very important because we are only interested in calculating the standard deviations and correlations), we can calculate the correspondences between the credit migration probabilities of the asset value model and those of the migration tables.

Table 13.13 shows the relationship between the transition probabilities of a BB firm (Table 13.1) and those obtained from the assets of the same firm by supposing that the assets' returns (based on the returns of listed stocks) follow a standard normal distribution. For example, we know that the default probability for this type of firm is 1.06% (Table 13.1). This default probability can be written as in equation (13.3), where Z is the return on the firm's assets:

$$\Pr(\text{default}) = \Pr(Z < Z_{def}) = \Phi(Z_{def}/\sigma) = 1.06 \tag{13.3}$$

where:

Φ represents the distribution function of a standard normal distribution ($\mu = 0$);
Z_{def} is the default threshold;
Z_{def}/σ is the standard normal value of Z_{def}.

If we take the inverse function of Φ, we obtain:

$$Z_{def} = \Phi^{-1}(1.06\%) = -2.30\sigma \tag{13.4}$$

where −2.30 is obtained from the table of a standard normal distribution. This value is shown in Table 13.14 (panel A). We find that assets' returns must be downgraded to -2.30σ to reach the default threshold. To become a CCC firm, the probability is 2.06% (1.06 + 1.00) in Table 13.13, which corresponds to a value of -2.04σ in Table 13.14, namely the value ($Z_{CCC} = \Phi^{-1}(2.06\%)$).

We can subsequently obtain all the threshold values associated with the zones of a BB firm. Figure 13.9 represents the different zones of values that a BB firm may

TABLE 13.13 Transition probabilities for a BB bond.

Rating	Transition probability	Probability according to the firm value model
AAA	0.03	$1 - \Phi(Z_{AA}/\sigma)$
AA	0.14	$\Phi(Z_{AA}/\sigma) - \Phi(Z_{A}/\sigma)$
A	0.67	$\Phi(Z_{A}/\sigma) - \Phi(Z_{BBB}/\sigma)$
BBB	7.73	$\Phi(Z_{BBB}/\sigma) - \Phi(Z_{BB}/\sigma)$
BB	80.53	$\Phi(Z_{BB}/\sigma) - \Phi(Z_{B}/\sigma)$
B	8.84	$\Phi(Z_{B}/\sigma) - \Phi(Z_{CCC}/\sigma)$
CCC	1.00	$\Phi(Z_{CCC}/\sigma) - \Phi(Z_{Def}/\sigma)$
Default	1.06	$\Phi(Z_{Def}/\sigma)$

Source: Gupton, Finger, and Bhatia (1997). Reproduced with permission of Greg Gupton.

TABLE 13.14 Threshold values of a BB firm (panel A)and an A firm (Panel B).

Threshold	Value: Panel A	Value: Panel B
Z_{AA}	3.43 σ	3.12 σ'
Z_{A}	2.93 σ	1.98 σ'
Z_{BBB}	2.39 σ	−1.51 σ'
Z_{BB}	1.37 σ	−2.30 σ'
Z_{B}	−1.23 σ	−2.82 σ'
Z_{CCC}	−2.04 σ	−3.19 σ'
Z_{Def}	−2.30 σ	−3.24 σ'

Source: Gupton, Finger, and Bhatia (1997). Reproduced with permission of Greg Gupton.

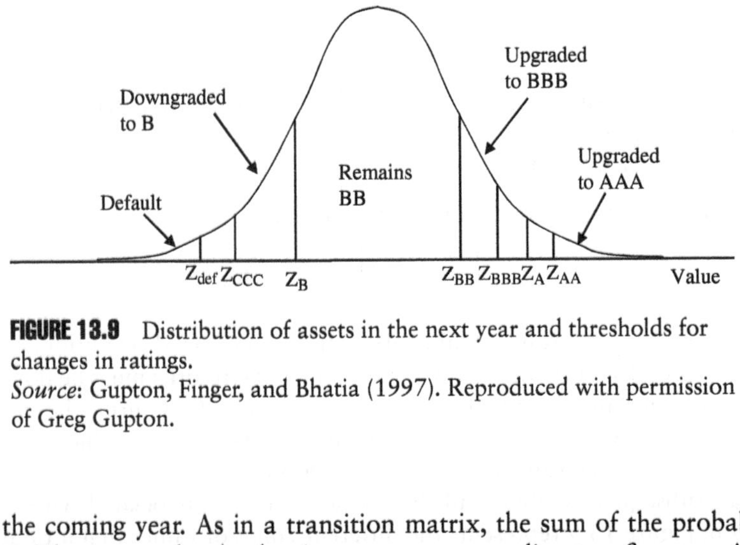

FIGURE 13.9 Distribution of assets in the next year and thresholds for changes in ratings.
Source: Gupton, Finger, and Bhatia (1997). Reproduced with permission of Greg Gupton.

have in the coming year. As in a transition matrix, the sum of the probabilities is equal to 1. The area under the density curve corresponding to a firm remaining at a BB rating is equal to 80.53%; that of default is equal to 1.06%; and that of transition from default to CCC is 1.00%.

These calculations can be done for each rating. Table 13.14 also reports the possible values of an A firm (Panel B). Knowing the asset distributions and the corresponding correlation coefficients, we can calculate the variance-covariance matrices (like that given in equation (13.5)), where σ' represents the standard deviation of an A firm's values and ρ the correlation coefficient between the BB and A firms' stock values. While continuing to assume that the mean values of returns are zero, with this information we can now calculate the joint probability that the first bond remains BB and that the second remains A.

This probability is given in a cell of a joint probability matrix, like that presented in Table 13.15, where ρ is equal to 20%; it is equal to 73.65%. This joint probability is obtained from equation (13.6), where $f(r, r'; \Sigma)$ is the density of a bivariate normal distribution that has a variance-covariance matrix Σ and R (R′)

TABLE 13.15 Joint probabilities of rating changes for BB and A bonds (%).

	Bond rating A								
Bond rating B	AAA	AA	A	BBB	BB	B	CCC	Default	Total
AAA	0.00	0.00	0.03	0.00	0.00	0.00	0.00	0.00	0.03
AA	0.00	0.01	0.13	0.00	0.00	0.00	0.00	0.00	0.14
A	0.00	0.04	0.61	0.01	0.00	0.00	0.00	0.00	0.67
BBB	0.02	0.35	7.10	0.20	0.02	0.01	0.00	0.00	7.69
BB	0.07	1.79	73.65	4.24	0.56	0.18	0.01	0.04	80.53
B	0.00	0.08	7.80	0.79	0.13	0.05	0.00	0.01	8.87
CCC	0.00	0.01	0.85	0.11	0.02	0.01	0.00	0.00	1.00
Default	0.00	0.01	0.90	0.13	0.02	0.01	0.00	0.00	1.07
Total	0.09	2.29	91.06	5.48	0.75	0.26	0.01	0.06	100

Source: Gupton, Finger, and Bhatia (1997). Reproduced with permission of Greg Gupton.

represents the random variables of BB (A) firms, and r and r' represent the corresponding observed returns.

$$\Sigma = \begin{pmatrix} \sigma^2 & \rho\sigma\sigma' \\ \rho\sigma\sigma' & \sigma'^2 \end{pmatrix} \tag{13.5}$$

$$\Pr\{Z_B < R < Z_{BB}, Z'_{BBB} < R' < Z'_A\} = \int_{Z_B}^{Z_{BB}} \int_{Z'_{BBB}}^{Z'_A} f(r, r'; \Sigma)\ dr'dr. \tag{13.6}$$

If we suppose that we can calculate all the correlations of the pairs of bonds of different risk classes, we must calculate 28 tables as in Table 13.15. However, this means that we assume that all firms in all pairs of A and BB firms have the same correlations, which seems to be a strong hypothesis. The remainder of the chapter describes how to evaluate the correlations between firms of different countries and different industries.

In section 8.5, CM discusses the practical problem of measuring correlations between assets of different firms. Banks that have sufficiently large databases may calculate them directly. For a portfolio of 100 bonds, this implies calculating 4,950 individual correlations. The correlations may also be estimated using different stock indices by country and by industry.

We will now describe this method. The main source of data is the stocks returns for rated firms and their correlations. These correlations are used to estimate those between the firm assets. To obtain an evaluation of the correlations between different firms in different countries, CM uses:

- The stock indices of different firms and different countries;
- Detailed information on each firm, using the weight of its activities in different countries and different industries.

Stock indices of countries concerned, along with those of main industries, are discussed in chapter 8 of CM. For countries that do not have detailed industrial indices, CM combines information from the country index with that of an International Industrial Index. CM constructed 152 country-industry indices, 28 country indices, 19 global industry indices, and 6 regional indices.

Banks can thus calculate the monthly returns on these indices, along with their standard deviations and covariances, to obtain the correlation indices for all indices constructed.

To apply these correlations to pairs of firms in a bond portfolio, CM:

- Assigns a weight to each firm depending on its industry and country;
- Calculates the returns of each firm by weighting the variations of firm-specific indices;
- Uses weights to calculate the correlations.[4]

13.5 CONCLUSION

In this chapter, we analyze how to calculate the credit risk of a bond portfolio. Correlations between defaults and credit rating movements should be considered for the following reasons:

1. Taking these correlations into account is important when carrying out credit risk portfolio management. We saw in section 13.2 that the analysis of correlations reduces capital. The empirical evidence affirms that correlations are important.
2. Generally, asset values can determine a firm's capacity to repay its debt. We should therefore use these values for the levels and variations of default probabilities. Because firm assets are not directly observable, we can use listed stocks to evaluate correlations between assets.
3. When we know the correlations between the stock returns of median firms (2×2), we can calculate the joint transition matrices using these correlations. We can repeat this exercise for each pair of firms whose bonds are in the portfolio. If all the correlations are equal between firms within the same risk class, we would need to calculate 28 joint matrices for the whole portfolio.
4. In practice, to calculate variance-covariance matrices of pairs of firms, we use correlations between stock indices of countries and industries because doing so for each pair of firms would be too painstaking. For instance, for a portfolio of 100 bonds we would need to calculate 4,950 correlations.
5. In chapter 10 of the CM document, the authors use the Monte Carlo simulation method to calculate a three-assets portfolio's VaR. They then do the same with an example of 20 assets.

REFERENCES

Alinasab, S., 2010. "Estimation of Default Correlation in a Loan Portfolio of Canadian Public Firms." Master thesis, HEC Montréal, Montreal, Canada.

Carty, L.V., and Lieberman, V., 1996. "Corporate Bond Defaults and Default Rates 1938–1995." Moody's Investors Service, Global Credit Research.

CreditMetrics, 2007. "Errata to the CreditMetrics Document." RiskMetrics Group, Inc.

CreditMetrics, 2007. "Technical Document." RiskMetrics Group, Inc.

[4]For an application to Canadian firms, see Alinasab (2010).

Dionne, G., Hammami, K., Gauthier, G., Maurice, M., and Simonato, J.G., 2010. "Default Risk in Corporate Yield Spreads." *Financial Management* 39, 707–731.
Dowd, K., 1998. *Beyond Value at Risk*. Chichester, UK: John Wiley & Sons, Inc.
Jorion, P., 2001. *Value at Risk*. McGraw Hill.
Fons, J.S., and Carty, L.V., 1995. "Probability of Default: A Derivatives Perspective." In: *Derivative Credit Risk*. London: The Risk Library, Risk Publications, 3–46.
Gupton, G.M., Finger, C.C., and Bhatia, M., 1997. CreditMetrics – Technical Document. JPMorgan, chapters 2, 3, and 8.
Merton, R.C., 1974. "On the Pricing of Corporate Debt: The Rate Structure of Interest Rates." *Journal of Finance* 29, 449–470.
Saunders, A., and Allen, L., 2002. *Credit Risk Measurement: New Approaches to Value at Risk and Other Paradigms*, 2nd ed. New York: John Wiley & Sons, Inc.
Standard & Poor's Corporation, 1996. Standard & Poor's *Creditweek*, vol. 16, nos. 45–51.

CHAPTER 14

Quantification of Banks' Operational Risk

This chapter covers operational risk, which is very different from the other risks previously discussed.[1] Operational risk is more similar to a pure risk rather than a financial risk intended to obtain a future return, such as market risk or credit risk. Although operational risk is also insurable, very few forms of insurance coverage for several components of operational risk exist on the market. Financial institutions must therefore opt for self-protection (prevention) and self-insurance to limit this risk. One form of self-insurance is to establish a capital reserve. This chapter will present models for calculating optimal capital for operational risk to satisfy regulatory requirements.

14.1 CONTEXT AND PRESENTATION OF OPERATIONAL RISK

Operational risk for banks and insurance companies is now regulated. We will discuss these regulations in relation to Basel II, which introduced the regulation of bank capital for operational risk in 2004.

In Europe, the regulation of operational risk for insurance companies is also well defined under Solvency II. Regulation of implementation procedures was discussed in Canada, and the rules took effect in 2017. In the United States, a task force (Capital Adequacy (E) Task Force) was put in place in 2013 by the NAIC (National Association of Insurance Commissioners) to evaluate how operational risk could be integrated in insurers' risk capital management.

14.1.1 Basel Accord and Regulation of Operational Risk

In 1988, the first rules for capitalization under Basel I were introduced by G10 countries. However, this regulation applied only to credit risk, also called counterparty risk. In 1996, Basel I was amended to take market risk into account.

It was only in 2004, under Basel II, that operational risk began to be regulated. The Basel II accord took effect in 2006 at the beginning of a period of financial difficulties for banks, which led to the major financial crisis that began in 2007.

[1]The research projects discussed in this chapter were conducted with Héla Dahen and Samir Saissi Hassani.

This second accord conserves the fundamental elements of the 1988 mechanism for credit risk but adds standards and measures that are more risk sensitive for credit and operational risks, underpinned by proven concepts, and that consider the local specificities of national oversight and accounting systems.

A new accord, Basel III, was proposed in 2010 to increase banks' Tier 1 regulatory capital and to put in place a mechanism to formally introduce liquidity risk in the regulation. Basel III does not significantly modify the regulation of market risk, credit risk, or operational risk. In this chapter, we focus on the regulation of operational risk under Basel II, although important modifications regarding calculations for capital based on advanced internal methods have been rethought.

Definition of Operational Risk

The operational risk of a bank is defined as the risk of losses resulting from inadequacy or failed internal processes (error) attributable to people, management and decision processes, technological systems, and external events. Operational risk is linked to the risks inherent in settlements or payments, to an unanticipated interruption of activities, and to administrative and legal risks. Strategic risks and those affecting reputation are not considered. Operational risk is very complex and, by definition, omnipresent.

Seven types of operational risk are part of the regulation's nomenclature:

1. Internal fraud (IF): theft by an employee, dishonest acts committed by employees acting on their own behalf, etc.
2. External fraud (EF): computer hacking, credit card theft, etc.
3. Employment practices and workplace safety (EPWS).
4. Clients, products, and business practices (CPBP): money laundering, sale of unauthorized products, incorrect pricing of a financial product, etc.
5. Damage to physical assets (DPA): vandalism, terrorism, earthquake, fire, flood, etc.
6. Execution, delivery, and process management (EDPM): error in recording data, gap in legal documentation, supplier failure, etc.
7. Business disruption and system failure (BD): breakdown of IT software and hardware, telecommunications malfunction, etc.

Banks must identify and evaluate each of these risks. They must therefore put in place a risk follow-up process within their administration, record losses, apply prevention, repair and control measures, and calculate a capital amount to cover net losses of insurance coverage.

A widespread procedure is to prepare a chart similar to that shown in Figure 14.1, in which the seven types of risk are associated with the eight main lines of business of a bank:

1. Corporate finance (CF)
2. Sales and trading (ST)
3. Retail banking (RB)
4. Commercial banking (CB)
5. Payment and settlement (PS)
6. Agency services (AS)

Line of business	Risk type						
	Internal fraud	External fraud	Job safety	Clients, products	Physical assets	Execution, process	System failure
Corporate finance							
Sales and trading							
Retail							
Commercial							
Settlement							
Agency							
Brokerage							
Asset management							

FIGURE 14.1 Management chart for banks' operational risk.

7. Retail brokerage (RBr)
8. Asset management (AM)

Banks must correctly define and measure the different types of risk associated with each of their lines of business and aggregate them to obtain their global exposure to operational risk, and thus calculate the optimal protection capital. Consequently, a mechanism must be put in place to give all bank employees incentives to not only reduce losses, but also to monitor, anticipate, control, and report them.

Operational risk management nonetheless faces several obstacles. For one, banks need historical data on operational losses to implement the mechanism described above; they did not really possess such data before the year 2000. This is true for many businesses, including insurance companies, which do not always keep their historical data. Another major difficulty is linked to the heterogeneity of loss distributions. Some losses, like those associated with poor pricing of structured financial products, are very rare but may collectively add up to several million dollars. Other losses are much more frequent, particularly those linked to credit card theft, but when considered individually, they represent only a few hundred or thousand dollars. The losses observed for one year therefore form a very heterogeneous set. We observe few extreme losses because they seem to be attached to rare events. Conversely, many small losses are caused by very frequent events. It is thus possible to observe totally different loss distributions from one cell to another (even within certain cells) in the chart shown in Figure 14.1.

14.1.2 Examples

The main losses associated with an operational risk are often categorized as follows:

- A loss is direct (identified as an operational loss) because it never would have been recognized if the operational event had not materialized itself. These losses include those related to operations, regulation, legal compliance, recourse, restitutions, and write-offs.
- A loss is indirect (not identified as an operational loss) if it is associated with improvements made to a process or an addition to post-event controls, or if it represents an opportunity cost.

Consider the example of a financial institution forced to partly interrupt its services for several days due to a major computer problem. Here is a list of losses the bank should potentially incur following this unexpected interruption. Note that by regulation, some of these losses cannot be recognized as operational losses.

Costs of restoring the system may be internal or external:

- Internal costs, which may be recognized as operational losses, are:
  - Wages of bank employees who work to correct and solve the failure (normal work hours) and wages of employees who do not work while the system is being repaired;
  - Overtime pay of bank employees who work on solving the failure.
- External costs, that may be recognized, are:
  - Fees charged by external consultants who help repair the failure;
  - Compensation offered to aggrieved clients;
  - Legal losses linked to lawsuits by aggrieved clients.
- Costs of improving the system that cannot be recognized are:
  - Putting in place additional controls to prevent and detect future system failures;
  - Developing a new, more effective IT system.

International banks have undergone major operational losses in the last 20 years. Here are some examples of extreme losses linked to operational risk:

- Damage to physical assets and business disruption following the September 11, 2001, attack in New York: $27 billion.
- Unauthorized transactions.
  - Allied Irish Bank (Ireland): $690 million;
  - Barings Bank (England): $1.3 billion in losses and bankruptcy of the bank;
  - Société Générale bank (France): 4.9 billion euros;
  - CIBC (Canada): $2.4 billion from the Enron bankruptcy.
- Mismanagement of mortgage loans and poor pricing of structured financial products during the financial crisis:
  - Wachovia Bank (United States): $8.4 billion;
  - CFC-Bank of America (United States): $8.4 billion.

14.2 MEASUREMENT OF REGULATORY CAPITAL

Three approaches are used to calculate banks' regulatory capital under Basel II.

14.2.1 Basic Approach

Although very simple, this method locks in a large portion of the capital. The minimum required capital for a bank is calculated by taking a given percentage of the gross income during one period (gross income × 15%). Note that gross income is defined here by the moving average of the last three years. However, this method does not really consider the real risk exposure of a bank, even though the bank's gross income may represent its volume of business or operations. Banks that use this approach must also follow the Basel Committee's recommendations that appear in the document "Sound Practices for the Management and Supervision of Operational Risk" (February 2003). Their choices must also be approved by local regulatory authorities.

14.2.2 Standardized Approach

The second approach involves calculating a minimal amount per line of business by using Gross income × Beta for each line of business. This capital largely integrates the distribution of a bank's risky operations among its lines of business, whose average risks may differ. The Beta is interpreted as a weight reflecting an approximation of the level of relative operational risk of a line of business. The Betas are set by the Basel Accord and vary between 12% and 18% depending on the line of business. Therefore, because the weights are exogenous to the bank, it can control the capital amount only with regard to the distribution of the level of its operations between lines of business. Each activity of a line of business implicitly represents a similar risk with this method. The total minimum capital amount of a bank equals the sum of the minimum capital required by each line of business.

14.2.3 Advanced Measurement Approach (AMA)

The advanced approach is more similar to an internal method of calculating regulatory capital, whereas the two previous approaches correspond more to standard methods. The advanced approach is divided into three mutually exclusive groups:

1. The loss distribution approach (LDA);
2. The internal measure approach (IMA);
3. The scorecard approach (SCA).

To apply these three approaches, banks must follow numerous rules defined by Basel II. Although the approaches are difficult to put in place because the bank data are not always adequate, each approach indicates the real risk exposure of the bank more accurately than the so-called standard approaches do. In addition, for some types of risk in lines of business, loss distributions have thick tails and few observations. The extreme examples mentioned above are probable for a bank but are rarely realized. One way to improve data quality is to share extreme loss data in the same industry or to use international external data.[2] The analysis and modeling of the loss distribution for a line of business is complicated by the fact that the same line of business may include heterogeneous losses, ranging from a few extreme losses to thousands of records of small losses. We will return to this particular aspect of the data in the following sections.

The degree of confidence that Basel II requires for regulatory capital calculations raises another difficulty concerning the loss distribution approach. The VaR used must be calculated at a 99.9% degree of confidence instead of 99% for market and credit risk. This rule therefore requires considerable capital. For example, Dahen, Dionne, and Zadenweber (2010) calculated the annual VaR of operational

[2]In Canada, banks share information on large losses to improve the estimation of these infrequent events.

risk for the American Bank Merrill Lynch according to the LDA approach, using the bank's losses of $1 million or more. They obtained a VaR at 99% of approximately $1 billion, whereas the VaR at 99.9% was $11.6 billion. Note that two American banks, mentioned above, each lost $8.4 billion in the last financial crisis due to operational risk, which seems to support the 99.9% rule. However, this does not resolve the main difficulties of applying the rule.

We will now describe the LDA approach in greater detail using American data for operational losses of over $1 million.

14.3 CALCULATION OF REGULATORY CAPITAL FOR LOSSES OF OVER $1 MILLION (LDA)

We present the results of two studies that use the LDA approach, conducted by Dahen and Dionne (2010) and by Dionne and Saissi Hassani (2017). The model of Dahen and Dionne (2010) shows how to quantify optimal capital for banks' operational risk by adding external data to the bank data. Two main difficulties are linked to operational risk measurement; loss data are still rare, and historical evidence is lacking. Many banks do not really have data on their losses prior to the 2000s. Because extreme losses are very rare, it is practically impossible to apply advanced statistical models that exclusively use internal data. The limited history of internal losses is not representative of a bank's real exposure. In addition, for cost reasons, losses are recorded by financial institutions only starting from a certain threshold. Truncated statistical distributions are thus necessary. Lastly, for many types of risk, losses are not normally distributed, and their modeling requires the use of distributions intended for the study of rare or extreme events.

The objective of Dahen and Dionne (2010) is to obtain a measure of operational regulatory capital by risk type and line of business that reflects a bank's risk level by integrating external loss data and internal bank data to improve the statistical reliability of the model used. The study results can answer several questions that banks have asked about the Basel II Accord, particularly concerning the use of external loss data of other institutions. The study also shows how to obtain a good fit of statistical distributions by using extreme loss data while controlling for the fact that the loss data are truncated.

The contribution by Dionne and Saissi Hassani (2017) proposes an extension of the previous study by adding the possibility that operational losses may be cyclical. The authors show that operational loss data from American banks are indeed characterized by a Markov model. Monthly losses follow a symmetrical normal distribution in low regimes and an asymmetric distribution with thick tails in high regimes. Various statistical tests do not reject this asymmetry. The regimes obtained are integrated in the estimation of operational losses, and the authors show that their presence affects loss distributions significantly. These results are particularly important for some operational losses, including those related to errors in pricing financial products, for which several large banks have been sued during and after the most recent financial crisis.

The study by Dionne and Saissi Hassani (2017) notably documents the presence of temporal heterogeneity within the data. If this heterogeneity is not considered in risk management models, the estimations of regulatory risk capital will be biased. Levels of capital set aside will be overestimated during periods where loss amounts are normal, corresponding to low regimes, and underestimated in periods of high regimes.

14.3.1 Scaling Model in LDA Models

Literature

Before the study by Dahen and Dionne (2010), scaling of external data in the bank or financial literature was scant. Shih, Samad-Khan, and Medapa (2000) and Na (2004) proposed scaling models for loss severity based on a nonlinear relationship between firm size and loss amounts observed. Na et al. (2006) assert that the loss amount can be broken down into a common component and an idiosyncratic component. However, this approach was not really based on a theoretical model. Accordingly, the portion designated as common contained banks' idiosyncratic components. Hartung (2004) also suggested adding bank-specific variables (revenues, number of employees, quality of risk management) to the regressions explaining conditional loss distributions along with adjustment factors to improve information limited to bank size.

Na (2004) proposed the first model for scaling loss frequencies. More recently, Cope and Labbi (2008), Wei (2007), and Chappelle et al. (2008) analyzed the effects of using the advanced approach on bank capital, and Allen and Bali (2007) studied the effect of economic cycles on loss distribution. However, they did not analyze the endogenous cyclicity of operational loss data. Other works on operational risk include those by Cruz (2002), Lewis (2003), Wei (2007), Chernobai and Yildirim (2008), and Jarrow (2008).

Model

Figure 14.2 presents the general model developed by Dahen (2010). On the left side of the figure, Dahen (2010) provides the study plan that will be described in the following pages. The study analyzes operational losses of $1 million or more. The scarcity of these losses for most banks requires the use of external data that can supplement the statistical information, thus allowing robust estimations for the distribution parameters. The availability of external data use is limited to losses of $1 million or more. It therefore requires the use of left truncated statistical distributions. In addition, the external data come from banks whose size, risk types, and lines of business differ. Specifically, the data originate from the United States, where banks are very heterogeneous. Some banks are very large and mainly act as investment banks, whereas others are small or regional, and focus on retail banking. The study therefore offers a methodology that can scale, for a single bank, the entire bank data included in the sample. The scaling affects two distributions, that of conditional losses and that of loss frequencies.

The general model on the right-hand side of Figure 14.2 shows how to integrate estimations for external losses with other bank data to obtain losses that were unanticipated by the risk type. These unanticipated losses can be used to calculate the VaR of the bank for a risk type. Further, the addition of different VaRs lets us calculate the total required capital.

The study by Dahen and Dionne (2010) makes the first methodological contribution by improving existing models of loss severity scaling (Shih, Samad-Khan, and Medapa, 2000; Na, 2004). The authors introduce factors other than bank size

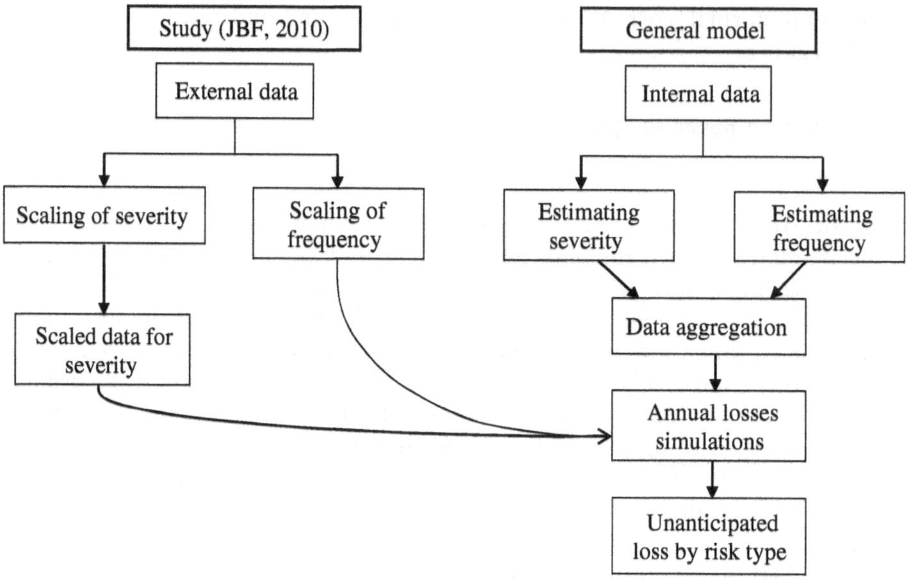

FIGURE 14.2 Diagram of a model for the integration of external data in the calculation of capital for banks' operational risk.

(such as bank-specific risk types and lines of business) and control for potential selection bias in the data of banks studied. The second contribution is the development of the first model for adjustment and scaling of external loss frequencies using Poisson (Zero Inflated Poisson, ZIP) and negative binomial (ZINB) distribution models with a regression component (Hausman, Hall, and Griliches, 1984; Cameron and Trivedi, 1986; Dionne and Vanasse, 1992). They adjust the models for excess zeros in the data, which makes a correction for the selection bias mentioned above. The sample studied cannot be limited to banks that sustained losses, which could present specific characteristics that differ from banks overall. Because the 300 losses studied are over $1 million, the researchers decided to retain the population of all banks with assets of $1 billion or more.

The operational loss data for American banks mainly come from the Fitch database and the Algo OpData Quantitative Database, and include 300 losses over US$1 million during the 1994–2003 period. The database on characteristics of US banks comes from the Federal Reserve Bank of Chicago and includes 3,650 observations of operational banks that held assets of at least $1 billion during this period (Bank Holding Companies). The use of zero-inflated models lets the author correct for the overrepresentation of zeros in the database (3,350 in total) and is justified by the scarcity of loss events over $1 million. The database contains information for each loss event, such as place, date, line of business, risk type, and identification of the institution that sustained the loss. The data used for banks to study loss frequencies include assets, stock capitalization, and mean employee salary.

Dahen and Dionne (2010) initially propose a model for scaling the 300 external loss amounts observed. The authors use Heckman's (1979) approach to control for potential selection bias that would affect the estimators of the loss distribution, obtained from an OLS regression. The model is estimated in two steps. First, a Probit regression is done to determine whether the banks that incurred the 300 losses differ from other banks. The Probit model therefore evaluates the probability that a bank sustains a loss. The regression component associated with this Probit model can be written as follows:

$$\begin{aligned} z^*_{it} &= w'_{it}\beta + e_{it} \\ z_{it} &= 0 \ \text{ si } \ z^*_{it} \le 0 \\ z_{it} &= 1 \ \text{ si } \ z^*_{it} > 0 \end{aligned} \tag{14.1}$$

where:

z_{it} is a discrete variable that takes the value of 1 if bank *i* had an operational loss during the period *t* or if the latent variable z^*_{it} is positive during this period;

w_{it} is the vector of observable variables of banks;

β is the vector of coefficients to estimate;

e_{it} is the error term.

The residuals e_{it} are supposed to be normally distributed. This first regression lets us calculate the inverse Mills ratio for each loss observation:

$$\text{inverse Mills ratio} = \frac{\dfrac{f(\alpha_{it} - \mu)}{\sigma}}{1 - F\left(\dfrac{\alpha_{it} - \mu}{\sigma}\right)} \tag{14.2}$$

where $\alpha_{it} = -w'_{it}\beta$ and f and F represent the density and distribution functions of the normal distribution. Since the error term in (14.1) is N(0,1) μ is equal to 0 and σ is equal to one.

In the second step, the regression coefficients associated with different factors that explain loss distributions are obtained by the ordinary least squares (OLS) method. Note that the main factors used are the bank size, risk type, and line of business variables. As we will see in the following section, several of these variables have a significant impact on loss variability. The inverse Mills ratio is added as an explanatory variable. If the coefficient of this variable is significant, this indicates that there was a selection bias in the data and that the estimators obtained by OLS must be corrected.

$$\begin{aligned} y^*_{it} &= x'_{it} b + u_{it} \\ y_{it} &= y^*_{it} \quad \text{if } z_{it} = 1 \\ y_{it} &\ \text{non observed if } z_{it} = 0 \end{aligned} \tag{14.3}$$

where:

x_{it} is the vector of observable variables;

b is the vector of coefficients;

u_{it} is an error term.

The results of the estimation of these two equations are not presented here. We will revisit them when we present the model of Dionne and Saissi Hassani (2017).

Loss Scaling

Once the parameters are estimated, we can scale the 300 observations to one bank for which we want to calculate the regulatory capital. We can thus create 300 loss observations for a single bank based on the 300 observations from all banks. The model proposed by Dahen and Dionne (2010) proceeds as follows: a loss (Loss) is defined as a nonlinear function of bank size (Size) weighted by a function $f(\cdot)$ that considers the particularities of the bank like its lines of business and risk types.

$$\text{Loss}_{it} = \psi \times \text{Size}_i^{\alpha} \times f(\omega, \theta_i) \tag{14.4}$$

where:

θ_i is the vector of the explanatory variables;
ω is the vector of the parameters;
Size is the bank size;
ψ is the constant;
α is the parameter of the functional form of the size variable.

To obtain a linear relationship of the loss function, we take the logarithm of equation (14.4), which gives:

$$\text{Log}(\text{Loss}_{it}) = \log(\psi) + \alpha \log(\text{Size}_{it}) + \sum_{k=1}^{7} \delta_k \text{RT}_{ikt} + \sum_{j=1}^{8} \beta_j \text{LB}_{ijt} \tag{14.5}$$

where the function $f(\cdot)$ in (14.4) is explicitly defined as a linear function of the risk types (RT) and the lines of business (LB).

The estimated regression coefficients let us calculate the values of Loss_i of a bank, $i = A, B$, by applying the following standardization formula:

$$\text{Loss}_B = \text{Loss}_A \frac{\text{Size}_B^{\alpha} \times f(\omega, \theta_B)}{\text{Size}_A^{\alpha} \times f(\omega, \theta_A)}. \tag{14.6}$$

We can therefore scale the loss of bank A to generate a loss for bank B, and so on for the 300 losses. Of course, some losses reported by bank B may appear among the 300 loss observations. Table 14.1 presents a validation of the scaling model for the bank US Bancorp. This table compares different statistics regarding the 15 losses observed at the bank compared with external losses scaled with the preceding formula. The fourth column does not give satisfactory results because several scaled losses among the 300 losses were too high for this bank (maximum of \$310 million versus a maximum for the bank of \$84 million). The third column limits the number of losses to 258 by setting upper and lower limits on the minimum and maximum losses sustained by the bank. In fact, the two limit values come from the 15 losses of the bank. Note that the 258 losses have fairly similar statistics to the 15 losses incurred although the kurtosis and standard deviation are smaller.

To obtain the global loss distribution that will let us calculate the VaR, we must estimate the loss frequencies of the banks and recalculate the frequencies obtained according to the bank's scale. Dahen and Dionne (2010) modeled the number of

TABLE 14.1 Statistics on scaled losses: US Bancorp.

	Observed losses	Scaled losses within same interval	Scaled losses
Average ($M)	13.152	12.113	19.414
Median ($M)	5.448	6.099	5.719
Standard deviation ($M)	21.281	15.185	39.906
Kurtosis	9.628	6.453	22.066
Skewness	2.984	2.447	4.270
Minimum ($M)	1.355	1.355	0.788
Maximum ($M)	83.681	83.681	309.953
Number of losses	15	258	300

losses per company for the 1994–2004 period using the Zero-Inflated Poisson (ZIP) and Zero-Inflated Negative Binomial (ZINB) models. Once again, the frequency depends on bank size and on different variables related to banks' characteristics. The authors could not use loss characteristics here because they are not observable in states of non-loss. After the frequencies are estimated, the authors obtained a distribution of expected bank losses and could use the appropriate percentile to calculate the required capital. They then backtested the VaR and obtained very satisfactory results. This approach will be discussed in the following section.

In conclusion, apart from bank size, several other factors, such as line of business and risk type, have a significant impact on the loss level and are considered in severity scaling. Bank size, economic conditions, and average salary of bank employees are factors that can determine the distribution parameters that generate the frequencies of scaled losses.

14.3.2 Adding Business Cycles

Dionne and Saissi Hassani (2017) use the Algo OpData Quantitative Database to update the data from Dahen and Dionne (2010) on operational losses over $1 million for American banks. They also use the data from the Federal Reserve Bank of Chicago to update the data on bank characteristics. Their study period ranges from January 2001 to December 2010, including the recent financial crisis period. Before examining the loss distribution and calculation of capital, they verified whether the data contained operational loss regimes linked to economic cycles.

Identification of Regimes

The hatched area in Figure 14.3 identifies two periods of recession of the NBER: The dot-com recession in 2001 and that corresponding to the financial crisis that began in 2007. The number of monthly operational losses increased significantly during and after the last financial crisis, but much less than during the 2001 recession. We observe another spike in the number of losses in 2010, one year after the recession ended. The losses in 2010 may be explained by delays linked to lawsuits. Indeed, several banks were sued during and after the financial crisis because they sold structured financial products with incorrect prices and dubious ratings issued by rating agencies whose objectivity was questionable according to some experts. Poor management of

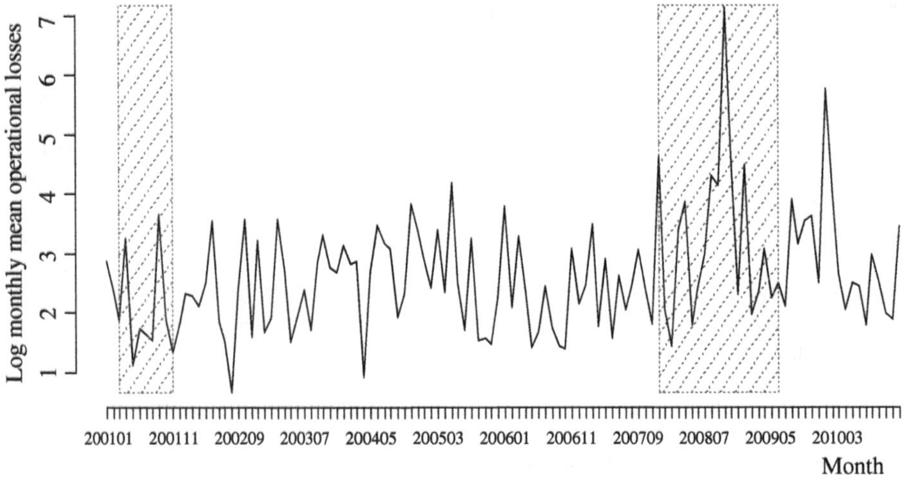

FIGURE 14.3 Changes in monthly mean operational losses.

subprime mortgage loans was also alleged by aggrieved client groups. The authors confirm similar variations concerning loss volatility.

Dionne and Saissi Hassani (2017) propose a model to identify the effect of potential regimes on operational loss distributions. They suppose that the evolution of losses over time could be linked to two possible distinct states. Hypothetically, the data thus fall in either state at any given moment. Two probabilities describe each state: that of staying and that of leaving. For a given state, the system could move toward the other state or remain in place. Because the states cannot be observed by the researchers, the model is called Hidden Markov, or HM. The data allow one to identify the states. The primary objective of the research is to characterize periods of high losses (regime 2, for example) and dissociate them from periods of normal losses (regime 1) in an endogenous manner. The second objective is to identify the conditional loss distributions in each regime to calculate bank capital.

Dionne and Saissi Hassani (2017) presume that losses follow a symmetrical normal distribution in the normal loss regime and an asymmetric distribution in the high loss regime. Three models were tested. In two of the three cases, they used splicing of symmetric distributions to obtain empirical measures of skewness and kurtosis that may be close to the observed moments of asymmetry and staggering of distributions. The three candidate distributions are N + N, N + SN, and N + ST4, where N is for Normal, SN is for Skew Normal, and ST4 is for Skew-t type 4. The base model N + N, used as a reference, supposes that operational losses are distributed normally in each regime.[3] The model N + SN supposes that the data follow a splicing of two normal distributions (SN) with different variances in the high loss regime. Lastly, the model N + ST4 (Skew-t type 4) presumes that the two distributions in the high loss regime are Student's *t* distributions with different degrees of freedom.

[3]Dionne and Saissi Hassani (2017) also estimated the GB2 distribution, a four-parameter distribution in the high regime. The results underestimate the skewness and kurtosis. This is why they needed to use splicing of distributions to obtain a better evaluation of these moments. The results for the GB2 are presented in the appendix to their paper.

TABLE 14.2 Estimation from the Markov Model.

	Model 1 N + N		Model 2 N + SN		Model 3 N + ST4	
	Variable	Coefficient	Variable	Coefficient	Variable	Coefficient
Probability of transition to high regime						
	Intercept	0.2879 (0.7392)	Intercept	0.3318 (0.7648)	Intercept	0.9772 (0.8161)
	L_1	−1.4853*** (0.2001)	L_1	−1.5468*** (0.2766)	L_1	−1.7371*** (0.2798)
Probability of staying in high regime						
	Intercept	−25.3101*** (4.6082)	Intercept	−28.1742*** (5.2129)	Intercept	−25.7285*** (4.5707)
	L_2	11.5681*** (2.5745)	L_2	12.9137*** (3.1253)	L_2	11.7434*** (2.4739)
Response distributions						
Low regime	Normal law		Normal law		Normal law	
	μ_1	2.4277*** (0.4366)	μ_1	2.4570*** (0.4546)	μ_1	2.4172*** (0.5876)
	σ_1	0.7685*** (0.2214)	σ_1	0.7979*** (0.2494)	σ_1	0.7653*** (0.2006)
High regime	Normal law		SN		ST4	
	μ_2	4.0294*** (6.5251)	μ_2	3.3991** (1.5123)	μ_2	3.7872*** (0.5449)
	σ_2	1.2968*** (0.1683)	σ_2	1.0207*** (0.2370)	$\log(\sigma_2)$	−0.0415 (0.2546)
			$\log(\gamma)$	0.5401 (0.7609)	$\log(\nu)$	2.7734* (1.4299)
					$\log(\tau)$	0.9492 (0.8007)
Log likelihood		−152.566		−151.863	−148.838	
AIC criterion		323.132		323.726	319.677	
Number of observations		120		120	120	

Notes: Standard deviations in parentheses. ***$p < 0.01$, **$p < 0.05$, *$p < 0.1$.

The results of the estimation of the different models are presented in Table 14.2. We discuss the parameters of Model 3 in detail, because this model dominates according to the information criterion of Akaike (AIC) and that of log likelihood. The normal distribution, which corresponds to phases of low losses, has an estimated mean of 2.4172 and an estimated standard deviation of 0.7653. These two coefficients are very significant and are fairly stable among the three models. Regarding the ST4 distribution, its mean is estimated at 3.7872, whereas its standard deviation can be fixed at 1 (its log can be considered statistically null because it is non-significant). In the high regime, the mean and the standard deviation increase significantly and simultaneously. In addition, the asymmetry of the Skew-t type 4 is confirmed by the coefficient of $\log(\nu)$, significant at 10%. We will validate these distributions below by performing a robustness analysis of the statistical results using different tests.

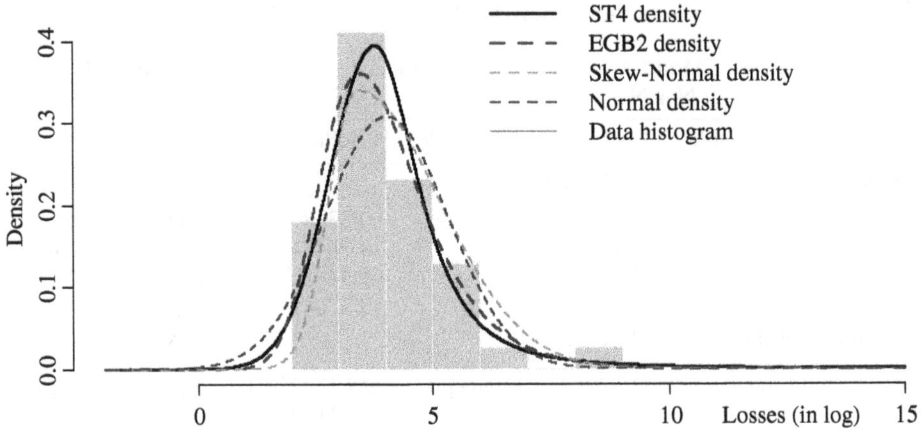

FIGURE 14.4 Estimated frequency of the logarithm of losses in the high regime.

The estimation from model 3 gives a value for the two parameters that measure the degrees of freedom, namely $v = \exp(2.7734) = 16.013$ and $\tau = \exp(0.9492) = 2.584$, which gives a very large thickness of ST4 distribution tails. Nonetheless, given that the estimation of $\log(\tau)$ in Table 14.2 is non-significant, $\log(\tau)$ can be considered null, and therefore $\tau = 1$. In this case, the right distribution tail would be even thicker. Given that these two estimated degrees of freedom are markedly below 30 in the high regime, this is another confirmation that we are far from a normal law where $v > 30$ and $\tau > 30$.

Figure 14.4 clearly shows how the ST4 accounts for the distribution tail when it is compared with the other distributions, notably the exponential GB2 (EGB2), which underestimates skewness and kurtosis.

Figure 14.5 presents another way to verify the fit of the data with the ST4. The upper panel compares the histogram of losses in the high regime with the frequency of a normal distribution (Model 1 in Table 14.2). We see that the frequency associated with the distribution does not correctly capture extreme losses (namely those that are higher than the log of monthly losses, equal to 4.5). The middle panel represents the two frequencies of the Student's *t* (ST4) in the high regime. The loss frequency is clearly captured well in the two ST4 distribution tails obtained from splicing the two Student's *t* distributions that have different degrees of freedom (Model 3 of Table 14.2). Lastly, the bottom panel illustrates the residuals from Model 3 that are found in Table 14.2. Various tests (Kolmogorov-Smirnov, Anderson-Darling, and Shapiro-Wilk) do not reject the normality of the residuals, which seems to indicate that Model 3 produces a good estimation of the loss distribution.

We now consider Figure 14.6, which shows the Markov states detected.

Three facts emerge from the figure:

1. First, there was almost no reaction to the recession of 2001 (which ranges from March 2001 to November 2001).
2. Only a few fluctuations in probability transition around 2003–2005 were observed.
3. In contrast, there is indeed a high regime detected during the recession starting in 2007 (December 2007 to June 2009), with a first impetus lasting one month in December 2007, followed by two other variations. The first lasts five months,

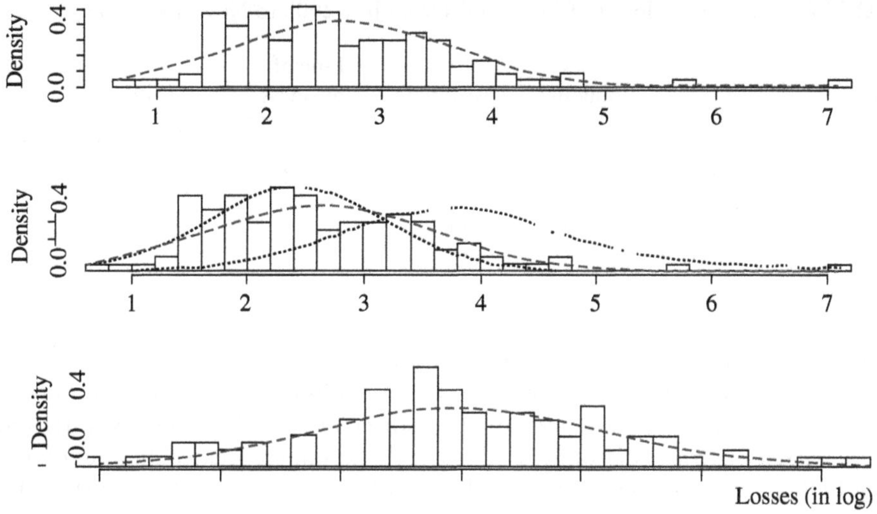

FIGURE 14.5 Estimated distribution of the logarithm of losses and the residuals in the high regime.

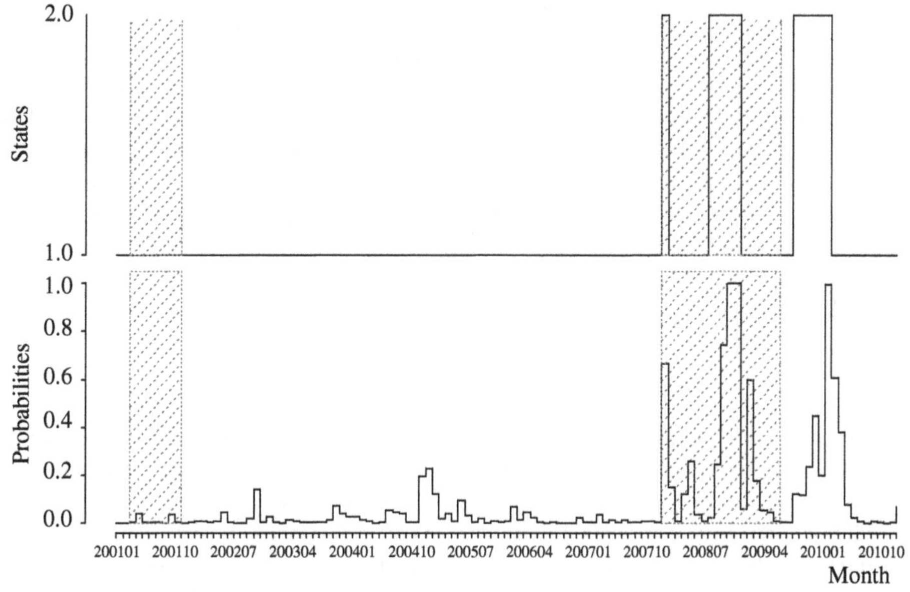

FIGURE 14.6 Markov regimes detected from January 2001 to December 2010.

from July to November 2008 inclusively, and the second lasts six months, from August 2009 until January 2010 inclusively. Note that the last impetus happens after the end of the recession.

Major Losses

To examine what happened in the last two variations presented above,[4] we analyze the most important individual losses, which represent at least 80% of the total loss

[4]See Saissi Hassani (2015) and Robertson (2011) for more details.

TABLE 14.3 Summary of losses of BHC Banks from July 2008 to November 2008.

Bank	Loss (billions)	Risk type	Line of business	Date	% loss
Wachovia Bank	8.4	CPPC	SBP	2008-07-21	40.73
CFC–Bank of America	8.4	CPPC	SBP	2008-10-06	40.73
Other losses (<80%)	3.8	30 losses			
All	20.6	32 losses			

during each period. The information about these losses is obtained from comments inserted in the loss database and from sites such as Bloomberg or that of the SEC (US Securities and Exchange Commission). As reported in Table 14.3, the first variation is characterized by two losses of $8.4 billion each, an unprecedented amount of losses for a BHC (Bank Holding Company). The first loss concerns the Wachovia bank, in July 2008 and results from a series of definitive write-downs linked to mortgages. The class action suit filed in federal court in California on June 6, 2008, alleges that the bank used improper standards for underwriting adjustable-rate mortgage loans. The second loss was suffered by CFC–Bank of America in October 2008 and results from illegal practices concerning products related to bank loans; 400,000 buyers were affected. CFC–Bank of America had to agree to settle the lawsuits filed against it by a group of attorney generals in 11 states, including California, Florida, Illinois, Connecticut, and Washington. In both cases, these losses result from problems linked to subprime loans and represent more than 80% of the $20.6 billion lost during this first variation, which lasted from July to November 2008. The two banks settled the class action suits before the cases could be decided in court. Therefore, there was no gap in time between the problems observed and the date the losses were declared.

We will see that this is not the case for most losses greater than a certain amount incurred during the last variation, namely between August 2009 and January 2010.

As in the previous variation, Table 14.4 describes six major losses observed during the last variation (from August 2009 to 2010), which independently accounts for over 80% of the total losses.

We begin with Citibank, which announced a loss of $840 million in January 2010 resulting from an accounting error linked to the way the bank calculated its CVA (Credit Value Adjustment) during the financial crisis.

The second loss concerns Discover Financial Services, which announced on February 12, 2010, that it would pay its former parent company Morgan Stanley $775 million following a violation of a contractual agreement. This violation dates back to October 2008, when Morgan Stanley filed a complaint against Discover Financial Services concerning the distribution of proceeds from the settlement of an antitrust dispute against rival credit card issuers Visa and MasterCard.

A third loss was incurred by JP Morgan Securities, which was forced to pay a total fine of $722 million. On November 4, 2009, the SEC announced a settlement whereby JP Morgan Securities would pay a fine of $25 million to the SEC and $50 million to Jefferson County. It also waived $647 million in windup fees linked to bonds and interest rate swap contracts.

Also, in February 2010, the SEC and the Massachusetts authorities announced that the State Street Bank and Trust had agreed to pay damages and fines following

TABLE 14.4 Summary of losses of BHC Banks from August 2009 to February 2010.

Bank	Loss (billions)	Risk type	Line of business	Date	% loss
Citibank N.A.	840	GELP	NV	2010-01-19	20.77
Discover Financial Services	775	CPPC	SBE	2010-02-12	19.16
JP Morgan Securities Inc.	722	CPPC	FE	2009-11-04	17.85
State Street Bank and Trust	663	CPPC	GA	2010-02-04	16.39
Merrill Lynch[1]	150	CPPC	FE	2010-02-22	3.71
Bank of America	142	FE	SBE	2009-09-21	3.51
Other losses (<80%)[2]	753	21 losses			
All	4,050	27 losses			

[1]Our data source attributes this loss to Merrill Lynch, although it was the new parent company Bank of America that paid the loss.
[2]It includes Citigroup ($75 million) and HSBC ($75 million).

a judgment on allegations that the bank misled investors regarding bonds in the "Limited Duration Bond Fund" of 2007. The SEC also accused the bank of having disclosed selective information to certain investors. As a result, these investors quickly redeemed their investment, to the detriment of other investors who lacked access to this information.

For the fifth loss, according to the SEC, Bank of America allegedly omitted to disclose to its shareholders some bonus payments by Merrill Lynch before the definitive ratification vote on the acquisition of Merrill Lynch. The bank consequently had to pay the SEC $150 million.

A large-scale fraud affecting Bank of America ($142 million), Citigroup ($75 million), and HSBC ($75 million) was observed, in September 2009; the culprit received a 12-year prison sentence after pleading guilty. Apart from this latter case of external fraud, the other losses cited are mainly linked to problems with disseminated information or risk management errors concerning financial products, like poor pricing of products during the financial crisis. Many of these losses were delayed to varying extents due to lawsuits.

In conclusion, a significant percentage of losses belong to the CPPC category (clients, products, and business practices) of operational risk and are associated with two lines of business: Corporate banking and Retail banking: 80% of the amounts in question come from extreme cases, two of which appear in Table 14.3 and six in Table 14.4. Most often, the same banks are involved.

Measurement of Regime Effects Detected on Loss Distributions

Starting with the modeling of log (Loss) estimation of Dahen and Dionne (2010), Dionne and Saissi Hassani (2017) estimate the parameters of the following equation:

$$\log(\text{Loss}) = \alpha + \beta \log(\text{Asset}) + \gamma \text{LB} + \delta \text{RT} + \text{time effects} + \varepsilon \qquad (14.7)$$

where:

LB is a vector identifying lines of business and γ is a corresponding vector of parameters;

RT is a vector identifying types of risk and δ is a corresponding vector of parameters;
ε is an error term.

The dependent variable is the log(Loss). The explanatory variables are log(Asset), a vector of the variables of the Line of business categories, and a vector of the variables of the Risk type categories. The analysis takes into account the time fixed effects using dichotomous variables that indicate different years. All of the standard variations and *p*-values are robust to the presence of heteroscedasticity and clustering, in line with the White methodology.

Results of the regressions are presented in Table 14.5. Model 1 is used as a reference, which corresponds to that of Dahen and Dionne (2010a) apart from being estimated with updated data, namely 508 observations. To simplify the estimation presentation, the authors do not report the coefficients for yearly fixed effects, present in the three models. In Model 2, they add the variable Regime (1 indicating a high regime) only, then they add its interactions with the Line of business and the Risk type variables in Model 3.[5]

Similar to the results commonly found for this type of model, the coefficient for the variable log (Asset) is highly significant. In addition, it is stable in the three models. Similarly, the coefficients associated with the Line of business and Risk type variables tend to conserve a relatively similar magnitude in the regressions of the three models. The coefficient of the Regime variable is highly significant, at 1% in Model 2, but is less so in Model 3, where it is significant at 10%. In contrast, three interaction variables are significant at 1%. Note that considering the annual fixed effects does not reduce the significance of the regimes. This suggests that the regimes detected cannot be explained uniquely by time. The comparison of the adjusted R^2 of the models shows that there is improvement adding the regime variable in Model 2 or with interactions in Model 3. Further, note the absence of observations concerning BD and DPA when the regime is high (in other words, when the indicator variable Regime is equal to 1 in the loss database). This is the reason why the coefficients corresponding to the interactions of the two variables are not presented in Model 3.

Estimation of Loss Frequency

To calculate the VaR, loss frequencies must be estimated. We can also measure the effect of the regimes on frequencies. The authors have retained the Zero-Inflated Negative Binomial (ZINB) model, which Dahen and Dionne (2010) did not reject. The estimations are presented in Table 14.6. The dependent variable is the number of annual losses in the counting model and is a dichotomous variable that takes the value of 1 if a zero is observed, and 0 otherwise in the excess zero model (Zero-Inflated model). The authors wanted to measure the effect of the regimes (1 for high regime) in both the counting estimation portion and in the presence of zeros. The idea is to see whether inflated zeros are more numerous or not in a particular regime and if the number of losses is significantly affected by the high regime.

Model 1 is the benchmark model to compare the effect of adding regimes. The authors used 4,329 observations from January 2001 to December 2010. Model 2 adds the regime dimension in both models. In the counting part, the High Regime variable is negative and significant at 10% and very significantly positive for the

[5]The model was also estimated using Heckman's methodology to take into account the potential endogeneity of companies that sustained losses, as in Dahen and Dionne (2010a). The results indicate that the inverse Mills ratio is not significant in the second step, and the other results remain stable.

TABLE 14.5 Effect of regimes detected on log(Loss).

	Model 1 Reference model	Model 2 Regime added	Model 3 Regime and cross-tabulation added
Constant	−0.297 (0.433)	−0.260 (0.446)	−0.160 (0.436)
Log(assets)	0.139*** (0.037)	0.139*** (0.038)	0.126*** (0.036)
Regime		0.977*** (0.331)	1.538* (0.791)
PS	1.261*** (0.438)	1.199*** (0.438)	1.196** (0.466)
ST	1.104*** (0.290)	1.026*** (0.304)	0.906** (0.372)
CB	1.182*** (0.167)	1.117*** (0.164)	1.159*** (0.172)
RB	0.930*** (0.207)	0.867*** (0.207)	0.827*** (0.171)
AS	1.223*** (0.413)	1.161*** (0.435)	1.532*** (0.443)
CF	2.056*** (0.237)	2.063*** (0.250)	1.999*** (0.294)
AM	1.358*** (0.274)	1.321*** (0.254)	1.307*** (0.283)
BD	−1.080 (0.687)	−0.926 (0.569)	−0.878 (0.630)
DPA	−0.086 (1.925)	−0.044 (1.923)	0.047 (1.953)
EPWS	−0.676*** (0.252)	−0.622** (0.254)	−0.476** (0.224)
EF	−0.502*** (0.157)	−0.489*** (0.161)	−0.433** (0.170)
IF	−0.593*** (0.227)	−0.524** (0.226)	−0.304 (0.211)
EDPM	−0.214 (0.228)	−0.217 (0.230)	−0.130 (0.256)
EPWS × Regime			−2.321*** (0.513)
EF × Regime			0.120 (1.088)
IF × Regime			−3.314*** (0.547)
EDPM × Regime			0.115 (1.228)
PS × Regime			−0.561 (1.584)
ST × Regime			0.317 (1.248)

(*continued*)

TABLE 14.5 (*Continued*)

	Model 1 Reference model	Model 2 Regime added	Model 3 Regime and cross-tabulation added
CB × Regime			−1.511 (1.266)
RB × Regime			0.401 (1.075)
AS × Regime			−4.491*** (1.114)
CF × Regime			0.645 (1.565)
AM × Regime			−0.249 (0.963)
Year effects	yes	yes	yes
Adjusted R^2	0.170	0.186	0.223
Number of observations	508	508	508

zero-inflated model. Apparently, during high levels of the Markov regime, fewer losses would occur because the zeros usually came from the inflation of the zeros (outside the negative binomial). The variable GDP is also very significant to explain the excess zeros. To measure whether the deflation of zeros provides statistical value, the authors compare Model 2 with the base model (Model 1). Given that the models are embedded, they perform the likelihood ratio test, and its results also appear in the same table. The likelihood ratio test of Model 2 versus Model 1 is conclusive, with a statistical value of 46.53 and a p-value of almost 0. Model 2 using the Markov regime seems to provide more information than the reference model, given the substantial decrease in the AIC criterion. A final comment concerns the values of the log(δ) dispersion parameter of the negative binomial model. Starting with a value of 2.097 in Model 1, it reaches 1.085 for Model 2, which is a clear improvement in the specification in the sense that there is less unobserved heterogeneity in Model 2. We can now proceed to the backtesting of the models.

Backtesting and Computation of Capital

This section has a dual objective. First, Dionne and Saissi Hassani (2017) want to construct a backtesting procedure for their models with regimes to determine their validity. They also want to measure the extent to which ignoring the existence of additional regimes in their operational loss data biases calculation of reserve capital. They number their two models as follows: Model 1 is the base model, and Model 2 is the Markov regime + interactions with Business Lines and Event Types. To construct the backtesting, they use the methodology from Dahen and Dionne (2010) and take the detected regimes into account. In addition, they perform an out-of-sample backtesting, which, by definition, does not include the period covered in the history. The history lasts from January 2001 to December 2009 and is denoted by H. The period selected to calculate coverage is January 2010 to December 2010 and is denoted by C. The regime is high for the month of January and low for the 11 other months during this period. For each model, the data from the periods H and C are scaled by the coefficients estimated in the regressions.

TABLE 14.6 Effect of regimes on frequencies.

	Model 1 Reference Model	Model 2 Adding HMM regime
Count model		
Constant	−10.969***	−11.370***
	(0.741)	(0.424)
Log(actifs)	0.885***	0.916***
	(0.053)	(0.034)
High regime		−0.531*
		(0.291)
GDP	0.018	0.011
	(0.034)	(0.039)
Bank capitalization	4.428***	4.103***
	(0.933)	(0.705)
Mean salary	−0.751	−1.642*
	(0.913)	(0.841)
Log(δ)	2.097***	1.085***
	(0.634)	(0.417)
Zero-inflated model		
Constant	1.176	−4.580*
	(1.681)	(2.712)
Log(actifs)	−0.176	−0.149
	(0.120)	(0.202)
High regime		7.888***
		(2.502)
GDP	0.001	2.734***
	(0.109)	(0.787)
Mean salary	1.466	−48.468**
	(2.569)	(23.625)
AIC	1,640.089	1,597.558
Log likelihood	−810.044	−786.779
Test of likelihood ratio		46.530
Number of observations	4,329	4,329

Note: Standard deviations between parentheses. ***p < 0.01, **p < 0.05, *p < 0/1.

They draw 200,000 observations from the loss distribution (Table 14.5), for which they compute the convolutions for 2,000 losses obtained from the negative binomial of the frequency model obtained in Table 14.6. This gives an aggregate distribution for which they calculate the reserve capital for four degrees of confidence: 95%, 99%, 99.5%, and 99.9%. The 99.5% degree of confidence lets them evaluate the thickness of the distribution tail and gives them an idea of what is happening when the VaR at 99.9% is not exceeded.

They performed the statistical tests below:

- The Kupiec test (1995), which evaluates the number of values in excess of VaR.
- The Christoffersen test (CT, 1998), which measures the independence of these values.

- The total Christoffersen test (TCT, 1998), which determines the conditional simultaneous coverage of frequency and independence of the values in excess of VaR.

These tests give them a complete and robust picture of the validity of their backtesting.

They have 445 losses recorded for the period H and 63 for the period C, which gives 508 losses. They must calculate the probable losses that a given bank incurs during period C. Accordingly, the C's 63 losses are scaled to the size of the bank, and each loss is multiplied 56 times by the scaling of the models to simulate all 8 Business Lines and 7 possible Risk Types according to the Basel nomenclature. This allows to manage operational risk in all possible cases. The 63 losses therefore generate 3,528 possible losses, on which they perform statistical backtesting. Note that the scaling covers all historical losses of H and the possible losses in period C. Consequently, the model that passes the backtesting will automatically be the one that can simultaneously scale all loss observations and their frequencies.

Calculations are performed for two banks, the first being US Bancorp (as found in Dahen and Dionne, 2010). Results in Table 14.7 show that only one test value, that of the CT test that measures the independence of values, rejects the VaR at 99.9% with a p-value of 1%. The bank's total assets are $290.6 billion, and reserve capital represents 1.02% of assets. Further, the estimated capital reserve is lower in Model 2 than for the benchmark Model 1, at $2,060.7 million versus $2,480.5 million for VaR at 99.9%.

They notice that the capital calculated at different degrees of confidence (VaR) is less than that calculated for Model 1, which does not consider the existence of regimes. These results confirm the existence of an endogenous regime in the data and that ignoring it creates a positive bias in the calculation of regulatory capital during low regimes and the opposite during high regimes. Using the calculation of Model 2, this bias for US Bancorp is (2,957.4 – 2,060.7)/2957.4, which is very high, at 30.3%.

As further proof, they do the same process for a second BHC bank: Fifth Third Bancorp. Its size is $111.5 billion. They largely obtain the same pattern by analyzing Table 14.8. Model 2 is still the least capital-expensive. This model allows savings

TABLE 14.7 Backtesting of US Bancorp Bank.[1]

Backtesting	Confidence level	Frequency		VaR[2]	Kupiec test		CT		TCT	
		Theoretical	Observed		Stat.	*p*-value	Stat.	*p*-value	Stat.	*p*-value
Reference model	95%	0.050	0.043	269.7	1.760	0.1846	2.359	0.6701	2.550	0.2795
Model 1	99%	0.010	0.012	842.3	0.479	0.4887	1.404	0.8434	0.479	0.7869
	99.5%	0.005	0.008	1,289.7	2.385	0.1225	14.792	0.0052	5.027	0.0810
	99.9%	0.001	0.002	2,957.4	1.991	0.1583	2.751	0.6003	1.991	0.3696
HMM regimes and interactions										
Model 2	95%	0.050	0.043	209.0	1.760	0.1846	3.430	0.4886	1.844	0.3977
	99%	0.010	0.016	619.3	5.730	0.0167	9.258	0.0550	5.730	0.0570
	99.5%	0.005	0.004	913.6	0.116	0.7334	0.208	0.9949	0.116	0.9436
	99.9%	0.001	0.002	2,060.7	0.666	0.4145	0.826	0.9349	0.666	0.7169

[1]Value in bold means model rejected at 1%.
[2]In millions of US dollars.

TABLE 14.8 Backtesting of Fifth Third Bancorp Bank.

Backtesting	Confidence level	Frequency		VaR[2]	Kupiec test		CT		TCT	
		Theoretical	Observed		Stat.	*p*-value	Stat.	*p*-value	Stat.	*p*-value
Reference model	95%	0.050	0.038	115.0	5.590	0.0181	7.547	0.1097	5.816	0.0546
Model 1	99%	0.010	0.007	430.7	1.553	0.2127	1.614	0.8063	1.553	0.4600
	99.5%	0.005	0.004	689.8	0.484	0.4867	0.511	0.9724	0.484	0.7851
	99.9%	0.001	0.003	1,722.6	3.822	0.0506	5.812	0.2137	3.822	0.1479
HMM regimes and interactions										
Model 2	95%	0.050	0.042	94.4	2.783	0.0953	4.984	0.2889	2.804	0.2461
	99%	0.010	0.013	338.1	1.829	0.1762	3.369	0.4980	1.829	0.4007
	99.5%	0.005	0.007	522.6	1.570	0.2102	2.205	0.6981	1.570	0.4562
	99.9%	0.001	0.003	1,291.5	6.057	0.0138	10.012	0.0402	6.057	0.0484

[1]In millions of US dollars.

of 25% in reserve capital at 99.9%, namely (1,722.6 – 1,291.5)/1,722.6. Further, the cross-loading of regimes with Business Lines and Event Types seems to capture the fact that these variables do not have the same effects during different phases of the regimes. Consideration of Markov regimes therefore undeniably improves the analysis.

14.4 CONCLUSION

In this chapter, we analyzed banks' operational risk, which many consider unusual. After presenting its characteristics and how it is regulated, we discussed models for optimal calculation of banks' capital to cover this risk. We confirm the importance of using external sources of statistical information to supplement a bank's extreme loss observations and present a loss-scaling methodology. We illustrated scaling with an example that covered two American banks.

We also analyzed the effect of economic cycles on operational loss data and on banks' optimal capital. We demonstrated that considering business cycles can reduce capital for operational risk by redistributing it between high regime and low regime cycles. We also provide evidence that court settlements affect the temporal distribution of losses significantly. Several large losses were reported after the financial crisis of 2007–2009 owing to these delays. This phenomenon is not new; it is also observed in large losses for insurance companies whose monetary settlements are often decided by the court.

Several extensions of these findings are possible. The most promising would be to test the stability of the results using different regime detection methods such as those used by Maalaoui-Chun, Dionne, and François (2014). Specifically, how could a real-time regime detection approach improve the results, particularly given the asymmetry observed in the data? This approach would notably allow separate analysis of level and volatility regimes.

Another possible extension of these findings is to use a different approach than the scaling of operational losses to generate a larger number of observations for each bank. Some banks use the Change of Measure Approach proposed by Dutta and Babbel (2013). This method combines scenario analysis with the use of historical data. It would be interesting to examine whether the results of this approach can remain stable after cycles are introduced in the data. An extension of the analyses to stress-testing of models could also be informative.

Finally, the results of this chapter can be compared with those from the new Standardised Measurement Approach (SMA) proposed by the Basel Committee.

REFERENCES

Acharya, V.V, Schnabl, P., and Suarez, G., 2013. "Securitization without Risk Transfer." *Journal of Financial Economics* 107, 515–536.

Allen, L., and Bali, T.G., 2007. "Cyclicality in Catastrophic and Operational Risk Measurements." *Journal of Banking and Finance* 31, 1191–1235.

Ames, M., Schuermann, T., and Scott, H.S., 2014. "Bank Capital for Operational Risk: A Tale of Fragility and Instability." Available on SSRN. https://papers.ssrn.com/sol3/papers.cfm?abstract_id=2396046.

Azzalini, A., 1985. "A Class of Distributions Which Includes the Normal Ones." *Scandinavian Journal of Statistics* 12, 171–178.

Baum, L.E., and Petrie, T., 1966. "Statistical Inference for Probabilistic Functions of Finite State Markov Chains." *The Annals of Mathematical Statistics* 37, 1554–1563.

Baum, L.E, Petrie, T., Soules, G., and Weiss, N., 1970. "A Maximization Technique Occurring in the Statistical Analysis of Probabilistic Functions of Markov Chains." *The Annals of Mathematical Statistics* 41, 164–171.

Bhamra, H.S., Kuehn, L.A., and Strebulaev, I.A., 2010. "The Levered Equity Risk Premium and Credit Spreads: A Unified Framework." *Review of Financial Studies* 23, 645–703.

Bulla, J., 2011. "Hidden Markov Models With T Components: Increased Persistence and Other Aspects." *Quantitative Finance* 11, 459–475.

Cameron, A.C., and Trivedi, P.K., 1986. "Econometric Models Based on Count Data: Comparisons and Applications of Some Estimators and Tests." *Journal of Applied Economics* 1(1), 29–53.

Cameron, A.C., Trivedi, P.K., Milne, F., and Piggott, J., 1988. "A Microeconometric Model of the Demand for Health Care and Health Insurance in Australia." *Review of Economic Studies* 55, 85–106.

Chapelle, A., Crama, Y., Hübner, G., and Peters, J.P., 2008. "Practical Methods for Measuring and Managing Operational Risk in the Financial Sector: A Clinical Study." *Journal of Banking and Finance* 32, 1049–1061.

Chavez-Demoulin, V., Embrechts, P., and Nešlehová, J., 2006. "Quantitative Models for Operational Risk: Extremes, Dependence and Aggregation." *Journal of Banking and Finance* 30, 2635–2658.

Chernobai, A. and Yildirim, Y., 2008. "The Dynamics of Operational Loss Clustering." *Journal of Banking and Finance* 32, 2655–2666.

Christoffersen, P.F., 1998. "Evaluating Interval Forecasts." *International Economic Review* 39, 841–862.

Chen, H., 2010. "Macroeconomic Conditions and the Puzzles of Credit Spreads and Capital Structure." *Journal of Finance* 65, 2171–2212.

Cope, E., and Labbi, A., 2008. "Operational Loss Scaling by Exposure Indicators: Evidence from the ORX Database." *Journal of Operational Risk* 3, 25–45.

Cruz, M.G., 2002. *Modeling, Measuring and Hedging Operational Risk*. Chichester, UK: John Wiley & Sons.

Cummins, J.D., Dionne, G., McDonald, J.B., and Pritchett, B.M., 1990. "Applications of the GB2 Distribution in Modeling Insurance Loss Processes." *Insurance: Mathematics and Economics* 9, 4, 257–272.

Dahen, H., 2007. "La quantification du risque opérationnel des institutions bancaires." Ph.D. thesis, HEC Montréal, Montreal, Canada.

Dahen, H., 2010. "La quantification du risque opérationel des institutions bancaires." Presentation at HEC Montréal, Montreal, Canada.

Dahen, H., and Dionne, G., 2010. "Scaling Models for the Severity and Frequency of External Operational Loss Data." *Journal of Banking and Finance* 34, 1484–1496.

Dahen, H., Dionne, G., and Zajdenweber, D., 2010. "A Practical Application of Extreme Value Theory to Operational Risk in Banks." *Journal of Operational Risk* 5, 63–78.

Dionne, G., 1992. *Contribution to Insurance Economics*. Boston: Kluwer Academic Press.

Dionne, G., and Saissi Hassani, S., 2017." Hidden Markov Regimes in Operational Loss Data: Application to the Recent Financial Crisis." *Journal of Operational Risk* 12, 23–51.

Dionne, G., and Vanasse, C., 1989. "A Generalization of Actuarial Automobile Insurance Rating Models: The Negative Binomial Distribution with a Regression Component." *ASTIN Bulletin* 19, 199–212.

Dionne, G., and Vanasse, C., 1992. "Automobile Insurance Ratemaking in the Presence of Asymmetrical Information." *Journal of Applied Econometrics* 7, 149–165.

Dutta, K.K., and Babbel, D.V., 2014. "Scenario Analysis in the Measurement of Operational Risk Capital: A Change of Measure Approach." *Journal of Risk and Insurance* 81, 303–334.

Engle, R.F., and Manganelli, S., 2004. "Caviar: Conditional Autoregressive Value at Risk by Regression Quantiles." *Journal of Business and Economic Statistics* 22, 367–381.

Fernandez, C., Osiewalski, J., and Stell, M.F.J., 1995. "Modeling and Inference with V-Spherical Distributions." *Journal of the American Statistical Association* 90, 1331–1340.

Frachot, A., and Roncalli, T., 2002. "Mixing Internal and External Data for Managing Operational Risk." Working paper. Groupe de Recherche Opérationnelle, Crédit Lyonnais.

Gatzert, N., and Kolb, A., 2014. "Risk Measurement and Management of Operational Risk in Insurance Companies from an Enterprise Perspective." *Journal of Risk and Insurance* 81, 683–708.

Hamilton, J.D., 1989. "A New Approach to the Economic Analysis of Nonstationary Time Series and the Business Cycle." *Econometrica* 57, 357–384.

Hartung, T., 2004. "Operational Risks: Modelling and Quantifying the Impact of Insurance Solutions." Working paper. Ludwig-Maximilians-University.

Hausman, J., Hall, B., and Griliches, Z., 1984. "Econometrics Models for Count Data with an Application to the Patents-R&D Relationship." *Econometrica* 52, 909–938.

Heckman, J., 1979. "Selection Bias as a Specification Error." *Econometrica* 47, 153–161.

Jarrow, R.A., 2008. "Operational Risk." *Journal of Banking and Finance* 32, 870–879.

Kindelberger, C.P., and Aliber, R.Z., 2011. *Manias, Panics and Crashes: A History of Financial Crisis*. Palgrave Macmillan.

Korolkiewicz, M.W., and Elliott, R.J., 2007. "Smoothed Parameter Estimation for a Hidden Markov Chain of Credit Quality." In: R.S. Mamon and R.J. Elliott (Eds), *Hidden Markov Models in Finance*. Springer, 69–90.

Kroszner, R.S., and Strahan, P.E., 2013. "Regulation and Deregulation of the US Banking Industry: Causes, Consequences and Implications for the Future." In: N.L. Rose (Ed.), *Economic Regulation and Its Reform: What Have We Learned?* Chicago: University of Chicago Press, 485–543.

Kupiec, P.H., 1995. "Techniques for Verifying the Accuracy of Risk Measurement Models." *The Journal of Derivatives* 3, 73–84.

Lewis, M.A., 2003. "Cause, Consequences and Control: Towards a Theoretical and Practical Model of Operational Risk." *Journal of Operations Management* 21, 205–224.

Liechty, J., 2013. "Regime Switching Models and Risk Measurement Tools." In: J.P. Fouque and J.A Langsam (Eds.), *Handbook on Systemic Risk*. Cambridge University Press, 180–192.

Maalaoui-Chun, O., Dionne, G., and François, P., 2014. "Detecting Regime Shifts in Credit Spreads." *Journal of Financial and Quantitative Analysis* 49, 1339–1364.

Mitra, S., and Date, P., 2010. "Regime Switching Volatility Calibration by the Baum-Welch Method." *Journal of Computational and Applied Mathematics* 234, 3243–3260.
Na, H.S., 2004. "Analysing and Scaling Operational Risk." Master thesis, Erasmus University.
Na, H.S., van den Berg, J., Couto Miranda, L., and Leipoldt, M., 2006. "An Econometric Model to Scale Operational Losses." *The Journal of Operational Risk* 1, 11–31.
Nešlehová, J., Embrechts, P., and Chavez-Demoulin, V., 2006. "Infinite Mean Models and the LDA for Operational Risk." *Journal of Operational Risk* 1, 3–25.
Peters, G.W., Shevchenko, P.V., Hassani, B., and Chapelle, A., 2016. "Should AMA Be Replaced with SMA for Operational Risk?" Mimeo, University College London, London, UK.
Psaradakis, Z., and Sola, M., 1998. "Finite-Sample Properties of the Maximum Likelihood Estimator in Autoregressive Models with Markov Switching." *Journal of Econometrics* 86, 369–386.
Rabiner, L., 1989. "A Tutorial on Hidden Markov Models and Selected Applications in Speech Recognition." Proceedings of the IEEE 77, 257–286.
Rigby, B., Stasinopoulos, M., Heller, G. and Voudouris, V., 2014. "The Distribution Toolbox of GAMLSS." http://www.gamlss.org/wp-content/uploads/2014/10/distributions. pdf.
Robertson, B., 2011. "So That's Operational Risk!" OCC Economics working paper 2011-1.
Saissi Hassani, S., 2015. "Risque opérationnel des institutions bancaires: modélisation et validation." PHD thesis, HEC Montréal, Montreal, Canada.
Shih, J., Samad-Khan, A., and Medapa, P., 2000. "Is the Size of an Operational Loss Related to Firm Size? *Operational Risk Magazine* 2, 1–2.
Siu, K.B., and Yang, H., 2007. "Expected Shortfall under a Model with Market and Credit Risks." In: R.S. Mamon and R.J. Elliott (Eds.), *Hidden Markov Models in Finance.* Springer, 91–100.
Siu, T.K., 2007. "On Fair Valuation of Participating Life Insurance Policies with Regime Switching." In: R.S. Mamon and R.J. Elliott (Eds.), *Hidden Markov Models in Finance.* 000: Springer, 31–43.
Visser, I., and Speekenbrink, M., 2010. "depmixS4: An R-Package for Hidden Markov Models." *Journal of Statistical Software* 36, 1–21.
Wei, R., 2007. "Quantification of Operational Losses Using Firm-Specific Information and External Database." *The Journal of Operational Risk* 1, 3–34.
Zucchini, W., and MacDonald, I.L., 2009. *Hidden Markov Models for Time Series: An Introduction Using R.* CRC Press.

CHAPTER 15

Liquidity Risk

Liquidity risk became very important during the last financial crisis (2007–2009). Many financial instruments like bonds, CDOs (collateralized debt obligations), commercial papers, and CDSs (credit default swaps) were strongly affected by this risk.[1] This chapter focuses on corporate bonds and CDSs.

The first question raised by Longstaff, Mithal, and Neis (2005) is: What proportion of bonds' yield spreads is due to default risk? There are many analytical methods to answer this question. The first, proposed by Elton et al. (2001), is to estimate default risk and determine which fraction of the corporate bonds' total credit spread (credit spread below) is due to default risk.[2] This analysis of default risk was extended by Dionne et al. (2010, 2011). In all three studies, the authors estimate the default probabilities, recovery rates, and risk exposure at default, and then evaluate the proportion of yield spreads explained by estimated default risk. Another approach uses CDSs to measure default risk because the CDS premiums include all this information.

This question, addressed by Longstaff, Mithal, and Neis (2005), is important for corporate finance. The party associated with non-default in yield spreads may affect decisions related to capital structure, asset issues, and risk management of financial institutions. Considering only the default portion may therefore lead to an undervaluation of the required capital.

As Longstaff, Mithal, and Neis (2005) would assume, the CDS premium is an appropriate measure of default risk if the CDSs are not exposed to liquidity risk. Because their article was published before the financial crisis, this assumption was probably not challenged at the time. However, the major evolution of markets since the crisis has made a detailed analysis of CDSs' liquidity risk quite pertinent today. This chapter thoroughly describes the approach of Longstaff, Mithal, and Neis (2005) and presents an extension of their contribution by analyzing the evolution of corporate credit spreads during the last financial crisis.

A CDS provides insurance against the default risk of a bond. Three actors are involved in managing a CDS: The bond issuer, the bondholder (insured, who may request protection), and the CDS issuer (the insurer, generally an investment bank). We assume that the insured hold his bonds when he requests protection. He may purchase the two assets at the same time, or even make more complex decisions since

[1]The research discussed in this chapter was conducted with Olfa Maalaoui-Chun.

[2]See also Collin-Dufresne, Goldstein, and Martin (2001); Lando (2004) and Huang and Huang (2012) for other approaches, including the structural approach. Giesecke et al. (2011) present a historical analysis of default risk.

arbitrage behaviors may occur when pricing CDSs is not optimal, or when bonds' liquidity is inadequately considered. We do not consider arbitrage in this chapter.

A bondholder requests a coverage when he thinks that protecting his security is more advantageous than selling it. He is thus willing to periodically pay the CDS seller a premium to receive protection should the bond default. He pays the premium until the CDS expires, generally over five years, or until the bond defaults. In return, the insurer (which sells the CDS) commits to buy the bond from the insured at face value when default occurs (other forms of contractual arrangements are also possible). The insurer receives the recovery value from the defaulted bond issuer and loses the loss given default value, or LGD value. The CDS premium therefore covers the average potential loss. It is important that this loss be adequately anticipated by the CDS issuer.

There are many ways to calculate the bond's default premium using a CDS. Longstaff, Mithal, and Neis (2005) propose two approaches. First, they directly use the measure of the bond yield spread for default risk given by the observed value of the CDS premium. However, this direct measure may be biased. Second, they estimate the CDS premium using a reduced-form model. They show that the default risk portion represents more than 50% of the analyzed bond yield spreads. This result predates the financial crisis and corroborates those of Dionne et al. (2010, 2011) who show that the previous approaches, which limited default risk to less than 25% of yield spreads, underestimated this risk by failing to use appropriate transition matrices, for example. Nonetheless, 50% of the total spread is far from the total yield spread traditionally attributed to default risk.

In a subsequent step, Longstaff, Mithal, and Neis (2005) analyze factors other than default to explain yield spreads. They discuss taxes on bond coupons, as suggested by Elton et al. (2001), and liquidity risk using cross-section and time-series regressions. More recently, Dick-Nielsen, Feldhütter, and Lando (2012) and Dionne and Maalaoui-Chun (2013) extended the analysis of bond liquidity using a principal component approach and evaluated its cyclical evolution. Dick-Nielsen, Feldhütter, and Lando (2012) estimated that liquidity risk represented about 40% of corporate credit spreads during the financial crisis, whereas Dionne and Maalaoui-Chun (2013) show that default and liquidity risks had undergone major regime changes during the same period.

15.1 THEORETICAL MODELING OF CDSs

Credit derivatives are contingent assets whose payoffs are associated with the default risk of the firms or securities they cover. The first party to a CDS contract, namely the insured, wants to obtain protection from the default of a bond issued by a private firm. The firm that issued the bond is called the reference entity or bond seller. The second party to the contract, the seller of the protection (insurer), agrees to assume the risk associated with the reference entity or bond defaults. In case of default, the insurer agrees to buy the bond from the insured at face value.

In return, the insurer periodically receives a premium from the insured, called the CDS premium. At default, the insured remits the bond to the insurer, and the insured stops paying the premium. If the reference entity does not default, the insured pays the premium until the CDS contract expires. Figure 15.1 presents a numerical example of a contract. This contract protects the buyer from the default risk of Worldcom, which

Risk exposure	10,000 bonds at $1,000, 7.75% yield, 5-year maturity. Total notional value: $10,000,000.
Premium	Annual premium: 169 basis points, or 1.69%. Premium per quarter: $169 \times \frac{A}{360} \approx 42.25$ basis points, where A is the number of days per quarter. Quarterly premium in \$ $= \$10{,}000{,}000 \times 0.0169 \times \frac{A}{360} = \$169{,}000 \times \frac{A}{360} = \$42{,}250$ Premium is paid at the beginning of each quarter.
Default payment	If default occurs at the beginning of the quarter, the insured receives 10,000,000. If default occurs during a quarter, the insured receives $10,000,000 adjusted for premium accrued since the last payment.

FIGURE 15.1 Payoff of a CDS contract.
Source: Reproduced from Longstaff, Mithal, and Neis (2005). © John Wiley & Sons, Inc. Reproduced with permission.

went bankrupt in 2002. The insured holds 10,000 Worldcom bonds, each with a face amount of $1,000, for a total value of $10 million. The bond matures in five years, and the coupon rate is 7.75%. Premiums are generally paid ex ante with quarterly payments. The insurer charges a quarterly premium of $42,250 to cover the default risk. This premium is paid until default or maturity. The total annual premium of $169,000 corresponds to an evaluation of default risk of 169 basis points. In case of default, the insurer will pay the insured $10 million and recover (1 − LGD) × 10 million from Worldcom. Its loss will be LGD × 10 million.

15.2 BOND YIELD SPREAD'S DEFAULT PORTION

The price of a corporate bond CB (c, w, T) with a unit face value is a function of the coupon *c*, the LGD *w*, and the maturity T. It can be calculated as follows:

$$\begin{aligned} CB(c,w,T) = {} & E\left[c\int_0^T \exp\left(-\int_0^t (r_s+\lambda_s+\gamma_s)ds\right)dt\right] \\ & + E\left[\exp\left(-\int_0^T (r_t+\lambda_t+\gamma_t)dt\right)\right] \\ & + E\left[(1-w)\int_0^T \lambda_t \exp\left(-\int_0^t (r_s+\lambda_s+\gamma_s)ds\right)dt\right] \end{aligned} \tag{15.1}$$

where the first line of equation (15.1) gives the expected value of coupons receivable and *t* is the default date. The second line is the expected value of capital recovery with a value of $1 at maturity. The third line indicates the expected value of payments linked to recovery (1 − w), conditional on default at date *t*. These values are discounted at the total random rate $g_s = r_s + \lambda_s + \gamma_s$, where r_s is the Treasury bill rate, λ_s the premium rate for default risk and γ_s the premium rate for the bond's liquidity risk.

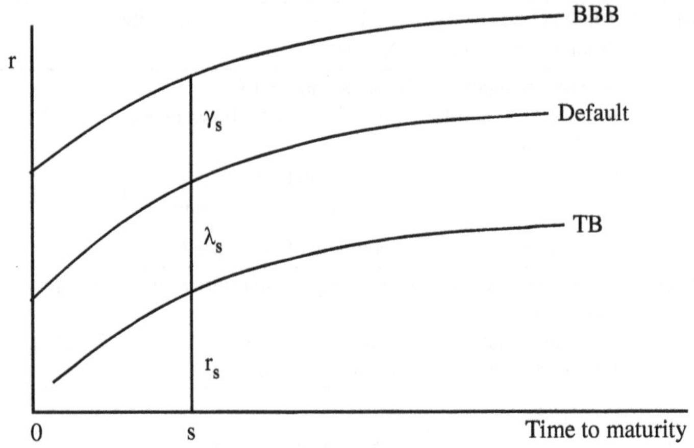

FIGURE 15.2 Default and liquidity risk of a BBB bond.

Figure 15.2 represents the three rates for a BBB bond at a given time *s*, where the TB curve is the curve of Treasury bills, the Default curve corresponds to the yield curve linked to the default risk of a BBB, and BBB is the total credit risk curve (Treasury bill rate plus default risk rate plus liquidity risk rate) of the BBB bond.

We will now analyze the pricing of a CDS. P(p, T) is the expected present value of premiums receivable, and *p* is the premium for a given period of time.

$$P(p,T) = E\left[p\int_0^T \exp\left(-\int_0^t (r_s+\lambda_s)ds\right)dt\right]. \tag{15.2}$$

Note that in (15.2) the term γ_s is not present because Longstaff, Mithal, and Neis (2005) suppose that the CDS is not exposed to liquidity risk.

Similarly, we can calculate the expected present value of the non-recovery part of the bond that the insurer will lose at default (NR(w, T)), where *w* is the LGD, considered here as non-random:

$$NR(w,T) = E\left[w\int_0^T \lambda_t \exp\left(-\int_0^t (r_s+\lambda_s)ds\right)dt\right]. \tag{15.3}$$

At market equilibrium, economic profits are zero, and this implies that (15.2) is equal to (15.3). Because *p* is not random, we can isolate it and obtain:

$$p = \frac{E\left[w\int_0^T \lambda_t \exp\left(-\int_0^t (r_s+\lambda_s)ds\right)dt\right]}{E\left[\int_0^T \exp\left(-\int_0^t (r_s+\lambda_s)ds\right)dt\right]}. \tag{15.4}$$

In the simple situation where λ_t is not random, we can take its value out of the integral and obtain $\lambda_t = \lambda$, which implies that $p = \lambda w$. We thus obtain the result that the premium is equal to the expected loss for a \$1 bond measured by the product of the default intensity (λ) and the LGD.

More generally, if λ_t is random along with $\lambda_t w$, the premium p can be interpreted as the mean present value of $\lambda_t w$. However, this is an approximation because we generally observe a negative correlation between λ_t and $\exp\left(-\int_0^t \lambda_s ds\right)$. The premium should therefore be less than the mean value of $\lambda_t w$. This premium does not consider the default risk of the protection seller. Suppose this risk has a probability equal to d and is independent of the bond default. Then, the premium becomes $(1 - d)p$ in OTC markets. In central clearing markets, it will remain close to p (Akari et al., 2018).

If we suppose that the intensity λ_t follows square-root dynamics and that the liquidity process γ_t follows Gaussian dynamics, we can obtain the exact solutions for the values calculated in (15.1) and (15.4) (Duffie, Pan, and Singleton, 2000). The model is presented in Longstaff, Mithal, and Neis (2005) and is used to calculate the parameter values of the CDS premium. We will revisit this model later in this chapter.

15.3 EMPIRICAL MEASUREMENT OF YIELD SPREADS' DEFAULT PORTION

Table 15.1 reports the mean CDS premiums observed (CDS), the total average credit yield spreads (Δ Sprd) and the mean ratios of the two values for the different bonds studied (Ratio). The data were obtained from Citigroup, and it corresponds to the five-year CDS bonds contracts of 68 American firms. The Ratio columns present the observed ratio of the CDS premium to the total yield spread. This is a first approximation of the total bond spread's default portion. The total yield spread is calculated using three approximations for the risk-free rate: Treasury bills, Refcorp rates and the rate of an interest rate swap. Refcorp is an American public firm considered to have no default risk. Asterisks denote ratios that differ significantly from 1 at the 5% level, meaning that total credit spread is higher than default spread. N gives the number of observations for each firm. Prices were obtained weekly from CDS data between March 15, 2001, and October 9, 2002.

We can observe that the ratios are below 1 for most bonds. Their means by rating are also below 1, even if they are not all significantly different at 5%. We also observe that the ratios increase when the rating quality decreases, which seems to indicate that the default portion of total yield spreads is larger for these bonds. In the rest of the chapter, we will focus on the interpretation of the results linked to Treasury bills.

Longstaff, Mithal, and Neis (2005) also evaluate default and liquidity risk premiums using the method proposed by Duffie, Pan, and Singleton (2000). For each firm in the sample, they obtain (risk-neutral) values for γ_t and λ_t. The results are presented in Table 15.2. This table provides the estimated values of the parameters and the ratio $\lambda_t/(\gamma_t + \lambda_t)$. Once again, an asterisk indicates that the ratio is below 1 or that γ_t is statistically different from zero.

Table 15.3 presents a more direct comparison of the results from Table 15.1. Similar total yield spreads (Δ spreads) are reported. However, those related to default risk are measured by CDS premiums estimated with the parameter λ_t. We can observe that the mean ratios do not differ much between the two tables, regardless of the reference rate used. It seems that pricing of CDSs during this period was fairly accurate

TABLE 15.1 Ratio of observed CDS premium to total corporate yield spread.

		Treasury bill curve			Refcorp curve			Swap curve			
Rating	Firm	CDS	Δ Sprd	Ratio	CDS	Δ Sprd	Ratio	CDS	Δ Sprd	Ratio	N
AAA	GE Capital	46.8	92.0	0.51*	46.8	73.4	0.64*	46.8	31.8	1.47*	69
AA	Citigroup	40.9	106.8	0.38*	40.9	88.3	0.46*	40.9	46.1	0.89*	70
AA	Dupont	38.2	74.2	0.51*	38.2	60.4	0.63*	38.2	22.5	1.70*	52
AA	Merrill Lynch	66.7	130.9	0.51*	66.7	112.5	0.59*	66.7	71.1	0.94*	70
AA	Morgan Stanley	55.5	133.8	0.41*	55.5	112.8	0.49*	55.5	73.7	0.75*	70
AA	SBC	81.7	113.0	0.72*	81.7	100.0	0.82*	81.7	58.3	1.40*	52
AA	Wal-Mart	23.5	74.4	0.32*	23.5	54.0	0.44*	23.5	14.8	1.59*	70
A	AON	80.2	188.3	0.43*	80.2	167.5	0.48*	80.2	125.1	0.64*	42
A	Alcoa	40.6	110.5	0.37*	40.6	92.2	0.44*	40.6	53.4	0.76*	52
A	Bank One	44.4	116.1	0.38*	44.4	100.5	0.44*	44.4	60.2	0.74*	52
A	Bank of America	39.2	109.6	0.36*	39.2	90.9	0.43*	39.2	49.8	0.79*	70
A	Bear Stearns	74.0	163.1	0.45*	74.0	143.3	0.52*	74.0	103.3	0.72*	70
A	Boeing	59.4	127.9	0.46*	59.4	108.1	0.55*	59.4	71.9	0.82*	70
A	CIT Group	208.7	251.5	0.83*	208.7	237.6	0.88*	208.7	196.5	1.06*	47
A	Caterpillar	48.6	158.8	0.31*	48.6	134.5	0.36*	48.6	90.2	0.54*	70
A	Con Edison	48.1	129.7	0.37*	48.1	115.5	0.42*	48.1	74.4	0.65*	52
A	Conoco	66.4	123.7	0.54*	66.4	110.5	0.60*	66.4	72.0	0.92*	52
A	Countrywide Cr.	88.2	144.5	0.61*	88.2	130.3	0.68*	88.2	91.2	0.97	52
A	Deere	68.0	143.5	0.47*	68.0	123.3	0.55*	68.0	86.9	0.78*	69
A	Dow Chemical	98.0	158.1	0.62*	98.0	143.3	0.68*	98.0	105.7	0.93*	52
A	Duke Capital	85.1	144.7	0.59*	85.1	128.5	0.66*	85.1	90.6	0.94	39
A	Goldman Sachs	60.1	142.9	0.42*	60.1	121.1	0.50*	60.1	82.4	0.73*	70
A	Hewlett Packard	111.4	166.8	0.67*	111.4	152.1	0.73*	111.4	111.2	1.00	42
A	Household Fin.	171.4	210.6	0.81*	171.4	196.2	0.87*	171.4	154.2	1.11*	58
A	IBM	54.7	93.1	0.59*	54.7	77.8	0.70*	54.7	35.6	1.54*	70
A	JP Morgan Chase	54.8	132.8	0.41*	54.8	114.9	0.48*	54.8	74.2	0.74*	70
A	Lehman Brothers	75.4	153.0	0.49*	75.4	133.1	0.57*	75.4	94.2	0.80*	70
A	Nordstrom	130.7	239.4	0.55*	130.7	225.5	0.58*	130.7	184.8	0.71*	52
A	Philip Morris	106.5	162.4	0.66*	106.5	143.7	0.74*	106.5	102.2	1.04	70
A	Rohm&Haas	50.4	121.2	0.42*	50.4	108.8	0.47*	50.4	72.3	0.70*	52
A	Sears-Roebuck	101.1	177.8	0.57*	101.1	157.6	0.64*	101.1	120.5	0.84*	70
A	United Tech.	50.3	104.0	0.48*	50.3	87.2	0.58*	50.3	49.7	1.01	52
A	Viacom	74.9	147.1	0.51*	74.9	122.8	0.61*	74.9	86.9	0.86*	71
BBB	AT&T	270.5	321.2	0.84*	270.5	304.3	0.89*	270.5	262.9	1.03	69
BBB	Abitibi	250.8	316.6	0.79*	250.8	304.0	0.83*	250.8	261.7	0.96*	52
BBB	Albertson's	74.2	165.4	0.45*	74.2	142.8	0.52*	74.2	106.8	0.69*	70
BBB	Amerada Hess	81.1	150.7	0.54*	81.1	135.2	0.60*	81.1	98.0	0.83*	52
BBB	Daimler Chrysler	133.5	200.7	0.67*	133.5	179.1	0.75*	133.5	139.8	0.96*	73
BBB	Delphi Automotive	137.9	219.5	0.63*	137.9	204.1	0.68*	137.9	164.8	0.84*	61
BBB	Enron	173.6	197.5	0.88*	173.6	170.2	1.02	173.6	117.9	1.47*	31
BBB	Federated	103.1	174.6	0.59*	103.1	166.0	0.62*	103.1	127.4	0.81*	52
BBB	Fedex	73.3	176.9	0.41*	73.3	160.4	0.46*	73.3	124.5	0.59*	52
BBB	Ford Motor Credit	204.3	258.2	0.79*	204.3	238.1	0.86*	204.3	197.7	1.03	71
BBB	GMAC	154.9	213.2	0.73*	154.9	194.4	0.80*	154.9	152.7	1.01	71
BBB	Hilton Hotels	299.1	372.7	0.80*	299.1	363.8	0.82*	299.1	321.2	0.93*	52
BBB	Ingersoll-Rand	76.8	178.1	0.43*	76.8	154.6	0.50*	76.8	110.0	0.70*	52
BBB	Int. Paper	95.0	177.6	0.53*	95.0	158.1	0.60*	95.0	116.5	0.82*	70
BBB	Lockheed Martin	76.4	139.8	0.55*	76.4	117.8	0.65*	76.4	83.8	0.91*	69
BBB	MBNA	171.9	252.7	0.68*	171.9	241.1	0.71*	171.9	198.5	0.87*	52
BBB	MGM Mirage	278.1	359.7	0.77*	278.1	347.5	0.80*	278.1	305.1	0.91*	51
BBB	Marriott	128.8	237.7	0.54*	128.8	223.3	0.58*	128.8	185.4	0.69*	52
BBB	Motorola	288.9	348.6	0.83*	288.9	335.0	0.86*	288.9	290.4	0.99*	70
BBB	Norfolk Southern	79.3	143.3	0.55*	79.3	128.5	0.62*	79.3	89.3	0.89*	52

TABLE 15.1 (*Continued*)

		Treasury bill curve			Refcorp curve			Swap curve			
Rating	Firm	CDS	Δ Sprd	Ratio	CDS	Δ Sprd	Ratio	CDS	Δ Sprd	Ratio	N
BBB	Occidental	78.4	165.5	0.47*	78.4	150.3	0.52*	78.4	110.8	0.71*	52
BBB	Park Place Ent.	283.0	403.0	0.70*	283.0	388.7	0.73*	283.0	348.0	0.81*	52
BBB	Qwest Capital	240.1	271.8	0.88*	240.1	252.0	0.95	240.1	209.3	1.15*	16
BBB	Raytheon	153.5	189.4	0.81*	153.5	169.1	0.91*	153.5	133.0	1.15*	70
BBB	Sprint	140.0	204.3	0.69*	140.0	177.1	0.79*	140.0	140.0	1.00	33
BBB	Sun Microsystems	186.7	262.3	0.71*	186.7	247.3	0.76*	186.7	210.0	0.89*	52
BBB	TRW	158.8	244.3	0.65*	158.8	224.2	0.71*	158.8	185.0	0.86*	70
BBB	The Gap	107.8	213.1	0.51*	107.8	191.7	0.56*	107.8	153.7	0.70*	19
BBB	Union Pacific	75.1	134.3	0.56*	75.1	122.2	0.61*	75.1	81.3	0.92*	52
BBB	Visteon	187.5	268.4	0.70*	187.5	244.6	0.77*	187.5	206.0	0.91*	71
BBB	Walt Disney	80.4	140.6	0.57*	80.4	120.7	0.67*	80.4	77.0	1.04	70
BBB	Worldcom	162.0	235.4	0.69*	162.0	205.1	0.79*	162.0	168.0	0.96*	33
BB	Capital One	266.2	349.4	0.76*	266.2	328.2	0.81*	266.2	284.6	0.94	30
BB	Georgia Pacific	461.0	472.7	0.98*	461.0	460.9	1.00	461.0	417.8	1.10*	52
BB	Goodyear	346.0	461.4	0.75*	346.0	444.7	0.78*	346.0	401.6	0.86*	68
Average AAA/AA		50.5	103.6	0.49*	50.5	85.9	0.59*	50.5	45.5	1.11	65
Average A		80.4	150.8	0.53*	80.4	133.3	0.60*	80.4	93.8	0.86*	59
Average BBB		156.4	229.3	0.68*	156.4	211.3	0.74*	156.4	171.1	0.91*	55
Average BB		357.7	427.8	0.84*	357.7	411.3	0.87	357.7	368.0	0.97	50

Source: Reproduced from Longstaff, Mithal, and Neis (2005). © John Wiley & Sons, Inc. Reproduced with permission.

and that the authors' fears about biases caused by the use of observed premiums rather than estimated premiums were unfounded.

The authors also performed linear regressions to estimate the degree of default risk in total credit yield spreads. The dependent variable is the yield spread observed for each firm, and the independent variable is the estimated CDS premium. Using Treasury bills as default riskless rates, they obtained a R^2 of 0.37 for AAA/AA, 0.43 for A, 0.57 for BBB and 0.62 for BB, which confirms the previous results regarding levels by rating and comparisons between ratings.

15.4 NON-DEFAULT PORTION OF YIELD SPREADS

Longstaff, Mithal, and Neis (2005) also analyze the composition of the non-default portion of corporate credit spreads. This portion is measured by the difference between the observed bond yields and the portion associated with default risk, measured by the estimated CDS premiums. These values are presented in Table 15.3 (CDS and Δ Sprd column). The values of the differences range from 15.8 to 104.5 basis points, with a mean of 65 points when the Treasury bill curve is used as a reference.

To determine which factors can explain the non-default portion of yield spreads, the authors make a regression analysis using the non-default portion of rate spreads as a dependent variable. Different explanatory variables are used. We can write the regression equation as follows:

$$\text{Non-default spread} = \beta_0 + \beta_1\text{coupon} + \beta_2\text{bid-ask} + \beta_3\text{principal amount} + \beta_4\text{age} + \beta_5\text{maturity} + \beta_6\text{financial sector} + \beta_7\text{AAA/AA} + \varepsilon$$

where ε is an error term.

TABLE 15.2 Ratio of default intensity (λ) divided by instantaneous spread ($\lambda+\gamma$).

		Treasury bill curve			Refcorp curve			Swap curve			
Rating	Firm	λ	γ	Ratio	λ	γ	Ratio	λ	γ	Ratio	N
AAA	GE Capital	77.0	43.6	0.64*	77.1	25.0	0.75*	77.1	−16.3	1.27*	69
AA	Citigroup	42.4	63.4	0.40*	42.5	46.3	0.48*	42.1	4.0	0.91*	70
AA	Dupont	35.4	32.1	9.52*	35.5	20.2	0.64*	37.6	−16.9	1.82*	52
AA	Merrill Lynch	76.4	58.2	0.57*	76.1	40.8	0.65*	76.2	0.2	1.00	70
AA	Morgan Stanley	52.4	72.1	0.42*	52.0	53.4	0.49*	52.2	14.4	0.78*	70
AA	SBC	233.3	17.7	0.93*	209.6	8.6	0.96	207.7	−30.3	1.17*	52
AA	Wal–Mart	13.7	44.0	0.24*	13.8	26.6	0.34*	13.9	10.6	4.25*	70
A	AON	119.3	100.7	0.54*	147.5	81.9	0.64*	164.6	42.8	0.79*	42
A	Alcoa	44.5	69.7	0.39*	44.5	51.2	0.47*	44.3	13.4	0.77*	52
A	Bank One	32.9	71.5	0.31*	32.9	55.6	0.37*	33.1	16.7	0.67*	52
A	Bank of America	28.0	69.9	0.29*	28.1	53.2	0.35*	27.8	11.7	0.70*	70
A	Bear Stearns	59.6	84.9	0.41*	47.2	67.0	0.41*	69.3	26.3	0.72*	70
A	Boeing	100.4	68.8	0.59*	100.5	50.6	0.67*	100.0	14.2	0.88*	70
A	CIT Group	534.0	52.2	0.91*	533.3	39.5	0.93*	530.1	−0.7	1.00	47
A	Caterpillar	44.8	70.4	0.39*	44.7	50.9	0.47*	44.4	15.2	0.74*	70
A	Con Edison	42.3	82.7	0.34*	42.2	68.4	0.38*	42.4	29.1	0.59*	52
A	Conoco	42.8	56.0	0.43*	53.9	43.2	0.56*	63.6	5.0	0.93*	52
A	Countrywide Cr.	118.6	57.3	0.67*	118.6	44.1	0.73*	118.3	6.5	0.95*	52
A	Deere	74.0	75.2	0.50*	73.6	57.6	0.56*	82.6	20.0	0.81*	69
A	Dow Chemical	147.6	66.8	0.69*	151.4	52.5	0.74*	147.2	15.4	0.91*	52
A	Duke Capital	110.6	57.0	0.66*	119.9	40.9	0.75*	127.3	3.7	0.97	39
A	Goldman Sachs	61.6	85.4	0.42*	61.2	64.6	0.49*	61.4	25.3	0.71*	70
A	Hewlett Packard	222.5	53.5	0.81*	231.4	39.7	0.85*	241.2	−0.3	1.00	42
A	Household Fin.	411.9	44.2	0.90*	411.5	31.3	0.93*	408.2	−9.7	1.02	58
A	IBM	49.8	32.1	0.61*	49.9	17.9	0.74*	50.0	−25.2	2.02*	70
A	JP Morgan Chase	70.3	79.4	0.47*	69.9	62.7	0.53*	69.9	21.6	0.76*	70
A	Lehman Brothers	50.0	74.5	0.40*	50.1	56.2	0.47*	60.6	16.9	0.78*	70
A	Nordstrom	163.8	110.3	0.60*	163.9	97.6	0.63*	163.9	57.8	0.74*	52
A	Philip Morris	116.0	51.9	0.69*	123.2	32.9	0.79*	132.6	−6.5	1.05	70
A	Rohm&Haas	36.0	71.6	0.33*	41.0	59.5	0.41*	49.3	23.6	0.68*	52
A	Sears-Roebuck	235.6	75.7	0.76*	235.0	57.1	0.80*	233.6	20.9	0.92*	70
A	United Tech.	35.6	53.6	0.40*	44.8	36.8	0.55*	45.0	−0.2	1.00	52
A	Viacom	90.4	69.3	0.57*	90.2	46.6	0.66*	122.4	9.6	0.93*	71
BBB	AT&T	708.0	81.8	0.90*	707.3	67.0	0.91*	706.5	25.1	0.97*	69
BBB	Abitibi	398.7	79.3	0.83*	381.7	66.2	0.85*	375.0	26.3	0.93*	52
BBB	Albertson's	111.3	87.0	0.56*	122.5	65.6	0.65*	132.4	29.2	0.82*	70
BBB	Amerada Hess	78.8	68.2	0.54*	98.2	52.6	0.65*	100.1	16.1	0.86*	52
BBB	Daimler Chrysler	184.1	61.9	0.75*	190.7	40.9	0.82*	191.0	2.8	0.99	73
BBB	Delphi Automotive	236.6	88.9	0.73*	248.5	74.4	0.77*	261.1	35.0	0.88*	61
BBB	Enron	325.6	8.1	0.98	320.6	−27.0	1.09*	331.8	−66.4	1.25*	31
BBB	Federated	145.3	78.3	0.65*	178.2	68.8	0.72*	177.8	32.4	0.85*	52
BBB	Fedex	120.8	100.4	0.55*	157.0	83.2	0.65*	153.2	48.0	0.76*	52
BBB	Ford Motor Credit	523.4	62.1	0.89*	522.9	44.3	0.92*	519.1	4.2	0.99	71
BBB	GMAC	297.1	51.9	0.85*	297.2	34.1	0.90*	296.2	−6.5	1.02	71
BBB	Hilton Hotels	464.2	94.4	0.83*	462.6	78.2	0.86*	460.7	40.5	0.92*	52
BBB	Ingersoll-Rand	47.4	76.0	0.38*	47.3	64.2	0.42*	55.7	30.2	0.65*	52
BBB	Int. Paper	133.6	76.2	0.64*	114.6	59.5	0.66*	123.1	17.9	0.87*	70
BBB	Lockheed Martin	135.4	56.7	0.70*	111.0	38.3	0.74*	183.1	1.7	0.99	69
BBB	MBNA	264.8	75.8	0.78*	264.1	64.9	0.80*	261.3	23.1	0.92*	52
BBB	MGM Mirage	401.3	84.5	0.83*	287.8	72.0	0.80*	342.9	32.2	0.91*	51
BBB	Marriott	185.0	108.5	0.63*	218.9	92.6	0.70*	218.9	56.0	0.80*	52
BBB	Motorola	503.3	92.6	0.84*	502.9	75.5	0.87*	500.1	34.1	0.94*	70
BBB	Norfolk Southern	106.1	60.3	0.64*	128.2	45.6	0.74*	115.1	7.5	0.94*	52

TABLE 15.2 (*Continued*)

Rating	Firm	Treasury bill curve λ	Treasury bill curve γ	Treasury bill curve Ratio	Refcorp curve λ	Refcorp curve γ	Refcorp curve Ratio	Swap curve λ	Swap curve γ	Swap curve Ratio	N
BBB	Occidental	158.6	81.4	0.66*	147.8	67.5	0.69*	151.9	28.5	0.84*	52
BBB	Park Place Ent.	636.0	115.1	0.85*	622.3	101.4	0.86*	613.7	62.7	0.91*	52
BBB	Qwest Capital	582.4	31.5	0.95*	546.6	13.5	0.98	570.7	−28.1	1.05*	16
BBB	Raytheon	274.9	33.0	0.89*	286.0	13.6	0.95*	317.3	−23.5	1.08*	70
BBB	Sprint	285.3	75.3	0.79*	284.6	48.7	0.85*	285.6	11.2	0.96	33
BBB	Sun Microsystems	263.0	72.2	0.78*	263.4	58.7	0.82*	277.4	21.5	0.93	52
BBB	TRW	260.4	82.8	0.76*	252.4	64.7	0.80*	283.5	24.7	0.92*	70
BBB	The Gap	180.8	75.1	0.71*	180.7	49.2	0.79*	180.3	22.5	0.89*	19
BBB	Union Pacific	228.6	54.7	0.81*	226.3	43.1	0.84*	266.5	2.5	0.99	52
BBB	Visteon	352.5	89.6	0.80*	351.9	66.8	0.84*	351.1	28.5	0.92*	71
BBB	Walt Disney	136.7	50.8	0.73*	136.6	31.7	0.81*	143.0	−5.8	1.04*	70
BBB	Worldcom	201.9	70.4	0.74*	184.9	42.3	0.81*	256.8	2.9	0.99	33
BB	Capital One	447.1	82.6	0.84*	446.8	66.9	0.87*	446.4	26.2	0.94*	30
BB	Georgia Pacific	1545.2	139.0	0.92*	1542.3	125.5	0.92*	1526.6	85.6	0.95*	52
BB	Goodyear	898.9	130.1	0.87*	898.0	114.8	0.89*	894.1	74.0	0.92*	68
Average AAA/AA		75.8	47.3	0.62*	72.3	31.6	0.70*	72.4	−7.9	1.12	65
Average A		117.0	68.6	0.63*	119.6	52.3	0.70*	124.3	13.6	0.90*	59
Average BBB		279.2	72.6	0.79*	276.4	55.1	0.83*	287.6	16.8	0.94*	55
Average BB		963.7	117.2	0.89*	962.4	102.4	0.90*	955.7	61.9	0.94*	50

Source: Reproduced from Longstaff, Mithal, and Neis (2005). © John Wiley & Sons, Inc. Reproduced with permission.

The first independent variable measures the effect of the bond coupon, which is in fact an indirect variable to measure rating. A positive sign will indicate that the liquidity risk increases as the bond quality worsens. The dummy variable AAA/AA has a similar function except that it qualitatively distinguishes these two bond categories from other categories. As we will see in the results analysis, the coupon variable can also indirectly measure the effect of taxes on corporate bond coupons to explain yield spreads that are not linked to default.

The second variable is the bid-ask spread of bond prices, measured in basis points. The spreads are obtained from Bloomberg and vary between 4 and 15 basis points. A larger spread indicates lower liquidity because bond issuers often have difficulty finding investors who are willing to pay their prices. A positive sign is therefore predicted for this variable.

The variable principal amount measures the availability of the bond on markets. The larger the amount issued (or transaction value) the greater the liquidity of the bond and the narrower the residual yield spread.

The fourth variable is the age of the bond. In general, recently issued bonds (on-the-run) are more liquid than off-the-run bonds, as observed for Treasury bills. If the same is true for private bonds, we should observe a positive sign. However, because Treasury bills are used to calculate spreads, it is not clear that there will be a net effect.

Another variable to consider is bond maturity. The authors hypothesize that bonds with shorter maturities are more liquid, so a positive sign is anticipated, indicating that the longest maturities are less liquid. Still, this variable could be correlated with the age variable.

TABLE 15.3 Ratio of estimated CDS premium to observed Δ spread.

		Treasury bill curve			Refcorp curve			Swap curve			
Rating	Firm	CDS	Δ Sprd	Ratio	CDS	Δ Sprd	Ratio	CDS	Δ Sprd	Ratio	N
AAA	GE Capital	49.6	92.0	0.54*	49.4	73.4	0.67*	49.1	31.8	1.54*	69
AA	Citigroup	43.0	106.8	0.40*	43.0	88.3	0.49*	42.7	46.1	0.92*	70
AA	Dupont	40.2	74.2	0.54*	40.1	60.4	0.66*	40.0	22.5	1.78*	52
AA	Merrill Lynch	70.0	130.9	0.53*	69.9	112.5	0.62*	69.4	71.1	0.98	70
AA	Morgan Stanley	58.2	133.8	0.44*	58.0	112.8	0.51*	57.7	73.7	0.78*	70
AA	SBC	87.6	113.0	0.78*	86.7	100.0	0.87*	85.7	58.3	1.47*	52
AA	Wal-Mart	24.6	74.4	0.33*	24.5	54.0	0.45*	24.4	14.8	1.65*	70
A	AON	86.4	188.3	0.46*	86.2	167.5	0.51*	85.7	125.1	0.69*	42
A	Alcoa	42.8	110.5	0.39*	42.6	92.2	0.46*	42.3	53.4	0.79*	52
A	Bank One	46.9	116.1	0.40*	46.8	100.5	0.47*	46.6	60.2	0.77*	52
A	Bank of America	41.1	109.6	0.37*	41.0	90.9	0.45*	40.8	49.8	0.82*	70
A	Bear Stearns	78.0	163.1	0.48*	77.5	143.3	0.54*	77.6	103.3	0.75*	70
A	Boeing	61.8	127.9	0.48*	61.5	108.1	0.57*	61.0	71.9	0.85*	70
A	CIT Group	215.3	251.5	0.86*	214.4	237.6	0.90*	212.2	196.5	1.08*	47
A	Caterpillar	54.4	158.8	0.34*	54.4	134.5	0.40*	54.1	90.2	0.60*	70
A	Con Edison	50.6	129.7	0.39*	50.5	115.5	0.44*	50.2	74.4	0.67*	52
A	Conoco	68.2	123.7	0.55*	68.4	110.5	0.62*	68.3	72.0	0.95	52
A	Countrywide Cr.	91.1	144.5	0.63*	90.8	130.3	0.70*	90.1	91.2	0.99	52
A	Deere	69.6	143.5	0.49*	69.3	123.3	0.56*	69.1	86.9	0.80*	69
A	Dow Chemical	100.3	158.1	0.63*	99.9	143.3	0.70*	99.2	105.7	0.94	52
A	Duke Capital	88.9	144.7	0.61*	88.8	128.5	0.69*	88.6	90.6	0.98	39
A	Goldman Sachs	63.3	142.9	0.44*	63.0	121.1	0.52*	62.7	82.4	0.76*	70
A	Hewlett Packard	115.4	166.8	0.69*	115.0	152.1	0.76*	113.8	111.2	1.02	42
A	Household Fin.	178.5	210.6	0.85*	177.9	196.2	0.91*	175.9	154.2	1.14*	58
A	IBM	57.2	93.1	0.61*	57.2	77.8	0.74*	56.9	35.6	1.60*	70
A	JP Morgan Chase	57.3	132.8	0.43*	57.2	114.9	0.50*	56.8	74.2	0.77*	70
A	Lehman Brothers	78.3	153.0	0.51*	78.1	133.1	0.59*	78.0	94.2	0.83*	70
A	Nordstrom	136.0	239.4	0.57*	135.8	225.5	0.60*	134.6	184.8	0.73*	52
A	Philip Morris	112.7	162.4	0.69*	112.7	143.7	0.78*	112.0	102.2	1.10*	70
A	Rohm&Haas	51.5	121.2	0.43*	51.7	108.0	0.48*	51.8	72.3	0.72*	52
A	Sears-Roebuck	109.4	177.8	0.62*	109.0	157.6	0.69*	107.8	120.5	0.89*	70
A	United Tech.	52.0	104.0	0.50*	52.1	87.2	0.60*	51.8	49.7	1.04	52
A	Viacom	78.4	147.1	0.53*	78.0	122.8	0.63*	78.7	86.9	0.91*	71
BBB	AT&T	271.6	321.2	0.85*	270.5	304.3	0.89*	267.6	262.9	1.02	69
BBB	Abitibi	258.9	316.6	0.82*	258.1	304.0	0.85*	255.7	261.7	0.98	52
BBB	Albertson's	78.4	165.4	0.47*	78.5	142.8	0.55*	78.2	106.8	0.73*	70
BBB	Amerada Hess	83.6	150.7	0.56*	84.0	135.2	0.62*	83.5	98.0	0.85*	52
BBB	Daimler Chrysler	139.4	200.7	0.69*	139.2	179.1	0.78*	138.1	139.8	0.99	73
BBB	Delphi Automotive	143.1	219.5	0.65*	143.0	204.1	0.70*	141.9	164.8	0.86*	61
BBB	Enron	178.7	197.5	0.90*	178.3	170.2	1.05	175.7	117.9	1.49*	31
BBB	Federated	105.5	174.6	0.60*	106.7	166.0	0.64*	105.8	127.4	0.83*	52
BBB	Fedex	77.6	176.9	0.44*	78.5	160.4	0.49*	77.8	124.5	0.62*	52
BBB	Ford Motor Credit	214.8	258.2	0.83*	214.0	238.1	0.90*	211.6	197.7	1.07*	71
BBB	GMAC	160.1	213.2	0.75*	159.7	194.4	0.82*	158.0	152.7	1.03*	71
BBB	Hilton Hotels	309.8	372.7	0.83*	310.0	363.8	0.85*	306.9	321.2	0.96*	52
BBB	Ingersoll-Rand	83.1	178.1	0.47*	82.9	154.6	0.54*	82.3	110.0	0.75*	52
BBB	Int. Paper	102.8	177.6	0.58*	102.3	158.1	0.65*	101.7	116.5	0.87*	70
BBB	Lockheed Martin	82.7	139.8	0.59*	80.9	117.8	0.69*	83.8	83.8	1.00	69
BBB	MBNA	180.0	252.7	0.71*	179.7	241.1	0.75*	178.0	198.5	0.90*	52
BBB	MGM Mirage	286.3	359.7	0.80*	285.6	347.5	0.82*	283.4	305.1	0.93*	51
BBB	Marriott	135.7	237.7	0.57*	136.4	223.3	0.61*	135.5	185.4	0.73*	52
BBB	Motorola	288.0	348.6	0.83*	288.0	335.0	0.86*	284.5	290.4	0.98	70
BBB	Norfolk Southern	84.3	143.3	0.59*	84.7	128.5	0.66*	83.8	89.3	0.94*	52

TABLE 15.3 *(Continued)*

Rating	Firm	Treasury bill curve CDS	Δ Sprd	Ratio	Refcorp curve CDS	Δ Sprd	Ratio	Swap curve CDS	Δ Sprd	Ratio	N
BBB	Occidental	85.6	165.5	0.52*	85.0	150.3	0.57*	84.5	110.8	0.76*	52
BBB	Park Place Ent.	302.2	403.0	0.75*	301.1	388.7	0.77*	298.2	348.0	0.86*	52
BBB	Qwest Capital	250.4	271.8	0.92*	249.1	252.0	0.99	246.5	209.3	1.18*	16
BBB	Raytheon	159.7	189.4	0.84*	159.4	169.1	0.94*	159.4	133.0	1.20*	70
BBB	Sprint	147.8	204.3	0.72*	147.2	177.1	0.83*	145.3	140.0	1.04	33
BBB	Sun Microsystems	193.0	262.3	0.74*	192.3	247.3	0.78*	191.6	210.0	0.91	52
BBB	TRW	167.0	244.3	0.68*	166.3	224.2	0.74*	165.6	185.0	0.90*	70
BBB	The Gap	111.9	213.1	0.52*	112.0	191.7	0.58*	110.6	153.7	0.72*	19
BBB	Union Pacific	81.8	134.4	0.61*	81.5	122.2	0.67*	81.4	81.3	1.00	52
BBB	Visteon	201.8	268.4	0.75*	200.7	244.6	0.82*	199.1	206.0	0.97	71
BBB	Walt Disney	84.9	140.6	0.60*	84.7	120.7	0.70*	83.8	77.0	1.09*	70
BBB	Worldcom	166.8	235.4	0.71*	165.4	205.1	0.81*	166.7	168.0	0.99	33
BB	Capital One	264.4	349.4	0.76*	263.3	328.2	0.80*	260.2	284.6	0.91*	30
BB	Georgia Pacific	446.8	472.7	0.95*	445.4	460.9	0.97	439.9	417.8	1.05*	52
BB	Goodyear	356.8	461.4	0.77*	355.6	444.7	0.80*	351.1	401.6	0.87*	68
Average AAA/AA		53.3	103.6	0.51*	53.1	85.9	0.62*	52.7	45.5	1.16	65
Average A		84.0	150.8	0.56*	83.8	133.3	0.63*	83.3	93.8	0.89*	59
Average BBB		163.3	229.3	0.71*	162.7	211.3	0.77*	161.4	171.1	0.94*	55
Average BB		356.0	427.8	0.83*	354.8	411.3	0.86*	350.4	368.0	0.95	50

Source: Reproduced from Longstaff, Mithal, and Neis (2005). © John Wiley & Sons, Inc. Reproduced with permission.

Financial sector is a dummy variable that takes the value of 1 for bonds from the financial sector and 0 otherwise. The authors foresee a negative sign because financial firms are more connected to the capital market than are nonfinancial firms, which makes their bonds more liquid.

The last variable used to measure liquidity risk, discussed above, is the combined rating AAA/AA under the assumption that these bonds are more liquid than other bonds because they represent a type of safe investment. A negative sign is predicted.

As anticipated, Table 15.4 shows that coupon rates have a positive coefficient in the three models but a less significant one for the Refcorp curve regression. This result partly rejects the argument of a tax on private bond coupons with respect to TB coupons to explain residual spread. In fact, interest income, as defined by the coupon rates in the Swap curve, is not taxed and has a significantly positive effect. Therefore, we cannot conclude that the coupon variable only measures the effects that Elton et al. (2001) report on the effect of tax on bond spread. There is, however, a non-negligible difference between the two coefficients (5,441 vs. 3,637), which may be partly attributable to differences in the taxes on coupons. The coupon variable also seems to capture a residual effect that can be associated with a greater liquidity risk for bonds that pay higher coupons or that have lower ratings.

As suggested by the authors, the other variables used tend to be associated with liquidity risk. The bid-ask spread variable has a significant positive coefficient, whereas the amount issued and maturity variables have negative and positive coefficients respectively. This seems to indicate that these variables measure illiquidity differences well. The age variable is not significant, but its effect may be captured by the maturity variable.

The financial sector variable is highly significant, but with an effect contrary to that predicted by the authors. Lastly, the AAA/AA variable has a significant

TABLE 15.4 Regression of the non-default component of yield spreads according to coupons and different liquidity measures.

Variable	Treasury bills curve		Refcorp curve		Swap curve	
	Coefficient	*t*-Statistic	Coefficient	*t*- Statistic	Coefficient	*t*-Statistic
Intercept	5.576	0.48	3.190	0.27	−33.913	−2.93
Coupon	5.441	3.35	3.178	1.90	3.637	2.19
Bid-Ask spread	0.369	1.96	0.510	2.47	0.549	2.77
Principal amount	−0.622	−3.16	−0.706	−3.67	−0.691	−3.81
Age	−0.336	−0.47	−0.623	−0.77	−0.777	−1.00
Maturity	2.947	3.25	2.860	3.10	2.055	2.46
Financial	12.399	2.40	12.867	2.67	10.938	2.32
AAA/AA rating	−13.242	−2.17	−12.024	−2.19	−12.630	−2.29
	$R^2 = 0.234$	N = 356	$R^2 = 0.212$	N = 356	$R^2 = 0.210$	N = 356

Source: Reproduced from Longstaff, Mithal, and Neis (2005). © John Wiley & Sons, Inc. Reproduced with permission.

negative sign, which seems to suggest that the bonds in these two categories are more liquid than those of other categories. This result corroborates that obtained by Dick-Nielsen, Feldhütter, and Lando (2002), who observed a shift in demand for these bonds during the financial crisis (flight to quality).

Results are stable between regressions and the R^2 of the three regressions are situated between 21% and 23%, which seems reasonable. The authors also propose a time series analysis; however, they do not obtain satisfactory results owing to both their data and the very short period of analysis.

15.5 ILLIQUIDITY INDEX

In this section, we present other research findings on liquidity risk (Dick-Nielsen, Feldhütter, and Lando, 2012; Dionne and Maalaoui-Chun, 2013). Dick-Nielsen, Feldhütter, and Lando (2012) were the first to introduce a corporate bond illiquidity index in the literature. Their period of analysis includes the financial crisis of 2007–2009, marked by a major lack of liquidity for several financial products. Their model uses different illiquidity measures proposed in the literature to build an index from a principal component approach. The eight measures of illiquidity are:

1. Amihud measure

   For each individual bond *i*, we calculate the daily measure of illiquidity defined by the following equation:

$$\text{Amihud}_t^i = \frac{1}{N_t^i}\sum_{j=1}^{N_t^i}\frac{1}{Q_{j,t}^i}\frac{|P_{j,t}^i - P_{j-1,t}^i|}{P_{j-1,t}^i}$$

   where:

   N_t^i is the number of returns observed on day *t*;

   $P_{j,t}^i$ is the price of the jth transaction of bond *i* on day *t*;

   $Q_{j,t}^i$ is the trading volume of the jth transaction of bond *i* on day *t*.

$Amihud_t^i$ measures the effect of illiquidity on the bond price per unit traded. It is a price-volume measure of illiquidity. The larger the $|P_{j,t}^i - P_{j-1,t}^i|$ spread, the less liquid the bond on the market. Conversely, the higher the transaction volume $Q_{j,t}^i$, the more liquid the bond.

Below are two measures of price spread:

2. Imputed roundtrip cost (IRC)

This cost, defined by Feldhütter (2012), is measured as follows:

$$IRC_t^i = \frac{P_{max}^i - P_{min}^i}{P_{max}^i}$$

where P_{max} and P_{min} respectively refer to the maximum and minimum transaction prices of a bond during a one-day period. The maximum price represents the highest price paid by a purchasing investor during the time period, and the minimum price corresponds to the lowest price received by a selling investor during the same period. These price spreads are calculated for a similar trading volume during the period considered, which implies that this illiquidity measure is a pure measure of price spread. It indirectly indicates the transaction costs that brokers charge for a given volume.

3. Roll measure of bid-ask spread

$$Roll_t^i = 2\sqrt{-cov(R_t^i, R_{t-1}^i)}$$

Covariance measures dependence between two consecutive returns of the same financial instrument. The greater the measured spread, the less liquid the asset. It is an indirect measure of illiquidity linked to observed spreads. Negative covariance between two returns of the price for a bond *i* indicates that price variations vacillate around a mean based on purchase and sale orders. Covariance is always negative or zero in the Roll model, and its intensity depends on price spreads or market illiquidity.

4. Amihud risk measure

The first measure of illiquidity risk is equal to the standard deviation of the variations of the Amihud illiquidity measure presented above.

5. IRC risk measure

The second measure of illiquidity risk is equal to the standard deviation of the variations of the IRC measure.

6. *Turnover of transactions*

$$Turnover_t^i = \frac{\text{Total trading volume}_t^i}{\text{Amount outstanding}_t^i}.$$

The higher the relative trading volume in a period, the more liquid the security. The inverse of $Turnover_t^i$ may be interpreted as a measure of illiquidity, implying that investors hold bonds for long periods of time.

7. *Zero trading days for an instrument during period t*

$$Bond_t^i\ zero = \frac{\text{Number of bond}_t^i \text{ zero trades within the rolling window}}{\text{Number of days in the rolling window}}.$$

8. *Zero trading days for a firm during period t*

$$\text{Firm}_t^{ki}\ \text{zero} = \frac{\text{Number of firm}_t^k\ \text{bond}^i\ \text{zero trades within the rolling window}}{\text{Number of days in the rolling window}}.$$

The first measure is specific to a given bond, whereas the second is linked to the firm *k* that issues the bond *i*.

15.6 ILLIQUIDITY PREMIUM

The illiquidity premium ς_{it} is the weighted sum of illiquidity measures *j* selected from a principal component analysis. Dick-Nielsen, Feldhütter, and Lando (2012) define a specific measure for the illiquidity of a bond *i* as the weighted sum of the standardized measures $\bar{I}_{jt}^{i}$ for bond *i* over period *t*:

$$\varsigma_{it} = \sum_{j=1}^{J} \bar{I}_{jt}^{i}\, \theta_j$$

where:

I_{jt}^{i} is the non-standardized measure of one of the eight definitions in the previous section;

$\bar{I}_{jt}^{i}$ is the standardized *j* measure, $\frac{I_{jt}^{i} - \mu_j}{\sigma_j}$;

θ_j is the weight of the *j* measure obtained from the principal component analysis;

μ_j is the mean of the *j* measure for the period;

σ_j is the standard deviation of the *j* measure for the period;

J is the number of illiquidity measures retained from the principal component analysis.

15.7 DATA

15.7.1 TRACE Database

The TRACE database reports high-frequency data about trades in the secondary over-the-counter market for corporate bonds and accounts for 99% of the total trading volume. The data used in the study by Dionne and Maalaoui-Chun (2013) cover the period of 2002 to 2012. The authors use the Dick-Nielsen (2009) filter to eliminate duplications (buy/sell) and that of Han and Zhou (2008) to eliminate price variations with no economic meaning.

15.7.2 Markit Database

Data on CDS contracts come from Markit. This study includes all CDS contracts in North America for which information can be linked to bonds. Maturities are from 6 months to 10 years. The data have a daily frequency and cover the period from 2002 to 2012. The authors use the whole term structure to extract the default intensities for each bond. Given that bonds have several maturities, the Duan and Simonato (1998) filter was used to standardize the information. The number of trading dates is defined by the New York Stock Exchange time schedule.

15.8 PRINCIPAL COMPONENT ANALYSIS OF LIQUIDITY RISK

Table 15.5, panel A, presents the principal component results for the eight illiquidity variables presented above. The procedure consists of building new non-correlated variables (or principal components) to explain the total illiquidity variance. The exercise also reduces the number of variables to measure illiquidity. The eight principal components obtained are ranked by their ability to explain the total variance of illiquidity. Accordingly, PC1 explains 41.84% of the variance, and the first five principal components explain 95% of the variance.

Now, if we look at the results of Table 15.5, panel B, we can see that the variables that best explain the variance in PC1 are IRC, IRC Risk, and Roll, while those that best explain the variance in PC2 are Amihud and Amihud Risk. PC3 is mainly explained by the two zero trading variables. Below, we will use PC1 only and assign equal weight to the three variables that make up this illiquidity index: IRC, IRC Risk, and Roll, which represent pure price spread variables.

TABLE 15.5 Principal component analysis of liquidity risk.

Panel A: Eigenvalues of the eight principal components

PC	Eigenvalue	Difference	Proportion	Cum. % explained
PC1	3.3470		0.4184	0.4184
PC2	1.8761	1.4709	0.2345	0.6529
PC3	0.9916	0.8845	0.1239	0.7768
PC4	0.9314	0.0602	0.1164	0.8933
PC5	0.4427	0.4887	0.0553	0.9486
PC6	0.2572	0.1855	0.0321	0.9807
PC7	0.1151	0.1421	0.0144	0.9951
PC8	0.0390	0.0761	0.0049	1.0000

Panel B: Eigenvectors of the Eight Principal Components

	PC1	PC2	PC3	PC4	PC5	PC6	PC7	PC8
Amihud	0.1623	0.6102	0.2803	−0.0839	−0.1056	−0.683	0.1785	0.0786
IRC	0.5037	−0.1887	0.1357	0.1064	0.1837	0.0047	0.4456	−0.6698
Amihud risk	0.1791	0.5701	0.376	−0.1321	0.1392	0.6735	−0.1054	0.002
IRC risk	0.5105	−0.201	−0.0016	0.1075	0.0513	0.1034	0.3825	0.7265
Roll	0.3725	−0.3161	0.5047	0.1502	−0.222	−0.1388	−0.6446	0.0046
Turnover	−0.1031	0.2389	−0.0557	0.9534	−0.118	0.072	0.0268	−0.0187
Zero bond	−0.3671	−0.171	0.4806	0.1344	0.7389	−0.1437	0.0568	0.1303
Zero firm	−0.3783	−0.2011	0.5223	−0.0544	−0.5691	0.1549	0.439	0.0064

Source: Reproduced from Dionne and Maalaoui-Chun (2013).

15.9 EMPIRICAL ANALYSIS OF CREDIT CYCLES

As already mentioned, the analysis completed by Dionne and Maalaoui-Chun (2013) covers the years 2002 to 2012. This period includes the financial crisis of 2007–2009. Figure 15.3 shows the evolution of the index for mean corporate bond yield spreads according to the main dates linked to this crisis.

The financial crisis began in the summer of 2007 with the deterioration of CDO products, triggered by the default of subprime mortgage loans. These defaults also affected the liquidity of commercial paper (ABCP). Bear Stearns was the first bank to default, in March 2008, and the American government-sponsored agencies Fannie Mae and Freddie Mac incurred major losses (explained by the default of subprime mortgages). However, it was Lehman Brothers' bankruptcy in September 2008 that caused the index to rise sharply, as shown in Figure 15.3. Some specialists maintain that the financial institutions' default risks amplified considerably after that date and that the variation of the index before fall 2008 was linked mainly to market liquidity risk. Lastly, starting in October 2008, the US Federal Reserve started to massively inject liquid assets into financial markets to end the financial crisis (TARP, Troubled Asset Relief Program).

Figure 15.4 presents variations on bond default intensities (λ in %) for the main US banks and the American Insurance Group (AIG) during the period of interest. The curves cover different maturities from 2 to 10 years. The hatched portion indicates the economic recession of December 2007 to June 2009. It is interesting to note that

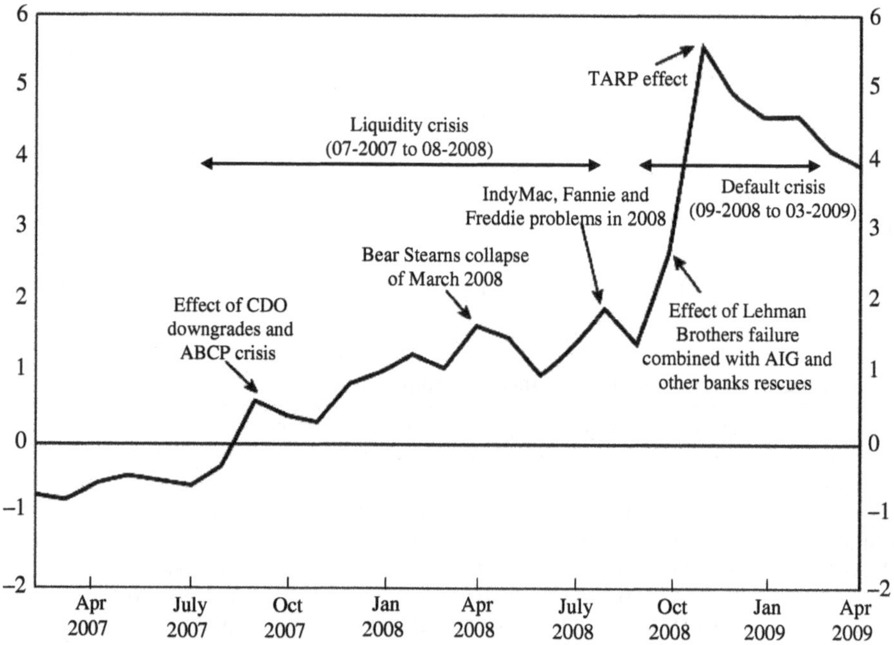

FIGURE 15.3 The dynamics of average credit spreads and major financial events during the years 2007–2009.
Source: Reproduced from Dionne and Maalaoui-Chun (2013). © John Wiley & Sons, Inc. Reproduced with permission.

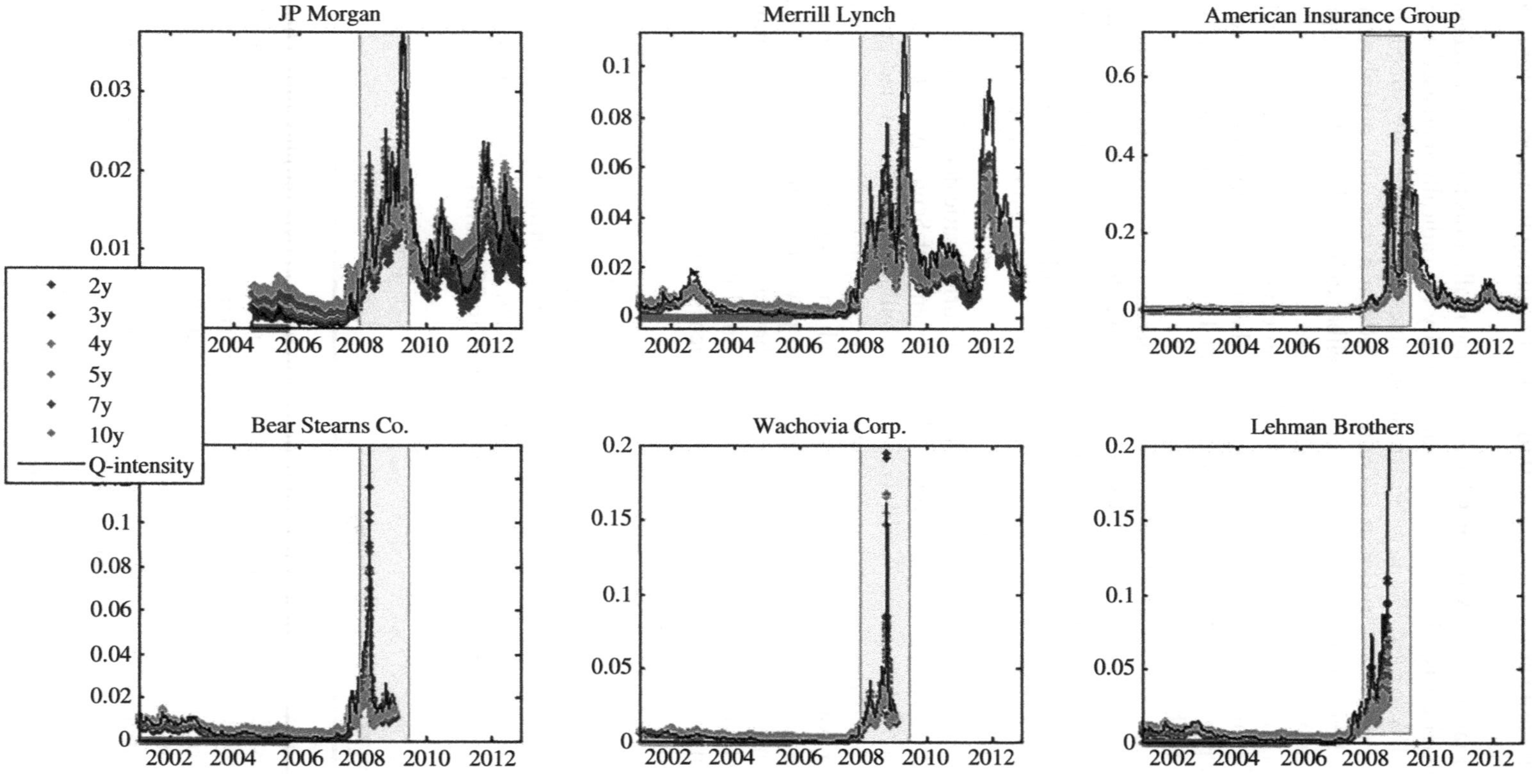

FIGURE 15.4 Default risk of bonds for some financial institutions during the 2007–2009 crisis.

the default intensity goes from almost 0 to over 20% during the recession for several banks, and over 60% for AIG.

J.P. Morgan (now JPMorgan Chase) was not really affected by the recession or the financial crisis, although its default intensity (λ) radically increased from a value below 1% to over 3%. Bear Stearns Companies was another investment bank that offered brokerage services. It defaulted in 2008 and was subsequently sold to J.P. Morgan. Bear Stearns was sued for having deliberately marketed financial products whose values were well below those advertised.

Merrill Lynch, another investment bank, also experienced financial difficulties related to the subprime crisis. It was acquired by Bank of America in 2008, yet the subsidiaries retained their original name. Merrill Lynch was a leader in the CDS market during the 2000s.

Wachovia, a diversified US bank, was quite active in 21 states during the early 2000s. Even so, it experienced serious financial difficulties in 2008 and was forced into a buyout by Wells Fargo, a transaction that it preferred to the offer by Citigroup.

Lehman Brothers (the fourth-largest investment bank before the financial crisis after Goldman Sachs, Morgan Stanley, and Merrill Lynch) filed for bankruptcy and insolvency protection on September 15, 2008, because of its heavy involvement in the subprime mortgage crisis. Figure 15.4 shows a fairly erratic default risk between 2001 and 2003. The bank was affected by the events of September 11, 2001; it occupied three floors in the World Trade Center building. It also clashed in 2003 with the US Securities and Exchange Commission (SEC) and other financial market regulators; it was accused of influencing financial analysts by compensating them based on the bank's revenues and was ordered to pay a large fine. In 2010, it was accused of intentionally producing documents that falsified its financial condition before its default. During the financial crisis, it found it difficult to sell the inferior tranches of its CDOs. Forced to retain these tranches, it incurred huge losses when subprime mortgages defaulted.

American Insurance Group (AIG) is an insurance company that displayed uncommon investor behavior in the 2000s. Some said that AIG had become a hedge fund rather than an insurance company (Kessler, 2014). The US government rescued AIG with a $182 billion bailout and took control of the firm. AIG was accused of selling a very large quantity of CDSs without setting aside the capital required to protect its commitments. It repaid the government in 2012 after selling off many of its subsidiaries.

15.10 REGIME DETECTION MODEL

In this section, we present a new regime detection method (Maalaoui-Chun, Dionne, and François, 2014a). This procedure is based on Student's t sequential tests for changes in levels and on F tests for changes in variance or volatility. The model is nonparametric. The procedure considers regimes to be random in the sense that on each date t, it is not possible to predict the existence of a regime change. This procedure can separate the analysis of level regimes (means) and volatility regimes. The two moments may behave independently in time. In the Markov model, they are estimated simultaneously. For an analysis of liquidity regimes with the Markov model, see Anténor-Habazac, Dionne, and Guesmi (2018).

Another characteristic of the method is that it can take into account abrupt changes in time series. It is a real-time method in the sense that changes can be detected when new data are observed. It does not make assumptions about the number or distribution of future regime changes. This method originates in the literature on regime changes in the ecosystem[3] and was first applied in finance by Maalaoui-Chun, Dionne, and François (2014a). Regimes are detected in two steps: the first identifies the regime levels in time series, and the second identifies volatility regimes. Below, we discuss the regime levels exclusively.

Consider the following time series:

$$\{Y_t, t = 1, \ldots, n\}.$$

Suppose that Y_t is described by the autoregressive model below:

$$Y_t - f_t = \rho(Y_{t-1} - f_{t-1}) + \varepsilon_t,$$

where:

f_t and f_{t-1} are time-varying means;

ρ is an autocorrelation coefficient;

$\varepsilon_t \sim N(0, \sigma^2)$.

Before applying the regime detection model, we must estimate $\hat{\rho}$ to remove the red noise in the data and work with a filtered time series such that the time series used will be $Y_t - \hat{\rho}Y_{t-1}$. We define c as a breakpoint where the distribution of data changes regime. We can then define f_t as:

$$f_t = \begin{cases} \mu_1, t = 1, 2, \ldots, c-1, \\ \mu_2, t = c, c+1, \ldots, n. \end{cases}$$

The null hypothesis H_0 is that $\mu_1 = \mu_2$, which signifies that we reject a change in the regime level.

We start with a mean $\overline{Z}_{cur}$ for the first observed sequence in the data containing m periods. By assumption, this is the initial mean of the current regime. We can define a confidence interval for this initial mean using Δ such that:

$$\Delta = t_{\alpha_{mean}}^{2m-2}\sqrt{2\bar{s}_m^2/m},$$

where:

m is the number of observations for the sequence chosen;

$\bar{s}_m^2$ is the sample variance of the data;

t is the value of the Student's t-distribution's two-tailed statistic with $(2m - 2)$ degrees of freedom;

α_{mean} is the level of confidence chosen.

[3]Rodionov (2004, 2005, 2006).

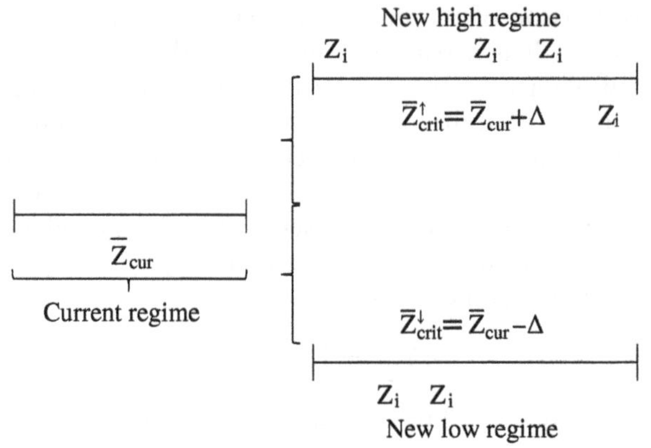

FIGURE 15.5 Diagram of the regime detection model.

We can graphically represent the regime change procedure, as shown in Figure 15.5.

Let Z_i be the new observations of the random variable, and let $\overline{Z}^{\uparrow}_{crit}$ and $\overline{Z}^{\downarrow}_{crit}$ designate the upper and lower bounds respectively. The Z_i included in the interval are not candidates for regime change, whereas those outside the interval may be. We can define this interval as $]\overline{Z}^{\uparrow}_{crit}, \overline{Z}^{\downarrow}_{crit}[$, where:

$$\overline{Z}^{\uparrow}_{crit} = \overline{Z}_{cur} + \Delta$$
$$\overline{Z}^{\downarrow}_{crit} = \overline{Z}_{cur} - \Delta,$$

and where $\overline{Z}^{\uparrow}_{crit}$ is the critical mean for an upward regime change and $\overline{Z}^{\downarrow}_{crit}$ is the critical mean for a downward regime change. We must test whether the change observed is a real regime change or a simple accident observed in the data.

We define RSI as an index of regime change equal to the value representing the cumulative sum of the standardized Z_i values relative to a critical mean measure $\overline{Z}_{crit}$:

$$RSI = \frac{1}{m\bar{s}_m} \sum_{j=t_{cur}}^{j=t_{cur}+m-1} (Z_i - \overline{Z}_{crit}), j = \ t_{cur}, t_{cur} + 1, \ldots, t_{cur} + m - 1.$$

Now, suppose that we observe some Z_i outside the interval and that they are higher than $\overline{Z}^{\uparrow}_{crit}$, as illustrated in Figure 15.5. The upward regime change will be confirmed, and H_0 will be rejected if RSI or the positive value of the sum does not change signs in the interval t_{cur} to $t_{cur} + m - 1$. Conversely, a downward regime change will be confirmed if some Z_i are less than $\overline{Z}^{\downarrow}_{crit}$ and the negative sum does not change signs in the same interval.

15.11 DETECTION OF DEFAULT AND LIQUIDITY REGIMES

The objective of this section is to explain the variations in bond yield spreads according to credit cycles and to determine how default and liquidity risks affect these

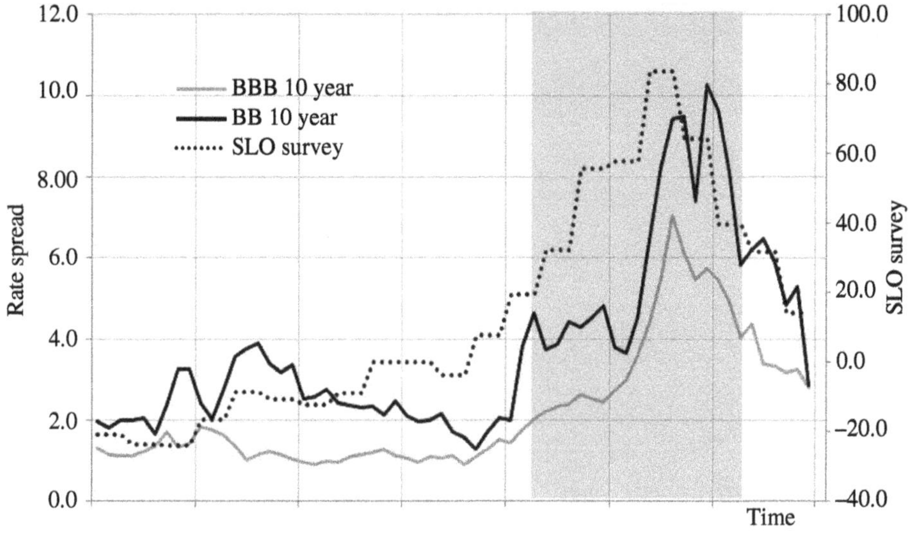

FIGURE 15.6 BBB and BB rate spread and SLO survey.

variations. Figure 15.6 represents total yield spreads of BBB and BB bonds with a 10-year maturity along with the evolution of the SLO (senior loan officer) opinion survey, an index for the state of the economy published by the US Federal Reserve. The shaded part corresponds to the financial crisis of 2007–2009.

We can see that yield spreads have a predictive effect on the financial crisis period. The BB curve has two levels during the crisis: one before the default of Lehman Brothers and a second one after the default, which seems to suggest that the default portion of the yield spread may be more accentuated after September 2008.

Figure 15.7 confirms this assumption. It describes the changes in default risk regime measured by the mean CDS premium of bonds in the sample, made up of all bonds with a 10-year maturity. The figure shows that default risk changed regimes in 2008 and demonstrated strong persistence after 2009.

Figure 15.8 presents the changes in liquidity risk regime for PC1 during the same period. It is interesting to note that liquidity risk experienced one shock at the start of the financial crisis and another one during the second part of 2008, namely after the Lehman Brothers bankruptcy. This risk lasted several months after the financial crisis and returned to its initial level in 2012. Figures 15.7 and 15.8 clearly show that the variation of the BB curve in Figure 15.6 may well be explained by the sum of default and liquidity risk variations.

15.12 CONCLUSION

This chapter presents important lessons and findings regarding liquidity risk. Liquidity risk has amplified since the last financial crisis; the Basel Committee consequently made it a priority in Basel III.

Many research questions on liquidity risk will be explored in the coming years. Even if new illiquidity measures have begun to provide results for fixed-income securities, the importance of illiquidity to explain bond yield spreads is still not measured

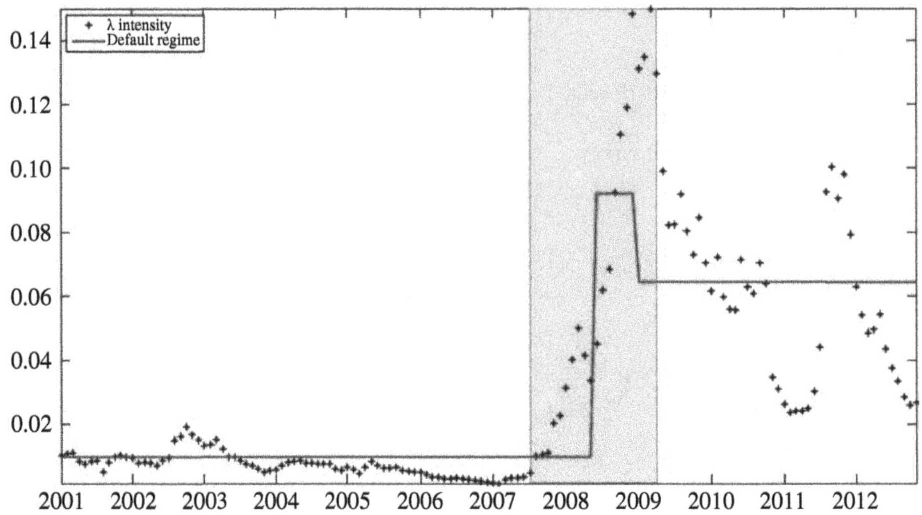

FIGURE 15.7 Default risk regimes.

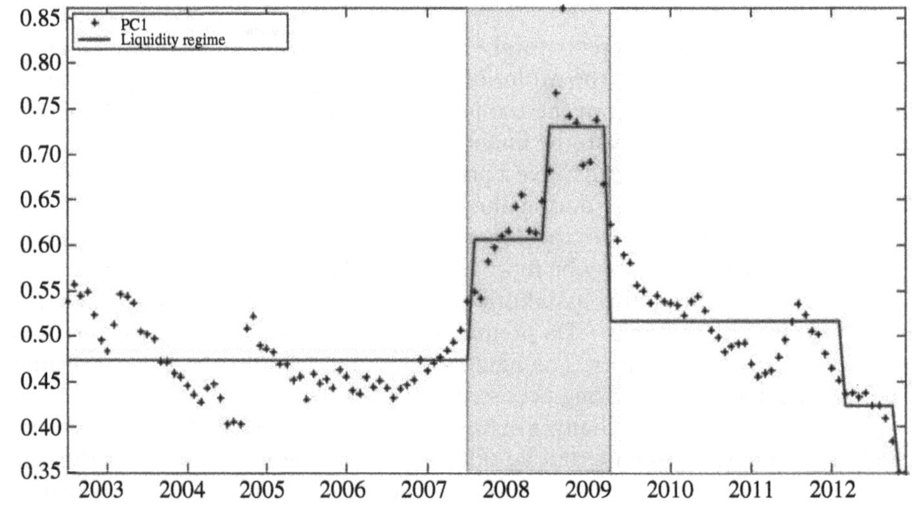

FIGURE 15.8 Liquidity risk regimes.

with strong precision. We know that a lack of liquidity is present, but its exact scope is not yet confirmed. It seems to vary with economic cycles. In addition, the pricing of bonds and CDSs does not yet integrate liquidity risk satisfactorily. Many models are still limited to default risk. A major challenge would therefore be to integrate liquidity risk in a structural model, which is already well defined for default risk.

REFERENCES

Akari, M.A., Ben-Abdallah, R., Breton, M., and Dionne, G., 2018. "The Impact of Central Clearing on the Market for Single-Name Credit Default Swaps." Working paper 18-01, Canada Research Chair in Risk Management, HEC Montréal.

Anténor-Habazac, C., Dionne, G., and Guesmi, S., 2018. "Cyclical Variations in Liquidity Risk of Corporate Bonds." Working paper 18-03, Canada Research Chair in Risk Management, HEC Montréal.

Collin-Dufresne, P. Goldstein, R.S., and Martin, J.S., 2001. "The Determinants of Credit Spread Changes." *Journal of Finance* 56, 2177–2208.

Dick-Nielsen, J., 2009. "Liquidity Biases in TRACE." *Journal of Fixed Income* 19, 43–55.

Dick-Nielsen, J., Feldhütter, P., and Lando, D., 2012. "Corporate Bond Liquidity before and after the Onset of the Subprime Crisis." *Journal of Financial Economics* 103, 471–492.

Dionne, G., Gauthier, G., Hammami, K., Maurice, M., and Simonato, J.G., 2011. "A Reduced Form Model of Default Spreads with Markov-Switching Macroeconomic Factors." *Journal of Banking and Finance* 35, 8, 1984–2000.

Dionne, G., Hammami, K., Gauthier, G., Maurice, M., and Simonato, J.G., 2010. "Default Risk in Corporate Yield Spreads." *Financial Management* 39, 707–731.

Dionne, G., and Maalaoui-Chun, O., 2013. Default and Liquidity Regimes in the Bond Market during the 2002–2012 Period." *Canadian Journal of Economics* 46, 1160–1195.

Duan, J.C., and Simonato, J.G., 1998. "Estimating and Testing Exponential Affine Term Structure Models by Kalman Filters." *Review of Quantitative Finance and Accounting* 13, 111–135.

Duffie, D., Pan, J., and Singleton, K., 2000. "Transform Analysis and Asset Pricing for Affine Jump-Diffusions." *Econometrica* 68, 1343–1376.

Elton E. J., Gruber, M.J., Agrawal, D., and Mann, C., 2001. "Explaining the Rate Spread on Corporate Bonds." *The Journal of Finance* 56, 247–277.

Feldhütter, P., 2012. "The Same Bond at Different Prices: Identifying Search Frictions and Selling Pressures." *Review of Financial Studies* 25, 1155–1206.

Giesecke, K., Longstaff, F.A., Schaefer, S., and Strebulaev, I., 2011. "Corporate Bond Default Risk: A 150-Year Perspective." *Journal of Financial Economics* 102, 233–250.

Han, S. and Zhou, H., 2008. "Effect of Liquidity on the Nondefault Component of Corporate Bond Spreads: Evidence from Intraday Transactions Data." *Finance and Economics Discussion Series* 2008-40, Federal Reserve System.

Huang, J.Z., and Huang, M., 2012. "How Much of the Corporate-Treasury Yield Spread Is Due to Credit Risk?" *Review of Asset Pricing Studies* 2, 153–202.

Kessler, D., 2014. "Why (Re)Insurance Is Not Systemic." *The Journal of Risk and Insurance* 81, 477–487.

Lando, D., 2004. *Credit Risk Modeling – Theory and Applications.* Princeton, NJ: Princeton University Press.

Longstaff, F.A., Mithal, S., and Neis, E., 2005. "Corporate Yield Spreads: Default Risk or Liquidity? New Evidence from the Credit Default Swap Market." *Journal of Finance* 60, 2213–2253.

Maalaoui-Chun, O., Dionne, G., and François, P., 2014a. "Detecting Regime Shifts in Credit Spreads." *Journal of Financial and Quantitative Analysis* 49, 1339–1364.

Maalaoui Chun, O., Dionne, G. and François, P., 2014b. "Credit Spread Changes within Switching Regimes." *Journal of Banking and Finance* 49, 41–55.

Rodionov, S.N., 2004. "A Sequential Algorithm for Testing Climate Regime Shifts." *Geophysical Research Letters* 31, L09204.

Rodionov, S.N., 2005. "Detecting Regime Shifts in the Mean and Variance: Methods and Specific Examples." Workshop on Regime Shifts, Varna, Bulgaria, 68–72.

Rodionov, S.N., 2006. "Use of Prewhitening in Climate Regime Shift Detection." *Geophysical Research Letters* 33, L12707.

CHAPTER 16

Long-Term Capital Management

This chapter analyzes the turbulent saga of Long-Term Capital Management (LTCM), a private American fund run very speculatively, although it was initially designated as a hedge fund. This fund began in 1994 and was rescued by the Federal Bank of New York in September 1998.

The problem with this fund, as Jorion (2000) and Shirreff (1999) argue, was that it took highly risky positions and neglected risk management. The fault lies both with the managers of LTCM and their financial backers, who not only lacked vision but also managed their risks ineffectively. The fund managers gave little information to financial backers. The backers did not even know the aggregate makeup of the portfolio.

The risk management of this fund was not regulated, although it should have been reported to the SEC (Securities and Exchange Commission). Consequently, the fund did not have to set aside minimum required capital. In fact, hedge funds are not really constrained in the formation of their portfolios or in their choice of leverage. Shirreff (1999) explains that LTCM managed default risk by assuming that markets were able to absorb all hedging positions within manageable limits. The fund offset a long position in one financial instrument with a short position in a similar instrument or its derivative. The problem is that the fund managers undervalued the limits of these activities. When the limits were reached, the partners insisted that it was too late to request more money.

The LTCM managers traded on their reputation to manage risks and failed to set aside the necessary margins. As a result, they borrowed without collateral and used these funds to buy assets, which they used as future collateral. In two years, they thus accumulated investment capital of $7 billion.

Jorion (2000) emphasizes that it is not the concept of VaR that was inadequate for computing capital; rather, VaR was misused by the LTCM managers. Specifically, they underestimated the credit and liquidity risks of their portfolio. The portfolio was undercapitalized because the VaR did not sufficiently take into account credit risk. The fund managers did not see, or want to see, the credit risk of their portfolio and consequently retain the necessary capital. They thought that this risk would be covered by their hedging activities, which were not always successful. In addition, they presumed that the returns followed a normal and stable distribution, which led them to underestimate the credit risk of the portfolio. This portfolio management approach biased the use of the VaR toward a very-short-term maturity, by supposing that the correlations observed between the assets would remain stable.

Based on very high positive correlations between assets, the LTCM managers took very large short arbitrage positions. Gradually, the decrease in correlations increased the portfolio risk. It is also possible that these correlations contained estimation errors when the initial positions were taken. Lastly, liquidity risk played a major role in the fund's final disastrous months because of insufficient reserve capital. This liquidity risk thus transformed into default risk.

Jorion (2000) also discusses the problem of the use of the same variance-covariance matrix to measure risk and optimize portfolio positions. This procedure creates a biased measure of portfolio risk when the number of observations is not high enough for the number of positions or instruments in the portfolio, as we have seen in detail for market risk.

This short-term bias introduced incentives to take biased arbitrage positions based on the recent history of returns and on extreme values rather than more stable long-term data. This critique highlights the importance of separating risk management and investment functions. Analysts who estimate risk must work independently from brokers and must be able to intervene (via the CRO, for example) when the situation becomes critical.

16.1 BRIEF HISTORY OF THE FUND

LTCM was founded in 1994 by John Meriwether, who left his position as head of fixed-income trading at Salomon Brothers in 1991 following a trading scandal. LTCM's main activity was to offer private diversification services for portfolios of bonds and other financial assets. To boost the firm's credibility and respect on Wall Street, Meriwether partnered with two Nobel laureates, Robert Merton and Myron Scholes, along with former regulator David Mullins. He also brought along a team of the best brokers from his former arbitrage group at Salomon Brothers (Shirreff, 1999).

In general, hedge funds are accessible only to investors with large portfolios and some knowledge of finance. These investors hire specialized hedging firms to manage their portfolios partly or fully. In return, these firms promise very high returns permitted by their large volumes and risky positions.

LTCM managed assets valued at about $125 billion, whereas its capital base was $7 billion. By comparison, the US budget surplus proposed by President Bush in 1999 was $231 billion. The fund had positions in off-balance-sheet derivative products of $1 trillion, but according to Jorion (2000) these positions were all offset. They consequently did not really represent an additional risk in the portfolio as long as there was liquidity. These positions nonetheless illustrated the scale of the transactions that the fund managed. In fact, the LTCM managers overexploited the leverage effect and lacked capital in their last months of operation to hedge against illiquidity.

At first, the fund obtained financing easily, avoiding the need to provide collateral in its liquidity search activities by using repos.[1] In general, banks ask for collateral to protect themselves from the depreciation of assets placed as guarantees. However, they did not do so with LTCM. Instead, they over-relied on the reputation of some partners. This blind trust by the lenders significantly reduced the financial constraint on LTCM managers.

[1]A repo is a deposit of some assets at a bank in exchange for liquid cash, with a promise to buy back the assets later.

Bond-related risk was taken as follows. The fund offered large-scale bond arbitrage services by writing and offering bond interest-rate swaps. The fund managers also sold government bonds, with a yield of 7%, for example. With the funds obtained, they bought private bonds with a 9% yield, but underestimated the default risk of private bonds or considered it to be zero. The fact that yield spreads could be explained by a potential default risk was not considered.

LTCM also engaged in arbitrage trading in bonds of the same issuer. For example, fund managers bought bonds yielding 6.1% near maturity, in return for recently issued bonds with a 6% yield. The yield spread was due to a liquidity risk, which was underestimated by LTCM. In general, more mature bonds are less liquid. The two values converge when liquidity risk disappears because the default risk does not change. Even if the spread was small, the high volume of transactions could generate sizable gains. The managers relied heavily on the convergence of the two prices, but this was a very risky arbitrage strategy. Another important activity was the management of stock options. The fund managers charged 2% in management fees on invested capital and 25% on profits, compared to 1% and 20% for other funds. In 1997, they received $1.5 billion in fee revenue (Prabhu, 2001).

Another frequently used strategy was position arbitrage with low price spreads. For instance, the managers bought Italian government bonds and sold futures on German bonds (Shirreff, 1999). They speculated on the fact that some assets with the same value were poorly priced. They bought those that were undervalued and sold those that were overvalued, hoping that the prices of the two assets would converge when other market agents would close the gap. This strategy, mainly applied on European bonds, became less profitable after the arrival of the euro in 1998, because bond yield spreads narrowed, reducing possible gains. Equity portfolios were very profitable at that time, so managers had to invent other means to outperform the market.

Consequently, the LTCM managers created pseudo-diversified portfolios, while considerably increasing the credit and liquidity risk of their global portfolio. As long as the asset issuers do not default, this strategy is very profitable but also very risky. We saw a similar situation with CDSs in the early 2000s. History was clearly repeating itself.

The LTCM managers' strategy was very profitable at first. It generated returns of over 40% in 1995 and 1996, as Figure 16.1 demonstrates. The fund even used its equity to maintain its high return of 40% because it had to fulfill its promise to deliver higher returns compared to other funds.

In 1997, LTCM returned billions of dollars to its investors, which reduced the fund's capital to $4.7 billion. This amounted to a staggering level effect relative to capital of 28! This leverage level began to worry observers, and profitability problems accentuated starting in 1997. The fund's return that year was only 17%, well below the 31% of the Standard and Poor's index.

In August 1998, the Russians defaulted on their debt, a risk that the fund had not anticipated. Investors consequently became much more prudent, which in turn widened the yield spreads of some on-the-run and off-the-run government bonds. LTCM, which had speculated on the narrowing of these spreads, lost $550 million in a few days. In addition, stock volatility increased, causing a loss of another $500 million a few days later on five-year stock options (Lewis, 1999).

The value of the fund's capital subsequently plunged by 50% in six months, whereas its investments stayed at approximately $125 billion. The leverage effect for

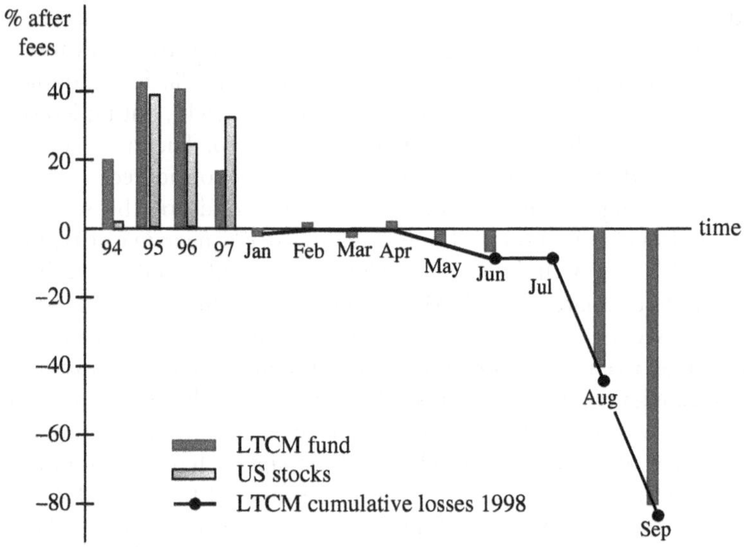

FIGURE 16.1 LTCM's returns.
Source: Reproduced from Jorion (2000). © John Wiley & Sons, Inc. Reproduced with permission.

equity soared to 55, whereas that of a typical hedge fund is about 11 (Prabhu, 2001). LTCM lacked liquidity to meet its purchasing obligations associated with its hedging positions. The managers appealed to their partners for a quick capital infusion, but no one replied. The end was approaching quickly.

To protect financial markets from potential systemic risk, the Federal Bank of New York formed a group of investors (14 banks) that acquired 90% of the firm for $3.65 billion, a capital injection that saved the fund. Many experts thought this intervention was necessary to protect financial markets because LTCM held an enormous fund and maintained close ties with several large financial institutions.

Shirreff (1999) lists the biggest losses: the LTCM partners ranked first with over $1 billion; the Bank of Italy forfeited $100 million; Sumitomo Bank $100 million; Merrill Lynch $22 million; Credit Suisse $55 million; UBS $690 million; Dresdner Bank $145 million, and so on. This partial list clearly demonstrates the international scale of the fund's activities. Jacobs (1999) asserts that the intervention by the Federal Reserve Bank of New York probably reduced the potential systemic risk, given the involvement of the fund in several assets, its international scope, and its very close financial ties with several large investment banks. Others are more skeptical because the amounts cited above are not that large relative to the total assets of these banks.

16.2 RISK MANAGEMENT, VaR, AND REQUIRED CAPITAL

As presented in previous chapters, VaR can be used in different ways to calculate the required capital for banks or other investors for market and credit risk.

For market risk, the time horizon is generally 10 days, and a 99% degree of confidence is usually employed. In addition, the Basel formula asks banks to multiply VaR calculated by 3. However, this definition of VaR is valid only for market risk of regulated banks. LTCM was not subject to this type of constraint, which explains its low capital. In the case of LTCM, we must also take credit risk into account because the portfolio contained multiple private bonds and the fund did not reserve capital for this type of risk. In addition, we have seen that the typical time horizon for credit risks is one year. Lastly, LTCM considered its liquidity risk to be nonexistent.

VaR measures economic capital, that is, protection capital required to cover an unanticipated loss and, in the extreme case, a default. In other words, the VaR is the amount of a firm's self-insurance. An important point is the distinction between the different roles of VaR. If the VaR is solely intended to allow evolution comparisons of the portfolio risk over time, its estimation must be precise, but not as precise as the calculation of the required reserve capital to protect the fund.

The degree of confidence and the time horizon are particularly important parameters. When setting the degree of confidence, it is important to keep in mind that it may affect the real default probability because it influences the economic capital that will be set aside for difficult times. However, an overly high degree of confidence will incur a high required capital cost.

More directly, the calculation of VaR affects the rate of return on equity set aside when the debt level is very high and the assets are derivatives such as futures. If we have an expected profit of \$5 million with \$100 million in investments (notional value) and the VaR is equal to \$20 million (economic capital), the return on capital is 25% (5/20). However, if we only have \$10 million in VaR, the return is 50%. The LTCM managers often claimed that they could deliver potential returns of this magnitude.

The choice of the hedging period is also important. This choice must consider the time that the company will need to obtain additional funds in difficult periods, which may be much longer for a hedge fund than for a bank. Basel regulation sets the hedging period used to estimate banks' market risk at 10 days. This is a reasonable period for a bank that had a setback to be able to refinance its capital by seeking new funds or by liquidating some assets in an orderly fashion. This example shows the importance of considering asset liquidity. For a hedge fund, a 10-day horizon is very short: LTCM could not replenish its funds within this time frame.

Daily volatility of the fund was estimated at \$100 million by some experts, whereas others compute it at \$45 million. According to the Basel formula for banks, the VaR at 99% is 100 times 2.33, which gives \$233 million on a daily basis. If we multiply the VaR by 9.50 $\left(\sqrt{10}\times 3\right)$, this gives \$2.2 billion in required capital for 10 days, an amount below the \$4.7 billion in capital that LTCM held (\$995 million according to the 45 million volatility figure of other experts). By excluding the factor of 3 imposed on banks, the respective values for 10 days become \$733 million and \$332 million (Jorion, 2000).

The capital required according to the 10-day VaR without weighting credit risk is completely unrealistic for this type of portfolio (Jorion, 2000). Let us consider a one-year horizon by integrating credit risk: Daily volatility of \$100 million over 252 days represents annual volatility of about \$1.6 billion (equal to \$100 million multiplied by $\sqrt{252}\approx 16$). The corresponding annual VaR at 99% for credit risk is \$3.7 billion if we do not consider the factor of 3 imposed on banks, which implies that total capital is still below \$4.7 billion. However, we supposed that total risk follows a normal distribution using 2.33 as a weight for a VaR at 99%.

By applying Moody's approach and by supposing that the credit rating is Aa2, the multiplier becomes 3.5 (instead of 2.33) for required capital of \$5.6 billion

($1.6 billion × 3.5) for credit risk, which is now much higher than $4.7 billion. However, the same hypothesis of a normal distribution for total risk is used, which underestimates the default probability. By using Student's law with 6 degrees of freedom, the required capital increases to $12.5 billion, which represents more than double the capital available for the two risks.

Jorion (2000) states that fund managers probably did their calculations as follows: they used the annual average volatility of 15% of the Standard and Poor's index for the years 1997 and 1998. By applying this very short-term percentage to the capital amount of $4.7 billion and by converting it to a daily value ($705 million divided by 16), we obtain an implied volatility of $44 million instead of $100 million.

Using $105 million (44 × 2.33) as a daily VaR without taking credit risk into account, the monthly VaR equals to $480 million $\left(105 \times \sqrt{21}\right)$. By removing the expected return of $71 million (expected monthly profit supposing an annual return of 18%) to derive the absolute VaR, we obtain $409 million as a maximum monthly loss once every 100 months. In May and June 1998, the fund lost $310 million and $450 million respectively and in August 1998 it lost $550 million.

Evidently, the approach used was not adequate for this portfolio. The first two losses should have alerted the managers that there was a problem. Lastly, their stress-testing calculations gave them a worst-case scenario of $2.3 billion in losses, whereas they lost over $4 billion.

Shirreff (1999) argues that the LTCM fund did not really use stress testing in its risk management policy and it underestimated liquidity risk. The managers assumed that the assets of their international portfolio had very weak correlations. LTCM's partners were also very negligent because they did not ask for collateral for their interest-rate swap and repo activities. The lack of transparency linked to these major transactions (including the lack of initial margins) was also criticized in several expert analyses of the LTCM bailout by the Federal Bank of New York. In addition, the SEC was accused of insufficient oversight of the banks that traded with LTCM.

16.3 PORTFOLIO OPTIMIZATION AND LEVERAGE EFFECT

Consider a portfolio with two highly correlated risky assets, like two types of bonds similar to those used in the LTCM portfolio. Table 16.1, taken from Jorion (2000), provides the data for a private BAA bond and a 10-year government bond. The two bonds have similar volatilities and a correlation of 0.9654.

The portfolio places $19.66 in private bonds and sells $15.60 in Treasury bills (per $ of equity). The difference is $4.06, which requires a loan of $3.06 at the risk-free rate. The expected monthly return is 3.1%, which gives an expected annual return of nearly 40% for LTCM. The leverage ratio is close to 20.

One problem with this type of strategy is that the portfolio volatility is very sensitive to the correlation of 0.9654. Jorion (2000) shows that the monthly volatility is 8.1% with the initial correlation of 0.9654 and that it can reach 19.24% with a correlation of 0.80. He also affirms that the correlation in 1998 was approximately 0.80. From 1994 to 1998, it was about 0.94, but before this period it was much

TABLE 16.1 Portfolio optimization with two assets.

Panel A: data	Corporate bond		Government bond	Risk-free asset
Input data (annual)				
Expected return	7.28%		5.75%	5.36%
Volatility of return	1.58%		1.90%	
Correlation		0.9654		
Output data:				
Position (for $1 equity)	$19.66		–$15.60	–$3.06

Panel B: Optimal portfolio	Return	Million $
Initial equity		4,700
Expected return (monthly)	3.1%	145
Volatility of return (monthly)	8.1%	382
Expected return (annual)	37.0%	1,740
Volatility of return (annual)	28.1%	1,322
Volatility of return (daily)	1.8%	83
Ratio of equity to standard deviation	12.31	

Source: Reproduced from Jorion (2000). © John Wiley & Sons, Inc. Reproduced with permission.

lower and reached a level of 0.75 in 1992. This clearly illustrates that one must not be too short-sighted and must always consider the evolution of volatility over the longer term by using historical data to decide on positions.

Lastly, Jorion (2000) shows that VaR should be used prudently when formulating portfolio strategies. It may be tempting to overweight recent observations and neglect the more distant ones, yet this would create significant biases.

16.4 CONCLUSION

The history of LTCM is not an indictment of VaR; rather, it was the misuse of the concept of VaR that caused the fund's collapse.

Managers neglected both liquidity risk and credit risk of the portfolio. They focused on market risk exclusively, although the two other risks were strongly present. They also took reckless arbitrage positions.

Ultimately, the fund's arbitrage strategies made it vulnerable. The failure of Russian bonds disrupted its profitability scenarios by triggering changes in market behaviors that defied their predictions. The other factor that caused a loss in a record time is the overuse of leverage. Regulatory authorities should be more stringent in this area, even if the main clients are large investors. It is not uniquely the financial health of these investors that is at stake, but the entire financial system, owing to the potential systemic effects.

REFERENCES

Jacobs B., 1999. *Capital Ideas and Market Realities*. Wiley-Blackwell.

Jorion P., 2000. "Risk Management Lessons from Long-Term Capital Management." *European Financial Management* 6, 277–300.

Lewis M., 1999. "How the Eggheads Cracked." *New York Times*, January 24, 1999.

Prabhu S., 2001. "Long-Term Capital Management: The Dangers of Leverage." Working paper, Duke University, Durham, NC.

Shirreff D., 1999. "Lessons from the Collapse of Hedge Fund, Long-Term Capital Management." Working paper, International Financial Risk Institute.

CHAPTER 17

Structured Finance and the Financial Crisis of 2007–2009[1]

Structured finance includes all advanced financial arrangements intended to refinance and effectively manage and cover credit risk of all economic activities. It has changed the role of banks and the functioning of financial and monetary markets. In many countries, structured finance has become a very important economic activity that has radically transformed the links among borrowers, lenders, and investors. Yet structured finance is also often cited as a major cause of the most recent financial crisis.

The objective of this chapter is to show that structured finance (and its complex products) did not cause the financial crisis. Rather, the problem stems from poor risk management in the years leading up to the crisis. We will look at the following examples: Agency problems in the securitization market, poor rating and pricing of structured financial products, lack of incentives for rating agencies to make objective evaluations, lack of market transparency, quest for high short-term returns by top management not motivated by the long-term financial stability of their companies, and the failure of regulators and central banks to understand the implications of a constantly evolving financial environment.

As a result of the crisis, several major banks declared bankruptcy, and governments and central banks had to rescue many other financial institutions. These bailouts protected financial markets in the short term, but did not solve the fundamental problems associated with this crisis. This chapter will highlight the role of risk management in restoring market confidence.

17.1 STRUCTURED FINANCE

Structured finance is a multifaceted concept. For many years, it was associated with derivative products and was considered marginal in economic and financial markets. In the 1990s, it became very prominent in the economy and raised concerns during the last financial crisis.

[1]The material in this chapter was presented at Advancing Canada's Competitive Advantage, a national *forum* on *management* held in Montréal on September 30, 2009. The comments by Shady Aboul-Enein, Richard Guay, and Nicolas Papageorgiou helped us improve the content. A previous version of the document was also published in French in the journal *Risques* (80, December 2009, 122–127) and in English in *Ivey Business Journal*, November–December 2009.

Structured finance has improved market liquidity and credit management. Its influence on trading in financial products has had major effects on retail credit organization and its extension in financial markets. These effects have begun to be better explained and understood. They have varied over time and often generated unanticipated complex consequences.

Structured finance has affected the nature of financial products by introducing new, increasingly complex products like those linked to credit risk securitization by banks such as CDOs (collateralized debt obligations) and ABCP (asset-backed commercial paper). These financial products imply the use of advanced mathematics and the formulation of new types of assets and sophisticated contracts that require collaboration from stakeholders in several disciplines (mathematicians, attorneys, tax specialists, financial analysts, etc.). They also require high IT capacities for performing calculations and managing large databases effectively. Owing to their liquidity, these products call into question the traditional methods of financial market regulation and monetary policy management.

Structured finance has been motivated mainly by credit risk hedging through the use of credit derivatives (CDSs, credit default swaps) and securitization of bank loans to investors. For example, securitization of a basket of bank loans for trusts is intended to transfer banks' credit risk to different investor groups such as pension funds, industrial and service firms, hedge funds, insurance companies, and even other banks. These trusts restructure baskets of loans (whose average rating is BBB, for example) into different asset tranches representing various risks, sold according to buyers' risk preferences. Note that the restructuring of asset baskets into tranches resembles the setting up of a firm's capital structure. The riskiest tranche, called equity, is the first to be exposed to default risk and yields a higher return. Superior, less risky tranches can even obtain an AAA rating if the default risk correlations between the tranches are very weak.

The CDO market has grown rapidly since the year 2000. Despite the growing importance of insurance companies, pension funds, and hedge funds, banks represent the most active players in this market. With the development of hedge funds, together with their demand for assets with high returns, structured products sellers accelerated their transfer of credit risk, particularly that of the riskiest tranches. Low interest rates in money markets motivated these sellers to build more and more AAA tranches of structured products using baskets of products of inferior risk classes to satisfy pension fund managers' needs. This exercise often neglected real correlations between different risk tranches.

Securitization of credit risk by banks was motivated by the need for liquidity and regulatory arbitrage possibilities under Basel I. Banks thus wanted to sell assets to reduce their regulatory capital. The Basel II Accord diminished the motivation for regulatory arbitrage, but the new capital rules for AAA financial products distorted bank capital allocation.

17.2 POOR RISK MANAGEMENT LINKED TO THE STRUCTURED FINANCE MARKET

Starting in the year 2000, financial markets rapidly underwent a major transformation. American banks and other retail credit institutions began to use different instruments to transfer their barely solvent (subprime) mortgage loans to financial markets via securitization. During this period, rating agencies' attribution of AAA ratings to tranches of these very risky products was an evident mistake because many of these products defaulted in 2007 during the early days of the financial crisis. Subsequently, some of these structured products were downgraded by the rating agencies, but it was too late: the damage had largely been done.

During this period, poor-quality mortgage assets were transformed into financial assets that had a risk considered acceptable to investors. This tranching of ABCP and CDOs concealed effective default risk tranches that were much higher than those suspected, which were not comparable to traditional bonds with the same risk rating. The financial crisis accelerated because retail banks faced pressure from investment banks to increase their high-risk mortgage loan offerings and generate structured assets with high returns during a period of low interest rates. This repackaging of financial instruments was very lucrative and prompted the issue of a second generation of CDOs (CDO squared). This heightened demand for the first issue and for mortgage-backed securities (MBS). When subprime mortgage loans began to default, these financial products externalized the damage to international financial markets. The financial crisis also caused external damage to the real economy in the form of unemployment and to the monetary economy by reducing banks' liquidity and creating difficult credit conditions for consumers and businesses, even though central banks' interest rates were very low. The crisis also undermined consumer confidence in financial institutions and rating agencies, and drove investors to take overly high risks. We can identify four major risk management problems linked to the structured finance market during this period.

17.2.1 Lack of Incentive Contracts in the Presence of Information Asymmetry

Banks and real estate mortgage brokers had little incentive to be vigilant and monitor borrowers' risks because much of their loans were securitized without an optimal contractual clause in the presence of moral hazard. They could even transfer all default risks from their assets to financial markets. Most often, the banks did not retain any credit risk retention or equity tranche. The same incentive problem existed (to a lower extent) for insurers and other market actors that diversified their risk portfolio and managed their capital using securitization. Because their potential losses were transferred to financial markets, these front-line institutions had little motivation to be vigilant regarding their clients' default or disaster risk. An adverse selection problem also existed; some BBB financial products (minimum rating to have access to CDOs) were sold to trusts even though they were in fact BB.

17.2.2 Poor Evaluation of Structured Products by Rating Agencies

As securitization stakeholders, intermediaries bought long-term assets like mortgage loans and financed them with asset-backed securities like ABCP and CDOs. Obtaining a high rating from rating agencies is essential to make profits. When the financial crisis began in 2007, ABCP was downgraded, and intermediaries could no longer roll their commercial paper. They consequently requested financing from their sponsors, namely investment banks, causing a decline in several banks' liquidity and then a liquidity crisis in many markets like that of commercial paper in Canada. This market was suspected of being contaminated by American mortgage products. During the same period, CDOs generated profits by reformatting pools of risky loans and commercializing them in the form of bond tranches. The profits associated with this structuring activity increased when the products had a high credit rating. However, it was difficult for rating agencies to appraise these increasingly complex assets because they lacked appropriate models and data. They therefore rated these tranches as they would for regular bonds, without considering the real correlations between tranches of structured products. It was also very difficult for buyers of these tranches to monitor and replicate the ratings of these structured products because they too lacked appropriate models and data.

17.2.3 Poor Pricing of Complex Financial Products

Another cause of the recent crisis lies in the price of these structured financial instruments, which often did not reflect their real risk exposure. These products contained systemic risk that was not considered in pricing. A systemic risk arises when the events in one market affect other markets. For example, when ABCP caused problems, many money market managers transferred their orders to the Treasury bill market, thus raising prices and lowering returns. These externalities were amplified by market opacity. In the case of ABCP in Canada, many investors did not know whether these products were contaminated by American or other subprime products, but rumors were flying. We now know that only a few trusts involved in the Montreal Accord held contaminated products, representing 6% of the total risk exposure. Rumors of their presence lowered market liquidity, forcing many investors, like pension funds and hedge funds, to sell good assets at a discount, which diminished their value.

17.2.4 Poor Regulation of Structured Finance

It is important to emphasize that risk regulation is currently limited to banks and insurance companies. Pension funds and hedge funds are not regulated in most countries. The Basel II regulation is even partly to blame because it significantly reduced required capital for AAA-rated assets. Whereas investors were attracted to the new structured AAA products, sellers were motivated to obtain the AAA rating for these products. This phenomenon intensified the pressure on rating agencies. AAA ratings of these products also significantly affected the purchasing behavior of pension funds, insurance companies, and mutual funds. Treasury bills offered lower interest rates, although they did not really represent lower risks for investors who based their decisions on the choice of structured products solely on the AAA ratings of rating agencies.

17.3 CONCLUSION

“”Why did investors buy these risky products, and why were they offered? Before 2007, structured products rarely defaulted, and there was no apparent cause for concern. However, when low interest rates plunged, investors became strongly drawn to the returns offered by structured products, which narrowed interest rate spreads. This narrowing may be attributable to strong demand for AAA structured products, which propelled prices upward and consequently lowered returns. Simultaneously, investors’ growing disinterest in traditional products translated into short selling, which triggered a drop in prices. This increased the returns of these products. Although structured products still offered slightly higher returns than traditional short-term assets, they did not compensate investors appropriately for risks incurred because the prices did not reflect the exposure to systemic risk associated with these products. As described above, the structured product market grew exponentially in the 2000s, and banks generated sizable profits by developing and structuring these new products. Rating agencies' mistakes are also well documented. These firms faced a conflict of interest because the issuers of structured products were suspected of having paid for the ratings. Some even believe that rating agencies helped set up these products. Regulators and central banks neither anticipated nor noticed these problems.

Many investors lost large sums during the financial crisis by failing to apply basic risk management principles:

1. Top managers' risk appetite was not defined in many companies
2. Risk management was not well established in many companies
3. Risk management policies were not supported by top management

In many organizations, emphasis on risk management seems to be cyclical, peaking after crises.

Before the financial crisis, underestimation of default and liquidity risks of the new structured financial products signaled poor risk management. Many products were introduced in the years preceding the crisis, and many investors adopted them without clearly understanding the risks because they did not have appropriate instruments to evaluate them. They therefore bought these complex financial products as if they were standard products, without analyzing the distribution tails of returns or performing backtesting and stress testing on the real risks that these products represented. Risk management had become pointless for top management of several funds and financial institutions, which effectively delegated their credit risk analyses to rating agencies and also experienced ethics and independence problems. Several lessons can be drawn from this crisis.

For the structured finance system, issuers of structured products must be held more liable. They must retain a large portion of the baskets of loans that they issue for the purposes of credit risk retention; possibly the complete equity tranche and a fraction of the more senior tranches in the presence of risk correlation between tranches. This should result in a greater incentive to apply better risk management in loan issuance, along with improved loan portfolios to securitize.

The makeup of structured products must be more transparent. Market participants and researchers must be able to replicate the composition of structured products. Public databases must be available for this purpose. The growing complexity of structured financial products poses major challenges in terms of effective management and dissemination of information. Greater transparency is therefore indispensable in the credit market, particularly when loans are securitized.

The rating of these products must also be more transparent. Any good researcher or investor can confirm standard bond ratings because the data are available and the rating methods can be replicated. This should also be true for structured products. In other words, we also need more transparency in the pricing of these products.

Institutional changes in several countries are necessary to reinforce independence or reduce vulnerability to externalities from international markets. Institutions must understand the technology available. Shared data collection and inexpensive communication methods between financial institutions should generate effective tools to verify and replicate the analyses by rating agencies and the formatting of trusts' structured products. Such data should be available to all investor groups, similar to market data. The ABCP market in Canada would not have collapsed in 2007 if it had been more transparent.

Concerning investors, top management and companies' boards of directors must ensure that their investment decisions are dictated by proper risk management. They must use detailed information on risk management for their business and weigh these risks against those of new investments. The board of directors must be made up of individuals who understand the risks incurred by structured products. The risk committee must monitor the firm's risks very actively. Top managers' risk appetite must be defined, known, and monitored by the board.

The chief risk officer (CRO) (senior VP, risk management, or the equivalent) must play a decision-making role rather than being limited to passive monitoring of risk measurement and analysis. This officer must report to the CEO and meet with the board of directors periodically. Some experts even argue that the CRO should have veto rights over some transactions that are considered overly risky. The CRO's office must be independent from all the firm's business units. All important transactions must be analyzed rigorously ex ante with appropriate data and models designed for rating, pricing, and testing of financial products. This implies more involvement in risk management for many investors, including pension and hedge funds, along with better transparency and appropriate risk disclosure.

These recommendations may seem difficult to apply for money market investors who have to manage a large number of assets with 30-day maturities. However, appropriate risk management is even more crucial for these investors. If necessary, new forms of risk analysis must be developed in cooperation with independent and transparent agencies that are sheltered from all situations linked to real or perceived conflict of interest.

To summarize, diligent risk monitoring is crucial.

REFERENCES

Aboul-Enein, S., Dionne G., and Papageorgiou, N., 2013. "Performance Analysis of a Collateralized Fund Obligation (CFO) Equity Tranche." *The European Journal of Finance* 19, 518–553.

Coval, J.D., Jurek, J., and Stafford, E., 2009. "The Economics of Structured Finance." Working paper 09-060, Harvard Business School, Boston, MA.

Crouhy M., Jarrow R.J., and Turnbull M.T., 2008. "The Subprime Credit Crisis of 07." *Journal of Derivatives* 16, 81–110.

Dionne, G., 2009a. "Finance structurée, gestion des risques et récente crise financière." *Risques* 80, 122–127.

Dionne, G., 2009b. "Structured Finance, Risk Management, and the Recent Financial Crisis." *Ivey Business Journal.*

Dionne, G., and Harchaoui, T.M., 2008. "Banks' Capital, Securitization and Credit Risk: An Empirical Evidence for Canada." *Insurance and Risk Management* 75, 459–485.

Dionne, G., and Malekan, S., 2017. "Optimal Form of Retention for Securitized Loans under Moral Hazard." *Risks* 5, 55–67.

Malekan, S., and Dionne, G., 2014. "Securitization and Optimal Retention under Moral Hazard." *Journal of Mathematical Economics* 55, 74–85.

Society of Actuaries, the Casualty Actuarial Society and the Canadian Institute of Actuaries, 2008. "Risk Management: The Current Financial Crisis, Lessons Learned and Future Implications." http://www.soa.org/library/essays/rm-essay-2008.pdf.

APPENDIX: HOW TO CREATE AN AAA CDO TRANCHE FROM BBB LOANS

Below is an example of a CDO obtained from different bank loans in a securitization transaction. Suppose that the bank securitizes 100 loans of \$1 million each, with a 10-year maturity. The average rating for the initial pool of loans is BBB. Using different tranches of the CDO, the bank can create financial products representing different risks that have an average rating of BBB (see Coval, Jurek, and Stafford, 2009, for more details on the examples presented in this appendix).

Tranching consists of separating the loan pool into asset tranches corresponding to different default risks. The three best-known tranches are equity, mezzanine, and senior. Similar to a business's capital structure, the equity tranche absorbs the first loan defaults, the mezzanine tranche takes the second wave (as does junior debt), and the senior tranche takes the rest. The mezzanine tranche's rating is often equal to the mean of the loan pool, so the equity tranche must have a rating below BBB (say B), and the senior tranche needs a higher rating, such as AAA. Generally, hedge funds invest in the equity tranche, and pension funds invest in the senior tranche.

Suppose that the equity tranche is worth \$10 million. It will then absorb the first 10% of loan defaults whatever their location in the different tranches. If two loans default without recovery, its value will be reduced to \$8 million. If 12 loans default, it will lose all its value, and the mezzanine tranche will lose \$2 million.

Now, suppose that we group loans into two groups of \$50 million each. We want to create two asset tranches: a junior (or equity) tranche and a senior tranche. Each tranche gives investors a return on the \$50 million invested if there is no default, and a lower return otherwise. To simplify, suppose that the default probability of each loan group is 10% and the recovery rate is nil.

The junior tranche (B) is the first to default, and the senior tranche (A) defaults only if the junior tranche already defaulted. The probabilities of the two tranches are independent. Under these assumptions, the default probability of the senior tranche is:

$$1\% = P(A) \times P(B).$$

Both tranches must default for the senior tranche to lose. That of the junior tranche becomes:

$$19\% = P(B) + (1 - P(B))P(A),$$

Namely, the probability that it defaults P(B) plus the probability that it does not default multiplied by the probability that loans in A default. Given the hierarchical structure, the junior tranche loses even if a loan in the senior tranche defaults.

If the default probabilities of the two loan groups are correlated (systemic risk), the default risks of the two tranches change radically. If they are perfectly correlated, the default probability of the senior tranche reverts to 10%, and, in general, its probability of default is determined by the value of the correlation coefficient (ρ).

$$P(A) = \rho P(B)(1 - P(B)) + P(B)^2$$

If $\rho = 0 : P(A) = P(B)^2 = 0.01$

If $\rho = 1 : P(A) = P(B)(1 - P(B)) + P(B)^2 = 0.09 + 0.01 = 0.10$

If $\rho = 0.5 : P(A) = 0.5\ P(B)(1 - P(B)) + P(B)^2 = 0.055$

etc.

Another way to redo the calculations is as follows:

P(A) is the probability that tranche A defaults or that both tranches default;

P(B) is the probability that tranche B defaults; the correlation coefficient of the defaults is equal to:

$$\rho = (P(A) - P(B)^2)/P(B)(1 - P(B)).$$

Note that the dependence between the default risks of loan groups increases the default probabilities of the tranches significantly, a fact that was neglected during the last financial crisis. Instruments ranked AAA (CDOs, commercial paper) were sold as if they were risk-free (no correlation was assumed), whereas they were in fact strongly correlated, meaning that loans' defaults in B would affect those in A. One example is AAA-rated commercial paper sold in Canada, which caused the *Caisse de dépôt et placement du Québec* to lose over $10 billion.

Another way to reduce the default probabilities when creating AAA tranches is to increase the number of tranches. Now, suppose that we can create three tranches (Senior, Mezzanine, Junior: abbreviated by S, M, and J) with three groups of initial loans of $50 million, always considered independent. The default probability for each group is 10%. In this case, the default probability of the senior tranche becomes 0.1% (10 % × 10 % × 10 %)! That of the mezzanine tranche is 2.8%. Either the three tranches default or at least two default; S with J, J with M, or S with M:

$$10\% \times 10\% \times 90\% \times 3 + 10\% \times 10\% \times 10\% = 2.8\%.$$

Lastly, the default probability of the junior tranche is 27.1% because it corresponds to the case where at least one tranche defaults:

$$10\% + 90\% \times 10\% + 90\% \times 90\% \times 10\% = 27.1\%$$

$$P(C) + (1 - P(C))\ P(B) + (1 - P(C))(1 - P(B))P(A).$$

The two superior tranches have default probabilities below 10%, whereas the junior tranche has a much higher default probability. With CDOs, we can do more with two CDOs obtained from three groups of loans as above. We can create CDOs–Squared by combining the junior tranches of the two CDOs. The two junior tranches have default probabilities of 27.1%. If we use them to create a third CDO, the senior tranche will have a default probability of 7.3%, which is still below 10%.

The default probabilities of AAA–BBB bonds vary between 0.2% and 0.75%, and those of more speculative bonds vary between 1% and 30%. Clearly, with tranching, it is possible to create all possible risk classes. But should standard bond ratings be used for CDOs and commercial paper? This was the case during the last financial crisis, but rating agencies adjusted. At the time, they did not have historical data to let them directly rate structured financial products; instead, they used standard bonds methodology. This generated very imprecise and even false ratings.

CHAPTER 18

Risk Management and Corporate Governance

The objectives of the risk management policy and those of maximizing firm value (or the value of shareholder's equity) reveal a potential conflict of interest that is directly linked to the question of corporate governance.[1] In fact, the board of directors must approve the objectives outlined by the firm's risk management policy, define the firm's risk appetite, and oversee the means used to attain the objectives set, including the controls of the risk management activities. We can then ask whether the board of director's risk and audit committees should be made up of independent directors only, as in other committees, according to the new rules discussed or already applied in many countries following the Enron affair and the 2007–2009 financial crisis.

This topic is relevant because many firms, particularly banks and insurance companies, have specific risk committees on the board. However, as we will see below, most documents that proposed new governance rules in 2002 regulated only the audit committee regarding all aspects of risk management. This decision underestimates the importance of risks in many business sectors along with governance conflicts that may arise from risk management. In addition, the requirements related to the members of risk committees' competencies may differ.

18.1 ENRON AND CORPORATE GOVERNANCE

The board of directors' main role is to represent shareholders' interests. The board thus aims to maximize the firm's value or its stock. The board oversees the recruitment, compensation, and activities of senior managers. Consequently, the roles of compensation and audit committees have received particular scrutiny since 2002. The makeup of the Board and its committees has also been discussed extensively because the prominence of non-independent members on a board or its committees may affect the way the board functions.

Below we analyze the Enron case, but similar conclusions could be drawn from other cases like that of WorldCom. The Enron case raised many questions about corporate governance, which we can define as a management or control system

[1]The research presented in this chapter was conducted with Danielle Blanchard, Olfa Maalaoui-Chun, Thouraya Triki, and Thi-Thanh-Nga Nguyen.

that can reduce conflicts of interest between shareholders and senior managers (or officers). Manipulation of information by senior managers was an important element in the events leading up to the Enron bankruptcy in December 2001. Enron used several risk management tools including derivatives, and was an important intermediary in the trading of these products.

Even specialists generally find it difficult to assess the total risk of a firm, particularly when financial statements use mark-to-market value rather than historical book value. It seems that the capital market as a whole could not identify many potential management problem signals or problems with information disclosure in the months preceding the Enron's bankruptcy. Also, they could not anticipate its financial difficulties.

Arthur Andersen faced several accusations and found itself in a conflict of interest because it had simultaneously assumed the role of independent auditor for Enron while serving as a consultant for the firm. To correct this type of situation, the US Congress created the Public Company Accounting Oversight Board (PCAOB) via the Sarbanes-Oxley Act of 2002. The PCAOB's roles include requiring external audit firms to register with it and setting standards for audit, quality control, ethics, and independence of these firms.

According to several observers (e.g., Healy and Palepu, 2003), Enron's board of directors also failed in its role of protecting shareholders and contributed to the firm's bankruptcy. Several board members held information on Enron's management practices such as very high compensation of senior managers and of some board members, and disclosure of false statistics on the company's growth potential to increase the value of stock and options. These board members chose to ignore them or did not disclose them to shareholders.

The Enron executives were compensated largely by a system based on the firm's stock options. For example, the CEO received over \$140 million in compensation during the year 2000, whereas his base salary was slightly higher than \$1 million (Demski, 2003). This form of compensation was a major factor in distorting managers' behavior. Stocks' market value is heavily influenced by expected future income. In the Enron case, top managers manipulated earnings reports to influence share value. They also overvalued assets and undervalued debt.

Researchers recently showed, using data from 31 countries, that managers' manipulation of earnings is positively correlated with the benefits they derive from this practice (on manipulation of earnings by firms, see Lev (2003) and the references in the article). The authors were surprised to note the extent that Enron's executive compensation committees kept silent about data manipulation by senior managers. Were these directors really incompetent? Were they in a conflict of interest because they were paid themselves by stock options? Did they have holdings in other companies that were doing business with Enron?

Evidently, the Enron case hinges more than the agency relationship between executives and their shareholders via directors. As mentioned above, the independent audit firm was questioned, along with the internal audit committee. Yet it is possible that financial analysts, brokers, consultants, bankers, attorneys, and investors were not all independent. Even the regulation may have introduced distortions. As Demski (2003) explains, a general analytical framework that covers all these players could be used to evaluate the situation more precisely. However, no such framework exists.

18.2 FINANCIAL CRISIS AND CORPORATE GOVERNANCE

Despite the regulatory attention given to corporate governance through the rules set by the Sarbanes-Oxley Act (SOX) and the New York Stock Exchange (NYSE) in 2002, a report of the Organisation for Economic Co-operation and Development (OECD) attributes the 2007 financial crisis to the failure of the boards in overseeing risk management systems, the reason often being the board's limited knowledge and understanding of the risks involved when using complex financial assets.

The OECD report does not limit the importance of qualified board oversight or the need for robust risk management of financial institutions (Kirkpatrick, 2009, p. 2). Drawing lessons from the 2007 crisis, the report emphasizes the necessity of certifying a minimum level of financial knowledge for the directors on boards and those composing the audit committees to ensure that they understand issues related to risk exposure and risk management.

In Section 18.7 of this chapter, we explore different dimensions of financial knowledge and test whether they add value to the firm through the channel of risk management activities. Given the importance regulators have placed on directors' independence, we also address the benefit of independent directors on the board or the audit committee and whether this requirement adds to firm value. More details on this research can be found in Dionne, Maalaoui-Chun, and Triki (2018).

18.3 NEW 2002 GOVERNANCE RULES

Since Enron declared bankruptcy in December 2001, several governance rules have been discussed and applied around the world (at the New York Stock Exchange, for example).

The Sarbanes-Oxley (SOX) Act, signed on July 30, 2002, by the US president, amends the Securities and Exchange Act of 1934 and urges the Securities and Exchange Commission (SEC) to enforce compliance with the amendments, enact regulations, and apply controls to protect the public and investors when the legislation is applied. This law also created the PCAOB, defined above, which reports to the SEC. The PCAOB currently studies various recommendations submitted by the public, along with several organizations and associations, including the NYSE and NASDAQ, in order to draft new regulations. Accordingly, the SEC has set forth minimal requirements concerning the audit committee, which must be made up of independent board members exclusively. As required by the SOX, the SEC and the Comptroller General of the United States pursued studies to clarify and modify the standards for listing on an exchange.

On February 13 2002, the SEC asked the New York Stock Exchange (NYSE) to revise its policy concerning the governance standards and requirements for firms listed on that exchange. On August 1 2002, the NYSE board approved the following measures:

1. The composition of boards of directors must consist of a majority of independent directors.
2. The nominating/corporate governance committee and the compensation committee must be composed entirely of independent directors.

3. Each listed company must include a minimum of three people on its audit committee, composed exclusively of independent directors.
4. Each listed company must have an internal audit function.
5. Listed companies must adopt minimum standard rules and disclose their guidelines concerning corporate governance.

The notion of independence is technical, and its definition is lengthy. There is insufficient space to present it here. Interested readers should consult Jenner and Block (2003). However, this contribution does not specify anything about the risk committee, although it mentions that according to the new regulations, the audit committee must discuss risk management assessment and policies.

Below we interpret the meaning of risk assessment and management control policy as perceived by different stakeholders, including the NYSE. According to this interpretation, company management is responsible for risk management. It must evaluate and manage the firm's exposure to different risks. The audit committee must discuss policies and guidelines governing the process for assessing the main risks that the company faces, as well as the risk management measures applied.

Several companies, particularly financial firms, approve and monitor their risks using means other than that of the audit committee, for example, with risk committees. In these cases, the audit committee is not required to be the sole entity responsible for risk assessment and management, but must perform risk assessment procedures of the company, including its internal control. In other words, the risk assessment processes that these firms have put in place must be generally reviewed by the audit committee, but all risk management activities do not need to be evaluated in detail by this committee.

18.4 RISK MANAGEMENT AND GOVERNANCE

Risk assessment and management instruments are difficult to use and monitor. Understanding them requires extensive knowledge of finance, mathematics, and statistics. Thus, audit committee members who lack specialized training may not be able to correctly monitor the hedging and especially the speculation issues presented to them, often quickly and very broadly. For example, at the Enron audit committee meeting on February 12, 2001, nine important points were on the agenda, including two related to risk assessment and management. Yet the meeting lasted only 95 minutes! Although this committee was made up of experts in management and university educators (the points discussed and committee members are listed in Healy and Palepu, 2003), it is unlikely that all these subjects were covered in depth, particularly those related to transactions that may appear questionable or cause conflicts of interest.

Researchers have shown that conflicts of interest may arise between senior managers and shareholders regarding risk management, notably when executives are paid by stock options (Smith and Stulz, 1985).

Consider the example of risk management in gold mines, which has been long studied in detail (Tufano, 1996; Dionne and Triki, 2013). The main random variable linked to firms' financial risks is the sale price of an ounce of gold. The three main questions that mining company executives constantly ask are:

1. Should we hedge the sale price from future fluctuations?
2. If so, in which proportions?
3. With which instruments?

Aside from the main objective of maximizing firm value, risk management can also maximize executive welfare. However, this second objective may clash with the first and thus create governance problems, especially when executive compensation is heavily weighted in stock options. Tufano (1996) showed that executives in the North American gold production industry whose pay includes stock options invest much less in risk management than do other executives (also see Dionne and Triki (2013) who obtained similar results with updated data and different econometric specifications, and Rodgers (2002), who reached the same conclusion with a different database).

This result is explained by the fact that the value of executives' options increases with stock or firm value volatility. Even if managers are risk averse concerning their personal wealth, they have convex preferences (that is, high risk tolerance) based on firm value when they hold stock options from the firm they run. They may consequently undertake fewer risk management activities because more risk management would reduce the volatility of firm value and hence the value of their options and the probability of exercising them, particularly when they are out of the money.

A theoretical counterargument was presented by Carpenter (2000). The author argues that holding options creates two consequences regarding senior managers' wealth. The first, described above, is that officer wealth increases with the volatility of the options held, particularly when options are out-of-the-money.

The second consequence is related to the fact that the value of the option portfolio may decrease proportionately with the total portfolio value or when the evaluation date is far away. We therefore have a theoretical arbitrage relationship, but the empirical results mentioned above seem to confirm the dominance of the convexity of manager preferences and the source of conflict of interest between executives and shareholders, especially when options are not in-the-money.

Further, these results reveal another potential conflict of interest involving board members and committees, which raises questions about the makeup of the risk committee. Several directors may also hold options on the stock of the company on whose boards they sit. This is why the board of director's risk committee should also be made up of independent directors only, and especially directors who do not hold stock options for these companies. Simple regulation for the makeup of an audit committee is surely insufficient to limit potential conflicts linked to risk evaluation and management, particularly for companies that have committees dedicated to these tasks.

This question is important because the general risk management policy must be approved and monitored by the board of directors. Some studies have shown that firms with a larger number of external directors engage in more risk hedging (Borokhorich et al., 2001; Dionne and Triki, 2013).

18.5 ADMINISTRATIVE COMPETENCE OF BOARD MEMBERS

Individuals and businesses face risks on a daily basis. For investors, higher risk is often associated with higher returns. However, excessive risk-taking may cause major losses and even bankruptcy. Corporate risk management has evolved considerably in the past 25 years, and includes several dimensions such as prevention, prudence, financial management, and use of derivatives and insurance.

Following the 2007 financial crisis, an OECD report (Kirkpatrick, 2009) mentioned that one of the causes of this crisis was linked to limited knowledge of risk management and a poor understanding of various risks to which the financial institutions' boards of directors were exposed. Several of these firms used very complex structured financial products like commercial paper (ABCP), CDOs (collateral debt obligation), and CDSs (credit default swap). Often, board members were unaware that the company was using these products, or that they were responsible for defining the risk appetite of the enterprise. This diagnosis emphasizes that board members from firms exposed to major risks need sufficient financial knowledge to oversee risk management effectively. Therefore, even if several board members are independent, they may not have adequate expertise to monitor these firms' risk management effectively.

In a recent study on governance of risk management within North American gold mining companies, Dionne, Maalaoui-Chun, and Triki (2018) examined, over a 10-year period, how board and audit committee members' independence and financial knowledge could affect firm value via the risk management policy. The researchers analyzed very detailed data on financial knowledge of audit committee members and board members for each firm, measured by three components; financial training, financial experience, and accounting education. Financial education is defined as holding a university degree in finance (BBA, MBA or MSc, PhD, etc.); financial experience is determined by whether a director is active in a financial environment, such as a manager of an insurance company or bank, or a financial analyst. Directors are considered to have an accounting education if they hold a university degree in accounting. The authors also obtained information on the university degrees held by each board member.

They show that the 2002 rules stipulated by the SOX and NYSE, based mainly on director independence, did not significantly influence firm value during the studied period. They also demonstrated that the variables of director independence and financial knowledge can influence risk management policy and that the effects of this policy on firm value are highly interrelated. The holding of a master's or doctorate degree in finance also significantly influences the firm's risk management policy. Lastly, the authors constructed governance indices for the board and the audit committee, made up of different variables, including financial knowledge, independence, master's and PhD degrees in finance, and separation of the roles of CEO and chairman of the firm's board. They showed that these indices have a significant effect on firms' risk management policy and value. More details regarding this study are presented in Section 18.7.

18.6 NEW REGULATION FOR FINANCIAL INSTITUTIONS

Recently, American, Canadian, and European regulatory agencies adopted new governance rules concerning banks and insurance companies. The Canadian rules (2013) require these institutions to have a risk committee on their board, made up of independent members only. The rules also specify that for large institutions with sophisticated risk management policies, the members of this new committee must be competent. The notion of competence is now part of the federal guideline on corporate governance issued by the Office of the Superintendent of Financial Institutions (OSFI). This guideline, summarized in Appendix A, calls on all directors to play an effective role. Although their individual contributions may vary, competencies must be interpreted collectively. Accordingly, the board of directors must collectively form a "balanced set of competencies, expertise, skills, and experience." The OSFI is not asking each director to be competent solely in finance. Rather, the members' collective competencies represent the combination of competencies from each board member. To evaluate these competencies, the guideline states that the board of directors must put in place an annual process to evaluate the effectiveness of its practices and to use external consultants as needed. In addition, directors must seek internal or external education opportunities in order to fully understand the risks that a federal financial institution takes.

To summarize, risk management has become a crucial responsibility for the board of directors of firms with high exposure to different risks. For large banks and insurance companies, a risk committee must oversee risk management. It must be made up of independent members who are knowledgeable about risk management. If possible, this committee should also include directors with technical knowledge in disciplines related to the risks that the firm faces.

Regarding the new European prudential regulations in the banking and financial sector, analyzed by Speroni (2014), a statute introduced on February 21, 2014 has brought about a large-scale reform of the banking sector. This reform also emphasizes governance and compensation in credit institutions, financial corporations, investment firms, and portfolio management firms. For example, the monetary and financial code now imposes the obligatory separation of the functions of CEO and chairman of the board, and requires boards of directors to create a risk committee and an appointment committee in addition to the compensation and audit committees. Lastly, the European order foresees balanced representation of males and females on boards of directors.

On March 27, 2014, the Board of Governors of the US Federal Reserve System promulgated Enhanced Prudential Standards (EPS) for large US bank holding companies (BHCs) and foreign banking organizations (FBOs). BHCs with total consolidated assets of $50 billion or more must have a distinct risk committee to oversee the risk management of the financial institution. The EPS rules require that the risk committee include at least one risk expert who has experience managing risk in line with the size and complexity of the organization.

The Office of the Comptroller of the Currency (OCC) has also analyzed risk management of large banking organizations following the financial crisis. On September 11, 2014, the OCC established new standards for the risk management of certain large banks. The OCC's standards emphasize independent risk management and require banks to establish a framework that manages and controls the bank's risk taking.

18.7 ECONOMIC ANALYSIS OF GOVERNANCE EFFECT

18.7.1 Testable Hypothesis

The main hypothesis to be tested is that corporate governance indexes for the board and the audit committee constructed using independence and financial knowledge of the directors should improve firm value through the risk management channel.

The Board as a Corporate Governance Mechanism

The board of directors plays a central role in any corporate governance system and is viewed as a primary means for shareholders to exercise control over higher management (Tirole, 2006). Specifically, board composition, independence, and engagement are key features in enhancing a firm's corporate governance system and achieving its performance goals. For instance, Armstrong, Core, and Guay (2014) showed how the structure of a board dominated by related directors increases both the level of information asymmetry between shareholders and higher management and uncertainty about firm value. A board structure dominated by independent directors has the opposite effect and leads to an increase in firm transparency and an increase in firm value.

A tremendous amount of the literature focuses on board structure, specifically member independence but with little emphasis on the value of the board's financial knowledge. Moreover, the 2002 regulations provided by SOX and the NYSE do not explicitly require financial knowledge for the board members; it is only explicitly required for audit committees.

The following analyses focuses on the importance of the financial knowledge dimension in board structure. Specifically, it examines the effect of having directors on the board and audit committee with relevant experience and/or education in finance on the firm's risk management activity and its performance.

Benefit of Financial Knowledge for the Board

The few papers that have investigated the financial knowledge argument for board members support the idea that the financial knowledge of directors adds value to the firm. Indeed, Guner, Malmendier, and Tate (2005) showed that boards composed of members with relevant and related financial and accounting knowledge obtained credible and high-quality financial statement evaluations. Agrawal and Chadha (2005) supported the benefit of having independent board directors who have financial knowledge. They found that the probability of earnings restatements is lower in firms whose boards have an independent director with a background in accounting or finance. Interestingly, the independence argument taken alone seems to have no explanatory power in their model, which suggests that directors' independence becomes more effective when they also have financial knowledge.

To the extent that financially knowledgeable directors have a better understanding of the sophisticated financial tools involved in risk management activities, we may expect firms whose boards are composed of financially knowledgeable directors to engage more actively in hedging the firm's exposure to risk and enhance its performance.

Different arguments support the conjecture that financial knowledge should benefit the firm and its shareholders, particularly in the energy industry. First, derivatives are sophisticated instruments, and directors need a minimum level of financial knowledge to understand them and adequately monitor their management: that is, fixing the optimal level of risk management and choosing appropriately between options or futures instruments in different risky environments. In addition, directors overseeing risk management need to understand that derivatives can affect officers' incentives (CFO and CEO) to act in line with shareholder welfare.

Second, financial knowledge is often measured by directors' experience in finance and their background in accounting. There is no explicit consideration of the financial education dimension, which may be relevant to the usage of hedging instruments. For instance, some directors have knowledge related to their business activities (engineers, communication specialists, lawyers, etc.) but not to finance. These directors may not be aware of all the available instruments to hedge a firm's exposure to risk and may not even fully understand the costs and benefits of the effective usage of sophisticated financial instruments.

Benefit of Financial Knowledge for the Audit Committee

The audit committee's primary task is to oversee the firm's corporate reporting and ensure the reliability of its financial reporting. Periodic review of the firm's risk assessment system and the managerial actions used to manage its risks is a critical step toward fulfilling this task. We would expect audit committees satisfying the SOX and/or NYSE rules to provide effective monitoring. Moreover, the NYSE's rules require the audit committee to discuss the guidelines and policies for risk assessment and risk management.

No study establishes a relationship between the composition of the audit committee, the backgrounds of its members, and corporate hedging. Dionne, Maalaoui-Chun, and Triki (2018) is the first contribution to have established such a link. Because audit committee members with financial backgrounds have the experience and training to understand risk management operations, we expect firms with financially knowledgeable directors to engage more actively in risk management when it increases firm value. The audit committee, through its monitoring role, should be qualified to deal with the financial environment, especially in critical financial episodes.

Independence Argument

In corporate finance, the standard approach is to view the board's independence as being closely related to its efficiency. Following the same reasoning, Section 303A.01 of the NYSE's listed companies manual requires a majority of independent directors on the board. Indeed, outside directors are viewed as superior monitors because their careers are not tied to the firm's CEO. Consequently, they are free to take decisions that may go against the CEO without being afraid for their positions or future compensation. This view is often referred to as the monitoring effect theory.

Outside directors also have incentives to build their reputation as expert monitors to obtain additional director appointments. Thus, they are more likely to maintain proper control over the firm's higher management. However, they are faced with the challenge of understanding the firm's operations, which puts their reputation in play in case of failure. The most recent study by Armstrong, Core, and Guay (2014) showed that firms with more independent directors sitting on the board are more transparent. This has the effect of reducing the uncertainty about the firm's cash flows and thus increasing its value.

The independence argument is also a concern for members of the audit committee. A large body of academic literature has investigated the extent to which the independence and financial literacy/expertise of the audit committee members are beneficial to shareholders, specifically members with an accounting background.

However, another strand in the literature questions the benefits of having independent directors on the audit committee. The reason is that there is no consensus that the presence of outside auditors provides additional benefits to the firm. For instance, Agrawal and Chadha (2005) provided arguments against the benefits of having independent auditors, while Carcello and Neal (2000) showed that the presence of independent auditors is beneficial to the firm.

Few papers link board composition to firm risk management activity. Again, the literature has not arrived at a clear consensus on the effect of outside directors on a firm's risk management policy. For instance, Mardsen and Prevost (2005) reported no effect on risk management activities of having outside directors. However, Fields and Keys (2003) claimed overwhelming support for outside directors providing superior monitoring and advisory functions to the firm. Dionne and Triki (2013) found that hedging increases with outside directors.

Since risk management is a complex activity, Dionne, Maalaoui-Chun, and Triki (2018) argued that the requirement of director independence is necessary but not sufficient. Independent members of the board and the audit committee also need a minimum level of financial knowledge (education, experience, and accounting) to monitor risk management activities. Many analysts of the 2007 financial crisis have mentioned that existing regulations are more focused on independence and accounting education than on financial knowledge.

18.7.2 Data and Variables

Sample Construction (1992–1999)

Observations on the composition of the board and the audit committee are published only on an annual basis in the firm proxy statement. Dionne, Maalaoui-Chun, and Triki (2018) assumed that the characteristics of corporate governance for the firm remained constant between two consecutive general annual meetings. They argued that this assumption is reasonable since, at the general annual meeting, directors are usually elected for terms of at least one year. Moreover, the main issues of corporate governance (risk appetite, risk management policy, risk management strategy, control process) are usually discussed once a year with the board.

Compustat Quarterly is used to collect firm-specific data, such as the market and book values of assets, the total value of debt, the value of sales, operating income, acquisition expenses, selling and general expenses, depreciation and amortization, and other data needed to compute variables describing firms' general characteristics. Firms' proxy statements and annual reports provide hand-collected information about the size and composition of the board and the audit committee, the name of each director sitting on the board and on the audit committee, the education level of each director, the current and former functions of each director, the age of the CEO, and the CEO's portfolio holding of common shares and exercisable options.

Data relative to firms' operating cash costs and exploration expenditures were obtained from quarterly reports. They proxy taxable income by taxable accounting earnings before extraordinary items and discounted operations. This information is needed to construct the Tax_save variable. Data about institutional shareholding are from the 13-F and 13-G forms available on the US Securities and Exchange Commission website and from proxy statements.

Directors are independent if they are not related to the management of the firm and are free from any interest or relationship that could conceivably affect their ability to act in the firm's best interest, other than interest arising from shareholdings.

Directors are financially active or have experience if they presently or formerly occupied a position as chief financial officer, treasurer, officer of an insurance or investment company or a mutual fund, financial analyst, financial consultant, banker, or any other position related to finance.

Directors are financially educated if they hold a finance degree or were enrolled in a program offering finance courses (BBA, MBA, CA, BCom, etc.). Several directors in the sample had been enrolled in qualified professional programs. Finally, directors are accountants if they have an accounting background or are Chartered Accountants (CA, CPA) or have an education or activities related to accounting. The final sample consists of 325 observations with complete information about the educational background of the directors and 348 observations with complete information about all the other variables used in the analysis. The sample contains 36 North American gold mining companies, composed of 20 Canadian firms and 16 U.S. firms.

Variable Definitions

Dependent Variable Following Tufano (1996), a firm's risk management activity is measured by the delta percentage, as discussed in previous chapters. Firm value variables are discussed below.

Independent Variables The main research question aims to evaluate the impact of directors' independence and financial knowledge when sitting on the board and/or the audit committee on firm value through corporate hedging behavior. Therefore, the choice of key independent variables is dictated by the two sets of regulations.

Two governance indexes are then constructed to account for all of these governance features and test the effect of governance on the firm's risk management behavior. Specifically, the authors used a scoring system to assess the quality of the audit committee and the board. The score is built such that it increases with each dimension of financial knowledge. It also increases with compliance with the SOX and NYSE requirements of independence and their definition of financial knowledge. However, the score decreases with the CEO's level of entrenchment and with directors' tenure. Tenured directors who have served the same company for at least 10 years should have acquired relevant experience and learned from the different challenges across various economic regimes. However, derivative instruments were relatively new during the sample period, and the authors were thus inclined to discount the high numbers of tenured directors simply because they may not have developed enough knowledge and experience with these new instruments. They documented the construction of both indexes—one for the audit committee and one for the board (*GovIndexAud* and *GovIndexBor*, respectively)—see Appendix B for details. In the robustness section of their research, they reconstructed the two governance indexes using Principal Component Analysis (PCA), and they discuss the issue of potential endogeneity.

Control Variables They use different determinants of risk management that are well documented in the literature (e.g., Tufano, 1996; Adam and Fernando, 2006; Dionne and Triki, 2013). Specifically, firm size (ln(size)), the market-to-book ratio of assets (market-to-book), the dividend policy (dividend policy), and the existence of financial slack (quick ratio) are used. The firm's expected financial distress costs using leverage (leverage) and the firm's operating cash costs (cash cost) are also included. Financial distress costs should increase firm's incentives to hedge (Tufano, 1996). Similarly, they control for the firm's investment opportunities using its exploration expenditures (exploration). Firms with attractive investment opportunities should hedge more extensively to ensure the availability of internal funding necessary to undertake these investments (Froot, Scharfstein, and Stein, 1993). Finally, the firm's home country is considered by including a variable (dummy US) that equals to one if the firm's country of origin is the United States.

As in Graham and Rogers (2002), the percentage of shares held by institutions (*%inst*) is used as a proxy for information asymmetry between the CEO and shareholders. This variable can also indicate that these shareholders are more diversified. Risk management activities should decrease with the importance of the firm's institutional holdings as they are willing to take more risk than other stakeholders do.

A firm with a convex tax function should have more incentives to hedge (Smith and Stulz, 1985; Graham and Rogers, 2002; Dionne and Triki, 2013). Hedging allows the firm to lock the level of taxable income, thus reducing the variability of the pre-tax assets value and tax liability, and increasing the after-tax value of assets. To capture the benefits of a convex tax function on hedging, the tax save variable (Tax_save) proposed by Graham and Smith (1999) is constructed. The definition is extended to include the country of origin's legislation and tax code.

Managerial risk aversion is another important determinant of risk management policy in the gold mining industry (Tufano, 1996). Two proxies for managerial risk aversion are used: the number of the firm's common shares held by the CEO (CEOCS) and the value of options held by the CEO (ValCEOOp). The two variables capture Smith and Stulz's (1985) argument that compensation packages leading to a concave (convex) function between the managers' expected utility and the firm's value encourage managers to hedge more (less).

The variable CEO age potentially captures the interplay between experience and education. The literature argues in favor of positive and negative relationships between director age and hedging activity. Younger directors may be more inclined to hedge, and older directors facing imminent retirement might prefer to reduce fluctuations in a firm's value and hence hedge more extensively. But some may find derivatives dangerous. The variables definitions are presented in Table 18A.1 in Appendix C.

18.7.3 Model

The dependent variable, the hedge ratio, has non-negative values. In about 15% of the observations in the sample, the hedge ratio is equal to zero. An observed hedge ratio of zero reflects managements' decision not to hedge. When the observed hedge ratio is positive, it reflects the firm's propensity to hedge. Therefore, the Heckman (1979) two-stage model is best suited to represent the data. Specifically, the first stage models the decision to hedge, and the second stage models the intensity of the hedge.

When estimating the effect of hedging on firm value, we are faced with an endogeneity problem. Adams, Hermalin, and Weisbach (2010) document this issue and report a lack of sufficient instrumental analyses in the corporate governance literature. Many results must be interpreted as the joint selection of governance policy and the policy's effect on firm performance. For example, a firm's hedging activity can be correlated with the unobservable characteristics of the firm, in which case the ordinary least square estimates of the parameters in the firm value equation could be biased. Dionne, Maalaoui-Chun, and Triki (2018) addressed this endogeneity issue using three complementary approaches. One approach is to find a suitable instrument for the hedging equation and use the predicted value of hedging in the firm value equation. Like Campello, Lin, Ma and Zou (2011) and Dionne and Triki (2013), they used the government rules on corporate taxes that capture tax convexity. This measure will then serve as an instrument in the hedging equation and it is measured as the variation in expected tax savings from a 5% reduction in the volatility of taxable income (Graham and Smith, 1999). The key argument is that tax convexity provides incentives to increase hedging, but there is no reason to expect it to directly affect the value of the firm; it is more the level of tax that affects firm value. Under this premise, tax convexity should be an adequate instrument for hedging.

Second, the governance variables change annually while the hedge ratio variable is measured quarterly. More importantly, in the two-stage regression analysis, the authors used their governance indexes to represent a weighted average of potential explanatory variables. They also apply principal component analysis (PCA) to construct two principal factors accounting for most of the total variance in their set of governance variable candidates for the board and audit committee. By means of orthogonal transformation, PCA converts their observations set of possibly correlated variable candidates into a linearly uncorrelated variable set represented by the principal component. The two principal component factors are chosen by the model and should be exogenous.

18.7.4 Empirical Results

In Table 18.1, the effect of the governance indexes on the firm's risk management behavior is tested using multivariate regressions in panel A and the Heckman two-stage model in panel B. Columns (1) to (3) for both panels refer to the effects of adding the governance index for the audit, the board, or both, respectively. In all cases, we observe that the quality of the audit committee and board significantly affects the observed hedging behavior for the firms in the sample. The higher the governance index, the higher the firm's hedging activity. These results are robust to the model specification. The control variables, not documented here, remain stable between the different equations.

Thus, consistent with the previous conclusions, a firm with sound corporate governance is actively hedging its gold position using the derivatives market. Consequently, financial knowledge and independence are important indicators of corporate governance in building indexes. It would be interesting to verify whether sound corporate governance based on the financial knowledge dimensions also increases shareholder value through the risk management channel.

Hedging Behavior and Firm Performance

Several studies address the question of whether hedging increases shareholder value. They are discussed in Chapter 20 of this book. In line with the literature, we may question whether the governance indexes accounting for the quality of directors in terms of financial expertise and independence increase firm value through the risk management channel. Table 18.2 reports the results of simultaneous estimation.

TABLE 18.1 Effect of governance indexes on hedging activities.

	Panel A: Multivariate regression			Panel B: Heckman second-stage regression		
	(1)	(2)	(3)	(1)	(2)	(3)
Gov_index_audit	0.043***		0.041***	0.053***		0.051***
	(2.95)		(2.83)	(3.31)		(3.21)
Gov_index_board		0.023**	0.021*		0.025***	0.023**
		(2.11)	(1.94)		(2.40)	(2.27)
Inverse Mills				−0.285	−0.098	−0.259
				(−1.06)	(−0.37)	(−0.97)
Controls & Intercept	Yes	Yes	Yes	Yes	Yes	Yes
R-Squared	0.22	0.21	0.23	0.26	0.24	0.27
F-Value (*p*-value)	5.78	5.40	5.70	5.59	5.15	5.66
Observations	(0.00)	(0.00)	(0.00)	(0.00)	(0.00)	(0.00)
	342	342	342	290	290	290

Note: The effect of director quality on firm hedging behavior is reported. Director quality is measured by two indexes: Gov_index_board (for the board) and Gov_index_audit (for the audit committee). The construction of both indexes is detailed in Appendix B. The table reports the partial results of the multivariate regressions (panel A), along with the partial results for the second stage using the Heckman selection model (panel B). The complete results for all the models are available in Dionne, Maalaoui-Chun, and Triki's (2018) Appendix E-3. The dependent variable is the delta percentage of the firm in panel A. Panel B reports the results of a Heckman two-stage model in which the dependent variable is the intensity of the hedge. All the regressions have firm fixed effects and include a dummy variable for each quarter to control for seasonal effects in the data. The *t*-statistics are in parentheses. The superscripts ***, **, and * denote significance at the 1%, 5%, and 10% levels, respectively.

Four measures of firm performance are used; Return on Equity (ROE), Return on Assets (ROA), Tobin's *q*, and Market-to-Book (MB).

There is no evidence of feedback effects between observed hedging and firm performance. As shown in Table 18.2 panel A, firm performance does not seem to affect hedging levels. Hedging activities in firms with qualified boards and audit committees increase both the firms' accounting and market performance (panel B). This result supports the views suggesting that risk management is beneficial to firms and their shareholders, while risk management is not endogenously affected by firm performance.

The measures for governance indexes (panel A) are always positive and significant, suggesting that the directors' financial expertise affects hedging behavior and leads firms to hedge more. The positive relationship between the price of gold and firm performance is intuitive since firms make more profits when the gold market is bullish because they can close up their positions and sell the gold at a higher price in the spot market. The instruments in the hedge equation are positive and significant, suggesting that the model does not suffer from endogeneity issues. Since firm performance is not significant in the hedging equation, the potential endogeneity effect of firm performance does not really matter.

TABLE 18.2 Simultaneous hedging and firm performance estimation.

	ROE	ROA	Tobin's *q*	MB
Panel A: The hedge ratio is the dependent variable				
Firm_performance	0.183	0.181	−0.015	−0.009
	(1.01)	(0.45)	(−0.33)	(−0.20)
Ln(size)	0.121***	0.122***	0.105***	0.102***
	(3.09)	(2.90)	(2.44)	(2.36)
Market-to-book	−0.035*	−0.038**		
	(−1.76)	(−1.97)		
Leverage	0.102***	0.099***	0.081***	0.080***
	(3.18)	(2.46)	(2.92)	(2.89)
Quick_ratio	−0.003	−0.005	−0.004	−0.004
	(−0.62)	(−1.00)	(−0.086)	(−0.86)
Dividend-policy	−0.001	−0.004	−0.008	−0.007
	(−0.02)	(−0.15)	(−0.30)	(−0.29)
Tax_save	0.172***	0.186***	0.173***	0.173***
	(3.85)	(4.18)	(4.01)	(4.04)
CEO_CS	0.089***	0.101***	0.114***	0.112***
	(2.48)	(2.87)	(2.96)	(2.96)
ValCEO_op	−0.006***	−0.006***	−0.008***	−0.008***
	(−3.02)	(−2.93)	(−3.540)	(−3.58)
%_inst	−0.556***	−0.603***	−0.591***	−0.588***
	(−3.71)	(−4.11)	(−4.04)	(−4.03)
CEO-*age*	0.002	0.001	0.001	0.001
	(0.74)	(0.68)	(0.54)	(0.54)
US_dummy	1.965***	−0.414	−0.307	−0.289
	(2.90)	(−1.51)	(−0.98)	(−0.93)
Gov_index_audit	0.041***	0.043***	0.050***	0.050***
	(3.24)	(3.39)	(3.76)	(3.88)
Gov_index_board	0.018*	0.020**	0.019*	0.019*
	(1.77)	(2.14)	(1.87)	(1.89)
Gold_price	−0.001*	−0.001*	−0.001	−0.00071
	(−1.74)	(−1.67)	(−1.40)	(−1.52)
Intercept	−2.340***	−0.502	−0.425	−0.406
	(−3.29)	(−1.60)	(−1.21)	(−1.16)
Chi-2 (*p*-value)	1293.52	2514.96	2544.04	2551.75
Observations	(0.00)	(0.00)	(0.00)	(0.00)
	339	341	341	342
Panel B: The firm performance is the dependent variable				
Hedge_ratio	0.625***	0.259***	0.848**	0.822**
	(2.40)	(2.73)	(2.03)	(2.00)
Ln(size)	−0.083	−0.070***	0.370***	0.384***
	(−1.08)	(−2.51)	(3.26)	(3.44)
Market-to-book	−0.024	<0.001		
	(−0.62)	(0.01)		

TABLE 18.2 (*Continued*)

	ROE	ROA	Tobin's q	MB
Leverage	−0.130***	−0.094***	0.132	0.140*
	(−2.37)	(−4.74)	(1.60)	(1.72)
Quick_ratio	−0.008	0.001	−0.007	−0.008
	(−0.82)	(0.17)	(−0.45)	(−0.57)
Dividend_policy	−0.029	−0.002	0.118	0.088
	(−0.61)	(−0.12)	(1.64)	(1.26)
Exploration	1.312	−1.578***	0.407	0.050
	(1.00)	(−3.20)	(0.19)	(0.02)
Cash_cost	<0.001	<0.001	−0.002***	−0.0002***
	(−1.32)	(−1.07)	(−3.73)	(−3.31)
%_inst	−0.138	0.118	−1.631***	−1.624***
	(−0.42)	(0.99)	(−3.24)	(−3.28)
%_blockholders	0.490	0.129	3.332***	3.415***
	(1.58)	(1.20)	(6.84)	(7.13)
Maj_indep_bor	−0.058	0.001	−0.174*	−0.197*
	(−0.87)	(0.04)	(−1.65)	(−1.92)
CEO_age	−0.007	−0.001	−0.006	−0.006
	(−1.33)	(−0.54)	(−0.79)	(−0.75)
CEO_change	0.022	0.032	−0.151	−0.148
	(0.30)	(1.25)	(−1.32)	(−1.32)
CEO_COB	0.010	0.001	0.022*	0.019
	(1.16)	(0.41)	(1.69)	(1.44)
CEO_tenure	−0.029	0.004	−0.203**	−0.215**
	(−0.49)	(0.19)	(−2.12)	(−2.31)
US_dummy	−1.546***	0.223	0.204	0.833
	(−3.61)	(1.16)	(0.31)	(1.28)
Gold_price	0.002***	<0.001	0.010***	0.010***
	(2.35)	(1.07)	(11.26)	(11.13)
Intercept	1.862***	0.260	−3.954***	−4.618***
	(3.24)	(1.38)	(−4.62)	(−5.48)
Chi-2 (p-value)	152.49	123.32	1780.99	1737.57
Observations	(0.00)	(0.00)	(0.00)	(0.00)
	339	341	341	342

Note: This table reports the effect of having qualified directors sitting on the board and the audit committee on the hedging behavior and performance of the firm. Simultaneous estimation of hedging and firm performance is made to account for endogeneity between the two variables. The system is based on Zellner's SURE combined with a two-stage least squares estimation for each equation. The return on equity (ROE) and return on assets (ROA) measure the firm's accounting performance. Tobin's q (Tobin's q) and the market-to-book (MB) measure firm market performance. Panel A reports hedge ratio equation estimates, and panel B reports firm performance equation estimates. Independent variable definitions are reported in Appendix C. All the regressions have firm effects and include a dummy variable for each quarter to control for seasonal effects in the data. The t-statistics are in parentheses. The superscripts ***, **, and * denote significance at the 1%, 5%, and 10% levels, respectively.

Policy Implications

Dionne, Maalaoui-Chun, and Triki (2018) also focused on the policy implications of the testable hypotheses. Even though the independence and accounting knowledge of directors are accounted for in the current regulation of nonfinancial institutions, it is not clear that these rules are achieving the goal of the regulation. The 2002 regulators have left the notion of financial literacy open to interpretation by the firm, and the concept is rather vague without an explicit regulatory requirement for the financial knowledge of board members. Under some circumstances, the concept is defined endogenously by the board members themselves. During the 2007 financial crisis, it became clear that board members were missing the necessary knowledge to understand the complexity of the financial markets, and necessary amendments to current regulations are still needed in the nonfinancial sector. Although the NYSE requires that at least one member of the audit committee have an accounting background, this requirement does not seem to have been very effective.

Dionne, Maalaoui-Chun, and Triki (2018) then tested the effect of the SOX and NYSE regulations on risk management activities in Table F-3 of their paper. As explanatory variables in the hedging equation, they add the variables measuring each of the corresponding rules. They also construct six compliance indexes: two for SOX rules, two for NYSE rules, and two indexes for both rules (see Appendix B for definitions). For each set of rules, they add the variables measuring each of these rules.

The results show that the SOX compliance index always has an effect on risk management activities; however, the NYSE compliance index is not significant in most cases. When they test the model using the index constructed for both the SOX and NYSE regulations, they find a significant regulation effect on risk management activities that is mainly due to SOX.

To test the effect of the regulations on firm performance, they use a two-stage system of simultaneous equations, thus addressing endogeneity issues. They find that SOX regulation remains positively significant in the hedging equation. However, this positive effect on hedging is not transmitted to shareholders since they do not find that risk management has any significant effect on firm performance. The results for the NYSE regulation remain consistent with a lack of significant effect on hedging.

Effect of Option Holdings on Risk Management

Dionne, Maalaoui-Chun, and Triki (2018) obtained two important results in relation to this literature on hedging. They first confirm that CEOs (or all executives) with call options on the firm's shares hedge less (effect on hedging is always significantly negative), while those with shares hedge more (effect on hedging always significantly positive); the results are reported in Table 18.2. Second, they find that less hedging reduces the value of the firm. This suggests that when hedging decisions are motivated by the officers' interests instead of those of the shareholders, the result is a negative effect on the firm. These results are obtained with different econometric specifications and are stable with the observed hedging behavior in this industry. These results extend Tufano's (1996) results. Without an explicit empirical test, Tufano argues that hedging less to increase the volatility of share prices and the value of personal option holdings may have no consequences on firm value when hedging is costless. Empirical results suggest that less hedging based on personal motives reduces the firm's value and thus becomes costly to shareholders. Still, this result should be stronger when options are out-of-the-money.

Dionne, Maalaoui-Chun, and Triki (2018) collected the strike prices from firms' proxy statements and corresponding share prices in the quarter the option was granted. They then computed the option's value and documented its moneyness. Among all options granted to officers, 66% were deeply out-of-the-money, 26% were in-the-money, and about 8% were at the money. These statistics support the conjecture that officers with more option holdings hedge less to increase their option holding value. They are consistent with Carpenter's (2000) conjecture, which suggests that officers may have increased incentives to hedge less if their option holdings are out-of-the-money. The results also support the need for better governance at the board with respect to this additional governance issue.

In this section, we presented the main results from the Dionne, Maalaoui-Chun, and Triki (2018) study of risk management and corporate governance. Two lessons should be retained from this analysis: (1) board member independence does not guarantee optimal risk management oversight; and (2) director expertise is instrumental to the good governance of risk management.

18.8 CONCLUSION

Boards of directors of large financial institutions now have risk committees that help the board define the firm's risk appetite, formulate risk management strategies, oversee firm management using adequate and robust risk measures, and put in place risk management control mechanisms. It would be preferable for pension funds, hedge funds, or investment funds managers to willingly adopt these governance rules to better protect their stockholders and clients.

One important aspect recently mentioned by Stulz (2013) is the fact that risk management audit differs from accounting statements audit. Financial statement audits mainly have a compliance role. Risk management audits have a compliance role, but the risk committee must also evaluate whether the current risk management policy, although compliant, maximizes the firm's value. This distinction justifies the creation of two distinct committees in large financial institutions and in nonfinancial institutions with high risk exposure. It also justifies the need for having independent members on the risk committee that have sufficient financial knowledge to accomplish the dual role of their audit.

REFERENCES

Adam, T.R., and Fernando, C.S., 2006. "Hedging, Speculation, and Shareholder Value." *Journal of Financial Economics* 81, 283–309.

Adams, R.B., Hermalin, B.E., and Weisbach, M.S., 2010. "The Role of Boards of Directors in Corporate Governance: A Conceptual Framework and Survey." *Journal of Economic Literature* 48, 58–107.

Aebi, V., Sabato, G., and Schmid, M., 2012. "Risk Management, Corporate Governance, and Bank Performance in the Financial Crisis." *Journal of Banking and Finance* 36, 3213–3226.

Aggarwal, R.K., 2008. "Executive Compensation and Incentives." In: *Handbook of Corporate Finance: Empirical Corporate Finance*. B.E. Eckbo (Ed.). Amsterdam: Elsevier, North-Holland, 497–538.

Agrawal, A., and Chadha, S., 2005. "Corporate Governance and Accounting Scandals." *Journal of Law and Economics* 48, 371–406.

Armstrong, C., Core, J., and Guay, W., 2014. "Do Independent Directors Cause Improvements in Firm Transparency?" *Journal of Financial Economics* 113, 383–403.

Blanchard, D., and Dionne, G., 2004. "The Case for Independent Risk Management Committees." *Risk* 17, S19–S21.

Borokhovich, K.A., Brunarski, K.R., Crutchley, C.E., and Simkins, B.J., 2001. "Board Composition and Corporate Investment in Interest Rate Derivatives." Working Paper, Oklahoma State University.

Campello, M., Lin, C., Ma, Y., and Zou, H., 2011. "The Real and Financial Implications of Corporate Hedging." *Journal of Finance* 66, 1615–1647.

Carcello, J., and Neal, T., 2000. "Audit Committee Composition and Auditor Reporting." *The Accounting Review* 75, 453–467.

Carpenter, J.N., 2000. "Does Option Compensation Increase Managerial Risk Appetite?" *Journal of Finance* 55, 2311–2331.

Core, J.E., Guay, W.R., and Larcker, D.F., 2003. "Executive Equity Compensation and Incentives: A Survey." *Federal Reserve Bank of New York Economic Policy Review* 9, 27–50.

Demski, J.S., 2003. "Corporate Conflicts of Interest." *Journal of Economic Perspectives* 17, 51–72.

Dionne, G., 2013. "Risk Management: History, Definition and Critique." *Risk Management and Insurance Review*, 16, 147–166.

Dionne, G., and Garand, M., 2003. "Risk Management Determinants Affecting Firms' Values in the Gold Mining Industry: New Empirical Evidence." *Economics Letters* 79, 43–52.

Dionne, G., Maalaoui-Chun, O., and Triki, T., 2018. "The Governance of Risk Management: The Importance of Directors' Independence and Financial Knowledge." *Mimeo, HEC Montréal*, Montreal, Canada.

Dionne, G., and Triki, T., 2013. "On Risk Management Determinants: What Really Matters?' *European Journal of Finance* 19, 145–164.

Falato, A., Kadyrzhanova, D., and Lel, U., 2014. "Distracted Directors: Does Board Busyness Hurt Shareholder Value?" *Journal of Financial Economics* 113, 404–426.

Fields, A., and Keys, P., 2003. "The Emergence of Corporate Governance from Wall St. to Main St.: Outside Directors, Board Diversity, Earnings Management, and Managerial Incentives to Bear Risk." *Financial Review* 38, 1–24.

Froot, K., Scharfstein, D., and Stein, J., 1993. "Risk Management: Coordinating Corporate Investment and Financing Policies." *Journal of Finance* 48, 1629–1658.

Graham, J.R., and Rogers, D., 2002. "Do Firms Hedge in Response to Tax Incentives?" *Journal of Finance* 57, 815–839.

Graham, J.R., and Smith, C.W., 1999. "Tax Incentives to Hedge." *Journal of Finance* 54, 2241–2262.

Guner, B., Malmendier, U., and Tate, G., 2005. "The Impact of Boards with Financial Expertise on Corporate Policies." Working paper, National Bureau of Economic Research, Cambridge, MA.

Hall, B.J., and Murphy, K.J., 2003. "The Trouble with Stock Options." *Journal of Economic Perspectives* 17, 49–70.

Healy, P.M., and Palepu, K.G., 2003. "The Fall of Enron." *Journal of Economic Perspectives* 17, 3–26.

Heckman, J.J., 1979. "Sample Selection as a Specification Error." *Econometrica* 47, 153–161.

Jenner and Block, 2003. "Summary of Final NYSE Corporate Governance Rules." https://jenner.com/system/assets/publications/8438/original/Summary_of_Final_NYSE_Corporate_Governance_Rules.pdf?1327097748.

Kirkpatrick, G., 2009. "The Corporate Governance Lessons from the Financial Crisis." *OCDE Journal: Financial Market Trends* 66, 893–919.
Lev, B., 2003. "Corporate Earnings: Fact and Fiction." *Journal of Economic Perspectives* 17, 27–50.
Mardsen, A., and Prevost, A., 2005. "Derivatives Use, Corporate Governance, and Legislative Change: An Empirical Analysis of New Zealand Listed Companies." *Journal of Business Finance and Accounting* 32, 255–295.
Nguyen, T.T.N., 2015. "Effet de la rémunération des CEOs par options d'achat d'actions sur leur comportement de gestion du risque des entreprises d'énergie." Final Master report, HEC Montréal, Montreal, Canada.
Rogers, D.A., 2002. "Does Executive Portfolio Structure Affect Risk Management? CEO Risk-Taking Incentives and Corporate Derivatives Usage." *Journal of Banking and Finance* 26, 271–295.
Smith, C.W., and Stulz, R.M., 1985. "The Determinants of Firms' Hedging Policies." *Journal of Financial and Quantitative Analysis* 20, 391–405.
Speroni, J., 2014. "Nouvelles règles prudentielles dans le secteur bancaire et financier." *L'Argus de l'assurance*, February 21.
Stulz, R.M., 2013. "How Companies Can Use Hedging to Create Shareholder Value." *Journal of Applied Corporate Finance* 25, 21–29.
Tirole, J., 2006. *The Theory of Corporate Finance*. Princeton: Princeton University Press.
Tufano, P., 1996. "Who Manages Risk? An Empirical Examination of Risk Management Practices in the Gold Mining Industry." *Journal of Finance* 51, 1097–1137.

APPENDIX A: GOVERNANCE OF CANADIAN FEDERAL FINANCIAL INSTITUTIONS

The federal guideline on corporate governance (January 2013) recommends that all federally regulated financial institutions put in place exemplary governance practices (http://www.osfi-bsif.gc.ca/eng/fi-if/rg-ro/gdn-ort/gl-ld/Pages/CG_Guideline.aspx).

The guideline pertains primarily to the board of directors, which plays a pivotal role in formulating the overall business strategy. The board of directors must approve the policies proposed by upper management by ensuring that these policies comply with the strategy and risk appetite specified by the board. It must also put in place a periodic risk assessment process and supervise senior management and internal controls.

The guideline is intended to evaluate the board's effectiveness using specific criteria. The Office of the Superintendent of Financial Institutions (OSFI) thus expects that the board will form a balanced set of competencies, expertise, skills, and experience given the strategy, risk profile, and global activities of financial institutions.

The board of directors should not have any relations of dependence with upper management. It must have the capacity to act on its own accord. The recruitment of new directors should emphasize board member independence.

The roles of board chair and CEO must also be separated, a crucial step in maintaining board independence. Other aspects of the guideline cover the role of the CEO, the nature and framework of controls, and the supervision process of the board relative to operational management, along with periodic examination and assessment of the board's effectiveness with the help of independent external consultants.

In addition, the guideline contains a section on risk governance. Accordingly, financial institutions must have a risk appetite framework that is commensurate with their size, the scope of their activities and the nature of their risk exposure. Guided by this framework, the board must establish a risk committee that oversees and defines risk management.

The guideline also mentions the audit committee and specifies the nature of its mandate. It is the audit committee, not senior executives, that should make recommendations to shareholders regarding the appointment, removal, and compensation of the external auditor.

The guideline's last section is dedicated to oversight of federal financial institutions by the OSFI. Another very important document is the Guide to Integrated Risk Management produced by the Treasury Board of Canada Secretariat, intended for federal departments and organizations (http://www.tbs-sct.gc.ca/hgw-cgf/pol/rm-gr/index-fra.asp).

In addition, two guidelines have been produced by the *Autorité des marchés financiers (Québec)*: one on governance, and the other on integrated risk management. They were adopted in April 2009 (http://www.lautorite.qc.ca/fr/lignes-directrices-i-d-pro.html).

APPENDIX B: DETAILS ON THE CONSTRUCTION OF THE GOVERNANCE INDEXES

Measuring Governance Standards

For the audit committee, the following dummy variables were constructed:

A1 = 1 if the audit committee is entirely composed of independent directors, and 0 otherwise.

A2 = 1 if the audit committee contains at least three members, and 0 otherwise.

A3 = 1 if the average tenure in the audit committee for directors is greater than 10 years, and 0 otherwise.

A4 = 1 if at least 25% of the audit committee hold a master's degree or a PhD in finance, and 0 otherwise.

A5 = 1 if each member of the audit committee is financially literate, and 0 otherwise.

A6 = 1 if the majority of the audit committee is comprised of financially active directors, and 0 otherwise.

A7 = 1 if the majority of the audit committee is comprised of financially educated directors, and 0 otherwise.

A8 = 1 if the majority of the audit committee is comprised of directors with an accounting background, and 0 otherwise.

A9 = 1 if at least one director in the audit committee is considered financially knowledgeable, and 0 otherwise.

A10 = 1 if at least one director in the audit committee has an accounting background, and 0 otherwise.

For the board, the following variables were constructed:

B1 = 1 if the majority of directors in the board are independent, and 0 otherwise.

B2 = 1 if the CEO is the COB, and 0 otherwise.

B3 = 1 if the average tenure of directors in the board is greater than 10 years, and 0 otherwise.

B4 = 1 if at least 25% of directors in the board hold a master's or a PhD in finance, and 0 otherwise.

B5 = 1 if the majority of directors in the board are considered financially knowledgeable, and 0 otherwise.

B6 = 1 if at least 25% of directors in the board are financially active, and 0 otherwise.

B7 = 1 if at least 25% of directors in the board are financially educated, and 0 otherwise.

B8 = 1 if at least 25% of directors in the board have an accounting background, and 0 otherwise.

The Quality of the Audit Committee

For the audit committee, our index requires the independence of directors and gives a higher score to audit committees comprised of directors with different levels and types of financial knowledge.

$$\text{Gov\_index\_audit} = A1 + A2 - A3 + A4 + A5 + A6 + A7 + A8.$$

The Quality of the Board

Similarly, the following score index for the board was constructed.

$$\text{Gov\_index\_board} = B1 - B2 - B3 + B4 + B5 + B6 + B7 + B8$$

SOX Standards

Two compliance indexes to measure the SOX standards were constructed.

$$\text{Compliance\_SOX1} = A1 + A9,$$

or

$$\text{Compliance\_SOX2} = A1 \times A9.$$

NYSE Standards

Two compliance indexes to measure the NYSE standards were also constructed as follows.

$$\text{Compliance\_NYSE1} = B1 + A2 + A5 + A10,$$

or

$$\text{Compliance\_NYSE2} = \text{B1} \times \text{A2} \times \text{A5} \times \text{A10}.$$

SOX and NYSE Standards

To obtain the compliance index to both SOX and NYSE standards, the following two variables were constructed.

$$\text{Compliance\_SOX1\_NYSE1} = \text{A1} + \text{A9} + \text{B1} + \text{A2} + \text{A5} + \text{A10},$$

or

$$\text{Compliance\_SOX2\_NYSE2} = \text{A1} \times \text{A9} \times \text{B1} \times \text{A2} \times \text{A5} \times \text{A10}.$$

APPENDIX C: VARIABLES

TABLE 18A.1 Variable definitions.

Hedge_ratio	The delta of the risk management portfolio held by the firm divided by its expected production. The variable is measured at the quarter end.
Ln(size)	The market value of assets defined as the number of common shares outstanding multiplied by the end-of-year price per share plus the book value of assets minus the book value of equity. We use the logarithm of the firm size.
Market_to_book	The market value of total assets divided by the book value of assets.
Leverage	The total debt divided by the total of common equity plus preferred stocks.
Quick_ratio	The value of the cash on hand, short-term investments, and clients' accounts divided by the short-term liabilities.
Dividend_policy	A dummy variable equal to 1 if a firm pays cash dividends, and 0 otherwise.
Tax_save	The expected percentage savings in tax arising from a 5% drop in the volatility of taxable income (more details in Appendix B). The computation is based on annual data. To obtain quarterly data, we assume the same value of tax advantages during the four quarters of the year.
US_dummy	A dummy variable equal to 1 if the firm is a US firm, and 0 otherwise.
%_inst	The percentage of shares held by institutions.
%_blockholders	The percentage of shares held by blockholders (i.e., a non-managerial shareholder holding more than 10% of the firm's shares, Tufano, 1996).
Exploration	The firm exploration expenditures scaled to the firm's market value.
Cash_cost	The operating cost of producing one ounce of gold, excluding all non-cash items such as depreciation, amortization, and other financial costs.

TABLE 18A.1 (*Continued*)

Gold_price	The price of one ounce of gold in the spot market.
CEO_age	The age of the CEO (years).
CEO_tenure	A dummy variable equal to 1 if the CEO is tenured as CEO, and 0 otherwise.
CEO_COB	A dummy variable equal to 1 if the CEO is the chairman of the board, and 0 otherwise.
CEO_change	A dummy variable equal to 1 if the CEO changed during the year, and 0 otherwise.
CEO_CS	The net value of the firm's common shares held by the CEO (millions, USD).
ValCEO_op	The value of exercisable options held by the CEO (millions, USD).
ValAll_op	The value of exercisable options held by all directors (millions, USD).
Cash_fee_outsiders	The cash fee paid to outside directors for each meeting attended (thousands, USD).
Annual_fixed_fee	The annual fixed fee paid to outside directors for each meeting attended (thousands, USD).
CEO_Bachelor	A dummy variable equal to 1 if the CEO has a bachelor's degree in finance, and 0 otherwise.
CEO_High_Edu	A dummy variable equal to 1 if the CEO has a master's degree or a PhD in finance, and 0 otherwise.

CHAPTER 19

Risk Management and Industrial Organization

Does risk management affect competition between firms? This industrial organization question has not been covered extensively in the literature despite its significance, particularly in markets where risk management is not regulated. For example, risk management may become a matter of competition when it increases debt capacity by lowering debt cost. Risk management could also affect the entry cost in a new industry or help finance mergers and acquisitions in a more mature market. In these examples, risk management decisions become market strategic decisions.

Industrial organization links firms to markets. It is particularly significant in a world of imperfect competition arising from limited information, transaction costs, and entry barriers (Tirole, 1988). It covers price discrimination, collusion, entry and exit, mergers and acquisitions, product differentiation, and many other subjects related to firms' strategic behavior. Usually, being a strategic firm matters in concentrated markets or those limited to a few firms. This does not mean that there is no competition between firms, but the type of competition tends to be very far from perfect. In fact, in a world of perfect competition, risk management may not matter. As discussed in previous chapters, the main motivation behind risk management lies in real-world market imperfections such as default costs, agency costs, and taxes. Managers' risk behavior may also justify risk management for non-regulated firms.

Up to now we have considered non-strategic corporate risk management decisions for price-taking firms facing random cash flows or random prices such as the price of gold or oil. Thus, when firms make optimal hedging decisions, they do not consider decisions of other firms or the impact of their decisions on the market equilibrium. In this chapter we discuss two recent theoretical articles that treat risk management as a strategic decision in a world of imperfect competition. The two articles are complementary and are mainly related to the effect of risk management on competition.

19.1 ENTRY, PRODUCTION, AND HEDGING

Dionne and Santugini (2014) analyzed firms' entry, production, and hedging decisions under imperfect competition. The main motivation of their research is the well-known separation theorem under perfect competition where optimal output production is independent of price distribution and firm risk behavior. They assume that firms have a concave payoff function due to managerial risk aversion. Concavity can also be explained by different market imperfections (Froot, Sharfstein, and Stein, 1993).

In the separation theorem framework, price distribution and payoff concavity affect firms' involvement in futures trading exclusively. Hence, with access to the futures market a separation result is obtained: uncertainty does not affect production efficiency (Holthausen, 1979; Katz and Paroush, 1979). Paroush and Wolf (1992) showed, however, that the separation result does not hold in the presence of derivative basis risk, while Anderson and Danthine (1981) obtained a similar negative result with production uncertainty. Different extensions have been proposed by considering multiple risky inputs, background risk, joint output price, and input price uncertainty.

To add the entry decision to the basic framework of the separation theorem, Dionne and Santugini (2014) consider an oligopoly industry producing a homogeneous output in which risk-averse firms incur a sunk cost upon entering the industry, and then compete in a Cournot environment. Each firm faces uncertainty in the input price when making production decisions and has access to the futures market to hedge this cost.

There is only one source of risk in their analysis. One application of their model is the US airline market, in which the presence of Cournot competition has been confirmed (Brander and Zhang, 1990; Fisher and Kamerschen, 2003). In this market, airline companies face fuel price uncertainty when they make their optimal route decisions for the next few months and purchase futures contracts for jet fuel (Morrell and Swan, 2006). Carter et al. (2006) documented the strategic importance of fuel hedging in this industry. Over the 1992–2003 period, fuel price, with an annualized volatility of 27%, represented more than 13% of airlines' operating costs, as Léautier and Rochet (2014) demonstrated. Other costs are usually less volatile, so hedging fuel costs guarantees stable profits. Dionne and Santugini (2014) interpret entering or exiting the output market as route decisions. Airline companies can also purchase derivative products other than futures contracts, such as options and even collars. These options would introduce more flexibility for the firm but would not affect the main results of their study.

Dionne and Santugini (2014) report two main results. First, under general assumptions about risk preferences, demand, and uncertainty, they obtain a unique equilibrium. This equilibrium contrasts with previous results without entry activity in the market, in that production and output price now depend on uncertainty and risk behavior. In other words, when entry is an endogenous decision, access to the futures market does not lead to a separation between production and hedging decisions.

Second, to isolate the specific effect of access to the futures market on entry and production, the authors focus their attention on constant absolute risk aversion (CARA) preferences, linear demand, and a normal distribution for the spot input price. In general, the effect of having access to the futures market on the number of firms and production is ambiguous. However, when the model parameters lead to partial hedging, access to the futures market induces more firms to enter the market and to produce more.

19.2 COMMITMENT TO HEDGING

Léautier and Rochet (2014) study the effect of committing to a hedging strategy on production or pricing decisions. Specifically, they consider a two-stage game in which the firm commits to a hedging strategy in the first stage and then chooses production or pricing strategies in the second stage. As in the study by Dionne and Santugini (2014), firms have market power in the output sector but are perfectly competitive in the input market. There are, however, important differences in the setups of the two contributions as well as in the issues studied.

Léautier and Rochet (2014) consider a market with a fixed number of firms, whereas in the study by Dionne and Santugini (2014) entry is a decision variable in the first stage, and hedging and production are chosen simultaneously in the second stage. Beyond the differences in modeling, the two contributions study different and complementary aspects of the link between real and financial activities when firms exert market power. Léautier and Rochet (2014) show that strategic hedging (when used as a strategic commitment device) has a strong effect on Bertrand (price competition) or Cournot (quantity competition) equilibriums and consequently on firms' real decisions. Specifically, under actuarially fair pricing, hedging accentuates quantity competition but softens price competition. Committing to hedging is a dominant strategy for all firms. Accordingly, not committing to a hedging position can never be an equilibrium outcome: committing is always a best response relative to non-committing.

Let us consider first Cournot (quantity) competition. Léautier and Rochet (2014) prove that the equilibrium of the production game always exists in their theoretical framework. At this equilibrium, firms hedge more than their (anticipated) equilibrium production, and thus commit to producing more quantities of the good than if their costs were constant and equal to the expected cost under the physical probability measure.

Under differentiated Bertrand (price) competition, an equilibrium exists but with an opposite conclusion: commitment to hedging softens price competition. An increase in hedging reduces the firm's expected risk-adjusted cost and hence reduces the rival's equilibrium price. This effect is standard with differentiated Bertrand games. The crucial distinction with quantity competition is that a firm's commitment to hedging less than its (anticipated) equilibrium production entails committing to a higher price than if its cost was constant and equal to the expected cost under the physical probability measure.

The food-processing industry provides a good example of such a market. Food-processing firms are exposed to volatile input prices (e.g., grains). Although these firms may not exert market power in the feedstock markets, most empirical studies document their market power in their product markets (Sheldon and Sperling, 2003). Léautier and Rochet (2014) present an extensive review of the main results from the literature on the link between risk management and product market strategies.

19.3 CONCLUSION

We presented two contributions that provide analyses of firms' production and hedging decisions under imperfect competition. Dionne and Santugini (2014) show that entry removes the traditional separation result that has often been discussed in the literature. Although firms have access to the futures market, their production decisions now depend on uncertainty and risk preferences through the determination of the number of firms in the industry.

They also show that the use of futures contracts has an ambiguous effect on the market structure of the industry. For instance, when the futures input price is actuarially fair, access to the futures market increases or decreases the number of entering firms depending on the value of the sunk cost.

Many extensions of this research are possible. In their study of the interaction between entry and the futures market, the authors overlook two important aspects. First, they assume that the spot and futures prices are exogenous. However, these prices can be determined by market participants as well, which, in turn, could affect resource allocation, production decisions, and risk-taking. Extending the model to include suppliers of inputs along with speculators in futures markets is an avenue of future research.

Moreover, although the determination of spot and futures prices has already been studied by Turnovsky (1983), output producers are assumed to be passive: that is, the input for their demand is a given. In fact, output producers are active and forward-looking, and, as this article demonstrated, their output and input decisions are intertwined.

Second, Dionne and Santugini (2014) ignore the role of financial decisions in deterring entry. It would also be interesting to study how strategic hedging from an incumbent firm may alter the entry decision of a potential new competitor. For instance, Maskin (1999) considered a model in which capacity installation by an incumbent firm serves to deter others from entering the industry. Uncertainty about demand or costs forces the incumbent to choose a higher capacity level than it would under certainty. This higher requirement for capacity diminishes the attractiveness of deterrence. It would be interesting to study the incumbent's incentive to deter entry when it has access to futures markets.

Finally, an empirical extension would be to test the model in the airline industry or any industry with similar characteristics facing Cournot competition. Recent empirical tests on hedging were limited to the effect of determinants, such as CEO risk aversion, convexity of the tax function, corporate governance, distress costs, information asymmetry, and the effect of hedging on firm value.

To our knowledge, no empirical study has analyzed the effect of hedging on entry. The main question would be: Do airline companies that hedge (or speculate) enter different routes more aggressively? The theoretical results are ambiguous on this question, and an empirical hypothesis could be: Airline companies produce less in different routes when futures prices are high, which induces more firms to enter.

Léautier and Rochet (2014) examine how firms facing volatile input prices and holding some degree of market power in their product market link their risk management to their production or pricing strategies when the number of firms in the market is constant. They find that commitment to hedging modifies firms' pricing and production strategies. This strategic effect is channeled through the risk-adjusted expected cost: that is, the expected marginal cost under the probability measure induced by firm risk aversion. It has opposite effects depending on the nature of the product market competition: Commitment to hedging toughens quantity competition and softens price competition. Finally, not committing to the hedging position can never be an equilibrium outcome: committing is always the best response.

Léautier and Rochet discuss how their contribution can be extended in different directions. For example, it would be interesting to examine asymmetric situations where one firm is a market leader and announces its hedging strategy before the other, or when different firms have different costs. Another possibility would be to set pricing flexibility as a decision variable: that is, to determine when it is optimal for firms not to adjust their output prices to reflect the realization of their input costs.

Extending the model to capture richer dynamics is another research avenue. The first possibility would be to examine the impact of hedging on current product market competition and on investments, hence on future product market competition. Another possibility would be to revisit the notion of commitment under richer forward price dynamics, with the option of continuously reoptimizing the hedging portfolio.

Finally, testing the predictions as to how firms' hedging decisions influence their own and their competitors' pricing strategies is another challenge. This test naturally raises the question of which model of competition (Cournot vs. Bertrand) is more realistic when commitment to hedging exists. The most difficult task will be to observe this commitment.

REFERENCES

Alghalith, M., 2008. "Hedging and Production Decisions under Uncertainty: A Survey." Cornell University Library, Ithaca, NY. http://arxiv.org/abs/0810.0917.

Allaz, B., and Villa, J.L., 1993. "Cournot Competition, Forwards Markets and Efficiency." *Journal of Economic Theory* 59, 1–16.

Anderson, R.W., and Danthine, J.P., 1981. "Cross Hedging." *Journal of Political Economy* 89, 1182–1196.

Anderson, R.W., and Danthine, J.P., 1983. "Hedger Diversity in Futures Markets." *The Economic Journal* 93, 370–389.

Batra, R.N., and Ullah, A., 1974. "Competitive Firm and the Theory of Input Demand Under-price Uncertainty." *Journal of Political Economy* 28, 537–548.

Brander, J.A., and Zhang, A., 1990. "Market Conduct in the Airline Industry: An Empirical Investigation." *The RAND Journal of Economics* 21, 567–583.

Carter, D.A., Rogers, D.A., and Simkins, B.J., 2006. "Does Hedging Affect Firm Value? Evidence from the US Airline Industry." *Financial Management*, Spring, 53–86.

Danthine, J.P., 1973. "Information, Futures Prices, and Stabilizing Speculation." *Journal of Economic Theory* 17, 79–98.

Diamond, P.A., and Stiglitz, J.E., 1974. "Increases in Risk and in Risk Aversion." *Journal of Economic Theory* 8, 337–360.

Dionne, G., and Santugini, M., 2014. "Entry, Imperfect Competition, and Futures Market for the Input." *International Journal of Industrial Organization* 35, 70–83.

Dionne, G., and Triki, T., 2013. "On Risk Management Determinants: What Really Matters?" *The European Journal of Finance* 19, 145–164.

Eldor, R., and Zilcha, I., 1990. "Oligopoly, Uncertain Demand, and Forward Markets." *Journal of Economics and Business* 42, 17–26.

Ethier, W.J., 1973. "International Trade and the Forward Exchange Market." *The American Economic Review* 63, 494–503.

Feder, G., Just, R.E., and Schmitz, A., 1980. "Futures Markets and the Theory of the Firm under Price Uncertainty." *The Quarterly Journal of Economics* 94, 317–328.

Fisher, T., and Kamerschen, D.R., 2003. "Measuring Competition in the U.S. Airline Industry Using the Rosse-Panzar Test and Cross-Sectional Regression Analyses." *Journal of Applied Economics* 6, 73–93.

Freixas, X., and Rochet, J.C., 2008. *Microeconomics of Banking*. Cambridge, MA: MIT Press.

Froot, K.A., Sharfstein, D.A., and Stein, J.C., 1993. "Risk Management: Coordinating Corporate Investment and Financing Policies." *The Journal of Finance* 48, 1629–1641.

Holthausen, D.M., 1979. "Hedging and the Competitive Firm Underprice Uncertainty." *American Economic Review* 69, 989–995.

Katz, E., and Paroush, J., 1979. "The Effect of Forward Markets on Exporting Firms." *Economics Letters* 4, 271–274.

Laffont, J.J., 1989. *The Economics of Uncertainty and Information*. Cambridge, MA: MIT Press.

Léautier, T.O., and Rochet, J.C., 2014. "On the Strategic Value of Risk Management." *International Journal of Industrial Organization* 37, 153–169.

Losq, E., 1982. "Hedging with Price and Output Uncertainty." *Economics Letters* 10, 65–70.

Maskin, E.S., 1999. "Uncertainty and Entry Deterrence." *Economic Theory* 14, 429–437.

Morrell, P., and Swan, W., 2006. "Airline Jet Fuel Hedging: Theory and Practice." *Transport Reviews* 26, 713–730.

Moschini, G., and Harvey, L., 1992. "Hedging Price Risk with Options and Futures for the Competitive Firm with Production Flexibility." *International Economic Review* 33, 607–618.

Paroush, J., and Wolf, A., 1992. "The Derived Demand with Hedging Cost Uncertainty in the Futures Markets." *The Economic Journal* 102, 831–844.

Santos, J.A.C., and Tsatsarinis, K., 2003. "The Cost to Entry: Evidence from the Market for Corporate Euro Bond Underwriting." BIS working paper.

Sheldon, I., and Sperling, R., 2003. "Estimating the Extent of Imperfect Competition in the Food Industry: What Have We Learned?" *Journal of Agricultural Economics* 54, 89–109.

Tirole, J., 1988. *The Theory of Industrial Organization*. MIT Press.

Turnovsky, S.J., 1983. "The Determination of Spot and Futures Prices with Storable Commodities." *Econometrica* 51, 1363–1387.

Viaene, J.M., and Zilcha, I., 1998. "The Behavior of Competitive Exporting Firms under Multiple Uncertainty." *International Economic Review* 39, 591–609.

CHAPTER 20

Real Implications of Corporate Risk Management

Many contributions in the literature focus on hedging value and risk implications for firms (e.g., Guay, 1999; Allayannis and Westion, 2001; Jin and Jorion, 2006). Yet empirical findings on the value implications of risk management are fairly mixed and inconclusive.[1] Methodological problems related to endogeneity of derivative use and other firm decisions, sample selection, sample size, and the existence of other potential hedging mechanisms (e.g., operational hedge) are often blamed for this mixed empirical evidence.

This chapter revisits the question of hedging virtues in a more comprehensive and multifaceted manner for a sample of US oil producers while using a different econometric methodology. To better gauge the actual implications of hedging, we examine its effects on the following firm objectives:

1. Firm value: Measured by the Tobin's q to verify if hedging is associated with value creation for shareholders.
2. Firm risk: Measured by both idiosyncratic and systematic risk, and firms' stock returns sensitivity to oil price fluctuations. One would expect that hedging should attenuate firms' exposure to the underlying market risk factor, which leads to lower firm riskiness. We will analyze in particular whether firms are hedging or speculating by using derivatives.
3. Firm accounting performance: Measured by the return on equity (ROE). We will confirm whether hedging effects translate into higher accounting profits or not.

To overcome the major source of inconsistency from the empirical literature findings (i.e., endogeneity), we use an econometric approach based on instrumental variables applied to models with essential heterogeneity inspired by the work of Heckman, Urzua, and Vytlacil (2006). Their work controls for the individual-specific unobserved heterogeneity in the marginal treatment effects estimation from decision variables in the upper quartile versus those in the lower quartile. Heckman, Urzua, and Vytlacil (2006) confirm that the plain method of instrumental variables appears to be inappropriate when there are heterogeneous responses to treatment. In our application of the essential heterogeneity model, we identify a credible instrument arising from the economic literature pertaining to the macroeconomic responses to

[1]The research discussed in this chapter was conducted with Mohamed Mnasri.

crude oil price shocks; namely, the Kilian (2009) index, which gives a measure of the demand for industrial commodities driven by the economic perspective.

Our evidence suggests that marginal firm financial value (marginal treatment effect, MTE), as measured by the Tobin's q, is increasing in oil producers' propensity to hedge their oil production to a greater extent (i.e., upper quartile). This finding corroborates one strand in the previous literature that argues for the existence of a hedging premium for non-financial firms (Allayannis and Weston, 2001; Carter, Rogers, and Simkins, 2006; Adam and Fernando, 2006; Perez-Gonzales and Yun, 2013, among others). Consistent with the literature (e.g., Guay, 1999; Bartram, Brown, and Conrad, 2011), we find that marginal firm riskiness, as measured by its systematic and idiosyncratic risks, is decreasing with oil producers' propensity to be high-intensity hedgers rather than low-intensity hedgers. Oil beta, representing firms' stock returns' sensitivity to fluctuations in oil prices, is decreasing with the propensity to hedge to larger extents, albeit with no statistical significance. Altogether, these findings suggest that any potential positive effects associated with oil hedging should translate into value enhancement for shareholders because of the decrease in the required cost of equity. This is due to the lower riskiness of the oil producers, particularly lower systematic risk, as suggested by Gay, Lin, and Smith (2011). We also find that the firm's marginal accounting performance, as measured by the return on equity, is lower for oil producers that are low-intensive hedgers. Finally, we obtain a significant average treatment effect (ATE) for Tobin's q (positive), idiosyncratic risk (negative), and systematic risk (negative).

20.1 REAL IMPLICATIONS OF CORPORATE RISK MANAGEMENT: A REVIEW

One strand of the corporate hedging literature finds no support for the risk-reduction argument and firm value maximization theory. Using a sample of 425 large US corporations from 1991 to 1993, Hentschel and Kothari (2001) concluded that derivative users display economically small differences in their stock return volatility compared with non-users, even for firms with larger derivative holdings. Guay and Kothari (2003) studied the hedging practices of 234 large non-financial firms and found that the magnitude of the derivative positions is economically small compared with firm-level risk exposures and movements in equity values. Jin and Jorion (2006) revisited the question of the hedging premium for a sample of 119 US oil and gas producers from 1998 to 2001. Although they noted that oil and gas betas are negatively related to hedging extent, they also showed that hedging has no discernible effect on firm value. Fauver and Naranjo (2010) studied derivative usage by 1,746 US firms from 1991 to 2000 and asserted that firms with greater agency and monitoring problems exhibited an economically significant negative association of 8.4% between firms' Tobin's q and derivative usage.

In contrast, Tufano (1998) studied hedging activities of 48 North American gold mining firms from 1990 through March 1994, and found that gold firm exposures (i.e., gold betas) were negatively related to the firm's hedging production. Guay (1999) looked at a sample of 254 non-financial corporations that began using derivatives in the fiscal year of 1991, and reported that new derivative users experienced a statistically and economically significant reduction of 5% in stock return volatility compared with a control sample of non-users. Using a sample of S&P 500 non-financial firms for 1993, Allayannis and Ofek (2001) found strong evidence that foreign currency hedging reduces firms' exchange-rate exposure. Allayannis and Weston (2001) gave the first direct evidence of a positive relationship between currency derivative usage and firm value, (as defined by Tobin's *q*) and showed that for a sample of 720 non-financial firms, the market value of foreign currency hedgers is 5% higher on average than for non-hedgers. Hoyt and Liebenberg (2015) obtained that enterprise risk management increased the value of insurance firms. In their sample of 687 observations, they verified that insurers with ERM have a Tobin's *q* value 4% higher than other insurers.

Carter, Rogers, and Simkins (2006) investigated jet fuel hedging behavior of firms in the US airline industry during the period of 1993–2003 and found an average hedging premium of 12%–16%. Adam and Fernando (2006) examined the outstanding gold derivative positions for a sample of North American gold mining firms for the period of 1989–1999 and observed that derivative use translated into value gains for shareholders because there was no offsetting increase in firms' systematic risk. Bartram, Brown, and Conrad (2011) explored the effect of hedging on firm risk and value for a large sample of 6,888 non-financial firms from 47 countries in 2000 and 2001. Their evidence suggested that derivatives reduced both total and systematic risk, and are associated with higher firm value, abnormal returns, and larger profits.

Recently, Choi, Mao, and Upadhyay (2013) examined financial and operational hedging activities of 73 US pharmaceutical and biotech firms during the period of 2001–2006. They found that hedging was associated with higher firm value, and that this enhancement was greater for firms subject to higher information asymmetry and more growth options. For their sample, they estimated a hedging premium of approximately 13.8%. Perez-Gonzales and Yun (2013) exploited the introduction of weather derivatives in 1997 as a natural experiment for a sample of energy firms. As measured by the market-to-book ratio, they found that weather derivatives had a positive effect on firm value. Gay, Lin, and Smith (2011) investigated the relationship between derivative use and firms' cost of equity. From a large sample of non-financial firms during the two subperiods 1992–1996 and 2002–2004, they found that hedgers had a lower cost of equity than non-hedgers by about 24–78 basis points. This reduction mainly came from lower market betas for derivative users. Their results were robust to endogeneity concerns related to derivative use and capital structure decisions. Aretz and Bartram (2010) reviewed the empirical literature on corporate hedging and firm value.

More recently, Mnasri, Dionne, and Gueyie (2017) and Dionne, Gueyie, and Mnasri (2018) both demonstrated that using non-linear financial derivatives and short time–horizon derivatives increased firm value by considering a methodology similar to that described in this chapter. To our knowledge, this methodology has not yet been applied to analyze the effect of hedging intensity on firm value and risk.

20.2 METHODOLOGY

Endogeneity due to any reverse causality between firm hedging behavior and other firm financial decisions is a crucial concern in hedging studies; it is identified as the major source of inconsistency in past findings. To control for this endogeneity, we study the real effects of hedging using an instrumental variable applied to the essential heterogeneity model. We control for biases related to selection on unobservables and self-selection in the estimation of the Marginal Treatment Effects (MTEs) of hedging extent choice on firm value, risk, and accounting performance. A formal discussion of these models will be presented below. We also estimate the Average Treatment Effects (ATEs), which can be interpreted as the mean of the MTEs.

To obtain insight into the true implications of hedging activities on firm value, risk, and accounting performance, we classify positive hedging ratios for oil production during the current fiscal year as the following:

Low-intensity hedging: Below the 25th percentile, which corresponds to a hedging ratio of about 24%;

High-intensity hedging: Exceeds the 75th percentile, which corresponds to a hedging ratio of about 64%.

We create a dummy variable that takes the value of 1 for high-intensity hedging and zero for low- but positive-intensity hedging. We can thus attribute true implications of hedging to either low- or high-intensity hedging ratios.

20.2.1 Instrumental Variable

For the choice of our candidate instrument, we build on our previous research showing a significant impact of oil market conditions (oil spot price and volatility) on oil hedging design in terms of maturity and vehicles (Mnasri, Dionne, and Gueyie, 2017; Dionne, Gueyie, and Mnasri, 2018). Armed with this empirical evidence, we look for an instrument that can explain the fluctuations of the real oil price and that cannot directly affect the value, riskiness, and accounting performance of an oil producer. A large body of economic literature affirms that one of the most important fundamental factors that determines industrial commodity prices is demand pressures or shocks induced by real economic activity. Consequently, we chose the Kilian (2009) index as our instrument. This instrument measures the component of true global economic activity that drives demand for industrial commodities. This index is based on dry cargo (grain, crude oil, coal, iron ore, etc.), single-voyage ocean freight rates, and captures demand shifts in global industrial commodity markets. The Kilian index, constructed monthly, accounts for fixed effects for different routes, commodities, and ship sizes. It is also deflated with the US consumer price index and linearly detrended to remove the decrease in real term over time of the dry cargo shipping cost. Kilian (2009) shows that aggregate shocks for industrial commodities cause long swings in the real oil prices. This differs from the increases and decreases in the price of oil induced by oil market-specific supply shocks, which are more transitory. They also differ from shocks related to shifts in the precautionary demand for oil, which arise from uncertainty about expected supply shortfalls relative to expected demand. For our purposes, we calculate the changes in the Kilian (2009) index for each fiscal quarter in the sample. These changes in the index are calculated by taking the index's level at the end of the current fiscal quarter (i.e., at the end of the fiscal quarter's last month), minus its level at the end of the previous fiscal quarter. Figure 20.1 shows a high correlation of 76.7% between the Kilian index and the crude oil near-month futures contract price, meaning that an increase in demand for industrial commodities is correlated with an increase in futures contract prices. Consequently, oil hedging intensity should have a negative relationship with the Kilian index.[2]

[2]As a robustness check, we individualize our instrument by multiplying the changes in the Kilian aggregate index by the individual marginal tax rate, which represents the present value of current and expected future taxes paid on an additional dollar of income earned today as in Shevlin (1990). The marginal tax rate is used as a proxy for the firm's tax structure that measures the tax incentive for hedging (Haushalter, 2000). The marginal tax rate is constructed following the non-parametric procedure developed by Blouin, Core, and Guay (2010). Our results are qualitatively the same, albeit with lower MTEs statistical significance. They are available from the authors.

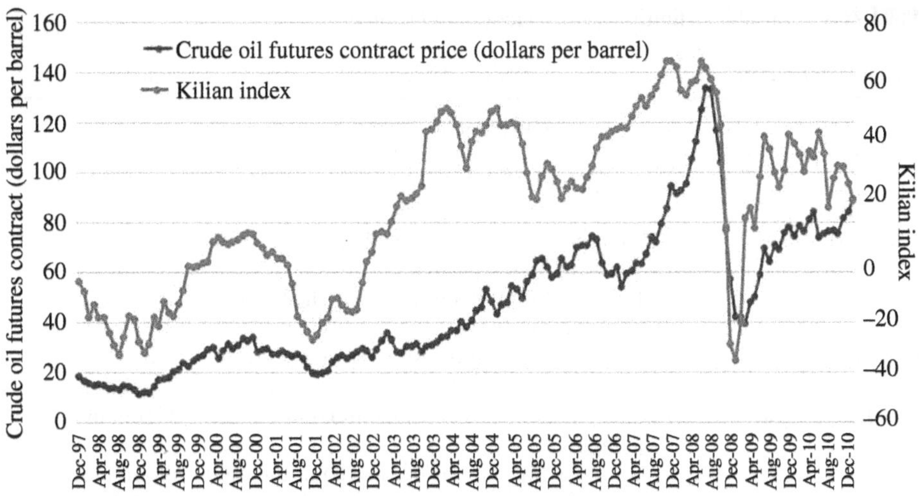

FIGURE 20.1 Kilian index versus crude oil futures contract price.

20.2.2 Essential Heterogeneity Model

The essential heterogeneity model usually begins with a Mincer-like equation (Mincer, 1974), as follows:

$$y_{i,t} = \alpha + \beta \times d_{i,t} + \sum \beta_i \text{ Control variables}_{i,t-1} + u_{i,t}, \tag{20.1}$$

where $y_{i,t}$ is the firm target or the risk and value of an oil producer i at the end of quarter t, and $d_{i,t}$ is the observed value of a dummy variable D = (0, 1) representing whether the oil producer i uses low (0) or high (1) intensity hedging during quarter t. The control variables include a set of observable covariates, namely the earnings per share from operations, investment opportunities, leverage ratio, liquidity, a dividend payout dummy, quantity of oil reserves, oil production uncertainty, geographical diversification in oil production, gas hedging ratio, gas reserves, gas production uncertainty, oil and gas spot prices and volatilities, institutional ownership, CEO shareholding and option-holding, and the number of analysts following the firm (see Table 20.1 for the definitions of these variables). The term $u_{i,t}$ is an individual-specific error term, and β represents the average return from using high-intensity hedging.

Two sources of bias could affect the estimates of β. The first is related to the standard problem of selection bias, when $d_{i,t}$ is correlated with $u_{i,t}$. However, it should be resolved using instrumental variable (IV) methods, among others. The second source of bias occurs if the returns from using high-intensity hedging vary across oil producers (i.e., β is random because of firm non-observed factors that can influence both the firm target and the hedging decision, such as governance or manager risk aversion), even after conditioning on observable characteristics leading to heterogeneous treatment effects. Moreover, oil producers make their hedging-level choice (low- versus high-intensity) with at least partial knowledge of the expected idiosyncratic gains from this decision (i.e., β is correlated with D), leading to selection into treatment or sorting on the gain problem.

Heckman, Urzua, and Vytlacil (2006) developed an econometric methodology based on IVs to solve the problem of essential heterogeneity (i.e., β is correlated with D) in the estimation of MTEs. Their methodology is built on the generalized

TABLE 20.1 Variable definitions, construction and sources

Variable definition	Construction	Source
	Independent variables	
EPS from operations	Earnings per share from operations calculated on a quarterly basis.	Compustat
Investment opportunities	Quarterly capital expenditure (CAPEX) scaled by net property, plant and equipment at the beginning of the quarter.	Compustat
Leverage ratio	Book value of total debts scaled by the book value of total assets.	Compustat
Liquidity	Book value of cash and cash equivalents divided by the book value of current liabilities.	Manually constructed
Dividend payout	Dummy variable for dividends declared during the quarter.	Manually constructed
Oil reserves	The quantity (in millions of barrels) of the total proved developed and undeveloped oil reserves (in logarithm). This variable is disclosed annually. We repeat the same observation for the same fiscal year quarters.	Bloomberg and 10-K reports
Institutional ownership	Percentage of firm shares held by institutional investors.	Thomson Reuters
Geographical diversification in oil (gas) production activities	Equals $1-\sum_{i=1}^{N}\left(\frac{q_i}{q}\right)^2$, where q_i is the daily oil (gas) production in region i (Africa, Latin America, North America, Europe, and the Middle East), and q is the firm's total daily oil (gas) production.	Manually constructed
Oil production risk	Coefficient of variation of daily oil production. This coefficient is calculated for each firm by using rolling windows of 12 quarterly observations. Daily oil production is disclosed annually. We repeat the same observation for the same fiscal year quarters.	Manually constructed Bloomberg and 10-K reports
Oil spot price	Oil spot price represented by the WTI index on the NYMEX at the end of the current quarter.	Bloomberg
Oil price volatility	Historical volatility (standard deviation) using daily spot prices during the quarter.	Manually constructed
Hedging ratio of the expected future gas production	The average hedging ratio of the expected future gas production over the subsequent five fiscal years. For each fiscal year, we measure the gas hedging ratio by the Fraction of Production Hedged (FPH) calculated by dividing the notional hedged gas quantity by the expected gas production. We then average these five hedging ratios.	Manually constructed
Gas spot price	Constructed as an average index established from principal locations' indices in the United States (Gulf Coast, Henry Hub, etc.).	Bloomberg
Gas price volatility	Historical volatility (standard deviation) using the daily spot prices during the quarter.	Manually constructed

TABLE 20.1 (*Continued*)

Variable definition	Construction	Source
Gas reserves	The quantity of the total proved developed and undeveloped gas reserves. This variable is disclosed annually. We repeat the same observation for the same fiscal year quarters. The raw value of this variable (in billions of cubic feet) is used in Table 20.2 (Summary Statistics). The logarithm transformation of this variable is used elsewhere.	Bloomberg and 10-K reports
Gas production risk	Coefficient of variation of daily gas production. This coefficient is calculated for each firm by using rolling windows of 12 quarterly observations. Daily gas production is disclosed annually. We repeat the same observation for the same fiscal year quarters.	Manually constructed Bloomberg and 10-K reports
CEO stockholding	The percentage of firm's stocks held by the CEO at the end of the quarter.	Thomson Reuters
CEO option holding	Number of stock options held by the firm's CEO (× 10, 000) at the end of the quarter.	Thomson Reuters
Number of analysts	Number of analysts following a firm that issued a forecast of the firm's quarterly earnings.	I/B/E/S
	Dependent variables	
Firm Tobin's q (in log)	Calculated by the ratio of the market value of equity plus the book value of debt plus the book value of preferred shares divided by the book value of total assets(in log).	CRSP/Compustat
Return on equity	Quarterly net income divided by the book value of common equity.	Compustat
Systematic risk	Measure of the oil producer stock return's sensitivity to the CRSP value weighted portfolio estimated using the Fama and French (1993) and Carhart (1997) four factors and the daily returns on the one-month crude oil futures and the one-month natural gas futures. The estimation is based on daily returns during each quarter in the sample.	CRSP/Bloomberg
Idiosyncratic risk	Measured by the Fama and French (1993) and Carhart (1997) four factors residual estimation's volatility and the daily returns on the one-month crude oil futures and the one-month natural gas futures. The estimation is based on daily returns during each quarter in the sample.	CRSP/Bloomberg
Oil beta	Measure of the oil producer stock return's sensitivity to the daily changes in the oil futures price estimated using the same methodology as that employed for the systematic risk.	CRSP/Bloomberg

Roy model, which is an example of treatment effects models for economic policy evaluation. The generalized Roy model involves a joint estimation of an observed continuous outcome and its binary treatment. In this model, let (Y_0, Y_1) be the potential outcomes observed under the counterfactual states of treatment (Y_1) and no treatment (Y_0); these outcomes are supposed to depend linearly upon observed characteristics X and unobservable characteristics (U_0, U_1) as follows:

$$Y_1 = \alpha_1 + \beta + \beta_1 X + U_1 \tag{20.2}$$

$$Y_0 = \alpha_0 + \beta_0 X + U_0 \tag{20.3}$$

where β is the benefit related to the treatment $D = 1$.

The selection process is represented by $I_D = \gamma Z - V$, which depends on the observed values of the Z variables and an unobservable disturbance term V. The selection process, related to whether low- or high-intensity hedging is used, is linked to the observed outcome through the latent variable I_D, which gives the dummy variable D representing the treatment status:

$$D = \begin{cases} 1 \text{ if } I_D > 0 \\ 0 \text{ if } I_D \leq 0 \end{cases} \tag{20.4}$$

where the vector of Z variables observed includes IV variables Z_{IV} and all the components of X in the outcome equation. The variables Z_{IV} satisfy the following constraints: $Cov(Z_{IV}, U_0) = 0$, $Cov(Z_{IV}, U_1) = 0$, and $\gamma \neq 0$. The unobservable set of (U_0, U_1, V) is assumed to be statistically independent of Z, given X. We must first estimate the probability of participation in high-intensity hedging or the propensity score and then analyze how this participation affects firm values and risk. To do so, we apply the parametric estimation method.

We can assume the joint normality of the outcome's unobservable components and decision equations $(U_0, U_1, V) \sim N(0, \Sigma)$, where Σ is the variance–covariance matrix of the three unobservable variables and $\sigma_{1V} = Cov(U_1, V)$, $\sigma_{0V} = Cov(U_0, V)$, and $\sigma_{VV} = 1$ following standard hypotheses. Under this parametric approach, the discrete choice model is a conventional probit with $V \sim N(0, 1)$ and where the propensity score is given by:

$$P(z) = Pr(D = 1|Z = z) = Pr(\gamma z > V) = \Phi(\gamma z), \tag{20.5}$$

where $\Phi(\cdot)$ is the cumulative distribution of a standard normal variable. The term P(z), called the probability of participation in hedging activity or propensity score, denotes the selection probability of using high-intensity hedging conditional on $Z = z$ (i.e., $D = 1$). We can therefore write:

$$\Phi(\gamma Z) > \Phi(V) \Longleftrightarrow P(Z) > U_D \tag{20.6}$$

where $U_D = \Phi(V)$ and $P(Z) = \Phi(\gamma Z) = Pr(D = 1|Z)$.

The term U_D is a uniformly distributed random variable between zero and one representing different quantiles of the unobserved component V in the selection process. These two quantities, P(Z) and U_D, play a crucial role in essential heterogeneity models. The quantity P(Z) could be interpreted as the probability of going into treatment and U_D, interpreted as a measure of individual-specific resistance to undertaking treatment (or, alternatively, the propensity to not being treated as a high-intensity hedger). In our case, the higher the P(Z), the more the oil producer is induced to hedging its oil production to a larger extent due to Z. Conversely, the higher the U_D, the more resistant the oil producer is to using higher hedging extents due to a larger unobserved component. $P(Z) = U_D$ is thus the margin of indifference for oil producers that are indifferent between low- and high-intensity hedging.

The marginal treatment effects (MTEs) can be defined as follows:

$$MTE(X = x, U_D = u_D) = (\alpha_1 + \beta - \alpha_0) + (\beta_1 - \beta_0)x + (\sigma_{1V} - \sigma_{0V})\Phi^{-1}(u_D) \quad (20.7)$$

In our application, estimation of the parameters follows the parametric method proposed by Brave and Walstrum (2014) by using the *MARGTE* command (see also Carneiro, Heckman, and Vytlacil, 2009, for a description of the different estimation techniques that allow the computation of treatment effects in the context of *essential heterogeneity* models). Under the assumption of joint normality, σ_{1V} and σ_{0V} are the inverse Mills ratio coefficients. They are estimated separately along with the other parameters in the two following equations:

$$E(Y|X = x, D = 1, P(Z) = p) = \alpha_1 + \beta + X\beta_1 + \sigma_{1V}\left(-\frac{\phi(\Phi^{-1}(p))}{p}\right) \quad (20.8)$$

$$E(Y|X = x, D = 0, P(Z) = p) = \alpha_0 + X\beta_0 + \sigma_{0V}\left(\frac{\phi(\Phi^{-1}(p))}{1 - p}\right) \quad (20.9)$$

to obtain the MTE values. Using the estimated propensity score:

$$MTE(X = x, U_D = u_D) = \alpha_1 + \beta - \alpha_0 + (\beta_1 - \beta_0)x' + (\hat{\sigma}_{1V} - \hat{\sigma}_{0V})\Phi^{-1}(u_D) \quad (20.10)$$

Intuitively, how the MTE evolves over the range of U_D informs us about the heterogeneity in treatment effects among oil producers. That is, how the coefficient β is correlated with the treatment indicator D in (20.1). Equivalently, the estimated MTE shows how the increment in the marginal firm value, risk, and performance by going from choice 0 to choice 1 varies with different quantiles of the unobserved component V in the choice equation. In our case, whether MTE increases or decreases with U_D tells us whether the coefficient β in (20.1) is negatively or positively correlated with the latent tendency of using high-intensity hedging for oil production.

20.3 US OIL PRODUCERS

20.3.1 Sample Construction

A preliminary list of 413 US oil producers with the primary Standard Industrial Classification (SIC) code 1311 (crude petroleum and natural gas) was extracted from Bloomberg. Only firms that met the following criteria were retained: they have at least five years of oil reserve data during the period 1998–2010, their 10-K and 10-Q reports are available from the EDGAR website, and the firm is covered by Compustat. The filtering process produced a final sample of 150 firms with an unbalanced panel of 6,326 firm-quarter observations.

Data on these firms' financial and operational characteristics were gathered from several sources. Data regarding financial characteristics were taken from the Compustat quarterly dataset held by Wharton Research Data Services (WRDS). Other items related to institutional shareholding were taken from the Thomson Reuters dataset maintained by WRDS. Data related to oil and gas reserves and production quantities were taken from Bloomberg's annual data set, and subsequently verified and supplemented by data hand-collected directly from 10-K annual reports. Quarterly data about oil producers' hedging activities were hand-collected from 10-K and 10-Q reports.

20.3.2 Descriptive Statistics

Descriptive statistics were computed for the pooled quarterly dataset. Table 20.2 gives the mean, median, first quartile, third quartile, and standard deviations for the 150 US oil producers in the sample. Table 20.2 shows that oil producers report average earnings per share from operations of $8 with a highly right-skewed distribution. Oil producers in the sample invest on average the equivalent of 13% of their net property, plant, and equipment in capital expenditure; however, there is a wide variation. Interestingly, statistics also indicate that oil producers have high leverage ratios and maintain high levels of liquidity reserves, as measured by cash on hand

TABLE 20.2 Summary statistics for firms' financial and operational characteristics

Variables	Obs	Mean	Median	First quartile	Third quartile	STD
EPS from operations	6,127	8.181	0.090	−0.030	0.490	284.693
Investment opportunities	6,295	0.129	0.062	0.035	0.107	2.333
Leverage	6,044	0.516	0.523	0.342	0.659	0.285
Liquidity	6,069	1.555	0.275	0.079	0.850	5.334
Dividend payout	6,326	0.265	0.000	0.000	1.000	0.442
Oil reserves (in log)	6,180	2.135	2.158	0.151	4.041	2.882
Institutional ownership	6,326	0.337	0.216	0.000	0.687	0.345
Geographic diversification (oil)	6,178	0.101	0.000	0.000	0.000	0.233
Geographic diversification (gas)	6,180	0.063	0.000	0.000	0.000	0.183
Oil price volatility	6,318	3.280	2.371	1.608	3.655	2.829
Oil spot price	6,318	49.265	43.450	26.800	69.890	28.044
Oil production risk	6,246	0.272	0.169	0.080	0.344	0.302
Gas hedge ratio	6,326	0.070	0.000	0.000	0.070	0.153
Gas spot price	6,318	5.139	4.830	3.070	6.217	2.617
Gas price volatility	6,318	0.733	0.500	0.289	1.111	0.560
Gas reserves (in log)	6,196	4.503	4.664	2.764	6.396	2.836
Gas production risk	6,222	0.273	0.181	0.092	0.360	0.281
CEO % of stockholding	6,028	0.004	0.000	0.000	0.002	0.017
CEO number of options (× 10,000)	6,326	17.439	0.000	0.000	12.000	68.176
Number of analysts	6,326	5.108	2.000	0.000	8.000	6.914

Note: This table provides financial and operational statistics for the 150 US oil producers, and oil price and volatility for the 1998 to 2010 period. See Table 20.1 for more details on the construction of these variables.

and short-term investments. The average leverage ratio liquidity is about 52%, and the average quick ratio (liquidity) is about 1.55. One-fourth of the oil producers in the sample pay dividends. The mean quantity of developed and undeveloped oil (gas) reserves, in log, is 2.135 (4.503), which corresponds to a quantity of about 276 million barrels of oil for oil reserves and 1,504 billion cubic feet for gas reserves.

The Herfindahl indices, which measure geographical dispersion of daily oil and gas production, have an average value of 0.10 for oil and 0.063 for gas, indicating that oil and gas–producing activities are highly concentrated in the same region. Table 20.2 further shows relatively stable oil and gas production quantities, with an average coefficient of variation in daily production of 0.27 for both oil and gas. Institutional ownership has a mean (median) of about 34% (22%), and varies from no institutional ownership for the first quartile to higher than 69% for the top quartile. On average, the CEO holds 0.4% of the oil producer's outstanding common shares and about 17,500 stock options, albeit with substantial dispersion as measured by the standard deviation. The mean (median) number of analysts following an oil producer on a quarterly basis is 5 (2) analysts.

Table 20.3 provides pairwise correlations of oil producers' characteristics. Except for the correlation coefficients for the number of analysts with respectively oil reserves, gas reserves and institutional ownership, all of the pairwise correlations are below 0.5.

20.3.3 Oil Hedging Activity

Oil hedging occurred in 2,607 firm-quarters, which represents 41.21% of the firm-quarters in the sample. Following Haushalter (2000), the oil hedging ratio for each fiscal year is calculated by dividing the hedged notional quantities by the predicted oil production quantities. We collect data relative to hedged notional quantities for each fiscal year from the current year to five years ahead. Oil production quantities are predicted for each fiscal year based on the daily oil production realized in the current fiscal year. Table 20.4 shows descriptive statistics for these hedging ratios by horizon and indicates an average hedging ratio for near-term exposures (i.e., hedging ratio for the current fiscal year, (*HR0*) of around 46%. Oil hedging for subsequent fiscal years is decreasing steadily across horizons in terms of extent and frequency. Figure 20.2 provides time series plots of median hedge ratios and shows that hedging intensities follow a median reverting process, particularly for near-term hedges (*HR0*). Figure 20.2 also indicates higher variability in the hedging intensities for subsequent years (*HR1* and *HR2*).

This figure plots how the median hedging ratios for the aggregate oil hedging portfolio evolved over time from quarter 4–1997 to 4–2010. *HR0* stands for the hedging ratio of the current fiscal year, *HR1* for the subsequent year and *HR2* for two years ahead.

20.3.4 Univariate Tests

Table 20.5 reports tests of differences between the means and medians of independent variables by oil hedging intensity. We classify the hedging ratios for the oil production over the current fiscal year (*HR0*) as (1) positive low hedging intensity, that is, below the 25th percentile, which corresponds to a hedging ratio of around 24%, and (2) high hedging intensity, which exceeds the 75th percentile and corresponds to a hedging ratio of around 64%. We also create a dummy variable that takes the value of 0 for low hedging intensity and 1 for high hedging intensity. The means are

TABLE 20.3 Correlation matrix

	EPS from operations	Investment opportunities	Leverage	Liquidity	Dividend payout	Oil reserves (in log)	Institutional ownership	Geographic diversification (oil)	Geographic diversification (gas)	Oil production risk
EPS from operations	1									
Investment opportunities	−0.000442	1								
Leverage	0.00731	−0.0233	1							
Liquidity	−0.00298	0.0261	−0.314***	1						
Dividend payout	−0.00862	−0.0560***	0.0486***	−0.0587***	1					
Oil reserves (in log)	0.00536	−0.0840***	0.239***	−0.231***	0.518***	1				
Institutional ownership	−0.0164	−0.0398**	0.168***	−0.174***	0.308***	0.575***	1			
Geographic diversification (oil)	−0.00573	−0.0438***	0.0258	−0.0660***	0.404***	0.525***	0.278***	1		
Geographic diversification (gas)	−0.00436	−0.0382**	0.0247	−0.0631***	0.353***	0.475***	0.185***	0.753***	1	
Oil production risk	−0.0105	0.118***	−0.00154	0.0422**	−0.193***	−0.300***	−0.175***	−0.159***	−0.147***	1
Gas hedge ratio	−0.00793	0.0284*	0.167***	−0.105***	0.0854***	0.0693***	0.0757***	−0.0859***	−0.104***	0.0719***
Gas reserves (in log)	0.00625	−0.0627***	0.335***	−0.312***	0.538***	0.759***	0.583***	0.352***	0.297***	−0.229***
Gas production risk	−0.0147	0.137***	−0.0757***	0.0526***	−0.245***	−0.232***	−0.219***	−0.173***	−0.165***	0.441***
CEO % of stockholding	−0.00427	−0.00617	−0.00320	−0.0326*	−0.0704***	−0.0287*	−0.0376**	−0.0372**	−0.0224	0.0349**
CEO number of options (× 10,000)	−0.00477	−0.0118	0.0226	−0.0427**	0.0260	0.0690***	0.0453***	0.0513***	0.0379**	0.0160
Number of analysts	−0.0116	−0.0569***	0.149***	−0.174***	0.493***	0.688***	0.647***	0.480***	0.346***	−0.194***
Oil price volatility	−0.00968	0.00680	−0.00430	0.0175	0.00975	0.0232	0.145***	−0.00447	0.00170	0.0306*
Oil spot price	−0.0149	0.0147	−0.0323*	0.0331*	0.00413	0.0375**	0.230***	0.00596	0.00365	0.0320*
Gas spot price	−0.0123	0.0585***	−0.0366**	0.0144	−0.0100	0.00497	0.149***	0.0136	−0.00450	0.0442***
Gas price volatility	−0.00973	0.0588***	−0.0335*	0.0168	−0.0184	0.00797	0.107***	0.00985	−0.00590	0.0167

	Gas hedge ratio	Gas reserves (in log)	Gas production risk	CEO % of stockholding	CEO number of options (× 10,000)	Number of analysts	Oil price volatility	Oil spot price	Gas spot price	Gas price volatility
Gas hedge ratio	1									
Gas reserves (in log)	0.215***	1								
Gas production risk	0.0554***	−0.269***	1							
CEO % of stockholding	−0.0109	−0.0338*	0.00917	1						
CEO number of options (× 10,000)	−0.00556	0.0721***	0.00593	0.815***	1					
Number of analysts	0.0813***	0.733***	−0.266***	−0.0856***	0.0440***	1				
Oil price volatility	0.182***	0.0307*	0.0500***	−0.0586***	−0.0259	0.110***	1			
Oil spot price	0.254***	0.0378**	0.0721***	−0.0758***	−0.0280*	0.150***	0.573***	1		
Gas spot price	0.0988***	0.0132	0.0749***	−0.00896	0.0362**	0.0904***	0.378***	0.635***	1	
Gas price volatility	0.0601***	0.0117	0.0469***	−0.00421	0.0292*	0.0553***	0.273***	0.388***	0.605***	1

Note: $^{*}p < 0.05$, $^{**}p < 0.01$, $^{***}p < 0.001$.

TABLE 20.4 Summary statistics for oil hedging ratios by horizon

Variables	Obs	Mean	Median	First quartile	Third quartile	STD
HR0	2,587	46.070%	44.564%	24.315%	63.889%	27.876%
HR1	1,723	38.328%	36.043%	16.437%	54.737%	27.338%
HR2	907	30.848%	26.798%	9.526%	46.392%	25.680%
HR3	431	27.352%	19.946%	7.340%	43.654%	25.777%
HR4	185	23.254%	14.686%	7.215%	33.860%	24.589%
HR5	61	21.887%	19.685%	4.563%	38.933%	18.171%

Note: This table reports summary statistics for oil hedging ratios (HR) by horizon (from the current fiscal year *HR0* to five fiscal years ahead *HR5*).

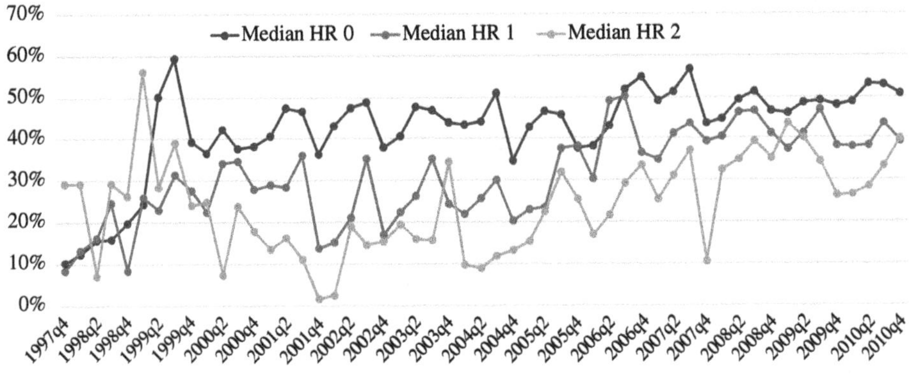

FIGURE 20.2 Median oil hedging ratios by horizon.

compared by using a t-test that assumes unequal variances; the medians are compared by using a non-parametric Wilcoxon rank–sum Z-test.

The univariate analysis reveals considerable differences in oil producers' characteristics between hedging intensities. Results show that oil producers with less operational profitability and higher investment opportunities hedge to a greater extent. These findings corroborate the prediction of Froot, Sharfstein, and Stein (1993) that firms hedge to protect their investment programs' internal financing. Results further indicate that oil hedging intensity is positively related to the level of financial constraints. In fact, oil producers with high hedging intensities have higher leverage ratios, lower liquidity levels, and pay smaller dividends. These findings corroborate the conjecture that financially constrained firms hedge more in order to decrease their default probability and increase their value. Univariate tests also show that oil producers that hedge to higher extents have lower oil and gas reserves, higher production uncertainty, and are less diversified geographically, thus suggesting that operational constraints motivate more hedging.

Regarding risk behavior and corporate governance, we find that managerial stockholdings are, on average, greater for oil producers using high-intensity oil hedging. Managers with greater equity stakes are poorly diversified (i.e., their human capital and wealth depend on firm performance) and tend to protect themselves by directing their firms to engage in risk management, as Smith and Stulz (1985) advance. The mean comparison for managerial options holding reveals no significant differences across hedging intensities. However, the median comparison indicates that managerial option holding is greater for low-intensity hedgers. This finding

TABLE 20.5 Oil producers' characteristics by oil hedging intensity

	(1) High quartile			(2) Low quartile			(1) vs. (2)
Variables	Obs	Mean	Median	Obs	Mean	Median	*t*-Stat Z-score
EPS from operations	626	0.257	0.180	631	0.425	0.370	1.889* 5.769***
Investment opportunities	629	0.099	0.062	632	0.080	0.059	−2.170** −0.330
Leverage	627	0.655	0.621	632	0.548	0.530	−8.449*** −10.245***
Liquidity	631	0.335	0.104	632	0.484	0.211	2.240** 8.057***
Dividend payout	641	0.282	0.000	632	0.523	1.000	9.045*** 8.778***
Oil reserves (in log)	641	3.498	3.464	632	4.137	4.292	6.384*** 5.600***
Institutional ownership	641	0.473	0.511	632	0.578	0.726	5.768*** 5.287***
Geographic diversification (oil)	641	0.046	0.000	632	0.227	0.000	13.997*** 12.662***
Geographic diversification (gas)	635	0.028	0.000	632	0.135	0.000	10.857*** 11.431***
Oil production risk	641	0.259	0.167	632	0.195	0.129	−4.816*** −3.940***
Gas hedge ratio	641	0.229	0.163	632	0.040	0.000	−17.498*** −17.556***
Gas reserves (in log)	632	5.623	5.586	630	6.364	6.382	7.245*** 8.043***
Gas production risk	641	0.268	0.193	632	0.193	0.142	−6.185*** −7.113***
CEO % of stockholding	626	0.007	0.000	630	0.003	0.000	−2.307** 2.755***
CEO number of options (in log)	641	30.123	0.000	632	20.798	6.000	−1.524 4.196***
Number of analysts	641	6.566	4.000	632	10.710	9.500	9.500*** 9.262***

corroborates Smith and Stulz's (1985) conjecture that risk-averse managers with higher option holdings will prefer less (or even no) hedging to increase the utility value of their options due to the convexity of the option's payoff. However, this depends on the moneyness of the option contracts. Looking at institutional ownership and the number of analysts, we find that they are, on average, lower for users with higher hedge intensities, suggesting that oil producers may engage in more hedging to alleviate problems related to weak governance and monitoring, and information asymmetry. With the exception of managerial stockholding, the comparison of medians gives the same results.

Table 20.6 reports tests of differences between the means and medians of dependent variables by oil hedging intensity. Our dependent variables are measures of firm value, riskiness, and profitability, using namely Tobin's q, systematic risk, idiosyncratic risk, oil beta or sensitivity to oil price fluctuations, and return on equity

TABLE 20.6 Oil producers' value and risk measures by oil hedging intensity

	(1) High quartile			(2) Low quartile			(1) vs. (2)
Variables	Obs	Mean	Median	Obs	Mean	Median	*t*-Stat Z-score
Tobin's q (in log)	615	0.339	0.302	629	0.386	0.376	2.405** 3.031***
Systematic risk	564	0.988	0.980	615	1.094	1.079	2.536** 2.626***
Oil beta	564	0.221	0.209	615	0.213	0.210	−0.609 −0.682
Idiosyncratic risk	564	0.026	0.021	615	0.025	0.019	−1.973** −3.768***
Return on equity	630	−0.018	0.025	624	−0.001	0.031	0.662 2.908***

(see Table 20.1 for more details on the construction of these variables). In short, we find that oil producers using high oil hedging intensities have lower firm value as measured by the Tobin's q, lower systematic risk, and greater idiosyncratic risk. The comparison of medians indicates that high-intensity hedgers have lower profitability as measured by the return on equity. Results show no significant differences in terms of the sensitivity to oil price fluctuations as measured by the oil beta.

20.4 MULTIVARIATE RESULTS

In Table 20.7, we estimate the choice equation by a probit model, leading to the estimation of the propensity score of using high-intensity oil hedging. The dependent variable is a dummy variable that takes the value of 1 for high-intensity hedging and 0 for low-intensity hedging, as defined previously. Regressors in the choice equation are our candidate instrument (the change in the Kilian index) and the set of control variables presented above. The results show that the Kilian index appears to be a strong predictor of hedging intensity choice, with an economically and statistically significant negative coefficient, suggesting that oil producers tend to use low-intensity hedging in periods of increasing aggregate demand for industrial commodities. This occurs because crude oil prices and, consequently, derivative prices are more likely to increase when driven by vigorous real economic activity. We also observe that many other firm variables are statistically significant, with signs consistent with risk management theory such as leverage, liquidity, dividend payout, oil reserves, geo-diversification, and market variables used as controls.

20.4.1 Firm Value

Table 20.8 reports the results of the outcome equation's estimation with respect to firm value. The output in Table 20.8 gives the estimations for both the treated and untreated groups.[3] The outcome equation also indicates the average treatment effect

[3]The treated group consists of high-intensity hedgers, whereas the untreated group consists of low-intensity hedgers. We obtain the parametric normal approximation of the MTE with bootstrapped standard errors corrected for within-firm clustering. We run 500 replications.

TABLE 20.7 First step of the essential heterogeneity models

	(1)	(2)	(3)	(4)	(5)
	Dependent variable is a dummy variable that takes the value of 1(0) when the hedging ratio is among the higher (lower) quartile				
Variables	Firm value	ROE	Systematic risk	Oil beta	Idiosyncratic risk
Δ Kilian index	−0.5910**	−0.6733**	−0.6283**	−0.6283**	−0.6283**
	(0.301)	(0.305)	(0.307)	(0.307)	(0.307)
EPS from operations	−0.0117	−0.0276	−0.0110	−0.0110	−0.0110
	(0.033)	(0.034)	(0.034)	(0.034)	(0.034)
Investment opportunities	0.3001	0.2723	0.2070	0.2070	0.2070
	(0.428)	(0.430)	(0.433)	(0.433)	(0.433)
Leverage	0.9687***	1.0191***	1.1282***	1.1282***	1.1282***
	(0.238)	(0.239)	(0.266)	(0.266)	(0.266)
Liquidity	−0.1451***	−0.1482***	−0.1449***	−0.1449***	−0.1449***
	(0.049)	(0.049)	(0.049)	(0.049)	(0.049)
Dividend payout	−0.3878***	−0.4002***	−0.3963***	−0.3963***	−0.3963***
	(0.115)	(0.115)	(0.116)	(0.116)	(0.116)
Oil reserves	0.2766***	0.2719***	0.2842***	0.2842***	0.2842***
	(0.040)	(0.041)	(0.042)	(0.042)	(0.042)
Institutional ownership	0.1037	0.1114	0.0197	0.0197	0.0197
	(0.170)	(0.171)	(0.175)	(0.175)	(0.175)
Geo diversification (oil)	−1.1723***	−1.1766***	−1.1884***	−1.1884***	−1.1884***
	(0.265)	(.266)	(0.266)	(0.266)	(0.266)
Geo diversification (gas)	−1.3415***	−1.3287***	−1.3203***	−1.3203***	−1.3203***
	(0.378)	(0.379)	(0.379)	(0.379)	(0.379)
Oil volatility	−0.0576***	−0.0529**	−0.0613***	−0.0613***	−0.0613***
	(0.021)	(0.021)	(0.021)	(0.021)	(0.021)
Oil spot price	0.0068***	0.0069***	0.0067**	0.0067**	0.0067**
	(0.002)	(.002)	(0.002)	(0.002)	(0.002)
Oil production risk	0.2000	0.1964	0.2490	0.2490	0.2490
	(0.239)	(0.239)	(0.244)	(0.244)	(0.244)
Gas hedging ratio	4.6209***	4.5688***	4.5824***	4.5824***	4.5824***
	(0.401)	(0.402)	(0.405)	(0.405)	(0.405)
Gas spot price	−0.0164	−0.0138	−0.0192	−0.0192	−0.0192
	(0.026)	(0.026)	(0.026)	(0.026)	(0.026)
Gas volatility	0.0006	−0.0061	0.0070	0.0070	0.0070
	(0.098)	(0.099)	(0.100)	(0.100)	(0.100)
Gas reserves	−0.1096**	−0.1035**	−0.1402***	−0.1402***	−0.1402***
	(0.045)	(.045)	(0.047)	(0.047)	(0.047)
Gas production risk	−0.2050	−0.1562	−0.2894	−0.2894	−0.2894
	(0.265)	(0.268)	(0.272)	(0.272)	(0.272)
CEO % of stockholding	10.6998	10.5728	10.8800*	10.8800*	10.8800*
	(6.546)	(6.556)	(6.592)	(6.592)	(6.592)
CEO number of options	0.0018	0.0018	0.0018	0.0018	0.0018
	(0.001)	(0.001)	(0.001)	(0.001)	(0.001)
Number of analysts	−0.0231**	−0.0235**	−0.0155	−0.0155	−0.0155
	(0.009)	(.009)	(0.010)	(0.010)	(0.010)

(continued)

TABLE 20.7 (*Continued*)

	(1)	(2)	(3)	(4)	(5)
	Dependent variable is a dummy variable that takes the value of 1(0) when the hedging ratio is among the higher (lower) quartile				
Variables	Firm value	ROE	Systematic risk	Oil beta	Idiosyncratic risk
Constant	−1.0224***	−1.0801***	−0.9402***	−0.9402***	−0.9402***
	(0.278)	(0.281)	(0.287)	(0.287)	(0.287)
Observations	1,178	1,173	1,133	1,133	1,133
R squared	0.3190	0.3237	0.3177	0.3177	0.3177

Note: This table provides the results of the probit regressions corresponding to the first step of the essential heterogeneity model related to oil hedging extent choice. The dependent variable takes the value of 1 if the oil producer has high-intensity oil hedging and 0 if it has positive low-intensity oil hedging. High-intensity oil hedging exceeds the 75th percentile, which corresponds to a hedging ratio of 64% of the oil production for the current fiscal year, and low-intensity hedging is below the 25th percentile, which corresponds to a hedging ratio of 24%. The instrument variable used is the changes in the Kilian index. All the variables are defined in Table 20.1. Independent variables are included in lagged values (first lag). Standard errors are reported in parentheses. The superscripts ***, **, and * indicate statistical significance at the 1%, 5%, and 10% levels, respectively.

(ATE), which captures the expected average benefit associated with the inducement in the treatment (i.e., high-intensity hedging in our case), conditional on observable independent variables. The ATE coefficient is positive and highly statistically significant, meaning that observable factors influence firm value. Further, Table 20.8 shows that oil volatility is significantly related to Tobin's q for both user types, as well as gas spot price and number of analysts. The negative sign for oil price volatility indicates that investors prefer lower exposure to oil price fluctuations. This negative effect is statistically similar for the two groups.

Importantly, gas spot price is significantly negatively related to firm value for oil producers using high-intensity hedging only. When gas price is higher, investors tend to penalize oil producers with high-intensity hedging that do not allow them to benefit from this upward potential. Importantly, the propensity of non-inducement in high-intensity oil hedging is positively affected by the inverse Mills ratio (K variable), and the difference in the sigma coefficients is statistically significant. Similar results are observed for the significance of observable variables in Table 20.8 for the risk measures (systematic risk, idiosyncratic risk, and oil beta) and ROE, but the average treatment effect (ATE) of hedging with intensity is not statistically significant for oil beta and ROE.

The differences between firms can be greater when non-observable factors are considered. Applying the standard IV approach with the two groups reveals only the effect of observable differences on firm value. All firms are considered homogeneous (with respect to unobserved factors) in deriving an average hedging intensity effect (one coefficient) on firm value. With the marginal treatment effect (MTE) methodology, we may find that the marginal effect differs between firms that have to be categorized in either group (high versus low-intensity hedgers) by adding the possibility of self-selection explained by unobserved factors.

TABLE 20.8 Second–step of the essential heterogeneity models

	(1) Firm value		(2) Systematic risk		(3) Idiosyncratic risk		(4) Oil Beta		(5) ROE	
Variables	Treated	Untreated	Treated	Untreated	Treated	Untreated	Treated	Untreated	Treated	Untreated
EPS from operations	0.0013	−0.0021	0.0305**	0.0457**	0.0004	−0.0004	0.0032	−0.0027	0.0051	0.0068
	(0.008)	(0.011)	(0.015)	(0.022)	(0.001)	(0.001)	(0.006)	(0.007)	(0.021)	(0.025)
Investment opportunities	0.0427	0.2631	0.2029	−0.2217	−0.0017	−0.0112	−0.1090*	−0.0750	−0.1432	0.1957
	(0.215)	(0.240)	(0.134)	(0.290)	(0.004)	(0.008)	(0.056)	(0.130)	(0.528)	(0.127)
Leverage	0.0941	−0.2703	−0.0257	0.6315*	0.0254***	0.0379***	0.0174	0.1644	0.2391*	−0.0857
	(0.196)	(0.215)	(0.238)	(0.370)	(0.009)	(0.007)	(0.096)	(0.101)	(0.134)	(0.201)
Liquidity	0.0379	0.0679	−0.1322**	−0.0530	−0.0002	−0.0017	−0.0133	−0.0171	−0.0170	0.0331
	(0.039)	(0.050)	(0.059)	(0.068)	(0.002)	(0.001)	(0.028)	(0.022)	(0.023)	(0.027)
Dividend payout	0.1049	0.0343	−0.2486**	−0.3112**	−0.0058*	−0.0081**	−0.0732**	−0.1026**	0.0062	0.0535
	(0.074)	(0.085)	(0.100)	(0.121)	(0.004)	(0.003)	(0.034)	(0.046)	(0.048)	(0.057)
Oil reserves	−0.0593*	−0.0391	0.0181	0.1034	−0.0018	−0.0001	−0.0035	0.0403	0.0802***	0.0025
	(0.031)	(0.042)	(0.055)	(0.066)	(0.001)	(0.002)	(0.016)	(0.026)	(0.028)	(0.023)
Institutional ownership	0.1735*	0.1145	0.2306	0.1319	−0.0022	−0.0111***	0.0669	0.0486	0.0326	−0.0226
	(0.091)	(0.097)	(0.190)	(0.132)	(0.003)	(0.004)	(0.044)	(0.039)	(0.054)	(0.065)
Geo diversification (oil)	−0.0610	0.2242	0.4692	−0.5295**	0.0047	−0.0001	−0.0093	0.0193	−0.2029	0.0120
	(0.212)	(0.161)	(0.310)	(0.239)	(0.007)	(0.006)	(0.114)	(0.085)	(0.124)	(0.120)
Geo diversification (gas)	0.1857	0.0600	−0.6668	−0.1478	−0.0100	−0.0128	0.0353	−0.1382	−0.3187	0.0106
	(0.237)	(0.164)	(0.975)	(0.298)	(0.026)	(0.009)	(0.731)	(0.106)	(0.585)	(0.098)
Oil volatility	−0.0292***	−0.0229***	0.0235**	0.0011	0.0021***	0.0017***	−0.0033	−0.0062*	−0.0467**	−0.0291***
	(0.008)	(0.006)	(0.011)	(0.012)	(0.000)	(0.000)	(0.004)	(0.003)	(0.020)	(0.010)
Oil spot price	0.0001	−0.0003	0.0034**	0.0038**	−0.0000	0.0000	0.0015***	0.0024***	0.0026	−0.0008
	(0.001)	(0.001)	(0.002)	(0.002)	(0.000)	(0.000)	(0.001)	(0.001)	(0.002)	(0.001)
Oil production risk	0.0112	−0.1408	−0.0896	0.2582	−0.0019	0.0017	−0.0152	0.0920	−0.0113	−0.0882
	(0.126)	(0.209)	(0.171)	(0.263)	(0.004)	(0.006)	(0.051)	(0.097)	(0.103)	(0.139)
Gas hedging ratio	−0.2422	−1.2567**	−0.5909	1.7059	0.0118	0.0322	−0.0448	0.3048	0.4432**	−0.2406
	(0.310)	(0.623)	(0.472)	(1.040)	(0.021)	(0.029)	(0.192)	(0.466)	(0.222)	(0.587)
Gas spot price	0.0312***	0.0413***	0.0215	−0.0062	−0.0015***	−0.0016***	−0.0044	−0.0026	0.0104	0.0227***
	(0.010)	(0.008)	(0.018)	(0.013)	(0.000)	(0.000)	(0.004)	(0.004)	(0.014)	(0.008)
Gas volatility	0.0164	−0.0435**	−0.0922	0.0524	0.0017	0.0031**	−0.0576***	−0.0359**	−0.0277	−0.0281
	(0.020)	(0.021)	(0.062)	(0.073)	(0.001)	(0.001)	(0.022)	(0.018)	(0.058)	(0.028)

(continued)

TABLE 20.8 *(Continued)*

	(1) Firm value		(2) Systematic risk		(3) Idiosyncratic risk		(4) Oil Beta		(5) ROE	
Variables	**Treated**	**Untreated**	**Treated**	**Untreated**	**Treated**	**Untreated**	**Treated**	**Untreated**	**Treated**	**Untreated**
Gas reserves	−0.0614**	−0.0003	0.1264**	−0.0177	−0.0031**	−0.0034***	−0.0270	−0.0209	−0.0286	0.0003
	(0.029)	(0.034)	(0.051)	(0.052)	(0.001)	(0.001)	(0.019)	(0.014)	(0.021)	(0.017)
Gas production risk	−0.0547	0.0628	−0.2068	−0.2472	0.0064	−0.0084	0.0367	−0.0857	0.0478	−0.0261
	(0.112)	(0.195)	(0.223)	(0.271)	(0.004)	(0.007)	(0.056)	(0.108)	(0.090)	(0.170)
CEO % of stockholding	−2.1151	0.8073	−7.7093	−1.9575	−0.0494	0.2422*	−4.7087**	1.4543	1.9361	−7.8252
	(4.411)	(4.332)	(6.837)	(6.221)	(0.129)	(0.137)	(1.968)	(2.524)	(3.248)	(7.453)
CEO number of options	0.0002	−0.0006	0.0034**	0.0010	0.0000	−0.0000	0.0006	0.0004	0.0004	0.0004
	(0.001)	(0.001)	(0.001)	(0.001)	(0.000)	(0.000)	(0.000)	(0.000)	(0.001)	(0.000)
Number of analysts	0.0153***	0.0142***	−0.0321***	−0.0138*	−0.0001	−0.0000	0.0043	−0.0007	−0.0016	−0.0001
	(0.005)	(0.005)	(0.008)	(0.007)	(0.000)	(0.000)	(0.003)	(0.003)	(0.004)	(0.004)
Constant	0.6511**	0.0650	0.2052	0.9264***	0.0307***	0.0468***	0.3455**	0.1459*	−0.5894**	0.0619
	(0.262)	(0.176)	(0.342)	(0.248)	(0.011)	(0.007)	(0.156)	(0.076)	(0.239)	(0.125)
K	0.1231	0.5185***	−0.0720	−0.7773**	−0.0073	−0.0168*	−0.0180	−0.1556	−0.3415***	0.0294
	(0.141)	(0.185)	(0.228)	(0.357)	(0.009)	(0.009)	(0.092)	(0.140)	(0.117)	(0.186)
$\hat{\sigma}_{1V} - \hat{\sigma}_{0V}$	−0.3954*		0.7053*		0.0096		0.1377		−0.3709*	
	(0.236)		(0.414)		(0.013)		(0.167)		(0.211)	
ATE	0.4970**		−0.7900**		−0.0238**		−0.1424		−0.2098	
	(0.207)		(0.393)		(0.011)		(0.162)		(0.218)	
Obs	1,193		1,148		1,148		1,148		1,188	

Note: This table provides the results of the second-step regressions (outcome equation) of the *essential heterogeneity* models. The dependent variables are 1) firm value represented by the Tobin's q, calculated by the ratio of the market value of equity, plus the book value of debt, plus the book value of preferred shares to the book value of total assets, 2) firms' systematic risk represented by its market beta, 3) firms' idiosyncratic risk represented by the standard deviation of the residuals, 4) oil beta representing the sensitivity of firms' stock returns to oil price fluctuations. Systematic risk, idiosyncratic risk, and oil beta are estimated simultaneously from a Fama-French 4-factor model supplemented by the changes in oil and gas 1-month futures contract prices. All the variables are defined in Table 20.1. Independent variables are included in lagged values (first lag). K is $\left(-\frac{\phi(\Phi^{-1}(p))}{p}\right)$ for the treated group (see equation (20.8)) and $\left(\frac{\phi(\Phi^{-1}(p))}{1-p}\right)$ for the untreated group (see equation (20.9)). $\hat{\sigma}_{1V}$ ($\hat{\sigma}_{0V}$) is K's coefficient for the treated (untreated) group. The term *ATE* stands for the average treatment effect. Treated is for users of high-intensity hedging, and untreated is for users of positive low-intensity hedging. Bootstrapped standard errors clustered at the firm level using 500 repetitions are reported in parentheses. The superscripts ***, **, and * indicate statistical significance at the 1%, 5%, and 10% levels, respectively.

Figure 20.3 plots the estimated MTEs with 95% confidence intervals, evaluated at the means of the independent (observable) characteristics of oil producers over different quantiles of the unobserved resistance to use high-intensity hedging (namely, U_D). The ATE is also plotted (dashed line) as a reference point. In addition, estimated MTEs on firm value with their respective standard errors are reported in Table 20A.1 for different evaluation quantile points of U_D, from 0.01 to 0.99. Estimated MTEs in the lower percentiles are positive and statistically significant. Figure 20.3 also shows that estimated MTEs are decreasing with different quantiles of U_D, implying that the marginal Tobin's *q* is highest for oil producers that are more likely to use high-intensity hedging (i.e., lower values of the unobserved component U_D). Table 20A.1 shows that estimated MTEs range from 1.42% for high propensities to using high-intensity hedging to −0.42% (not significant) for high propensities to using low-intensity hedging. Overall, our results show that marginal firm value increases with the propensity to use hedging, or equivalently, increases with the propensity to use high-intensity hedging.

In conclusion, the curvature of the depicted MTEs in Figure 20.3 with respect to the decision processes' different quantiles of unobserved components when using high-intensity hedging exhibits substantial heterogeneity in marginal treatment effects. This provides evidence of selection into treatment or a self-selection bias, indicating that the causal effects of the hedging intensity structure on firm value also vary across oil producers due to unobserved factors.

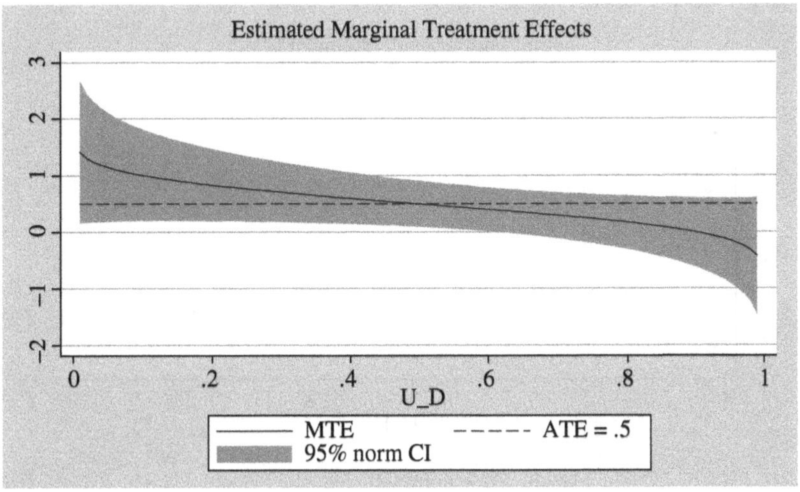

FIGURE 20.3 Estimated MTEs for firm value.
This figure plots the estimated MTE for firm value, measured by the Tobin's *q* with respect to the common support of the unobserved resistance among US oil producers to using high-intensity hedging represented by U_D. Average treatment effect (ATE) and 95% normal confidence interval are also plotted.

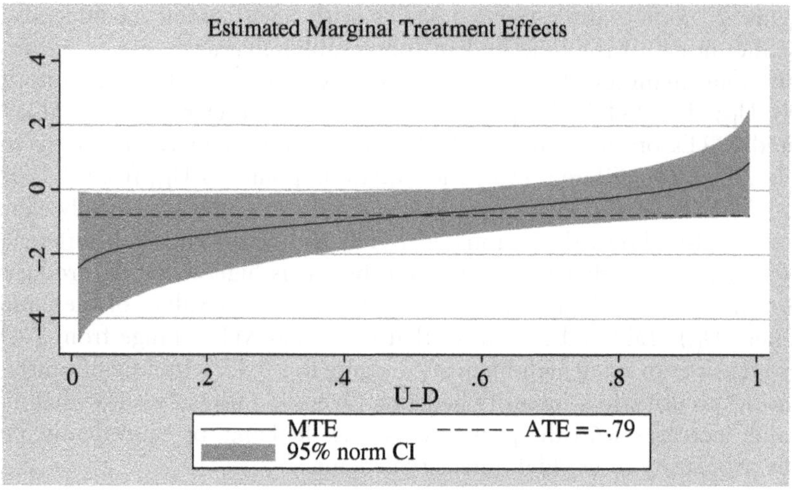

FIGURE 20.4 Estimated MTEs for firm systematic risk.
Figure 20.4 plots the estimated MTE for firm systematic risk with respect to the common support of the unobserved resistance among US oil producers to using high-intensity hedging represented by U_D. Average treatment effect (ATE) and 95% normal confidence interval are also plotted.

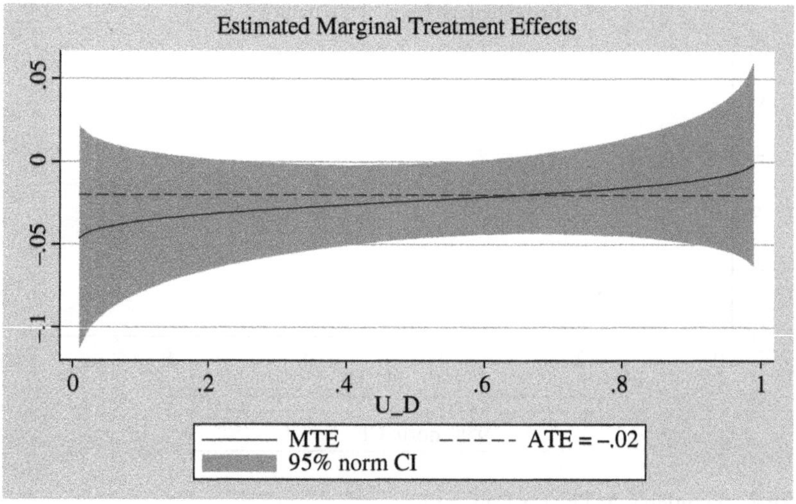

FIGURE 20.5 Estimated MTEs for firm idiosyncratic risk.
Figure 20.5 plots the estimated MTE for firm idiosyncratic risk with respect to the common support of the unobserved resistance among US oil producers to using high-intensity hedging represented by U_D. Average treatment effect (ATE) and 95% normal confidence interval are also plotted.

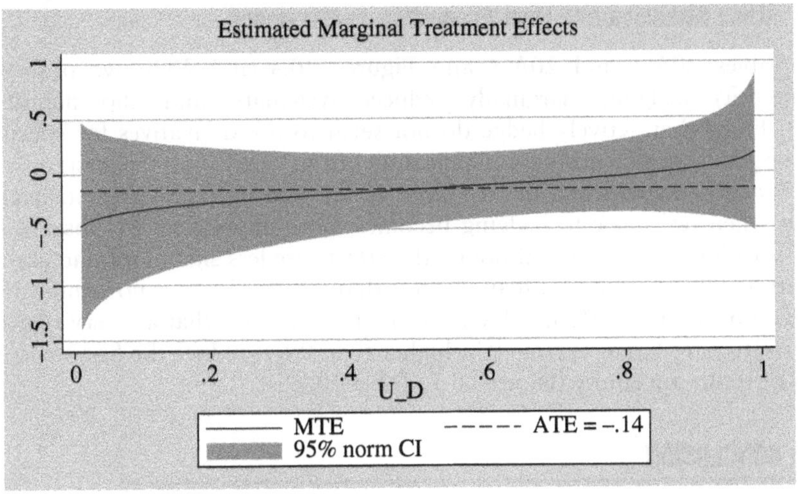

FIGURE 20.6 Estimated MTEs for oil beta.
Figure 20.6 plots the estimated MTE for firm oil beta with respect to the common support of the unobserved resistance among US oil producers to using high-intensity hedging represented by U_D. Average treatment effect (ATE) and 95% normal confidence interval are also plotted.

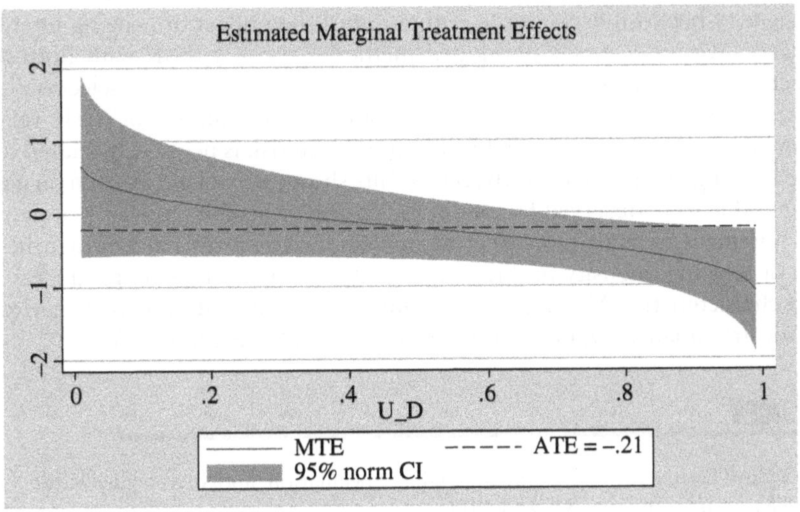

FIGURE 20.7 Estimated MTEs for ROE.
Figure 20.7 plots the estimated MTE for a firm's ROE with respect to the common support of the unobserved resistance among US oil producers to using high-intensity hedging represented by U_D. Average treatment effect (ATE) and 95% normal confidence interval are also plotted.

20.4.2 Firm Riskiness and Firm Accounting Performance

From Tables 20A.2 and 20A.3 and Figures 20.4 and 20.5, we observe that high-intensity hedging marginally reduces systematic and idiosyncratic risks (MTE). Firms that actively hedge do not seem to use derivatives for speculation. The marginal coefficients vary significantly from −2.4% at the first quartile to −0.60% at the sixtieth quartile in Table 20A.2 and become non-statistically significant when resistance to hedging becomes more important. We observe similar results for idiosyncratic risk, although the effects are less significant and are mainly concentrated between the tenth and sixteenth quartiles. There is no significant MTE for the oil beta (Figure 20.6, Table 20A.4), and managers that are very reluctant to use derivatives to larger extents (U_D higher than 0.64) reduce the firm's accounting results or return on equity (Figure 20.7, Table 20A.5).

20.5 CONCLUSION

A substantial body of theoretical corporate risk management literature has increased our understanding of the motivations, virtues, and value implications of hedging. This literature derives its theoretical and empirical predictions based on the extent of, or participation in, hedging activities. In this study, we go beyond the classical questions in the corporate hedging literature to investigate the real marginal effects of hedging activities on firm value and risk. We also measure the average effects obtained by computing the mean of the marginal effects.

To obtain further insight into the dynamics of these real implications, we consider heterogeneity between firms in the evaluation of the impact of hedging intensity on firm value. We use a newly developed methodology that deals with both sources of selection bias, namely, selection on unobservable variables and selection on gain into treatment. Our results show that marginal firm value is positively related to more intense hedging activities, while marginal firm risk is negatively related to more intense hedging. More importantly, our results show an evident selection on gain into treatment due to unobserved factors in the choice of hedging intensity design (high- versus low-intensity hedging). Selection on gain into treatment means that the causal effects of hedging intensity on firm value and risk vary across oil producers due to hidden characteristics. We also obtain significant results with the average treatment effect for firm financial value, idiosyncratic risk, and systematic risk.

REFERENCES

Adam, T., and Fernando, C.S., 2006. "Hedging, Speculation, and Shareholder Value." *Journal of Financial Economics* 81, 283–309.

Allayannis, G. and Ofek, E., 2001. "Exchange Rate Exposure, Hedging, and the Use of Foreign Currency Derivatives." *Journal of International Money and Finance* 20, 273–296.

Allayannis, G. and Weston, J.P., 2001. "The Use of Foreign Currency Derivatives and Firm Market Value." *Review of Financial Studies* 14, 243–276.

Aretz, K. and Bartram, S.M., 2010. "Corporate Hedging and Shareholder Value." *Journal of Financial Research* 33, 317–371.

Bartram, S.M., Brown, G.W., and Conrad, J., 2011. "The Effects of Derivatives on Firm Risk And Value." *Journal of Financial and Quantitative Analysis* 46, 967–999.

Blouin, J., Core, J.E., and Guay, W., 2010. "Have the Tax Benefits of Debt Been Overestimated?" *Journal of Financial Economics* 98, 195–213.

Brave, S. and Walstrum, T., 2014. "Estimating Marginal Treatment Effects Using Parametric and Semiparametric Methods." *Stata Journal* 14, 191–217.

Carhart, M.M., 1997. "On Persistence in Mutual Fund Performance." *Journal of Finance* 52, 57–82.

Carneiro, P., Heckman, J.J., and Vytlacil, E.J., 2009. "Evaluating Marginal Policies and the Average Treatment for Individuals at the Margin." NBER working paper 15211, National Bureau for Economic Research, Cambridge, MA.

Carter, D.A., Rogers, D., and Simkins, B.J., 2006. "Does Hedging Affect Firm Value? Evidence from the US Airline Industry." *Financial Management* 35, 53–87.

Choi, J.J., Mao, C.X., and Upadhyay, A.D., 2013. "Corporate Risk Management Under Information Asymmetry." *Journal of Business Finance and Accounting* 40, 239–271.

Dionne, G. and Garand, M., 2003. "Risk Management Determinants Affecting Firms' Values in the Gold Mining Industry: New Empirical Results." *Economic Letters* 79, 43–52.

Dionne, G., Gueyie, J.P., and Mnasri, M., 2018. "Dynamic Corporate Risk Management: Motivations and Real Implications." *Journal of Banking and Finance* 95, 97–111.

Dionne, G., Maalaoui Chun, O., and Triki, T., 2018. "*Risk Management and Corporate Governance: The Importance of Independence and Financial Knowledge.*" Working paper, Canada Research Chair in Risk Management, HEC Montréal, Montreal, Canada.

Dionne, G., and Triki, T., 2013. "On Risk Management Determinants: What Really Matters?" *European Journal of Finance* 19, 145–164.

Fama, E.F., and French, K.R., 1993. "Common Risk Factors in the Returns on Stocks and Bonds." *Journal of Financial Economics* 33, 3–56.

Fauver, L. and Naranjo, A., 2010. "Derivative Usage and Firm Value: The Influence of Agency Costs and Monitoring Problems." *Journal of Corporate Finance* 16, 719–735.

Froot, K.A., Scharfstein, D., and Stein, J., 1993. "Risk Management: Coordinating Corporate Investment and Financing Policies." *Journal of Finance* 48, 1629–1658.

Gay, G.D., Lin, C.M., and Smith, S.D., 2011. "Corporate Derivatives Use and the Cost of Equity." *Journal of Banking and Finance* 35, 1491–1506.

Guay, W.R., 1999. "The Impact of Derivatives on Firm Risk: An Empirical Examination of New Derivative Users." *Journal of Accounting and Economics* 26, 319–351.

Guay, W.R. and Kothari, S.P., 2003. "How Much Do Firms Hedge with Derivatives?" *Journal of Financial Economics* 70, 423–461.

Haushalter, D., 2000. "Financing Policy, Basis Risk, and Corporate Hedging: Evidence from Oil and Gas Producers." *Journal of Finance* 55, 107–152.

Heckman, J.J., Urzua, S., and Vytlacil, E.J., 2006. "Understanding Instrumental Variables in Models with Essential Heterogeneity." *Review of Economics and Statistics* 88, 389–432.

Hentschel, L. and Kothari, S.P., 2001. "Are Corporations Reducing or Taking Risks with Derivatives?" *Journal of Financial and Quantitative Analysis* 36, 93–118.

Hoyt, R.E. and Liebenberg, P., 2015. "Evidence of the Value of Enterprise Risk Management." *Journal of Applied Corporate Finance* 27, 1, 41–47.

Jin, Y. and Jorion, P., 2006. "Firm Value and Hedging: Evidence from U.S. Oil and Gas Producers." *Journal of Finance* 61, 893–919.

Kilian, L., 2009. "Not All Oil Price Shocks Are Alike: Disentangling Demand and Supply Shocks in the Crude Oil Market." *American Economic Review* 99, 1053–1069.

Mincer J., 1974. *Schooling, Experience and Earnings*. New York: National Bureau of Economic Research.

Mnasri, M., Dionne, G., and Gueyie, J.P., 2017. "The Use of Nonlinear Hedging Strategies by US Oil Producers: Motivations And Implications." *Energy Economics* 63, 348–364.

Perez-Gonzales, F., and Yun, H., 2013. "Risk Management and Firm Value: Evidence from Weather Derivatives." *Journal of Finance* 68, 2143–2176.

Shevlin, T., 1990. "Estimating Corporate Marginal Tax Rates with Asymmetric Tax Treatment of Gains and Losses." *Journal of the American Taxation Association* 12, 51–67.

Smith, C. W. and Stulz, R. M., 1985. "The Determinants of Firms' Hedging Policies." *Journal of Financial and Quantitative Analysis* 20, 4, 391–405.

Stulz, René M., 1996. "Rethinking Risk Management." *Journal of Applied Corporate Finance* 9, 8–24.

Tufano, P., 1998. "The Determinants of Stock Price Exposure: Financial Engineering and the Gold Mining Industry." *Journal of Finance* 53, 1015–1052.

APPENDIX: ESTIMATED MTEs

TABLE 20A.1 Estimated MTEs for firm value

(1) U_D	(2) Tobin's q	(3) U_D	(4) Tobin's q	(5) U_D	(6) Tobin's q	(7) U_D	(8) Tobin's q
u1	1.4168**	u26	0.7513***	u51	0.4871**	u76	0.2177
	(0.642)		(0.290)		(0.205)		(0.225)
u2	1.3090**	u27	0.7393***	u52	0.4771**	u77	0.2049
	(0.581)		(0.285)		(0.204)		(0.228)
u3	1.2406**	u28	0.7274***	u53	0.4672**	u78	0.1917
	(0.542)		(0.280)		(0.202)		(0.232)
u4	1.1892**	u29	0.7158***	u54	0.4573**	u79	0.1781
	(0.514)		(0.275)		(0.201)		(0.237)
u5	1.1473**	u30	0.7043***	u55	0.4473**	u80	0.1642
	(0.491)		(0.271)		(0.200)		(0.241)
u6	1.1117**	u31	0.6930***	u56	0.4373**	u81	0.1499
	(0.472)		(0.266)		(0.199)		(0.246)
u7	1.0805**	u32	0.6819***	u57	0.4272**	u82	0.1351
	(0.455)		(0.262)		(0.199)		(0.252)
u8	1.0525**	u33	0.6709***	u58	0.4172**	u83	0.1197
	(0.440)		(0.257)		(0.198)		(0.258)
u9	1.0271**	u34	0.6601***	u59	0.4070**	u84	0.1038
	(0.426)		(0.253)		(0.198)		(0.264)
u10	1.0037**	u35	0.6493***	u60	0.3968**	u85	0.0872
	(0.414)		(0.249)		(0.198)		(0.270)
u11	0.9819**	u36	0.6387***	u61	0.3865*	u86	0.0698
	(0.402)		(0.246)		(0.198)		(0.278)
u12	0.9615**	u37	0.6282***	u62	0.3762*	u87	0.0516
	(0.392)		(0.242)		(0.198)		(0.285)
u13	0.9423**	u38	0.6178***	u63	0.3658*	u88	0.0324
	(0.382)		(0.238)		(0.199)		(0.294)
u14	0.9241**	u39	0.6074***	u64	0.3552*	u89	0.0120
	(0.373)		(0.235)		(0.199)		(0.303)
u15	0.9068**	u40	0.5971***	u65	0.3446*	u90	−0.0097
	(0.364)		(0.232)		(0.200)		(0.313)
u16	0.8902**	u41	0.5869**	u66	0.3339*	u91	−0.0331
	(0.356)		(0.229)		(0.201)		(0.324)
u17	0.8742**	u42	0.5768**	u67	0.3230	u92	−0.0586
	(0.348)		(0.226)		(0.203)		(0.336)
u18	0.8589**	u43	0.5667**	u68	0.3121	u93	−0.0865
	(0.340)		(0.223)		(0.204)		(0.350)
u19	0.8441**	u44	0.5567**	u69	0.3009	u94	−0.1177
	(0.333)		(0.220)		(0.206)		(0.365)
u20	0.8297**	u45	0.5467**	u70	0.2896	u95	−0.1534
	(0.326)		(0.218)		(0.208)		(0.383)
u21	0.8158**	u46	0.5367**	u71	0.2782	u96	−0.1952
	(0.320)		(0.215)		(0.210)		(0.405)
u22	0.8023**	u47	0.5267**	u72	0.2665	u97	−0.2466
	(0.313)		(0.213)		(0.212)		(0.432)
u23	0.7891**	u48	0.5168**	u73	0.2547	u98	−0.3150
	(0.307)		(0.211)		(0.215)		(0.469)
u24	0.7762**	u49	0.5069**	u74	0.2426	u99	−0.4228
	(0.302)		(0.209)		(0.218)		(0.528)
u25	0.7637***	u50	0.4970**	u75	0.2303		
	(0.296)		(0.207)		(0.221)		

Note: This table gives the estimated MTEs related to the choice of oil hedging intensity, high versus low. The MTEs are for firm value measured by the Tobin's q. U_D reflects different estimation points of the unobserved resistance to using high-intensity hedging. The superscripts ***, **, and * indicate statistical significance at the 1%, 5%, and 10% levels, respectively.

TABLE 20A.2 Estimated MTEs for systematic risk

(1) U_D	(2) Systematic Risk	(3) U_D	(4) Systematic Risk	(5) U_D	(6) Systematic Risk	(7) U_D	(8) Systematic Risk
u1	−2.4307** (1.199)	u26	−1.2437** (0.569)	u51	−0.7723** (0.389)	u76	−0.2918 (0.364)
u2	−2.2385** (1.091)	u27	−1.2222** (0.559)	u52	−0.7546** (0.384)	u77	−0.2689 (0.368)
u3	−2.1165** (1.023)	u28	−1.2011** (0.549)	u53	−0.7369* (0.380)	u78	−0.2454 (0.373)
u4	−2.0247** (0.973)	u29	−1.1803** (0.540)	u54	−0.7191* (0.376)	u79	−0.2212 (0.379)
u5	−1.9501** (0.932)	u30	−1.1598** (0.531)	u55	−0.7014* (0.372)	u80	−0.1964 (0.385)
u6	−1.8866** (0.898)	u31	−1.1397** (0.522)	u56	−0.6835* (0.368)	u81	−0.1708 (0.391)
u7	−1.8308** (0.868)	u32	−1.1198** (0.513)	u57	−0.6656* (0.365)	u82	−0.1444 (0.399)
u8	−1.7810** (0.841)	u33	−1.1002** (0.505)	u58	−0.6476* (0.362)	u83	−0.1170 (0.407)
u9	−1.7356** (0.817)	u34	−1.0809** (0.497)	u59	−0.6295* (0.359)	u84	−0.0886 (0.416)
u10	−1.6939** (0.795)	u35	−1.0617** (0.489)	u60	−0.6113* (0.356)	u85	−0.0590 (0.425)
u11	−1.6550** (0.774)	u36	−1.0428** (0.481)	u61	−0.5930* (0.354)	u86	−0.0280 (0.436)
u12	−1.6187** (0.755)	u37	−1.0240** (0.473)	u62	−0.5745 (0.352)	u87	0.0045 (0.448)
u13	−1.5844** (0.737)	u38	−1.0054** (0.466)	u63	−0.5559 (0.351)	u88	0.0387 (0.461)
u14	−1.5519** (0.721)	u39	−0.9870** (0.459)	u64	−0.5372 (0.349)	u89	0.0751 (0.475)
u15	−1.5210** (0.705)	u40	−0.9687** (0.452)	u65	−0.5182 (0.348)	u90	0.1139 (0.491)
u16	−1.4914** (0.690)	u41	−0.9505** (0.445)	u66	−0.4991 (0.348)	u91	0.1556 (0.508)
u17	−1.4629** (0.675)	u42	−0.9324** (0.439)	u67	−0.4797 (0.348)	u92	0.2010 (0.528)
u18	−1.4356** (0.662)	u43	−0.9144** (0.432)	u68	−0.4601 (0.348)	u93	0.2509 (0.551)
u19	−1.4092** (0.648)	u44	−0.8965** (0.426)	u69	−0.4403 (0.348)	u94	0.3066 (0.576)
u20	−1.3836** (0.636)	u45	−0.8786** (0.420)	u70	−0.4201 (0.349)	u95	0.3701 (0.607)
u21	−1.3587** (0.624)	u46	−0.8608** (0.414)	u71	−0.3997 (0.351)	u96	0.4448 (0.643)
u22	−1.3346** (0.612)	u47	−0.8431** (0.409)	u72	−0.3789 (0.352)	u97	0.5365 (0.689)
u23	−1.3111** (0.601)	u48	−0.8254** (0.403)	u73	−0.3578 (0.355)	u98	0.6585 (0.752)
u24	−1.2881** (0.590)	u49	−0.8077** (0.398)	u74	−0.3362 (0.357)	u99	0.8508 (0.853)
u25	−1.2657** (0.579)	u50	−0.7900** (0.393)	u75	−0.3143 (0.360)		

Note: This table gives the estimated MTEs related to the choice of oil hedging intensity, high versus low. The MTEs are for firm systematic risk. U_D reflects different estimation points of the unobserved resistance to using high-intensity hedging. The superscripts ***, **, and * indicate statistical significance at the 1%, 5%, and 10% levels, respectively.

TABLE 20A.3 Estimated MTEs for idiosyncratic risk

(1) U_D	(2) Idiosyncratic Risk	(3) U_D	(4) Idiosyncratic Risk	(5) U_D	(6) Idiosyncratic Risk	(7) U_D	(8) Idiosyncratic Risk
u1	−0.0460	u26	−0.0299**	u51	−0.0235**	u76	−0.0170
	(0.034)		(0.015)		(0.011)		(0.014)
u2	−0.0434	u27	−0.0296**	u52	−0.0233**	u77	−0.0167
	(0.031)		(0.015)		(0.011)		(0.014)
u3	−0.0417	u28	−0.0293**	u53	−0.0230**	u78	−0.0164
	(0.029)		(0.015)		(0.011)		(0.014)
u4	−0.0405	u29	−0.0290**	u54	−0.0228**	u79	−0.0160
	(0.027)		(0.014)		(0.011)		(0.015)
u5	−0.0395	u30	−0.0288**	u55	−0.0226**	u80	−0.0157
	(0.026)		(0.014)		(0.011)		(0.015)
u6	−0.0386	u31	−0.0285**	u56	−0.0223*	u81	−0.0154
	(0.025)		(0.014)		(0.011)		(0.015)
u7	−0.0379	u32	−0.0282**	u57	−0.0221*	u82	−0.0150
	(0.024)		(0.014)		(0.011)		(0.016)
u8	−0.0372	u33	−0.0280**	u58	−0.0218*	u83	−0.0146
	(0.023)		(0.014)		(0.011)		(0.016)
u9	−0.0366	u34	−0.0277**	u59	−0.0216*	u84	−0.0142
	(0.022)		(0.013)		(0.011)		(0.016)
u10	−0.0360*	u35	−0.0274**	u60	−0.0213*	u85	−0.0138
	(0.022)		(0.013)		(0.012)		(0.017)
u11	−0.0355*	u36	−0.0272**	u61	−0.0211*	u86	−0.0134
	(0.021)		(0.013)		(0.012)		(0.017)
u12	−0.0350*	u37	−0.0269**	u62	−0.0208*	u87	−0.0130
	(0.021)		(0.013)		(0.012)		(0.018)
u13	−0.0345*	u38	−0.0267**	u63	−0.0206*	u88	−0.0125
	(0.020)		(0.013)		(0.012)		(0.018)
u14	−0.0341*	u39	−0.0264**	u64	−0.0203*	u89	−0.0120
	(0.020)		(0.013)		(0.012)		(0.019)
u15	−0.0337*	u40	−0.0262**	u65	−0.0201*	u90	−0.0115
	(0.019)		(0.012)		(0.012)		(0.019)
u16	−0.0333*	u41	−0.0259**	u66	−0.0198*	u91	−0.0109
	(0.019)		(0.012)		(0.012)		(0.020)
u17	−0.0329*	u42	−0.0257**	u67	−0.0195	u92	−0.0103
	(0.018)		(0.012)		(0.012)		(0.021)
u18	−0.0325*	u43	−0.0254**	u68	−0.0193	u93	−0.0096
	(0.018)		(0.012)		(0.012)		(0.021)
u19	−0.0321*	u44	−0.0252**	u69	−0.0190	u94	−0.0089
	(0.017)		(0.012)		(0.012)		(0.022)
u20	−0.0318*	u45	−0.0250**	u70	−0.0187	u95	−0.0080
	(0.017)		(0.012)		(0.013)		(0.023)
u21	−0.0315*	u46	−0.0247**	u71	−0.0185	u96	−0.0070
	(0.017)		(0.012)		(0.013)		(0.025)
u22	−0.0311*	u47	−0.0245**	u72	−0.0182	u97	−0.0058
	(0.016)		(0.012)		(0.013)		(0.026)
u23	−0.0308*	u48	−0.0242**	u73	−0.0179	u98	−0.0041
	(0.016)		(0.012)		(0.013)		(0.028)
u24	−0.0305*	u49	−0.0240**	u74	−0.0176	u99	−0.0015
	(0.016)		(0.012)		(0.013)		(0.031)
u25	−0.0302*	u50	−0.0238**	u75	−0.0173		
	(0.016)		(0.011)		(0.014)		

Note: This table gives the estimated MTEs related to the choice of oil hedging intensity, high versus low. The MTEs are for firm idiosyncratic risk. U_D reflects different estimation points of the unobserved resistance to using high-intensity hedging. The superscripts ***, **, and * indicate statistical significance at the 1%, 5%, and 10% levels, respectively.

TABLE 20A.4 Estimated MTEs for oil beta

(1) U_D	(2) Oil Beta	(3) U_D	(4) Oil Beta	(5) U_D	(6) Oil Beta	(7) U_D	(8) Oil Beta
u1	−0.4626	u26	−0.2309	u51	−0.1389	u76	−0.0451
	(0.477)		(0.227)		(0.160)		(0.159)
u2	−0.4251	u27	−0.2267	u52	−0.1355	u77	−0.0407
	(0.434)		(0.223)		(0.159)		(0.160)
u3	−0.4013	u28	−0.2226	u53	−0.1320	u78	−0.0361
	(0.407)		(0.220)		(0.158)		(0.163)
u4	−0.3834	u29	−0.2185	u54	−0.1285	u79	−0.0314
	(0.386)		(0.216)		(0.156)		(0.165)
u5	−0.3688	u30	−0.2146	u55	−0.1251	u80	−0.0265
	(0.370)		(0.212)		(0.155)		(0.168)
u6	−0.3564	u31	−0.2106	u56	−0.1216	u81	−0.0215
	(0.356)		(0.209)		(0.154)		(0.170)
u7	−0.3455	u32	−0.2067	u57	−0.1181	u82	−0.0164
	(0.344)		(0.206)		(0.153)		(0.174)
u8	−0.3358	u33	−0.2029	u58	−0.1146	u83	−0.0110
	(0.334)		(0.203)		(0.152)		(0.177)
u9	−0.3269	u34	−0.1991	u59	−0.1110	u84	−0.0055
	(0.324)		(0.200)		(0.151)		(0.181)
u10	−0.3188	u35	−0.1954	u60	−0.1075	u85	0.0003
	(0.315)		(0.197)		(0.150)		(0.185)
u11	−0.3112	u36	−0.1917	u61	−0.1039	u86	0.0063
	(0.307)		(0.194)		(0.150)		(0.189)
u12	−0.3041	u37	−0.1880	u62	−0.1003	u87	0.0127
	(0.300)		(0.191)		(0.149)		(0.194)
u13	−0.2974	u38	−0.1844	u63	−0.0967	u88	0.0194
	(0.293)		(0.188)		(0.149)		(0.199)
u14	−0.2911	u39	−0.1808	u64	−0.0930	u89	0.0265
	(0.286)		(0.185)		(0.149)		(0.205)
u15	−0.2850	u40	−0.1772	u65	−0.0893	u90	0.0340
	(0.280)		(0.183)		(0.149)		(0.212)
u16	−0.2793	u41	−0.1737	u66	−0.0856	u91	0.0422
	(0.274)		(0.180)		(0.149)		(0.219)
u17	−0.2737	u42	−0.1702	u67	−0.0818	u92	0.0510
	(0.268)		(0.178)		(0.149)		(0.227)
u18	−0.2684	u43	−0.1666	u68	−0.0780	u93	0.0608
	(0.263)		(0.176)		(0.150)		(0.236)
u19	−0.2632	u44	−0.1631	u69	−0.0741	u94	0.0717
	(0.258)		(0.174)		(0.150)		(0.246)
u20	−0.2582	u45	−0.1597	u70	−0.0702	u95	0.0841
	(0.253)		(0.171)		(0.151)		(0.258)
u21	−0.2534	u46	−0.1562	u71	−0.0662	u96	0.0986
	(0.248)		(0.169)		(0.152)		(0.273)
u22	−0.2487	u47	−0.1527	u72	−0.0621	u97	0.1165
	(0.244)		(0.167)		(0.153)		(0.292)
u23	−0.2441	u48	−0.1493	u73	−0.0580	u98	0.1403
	(0.239)		(0.166)		(0.154)		(0.317)
u24	−0.2396	u49	−0.1458	u74	−0.0538	u99	0.1779
	(0.235)		(0.164)		(0.155)		(0.358)
u25	−0.2352	u50	−0.1424	u75	−0.0495		
	(0.231)		(0.162)		(0.157)		

Note: This table gives the estimated MTEs related to the choice of oil hedging intensity, high versus low. The MTEs are for firm oil beta. U_D reflects different estimation points of the unobserved resistance to using high-intensity hedging.

TABLE 20A.5 Estimated MTEs for ROE

(1) U_D	(2) ROE	(3) U_D	(4) ROE	(5) U_D	(6) ROE	(7) U_D	(8) ROE
u1	0.6531	u26	0.0288	u51	−0.2191	u76	−0.4718**
	(0.631)		(0.310)		(0.215)		(0.191)
u2	0.5520	u27	0.0175	u52	−0.2284	u77	−0.4838**
	(0.576)		(0.305)		(0.213)		(0.193)
u3	0.4878	u28	0.0064	u53	−0.2377	u78	−0.4962**
	(0.542)		(0.300)		(0.210)		(0.195)
u4	0.4396	u29	−0.0045	u54	−0.2470	u79	−0.5089***
	(0.516)		(0.295)		(0.208)		(0.197)
u5	0.4003	u30	−0.0153	u55	−0.2564	u80	−0.5220***
	(0.495)		(0.290)		(0.206)		(0.199)
u6	0.3669	u31	−0.0259	u56	−0.2658	u81	−0.5354***
	(0.478)		(0.286)		(0.203)		(0.202)
u7	0.3376	u32	−0.0363	u57	−0.2752	u82	−0.5493***
	(0.463)		(0.281)		(0.201)		(0.205)
u8	0.3114	u33	−0.0466	u58	−0.2847	u83	−0.5637***
	(0.449)		(0.277)		(0.199)		(0.208)
u9	0.2875	u34	−0.0568	u59	−0.2942	u84	−0.5786***
	(0.437)		(0.273)		(0.198)		(0.212)
u10	0.2656	u35	−0.0669	u60	−0.3038	u85	−0.5942***
	(0.425)		(0.268)		(0.196)		(0.217)
u11	0.2451	u36	−0.0768	u61	−0.3134	u86	−0.6105***
	(0.415)		(0.264)		(0.194)		(0.221)
u12	0.2260	u37	−0.0867	u62	−0.3231*	u87	−0.6276***
	(0.405)		(0.261)		(0.193)		(0.227)
u13	0.2080	u38	−0.0965	u63	−0.3329*	u88	−0.6456***
	(0.396)		(0.257)		(0.192)		(0.233)
u14	0.1909	u39	−0.1062	u64	−0.3427*	u89	−0.6647***
	(0.388)		(0.253)		(0.191)		(0.239)
u15	0.1746	u40	−0.1158	u65	−0.3527*	u90	−0.6851***
	(0.379)		(0.249)		(0.190)		(0.247)
u16	0.1591	u41	−0.1254	u66	−0.3628*	u91	−0.7071***
	(0.372)		(0.246)		(0.189)		(0.255)
u17	0.1441	u42	−0.1349	u67	−0.3730**	u92	−0.7310***
	(0.364)		(0.242)		(0.188)		(0.264)
u18	0.1297	u43	−0.1444	u68	−0.3833**	u93	−0.7572***
	(0.357)		(0.239)		(0.188)		(0.275)
u19	0.1158	u44	−0.1538	u69	−0.3937**	u94	−0.7865***
	(0.351)		(0.236)		(0.188)		(0.288)
u20	0.1024	u45	−0.1632	u70	−0.4043**	u95	−0.8199***
	(0.344)		(0.232)		(0.187)		(0.302)
u21	0.0893	u46	−0.1725	u71	−0.4150**	u96	−0.8591***
	(0.338)		(0.229)		(0.188)		(0.320)
u22	0.0766	u47	−0.1819	u72	−0.4260**	u97	−0.9074***
	(0.332)		(0.226)		(0.188)		(0.343)
u23	0.0643	u48	−0.1912	u73	−0.4371**	u98	−0.9716***
	(0.326)		(0.223)		(0.188)		(0.374)
u24	0.0522	u49	−0.2005	u74	−0.4484**	u99	−1.0727**
	(0.321)		(0.220)		(0.189)		(0.425)
u25	0.0404	u50	−0.2098	u75	−0.4600**		
	(0.315)		(0.218)		(0.190)		

Note: This table gives the estimated MTEs related to the choice of oil hedging intensity, high versus low. The MTEs are for firm ROE. U_D reflects different estimation points of the unobserved resistance to using high-intensity hedging. The superscripts ***, **, and * indicate statistical significance at the 1%, 5%, and 10% levels, respectively.

CHAPTER 21

Exercises

EXERCISE 1 PORTFOLIO CHOICE AND THE NOTION OF VALUE AT RISK (VaR)[1]

The objective of this exercise is to clarify important points about VaR for market risk when choosing a portfolio. The same message applies for CVaR, but the formulas differ, as we will see in Exercise 5.

Calculating VaR

Suppose an individual has an expected utility function such that:

$$U(E, V) = E(R) - r\,V(R)$$

where:

E(R) is the expected portfolio return;

V(R) is the portfolio variance;

r is the risk aversion coefficient.

Answer the following questions by assuming that there are only three risky assets in the market and that the investor's portfolio may contain these three assets.

Question 1

What conditions must U and *r* verify to define a utility function of a risk-averse investor?

(a) Write the problem of maximization of the investor's utility in matrix form, given that the sum of the weights associated with the three risky assets is equal to 1.
(b) Find the first-order conditions of this portfolio choice problem.
(c) Give the analytical expression for the weight of an optimal portfolio.
(d) Suppose that the expected returns of the three risky assets are respectively:

$$E(R_1) = 14,\ E(R_2) = 13 \text{ et } E(R_3) = 12.$$

[1]This exercise was prepared in collaboration with Martin Lebeau, Samir Saissi Hassani, and Faouzi Tarkhani.

The matrix of the correlation coefficients is given by:

$$\begin{bmatrix} 1 & 0.25 & -0.5 \\ 0.25 & 1 & 0.45 \\ -0.5 & 0.45 & 1 \end{bmatrix}.$$

The variances associated with the assets are:

$$V(R_1) = 10,\ V(R_2) = 9 \text{ et } V(R_3) = 7,$$

and the risk aversion parameter is $r = 0.5$.

Calculate the optimal values of the weights associated with the three assets. Deduct the level of expected return for this portfolio and its variance. You may use Excel.

Question 2

Suppose that the investor possesses an initial wealth of \$10,000. Calculate the absolute VaR and the Relative VaR for this portfolio for a degree of confidence of 95% and 99%. Explain your results.

Question 3

Assume the following five situations:

(a) The variance of asset 2 increases from 9 to 14.
(b) The correlation coefficient of asset 1 and asset 2 becomes equal to 0.01.
(c) The correlation coefficient of asset 1 and asset 2 becomes equal to −0.5.
(d) The correlation coefficient of asset 1 and asset 3 changes from −0.5 to 0.8.
(e) The correlation coefficient of asset 2 and asset 3 becomes equal to 0.

Calculate in each case, for a 95% degree of confidence, the effect of each scenario on the values of Absolute VaR and Relative VaR. Explain your results.

Incremental VaR

Suppose that there are only two risky assets on the market with the following characteristics:[2]

$$C = \begin{bmatrix} 10\% \\ 12\% \end{bmatrix} \quad \Sigma = \begin{bmatrix} 0.16 & 0.1 \\ 0.1 & 0.25 \end{bmatrix}$$

where:

C is the vector of expected returns associated with each of the two risky assets;
Σ is the variance-covariance matrix of returns.

[2]On the topic of incremental risk, see Dowd (1998).

Question 4

Suppose that the investor's portfolio only contains these two assets.

(a) Given that $r = 0.5$, determine the composition of the portfolio that can maximize the investor's utility, if the sum of the weights associated with the assets is equal to 1.
(b) If the investor invests $W = \$100{,}000$. Calculate the Relative Value at Risk of his portfolio for a 95% degree of confidence.

Now suppose that a third risky asset is added to the portfolio, with the following characteristics:

$$E(R_3) = 5\%; \quad V(R_3) = 9\,\%; \quad \rho_{1.3} = 0.2; \quad \rho_{2.3} = -0.38$$

where:

$E(R_3)$ is the expected return of asset 3;
$V(R_3)$ is the variance of asset 3;
$\rho_{1,3}$ is the correlation coefficient between assets 1 and 3;
$\rho_{2,3}$ is the correlation coefficient between assets 2 and 3.

(c) Determine the value of the Beta for asset 3 using the capital asset pricing model (CAPM), considering a market premium equal to 20% and a return on the risk-free asset of 6%. What is your impression of asset 3?
(d) Calculate the incremental value at risk (IVaR) corresponding to asset 3 if the investor decides to allot \$20,000 to this asset. Use two approaches: the classic approach, which consists of comparing the VaRs of the two portfolios, and the approximation approach, which incorporates the Beta of the CAPM model.
(e) Assume this time that the market contains only the two risky assets and one risk-free asset with a return of 6%. Calculate the incremental value at risk (IVaR) associated with the risk-free asset by assuming an investment of \$10,000 in this asset. Use the classic approach. Comment on your results and compare them with the results obtained in question 4.d.

REFERENCE

Dowd, K., 1998. *Beyond Value at Risk*. Manchester, UK: John Wiley & Sons, Inc.

Solution for Exercise 1

Consider the equation:

$$U(E, V) = E(R) - rV(R).$$

Question 1

What conditions must U and *r* verify to define a utility function of a risk-averse investor?

E(R) and V(R) measure the expected return and the variance respectively. An investor is risk averse if and only if his utility level is a decreasing function of the risk incurred. In mathematical terms, if we suppose that the level of utility is an increasing function of the expected level of return and if we suppose that variance is a good measure of risk, we have:

$$U'_E > 0 \text{ et } U'_v < 0,$$

where U'_i is the partial derivative of U relative to the argument *i*, i = E, V. Consequently, r > 0.

(a) Write the problem of maximization of the investor's utility in matrix form, given that the sum of the weights associated with the three risky assets is equal to 1.

Let β_i be the weight associated to the risky asset *i*. We seek to maximize U(E, V) relative to the different β_i under the constraint $\sum_{i=1}^{3} \beta_i = 1$. We have the following expected portfolio return:

$$E(R) = \beta_1 E(R_1) + \beta_2 E(R_2) + \beta_3 E(R_3).$$

The portfolio variance equals:

$$V(R) = \beta_1^2 V(R_1) + \beta_2^2 V(R_2) + \beta_3^2 V(R_3) + 2\beta_1\beta_2 COV(R_1, R_2) + 2\beta_2\beta_3 COV(R_2, R_3) + 2\beta_1\beta_3 COV(R_1, R_3).$$

To simplify the notation, the portfolio variance can also be written as:

$$V(R) = \beta_1^2\,\sigma_{11} + \beta_2^2\,\sigma_{22} + \beta_3^2\,\sigma_{33} + 2\,\beta_1\,\beta_2\,\sigma_{12} + 2\,\beta_2\,\beta_3\,\sigma_{23} + 2\,\beta_1\,\beta_3\,\sigma_{13}.$$

We suppose that the return on assets follows a multivariate normal distribution. Their marginal distributions are given by $N(\mu_i, \sigma_i^2)$. The maximization problem in matrix form becomes:

$$E(R) = \begin{bmatrix}\beta_1 & \beta_2 & \beta_3\end{bmatrix}_{1\times 3} \times \begin{bmatrix}E(R_1)\\ E(R_2)\\ E(R_3)\end{bmatrix}_{3\times 1} = B'C$$

where:

$B = \begin{bmatrix}\beta_1\\ \beta_2\\ \beta_3\end{bmatrix}_{3\times 1}$ is the vector of the weights associated with the three risky assets;

B' is the transpose of vector B;

$C = \begin{bmatrix}E(R_1)\\ E(R_2)\\ E(R_3)\end{bmatrix}_{3\times 1}$ is the vector of expected returns associated with the three risky assets.

$$V(R) = \begin{bmatrix}\beta_1 & \beta_2 & \beta_3\end{bmatrix}_{1\times 3} \times \begin{bmatrix}\sigma_{11} & \sigma_{12} & \sigma_{13}\\ \sigma_{21} & \sigma_{22} & \sigma_{23}\\ \sigma_{31} & \sigma_{32} & \sigma_{33}\end{bmatrix}_{3\times 3} \times \begin{bmatrix}\beta_1\\ \beta_2\\ \beta_3\end{bmatrix}_{3\times 1} = B'\Sigma B.$$

Write Σ as the variance-covariance matrix of the returns. In matrix form we therefore have:

$$\underset{\beta_i}{\text{Max}}\left(B'\,C - r\,B' \sum B\right)$$

subject to

$$\sum_{i=1}^{3} \beta_i = 1.$$

(b) Find the first-order conditions of this portfolio choice problem.
The Lagrangian associated with the problem is:

$$L(\beta_1, \beta_2, \beta_3, \lambda) = \beta_1 E(R_1) + \beta_2 E(R_2) + \beta_3 E(R_3)$$
$$- r\begin{bmatrix} \beta_1^2\sigma_{11} + \beta_2^2\sigma_{22} + \beta_3^2\sigma_{33} + 2\beta_1\beta_2\sigma_{12} \\ +2\beta_2\beta_3\sigma_{23} + 2\beta_1\beta_3\sigma_{13} \end{bmatrix} - \lambda[\beta_1 + \beta_2 + \beta_3 - 1]$$

where λ is the Lagrange multiplier.
The four first-order conditions are written as:

$$\frac{\partial L}{\partial \beta_1} = E(R_1) - r[2\,\beta_1\,\sigma_{11} + 2\;\;\beta_2\,\sigma_{12} + 2\,\beta_3\,\sigma_{13}] - \lambda = 0$$
$$\frac{\partial L}{\partial \beta_2} = E(R_2) - r[2\,\beta_2\,\sigma_{22} + 2\;\;\beta_1\,\sigma_{12} + 2\,\beta_3\,\sigma_{23}] - \lambda = 0$$
$$\frac{\partial L}{\partial \beta_3} = E(R_3) - r[2\,\beta_3\,\sigma_{33} + 2\;\;\beta_2\,\sigma_{23} + 2\,\beta_1\,\sigma_{13}] - \lambda = 0$$
$$\frac{\partial L}{\partial \lambda} = -\beta_1 - \beta_2 - \beta_3 + 1 = 0.$$

(c) Give the analytical expression for the optimal portfolio.

$$E(R_1) = 2\,r\,\beta_1\,\sigma_{11} + 2\,r\,\beta_2\,\sigma_{12} + 2\,r\,\beta_3\,\sigma_{13} + \lambda$$
$$E(R_2) = 2\,r\,\beta_1\,\sigma_{12} + 2\,r\,\beta_2\,\sigma_{22} + 2\,r\,\beta_3\,\sigma_{23} + \lambda$$
$$E(R_3) = 2\,r\,\beta_1\,\sigma_{13} + 2\,r\,\beta_2\,\sigma_{23} + 2\,r\,\beta_3\,\sigma_{33} + \lambda$$
$$1 = \beta_1 + \beta_2 + \beta_3.$$

In matrix form:

$$\begin{bmatrix} E(R_1) \\ E(R_2) \\ E(R_3) \\ 1 \end{bmatrix} = \begin{bmatrix} 2\,r\,\sigma_{11} & 2\,r\,\sigma_{12} & 2\,r\,\sigma_{13} & 1 \\ 2\,r\,\sigma_{12} & 2\,r\,\sigma_{22} & 2\,r\,\sigma_{23} & 1 \\ 2\,r\,\sigma_{13} & 2\,r\,\sigma_{23} & 2\,r\,\sigma_{33} & 1 \\ 1 & 1 & 1 & 0 \end{bmatrix} \times \begin{bmatrix} \beta_1 \\ \beta_2 \\ \beta_3 \\ \lambda \end{bmatrix},$$

which is equivalent to writing the following system of equations:

$$\begin{cases} C = A\,B + \overline{1}\,\lambda \\ 1 = \overline{1}'\,B \end{cases}$$

with:

$$C = \begin{bmatrix} E(R_1) \\ E(R_2) \\ E(R_3) \end{bmatrix},\ B = \begin{bmatrix} \beta_1 \\ \beta_2 \\ \beta_3 \end{bmatrix},\ \bar{1} = \begin{bmatrix} 1 \\ 1 \\ 1 \end{bmatrix},\ \bar{1}' = \begin{bmatrix} 1 & 1 & 1 \end{bmatrix}$$

and

$$A = 2\,r \begin{bmatrix} \sigma_{11} & \sigma_{12} & \sigma_{13} \\ \sigma_{12} & \sigma_{22} & \sigma_{23} \\ \sigma_{13} & \sigma_{23} & \sigma_{33} \end{bmatrix}_{3\times 3} = 2\,r \sum;\ \text{so}\ A^{-1} = \frac{1}{2\,r} \sum^{-1}$$

$$\Leftrightarrow \begin{cases} A\,B = C - \bar{1}\,\lambda \\ 1 = \bar{1}'\,B \end{cases}$$

$$\begin{cases} B = A^{-1}\,C - A^{-1}\,\bar{1}\,\lambda & \text{(E1.1)} \\ 1 = \bar{1}'\,B. & \text{(E1.2)} \end{cases}$$

Let us replace (E1.1) in (E1.2):

$$1 = \bar{1}'\,A^{-1} C - \bar{1}'\,A^{-1}\,\bar{1}\,\lambda.$$

The solution to this system of equations solves:

$$\lambda = (\bar{1}'\,A^{-1}\,\bar{1})^{-1}\ [\bar{1}'\,A^{-1}\,C - 1]$$

$$B = A^{-1}\,C - A^{-1}\,\bar{1}\,\lambda.$$

To obtain the solution, we simply calculate the inverse variance-covariance matrix.

$$A^{-1} = \frac{1}{2\,r}\,\frac{1}{|\sum|} \begin{bmatrix} (\sigma_{22}\sigma_{33} - \sigma_{23}^2) & (\sigma_{13}\sigma_{23} - \sigma_{12}\sigma_{33}) & (\sigma_{12}\sigma_{23} - \sigma_{13}\sigma_{22}) \\ (\sigma_{13}\sigma_{23} - \sigma_{12}\sigma_{33}) & (\sigma_{11}\sigma_{13} - \sigma_{13}^2) & (\sigma_{13}\sigma_{12} - \sigma_{11}\sigma_{23}) \\ (\sigma_{12}\sigma_{23} - \sigma_{13}\sigma_{22}) & (\sigma_{13}\sigma_{12} - \sigma_{11}\sigma_{23}) & (\sigma_{22}\sigma_{11} - \sigma_{12}^2) \end{bmatrix}$$

where $|\sum|$ is the determinant of the matrix $\sum$ and by writing:

$$\left|\sum\right| = \sigma_{11} \times \begin{vmatrix} \sigma_{22} & \sigma_{23} \\ \sigma_{23} & \sigma_{33} \end{vmatrix} - \sigma_{12} \times \begin{vmatrix} \sigma_{12} & \sigma_{23} \\ \sigma_{13} & \sigma_{33} \end{vmatrix} + \sigma_{13} \times \begin{vmatrix} \sigma_{12} & \sigma_{22} \\ \sigma_{13} & \sigma_{23} \end{vmatrix}$$

$$\left|\sum\right| = \sigma_{11} \times [\sigma_{22}\sigma_{33} - \sigma_{23}^2] - \sigma_{12} \times [\sigma_{12}\sigma_{33} - \sigma_{23}\sigma_{13}] + \sigma_{13} \times [\sigma_{12}\sigma_{23} - \sigma_{22}\sigma_{13}].$$

(d) Consider the following values:

$$\Theta = \begin{bmatrix} 1 & 0.25 & -0.5 \\ 0.25 & 1 & 0.45 \\ -0.5 & 0.45 & 1 \end{bmatrix},\ C = \begin{bmatrix} 0.14 \\ 0.13 \\ 0.12 \end{bmatrix}\ \text{and}\ W = 10\,000.$$

where Θ is the matrix of the correlation coefficients.

We have:

$$V(R_1) = 10\%,\ V(R_2) = 9\% \text{ and } V(R_3) = 7\%.$$

Note that the solution to the problem depends on the parameter *r*, which measures the investor's risk aversion. For our example, we suppose that r = 0.5.

B* is the vector of optimal weights associated with the three risky assets:

$$B^* = \begin{bmatrix} \beta_1 \\ \beta_2 \\ \beta_3 \end{bmatrix} = \begin{bmatrix} 0.5804 \\ -0.1543 \\ 0.5738 \end{bmatrix}.$$

We deduce that the expected portfolio return given the optimal weights is:

$$E^*(R) = \begin{bmatrix} 0.5804 & -0.1543 & 0.5738 \end{bmatrix} \begin{bmatrix} 0.14 \\ 0.13 \\ 0.12 \end{bmatrix} = 13.01\%;$$

its variance is:

$$V^*(R) = 2.04\%.$$

Question 2

Suppose the investor possesses an initial wealth of \$10,000. Calculate the absolute VaR and the relative VaR for this portfolio for a degree of confidence of 95% and 99%. Explain your results.

Value at risk includes three components: time horizon, degree of confidence, and risk level of the portfolio. We have:

$$W = 10{,}000\ ; \quad E(R) = 13.01\%\ ; \quad V(R) = 2.04\%.$$

We use the following four definitions.

- Relative VaR in return:

$$\alpha \times \sigma \times \sqrt{\Delta t},$$

  where:

  α is the coefficient related to the level of confidence retained;

  $\sqrt{\Delta t}$ is an adjustment coefficient for time.

- relative VaR in \$:

$$\alpha \times \sigma \times \sqrt{\Delta t} \times W;$$

- absolute VaR in return:

  relative VaR − E(R) = $\alpha \times \sigma \times \sqrt{\Delta t} - E(R)$;

- absolute VaR in \$:

$$(\alpha \times \sigma \times \sqrt{\Delta t} - E(R)) \times W.$$

Calculate the value of the absolute VaR (VaR_a) and of the relative VaR (VaR_r) for a degree of confidence of 95%. We posit that:

$\sqrt{\Delta t} = 1$, because the time horizon of the data is the same as that of VaR;

$$VaR_a = (1.65 \times \sqrt{2.04\%} - 13.01\%) \times 10{,}000 = \$1,058.54;$$

$$VaR_r = (1.65 \times \sqrt{2.04\%}) \times 10{,}000 = \$2,359.20.$$

In this case, the investor will sustain a loss of less than $1058.54 in 95% of the cases. This value corresponds to the income that defines the extreme left part of the returns distribution and that also represents the lowest five centiles of revenues. The value of VaR_r, which is equal to $2,359.20, indicates the amount that the investor will lose (in 5% of the cases at the end of the period) relative to the average portfolio value, given its return.

We use the same process for the degree of confidence of 99% (α becomes 2.33):

$$VaR_a = (2.33 \times \sqrt{2.04\%} - 13.01\%) \times 10{,}000 = \$2,030.82;$$

$$VaR_r = (2.33 \times \sqrt{2.04\%}) \times 10{,}000 = \$3,331.48.$$

Note that for a degree of confidence of 99%, the values of absolute VaR and relative VaR are higher because at this level of confidence, there is only a 1% probability that the investor's loss will exceed $2,030.82. In contrast, in the first case there was a 5% probability that the loss would surpass $1,058.54. There is a lower probability of having a loss greater than the VaR with a higher degree of confidence, but the investor must set aside more capital.

Question 3

To compare the VaRs, we must calculate the new weight values in our portfolio each time the parameters that define the asset returns change. In other words, the VaR must always be calculated with an optimal portfolio.

Let us suppose the following five situations:

(a) Variance σ_2^2 goes from 9% to 14%

$$B^* = \begin{bmatrix} 0.5875 \\ -0.1774 \\ 0.5900 \end{bmatrix}$$

$$E^*(R) = 13\%$$

$$V^*(R) = 1.88\%$$

$$VaR_a = \$962.19$$

$$VaR_r = \$2,261.94$$

The two VaRs at 95% decrease because the optimal weights of the three assets change following the increase of σ_2^2.

(b) The correlation coefficient ρ_{12} goes from 0.25 to 0.01

$$B^* = \begin{bmatrix} 0.5000 \\ 0.0649 \\ 0.4351 \end{bmatrix}$$

$$E^*(R) = 13{,}06\ \%$$

$$V^*(R) = 2.25\%$$

$$VaR_a = \$1,168.96$$

$$VaR_r = \$2,475.45$$

The two VaRs increase because the optimal portfolio becomes more risky than in a).

(c) The correlation coefficient ρ_{12} goes from 0.25 to –0.5

$$B^* = \begin{bmatrix} 0.4808 \\ 0.3443 \\ 0.1749 \end{bmatrix}$$

$$E^*(R) = 13.31\ \%$$

$$V^*(R) = 1.75\%$$

$$VaR_a = \$851.40$$

$$VaR_r = \$2,181.99$$

The two VaRs decrease because the optimal portfolio becomes less risky than in b).

(d) The correlation coefficient ρ_{13} goes from −0.5 to 0.8

$$B^* = \begin{bmatrix} 0.7815 \\ 0.5788 \\ -0.3603 \end{bmatrix}$$

$$E^*(R) = 14.14\%$$

$$V^*(R) = 6.92\%$$

$$VaR_a = \$2,925.58$$

$$VaR_r = \$4,339.76$$

The two VaRs increase because the optimal portfolio becomes more risky than in c).

(e) The correlation coefficient ρ_{23} goes from 0.45 to 0

$$B^* = \begin{bmatrix} 0.4614 \\ 0.1091 \\ 0.4295 \end{bmatrix}$$

$$E^*(R) = 13.03\%$$
$$V^*(R) = 2.11\%$$
$$VaR_a = \$1,092.50$$
$$VaR_r = \$2,395.70$$

The two VaRs increase with respect to c) because the variance of the optimal portfolio increases.

Conclusion Regarding the Calculations for the VaR

In addition to showing how to calculate VaR for a simple portfolio, this exercise emphasizes the importance of recalculating the optimal portfolio and the weights of each asset in the portfolio before recalculating absolute and relative VaR. Note that the second-order conditions were also verified and that the solutions obtained correspond to a global maximum in the presence of risk aversion.

Incremental VaR

Question 4

Suppose that the investor's portfolio contains only two assets.

(a) Given that r = 0.5, determine the composition of the portfolio that maximizes the investor's utility if the sum of the weights associated with the assets is equal to 1.

We suppose that the return on each asset follows a normal distribution (μ_i, σ_i^2) with:

$$r = 0.5, \quad A = 2r\Sigma = \begin{bmatrix} 0.16 & 0.1 \\ 0.1 & 0.25 \end{bmatrix}; \ \Sigma\text{: variance-covariance matrix.}$$

As derived above, we obtain the vector B by calculating:

$$\begin{bmatrix} B \\ \lambda \end{bmatrix} = \begin{bmatrix} A & \overline{1} \\ \overline{1}' & 0 \end{bmatrix}^{-1} \times \begin{bmatrix} C \\ 1 \end{bmatrix} \text{ with } \overline{1} = \begin{bmatrix} 1 \\ 1 \end{bmatrix}.$$

Alternatively, we may use the two-step method:

$$\lambda = (\overline{1}'_{1x2}\, A^{-1}_{2x2}\, \overline{1}_{2x1})^{-1}\ [\overline{1}'_{1x2}\, A^{-1}_{2x2}\, C_{2x1} - 1].$$
$$B_{2x1} = A^{-1}_{2x2}\, C_{2x1} - \lambda A^{-1}_{2x2}\, \overline{1}_{2x1}.$$

The vector of optimal asset weights is $B^* = \begin{bmatrix} 0.6190 \\ 0.3810 \end{bmatrix}$.

The value of λ is -0.03714.

(b) If the investor invests W = \$100,000, calculate the relative Value at Risk of this portfolio for a 95% degree of confidence.

Below we determine the three elements required to calculate VaR:

1. Expected portfolio return:

$$E(R) = 0.6190 \times 10\% + 0.3810 \times 12\% = 10.76\%;$$

2. Portfolio variance:

$$V(R) = 0,619^2 \times 0.16 + 0.381^2 \times 0.25 + 2 \times 0.619 \ \times 0.381 \ \times 0.1 = 0.1448;$$

3. Standard deviation of the portfolio:

$$\sigma = (V(R))^{1/2} = 0.3805.$$

Relative VaR is written as:

$$VaR_r = \alpha \times \sigma \times W \quad \text{(E1.3)}$$

$$VaR_r = 1.65 \times 0.3805 \times \$100{,}000 = \$62,778.52. \quad \text{(E1.4)}$$

Now suppose that a third risky asset was added to the portfolio. It has the following characteristics:

$$E(R_3) = 5\%; \quad V(R_3) = 9\%; \quad \rho_{1.3} = 0.2; \quad \rho_{2.3} = -0.38.$$

(c) Calculating Beta

The capital asset pricing model is written as:

$$E(R_i) = R_f + \beta_i[E(R_m)–R_f]$$

where:

$[E(R_m)–R_f]$ is the market premium equal to 20%;

R_f is the risk-free rate equal to 6%.

We can then deduce the value of the asset's Beta:

$$\beta_3 = (0.05–0.06)/0.2 \qquad \beta_3 = -\ 0.05.$$

We obtain a Beta value of −0.05 for asset 3, which indicates that the return of this asset is weakly and negatively correlated with the market return. A negative (positive) variation of 1% in the market return will create a positive (negative) variation of 0.05% in the return of asset 3.

(d) Calculate the incremental value at risk for asset 3 if the investor decides to allot $20,000 to this asset.

The notion of incremental value at risk is very pertinent because it lets us:

- Identify the sources of risk that the investor faces, which will help in providing more information to manage positions taken on each asset;
- Obtain more information to adjust the return according to the risk level;
- Determine the impact of a decision to buy or sell an asset on the VaR of a portfolio.

Two approaches are possible to calculate the incremental VaR.

Classic approach

- For a decision to buy an asset:
  Incremental value at risk for an asset = VaR of the portfolio with a position on the asset – VaR of the portfolio without a position on the asset.
- For a decision to sell an asset:
  Incremental value at risk for an asset = VaR of the portfolio without a position on the asset – VaR of the portfolio with a position on the asset.

Approximation approach

Generally, incremental VaR (according to the first approach) may require fairly long calculations when many assets are considered. To resolve this, we can use an approximation to calculate the IVaR:

$$\text{IVaR of asset} = a \times \beta_{asset,p} \times \text{VaR of initial portfolio}$$

where:

a is the proportion of the asset's position relative to the initial portfolio;

$\beta_{asset,p}$ is the Beta of the asset, which measures its sensitivity to the initial portfolio *p*:

$$\beta_{asset,p} = \sigma_{asset,p}/\sigma_p^2.$$

Numerical application:

- Calculating the IVaR by the classic method
  Let us calculate the new VaR of the portfolio with a position of $20,000 on the third asset.

$$R_{new} = (R_{old} + a \times R_3)/(1 + a)$$

where:

R_{old} is the old portfolio return;

R_{new} is the new portfolio return,

hence:

$$\sigma_{pnew}^2 = (1 + a)^{-2}(\sigma_p^2 + a^2\sigma_3^2 + 2a\sigma_{3,p})$$

$$\sigma_{3,p} = \text{Cov}(R_3, R_P) = \text{Cov}(R_3, b_1R_1 + b_2R_2) = b_1\text{Cov}(R_3, R_1) + b_2\text{Cov}(R_3, R_2).$$

We must then determine the new variance-covariance matrix:

$$\text{Cov}(R_1, R_3) = \rho_{1.3} \times \sigma_1 \times \sigma_3 = 0.024;$$

$$\text{Cov}(R_2, R_3) = \rho_{2.3} \times \sigma_2 \times \sigma_3 = -0.057.$$

The new variance-covariance matrix becomes:

$$\Sigma_{new} = \begin{bmatrix} 0.16 & 0.1 & 0.024 \\ 0.1 & 0.25 & -0.057 \\ 0.024 & -0.057 & 0.09 \end{bmatrix}.$$

In this case:

$$a = 20{,}000/100{,}000 = 0.2; \quad \sigma_p = 0.3805; \quad \sigma_3 = 0.3;$$

$$\sigma_{3,p} = 0.619 \times 0.024 + 0.381 \times -0.057 = -0.0069;$$

$$\sigma^2_{pnew} = (1 + 0.2)^{-2} \times (0.3805^2 + 0.22 \times 0.3^2 + 2 \times 0.2 \times -0.0069) = 0.1011;$$

$$\sigma_{pnew} = 0.3180.$$

The VaR_r of the initial portfolio is $62,778.52, so we have:

$$VaR_r^{new} = 1.65 \times 0.3180 \times 120{,}000 = \$62{,}964.11;$$

IVaR of asset 3 = 62,964.11 − 62,778.52 = $185.58.

The unit VaR decreases from 0.6278 to 0.5247, but the portfolio value increases from $100,000 to $120,000. We then obtain a slight increase in VaR of $185.58. This is due to a diversification effect, even if the proportion of the investment in asset 3 is large (a = 20%) relative to the initial portfolio.

Figure E1.1 presents the evolution of the IVaR relative to the proportion of the portfolio invested in the additional asset.

- Calculating IVaR by the approximation method:
  IVaR of asset 3 = a × $\beta_{3,p}$ × VaR of the initial portfolio;

$$\beta_{3,p} = \sigma_{3,p}/\sigma_p^2 = -0.0069/0.3805^2 = -0.0477;$$

$$IVaR = 0.2 \times -0.0477 \times 62{,}778.52 = -\$594.74.$$

Incremental VaR may be negative because it is a variation of VaR. In our case, IVaR of −$594.74 would indicate that asset 3 contributes negatively to the initial portfolio risk: it would thus be a stronger form of portfolio hedging. However, the approximation method may appear quite imprecise when compared to the standard approach.

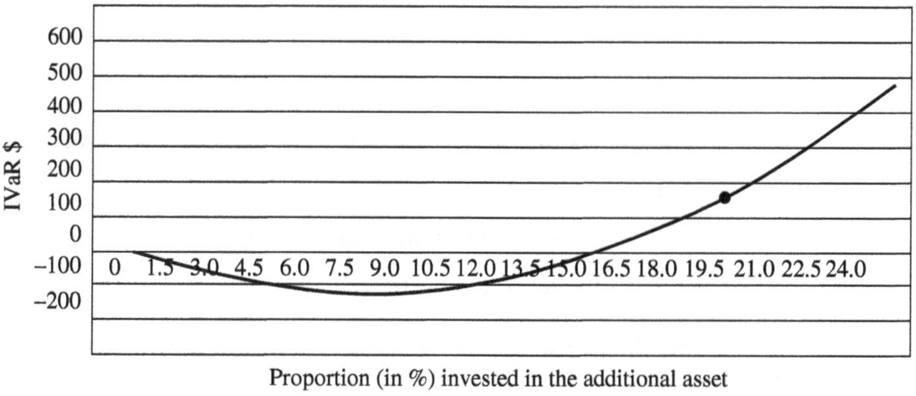

FIGURE E1.1 IVaR relative to the proportion invested in the additional asset.

It is possible to look at the sensitivity of the results according to the asset's Beta relative to the market: −0.05 instead of −0.0477 (found according to the CAPM, question 4.d with the incremental VaR approximation method).

IVaR = a × β_3 × VaR of the initial portfolio;

$$IVaR_r = 0.2 \times -0.05 \times 62,778.52 = -\$627.78.$$

Important: The two methods may produce different and even contradictory results. This is due to the approximations that method 2 assumes. The value of the proportion *a* must remain low if we want to apply this method. In other words, the amount invested in the new asset must be low relative to the initial portfolio.

For example, had we invested only \$2,000 (instead of \$20,000), *a* would be equal to 0.02, and we would have had a better approximation of IVaR:

$$VaR_r = \$62,778.52;$$

$$\sigma^2_{pnew} = (1 + 0.02)–2 \times (0.3805^2 + 0.02^2 \times 0.09 + 2 \times 0.02 - 0.0069)$$

$$= 0.138927;$$

$$\sigma_{pnew} = 0.3727;$$

$$VaR_r^{new} = 1.65 \times 0.3727 \times 102,000 = \$62,726.83.$$

Hence:

$$IVaR\ (classic) = 62,726.83 - 62,778.52 = -\$51.69;$$

$$IVaR\ (approximated) = 0.02 \times (-0.0477) \times 62,778.52 = -\$59.47.$$

(e) Assume this time that the market contains only the two risky assets and one risk-free asset with a return of 6%. Calculate the incremental value at risk (IVaR) associated with the risk-free asset by assuming an investment of \$10,000 in this asset. Use the classic approach. Comment on your results and compare them with the results obtained in question 4.d.

$$\sigma_p = 0.3805;$$

$$a = 10,000/100,000 = 0.1;$$

$$\sigma^2_{pnew} = (1 + 0.1)^{-2} \times (0.3805^2 + 0.1^2 \times 0 + 2 \times 0.1 \times 0) = 0.1196;$$

$$\sigma_{pnew} = 0.3459;$$

$$VaR_r^{new} = 1.65 \times 0.345887 \times 110,000 = \$62,778.49;$$

$$IVaR = 62,778.49 - 62,778.52 = 0.$$

The IVaR corresponding to a risk-free asset is equal to 0. The investment in this risk-free asset has no effect on IVaR. This result is predictable because the risk-free asset has a return with zero covariance.

EXERCISE 2 BACKTESTING OF VaR MODELS[3]

The Importance of Backtesting

Backtesting serves to validate VaR models relative to historical realizations. For example, if we say that VaR is $1 million at a 95% degree of confidence, is this amount exceeded only 5 times out of 100 in the model used? Should we accept or reject exceptions that occur 6 times out of 100? What if the exceptions happen only 2 times out of 100?

In this exercise, we will evaluate two VaR backtesting models: historical simulation (non-parametric) and the RiskMetrics model. Figure E2.1 presents the returns of a portfolio over time and the R* centile of VaR calculated according to the two models. The horizontal line (at around –2%) indicates VaR obtained from the historical simulations, whereas the other line, varying around the first horizontal line, indicates the RiskMetrics VaR.

- The RiskMetrics Model

  The return variance follows this calculation:

$$\sigma_n^2 = \lambda\sigma_{n-1}^2 + (1-\lambda)r_{n-1}^2 \quad \text{with} \quad \lambda = 0.94 \quad \text{and} \quad \text{VaR} = \alpha \times \sigma_n$$

where:

σ_n^2 is the variance of day n;

r_{n-1} is the daily market return of day n – 1 (end of previous day);

α is a weight corresponding to the degree of confidence selected.

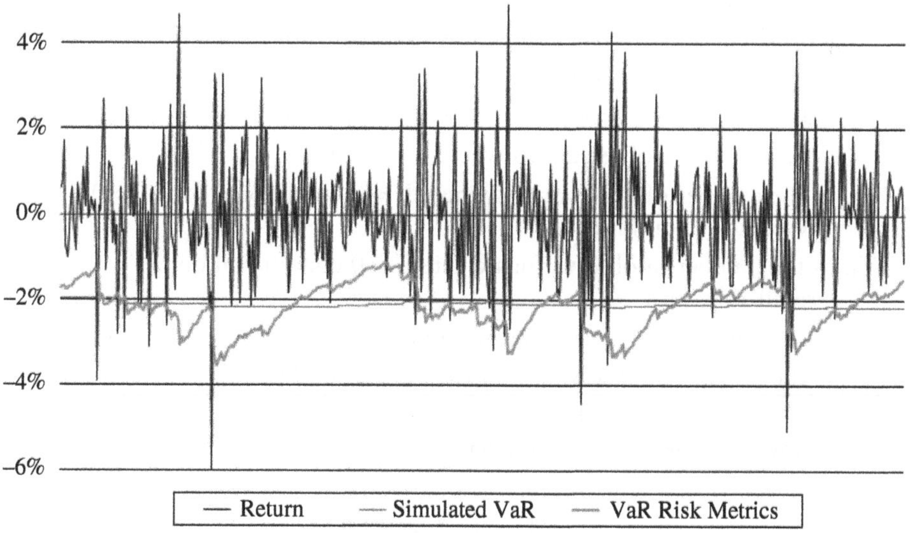

FIGURE E2.1 Comparison of Two VaR Models: RiskMetrics and Historical simulation.

[3]This exercise was produced in cooperation with Samir Saissi Hassani and Alain-Philippe Fortin. The data and basis of the calculations are heavily inspired by Christoffersen (2003).

- The Historical Simulation Model

  The historical simulation model does not make any assumptions about the return distribution (non-parametric). VaR is read directly at the desired centile.

Definitions for the Backtesting

(a) A hit is when the observed return becomes less than R*, which corresponds to the –VaR of the model.

(b) The proportion of hits should not be statistically different from the theoretical probability of the model. If there is an exception, the model will not cover the data as well. Conversely, if there are too few exceptions, the model would be outsized and therefore incur a high cost of capital to retain, which is also undesirable.

(c) Hits must be independent from one another over time.

(d) First, we define the indicator variable, I_t, which contains the series of hits, as follows:

$$I_t = \begin{cases} 1 & \text{if } R_t < R^* \\ 0 & \text{otherwise} \end{cases}$$

where R_t is the return at date *t*.

- Validation of a VaR model

$$H_0 : I_t \sim \text{iid of Bernouilli (p)}.$$

This amounts to doing two statistical tests:

- Kupiec Test (1995): I_t follows a Bernouilli law of the parameter p;
- Christoffersen Test (2003): the I_t are independent.

T is the number of observations;

T_0 is the number of observations where $I_t = 0$ (non-hit);

T_1 is the number of observations where $I_t = 1$ (hit);

T_{00} is the number of observations where $I_t = 0$ conditional on $I_{t-1} = 0$ (non-hit preceded by non-hit);

T_{10} is the number of observations where $I_t = 0$ conditional on $I_{t-1} = 1$ (non-hit preceded by hit);

T_{01} is the number of observations where $I_t = 0$ conditional on $I_{t-1} = 0$;

T_{11} is the number of observations where $I_t = 0$ conditional on $I_{t-1} = 1$.

- Kupiec Test: unconditional coverage

  We calculate the historical frequency of hits:

$$\pi = \frac{T_1}{T} = \frac{T_1}{T_0 + T_1}.$$

The probability function of a binomial law is written as:

$$L(p) = \binom{T}{T_1} (1 - p)^{T_0} (p)^{T_1}.$$

We compare π to the theoretical value $p : H_0 : p = \pi$. Asymptotically, if T is large enough, we have that the likelihood ratio (LR_{uc}) is equal to:

$$LR_{uc} = -2\ln[L(p)/L(\pi)] \sim \chi_1^2.$$

Important: There is a restriction that $p = \pi$. The degree of freedom (dof) of this Chi2 test is therefore 1. The Chi2 test helps us determine the validity of the VaR models. Usually we apply this test at a 10% degree of confidence. (This choice is not related to the confidence level of VaR.) The critical value at 10% is 2.705 for one degree of freedom (dof = 1).

In the case of the RiskMetrics model, the calculations for VaR at 1% are:

$$T_0 = 2{,}467, \quad T_1 = 54, \quad \pi = 0.02142.$$

We have:

$$LR_{uc} = 25.0216 > \text{Chi2}(10\%, \text{ddl} = 1) = 2.705.$$

H_0 is therefore rejected at 10%. We have 2,521 observations with 54 hits. For a VaR at 1%, if we are too far from 25 hits, H_0 must be rejected.

- Christoffersen Test: independence of hits

  Here we want to test the independence of the hits, I_t. The starting premise is that the sequence of hits follows a first-order Markovian process described by the transition matrix:

$$\Pi_1 = \begin{bmatrix} \pi_{00} & \pi_{01} \\ \pi_{10} & \pi_{11} \end{bmatrix}.$$

For example, the element $\pi_{11} = \Pr(I_t = 1 \text{ and } I_{t+1} = 1)$. The sum of the probabilities must equal 1, hence:

$$\Pi_1 = \begin{bmatrix} 1 - \pi_{01} & \pi_{01} \\ 1 - \pi_{11} & \pi_{11} \end{bmatrix}.$$

The probabilities are estimated by:

$$\hat{\pi}_{01} = \frac{T_{01}}{T_{00} + T_{01}}, \quad \hat{\pi}_{00} = 1 - \hat{\pi}_{01} \text{ and } \hat{\pi}_{11} = \frac{T_{11}}{T_{10} + T_{11}}, \ \hat{\pi}_{10} = 1 - \hat{\pi}_{11}.$$

The likelihood function in this case is:

$$L(\Pi_1) = (1 - \pi_{01})^{T_{00}} \pi_{01}{}^{T_{01}} (1 - \pi_{11})^{T_{10}} \pi_{11}{}^{T_{11}}.$$

Now, if we suppose that at date *t* the probability of obtaining a hit does not depend on the state of the previous day $t - 1$, we should have the same probability:

$$\pi_{01} = \pi_{11} = \pi,$$

hence:

$$\Pi = \begin{bmatrix} 1 - \pi & \pi \\ 1 - \pi & \pi \end{bmatrix}.$$

The test is summarized as:

$$H_0 : \pi_{01} = \pi_{11} \quad (= \pi).$$

If H_0 is true, the LR_{ind} statistic also follows a Chi2 distribution with a dof = 1 (one restriction):

$$LR_{ind} = -2\ln[L(\Pi)/L(\Pi_1)] \sim \chi^2_1.$$

In the case of the RiskMetrics model with a VaR at 1%, we obtain:

$$T_0 = 2{,}467,\ T_1 = 54,\ T_{00} = 2{,}418,\ T_{01} = 49,\ T_{10} = 49,\ T_{11} = 5;$$

$$\pi_{01} = 0.01986, \quad \pi_{11} = 0.09259, \quad \pi = 0.02142;$$

$$LR_{ind} = 7.5314 > \text{Chi2}(10\%,\ \text{ddl} = 1).$$

We therefore reject the null hypothesis, H_0. Consequently, the hits of this model should not be considered independent from one another over time.

- Simultaneous tests: conditional coverage

  To simultaneously test that the hits follow a binomial distribution and that they are independent over time we must write:

$$H_0 : \pi_{01} = \pi_{11} \quad \text{et} \quad p = \pi;$$

$$LR_{cc} = -2\ln[L(p)/L(\pi)] - 2\ln[L(\Pi)/L(\hat{\Pi}_1)] \sim \chi^2_2 (\text{two constraints here}).$$

Note that:

$$LR_{cc} = LR_{uc} + LR_{ind},$$

but the Chi2 test is done with a dof = 2. The critical value at 10% is 4.605 for two degrees of freedom.

$$LR_{cc} = 25.0216 + 7.5314 = 32.5530 > \text{Chi2}(10\%,\ \text{dof} = 2) = 4.605.$$

We again reject the null hypothesis, H_0. The simultaneous test at 10% rejects conditional coverage.

We can redo the calculations and apply the same logic to evaluate the validity of the RiskMetrics model at 5%. We follow the same procedure to evaluate the historical simulation model at 1% and at 5%. Table E2.1 indicates that we reject H_0 less often for a VaR at 5% than for a VaR at 1%.

Validation of the Model over a Longer Period

Up to now we have applied the tests over a very short period. However, the real test for practitioners concerns stability: is the model estimated with the current data stable for the future? The principle behind this type of validation is to verify whether we have a VaR model to cover us during the following 10 days (square root of 10). The hits obtained ex post would have met the same stability conditions as those we have just seen.

To do so, we choose as a test period from March 7, 1994 to December 31, 2001 (1,970 observations available from the database). At the beginning of each 10-day interval, we calculate VaR at 1% and 5% for our two models: RiskMetrics and Historical simulation. We define our projected VaR for the 10 days of the period. We thus obtain a new series of about 197 observations. Comparing the projected VaR of each 10-day period with the actual return realized ex post gives us the hits of the two models.

The calculations of the statistics and the test procedures are thus similar to the daily calculations done above.

Again, for the RiskMetrics model at 1%, we have:

$$LR_{uc} = 5.3886 > \text{Chi2}(10\%,\ 1) = 2.7055.$$

We therefore reject at 10% the hypothesis that the frequency of hits is statistically the same as the theoretical probability. Moreover:

$$LR_{ind} = 0{,}3770 < \text{Chi2}(10\%,\ 1) \quad \text{and} \quad LR_{cc} = 5.7656 > \text{Chi2}(10\%,\ 2) = 4.6052.$$

We cannot reject the hypothesis of independence. However, for this model, the joint test LR_{cc} lets us reject the hypothesis of conditional coverage at 10%. Details of calculations over a longer period are presented in Table E2.2.

We observe that the backtesting of RiskMetrics at 1% does not validate this model as in Table E2.1. Conversely, RiskMerics at 5% is validated more often just

TABLE E2.1 Comparison of two methods for calculating VaR.

RiskMetrics			Historical simulation		
VaR	1%	5%	VaR	1%	5%
T_0	2,467	2,395	T_0	2,485	2,376
T_1	54	126	T_1	36	145
T_{00}	2,418	2,279	T_{00}	2,451	2,240
T_{01}	49	116	T_{01}	34	136
T_{10}	49	116	T_{10}	34	136
T_{11}	5	10	T_{11}	2	9
π	0.021420	0.049980	π	0.014280	0.057517
π_{01}	0.019862	0.048434	π_{01}	0.013682	0.057239
π_{11}	0.092593	0.079365	π_{11}	0.055556	0.062069
LR_{uc}	25.021666	0.000021	LR_{uc}	4.118746	2.866314
LR_{ind}	7.531411	2.081109	LR_{ind}	2.589361	0.057494
LR_{cc}	32.553078	2.081130	LR_{cc}	6.708107	2.923808
Chi-test			Chi-test		
	10%	10%		10%	10%
LR_{uc}	Rejects VaR model	Does not reject VaR model	LR_{uc}	Rejects VaR model	Rejects VaR model
LR_{ind}	Rejects VaR model	Does not reject VaR model	LR_{ind}	Does not reject VaR model	Does not reject VaR model
LR_{cc}	Rejects VaR model	Does not reject VaR model	LR_{cc}	Rejects VaR model	Does not reject VaR model

TABLE E2.2 Comparison between the two methods of calculating VaR over a longer period.

RiskMetrics			Historical simulation		
VaR	1%	5%	VaR	1%	5%
T_0	191	188	T_0	193	186
T_1	6	9	T_1	4	11
T_{00}	185	179	T_{00}	190	177
T_{01}	6	9	T_{01}	3	9
T_{10}	6	9	T_{10}	3	9
T_{11}	0	0	T_{11}	1	2
π	0.030457	0.045685	π	0.020305	0.055838
π_{01}	0.031414	0.047872	π_{01}	0.015544	0.048387
π_{11}	0.000000	0.000000	π_{11}	0.250000	0.181818
LR_{uc}	5.388565	0.079411	LR_{uc}	1.627290	0.136405
LR_{ind}	0.377025	0.862032	LR_{ind}	3.657228	2.349031
LR_{cc}	5.765590	0.941442	LR_{cc}	5.284518	2.485436
Chi-test			Chi-test		
	10%	10%		10%	10%
LR_{uc}	Rejects VaR model	Does not reject VaR model	LR_{uc}	Does not reject VaR model	Does not reject VaR model
LR_{ind}	Does not reject VaR model	Does not reject VaR model	LR_{ind}	Rejects VaR model	Does not reject VaR model
LR_{cc}	Rejects VaR model	Does not reject VaR model	LR_{cc}	Rejects VaR model	Does not reject VaR model

as well in the two tables. This coherence is not generally observed, however. In certain situations it may occur that the two tests do not necessarily yield the same results.

Conclusion: Backtesting of RiskMetrics at 1% shows that this model is not suited to the data sample studied. For a model to be retained, it is better to perform simultaneous validation over different periods.

Linear Regression Approach

The linear regression approach can also verify whether the hits are autocorrelated or not. For information purposes, here is the principle behind this approach according to Christofferson (2003):

Consider the equation:

$$I_{t+1} = b_0 + b_1' X_t + e_{t+1}$$

where:

e_{t+1} is the error term;

X_t is the matrix generally containing 5 lags of I_t.

We have:

$$E[b_0 + b_1' X_t + e_{t+1} | X_t] = b_0 + b_1' X_t = p.$$

The test becomes:

$$H_0 : b_0 = p \quad \text{and} \quad b_1' = 0.$$

Intuitively, on average there is a percentage of *p* hits. Delayed hits do not contain information on the current hit. The statistical test is done by a standard Fisher test.

REFERENCES

Christoffersen P.F., 2003. *Elements of Financial Risk Management*. Amsterdam: Academic Press.

Kupiec, P., 1995. "Techniques for Verifying the Accuracy of Risk Measurement Models." *Journal of Derivatives* 2, 73–84.

EXERCISE 3 CALCULATION OF VaR WITH DIFFERENT DISTRIBUTIONS AND ACCURACY OF VaR

Calculating VaR using a Lognormal or Truncated Normal Distribution

Question 1

In this exercise we are interested in a random variable X that does not follow a normal distribution. We want to calculate VaR in two cases:

- X follows a lognormal distribution:

$$X \sim \text{LogN}(m, s^2) \quad \Longleftrightarrow \quad \log(X) \sim N(m, s^2)$$

We want to calculate VaR at quantile R* (i.e., degree of confidence equal to $1 - p = 0.95;\ 0.99$) from the right tail of the distribution.

1.a. Show that:

$$\text{VaR}_a = \text{Absolute VaR} = \exp(m + s\alpha')$$

$$\text{VaR}_r = \text{Relative VaR} = \exp(m + s\alpha') - \exp\left(m + \frac{s^2}{2}\right), \text{ where } \alpha' = \Phi^{-1}(1 - p).$$

- X follows a truncated normal distribution to the left of point *c* with a mean μ and variance σ^2.

1.b. Show that:

$$\text{VaR}_a = \mu + \sigma\Phi^{-1}\left[\Phi\left(\frac{c-\mu}{\sigma}\right) + (1-p)\left(1 - \Phi\left(\frac{c-\mu}{\sigma}\right)\right)\right]$$

$$\text{VaR}_r = \sigma\left[\Phi^{-1}\left[\Phi\left(\frac{c-\mu}{\sigma}\right) + (1-p)\left(1 - \Phi\left(\frac{c-\mu}{\sigma}\right)\right)\right] - \frac{\phi\left(\frac{c-\mu}{\sigma}\right)}{1 - \Phi\left(\frac{c-\mu}{\sigma}\right)}\right].$$

Estimating the Precision of the VaR Calculated

Question 2

The calculation of VaR is based on the determination of the return R. This depends on the distribution used to model the random variable in question. The estimation of the model is more or less precise depending on the number of observations available to be studied. The problem in this part of the exercise is to be able to determine the relative precision obtained when VaR is calculated according to a given model and based on a given sample size.

We suppose that the realizations of the random variable X come from the same non-negative distribution. We want to study two cases:

- A truncated normal distribution, $\mu = 1.3$, $\sigma = 0.9$, and $c = 0$.
- A lognormal $\text{LogN}(m = 0.0666,\ s = 0.6257)$.
  - 2.a In both cases, evaluate the precision to achieve a sample of 100 observations for absolute VaR at 95%. Determine the interval of uncertainty associated with the VaR for the two models; compare and discuss.
  - 2.b. Conversely, for each of the two models, calculate the minimum sample size required to calculate the absolute VaR with a relative precision of ±10%; compare and discuss.

We use Kiefer's approximation (1967) to evaluate the standard deviation of the empirical estimator of the quantile relative to R*.

Solution to Exercise 3

Question 1

1.a. X follows a lognormal distribution:

$$X \sim \text{LogN}(m, s^2) \quad \Longleftrightarrow \quad \log(X) \sim N(m, s^2).$$

We calculate the following probabilities:

$$p = \Pr(X \geq R^*) = \Pr(\ln(X) \geq \ln(R^*)) = \Pr\left(\frac{\ln(X) - m}{s} \geq \frac{\ln(R^*) - m}{s}\right)$$

$$= 1 - \Phi\left(\frac{\ln(R^*) - m}{s}\right)$$

$\ln(R^*) = m + \Phi^{-1}(1 - p) \times s \Rightarrow R^* = \exp(m + \alpha' \times s)$ where $\alpha' = \Phi^{-1}(1 - p)$.

Given that $E(X) = \exp\left(m + \frac{s^2}{2}\right)$:

Absolute VaR $= \exp(m + \alpha' s)$;

Relative VaR $= \exp(m + \alpha' s) - \exp\left(m + \frac{s^2}{2}\right)$.

Example: In Figure E3.1, on the continuous line, we have a normal distribution $x \sim N(\mu, \sigma^2)$ and on the dotted line, we have the lognormal distribution $X \sim \text{LogN}(m, s^2)$. The parameters are given in Table E3.1

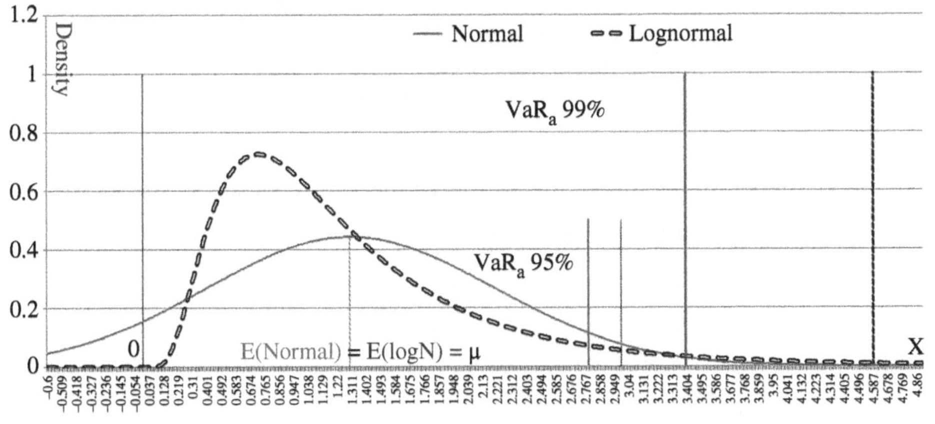

FIGURE E3.1 VaR with normal and lognormal distribution.

TABLE E3.1 Normal and lognormal distribution parameters.

	Normal		Lognormal	
Expected value	mu	1.3	m	0.0666
Standard deviation	sigma	0.9	s	0.6257
	VaR_a (95%)	2.785	VaR_a (95%)	2.9917
	VaR_a (99%)	3.397	VaR_a (99%)	4.5827
	VaR_r (95%)	1.485	VaR_r (95%)	1.6917
	VaR_r (99%)	2.097	VaR_r (99%)	3.2827

Note: If we want to calculate absolute VaR on the left tail, we can show that we have the following expression as a function of E(X) = m and standard deviation *s*: absolute VaR(left tail) = exp(m − α′s).

We can calculate the parameters of the lognormal with: $m = \ln\left[\frac{\mu^2}{\sqrt{\sigma^2+\mu^2}}\right]$ and $s = \sqrt{\ln\left[\frac{\sigma^2}{\mu^2}+1\right]}$.

1.b. X follows a truncated normal distribution at point *c*:

$$p = \Pr\left(\frac{X \geq R^*}{X \geq c}\right) = \frac{\Pr(X \geq R^*)}{\Pr(X \geq c)} = \frac{1-\Phi\left(\frac{R^*-\mu}{\sigma}\right)}{1-\Phi\left(\frac{c-\mu}{\sigma}\right)} = \frac{1-\Phi\left(\frac{R^*-\mu}{\sigma}\right)}{\delta},$$

$$\delta = 1-\Phi\left(\frac{c-\mu}{\sigma}\right)$$

$$\Phi\left(\frac{R^*-\mu}{\sigma}\right) = 1-\delta p \Rightarrow R^* = \mu + \sigma\Phi^{-1}(1-p\delta)$$

Further, we need to show that:

$$E\left(\frac{X}{X \geq c}\right) = \mu + \frac{\sigma}{\delta}\phi\left(\frac{c-\mu}{\sigma}\right).$$

Proof:

$$E\left(\frac{X}{X \geq c}\right) = E\left(\frac{X}{\frac{X-\mu}{\sigma} \geq \frac{c-\mu}{\sigma}}\right) = \int_{\frac{c-\mu}{\sigma}}^{+\infty} \frac{x\phi(x)}{\delta} dx.$$

Note that:

$$\frac{d\phi(x)}{dx} = -\frac{(x-\mu)}{\sigma}\phi(x) = \frac{-x}{\sigma}\phi(x) + \frac{\mu}{\sigma}\phi(x) \Rightarrow x\phi(x) = \mu\phi(x) - \sigma\frac{d\phi(x)}{dx};$$

$$\int_{\frac{c-\mu}{\sigma}}^{+\infty} \frac{x\phi(x)}{\delta} dx = \frac{\mu}{\delta}\int_{\frac{c-\mu}{\sigma}}^{+\infty} \phi(x)dx - \frac{\sigma}{\delta}\int_{\frac{c-\mu}{\sigma}}^{+\infty} d\phi(x) = \frac{\mu}{\delta}[\Phi(x)]_{\frac{c-\mu}{\sigma}}^{+\infty} - \frac{\sigma}{\delta}[\phi(x)]_{\frac{c-\mu}{\sigma}}^{+\infty};$$

$$\frac{\mu}{\delta}[F(x)]_{\frac{c-\mu}{\sigma}}^{+\infty} - \frac{\sigma}{\delta}[\phi(x)]_{\frac{c-\mu}{\sigma}}^{+\infty}$$

$$= \frac{\mu}{\delta}\left[1 - \Phi\left(\frac{c-\mu}{\sigma}\right)\right] - \frac{\sigma}{\delta}\left[0 - \phi\left(\frac{c-\mu}{\sigma}\right)\right] = \mu + \frac{\sigma}{\delta}\phi\left(\frac{c-\mu}{\sigma}\right);$$

which implies that:

$$E\left(\frac{X}{X \geq c}\right) = \mu + \frac{\sigma}{\delta}\phi\left(\frac{c-\mu}{\sigma}\right);$$

and

Absolute

$$\text{VaR} = \mu + \sigma\,\Phi^{-1}(1 - p\delta);$$

Relative

$$\text{VaR} = \mu + \sigma\,\Phi^{-1}(1 - p\delta) - \mu - \frac{\sigma}{\delta}\phi\left(\frac{c-\mu}{\sigma}\right) = \sigma\left[\Phi^{-1}(1 - p\delta) - \frac{\phi\left(\frac{c-\mu}{\sigma}\right)}{\delta}\right].$$

An example is presented in Table E3.2.

The gap between VaR_a at 95% of the two distributions (normal and truncated normal) is about that at 99%. This is due to the fact that the "truncation correction," which is a multiplicative coefficient, has a greater effect around the mode and almost no effect on the extreme values. Concerning the lognormal, the effect is precisely the

TABLE E3.2 Parameters of the normal and truncated normal distribution.

	Normal		Truncated normal	
			c	0
Expected value	mu	1.3	mu	1.4518
Standard deviation	sigma	0.9	delta	0.9257
	VaR_a (95%)	2.785	VaR_a (95%)	2.8138
	VaR_a (99%)	3.397	VaR_a (99%)	3.4197
	VaR_r (95%)	1.485	VaR_r (95%)	1.3620
	VaR_r (99%)	2.097	VaR_r (99%)	1.9678

Results are shown in Figure E3.2.

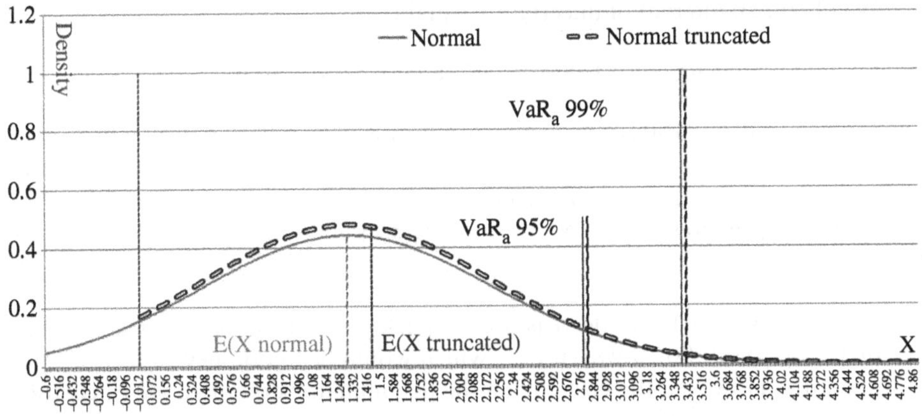

FIGURE E3.2 VaR with normal and truncated normal distribution.

inverse (compare the two figures). This is because the normal truncated distribution tail quickly joins that of the normal distribution, whereas the density of the lognormal always remains above the normal distribution.

As an exercise, analyze and discuss what happens to VaR_r in both cases.

Precision Estimation of the Calculated VaR

Question 2.a.

Suppose that $X > 0$. First we consider that the observations of X come from a normal truncated distribution. The estimation of the parameters of this model gives us $\mu = 1.3$, $\sigma = 0.9$, and $c = 0$. We have 100 observations. We want to evaluate the precision of the VaR obtained from this model.

Kiefer (1967) proposes an approximation for the empirical estimator's (R_p^*) of the standard deviation using the quantile evaluated at probability p:

$$\sigma(R_p^*) \approx \sqrt{\frac{p(1-p)}{n}}\frac{1}{f(R_p^*)},$$

where:

n is the number of observations;

$f(\cdot)$ is the density function of the estimated distribution.

We then calculate the precision of the estimation as a relative error, by writing $|\Delta R_p^*|/R_p^* = 2\sigma(R_p^*)/R_p^*$, hence:

$$\text{Relative precision} \approx 2\sqrt{\frac{p(1-p)}{n}}\frac{1}{f(R_p^*)}\frac{1}{R_p^*}.$$

For $p = 5\%$, $R_p^* = 2.8138$, hence a precision of R_p^* is approximated by:

$$\approx 2\sqrt{\frac{0.05(1-0.05)}{100}}\frac{1}{0.1164}\frac{1}{2.8138} = 13.3\%.$$

We obtain an interval of uncertainty equal to:

$$R_p^* = 2.8138 \pm 13.3\% \Rightarrow R_p^* \in [2.44;\ 3.19].$$

With a sample of 100 observations, we cannot guarantee a precision better than ±13.3%. All of the values included between 2.44 and 3.19 are possible as absolute VaR values at 95% degree of confidence!

In Kiefer's expression (1967), three factors influence the calculations of precision:

- The function $\sqrt{p(1-p)}$ decreases very quickly toward 0, in the area to the left of 1 ($(1-p) = 0.90$; 0.99, etc)…, which would be "good news" for the upper quantiles. However, the elements in the denominator dominate the calculations of precision for the VaR.
- Sample size is in the denominator and is expressed in $\sqrt{n}$. To double the desired precision, we must quadruple the sample size. This is very important when the study examines rare or difficult to find data, like credit risk and tail losses in operational risk modeling.
- $f(R_p^*)$ also appears in the denominator. This leads to two cases:
  - For the same distribution, $|R_{1\%}^*| > |R_{5\%}^*|$, therefore $f(R_{1\%}^*) < f(R_{5\%}^*)$. The necessary sample size then increases with the degree of confidence required for VaR.
  - For the same degree of confidence, the minimum sample size increases with the thickness of the distribution tail to achieve the same precision of VaR. If f and g are two densities where g has a thicker tail than f, then: $|R_{1\%}^*$ with $g| > |R_{1\%}^*$ with $f|$, therefore $f(R_{1\%}^*) > g(R_{1\%}^*)$.

We can verify this with our lognormal distribution ($s = 0.0666$, $m = 0.6257$). For $p = 5\%$, $R_p^* = 2.9917$, hence a precision of:

$$\approx 2\sqrt{\frac{0.05(1-0.05)}{100}}\ \frac{1}{0.0551}\ \frac{1}{2.9917} = 26.4\%.$$

The interval of uncertainty is equal to: $R_p^* = 2.9917 \pm 26.4\% \Rightarrow R_p^* \in [2.20;$ $3.78]$.

In practice, this result means that the imprecision is such that we obtain a value of R_p^* that may range between 2 and 4. If these figures correspond to the capital to cover a portfolio of millions of dollars, by modeling historical losses of the portfolio with a lognormal, the capital to retain may be $2 million or $4 million, which would be double in value. So, will you keep $2 million, $3 million, or $4 million in capital? These numbers illustrate the crucial importance of having a sufficient sample size. Overall, we should aim for precision of at least ±10%, to have a usable calculated VaR.

Table E3.3 clearly illustrates the importance of sample size in improving the precision of the calculated VaR. With 100 observations, a VaR at 99% calculated with a lognormal distribution becomes imprecise by about 50%, whereas for 99.9%, the calculation of this VaR has no meaning because imprecision exceeds 100%. With the Pareto distribution, it is even larger at 218%, and this distribution is often used for operational risk estimation.

TABLE E3.3 Effects of sample size for the precision of the calculated VaR.

Sample size	Pareto Parameters			Lognormal			Normal			Truncated Normal c = 0		
100	alpha = 2.8957			m = 0.0666 s = 0.6257			mu = 1.3000 sigma = 0.9000			mu = 1.4518		δ = 0.9257
1 − p	Precision	R_p^*	$f(R_p^*)$	Precision	R_p^*	$f(R_p^*)$	Precision	R_p^*	$f(R_p^*)$	Precision	R_p^*	$f(R_p^*)$
0.9	20.7%	2.21	0.1307	21.4%	2.38	0.1177	12.5%	2.45	0.1950	13.1%	2.51	0.1827
0.95	30.1%	2.81	0.0515	26.4%	2.99	0.0551	13.7%	2.78	0.1146	14.3%	2.86	0.1065
0.99	68.7%	4.91	0.0059	46.7%	4.58	0.0093	19.8%	3.39	0.0296	20.7%	3.52	0.0273
0.995	97.4%	6.23	0.0023	61.0%	5.36	0.0043	24.3%	3.62	0.0161	25.4%	3.77	0.0148
0.999	218.3%	10.86	0.0003	117.5%	7.39	0.0007	41.4%	4.08	0.0037	43.2%	4.27	0.0034

Question 2.b.

Calculate the minimum sample size required to guarantee a precision of ±10%.

This is the inverse calculation to that of the previous question. Table E3.4 shows how the minimum size *n* increases faster when the thickness of the distribution in question increases.

Now, let us look at Figure E3.3, which summarizes the essentials of the statistical intuition behind the calculations, where the areas are measured by $\sqrt{\frac{p(1-p)}{n}} \times \frac{1}{R_p^*}$ and R_p^* is either at 5% or at 1%.

Similarly, when we work with the same data sample and we want to test two distribution models, Figure E3.4 shows what happens if one of the distributions has a thicker tail than the other.

This last case clearly shows what happens in modeling with a distribution that does not suit the data. For example, suppose that the data presents realizations at extreme values, which seems to indicate the presence of a thick tail. If the model design does not take this into account, the calculation and precision of VaR may be very biased. This is why the number of observations is crucial. The more observations we have, the lower the likelihood of making a mistake when choosing a distribution to use. Further, with more observations, as seen in this exercise, we can expect more precision for our calculations of VaR. For more information on data modeling principles, see Tukey (1977) and Hoaglin, Mosteller, and Tukey (2011) on exploratory data analysis.

TABLE E3.4 Analysis of minimum sample size.

Precision required	Pareto Parameters			Lognormal			Normal			Truncated Normal c = 0		
10.00 %	alpha = 2.8957			m = 0.0666 s = 0.6257			mu = 1.3000 sigma = 0.9000			mu = 1.4518		δ = 0.9257
1 − p	n	R_p^*	$f(R_p^*)$	n	R_p^*	$f(R_p^*)$	n	R_p^*	$f(R_p^*)$	n	R_p^*	$f(R_p^*)$
0.9	429	2.21	0.1307	458	2.38	0.1177	157	2.45	0.1950	171	2.51	0.1827
0.95	906	2.81	0.0515	699	2.99	0.0551	187	2.78	0.1146	205	2.86	0.1065
0.99	4,723	4.91	0.0059	2,183	4.58	0.0093	392	3.39	0.0296	430	3.52	0.0273
0.995	9,493	6.23	0.0023	3,727	5.36	0.0043	589	3.62	0.0161	644	3.77	0.0148
0.999	47,656	10.86	0.0003	13,801	7.39	0.0007	1,714	4.08	0.0037	1,868	4.27	0.0034

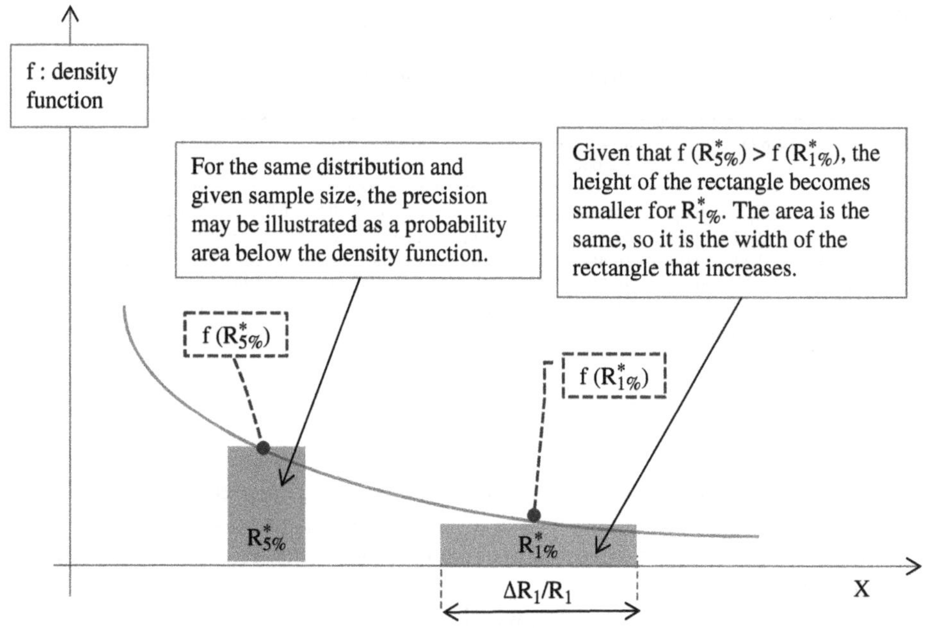

FIGURE E3.3 Representation of the effect of sample size.

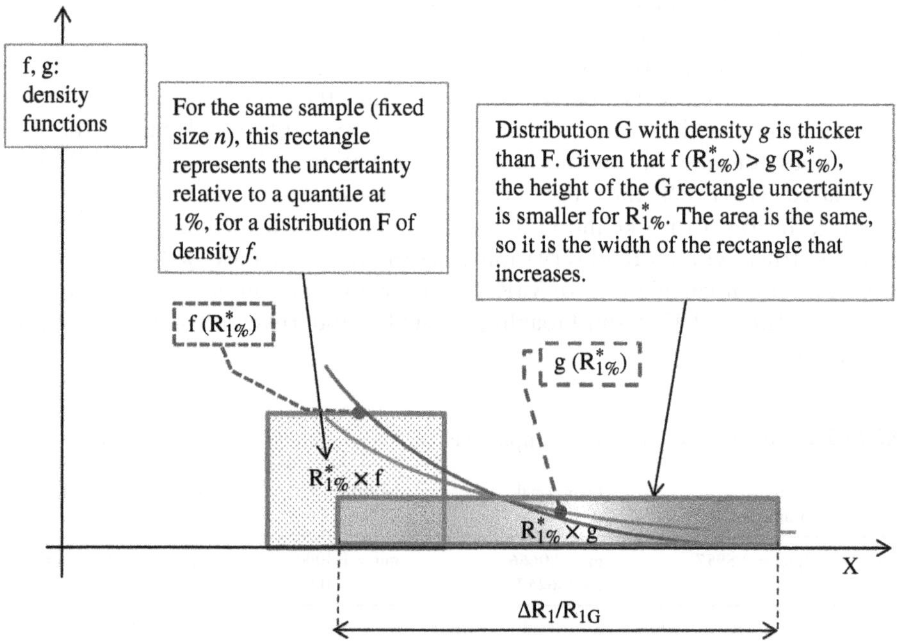

FIGURE E3.4 Comparison of two distributions with different tails.

REFERENCES

Hoaglin, D.C., Mosteller, F., and Tukey, J.W., 2011. *Exploring Data Tables, Trends, and Shapes*. Wiley.
Kiefer, J., 1967. "On Bahadur's Representation of Sample Quantiles." *Annals of Mathematical Statistics* 38, 1323–1342.
Tukey, J.W., 1977. *Exploratory Data Analysis*. Reading, MA: Addison-Wesley Publishing Co.

EXERCISE 4 VaR FOR AN EQUITY PORTFOLIO WITH OPTIONS

Part A Choosing a Portfolio Application of VaR Calculations with Real Data from a Stock Portfolio[4]

This exercise consists of applying and analyzing the results obtained with real data. With the same notations as in Exercise 1, the optimal weights of the assets are calculated by using:

$$\begin{bmatrix} B \\ \lambda \end{bmatrix} = \begin{bmatrix} A & \bar{1} \\ \bar{1}' & 0 \end{bmatrix}^{-1} \begin{bmatrix} C \\ 1 \end{bmatrix} \text{ where } A = 2\,r\,\Sigma.$$

We build a portfolio composed of five risky assets (see Table E4.1).

We want to calculate the optimal portfolios for six different agents, whose risk aversion is identified respectively by s = 0.01; 0.1; 0.3; 0.5; 0.7; and 1.

The evolution of these optimal portfolios will be followed and analyzed for four successive periods of five business days each.

1. Calculate the individual returns of the stocks.

   We take the data from the Bloomberg terminal (see references for the Excel file available online). For each period we need a series of 252 historical returns to calculate the expected value and the variance of the returns on each stock (therefore 253 observations of stock prices for each stock). The daily returns (R_i) are obtained by:

$$R_{i,t+1} = \frac{P_{t+1} - P_t}{P_t},$$

   with P_t, the closing price of the stock at day *t*. In the case of a dividend payment (D_{t+1}), the return at the ex-dividend date is:

$$R_{i,t+1} = \frac{P_{t+1} + D_{t+1} - P_t}{P_t}.$$

   Based on the series, we use the Excel functions *Mean*, *Variance*, and *Covariance* to calculate $E(R_i)$, Variance(R_i) and Covariance(R_i, R_j), respectively.

[4]This exercise was prepared in cooperation with Samir Saissi Hassani and Faouzi Tarkhani.

TABLE E4.1 Presentation of stocks used.

Wal-Mart	RBC	SNC-Lavalin	Coca-Cola	Rogers
WMT US Equity	RY CN Equity	SNC CN Equity	KO US Equity	RCI US Equity

2. Calculate the variance-covariance matrix for each period.
   Each matrix is based on a range of cells covering the day associated with the period's end and going back 252 days.
3. Calculate the optimal weights, and report the expected value, variance, and VaR of the portfolio for each level of risk aversion.
   Relative VaR (VaR_r) is calculated for 95% and 99%.
4. Present the calculations by showing the evolution of the VaR over time and relative to the six risk-averse agents.
5. Analyze and comment on the results.

We want to understand what is happening according to three axes:

- Axis 1: Evolution of the portfolio for a given agent ($r = 0.01$, for example).
- Axis 2: For a given period, analyze and justify the calculations of VaR_r for each of the six agents (relationship between the risk aversion parameter *s* and VaR_r).
- Axis 3: Discuss the degree of confidence (95% or 99%) that an agent may choose depending on their degree of risk aversion.

Part B Application of the Delta and Delta-Gamma Methods to Calculate VaR

Review of Options Theory

The variation in the value of a portfolio formed of *m* stocks and *n* options is given by this equation:

$$dV = \sum_{i=1}^{m}\left[\sum_{j=1}^{n}\omega_{ij}\, dC_{ij} + x_i\, dS_i\right] \tag{E4.1}$$

where:

dV is the variation in the value of stocks and options portfolio;

C_{ij} is the value or the price of the jth option on the ith stock;

ω_{ij} is the number of options *j* on the stock *i*;

x_i is the number of stocks *i* in the portfolio;

S_i is the price of stock *i*.

According to the option valuation model, the price of an European option (C_t), whose underlier is a stock that does not pay dividends, is a function of the five following variables:

$$C_t = f(S_t, K, \sigma, r, \tau)$$

where:

S_t is the spot price of the underlying stock;
K is the exercise price of the option;
σ is the volatility of the stock price;
r is the risk-free rate;
τ is the time remaining before the option expires ($\tau = T - t$);
T is the expiry date of the option and t is the valuation date of the option.

In general, we can use the Taylor development to express the variation in the option price j on stock i:

$$dC_{ij} = \frac{\partial C_{ij}}{\partial S_i} dS_i + \frac{1}{2} \frac{\partial^2 C_{ij}}{\partial S_i^2} (dS_i)^2 + \frac{\partial C_{ij}}{\partial \sigma_i} d\sigma_i + \frac{\partial C_{ij}}{\partial r_{ij}} dr_{ij} + \frac{\partial C_{ij}}{\partial \tau_{ij}} d\tau_{ij}. \quad \text{(E4.2)}$$

The Greek values are defined as:

$$\frac{\partial C_{ij}}{\partial S_i} = \Delta_{ij}; \quad \frac{\partial^2 C_{ij}}{\partial S_i^2} = \Gamma_{ij}; \quad \frac{\partial C_{ij}}{\partial \sigma_i} = \Lambda_{ij}; \quad \frac{\partial C_{ij}}{\partial r_{ij}} = \rho_{ij}; \quad \frac{\partial C_{ij}}{\partial \tau_{ij}} = \theta_{ij}. \quad \text{(E4.3)}$$

Therefore, by substituting equations (E4.2) and (E4.3) in equation (E4.1), we have:

$$dV = \sum_{i=1}^{m} \left[\sum_{j=1}^{n} \omega_{ij} \left[\Delta_{ij}\, dS_i + \frac{1}{2} \Gamma_{ij} (dS_i)^2 + \Lambda_{ij}\, d\sigma_i + \rho_{ij} dr_{ij} + \theta_{ij}\, d\tau \right] + x_i\, dS_i \right] \quad \text{(E4.4)}$$

hence, by factoring and aggregating:

$$\Delta_i = \sum_{j=1}^{n} \omega_{ij}\, \Delta_{ij} + x_i; \; \Gamma_i = \sum_{j=1}^{n} \omega_{ij}\, \Gamma_{ij}; \; \Lambda_i = \sum_{j=1}^{n} \omega_{ij}\, \Lambda_{ij}; \; \Theta_p = \sum_{i=1}^{m} \sum_{j=1}^{n} \omega_{ij}\, \theta_{ij}.$$

With these substitutions, the variation in the portfolio value becomes:

$$dV = \sum_{i=1}^{m} \left[\Delta_i\, dS_i + \frac{1}{2} \Gamma_i\, (dS_i)^2 + \Lambda_i\, d\sigma_i + \sum_{j=1}^{n} \omega_{ij}\, \rho_{ij}\, dr_{ij} \right] + \Theta_p\, dt. \quad \text{(E4.5)}$$

Note that the aggregation of time is more complete because time advances in the same way for an option as for a stock, but aggregating r_{ij} is impossible because ρ_{ij} varies according to the expiry dates of the options.

Risk Exposure of the Portfolio by the Delta Approach

The Delta method excludes all terms of the Taylor development, with the exception of the term dS. The linear approach by the Delta is only precise when it is far from the "in-the-money" zone. This approach supposes that the effect of nonlinearity or of convexity is negligible (moments of order 2 or more are assumed to be zero). Therefore, equation (E4.5) becomes:

$$dV = \sum_{i=1}^{m} \Delta_i dS_i.$$

In terms of return, the equation becomes:

$$\frac{dV}{V} = \sum_{i=1}^{m} \frac{\Delta_i S_i}{V} \frac{dS_i}{S_i}. \qquad \text{(E4.6)}$$

The portfolio return can be written as:

$$\mu_p = \sum_{i=1}^{m} \frac{\Delta_i S_i}{V} \mu_i$$

and the portfolio variance is equal to:

$$\sigma_p^2 = \sum_{i=1}^{m} \sum_{j=1}^{m} \frac{\Delta_i S_i}{V} \frac{\Delta_j S_j}{V} \sigma_{ij}.$$

Risk Exposure of the Portfolio by the Delta-Gamma Approach

The Delta-Gamma method excludes all terms of the Taylor development, with the exception of the terms dS and $(dS)^2$. According to this method, price variations relative to other factors of equation (E4.) are negligible. Therefore, equation (E4.5) becomes:

$$dV = \sum_{i=1}^{m} \left[\Delta_i dS_i + \frac{1}{2} \Gamma_i (dS_i)^2 \right].$$

In terms of return, the equation becomes:

$$\frac{dV}{V} = \sum_{i=1}^{m} \left[\frac{\Delta_i S_i}{V} \frac{dS_i}{S_i} + \frac{1}{2} \frac{\Gamma_i S_i^2}{V} \left(\frac{dS_i}{S_i} \right)^2 \right]. \qquad \text{(E4.7)}$$

If we hypothesize that the portfolio return follows a normal distribution, the portfolio return can be written as:

$$\mu_p = \sum_{i=1}^{m} \left[\frac{\Delta_i S_i}{V} \mu_i + \frac{1}{2} \frac{\Gamma_i S_i^2}{V} \mu_i^2 \right].$$

The portfolio variance becomes:

$$\sigma_p = \sum_{i=1}^{m}\sum_{j=1}^{m}\frac{\Delta_i S_i}{V}\frac{\Delta_j S_j}{V}\sigma_{ij} + \frac{1}{4}\sum_{i=1}^{m}\sum_{j=1}^{m}\frac{\Gamma_i S_i^2}{V}\frac{\Gamma_j S_j^2}{V}\sigma'_{ij}.$$

with σ_{ij} the covariance of returns and σ'_{ij} the covariance of the squared returns.

Question: How can we obtain the values of Delta and Delta-Gamma VaR?

We will build two portfolios and calculate VaR by the two methods. Portfolio A is initially made up of three risky stocks and one option:

- Short sale of 500 shares of Microsoft (MSFT)
- Long position on 500 shares of Toyota Motors Corp. (TM)
- Long position on 500 shares of Acura Pharmaceuticals Inc. (ACUR)
- A put option on 500 shares of Microsoft. The put option began on December 30, 2011; 30 days remain until expiry; and the exercise price is $25.70.

We make the calculations of VaR at a 95% degree of confidence.

- Approach

  Here are some useful tips to help you do the calculations.

$$\Delta_{put} = N(d_1) - 1;$$

$$\Gamma_{put} = \frac{N'(d_1)}{S \times \sigma \times \sqrt{\tau}} = \frac{e^{-(d_1)^2/2}}{S \times \sigma \times \sqrt{\tau} \times \sqrt{2 \times \pi}}.$$

- Calculating the return

  Value of portfolio A:

$$V = -500 \times S_{MSFT} + 500 \times Put_{MSFT} + 500 \times S_{TM} + 500 \times S_{ACUR}.$$

Delta method

$$\Delta_{MSFT} = 500 \times \Delta_{put} - 500; \quad \Delta_{TM} = 0 + 500; \quad \Delta_{ACUR} = 0 + 500$$

The delta of a stock is $dS/dS = 1$.

$$\mu_{pf}^{\Delta} = \frac{\Delta_{MSFT} \times S_{MSFT}}{V} \times r_{MSFT} + 500 \times \frac{S_{TM}}{V} \times r_{TM} + 500 \times \frac{S_{ACUR}}{V} \times r_{ACUR}.$$

Delta-Gamma method

$$\frac{dV}{V} = \frac{\Delta_{MSFT} \times S_{MSFT}}{V} \times r_{MSFT} + \frac{1}{2}\frac{\Gamma_{MSFT} \times S^2_{MSFT}}{V} \times (r_{MSFT})^2$$
$$+ \frac{\Delta_{TM} \times S_{TM}}{V} \times \ r_{TM} + \frac{1}{2}\frac{\Gamma_{TM} \times S^2_{TM}}{V} \times (r_{TM})^2 + \frac{\Delta_{ACUR} \times S_{ACUR}}{V}$$
$$\times r_{ACUR} + \frac{1}{2}\frac{\Gamma_{ACUR} \times S^2_{ACUR}}{V} \times (r_{ACUR})^2;$$

$$\Delta_{MSFT} = 500 \times \Delta_{put} - 500;$$
$$\Delta_{TM} = 0 + 500;$$
$$\Delta_{ACUR} = 0 + 500;$$
$$\Gamma_{MSFT} = 500 \times \Gamma_{put};$$
$$\Gamma_{TM} = 0;$$
$$\Gamma_{ACUR} = 0;$$

$$\mu^{\Delta-\Gamma}_{pf} = \frac{\Delta_{MSFT} \times S_{MSFT}}{V} \times r_{MSFT} + \frac{1}{2}\frac{\Gamma_{MSFT} \times S^2_{MSFT}}{V} \times (r_{MSFT})^2$$
$$+ 500 \times \frac{S_{TM}}{V} \times r_{TM} + 500 \times \frac{S_{ACUR}}{V} \times r_{ACUR}.$$

We calculate the daily returns for the last 252 days (*look-back-days*), to determine the expected return and variance.

- Calculating portfolio variance

  Delta method

$$\sigma_p = \text{Var}\,(\mu^{delta}_{pf})$$

Delta-Gamma method

$$\sigma_{pf} = \text{Var}\,(\mu^{\Delta-\Gamma}_{pf}) - 2 \times \text{Cov}\left(\frac{\Delta_{MSFT} \times S_{MSFT}}{V} \times \ r_{MSFT};\right.$$
$$\left.\frac{1}{2}\frac{\Gamma_{MSFT} \times S^2_{MSFT}}{V} \times (r_{MSFT})^2\right)$$
$$- 2 \times \text{Cov}\left(500 \times \frac{S_{TM}}{V} \times \ r_{TM} + 500 \times \frac{S_{ACUR}}{V} \times \ r_{ACUR};\right.$$
$$\left.\frac{1}{2}\frac{\Gamma_{MSFT} \times S^2_{MSFT}}{V} \times (r_{MSFT})^2\right).$$

Here, the third moment is supposed to be zero if we assume a normal distribution. We can calculate the relative and absolute VaR of our portfolio based on the preceding elements.

Solution to Exercise 4

Part A Optimal Portfolios Relative to Risk Aversion

We observe, in Table E4.2, that the relative VaR values decrease as risk aversion increases: More risk averse individuals chose less risky portfolios. Moreover, VaR_r values at 99% presented in Table E4.3 are always higher than those at 95% of Table E4.2 because they are located in a higher tail of the distribution where only 1% of the losses are located. These conclusions are very stable over time.

Part B Portfolio positions for the Delta-Gamma analysis.

The results in Table E4.4 show that the two methods give very similar values even if the put option is "in-the-money" to verify the impact of the Gamma in the calculations. For portfolio A, the Delta method is sufficient and effective to calculate VaR with simple expressions.

Now we analyze the second portfolio with different weights.

The new portfolio in Table E4.5 is made up of the same stocks and of the same option. What changed is the number of put options, which goes from 500 to 10,000 units. Additionally, the position on the underlier becomes long by 3,700 shares. The magnitude of the VaR remains comparable between the Delta and the Delta-Gamma methods. However, the Delta method is clearly less precise. According to our figures, relative VaR would have been underestimated by \$33, whereas absolute VaR would have been overestimated by \$33, which represents a correction

TABLE E4.2 Evolution of VaR_r at 95%.

s	2013-01-07	2013-01-14	2013-01-21	2013-01-28
0.01	5.67850	5.88722	4.99905	4.65505
0.1	0.56795	0.58885	0.50026	0.46587
0.3	0.18958	0.19657	0.16723	0.15579
0.5	0.11406	0.11826	0.10080	0.09396
0.7	0.08180	0.08480	0.07246	0.06760
1	0.05775	0.05985	0.05136	0.04799

Note: Relative VaR of the portfolio at a level of confidence of 95%, supposing a normal distribution.

TABLE E4.3 Evolution of VaR_r at 99%.

s	2013-01-07	2013-01-14	2013-01-21	2013-01-28
0.01	8.01873	8.31347	7.05926	6.57349
0.1	0.80201	0.83153	0.70643	0.65786
0.3	0.26770	0.27757	0.23616	0.21999
0.5	0.16106	0.16699	0.14235	0.13269
0.7	0.11551	0.11975	0.10232	0.09546
1	0.08156	0.08452	0.07252	0.06777

Note: Relative VaR of the portfolio at a level of confidence of 99%, supposing a normal distribution.

TABLE E4.4 Results of portfolio A.

Weight 1	Weight 2	Weight 3	Weight option
–500	500	500	500

				V$_0$ of portfolio: $21,945.46		
Mean	Variance	Standard deviation	Relative VaR (%)	Absolute VaR (%)	Relative VaR ($)	Absolute VaR ($)
Calculation of VaR: Delta method (only)						
–0.062321%	0.042100%	2.051839%	3.385534%	3.447855%	742.97	756.65
Calculation of VaR: Delta-Gamma method						
–0.048241%	0.042111%	2.052105%	3.385973%	3.434214%	743.07	753.65
Delta versus Delta-Gamma gaps						
0.014080%	0.000011%	0.000266%	0.000438%	–0.013641%	0.10	–2.99

TABLE E4.5 Results of portfolio B.

Weight 1	Weight 2	Weight 3	Weight option
3,700	500	500	10,000

				V$_0$ of portfolio: $135,809.26		
Mean	Variance	Standard deviation	Relative VaR (%)	Absolute VaR (%)	Relative VaR ($)	Absolute VaR ($)
Calculation of VaR: Delta method (only)						
0.032199%	0.001841%	0.429064%	0.707956%	0.675757%	961.47	917.74
Calculation of VaR: Delta-Gamma method						
0.081269%	0.001971%	0.443931%	0.732486%	0.651217%	994.78	884.41
Delta versus Delta-Gamma gaps						
0.049070%	0.000130%	0.014866%	0.024529%	–0.024541%	33.31	–33.33

of approximately 3.4%. Because the Gamma correction is of second order, this indicates a significant change in the degree of convexity of the "in-the-money zone" of portfolio B relative to the previous one (A). In other words, the effect of nonlinearity of the option was too diluted in portfolio A, whereas portfolio B would clearly be nonlinear. To intuitively illustrate this fact, we trace the payoff of a portfolio containing one Microsoft share that was sold (short) and one Microsoft option (same characteristics) in Figure E4.1.

As Figure E4.1 demonstrates, the curve of the European call option is much more convex in the region of the exercise price ($25.70) than in the extremes. Therefore, in these extreme regions, we can expect that only Delta suffices. In contrast, for a value of the underlier that is close to the exercise price (at the money zone), the Gamma component will make a sizable correction. As Figure E4.2 illustrates, the logic is equally valid for the put option.

We must now justify the gap between the expected portfolio returns calculated by the Delta and those of the Delta-Gamma. Equation (E4.7) has one additional term than does (E4.6). The gamma of a put or call option is still positive for long positions and is negative for short positions. The effect of the Gamma correction may then doubly affect relative VaR. It influences both the calculation of the expected return and the expression of the portfolio variance.

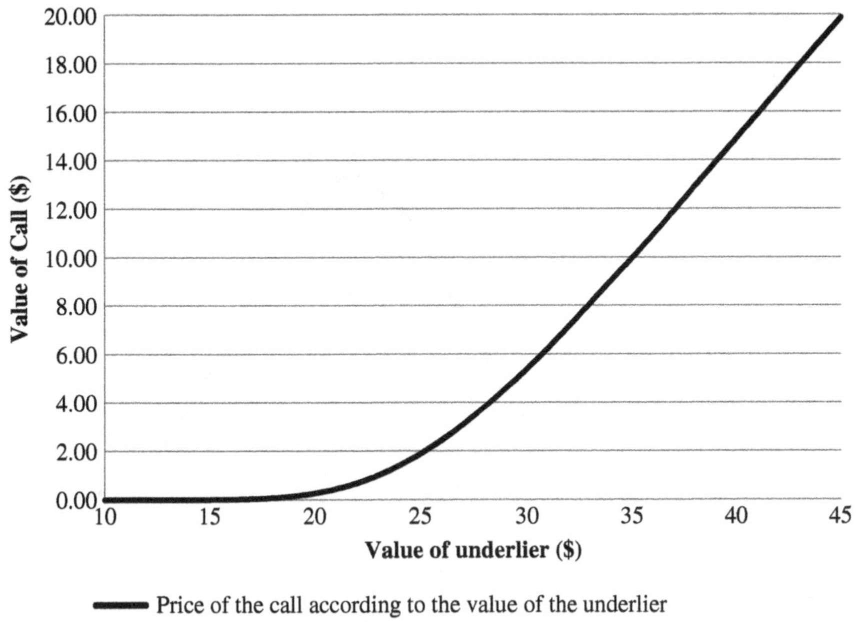

FIGURE E4.1 Convexity of the call.

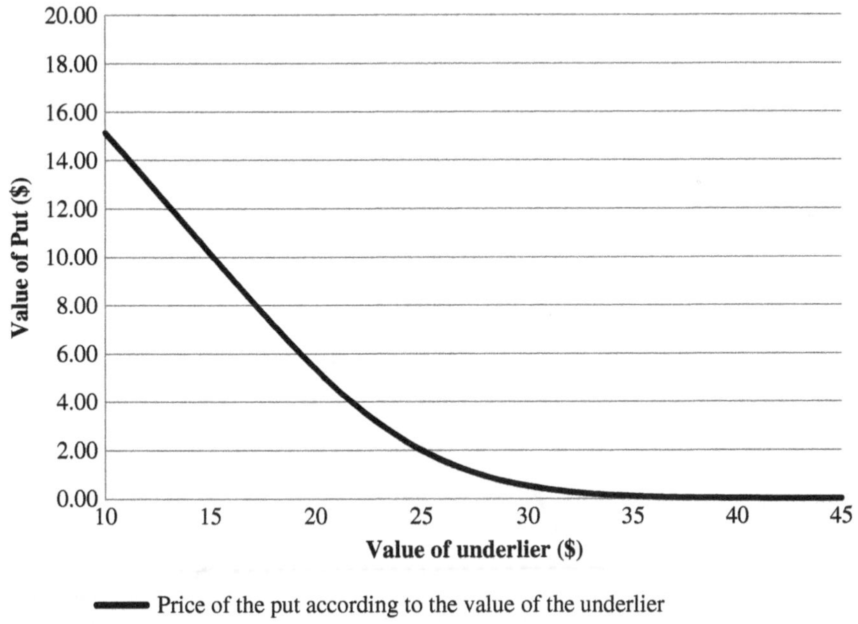

FIGURE E4.2 Convexity of the put.

The histograms in Figures E4.3 and E4.4 show the historical densities of portfolio B. The first histogram (Figure E4.3) is related to the Delta method only. Despite the excess Kurtosis of 0.7, the distribution observed does not seem to reject a normal distribution at 1%. In contrast, the second distribution (Figure E4.4) rejects the normal distribution at all degrees of confidence according to the

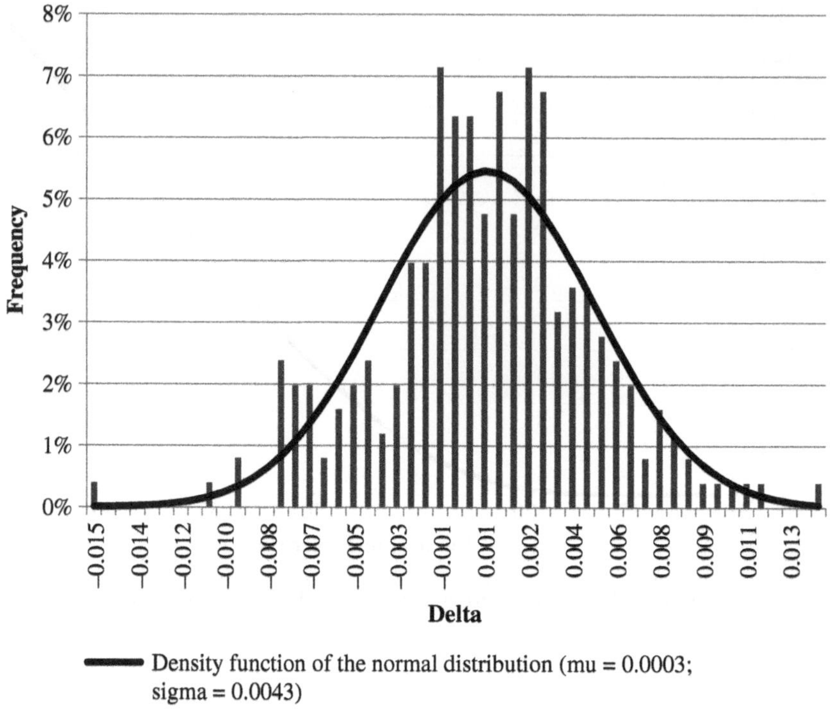

FIGURE E4.3 Distribution of Delta.

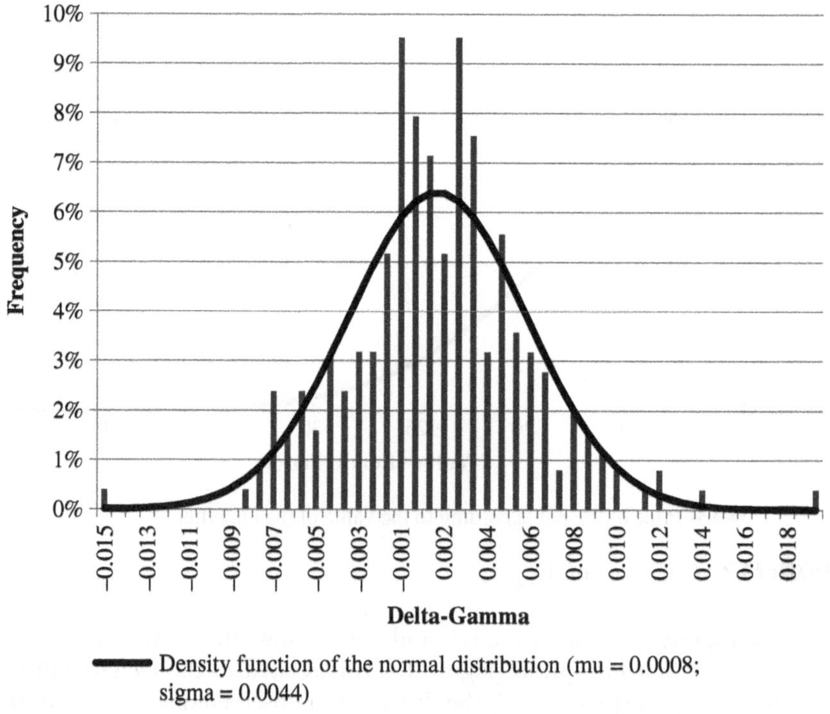

FIGURE E4.4 Distribution of Delta-Gamma.

Kolmogorov-Smirnov, Cramer-von Mises, and Anderson-Darling tests, not displayed here. We think this is linked to the nonlinear accentuated nature in portfolio B that is better captured by the Delta-Gamma method.

The Delta method is quite sufficient in many situations and is effective owing to the simplicity of its expressions. It is quite satisfactory far from the at-the-money area. The degree of convexity of the nonlinear portfolio should be examined in the at-the-money area to decide on which model to use.

The Delta-Gamma method provides a second-order term to take convexity into account. The cost of this method is a major issue when calculating VaR for a portfolio with several stocks and options.

Assignment

By following this example, create your own portfolio formed of at least three stocks and an option. Calculate Relative VaR and Absolute VaR. Comment on your charts and results.

EXERCISE 5 CVaR CONDITIONAL VALUE AT RISK[5]

The objective of this assignment is to clarify the important points about CVaR regarding market risk and portfolio choice, based on real data.

We are interested in three risky stocks: IBM, General Electric, and Wal-Mart. The daily prices are extracted from October 15, 2008, to August 31, 2009. Returns are calculated by supposing no dividends. We know that the returns during the financial crisis period exhibited sizable variance relative to the usual assumptions of normality. We want to see the limits of the VaR calculations and then evaluate the opportunity of using CVaR in the case of different hypotheses, including the following: the Student's *t*-distribution, a mixture of two normal distributions, and the calculations of $CVaR^-$ and $CVaR^+$ with a nonparametric historical simulation model (as in exercise 2 on backtesting). We will begin with some mathematical derivations that are useful for the calculations.

Mathematical Expressions of CVaR

1. The mathematical expression of CVaR for a normal distribution
   - Case of a normal variable $t \sim N(0,1)$

$$\frac{df(t)}{dt} = \frac{d}{dt}\left(\frac{1}{\sqrt{2\pi}}e^{-\frac{t^2}{2}}\right) = \frac{1}{\sqrt{2\pi}}e^{-\frac{t^2}{2}} \times -\frac{2t}{2} = -tf(t)$$

hence:

$$E(t|t < q_t) = \int_{-\infty}^{q_t} t\frac{f(t)}{F(q_t)}\,dt = \frac{1}{F(q_t)}\int_{-\infty}^{q_t} tf(t)\,dt = \frac{1}{F(q_t)}\int_{-\infty}^{q_t} \frac{-df(t)}{dt}\,dt$$

$$CVaR_{N(0,1)} = -\frac{1}{F(q_t)}\,[f(t)]_{-\infty}^{q_t} = -\frac{f(q_t)}{F(q_t)} \qquad \text{(E5.1)}$$

where $q_t = VaR < 0$.

[5]This exercise was produced in cooperation with Samir Saissi Hassani and Alain-Philippe Fortin.

- Case of a normal $x \sim N(\mu, \sigma)$

  We posit $t = \frac{x-\mu}{\sigma} \sim N(0,1)$; we replace x with its value $x = \mu + \sigma t$ in the definition:

$$\text{CVaR}_{N(\mu,\sigma)} = E(x|x < q) = E(\mu + \sigma t|\mu + \sigma t < q)$$

$$= \mu + \sigma E\left(t|t < \frac{q-\mu}{\sigma}\right) = \mu - \sigma \frac{f\left(\frac{q-\mu}{\sigma}\right)}{F\left(\frac{q-\mu}{\sigma}\right)} < 0.$$

  The last equality results directly from (E5.1).

2. The expression of CVaR in a Student's *t*-distribution

   If $x \sim$ Student's *t*-distribution where m is the mean, s^2 is a dispersion parameter and ν is the number of degrees of freedom:

$$\text{CVaR} = \int_{-\infty}^{q} x\frac{f(x)}{F(q)}\,dx = \frac{1}{F(q)}\int_{-\infty}^{q} x\frac{\Gamma\left(\frac{\nu+1}{2}\right)}{\Gamma\left(\frac{\nu}{2}\right)\sqrt{\pi s\nu}}\left(1+\frac{x^2}{s\nu}\right)^{-(1+\nu)/2} dx.$$

   By changing the variable: $y = x^2/s\nu$,

   $\text{CVaR} = -\frac{s\nu}{\nu-1}\left(1+\frac{q^2}{s\nu}\right)\frac{f(q)}{F(q)} < 0$ for the centered, reduced distribution, hence:

$$\text{CVaR} = m - \frac{s \times \nu + (q-m)^2}{\nu - 1}\frac{f(q)}{F(q)} < 0 \qquad \text{(E5.2)}$$

   where $q = \text{VaR} < 0$.

3. The expression of CVaR when the selected model is a mixture of normal distributions.

   In the case of a mixture of two normal distributions, $N(\mu_1, \sigma_1)$ and $N(\mu_2, \sigma_2)$ with the probability of the mixture p, the cumulative probability function of the mixture is written as $F_p(x) = pF_1(x) + (1-p)F_2(x)$ and the density is $f_p(x) = pf_1(x) + (1-p)f_2(x)$ for all values of x.

   We thus do a mixture of CVaRs by using the same calculations as for only one normal (Broda and Paolella, 2011):

$$\text{CVaR} = \sum_{j=1}^{2}\frac{p_jF_j(C_j)}{F_p(q)}\left(\mu_j - \sigma_j\frac{f_j(C_j)}{F_j(C_j)}\right). \qquad \text{(E5.3)}$$

   where:

$$C_j = \frac{q-\mu_j}{\sigma_j};$$

$$q = \text{VaR} < 0.$$

The explicit formula used for the calculations in the example can be found in the Excel file.

Data

For the three stocks, Table E5.1 presents the correlation matrix, the variance-covariance matrix, the expected return during the study period, and their variances.

Question 1

Calculate the optimal weights of portfolio A, which minimize the VaR under the constraint that the weights add up to 1. We suppose that the returns follow a normal distribution.

At the stated conditions, relative VaR is written as:

$$VaR_r = -\sigma_{portfolio} \times F^{-1}(p) = -\sqrt{\beta^T \Sigma \beta} \times q > 0$$

where β is the vector of the stocks' weights, β^T is the transpose of β, Σ is the variance-covariance matrix of the stocks, and $q < 0$ is the weight of the portfolio risk measure relative to the degree of confidence chosen $(1 - p)$. Excel's Solver gives the following results, in percentages.

The "Weighted sum" column in Table E5.2 represents the sum of the individual VaRs for the three stocks weighted by the previously calculated weights. This

TABLE E5.1 Portfolio characteristics.

	IBM	General Electric	Wal-Mart
IBM	1		
General Electric	0.575845	1	
Wal-Mart	0.546558	0.416497	1
IBM	0.06152 %	0.06293 %	0.02822 %
General Electric	0.06293 %	0.19411 %	0.03820 %
Wal-Mart	0.02822 %	0.03820 %	0.04334 %
Mean	0.11382 %	−0.14801 %	−0.03411 %
Variance	0.06152 %	0.19411 %	0.04334 %

TABLE E5.2 VaR, $q = -1{,}6448$.

	Portfolio	IBM 0.3590851	General Electric −0.0569328	Wal-Mart 0.6978477	Sum 1
Mean	0.02550	0.11382	0.14801	−0.03411	
Variance	0.03820				
Standard deviation	1.95457	2.48035	4.40574	2.08181	
					Weighted sum
VaR_a 5%	3.18949	3.96599	7.09879	3.45838	4.24171
VaR_r 5%	3.21499	4.07981	7.24680	3.42427	4.26720

gives us a direct idea of the coherence of the VaR measure in this example. The calculations show that absolute VaR and relative VaR clearly verify that $\text{Risk}(\beta_i R_i) \leq \Sigma\beta_i \times \text{Risk}(R_i)$, which means that the portfolio's VaR is smaller than the sum of individual VaRs.

Question 2

Calculate the optimal weights for portfolio B, which minimize CVaR (in absolute value), subject to the constraint that the weights must be equal to 1 and under the same assumptions of normality.

For CVaR, the choice of optimal portfolio is intended to minimize volatility. We obtain the same weights β_i as for VaR.

$$\text{CVaR}_r = \sigma_{\text{portfolio}} \times \frac{f(q)}{F(q)} = \sqrt{\beta^T \Sigma \beta} \times \frac{f(q)}{F(q)} > 0.$$

Excel's Solver gives the results (in percentages) presented in Table E5.3.

CVaR_r is consistent with 4.03172% < 5.35124%. CVaR_a gives the same results.

Question 3

Using historical simulations, estimate VaR_a and CVaR_a of a portfolio made up of the three stocks and weights given in Table E5.4. Comment on the coherence of the VaR_a, CVaR_a^-, and CVaR_a^+ measures of this portfolio.

TABLE E5.3 CVaR, $q = -1.6448$.

	Portfolio	IBM 0.3590851	General Electric −0.0569328	Wal-Mart 0.6978477	Sum 1
Mean	0.02550				
Variance	0.03820				
Standard deviation	1.95457	2.48035	4.40574	2.08181	Weighted sum
CVaR_a	4.00623	5.00243	8.93977	4.32828	5.32575
CVaR_r	4.03172	5.11625	9.08779	4.29418	5.35124

TABLE E5.4 VaR, CVaR^- and CVaR^+ (historical simulations) in percentages.

5 %	Portfolio	IBM 0.4259457	General Electric 0.10456364	Wal-Mart 0.4694906	Weighted sum	Difference
VaR_a nparam	3.74296	3.73551	8.08105	3.21677	3.94635	−0.20339
CVaR_a^- nparam	4.78451	5.22991	9.54917	4.52796	5.35199	−0.56748
CVaR_a^+ nparam	4.87919	5.36577	9.68264	4.64716	5.47977	−0.60058

Note: nparam signifies non-parametric.

The last column of the table shows the difference Risk($\beta_i R_i$) – $\Sigma\beta_i \times$ Risk(R_i). All these differences are strictly negative. The three risk measures are coherent for this portfolio. Note that CVaR$^+$ is equal to CVaR in this example.

Question 4

Table E5.5 presents the estimates of VaR$_a$, CVaR$_a^-$, and CVaR$_a^+$ non-parametric (in percentages) with the optimal weights calculated in question 2.

With the optimal weights from question 2, the three measures are equally coherent. They can thus be used to compare the risks and manage the portfolio diversification. They also give a smaller risk measure than the previous portfolio because this is the optimal portfolio.

In question 1, absolute VaR is 3.18949%, which is comparable to, but greater than, the value of 3.10716% found in the non-parametric model (Table E5.5). This suggests that VaR found by supposing a normal distribution would be underestimated slightly by the parametric approach. Nonetheless, CVaR$_a$ for a normal distribution should fall between CVaR$_a^-$ and CVaR$_a^+$, as seen in Chapter 8. Because we have a continuous density for the normal distribution CVaR$_a$ of Table E5.3, it would definitely be underestimated (4.00623) because it is not included in the interval CVaR$_a^-$ (4.35652) and CVaR$_a^+$ (4.47010) found in Table E5.5. Clearly, the normal distribution does not suit the data. This is because after the quantile of the VaR, there is still some risk to consider, which does not seem to be taken into account by the normal distribution for this portfolio.

We now start the search for a model that considers the risk measures identified by the two non-parametric measures: CVaR$_a^-$ and CVaR$_a^+$. Further, knowledge of these two non-parametric measures helps us choose a model that best fits our data.

Question 5

We want to see whether the estimation of the model with a Student's *t*-distribution provides a satisfactory correction. With the expression of the CVaR derived above, we show and comment on the results below.

The first important comment is that the "degree of freedom" parameter of the Student's *t* distribution is slightly lower than 3 in Table E5.6. This clearly illustrates some *leptokurtic* (thick-tailed) nature of our data, which, incidentally, concerns a very turbulent period, namely the 2008 crisis. With a degree of freedom lower

TABLE E5.5 VaR, CVaR$^-$ and CVaR$^+$ (historical simulations).

5 %	Portfolio	IBM 0.3590851	General Electric -0.0569328	Wal-Mart 0.6978477	Weighted sum	Difference
VaR$_a$ nparam	3.10716	3.73551	6.28336	3.21677	3.94391	−0.83675
CVaR$_a^-$ nparam	4.35653	5.22991	9.87618	4.52796	5.60009	−1.24356
CVaR$_a^+$ nparam	4.47010	5.36577	10.20280	4.64716	5.75065	−1.28055

Note: nparam signifies non-parametric.

TABLE E5.6 Student's t distribution, $p = 5\%$.

Parameter	Value	Quantile q	Density f(q)	Probability F(q)
m	0.00030			
s	0.01125			
ν	2.18900			
		−0.032550	0.029281	0.05
VaR_a	3.25498%		$CVaR_a^-$ nparam	4.35652%
$CVaR_a$	4.77%		$CVaR_a^+$ nparam	4.47010%

Note: nparam signifies non-parametric.

than 4, the Student's t has a fourth infinite moment. The VaR_a calculated with Student's t is 3.25498%, which is markedly superior to the one calculated with a parametric normal distribution (3.189%) and the non-parametric historical simulation (3.10716%). However, $CVaR_a$ (Student's t) does not seem to suit the data because it is too large to be included between $CVaR^-$ (4.35653%) and $CVaR^+$ (4.47010%). One possible interpretation may be that Student's t has a very low estimated degree of freedom, which may have overestimated the losses during the financial crisis.

Note that the estimations of the values $CVaR_a^-$ and $CVaR_a^+$ in Table E5.6 are those obtained with the non-parametric model in Table E5.5. The same comment applies to Table E5.7. These two values are added for reference purposes. We know that for the distributions contained in these two tables, $CVaR_a^- = CVaR_a = CVaR_a^+$, because the two distributions are continuous.

Question 6

We redo the previous question with a mixture of two normal distributions. The advantage of this mixture is that often, the calculations amount to what we can do on the Gaussian distribution, which implies simple calculations. One major benefit of this method is that we can estimate the parameters of the two normal components and the probability of the mixture separately, to create asymmetry in the resulting density. Consequently, with two more parameters than a Student's t-distribution, more precise modeling of asymmetry with important *kurtosis* is possible. We should

TABLE E5.7 Mixture of two normal distributions, $p = 5\%$.

		Quantile q	Density f(q)	Probability F(q)
N1: μ_1	−0.00380			
σ_1	0.03310			
N2: μ_2	0.00037			
σ_2	0.01180			
Probability	0.23400			
N1			0.281717	0.202095
N2			0.010611	0.003538
		−0.031411	0.002278	0.050000
VaR_a	3.14108%		$CVaR_a^-$ nparam	4.35652%
$CVaR_a$	4.86%		$CVaR_a^+$ nparam	4.47010%

Note: nparam signifies non-parametric.

obtain a better model with a mixture of two normal distributions. The results are presented in Table E5.7.

The first result is that VaR seems to resemble the non-parametric VaR the most. With 3.141%, we obtain the number closest to 3.10716% of the three adjusted models in this exercise. The CVaR obtained also seems to overestimate the data, because it is much higher than the non-parametric CVaR$^+$. More research remains necessary to find the appropriate parametric distribution.

Recapitulation of the Three Models: Normal Distribution, Student's *t*, and Mixture of Two Normal Distributions

Figures E5.1 and E5.2 illustrate what happens under the three models. Student's *t* and the normal mixture can seek out more information in the left tail of the distribution, whereas the normal stops at two-thirds of the height of the histogram (Figure E5.1). We can see the asymmetric adjustment of the mixture of the two normal distributions. Figure E5.2 shows a zoom of Figure E5.1 around the values of the risk measures in the left tail of the distributions. We see how the normal converges too quickly towards 0, whereas Student's *t* and the normal mixture still keep an area below the curve well after the VaR quantile. This conclusion seems to support the mixture of the two normal distributions even if it exceeds the CVaR$^+$. We can once again note the importance of the CVaR$^-$ and CVaR$^+$ measures in the optimization of the adjustment. Now that we have a parametric model that can almost replicate the non-parametric behaviour of our stocks, we can use it to infer VaR and CVaR relative to quantiles that are difficult to quantify, such as for degrees of confidence of 99% and 99.9%. This latter degree of confidence is particularly very difficult to estimate with sufficient precision in a non-parametric approach when the data is sparse. This may explain the instability of internal models for operational risk given that the Basel Accord requires the use of a 99.9% degree of confidence.

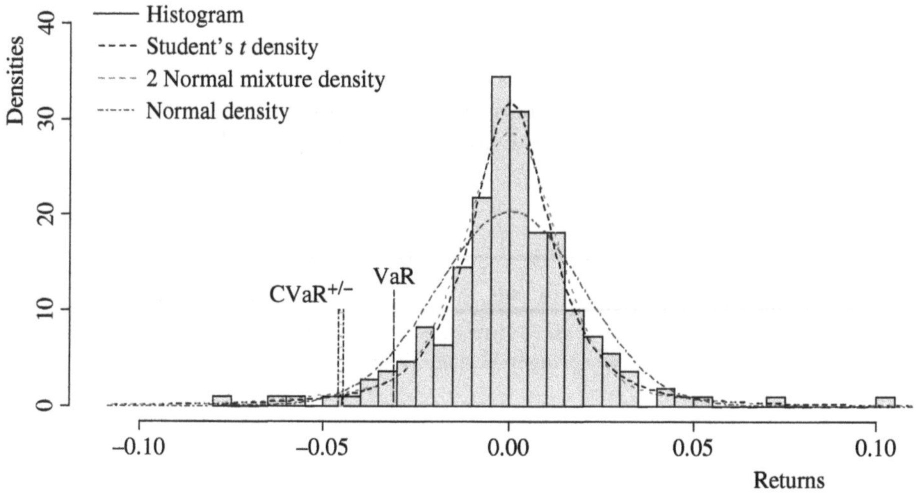

FIGURE E5.1 Histogram of portfolio returns, Normal density, Student's *t* density and a mixture of Normal distributions. The CVaRs are obtained from the non-parametric approach. VaR is from the Normal distribution.

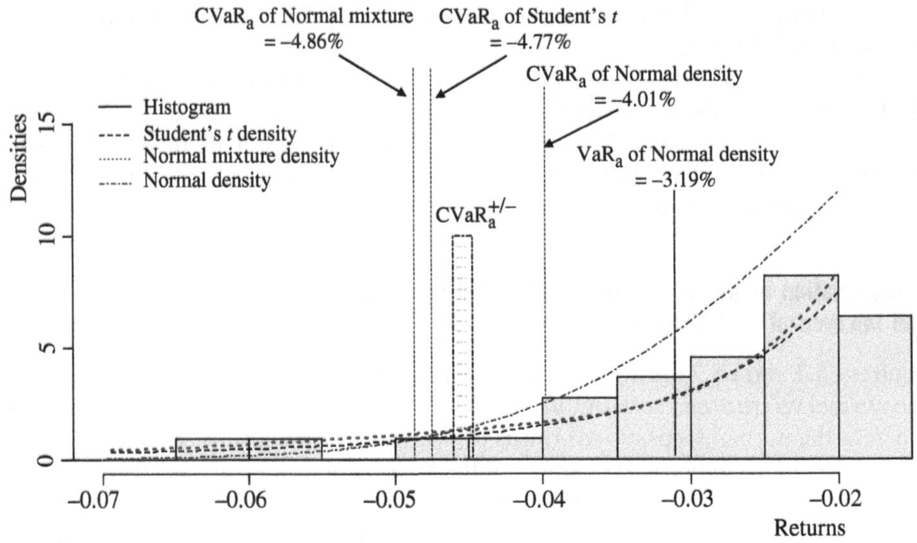

FIGURE E5.2 Details of the left tail for portfolio returns, Normal density, Student's t density and a mixture of Normal distributions.

Note: $CVaR_a^{+/-}$ values were obtained with the non-parametric approach. They are equal to −4.47% and −4.36%.

CONCLUSION

Based on real data we have built portfolios that illustrate the behavior of VaR and of CVaR in terms of risk measurement criteria, as seen in different chapters of the book, including the one that covers CVaR.

In the case of parametric calculations, CVaR modeled with a normal distribution does not seem to effectively explain what happens in the tail of the distribution. This is because the data imposes a thickness of the tail that the normal distribution cannot capture. The use of a Student's t-distribution improves the results. We then apply a mixture of two normal distributions with different means to better replicate the asymmetry. We obtain an overestimation of the CVaR with these two parametric distributions when compared with the non-parametric approach.

REFERENCE

Broda, S.A., and Paolella, M.S., 2011. "Expected Shortfall for Distributions in Finance." In: P. Cizek, W.K. Härdle, and R. Weron (Eds.), *Statistical Tools for Finance and Insurance*. Berlin and Heidelberg: Springer-Verlag, 57–99.

Conclusion

We have presented more than twenty subjects related to risk management. Several issues have not been covered in depth. In this short conclusion, we raise some important open questions to stimulate future research, teaching, and management.

Risk management is evolving at an accelerated pace to adapt to permanent changes in risks. For example, liquidity risk was not really considered before the last financial crisis. The first empirical result that caught researchers' attention is the fact that default risk represents only a fraction of the spread between corporate and government bonds. Several studies have now shown that liquidity risk partly explains residual spreads. This risk played a significant role in the last financial crisis and in the following years. Consequently, Basel III introduced a regulatory capital requirement to reduce the effects of liquidity risk on banks' financial health. Managing this risk is a formidable challenge and very few theoretical publications have examined this subject. The very definition of liquidity risk remains vague.

Integrated risk management is still very fragmented. Several firms' annual reports describe the implementation of an integrated risk management model. Organizational charts are quite stylized, but often superficial, because risks continue to be managed in silos. Very few banks consider correlations between market, default, and liquidity risk of the assets contained in their portfolios. This may be explained by the fact that these correlations are too weak to be modeled. Estimating these correlations would shed light on the empirical fundamentals inherent in an integrated form of risk management.

Environmental risks have also received scant attention. Is this due to the fact that we feel powerless to control them, or do we care little about future generations? Owing to indifference and the absence of government involvement in addressing these risks, individuals and businesses seem disinclined to sacrifice present resources to achieve long-term benefits that are difficult to internalize. More in-depth research is necessary to find an international approach to creating much-needed individual and collective incentives to reduce polluting emissions, for example.

The literature contains diverging empirical conclusions regarding the effects of risk management on firm value. The problem seems to be methodological: Risk management decisions are endogenous to firm value. We must therefore find an exogenous source in the variation of risk management or clearly instrument the estimation of the risk management equation. This task is very complex because almost all of the variables available are endogenous to firm value. In addition, the beneficial effect on corporate welfare brought by the Basel regulation on banks or more local regulations on insurance companies has not been demonstrated. The last financial crisis raised questions about the effectiveness of these regulations.

Measurement of systemic risk is also problematic. Researchers have difficulty proving that their measures differ from those of systematic risk.

Research on risk management of financial portfolios under high frequency trading is advancing slowly. Risk measures (e.g., VaR) have been defined, but their use in real time remains challenging. Estimating and testing models requires very powerful calculation capacities to obtain values in a few hours or minutes, whereas brokers trade in microseconds or even in nanoseconds! Studies of information asymmetry and arbitrage problems in these markets are also inconclusive, owing to inadequate methodologies.

Cyber risk is now a leading concern for many organizations. The frequency and severity of cyber-attacks increase even if all of them are not necessarily reported. Is insurance coverage for this risk the best risk management strategy? Prevention and mitigation of possible costs with optimal capital management must be investigated as complementary strategies to insurance coverage. The risk management of cyber risk data and information technology systems raises the same concerns for many firms.

Lastly, the Basel Committee has proposed to replace the advanced approach (AMA) to operational risk modeling and calculating required bank capital. Banks oppose this reform because the new approach restricts their freedom to use internal models, as was the case for credit risk under Basel I. One of the Basel Committee's arguments is that internal models are very heterogeneous, which makes them more costly to oversee. The new formula proposed, the SMA (Standardized Measurement Approach), also has flaws: 1) it is much less sensitive to banks' individual risk, which reduces incentives to manage this risk well; and 2) its stability is not yet proven.

GENERAL REFERENCES

Banks, E., 2004. *Alternative Risk Transfer*. Chichester, England: John Wiley & Sons,.

Dahen, H., and Dionne, G., 2010. "Scaling Models for the Severity and Frequency of External Operational Loss Data." *Journal of Banking and Finance* 34, 1484–1496.

Dionne, G., Pacurar, M., and Zhou, X., 2015. "Liquidity-Adjusted Intraday Value at Risk Modeling and Risk Management: An Application to Data from Deutsche Börse." *Journal of Banking and Finance* 59, 202–219.

Eling, M., 2018. "Cyber Risk and Cyber Risk Insurance: Status Quo and Future Research." Editorial, Special issue of the *Geneva Paper on Risk and Insurance—Issues and Practice on Cyber Risk and Cyber Risk Insurance*.

Gerlach, S., 2009. *Defining and Measuring Systemic Risk*. European Parliament's Committee on Economic and Monetary Affairs publication, Brussels, Belgium.

Gollier, C., and Tirole, J., 2015. *Effective Institutions against Climate Change*. Mimeo, Toulouse School of Economics, France.

Hampton, J.J., 2009. *Fundamentals of Enterprise Risk Management*. New York: Amacom.

Insurance Institute of Canada, 2012. *Enterprise Risk Management (ERM) in the Insurance Sector*. Mimeo, Toronto, Canada.

Nikolaou, K., 2009. *Liquidity (Risk): Concepts Definitions and Interactions*. Working paper no. 1008, European Central Bank, Germany.

Peters, G.W., Shevchenko, P.V., Hassani, B. and Chapelle, A., 2016. *Should AMA Be Replaced with SMA for Operational Risk?* Mimeo, University College of London, UK.

Index